Korean Crisis and Recovery

Editors

David T. Coe
and
Se-Jik Kim

INTERNATIONAL MONETARY FUND
KOREA INSTITUTE FOR INTERNATIONAL ECONOMIC POLICY

Production: Korea Institute for International Economic Policy, Korea
Typesetting and figures: Orom System, Korea

Cataloging-in-Publication Data

Korean crisis and recovery / editors, David T. Coe and Se-Jik Kim—Washington, D.C.:
    International Monetary Fund: Korea Institute for International Economic Policy, c2002

        p. cm.

Papers presented at a conference held May 17-19, 2001 at the Shilla Hotel in Seoul, Korea.
Sponsored by the International Monetary Fund and the Korea Institute for International Economic Policy.
Includes bibliographical references.
ISBN 1-58906-068-7
1. Financial crises—Korea (South)—Congresses. I. Coe, David T. II. Kim, Se-Jik, 1960-
III. International Monetary Fund.

    HG3330.5.A6K57 2002

Price: $32.00

Address orders to:
International Monetary Fund, Publication Services
700 19th Street, N.W., Washington, D.C. 20431, U.S.A.
Tel: (202) 623-7430   Telefax: (202) 623-7201
E-mail: publications@imf.org
Internet: http://www.imf.org

Cover Painting Credit: Tanwon Kim, Hong-to (1760-?, Chosun Dynasty), "Daejangkan" ("A Blacksmith's Workshop," genre painting), a light-colored picture on paper, 27cmx22.7cm, National Museum of Korea, Seoul, Korea.

Contents

Foreword

Four years after the outbreak of the Asian economic crisis and three and one-half years after the beginning of the IMF program with Korea, the International Monetary Fund (IMF) and the Korea Institute for International Economic Policy (KIEP) jointly sponsored a conference on the Korean crisis and recovery. The conference was held at the Shilla Hotel in Seoul on May 17-19, 2001.

The objective of the conference was to distill lessons from the Korean economic crisis and recovery, and the policies adopted by the government with support from the international community. The timing of the conference, coming after the three-year Stand-By Arrangement with the IMF ended on December 2, 2000, and following two years of remarkable economic recovery from the crisis, seemed appropriate for such an assessment. The conference brought together Korean and non-Korean economists with Korean policymakers and IMF and World Bank staff, some of whom were involved in designing and implementing the Korean program. Holding the conference in Seoul, with broadly equal participation by Koreans and non-Koreans, was considered essential to ensure that Korean perspectives on the crisis were well represented.

David Coe, who was IMF Senior Resident Representative in Seoul, and Se-Jik Kim, Visiting Research Fellow at KIEP, on leave from the Research Department of the IMF, proposed and organized the conference. Their proposal was strongly supported by Stanley Fischer, then First Deputy Managing Director of the IMF—whose planned participation in the conference, unfortunately, had to be cancelled at the last minute—by Kyung Tae Lee, then President of KIEP, and by the Asia and Pacific Department of the IMF.

This conference volume contains the 13 papers presented at the conference. Each paper is an important reference for scholars and policymakers seeking to understand the Korean crisis and recovery, and the policies adopted to address the crisis. We believe the conference accomplished its objective very successfully.

Yusuke Horiguchi
Director, Asia and Pacific Department
International Monetary Fund

Choong Yong Ahn
President, Korea Institute for
International Economic Policy

Acknowledgments

We are indebted to Stanley Fischer, Kyung Tae Lee, and Yusuke Horiguchi for their unwavering support. They, together with Professor Un-Chan Chung of Seoul National University, Dr. Jaebong Ro of KIEP, Professor Jong-Wha Lee of Korea University, and Ajai Chopra of the IMF's Asia and Pacific Department, gave generously of their time to help define the themes of the conference and identify potential authors and participants.

We are particularly grateful to Jung Woon Kim, Young-Mok Yang, and Hyong Kun Lee of KIEP, and to Hyeon-Sook Shim of the IMF's Seoul office for their superb assistance in making local conference arrangements and taking care of a myriad of organizational details. We are also indebted to Audrey K. Lee, Maryse Dubé, and Seonhee Bae for their excellent assistance in editing and coordinating the production of this volume.

Contributors and Participants

Contributors

Robert J. Barro is Professor in the Department of Economics at Harvard University.

Yangho Byeon is Director General of the Financial Policy Bureau at the Ministry of Finance and Economy.

Yoon Je Cho is Professor at the Graduate School of International Studies at Sogang University.

Ajai Chopra was Assistant Director, Asia and Pacific Department at the time of the conference and is currently Senior Advisor, European I Department at the International Monetary Fund.

Chae-Shick Chung was Research Fellow in the Korea Institute for International Economic Policy, and is currently Professor in the Department of Economics at Sogang University.

David T. Coe was the IMF's Senior Resident Representative in Seoul and is currently Assistant Director, Asia and Pacific Department at the International Monetary Fund.

Michael Dooley is Professor in the Department of Economics at the University of California at Santa Cruz.

Rudi Dornbusch was Professor in the Department of Economics at the Massachusetts Institute of Technology.

Barry Eichengreen is Professor in the Department of Economics at the University of California at Berkeley.

Eric Friedman is Professor of Economics at Rutgers and Cornell Universities.

Simon Johnson is Professor in the Sloan School of Management at the Massachusetts Institute of Technology.

Kenneth Kang is Senior Economist, Asia and Pacific Department at the International Monetary Fund.

Meral Karasulu is Economist, Monetary and Exchange Affairs Department at the International Monetary Fund.

Dae Il Kim is Professor in the Department of Economics at Seoul National University.

Se-Jik Kim is Visiting Research Fellow at the Korea Institute for International Economic Policy, on leave from the Research Department at the International Monetary Fund.

Woochan Kim is Professor at the Korea Development Institute's School of Public Policy and Management.

Anne O. Krueger was Professor of Economics at Stanford University and is currently First Deputy Managing Director of the International Monetary Fund.

Jong-Wha Lee is Professor in the Department of Economics at Korea University.

Hong Liang is Economist, Asia and Pacific Department at the International Monetary Fund.

Henry Ma is Economist, Asia and Pacific Department at the International Monetary Fund.

William P. Mako is Senior Specialist in the Private Sector Development Unit, East Asia and Pacific Region at the World Bank.

Todd Mitton is Professor of Business Management at Brigham Young University.

Gyutaeg Oh is Professor in the School of Business Administration at Chung-Ang University and Director, Korea Fixed Income Research Institute.

Yung Chul Park is Professor in the Department of Economics at Korea University.

Changyong Rhee is Professor in the Department of Economics at Seoul National University and Director, Korea Fixed Income Research Institute.

Anthony Richards was Deputy Chief, Asia and Pacific Department at the International Monetary Fund, and is currently Chief Manager for International Markets and Relations at the Reserve Bank of Australia.

Jungho Yoo is Director of the Center for Economic Information at the Korea Development Institute.

Participants

Charles Adams was Senior Economic Advisor at the Asian Development Bank and is currently Assistant Director, Regional Office for Asia and the Pacific (Tokyo) at the International Monetary Fund.

Bijan B. Aghevli was Managing Director of Asian Economic and Policy Research at Chase Manhattan Bank, Hong Kong and is former Deputy Director, Asia and Pacific Department at the International Monetary Fund.

*Choong Yong Ahn** was Professor at the Department of Economics at Chung-Ang University and is currently President of the Korea Institute for International Economic Policy.

*Michael Callaghan** is Executive Director for Korea in the International Monetary Fund.

*Young-Rok Cheong** is Professor in the School of International and Area Studies at Seoul National University.

*Jonghwa Cho** is Director of the Department of International Macroeconomics and Finance and Senior Research Fellow at the Korea Institute for International Economic Policy.

Won-Dong Cho is Advisor to the Executive Director for Korea at the International Monetary Fund and was formerly Deputy Director General for Policy Coordination at Korea's Ministry of Finance and Economy.

Myung-Chang Chung is Director of the Research Department at the Bank of Korea.

Stephen Grenville was Deputy Governor at the Reserve Bank of Australia.

*Kyttack Hong** is Professor in the Department of Economics at Chung-Ang University.

Yusuke Horiguchi is Director of the Asia and Pacific Department of the International Monetary Fund.

Hasung Jang is Professor of Business Administration at Korea University.

Nyum Jin was Deputy Prime Minister and Minister of Finance and Economy of Korea.

Sung Hee Jwa is President of the Korea Economic Research Institute.

Jun Il Kim was Research Fellow at the Korea Development Institute and is currently Senior Economist, Policy Development and Review Department at the International Monetary Fund.

Pyung Joo Kim is Professor in the Department of Economics at Sogang University.

*Sun Bae Kim** is Managing Director and Head of Asia-Pacific Economic Research, Goldman Sachs, Hong Kong.

*Sung-Min Kim** is Head of Bond Market Analysis Team in the Department of Financial Markets at the Bank of Korea.

Yong Jin Kim is Professor in the Department of Economics at Dongduk Women's University.

*Chon Pyo Lee** is Professor in the Department of Economics at Seoul National University.

*Doowon Lee** is Professor in the Department of Economics at Yonsei University.

Jang-Yung Lee is Senior Counselor to the Minister of Finance and Economy of Korea.

*Keun-Young Lee** is Research Advisor in the Institute for Monetary and Economic Research of the Bank of Korea.

Kye-Sik Lee* is Visiting Professor at the Korea Development Institute's School of Public Policy and Management.

Kyung Tae Lee was President of the Korea Institute for International Economic Policy and is currently Ambassador to the Organization for Economic Cooperation and Development, Paris.

Robert McCauley* is Deputy Chief Representative, Asian and Pacific Office of the Bank for International Settlements, Hong Kong.

Rachel McCleary* is Director of the Religion, Economic Performance, and Political Structure Project at Harvard University.

Tarrin Nimmanahaeminda is a former Minister of Finance of Thailand.

Kap-Soo Oh* is Assistant Governor of the Financial Supervisory Service of Korea.

Se-Il Park* is Professor in the School of International and Area Studies at Seoul National University.

Hak Kil Pyo is Professor in the Department of Economics at Seoul National University.

Zia Qureshi was Lead Economist and Country Program Coordinator for Korea at the World Bank and is currently Sector Manager, Economic Policy at the World Bank.

Jaebong Ro* is Senior Research Fellow at the Korea Institute for International Economic Policy and Executive Director of Asia-Pacific Economic Cooperation Education Foundation, Korea.

Eisuke Sakakibara is Professor at Keio University and Director of the Global Security Research Centre in Japan.

Il SaKong is Chairman and CEO of the Institute for Global Economics, Korea and a former Minister of Finance and Economy of Korea.

Richard Samuelson* is Head of Korean Equities at UBS Warburg, Seoul.

Kwanho Shin* is Professor in the Department of Economics at Korea University.

Michael Spencer* is Chief Economist, Asia for Deutsche Bank, Hong Kong.

Rak-Yong Uhm* is a former Vice Minister of Finance and Economy of Korea and is currently Advisor of Yoon & Partners and Research Fellow at the Korea Institute of Finance.

Yunjong Wang* is Senior Research Fellow at the Korea Institute for International Economic Policy.

Joseph Winder* is President of the Korea Economic Institute of America in Washington, D.C.

Doo Yong Yang* is Research Fellow at the Korea Institute for International Economic Policy.

* Invited observers.

1 Introduction

David T. Coe and Se-Jik Kim

Korea's rapid growth since the early 1960s has indeed been a wonder. Over three decades until the mid-1990s, annual real income growth in Korea averaged over 8 percent. If a country grows by 8 percent each year, its national income will double every decade; if that growth trend continues for thirty years, national income will record a stunning tenfold increase. The small city-state economies of Hong Kong SAR and Singapore also enjoyed rapid growth comparable to Korea's over the same period. But it was a much bigger accomplishment for a country of almost 50 million people to sustain such high growth for more than three decades.

In stark contrast to this remarkable achievement, the honor student of economic growth was down on its luck in the late 1990s when it suddenly faced a financial crisis and its economy crashed. In 1997, consecutive bankruptcies of several large chaebol (Korean industrial conglomerates), coupled with financial crises or foreign exchange instability in Thailand and other East Asian countries, weakened investor confidence in Korea. As a result, foreign banks refused to roll over credit lines to Korean financial institutions and foreign investors pulled out of Korea *en masse*. By mid-December 1997, Korea's foreign exchange reserves were almost depleted. Korea, like a number of other economically vulnerable crisis-hit countries, had no choice but to ask for a rescue package from the International Monetary Fund. The crisis led to a sharp contraction of economic activity in 1998—a *negative* 6.7 percent growth, the worst in modern Korean history. Many Koreans considered the 1997 crisis to be the most critical national crisis since the Korean War in the early 1950s, and the worst national disgrace since the 1910 Japanese Annexation.

How can this sharp contrast between high growth and economic debacle be explained? What caused Korea's three decades of high growth to come to an abrupt halt? Was the crisis a short-term liquidity shock that would be quickly overcome in the context of an otherwise strong economy, or did it reveal more fundamental underlying problems built up during the thirty-year period of rapid economic growth?

Regardless of the causes, Korea was on the brink of bankruptcy in November 1997. On December 3 of that year, Korea and the IMF signed a three-year Stand-By Arrangement. The arrangement included financing for a total of US$58 billion from the IMF, the World Bank, the Asian Development Bank, and a group of countries—the largest rescue package in the history of the IMF.

The financing was not provided unconditionally. The condition was that Korea had to agree with the IMF about macroeconomic as well as financial and corporate restructuring policies during the three years of the program. The Fund recommended to the Korean government a short-term macroeconomic policy focused on high interest rates to restore the plummeting confidence of overseas investors during the early months of the crisis. A concerted effort to persuade foreign creditors to roll over short-term debt was also launched in late December 1997, followed by a more comprehensive rescheduling of maturing debt. The Fund also recommended that the government implement various policies to restructure and reform the heavily indebted corporate sector dominated by the chaebol and the financial sector saddled with non-performing loans.

Were the policies agreed with the IMF and pursued during the crisis appropriate? For example, did the high interest rate policy induce a fast economic recovery by stabilizing the foreign exchange market, or did it deepen the crisis and delay economic recovery? Was it really necessary to restructure the financial and corporate sectors, which, after all, had contributed importantly to thirty years of rapid growth? Indeed, was not there the risk that potentially misguided changes to the fundamental structure of the economy in reaction to a transitory shock would damage Korea's long-run growth potential? Or was it necessary to exorcise long-standing weaknesses masked by rapid economic growth?

There are many questions about the nature of the Korean crisis and the effectiveness of the policies adopted to resolve the crisis. In the early stage of the crisis, IMF recommendations to Korea and other crisis-hit Asian countries sparked heated debates, both in Korea and abroad. The disparity between arguments in favor of and against the IMF's policy recommendations was as sharp as the contrast between the high-growth period and the crisis. During the crisis and the early post-crisis period, it was difficult to judge which side—the critics or supporters of the IMF program—was correct, since the full effects of the policies adopted during the program were not yet apparent. A considered evaluation of the effectiveness and appropriateness of the IMF's policy recommendations during the crisis would require the passage of a certain amount of time.

In May 2001, three and one-half years after the outbreak of the crisis, the Korea Institute for International Economic Policy and the IMF organized a conference on the Korean crisis and recovery. The objective of the conference was to distill lessons based on an analysis of the crisis and recovery, and the effects of the policies implemented under the IMF-supported program. At the time of the conference, considerable data on the effects of the policies under the program were available, enabling serious study and analysis. In addition, as the IMF program came to an end in December 2000, the conference was able to review all policies implemented during the three years of the program. It was recognized, of course, that the papers presented at the conference would not provide unambiguous answers to all, or indeed even to most, of the key questions about the nature of the Korean crisis and the policies recommended by the IMF and implemented by the Korean government during the program.

There were a number of features that distinguished the conference from other conferences on currency or financial crises. First, most of the papers presented in the conference focused on a single country. Second, a wide spectrum of authors contributed papers, ranging from economists who were critical of IMF policies to staff of the IMF and the World Bank and Korean government officials who participated in the design, development, and implementation of economic policies. The organizers of the conference intended to invite diverse views and methodologies that would allow a balanced perspective on policies recommended by the IMF. Third, one-half of the papers were written by Korean economists from the crisis-hit country and one-half by foreign economists, and similarly for the discussants. This arrangement was intended to enhance synergy between studies by foreign experts with a comparative advantage of looking at the Korean crisis from a global perspective, and those by Korean economists with a comparative advantage in understanding the Korean economy, institutions, political economy, culture, data, and so on.

Thirteen papers on the Korean crisis and policy issues were presented at the two day conference. The first session was an overview of the Korean crisis and recovery and an overall assessment of the policies implemented during the IMF program. To begin, an "umbrella" paper by Ajai Chopra, Kenneth Kang, Meral Karasulu, Hong Liang, Henry Ma, and Anthony Richards—members of the IMF's Asia and Pacific Department then working on Korea—reviews the origins of the crisis and the macroeconomic stabilization and structural reform policies of the IMF-supported program (Chapter 2). Based on their review of the crisis and policies, they suggest that the primary factors causing the 1997 crisis were structural weaknesses—notably a weak financial sector with limited ability to assess risk and an over-leveraged corporate sector with insufficient attention to profitability—that left the Korean economy vulnerable to external shocks. Regarding monetary policy, the authors conclude that the initial policy of high interest rates, quickly supplemented by the coordinated debt rollover, helped stabilize the exchange rate and financial markets. On financial sector reforms, the authors underline achievements, such as closures of nonviable financial institutions and reforms of prudential regulations and supervision, but stress the need for the government to privatize its stake in a number of large banks. Corporate sector reforms also made progress in terms of financial disclosure and corporate governance, but Korea's corporate sector remains highly leveraged and continues to suffer from low profitability, indicating the need for more operational reforms. Based on this review, the authors draw lessons from the Korean experience, focusing on crisis prevention and management and also the sequencing of structural reforms.

The second paper, reflecting a Korean scholar's view of the overall IMF program, was presented by Yoon Je Cho (Chapter 3). While agreeing that the Korean crisis mainly reflected deep-rooted structural problems, he raises several concerns about the program. First, he conjectures that the high interest rate policy recommended by the IMF during the early stage of the crisis may have deepened the financial crisis rather than stabilized the exchange rate. A second problem was that the financial restructuring focused primarily on the banks without also improving regulatory oversight of the investment trust companies (ITCs). The rapid expansion of the ITCs contributed to the quick recovery in 1999, but delayed corporate restructuring and deepened financial sector problems. Cho also notes that money growth in a crisis-hit country may be affected more strongly by the regulatory actions of the supervisory authorities than by the policies of the monetary authorities, since the strengthening of regulatory rules may limit money creation by financial intermediaries. Finally, he emphasizes that too ambitious a reform program, such as the rapid introduction of global standards into the banking system, may not be digestible by the political economy of the country, and hence may backfire.

Starting with the second session, the papers looked into specific issues related to the Korean crisis and policies during the IMF-supported program. The first was the high interest rate policy recommended by the IMF during the early months of the crisis, one of the most hotly debated issues in the Korean program. Advocates argued that the high interest rate policy would help stabilize exchange rates by restoring confidence and fostering needed corporate restructuring, while critics, including Cho, argued that the policy is more likely to destabilize the exchange rate by raising corporate bankruptcies.

Chae-Shick Chung and Se-Jik Kim's paper empirically evaluates the effectiveness of the high interest rate policy in stabilizing the won/dollar exchange rate during the Korean crisis (Chapter 4). Using daily data for the exchange rate and Korean and U.S. interest rates during 1995-98, they estimate the underlying nonlinear dynamics of the exchange rate. Based on a nonlinear impulse response function analysis within the estimated model, they find that high interest rates induce depreciation for several days, followed by a substantial appreciation for an extended period of more than three months. In contrast, a low interest rate policy would not have a substantial impact on the exchange rate for very long, indicating an asymmetry in the exchange rate response to an interest rate shock. From the impulse function analysis, they also find that a reduction of interest rates to the pre-crisis level would not induce another serious depreciation. Their findings suggest that the interest rate policy recommended by the IMF, which was characterized by a sharp increase in interest rates at the onset of the crisis followed by a cutback after several months, contributed to the stabilization of the exchange rate.

A second issue addressed in this session was the role of the Korean chaebol. The corporate system based on chaebol has often been cast as a key culprit in the Korean financial crisis. But the specifics of how and to what extent the chaebol contributed to the financial crisis have received little attention.

The paper by Anne Krueger and Jungho Yoo addresses the role of the chaebol in the Korean crisis (Chapter 5). They find that the corporate sector's profitability fell to very low levels in the 1990s. Despite this deterioration, banks continued to "evergreen," or roll over, the chaebol's outstanding debt. When favorable circumstances did not materialize, the needed increase in evergreening by the banks was larger than their balance sheets could tolerate. The authors argue that the chaebol's low profitability, high leverage, and economic dominance meant that the Korean crisis was a disaster waiting to happen. Given the magnitude of leveraging of the chaebol prior to the crisis, the increase in the interest rate, not the foreign exchange crisis itself, probably triggered the financial crisis. The authors conclude, however, that failure to raise the interest rate would have resulted in larger capital outflows and perpetuated the foreign exchange crisis.

Session 3 addressed the issue of corporate sector reforms that are often considered, together with financial sector reform, as key structural reform policies of the IMF-supported program in Korea. Given the Korean corporate sector's endemic low profitability and heavy debt burden, as emphasized by Krueger and Yoo, the government has taken various measures to encourage corporate sector restructuring to overcome the crisis and lay the foundation for a sustained recovery in the real economy.

William Mako, a World Bank specialist who participated in the Korean program, derives lessons from Korea's recent experience in corporate restructuring in his paper (Chapter 6). He sets out a framework for corporate restructuring in a systemic crisis that emphasizes the importance of operational restructuring through discontinuation or sales of less profitable or loss-making non-core businesses, layoffs of excessive labor, and other cost-reduction measures to reduce corporate debt from unsustainable levels. Mako then documents a recurring pattern of corporate problems and restructuring in Korea during 1997-2000. Based on the experience of Korean firms, including those put into workout programs, he ascribes the recurrence of corporate problems to the failure to move beyond temporary financial stabilization measures—such as term extensions, rate reductions, and debt-equity conversions—and make substantial progress on operational restructuring of distressed corporations. He underlines that relatively few large corporations have emerged from court-supervised reorganization or been sold or liquidated since 1997. The slow operational restructuring is attributed partly to the reluctance of under-provisioned creditors to take additional losses on the sale of over-valued assets at realistic prices.

This session also addressed the government's policy of financial restructuring, which focused on the restructuring of banks with little attention paid, at least initially, to the investment trust companies. The bank-focused restructuring policy helped reduce banks' exposure to large corporates but allowed weak chaebol such as the Daewoo group to issue large amounts of corporate bonds through the ITCs, which were not closely supervised. Although the issuance of these bonds helped avoid a credit crunch in the late 1990s, the proceeds were used largely for further business expansion rather than restructuring. As a result, the corporate bond market faced another credit crunch in 2001 when the bonds matured.

The paper by Gyutaeg Oh and Changyong Rhee evaluates the downside of the bank-focused financial restructuring policy by measuring the amount of defaulted corporate bonds (Chapter 7). They find that issuers defaulted on 22 percent of the total value of corporate bonds issued from December 1997 to December 1999, and that 78 percent of the defaulted bonds were from the Daewoo group. This suggests that the bank-focused financial restructuring had large negative side effects, and that short-run liquidity problems could have recurred if there had not been significant corporate restructuring. The authors also find that the total amount of corporate debt remained virtually unchanged as a result of the bank-focused restructuring policy and the associated replacement of bank loans by corporate bonds, not by equities, suggesting that the corporate sector would remain vulnerable to adverse shocks. Finally, the authors criticize the 2001 government program under which the Korea Development Bank bought corporate bonds issued by chaebol companies that had difficulty rolling over their debt.

The important issue of the impact of the crisis on the labor market was explored in Session 4. The economic crisis and the ensuing output decline resulted in hundreds of thousands of newly unemployed Koreans, with an attendant deterioration in living conditions.

The paper by Dae Il Kim investigates the pattern of changes in employment, wages, and inequality after the crisis (Chapter 8). He reports that unemployment rose by more than a million between October 1997 and July 1998, and decreased rapidly thereafter as the economy recovered. By October 2000, however, the number of jobless people was still 200,000 higher than in October 1997. The post-crisis rise in unemployment, he suggests, reflects the increase in labor market participation of middle-aged women who started job search to supplement household income, and job losers who kept searching for new jobs instead of exiting the labor market. In addition, Kim notes that the rise in the share of temporary and daily workers reflected both public work programs and private firms' efforts to cut labor costs by hiring non-regular workers. He also documents the decline in nominal wages during the crisis, reflecting increased wage flexibility. Finally, he finds widening income inequality during the crisis: the poorest 10 percent suffered a decline of more than 20 percent in total and labor income, while the richest 10 percent enjoyed a 10 percent increase in their total income and only a 2 percent decrease in their labor income.

Another issue addressed in this session was the role of weak corporate governance in the East Asian crises. As emphasized by Krueger and Yoo and others, the heavy debt burden of the corporate sector in Korea and other crisis-hit Asian countries was a key factor behind the severity of the 1997-98 financial crisis. The question then arises as to why so many corporations in East Asian countries chose to take on so much debt. An explanation that has recently started to receive much attention is that high debt levels may reflect weak corporate governance, especially weak protection of minority shareholders and creditors.

Eric Friedman, Simon Johnson, and Todd Mitton's paper evaluates the extent to which corporate governance in Korea and other East Asian countries affected their corporate debt levels before the crisis (Chapter 9). Using data related to corporate governance and corporate debt levels in 1996, they find evidence that Asian firms with weaker firm-level corporate governance or investor protection tend to be more indebted. This correlation is particularly strong in countries with weak country-level institutions for corporate governance or legal protection for minority shareholders. The empirical results suggest that weak country- and firm-level corporate governance arrangements appear to have directly undermined investors' confidence at the start of the crisis. In light of these results, the authors emphasize that measures to strengthen the institutions of corporate governance should be at the top of the policy agenda.

Session 5 addressed important issues related to the effects of the crisis on the dynamic path of the Korean economy and the economies of other crisis-hit East Asian countries, including the nature of post-crisis recoveries and implications for long-term growth prospects. A variety of questions were addressed in the two papers: Are the recovery patterns in Asia similar to or different from other crises? Will the crisis-stricken Asian countries, including Korea, be able to return to their previous path of high growth?

Robert Barro's paper looked at the effects of the Asian financial crises on rates of economic growth and investment ratios in East Asia (Chapter 10). In the Asian crisis countries, economic growth rebounded in 1999-2000. In Korea, for example, real GDP bounced back from a 6.7 percent decline in 1998 to increase by 10.9 percent in 1999 and by 8.8 percent in 2000. But investment ratios did not significantly rebound, which might suggest that the crisis would have an adverse effect on long-term growth prospects. Based on cross-country growth regressions using panel data for 67 countries, Barro finds a negative effect of a currency crisis dummy variable on contemporaneous income growth and investment ratios. However, he finds no evidence of an adverse effect of currency crises on economic growth and investment in the five-year period following the crisis. If extrapolated to the crisis-hit Asian countries, he argues, this evidence suggests that their growth rates and investment ratios would return to those that would have prevailed without the currency crises.

The paper by Yung Chul Park and Jong-Wha Lee establishes a stylized pattern of post-crisis recoveries (Chapter 11). Based on 160 previous episodes of currency crises from 1970 to 1995, they find that a V-shaped recovery of real GDP growth following a crisis was not unique to the East Asian countries. Using cross-country regressions, they also show that the speedy recovery can be attributed to the depreciation of the real exchange rate, expansionary macroeconomic policies, and a favorable global environment. The authors find, however, that East Asia experienced a far sharper contraction and recovery, which they attribute to more severe liquidity crises and weaker corporate and bank balance sheets. They also find no evidence of a direct impact of the number of currency crises in the previous decades on the growth of per capita incomes.

The final session of the conference focused on the implications of the crisis for future crisis management and for reform of the international financial architecture. The 1997-98 crises in East Asia, following the Mexican crisis in 1995, raised serious concerns among scholars and policymakers about the stability of the current international monetary and financial system, and spurred debate about reforming various aspects of the international financial architecture. An important issue concerns the restructuring of foreign debts and private sector involvement in the process. In Korea, the restructuring of foreign debt in early 1998 was often considered to have been the key to regaining international investors' confidence and overcoming the liquidity crisis. The Korean experience of foreign debt restructuring and private sector involvement during the crisis provides interesting and useful practical lessons for countries that might face similar problems in future.

Woochan Kim and Yangho Byeon, who participated in the debt-restructuring process as a Korean government official, present a detailed account of the Korean restructuring of short-term foreign debts from the debtors' perspective in their paper (Chapter 12). Based on internal Korean government documents, they report the events, explain major decisions and the reasons they were taken, and describe detailed administrative aspects. They focus on how the government set the strategy to successfully induce foreign creditor banks to participate in the debt-maturity extension program and win favorable terms from the creditors. The authors ascribe the success of the Korean debt restructuring to various factors, including the adoption of a sequential approach instead of simultaneously making exchange and new cash offers, the government's guarantee of rolled-over debts combined with guarantee fees, the employment of outstanding veterans on emerging market debt restructuring, aggressive road shows, and the linking of the financial support package with international banks' voluntary maturity extension.

Involving the private sector in debt restructuring is only one of the many areas where proposals have been made to strengthen the international financial architecture. Some reforms have already been adopted, and others are being considered by the international community. Barry Eichengreen's paper evaluates the post-Asian-crisis progress in reforming the international financial architecture (Chapter 13). He praises the progress made in setting international standards, particularly in macroeconomic policy, transparency, financial market infrastructure, and financial regulation and supervision, which will enhance the stability of the international financial system. Regarding exchange rate systems, Eichengreen considers that the recent tendency for countries to vacate the middle ground between hard pegs and relatively free floats to be a step in the right direction. He also suggests that the reform initiatives taken so far address Asia's concerns incompletely at best, and a more satisfactory outcome requires more effective representation of Asian views in the multilateral institutions—for example, through reform in voting procedures.

Exchange rate regimes are at the center of the international financial architecture. During the 1997-98 Asian crisis, regimes of tightly managed nominal exchange rates and relatively closed capital markets collapsed. This has led economists and policymakers to focus on the question of the type of exchange rate regime that best maintains financial stability. A number of recent studies, including Eichengreen's, suggest that the choice for emerging market economies comes down to either free floats or hard pegs, leaving little room for intermediate regimes.

For Korea, however, Michael Dooley, Rudi Dornbusch, and Yung Chul Park propose adopting a managed float combined with certain rules governing intervention (Chapter 14). In particular, they make a set of proposals for Korean exchange rate and monetary policies. First, they propose sterilized intervention to limit day-to-day volatility of the Korean won against a well-defined basket of major foreign currencies. They propose, however, that the intervention not aim to attain a target level of the exchange rate, but rather a target level for the government's net foreign exchange reserves, with deviations of the actual reserves from the target level eliminated according to an announced rule. Together with such an exchange rate system, they propose that a flexible inflation-targeting rule be established so that interest rate policy can be used to stabilize output in the short run and inflation in the long run.

*   *   *

Economic developments in Korea in the year since the conference have, in general, been broadly consistent with the conclusions of many of the papers presented at the conference. The rapidity of Korea's recovery from the crisis was highlighted on August 23, 2001 when Korea repaid the IMF in full.

It was apparent at the time of the conference that economic growth was slowing sharply following the high levels of growth in 1999 and 2000. The reduction in growth was exacerbated by a global economic slowdown in the second half of 2001, partly caused by the economic effects of the terrorist attack on the United States of September 11. The Korean economy, however, performed better than most in 2001, with economic growth of 3 percent. Most forecasters, including the IMF, progressively revised up their projections during the first half of 2002, and by mid-year the consensus forecast was for the Korean economy to expand by 6-7 percent in 2002, with relatively low inflation and a comfortable external position. During the past year, Korea's progress in financial and corporate reform has been increasingly recognized by the international community, including by rating agencies, which have steadily upgraded Korea's sovereign debt ratings.

2 From Crisis to Recovery in Korea: Strategy, Achievements, and Lessons

*Ajai Chopra, Kenneth Kang, Meral Karasulu, Hong Liang, Henry Ma, and Anthony Richards**

Korea's three-year stand-by arrangement with the IMF expired on December 3, 2000. Looking back, a tremendous amount was accomplished during the IMF-supported program. First, macroeconomic fundamentals have improved and vulnerability to a balance of payments crisis has been sharply reduced. The economy recovered very rapidly from the deep recession in the immediate aftermath of the 1997 crisis; unemployment has been reduced; inflation has been contained; exports have been strong (although they have softened recently with the global slowdown); foreign direct investment and portfolio inflows have increased markedly; and foreign reserves have been built to record levels. Second, a wide range of structural reforms have made Korea's economy more open, competitive, and market driven. Significant progress has been made in stabilizing the financial system; addressing corporate distress; strengthening the institutional framework for corporate governance and financial sector supervision; liberalizing capital markets and foreign investment; enhancing transparency; and creating an environment where market discipline plays an increasingly important role.

These are impressive achievements and they surpass those in other crisis-affected economies. The IMF-supported program has thus been very successful and its goals—namely, to restore confidence and stabilize financial markets, and also to lay the foundation for a sustained recovery in the real economy and lower the chances of future crises—have been met. Moreover, the reforms initiated since the crisis will continue to yield benefits for years to come, and

*This paper draws on work done by Peter Hayward, Nigel Chalk, Jeanne Gobat, and numerous other colleagues in the IMF. We would also like to thank David Coe, Stanley Fischer, Jim Gordon, Peter Hayward, and Wanda Tseng for valuable comments and insights. The authors, alas, are solely responsible for any remaining errors or shortcomings.

in many cases the benefits will increase as practices and ways of doing business change.

Notwithstanding these achievements, the reforms are far from complete and there are still important structural weaknesses. Confidence has declined amid the growing perception that corporate and financial sector restructuring has been slow. Worries about the health of the corporate sector, a large portion of which is still saddled with weak cash flow and poor profitability, have intensified. Further, financial sector risk will remain high as long as the corporate sector remains weak. The uncertainty about domestic restructuring has been exacerbated by the simultaneous weakening in the external outlook, notably slower world growth and lower equity prices.

The slow progress on the structural front will increasingly exert a drag on the economy. Commendably, the government has increased its efforts to provide new impetus to reform and restructuring. Weak banks are being pressed to restructure and recapitalize, and more public funds have been allocated to assist this process. Creditors, in turn, are beginning to take a tougher attitude toward weak companies, forcing some important ones into court-supervised insolvency and wresting control of others. These are positive steps, but many challenges still remain.

The paper is structured as follows.[1] The following section reviews the origins of the twin currency and financial sector crisis in Korea and provides a summary of the events leading to the outbreak of the crisis. The third section discusses the strategy followed in responding to the crisis and its rationale. Where relevant this strategy is contrasted with alternative approaches that have been proposed. The subsequent two sections examine the strategy for restructuring the corporate and financial sectors—the heart of the structural reforms being pursued in Korea—and the achievements in these two areas. The sixth section reviews the factors that contributed to the unexpectedly rapid economic recovery following the crisis. The final section concludes with some general lessons and summarizes the challenges ahead.

The Origins and Outbreak of the Crisis

Most observers in 1997 were shocked to see Korea—the world's eleventh largest economy with an impressive record of macroeconomic performance—

---

[1]This paper reflects information available through March 2001. For a discussion of developments and policy issues since then see IMF (2002). In addition, an earlier version of the current paper, Chopra *et al.* (2001), contains an appendix on IMF conditionality in Korea.

swept into the financial crisis that was spreading through Southeast Asia. In retrospect, however, Korea's remarkable growth masked a number of structural weaknesses that left the economy vulnerable to external shocks and adverse shifts in investor sentiment.

Although a severe international liquidity squeeze was the immediate trigger for the crisis, structural weaknesses—notably a weak financial sector with little commercial orientation and limited ability to assess risk, combined with an overleveraged corporate sector that had invested heavily to gain market share with insufficient attention to profitability—were at the core of the problem. These weaknesses left the economy exposed to external shocks, including financial contagion and the sudden reversal of capital flows, and exacerbated the severity of the crisis. This section describes these vulnerabilities and the macroeconomic conditions leading up to the "twin" currency and banking crisis.

The Buildup in Short-Term Debt and Foreign Currency Exposure

The rapid buildup in private short-term external debt created the potential for liquidity problems. In Korea, as in many other Asian countries, bank financing historically played a leading role in economic development, with relatively undeveloped equity and debt capital markets. In 1993, when the government expanded the scope for short-term overseas borrowing by removing controls

Figure 1. Korea: Short-term External Debt and its Ratio to Usable International Reserves, 1993 - 2000

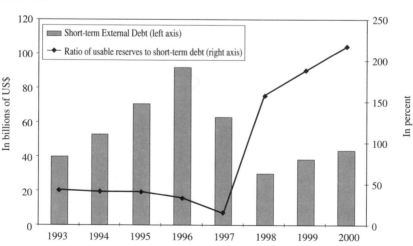

Source: Korean authorities and staff estimates.

on such borrowing by banks, it maintained tight restrictions on medium- and long-term capital and on direct access to capital markets by Korean corporations.[2] As a result, short-term external debt increased dramatically, creating a maturity mismatch, as Korean financial institutions borrowed short-term overseas in order to help finance long-term investments.[3] Short-term external debt rose from $40 billion in 1993 to $98 billion at end-September 1997, representing 54 percent of total external liabilities. Short-term external debt also quickly outpaced growth in usable reserves, creating the potential for liquidity problems and raising doubts about Korea's external position. The ratio of usable international reserves to short-term debt (on a residual maturity basis) fell from 42 percent in 1993 to 29 percent at end-1996.[4]

Prior to the crisis, strong macroeconomic performance and the relative stability of the exchange rate may have led both borrowers and lenders to

Figure 2. Korea: Exchange Rates, 1990 - 2000
(January 1990 = 100)

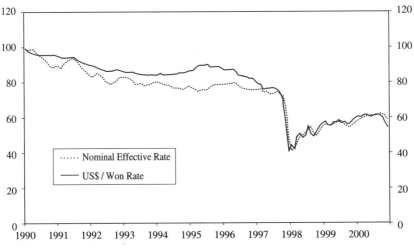

Source: Korean authorities and staff estimates.

---

[2]To limit possible takeovers by foreigners, foreign ownership of listed companies was restricted to 20 percent of capital with the limit on individual stakes set at 5 percent. See Johnston *et al.* (1999) for an overview of how capital account liberalization led to a buildup of short-term borrowing and a maturity mismatch in banks' balance sheets.

[3]At end-December 1997, short-term assets covered only 55 percent of short-term liabilities in commercial banks and only 25 percent in merchant banks.

[4]Reserves here exclude foreign exchange deposits lent to commercial banks accounts held abroad for liquidity support.

underestimate the risk of their foreign currency exposure. During the 1990s, Korea's exchange rate regime was essentially a tightly managed float with the won/dollar rate moving in a very narrow range. Together with the underdeveloped market for hedging, there was thus little incentive to hedge against exchange rate risk. The positive spread between domestic and foreign interest rates combined with the relative stability in the exchange rate also helped to draw large inflows of foreign capital.[5] Net capital inflows rose from around 2 percent of GDP during 1990-94 to around 5-6 percent in 1995-96, with much of these inflows being channeled through the banking system. The perceived low risk in Korean lending can be seen in the narrow international spreads, which in 1996 were around 65 basis points and rose only to about 80 basis points after the Thai baht devaluation in July 1997. The large unhedged foreign debt and its short maturity left Korea vulnerable to capital flight and a sharp devaluation.

Figure 3. Korea: Capital and Financial Account Balance, 1990 - 2000
(In percent of GDP)

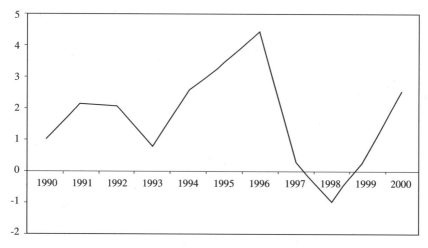

Source: Korean authorities and staff estimates.

---

[5]It should be noted, however, that the positive interest rate spread did not draw large inflows into the domestic bond and money markets, which were essentially closed to foreigners. A factor that contributed to the rise in overseas interbank lending to Korea was the more favorable capital requirement on lending to Korea when it became a member of the OECD in December 1996. Upon entry, the risk-weight for loans to Korean banks fell from 100 percent to 20 percent, which raised banks' return on capital and lowered the spreads for loans to Korean banks (Baliño and Ubide, 1999).

The Weak Financial System

Korea's weak financial system, lacking in market discipline and proper supervision, was ill-equipped to handle the large inflows. Liberalization of the financial system gained momentum in the early 1990s, leading to rapid growth in domestic credit and large capital inflows. A history of government intervention in the financial system (e.g., the directed credit policy of the 1970s and 1980s) not only left the financial system with large nonperforming loans, it also left it with little commercial orientation. In addition, weak regulatory and supervisory arrangements allowed banks to take on excessive risk without an adequate capital base to withstand shocks.[6]

Although the financial system was gradually liberalized in the early 1990s, substantial moral hazard remained, reflecting the legacy of government intervention and the perception that the government would not allow major banks or large Korean *chaebol* to fail.[7] Commercial banks were privatized starting in the mid-1980s, but the government still exerted significant control in the system through the appointment of senior management and through the large state-owned banks, such as the Korea Development Bank (KDB) and the Korea Export-Import Bank (KEXIM), which were important sources of financing for the large *chaebol*.

Government intervention in credit decisions also hampered the development of strong risk management and credit analysis skills. Because of the government's traditional role in guiding the allocation of credit and implicitly assuming the risk of directed lending, banks had little incentive to develop the necessary skills to assess risk and credit quality. Instead, lending decisions relied more upon collateral and inter-company guarantees rather than projected cash flows. Banks did not follow proper loan review processes, and management information systems were rudimentary. Financing was made available for large investment projects even when such investments added to overcapacity. Private sector credit grew during the 1990s at an average rate of close to 20 percent per year, helping to keep investment rates high. As a result, banks took on excessive risk in their lending and were under-capitalized.

---

[6]See Cho (1999) for discussion on how the sequencing of Korea's financial liberalization contributed to the buildup of these structural weaknesses in the system.

[7]Korea had a partial deposit insurance scheme but the funds were woefully insufficient to provide adequate coverage. Prior to the crisis, the government never allowed a bank to fail, which led depositors to believe that their deposits were implicitly insured. Insolvent banks were either taken over by the government, forced to restructure with public funds, or merged with a healthy bank.

The misallocation of credit was facilitated by a weak system of prudential controls. Loan classification standards and provisioning were less stringent in Korea than in many OECD countries and were based upon backward looking criteria that focused more on borrowers' prior loan servicing record and availability of collateral rather than their future capacity to repay.[8] Loose restrictions on banks' risk concentration led to large exposures to certain conglomerates that were heavily leveraged and dependent mainly upon bank financing. In addition, the bulk of corporate bonds issued carried a bank guarantee that exposed the financial system to even more corporate risk. Accounting and disclosure standards were also below international best practices, and market value accounting was not widely practiced. The lack of a liquid bond market and of transparency in the equity market also hindered the development of strong corporate governance and market discipline.

The problem of weak prudential controls was compounded by fragmented supervision and widespread forbearance. Supervision of the financial sector was split between the Office of Banking Supervision at the Bank of Korea (commercial banks) and Ministry of Finance and Economy (specialized banks and nonbank financial institutions). The lack of a unified supervisory framework created opportunities for regulatory arbitrage and permitted unsound banking practices to continue. Furthermore, regulatory forbearance made enforcement nontransparent and undermined the credibility of the system.

In addition, less stringent regulatory requirements on nonbanks triggered an expansion in their activities, cutting into the profitability of the banking sector. Merchant banks, as wholesale financial institutions engaging in underwriting, leasing, and unsecured short-term lending, competed directly with the commercial banks and attracted an increasing share of funds by offering a wide range of accounts and instruments. Many were owned by the large *chaebol* and invested their funds in short-term corporate paper. Banks also faced competition in their trust business from the growth of the investment trust sector. As a result, banks faced declining profits and were unable to generate sufficient income to strengthen their capital base.

---

[8]Nonperforming loans were defined as loans that had been in arrears for six months or more, compared with a more typical definition of three months or more. Official data, which showed nonperforming loans falling between 1993 and 1996, may have obscured the true health of banks' balance sheets. After accounting for insufficient provisioning of loan losses and the underreporting of nonperforming loans, Hahm and Mishkin (2000) show that banks' balance sheets deteriorated steadily throughout the 1990s. This assertion is partly supported by the poor performance of the bank stock price index beginning in late 1995, suggesting that the stock market was aware of the severity of the asset quality problem well before the crisis.

The result was an under-capitalized financial system that was highly vulnerable to external shocks and rising corporate distress. When export prices slumped and a number of *chaebol* went bankrupt in 1997, banks experienced a rapid deterioration in their asset quality and a loss of capital. By end-1997, 14 of the 27 commercial banks had measured capital adequacy ratios below 8 percent even under the lax accounting standards.[9]

A Highly Leveraged Corporate Sector

Structural weaknesses in the corporate and financial sector were closely intertwined because of firms' heavy reliance on bank financing. As a result, banks were taking on risks that in most countries were borne by shareholders. In view of their large exposure, both in terms of direct lending and through bond guarantees, banks faced a systemic risk from the growing problems in the corporate sector. Corporations, in turn, depended upon the health of the banks for their financing, and in some cases, their survival.

Prior to the crisis, the corporate sector was highly leveraged and suffering from poor profitability. The history of directed lending and government bailouts

Figure 4. Korea: Manfacturing Debt-Equity Ratios, 1988 - 2000

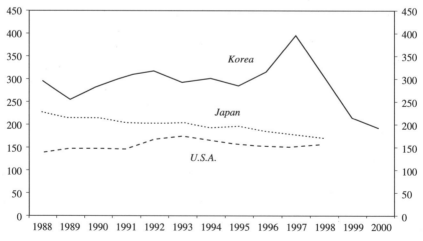

Source: Korean authorities and staff estimates.

---

[9]No doubt many of these would have shown much lower capital ratios had assets been valued appropriately.

of distressed companies encouraged excessive risk taking and overinvestment.[10] Between 1993 and 1996, Korean industrial conglomerates (*chaebol*) launched a series of ambitious investment projects, but these investments failed to generate adequate returns to cover the cost of capital.[11] Because of restrictions that favored debt over equity financing, *chaebol* financed much of their investment with short-term borrowing from banks. As a result, the debt-to-equity ratio of the manufacturing sector jumped from 300 percent to 400 percent— double the OECD average—between 1996 and 1997. Even worse, the average debt-to-equity ratio for the top-30 *chaebol* rose from 387 percent to 518 percent over the same period.[12]

The high level of corporate debt cut into profitability and left the sector vulnerable to a cyclical downturn or a cutoff in credit lines. Profitability indicators in the manufacturing sector, such as return on assets and net profit margins, already low relative to other countries, all exhibited sharp declines after 1995, and turned negative in 1997. One reason for the poor performance was the high interest expense on accumulated debt that was about three times higher than in Germany, Japan, Taiwan Province of China, and the United States. In addition, a major part of this debt was short-term (60 percent of total liabilities in 1996) in the form of commercial paper and promissory notes, creating the potential for a liquidity squeeze.

The overexpansion of the sector was associated with the perception that *chaebol* were "too big to fail." With few exceptions, the government repeatedly bailed out large failing companies instead of leaving their fate to the markets or the courts.[13] As a result of the implicit guarantee on their risky investments, companies faced an artificially low cost of capital that allowed excessive expansion. Even struggling companies faced little pressure to restructure through downsizing and divestiture of loss-making affiliates.

Poor corporate governance encouraged excessive risk taking and shielded managers from market discipline. The complex web of cross-guarantees and cross-equity investments within the Korean *chaebol* created soft-budget constraints for weaker affiliates and diluted accountability for poor business decisions. Cross-guarantees allowed weaker affiliates easy access to credit mar-

---

[10]See Graham (2001) for a discussion of Korea's policy of "socialization" of risk, starting in the 1960s, and its consequences (including excessive risk taking) over time.

[11]See Claessens *et al.* (1998) for an analysis of the financial structure and performance of the corporate sectors in the Asian crisis countries prior to 1997, and evidence that many of the now apparent vulnerabilities in the corporate sector can be traced as far back as the early 1990s.

[12]In addition to the rise in debt-financed investment, the spike in the debt-equity ratio in 1997 also reflected the overshooting of the exchange rate.

[13]With just two exceptions—Kukje in 1985 and Woosung Construction in 1996—the government did not allow a big business or nationwide bank to fail until 1997.

kets, and they also had the potential for bringing the whole group down by allowing financial distress in one affiliate to affect the rest of the group.[14] Further, cross-shareholdings shielded managers from market discipline and led to nontransparent corporate decision making by allowing a large investor, typically a family owner, to control the company with little of his own capital at risk. This lack of corporate transparency also deterred outsiders from investing in Korean companies.[15]

The lack of well-developed capital markets and adequate financial reporting and disclosure standards limited the role of market discipline. Korean corporate financial statements did not conform to internationally accepted accounting and auditing standards and prevented a clear assessment of a company's health.[16] Government restrictions on the capital markets and foreign direct investment limited corporations' access to nonbank funding and other longer-term instruments while protecting managers from hostile foreign takeovers. Mergers and acquisitions were rare because of regulations limiting takeovers.

Problems in the corporate sector began surfacing as early as January 1997 with a string of large bankruptcies. Hanbo Steel, Korea's second largest steel maker and fourteenth largest *chaebol* was the first to go under, followed by five more *chaebol* before the financial crisis struck in November. These large bankruptcies combined with the rising bankruptcies among small and medium-sized enterprises quickly eroded the asset position of financial institutions and raised doubt about the soundness of the entire financial system. It was ironic that these bankruptcies, which were the precursor to the crisis, were in some sense a manifestation of government policies to increase market discipline in the Korean economy, as part of the liberalization accompanying OECD membership.

---

[14]The total value of these cross-guaranteed debts for the top-30 *chaebol* amounted to W70 trillion at end-April 1997 or 91 percent of total equity of these affiliates. See Gobat (1998) for a discussion of corporate governance in Korea prior to the crisis.

[15]Johnson *et al.* (2000) find empirical evidence in crisis countries that weak corporate governance can also leave a country vulnerable to a sudden loss of investor confidence, resulting in a collapse in the exchange rate and a sharp fall in asset prices. Krueger (2000) notes that the declining rate of return on capital in the 1990s exposed the cost of favoritism to large firms (so called "cronyism"), resulting in a slower rate of economic growth. Shin and Park (1999) compare the financing constraints of the *chaebol* and non-*chaebol* firms and find that largely as a result of the soft budget constraint within the *chaebol* structure, *chaebol* firms were able to invest more than non-*chaebol* despite the poorer growth opportunities. Finally, Joh (2000) finds firm-level evidence that prior to the crisis, poor corporate governance, such as through conflicts of interest among shareholders and business groups, lowered firm performance.

[16]As combined financial statements were not required for the entire group, it was nearly impossible for investors to understand the internal finances of the *chaebol*, including the separation of strong and weak affiliates.

Macroeconomic Developments Before the Crisis

Korea's impressive macroeconomic record prior to the crisis may have blinded most observers to the structural weaknesses in the financial and corporate sector that left Korea vulnerable to an economic crisis. Macroeconomic fundamentals appeared sound and offered few clues as to the timing and severity of the crisis. As a result, foreign investors, attracted by high returns and the region's impressive growth record, failed to carefully assess the risks involved and continued to pour money into Korea with low spreads. However, as external conditions began to worsen in 1997, these financial vulnerabilities became evident and helped quickly turn market sentiment against Korea. Growth in Korea remained strong until shortly before the crisis (Table 1). Amid an investment boom, growth averaged 8 percent per year over 1994-96. It was in 1997 that growth fell to 5 percent due to a cut back in investment and slowing consumption. Although export volumes remained strong before the crisis, slumping export prices led to a sharp decline in export revenues. Korea's terms of trade fell by 22 percent from 1995 to 1997, driven largely by a worldwide slump in semiconductor prices, one of Korea's main export items.[17]

Neither inflation nor the real exchange rate showed signs of growing imbalance. During the boom of 1994-96, broad money and credit to the private sector grew at an average annual rate of 20 percent. The authorities tightened monetary policy starting in the second half of 1996 over concerns of the inflationary impact of the sustained expansion. The policy was successful in containing average inflation at $4\frac{1}{2}$ percent in 1997. Despite the inflation, the real exchange rate remained fairly stable. Although the exchange rate in real effective terms appreciated by about 5 percent between 1994 and 1996, it declined by 1 percent since 1990.[18]

Domestic investment rates were high before the crisis, but the overall efficiency of investment appeared to have declined. Gross domestic investment averaged over 37 percent of GDP during 1994-96, falling to 34 percent in

---

[17]See Corsetti *et al.* (1999) and IMF (1999) for an overview of the macroeconomic fundamentals in the Asian countries prior to the crisis. In Korea's case, as discussed in Gordon (2001), strong export volumes and slumping export prices were not unrelated—Korean producers played a major role in the oversupply of memory chips that emerged in the world market in 1996.

[18]Empirical studies of the degree of exchange rate misalignment prior to the crisis do not suggest that the won was overvalued. For example, Chinn (1999) finds that the won was substantially undervalued prior to the crisis, while Marquez (1999) finds that the real exchange rate was not misaligned through 1996.

Table 1. Korea: Summary Indicators, 1990-2000

	1990	1991	1992	1993	1994	1995	1996	1997	1998	1999	2000
Real GDP (percent change)	9.0	9.2	5.4	5.5	8.3	8.9	6.8	5.0	-6.7	10.9	8.8
Final domestic demand	14.5	9.8	3.3	5.7	8.4	9.5	7.3	1.2	-13.8	7.4	7.7
Consumption	9.2	7.9	5.6	5.4	7.1	8.2	7.2	3.2	-9.8	9.1	6.2
Gross fixed investment	25.9	13.3	-0.7	6.3	10.7	11.9	7.3	-2.2	-21.2	3.7	11.0
Stock building[1]	-1.4	0.6	-0.1	-1.1	1.2	-0.1	0.6	-2.0	-5.5	5.4	-0.9
Net foreign balance[1]	-2.1	-2.0	1.2	1.1	-1.5	0.2	-1.1	5.7	12.3	-0.8	3.5
Saving and investment (in percent of GDP)											
Gross national saving	36.9	37.0	36.1	35.8	35.5	35.4	33.5	32.5	33.9	32.7	31.1
Gross domestic investment	37.7	39.9	37.3	35.5	36.5	37.2	37.9	34.2	21.2	26.7	28.7
Prices (percent change)											
Consumer prices (average)	8.6	9.3	6.2	4.8	6.3	4.5	4.9	4.4	7.5	0.8	2.3
Consumer price (end-period)	9.4	9.2	4.6	5.8	5.6	4.7	4.9	6.6	4.0	1.4	3.2
GDP deflator	10.7	10.9	7.6	7.1	7.7	7.1	3.9	3.1	5.1	-2.0	-1.6
Employment and wages											
Unemployment rate	2.5	2.3	2.4	2.8	2.4	2.0	2.0	2.6	6.8	6.3	4.1
Wages, manufacturing (annual percent change)	20.1	16.9	15.6	10.8	15.4	9.9	12.3	5.1	-3.1	14.7	8.6
Consolidated central government (in percent of GDP)											
Revenues[2]	17.9	17.3	17.8	18.6	19.1	19.3	20.4	20.6	21.8	22.4	25.8
Expenditure	18.6	19.2	18.5	18.3	19.0	19.0	20.4	22.3	26.0	25.7	24.8
Balance[2][3]	-0.7	-1.9	-0.7	0.3	0.1	0.3	0.0	-1.7	-4.3	-3.3	1.1
Consolidated Central Government Debt[4]								8.8	12.7	24.7	33.2	30.8
Money and credit (end of period)											
M3	28.7	23.6	21.8	19.0	24.7	19.1	16.7	13.9	12.5	8.0	8.8
Yield on corporate bonds	16.4	18.9	16.2	12.6	12.9	13.8	11.9	13.4	15.1	8.9	10.0
Trade (percent change)											
Export volume	6.2	9.9	8.5	6.9	13.8	24.9	20.0	17.2	19.5	12.6	20.6
Import volume	12.0	16.7	2.1	6.4	21.5	21.2	17.2	4.1	-23.1	29.5	18.4
Terms of trade	-2.8	0.3	0.1	4.3	1.2	-3.5	-11.7	-11.4	-3.9	-2.1	-12.8
Balance of payments (in billions of U.S. dollars)											
Exports, f.o.b.	63.7	70.5	76.2	82.1	95.0	124.6	130.0	138.6	132.1	145.2	175.8
Imports, f.o.b	66.1	77.3	78.0	79.8	97.8	129.1	144.9	141.8	90.5	116.8	159.2
Current account balance	-2.0	-8.3	-3.9	1.0	-3.9	-8.5	-23.0	-8.2	40.4	24.5	11.0
Current account balance (in percent of GDP)	-0.8	-2.8	-1.3	0.3	-1.0	-1.7	-4.4	-1.7	12.7	6.0	2.4
Short-term debt cover	...	...	0.4	0.4	0.4	0.4	0.3	0.1	1.6	1.9	2.2
Usable gross reserves[5]											
In billions of U.S. dollars (end of period)	11.3	10.1	13.8	16.9	21.5	28.5	29.4	9.1	48.5	74.1	96.1
In months of imports of goods and services	1.8	1.4	1.8	2.1	2.2	2.2	2.0	0.6	5.1	6.2	6.0
External debt[6]											
In billions of U.S. dollars	...	...	62.9	67.0	88.7	127.1	164.4	159.2	148.7	137.1	136.3
In percent of GDP	...	...	20.0	19.4	22.0	26.0	31.6	33.4	46.9	33.8	29.8
Exchange rate (period average)											
Won per U.S. dollar	707.8	733.4	780.7	802.7	803.4	771.3	804.5	951.3	1,402.1	1,188.9	1,131.1
Nominal effective exchange rate (1995=100)	122.5	116.5	106.6	103.8	100.9	100.0	100.6	92.4	64.5	73.1	78.4

Sources: Data provided by the Korean authorities; and staff estimates and projections.

[1]Contribution to GDP growth.

[2]Excluding privatization receipts.

[3]Prior to 2000, the civil service pension fund is excluded.

[4]Including government guaranteed restructuring bonds issued by KDIC and KAMCO.

[5]Excluding deposits at overseas branches and subsidiaries of domestic banks.

[6]Includes offshore borrowing of domestic financial institutions and debt contracted by overseas branches of domestic financial institutions.

Figure 5. Korea: Real Effective Exchange Rate and Inflation, 1990 - 2000

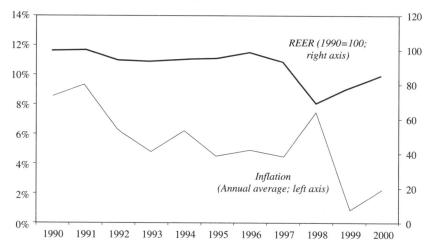

Source: Korean authorities and staff estimates.

1997. However, the incremental output to capital ratio (ICOR), a crude meas-ure of overall investment efficiency, declined from 0.24 in 1995 to 0.14 in 1997 suggesting that investment productivity was falling in the years prior to the crisis. This is consistent with the sharp decline in manufacturing profita-bility after the large *chaebol* launched their investment drive in 1995.

The current account deficit widened somewhat in 1996 but remained in a range that was considered sustainable given Korea's external debt position. Korea's current account deficit averaged 2 ½ -3 percent of GDP before the crisis, and external debt as a share of GDP was about 30 percent in 1996. At first glance, Korea's historically high domestic savings rate and low debt ser-vice burden (8 percent of export earnings in 1996) suggested that its external debt position was sustainable provided banks were able to refinance their short-term obligations. The current account deficit widened to 4.4 percent of GDP in 1996, largely because of the slowdown in exports. The deficit continued to widen in the first quarter 1997, but then fell sharply thereafter as import de-mand weakened and exports picked up.

The measured fiscal position appeared sound with the budget either in surplus or in balance in the four years prior to the crisis. Korea had a record of fiscal prudence such that the share of public sector debt in GDP was below 10 percent at end-1996—one of the lowest among OECD countries. The true fiscal position, however, may have been understated to some extent by the presence of large nonperforming loans and their implicit government guarantee that would have raised the public sector debt burden significantly if these implicit costs were included.[19]

The Outbreak of the Crisis

The changing external environment—including increased oil prices, falling semiconductor prices, and the depreciation of the yen—and slowing domestic economy gradually brought to the forefront the weaknesses in Korea's corporate and financial sectors that had been hidden behind its impressive growth record. The decline in equity prices was the clearest signs of growing problems in the corporate and financial sectors. The overall market index (KOSPI) fell by over 40 percent from its peak in November 1994 to end-1996. The decline in bank share prices was somewhat larger (46 percent over the same period), suggesting that the market was aware of the growing risks to the financial system from the difficulties in the corporate sector. Problems in the corporate sector began surfacing as early as January 1997 with a string of large bankruptcies.

The collapse of several large *chaebol,* combined with the rising failures among small and medium-sized enterprises, quickly spilled over to the banks, eroding their capital positions and raising doubt about the soundness of the entire financial system. Uncertainty about the true extent of nonperforming loans and declining corporate earnings contributed to the continued decline in equity prices. In July 1997, several Korean banks were placed on a negative credit outlook by credit rating agencies.

The devaluation of the Thai baht in July 1997 turned market sentiment against the region. International banks began to modestly reduce their exposure to Korean financial institutions and to cut back on their short-term credit lines because of concerns about the health of Korea's financial system. Accordingly, in August 1997, the government announced a blanket guarantee on overseas borrowing by Korean financial institutions.[20] Nonetheless, until mid-October, most observers thought that Korea would be spared from any major impact, and the rollover ratio for interbank credit lines averaged over 85 per-

---

[19]Burnside *et al.* (1999) argue that the large implicit guarantee to the failing financial sectors in Korea and Thailand was the primary cause of the crisis by raising the *prospective* fiscal deficits that would be needed to bailout the financial sector and casting doubt on the government's ability to finance these costs without resorting to higher seignorage.

[20]The government issued a public statement on August 25, 1997 that the "Korean Government will ensure the payment of debt liabilities by Korean financial institutions." The legal status of such a guarantee was, however, indeterminate as the procedure required for government guarantees (approval by the National Assembly) was not taken.

cent. However, in the second half of October a number of events combined to worsen sentiment against Korea. On October 17, the authorities in Taiwan Province of China abandoned their defense of the New Taiwan dollar leading to a substantial depreciation. Further, intense pressures on the Hong Kong SAR stock market in the second half of October spread to other regional markets and even the to U.S. and European markets. Then, on October 24, Standard and Poor's downgraded Korea from AA- to A+, citing corporate and financial problems and the government's response, including the rescue of Korea First Bank and the bailout of the Kia group. These developments struck a tremendous blow to market confidence in Korea, leading to capital flight and a rapid withdrawal of credit lines. Once market participants began to scrutinize Korea, the structural weaknesses of the economy began to look more stark. Capital flight took place as foreign investors started to pull out of Korea, and domestic residents shifted funds to foreign currency deposits.

The lack of transparency in key financial data contributed to the uncertainty in the markets and inflated the fears of international lenders. Official data provided incomplete disclosure on key variables, such as BOK's international reserves, forward exposure, and the amount of nonperforming loans. In addition, official data on external debt omitted debt contracted by offshore entities, which was estimated to have understated the true level of external indebtedness by a half. The lack of transparency served to undermine the government's attempt to stabilize the situation and exacerbated the severity of the crisis.

By November, Korea was confronted with a "twin crisis" —a banking and a currency crisis—that complicated the government's handling of the situation. The wave of corporate bankruptcies and rising nonperforming loans created doubts about the overall health of the financial system and drove foreign banks to withdraw their credit lines to Korea. The drying up of foreign credit lines in turn made it more difficult for Korean banks to roll over their large stock of short-term external debt, creating the potential for a currency crisis and contributing to capital flight and further falls in the value of the won. It should be noted, though, that the currency crisis in Korea was not a classic speculative attack. Capital controls in 1997 were such that the won was difficult to short, and the crisis reflected a foreign currency creditor panic, rather than an attack on the won by speculators. That is, the reason that the won came under pressure was not that spectators were selling it short, but rather that Korean banks were scrambling to find foreign currency to meet loans that were no longer being rolled over. Government support of distressed banks through foreign exchange deposits in overseas branches and intervention in the foreign exchange market were ineffective and served only to deplete the BOK's supply of usable reserves. Despite the sharp turn for the worse in the external financing situation in late October, the authorities waited until November 21 to approach the Fund.

The Crisis Resolution Strategy

The objectives of Korea's crisis resolution strategy were, first and foremost, to restore confidence and stabilize financial markets; and second, to lay the foundation for a sustained recovery in the real economy and lower the chances of future crises. The policy strategy was three-pronged, combining macroeconomic policy adjustment, structural reforms, and the largest financing package in IMF history. To ease the dislocations that inevitably accompany reforms, the program also contained a substantial expansion of the social safety net.

Stabilizing the Exchange Rate

At the onset of the crisis in November and December of 1997, the immediate priority was to stabilize the situation in financial markets and to bolster investor confidence, especially in the foreign exchange market. After trading at about W910 per U.S. dollar in September and early October, the won began to depreciate amid pressures on stock markets in Hong Kong SAR and beyond.

Figure 6. Reserves
(In billions of U.S. dollars)

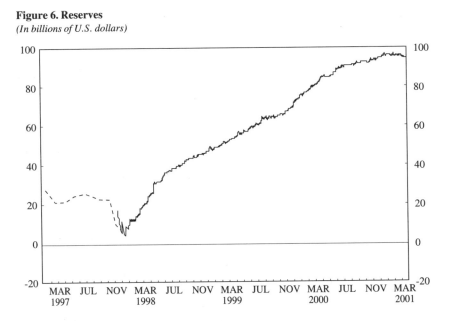

The depreciation was initially quite gradual, but by mid-November the won had weakened through the W1,000 level and by the time of the announcement of agreement on the stand-by arrangement with the IMF on December 3 it had fallen to about W1,150. At the same time, the authorities had absorbed much of the exchange market pressures through intervention; combined with Bank of Korea deposits being moved to offshore branches of Korean banks that were facing problems in rolling over international interbank credit lines, reserves fell from a reported $30 billion at end-September to only $6 billion of "usable" reserves by early December.[21]

The December 3 program was based on the expectation that a large financing package, comprehensive structural policy measures, and firm monetary and fiscal policies would be sufficient to restore market confidence. The monetary policy component was directed both at containing inflation to avoid an inflation-depreciation spiral and at limiting downward pressure on the won by raising nominal returns on won assets and thereby slowing capital outflows and limiting speculation. In operational terms this translated into an increase in interest rates and a reduction in monetary growth rates. The overnight call rate was immediately increased from 15 percent to 25 percent (and the legal ceiling on interest rates was increased and then removed). The intention was that the increase in interest rates would be only temporary and would be reversed once markets stabilized. In addition to the funds being made available

Figure 7. Won-Dollar and Overnight Call Rates

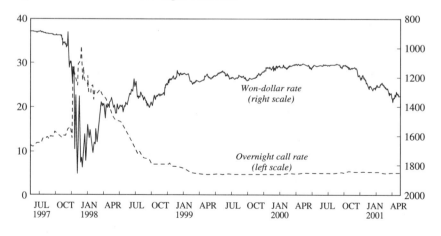

under the program, the foreign exchange constraint was to be further eased by an acceleration of the program to liberalize capital flows into the equity, bond and money markets. There was also to be close monitoring of the provision of foreign exchange to overseas branches of Korean commercial banks, with any further such financing to be at penal interest rates and to be discontinued by the end of December 1997.

Box 1. Literature on the Origins of the Crisis in Korea

Explanations on the origins of the crisis vary, from the lack of liquidity to problems of moral hazard and investor panic. Although almost all would agree that the rapid buildup of unhedged short-term external debt played a major role, many disagree to what extent underlying structural weaknesses in the Korean economy caused the crisis and contributed to its severity, and consequently, how policies to address the crisis should have been formulated.

A case of temporary illiquidity

Some view the crisis as mainly a case of "temporary illiquidity" brought upon by the rapid buildup in short-term external debt (Feldstein (1998, 1999)). Korea was solvent and its macroeconomic fundamentals were sound, but faced questions on whether it was liquid enough to meet its short-term obligations. The appropriate policy response would be to relieve the liquidity constraint either through massive up-front assistance or by coordinated action by creditor banks to restructure short-term debt. The argument goes one step further to claim that the IMF's early emphasis on structural reforms may have exacerbated the crisis by raising doubts as to whether Korea would be able to service its external debt without first resolving its deeply-rooted structural problems.

A self-fulfilling panic

Other explanations focus on the inherent instability in financial markets that led to a self-fulfilling panic by investors (Sachs and Radelet (1998, 1999)). As evidence, proponents point out that the underlying structural weaknesses in the economy have existed for some time, including during periods of rapid growth, and do not offer enough of an explanation for the severity of the crisis, i.e. "the scale of the punishment seems wholly disproportionate to the crime" (Krugman (1999)).

Under this scenario, rational investors have an incentive to pull their money out of a country if they feel that other investors are likely to do the same, pushing the economy into a "bad equilibrium" and causing a financial panic. The key precondition was Korea's high level of short-term external liabilities relative to its short-term assets that created the incentive to move before others in order to avoid being unpaid. In some sense, short-term borrowing imposed a negative externality on the economy by raising the probability of a liquidity crisis and speculative attack (Furman and Stiglitz (1998)).

Moral hazard

Some have used an asymmetric information framework to understand the causes of the crisis (Frankel (1999), Hahm and Mishkin (2000)). According to this line of thinking, the rising uncertainty and deterioration in the balance sheets of Korean banks and corporations prior to the crisis may have created asymmetric information problems that left Korea vulnerable to a financial crisis. In this environment, banks found it more difficult to distinguish between good and bad borrowers, and corporations with falling net worth had a greater incentive to make risky investments.

In addition, the impression that *chaebol* were "too big to fail" led banks to overlend to these large conglomerates and underestimate the riskiness of their loans. The combination of these factors worsened adverse selection and moral hazard problems and made the Korean economy highly susceptible to a financial panic. The relatively favorable macroeconomic fundamentals in the years before the crisis may have masked the underlying weaknesses and vulnerabilities in the economy, leading to overinvestment and an underestimation of the risk of a potential crisis.

Underlying Structural Weaknesses and Policy Distortions

Here, structural weaknesses in the corporate and financial sectors, in combination with a sharp build up in short-term external debt, were at the root of the crisis and made Korea vulnerable to a reversal of capital flows and financial contagion (Corsetti *et al.* 2000; Fischer 1998; Goldstein 1998; IMF 1999a, 1999b). These fundamental imbalances, brought about by a long history of policy distortions, triggered a "twin crisis" —a financial and currency crisis—and explain how market overreaction and investor panic could have had such a severe impact on economic activity, asset prices, and the exchange rates given the modest weakening of macro fundamentals prior to the crisis. This explanation is also more in line with the IMF's views on the origins of the crisis and formed the basis for the IMF program's approach which combined financing, macroeconomic policy adjustment, and structural reforms to resolve the crisis.

The magnitude of the financing made available to support the program—the largest in the history of the IMF—was notable. The IMF committed SDR 15.5 billion (or about $21 billion)—an unprecedented 19 times Korea's IMF quota. The funds were to be available over a three-year period, albeit with an expectation that if the situation was successfully stabilized some of the subsequent drawings would not be needed and repayments could occur early. The initial drawing was SDR 4.1 billion ($5.6 billion), with a further SDR 2.6 billion ($3.6 billion) to become available after two weeks upon the first program review. The program was approved under accelerated procedures established under the emergency financing mechanism and subsequent drawings were to be financed in part from the IMF's new Supplemental Reserve Facility (SRF).[22] The World Bank and Asian Development Bank pledged a further $ 14 billion, and a group of other countries pledged an additional $23 billion in a "second line of defense." The overall package of $58 billion was expected to contribute to stabilizing financial markets.

It soon became apparent that the December 3 program had not been successful in turning sentiment around. On several days during the second week of December, the won fell by the 10 percent daily limit (which was eliminated

---

[22]The SRF is designed to assist countries facing exceptional balance of payments problems created by large short-term financing needs, and provided funds at higher interest rates and shorter maturities than conventional IMF lending. Drawings under the SRF began on December 18, 1997, two weeks after the stand-by arrangement was approved. See Chopra *et al.* (2001) for the full schedule of drawings.

on December 16) and trading then essentially stopped for the day. By the end of this week, the currency traded at about W1,700 per dollar, a further depreciation of about 30 percent since the announcement of the program. By the time of the first review of the program on December 18, usable reserves had fallen to $4 billion.

The major reason for the failure to turn sentiment about was the overhang of Korea's massive short-term external debt.[23] Short-term interbank credit had been Korea's main source of external credit, and markets feared the worst about the magnitude of total short-term debt, with estimates of about $100 billion. Given the fragile situation, there were strong incentives for individual foreign banks to refuse to roll over credit lines. In these circumstances, increased official financing to bolster central bank reserves would simply allow further cutbacks in credit lines. On some days in mid-December, the rollover rate fell to 5-15 percent.

The pressures on the won in mid-December were also aggravated by sharp downgrades in Korea's external credit rating. The two major international

Figure 8. Short-term Debt Rollover Ratios
(In percent; 5-day rolling average)

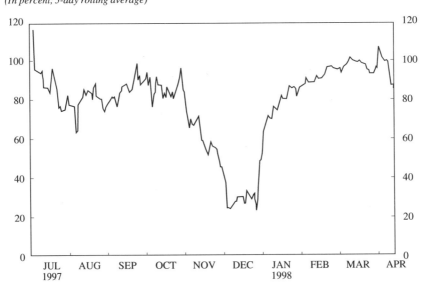

---

[23]The leak of IMF Executive Board documents also had a very damaging effect on market confidence. As markets digested the contents of the report, including the fact that official financing under the program was barely enough to cover short-term debts falling due, doubts about Korea's ability to repay heightened.

Figure 9. External Debt Ratings (Long-term)

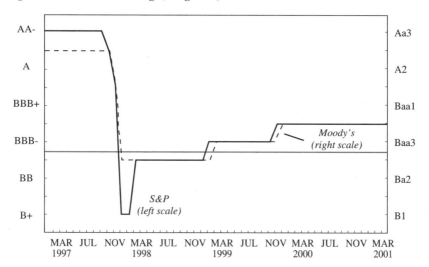

agencies had both cut Korea's long-term foreign currency debt rating in late November, to A-/A3. However, the agencies made far sharper cuts between December 10 and December 22 to subinvestment grade levels, with one agency moving the sovereign rating to four "notches" below the investment grade cutoff, a massive and unprecedented ten notch movement in less than two months. In both cases, the agencies cited the large short-term external debt of banks and the low level of usable external reserves. More so than with any of the other crisis countries, the Korean case raised widespread concerns about the role of the agencies, failing to foresee and then exacerbating the crisis.

The ongoing pressures on the won prompted a strengthening of the program in late December. With the won falling close to W2,000 per dollar on December 23, the Korean authorities on December 24 requested a rephasing of the financing under the program to bring forward a disbursement of SDR 1.5 billion ($2 billion) from January 8, 1998 to December 30. In doing so, they committed to strengthen and bring forward some of the measures in the program. Overnight interest rates were raised to 30 percent on December 24, and the authorities took new measures to ensure that liquidity was distributed through the financial system to prevent a liquidity crunch that could cause bankruptcies of viable firms. They also accelerated the liberalization of capital markets, and further increased the penal rate on Bank of Korea foreign currency loans to commercial banks. In addition, the program was strengthened in other areas including financial sector restructuring, trade policy, labor market policies, fiscal policy, and data publication.

However, given the problem of maturing short-term interbank debt, the most important factor in containing the crisis in late December was the roll-over agreement with international banks. With support and provision of information from the Fund, officials in the major economies convened meetings with the largest creditor banks and also made several phone calls to try to convince them to roll over their maturing interbank lines. It was pointed out that a failure to roll over enough of the credit lines would likely lead to systemic financial risk. On December 24, a temporary agreement was reached with U.S. banks to maintain interbank lines at existing levels for at least a week, while a longer-term solution was hammered out (see Box 2).

Exchange market pressures eased following the success in obtaining the informal standstill on short-term debt, allowing monetary policy to be eased from early 1998. By the end of January, the exchange rate had strengthened back to about W1,550 per dollar and usable reserves had grown to $12 billion. The overnight call rate peaked at about 35 percent in early January but was only briefly above 30 percent. Further, the current account swung sharply into surplus in the first quarter of 1998 due to the compression of imports, extraordinary gold exports (associated with donations made by individuals), and transfers from overseas Koreans. By the end of the first quarter, the call rate had fallen to 22 percent, as the won continued to strengthen. Usable reserves had recovered to $24 billion by end-March. The elimination of restrictions on foreign investment in domestic bonds and other capital account liberalization measures began to have an impact and contributed to a pickup in portfolio inflows from the first quarter of 1998.

By mid-1998, interest rates had been brought down to pre-crisis levels. As the recovery in foreign reserves continued, the overnight call rate was lowered below 10 percent in early August 1998, even in the face of Russia-driven turmoil in other emerging markets. After a period of continued reductions in the overnight call rate, which contributed to bringing down other interest rates, the Bank of Korea kept the call rate near 4 percent between May 1999 and February 2000, when the easing cycle ended with the first increase in official rates in more than two years.

Indeed, the major problem for monetary policy soon became the issue of how to manage capital inflows and pressures for appreciation. With the current account moving sharply into surplus in 1998, repayment of foreign debt, and healthy capital inflows (via direct and portfolio investment), there was substantial upward pressure on the exchange rate. The Bank of Korea absorbed much of this pressure through intervention, initially from a desire to rebuild its reserves, and then out of concern that the exchange rate not appreciate excessively. The intervention was partially sterilized through issuance of cen-

---

Box 2. "Bailing In" the Private Sector

Following the concerted efforts in late 1997 to persuade foreign creditors to roll over short-term debt, negotiations were also initiated on a more comprehensive rescheduling of the debt maturing in 1998 of 33 commercial and specialized banks and certain merchant banks. After difficult negotiations, agreement in principle was reached on January 16, and covered debt amounting to about US$24 billion. A key component in enforcing the agreement was a debt monitoring system set up by the IMF and the Bank of Korea, which helped solve the collective action problem inherent in any rollover operation. Rollover ratios quickly recovered, rising to over 80 percent by late January. Efforts were also undertaken to find mechanisms to maintain trade credits and derivatives exposure.

In early February 1998, negotiations commenced on a longer-term solution for the rolled-over foreign debt. On March, a debt restructuring agreement was signed, covering loans and deposits to 134 banks in 32 countries, and amounting to nearly US$22 billion (96 percent of eligible debt). The debt covered interbank deposit obligations, as well as short-term loans owed to foreign banks and financial institutions that matured in 1998. As a result of the restructuring, Korea's short-term debt declined from US$61 billion at end-March to US$42 billion at end-April.

Under the agreement, new claims carried an explicit guarantee by the Government of Korea. Creditor banks could choose from three options: (a) a one-year rescheduling at an interest rate of 225 basis points above six-month LIBOR (into which US$3.8 billion was transformed), (b) a two-year rescheduling at an interest rate of 250 basis points above six-month LIBOR (US$9.8 billion), and (c) a three-year rescheduling at an interest rate 275 of basis points above six-month LIBOR (US$8.3 billion). Individual creditors were not permitted to choose more than 20 percent of their exposure for the one-year rescheduling option. Korean debtor banks reserved the option to prepay the new two to three year loans, on any interest payment date, without premium or penalty, but no earlier than the first six months after the completion of the operation. Subsequently, several Korean banks availed themselves of this option.

In Korea's case, private sector involvement played a critical role in the successful resolution of a major foreign currency liquidity problem. The agreement was key to easing the foreign exchange constraint, and also facilitated an upgrade of Korea's sovereign credit ratings and its return to international capital markets. By early April 1998, the government was able to place two sovereign global bond issues totaling US$4 billion, demonstrating the turnaround in investor confidence.

By any reasonable ex post standard, the "bailing in" was creditor-friendly. Banks that agreed to coordinated rollovers incurred no losses, and in exchange for their claims on Korean banks received government-guaranteed claims carrying generous interest rates. Indeed, some critics have argued that the generosity of the rollover package—in contrast with the losses borne by holders of longer-term claims—was a bad precedent that provides an incentive to lenders to keep the maturity of lending to emerging markets as short as possible.

---

tral bank securities, and inflationary pressures have indeed been modest. At its peak in September 2000, the CPI-based real effective exchange rate was estimated at about only 10 percent below its pre-crisis level.

The Monetary Policy Debate

Notwithstanding the success in stabilizing the situation within only a few months after the onset of the crisis, the monetary policy response to the crisis has come under some criticism. Monetary policy in the middle of the crisis faced the difficult task of deciding which of two courses of action would be less costly in terms of output losses. On one hand, the high rates of leverage and exposure to bank debt made the corporate sector vulnerable to increases in interest rates. On the other hand, the high rates of exposure of financial corporations and business enterprises to short-term foreign currency borrowing meant that unchecked depreciation would have imposed substantial burdens on banks and corporations. In addition, an unchecked depreciation would have led to further overshooting of the exchange rate and, in turn, a depreciation-inflation spiral.[24] Hence, stabilizing the currency assumed a high priority in program design and a temporary hike in interest rates was viewed as necessary.[25] At the same time, the authorities were keenly aware of the disruption that this could bring to particular institutions. In response, a range of measures were adopted to mitigate these effects, including emergency liquidity support from the Bank of Korea, various structural measures such as increased provision of official export guarantees, financing for small and medium-sized enterprises, and purchase of subordinated debt from banks facing capital shortfalls.

In broad terms, the criticisms that have been raised against monetary policy can be summarized as follows: High interest rates were the cause of the slow turnaround in currency markets, because they raised debt servicing costs for firms, and hence the risk of default.[26] Thus, higher interest rates actually exacerbated capital outflows and contributed to a weakening of the currency. The program should instead have comprised a larger financial package to boost confidence, and less monetary tightening. Furthermore, even if tight monetary policy had been necessary to stabilize the exchange rate, interest rates were

---

[24]Krueger (2000) also discusses the dilemma at the height of the crisis. She notes that the crisis was a dual balance-of-payments and financial crisis, and that the traditional remedy for the former problem (tighter monetary and fiscal policy) was exactly the opposite of the traditional policy required for the latter problem. She concludes, however, that it is inevitable that the balance-of-payments crisis is addressed immediately, and that addressing the financial problems requires time, involving measures to improve the balance sheet of the corporate sector as well as the financial sector.

[25]Analysis by Claessens, Djankov and Ferri (1999) on the balance sheets of a large sample of Korean firms lends support to the focus on the exchange rate. They find that the exchange rate shock was sufficient to drive 20 percent of firms in their sample into insolvency and 38 percent into (their definition) of illiquidity. By contrast, the interest rate shock had an impact (in terms of insolvency or illiquidity) on a much smaller proportion of firms. As noted in Lane *et al.* (1999), the authors did not estimate an explicit trade-off between higher interest rates and a smaller depreciation.

[26]See, e.g., Furman and Stiglitz (1998), Feldstein (1998), and Radelet and Sachs (1998).

kept high for "too long" and resulted in a credit crunch, which exacerbated the output decline following the financial crisis.[27]

There have been numerous studies that have tried to assess empirically whether higher interest rates are useful in supporting the exchange rate during financial and currency crises.[28] The results are inconclusive, which may not be surprising since the degree of monetary tightening actually implemented may well be a function of the magnitude of the depreciation that would have occurred in the absence of the tightening. Although some studies find some support for the view that higher interest rates are associated with a strengthening of the currency, the evidence is not overwhelming or robust to changes in sample periods or countries. However, none of the studies finds any evidence to support the contention that monetary tightening has a perverse effect on exchange rates. In light of this lack of evidence, it seems hard to argue that the decision taken to defend the exchange rate was inherently flawed. The argument that higher interest rates were necessary to help stabilize the exchange rate does not, of course, imply that they were a sufficient condition or that they did not have a negative impact on corporate balance sheets. Indeed, given the high leverage of the corporate sector, IMF staff were well aware of the negative impact of high interest rates. Accordingly, very soon after the approval of the initial program, the IMF began to argue for action to deal with the rollover problem, to reduce the reliance on monetary policy.

The argument that Korea should have received a larger external financing package, and should have implemented less restrictive policies is not persuasive. Korea's was the largest financing package provided by the IMF and the official international community in the IMF's history, and the existence of the program enabled the agreement on the critical debt restructuring agreement with commercial banks. A larger financing package was simply not available, and there are indeed many critics who argue it was too large and—in conjunction with the generous terms on the rollover—involved too much of a "bailout," with implications for future moral hazard.

Consider next the argument that interest rates were kept too high for too long in Korea, plunging the economy into a vicious circle of declining output, increasing bankruptcies, and further weakening of the financial sector. Several points can be made in response to this line of argument. First, the magnitude of the peak in interest rates was not large for an economy that had seen its

---

[27]See Boorman *et al.* (2000) and Lane *et al.* (1999) for general discussions of the monetary policy response to the Asian crisis.

[28]See, e.g., Dekle, Hsiao, and Wang (1999); Furman and Stiglitz (1998); Goldfajn and Baig (1998); Goldfajn and Gupta (1998); Kraay (2000); Basurto and Ghosh (2000); and Flood and Rose (2001).

Table 2. A Comparison of Real Interest Rates During Crisis Periods[1] [2]
(In percent unless otherwise indicated)

Country	Nominal rate		Real rate		Threshold	No. of months
	Minimum	Maximum	Minimum	Maximum	rate[3]	Real 〉 Threshold
Korea	7.0	27.4	-0.2	19.1	7.7	7
Brazil	19.5	43.3	13.8	40.3	17.5	10
Thailand	15.6	24.9	7.5	17.7	5.4	12
Sweden	8.4	82.4	3.7	80.0	5.0	5
Mexico	29.9	70.3	-8.9	40.9	8.7	5

[1]Based on average monthly data of overnight interbank/call rate.

[2]The 12-month period for Korea is defined as Dec 97 to Nov 98; for Brazil Sep 98 to Aug 99; for Thailand Jul 97-Jun 98; for Sweden Sep 92 to Aug 93; for Mexico Jan 95 to Dec 95.

[3]The threshold real interest rate is defined as the average real interest rate during the 24 months proceeding the crisis period.

currency lose half its value in a two month period. In particular, the 35 percent peak in the call rate corresponds to a monthly rate of less than 3 percent, which is not the type of level that *per se* should have resulted in major dislocations in the economy. Second, the degree of tightening—measured by the number of months during which interest rates were maintained above the average level prevailing during the two years prior to the crisis—was not unusual compared to recent experience in other countries facing exchange rate crises (see Table 2). By June 1998—about seven months after the onset of the crisis—interest rates had been brought down to below the level prevailing before the crisis. Third, domestic demand collapsed independently of the spike in interest rates as there was a massive shock to confidence. This shock to confidence was related to the end of the prospect of life-time job security, combined with the damage sustained to the sense that Korea's model of development—which had delivered spectacular growth of per capita income in previous decades— also had its flaws and left it prone to a crisis. And fourth, the continued emergence of new cases of corporate distress after the period of high growth and low interest rates that prevailed in 1999 and 2000 suggests that the problem of nonperforming loans was related more to underlying weaknesses than to the spike in interest rates.

There are numerous studies that attempt to address the issue of whether the modest decline in bank credit in 1998 represented a "credit crunch" and was caused by tight monetary policy. Several papers have examined developments at an aggregate level and obtain results with different conclusions or that are open to alternative interpretations.[29] For example, it remains an open question as to whether the contraction in credit was due more to reduced supply or to reduced demand. Further, even if data suggested the former, it would still be unclear if this was due to appropriately tighter bank lending policies or to monetary policy being too tight and not attempting to offset the reduction in bank lending that occurred.

Some of the more robust conclusions on the credit crunch issue have come from studies that use disaggregated data for individual banks or enterprises. Ferri and Kang (1999) use individual bank data and find that capital-constrained banks experienced a more marked slowdown in loan expansion and disproportionately raised their lending rates. Ferri, Kang and Kim (1999) show that small and medium-sized enterprises (SMEs) with strong pre-crisis relationships with (surviving) banks were better able to maintain bank credit than other SMEs. Finally, Borensztein and Lee (2000) use firm-level data and find that there was a reallocation of credit away from nonprofitable firms to profitable ones. Furthermore they find that the disadvantage in fund raising that non-*chaebol* firms faced prior to the crisis disappeared in the aftermath of the

Figure 10. Issuance of Corporate Bonds
(In trillions of won)

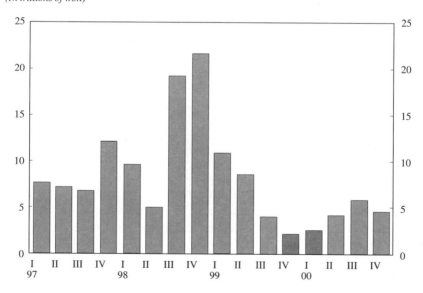

---

[29]E.g., Kim (1999), Ghosh and Ghosh (1999), Ding, Domac and Ferri (1998), Domac and Ferri (1999), and Hahm and Mishkin (2000).

crisis. Overall, these results suggest that the credit constraints suffered by certain sectors or firms might well be explained more by the adjustment by banks and enterprises to changes in creditworthiness and capital positions, rather than to tight monetary policy *per se*.

More generally, there are some important broader trends in corporate financing that are missed in analyses that focus purely on bank credit. In particular, while bank financing may have fallen in 1998, firms obtained increased financing from the equity markets and the corporate bond market. Increased equity financing was clearly a positive development given that high leverage was one of the factors that contributed to the crisis. The increased financing from the bond market was less clearly a positive development. It partly reflected the lax supervision of the investment trust company (ITC) sector, and the growth in this sector in 1998 magnified the problems that were seen in 1999. More broadly, the corporate bond rollover problems seen in late 2000 and in 2001 would suggest that some of the firms that raised funds in the bond market in the wake of the crisis were nonviable, or at least that the easy access to funds in this market delayed necessary restructuring.

Overall, it is difficult to argue that the decline in output that was observed was due primarily to monetary policy. Given the massive loss of confidence and the fundamental nature of restructuring that was required in both the corporate and financial sectors, it seems inevitable that the crisis that hit Korea in late 1997 would have had substantial real effects. It seems highly unlikely that different monetary policy choices would have been effective in avoiding all the dislocation that was observed.[30] Further, given the potential moral hazard if insolvent or undercapitalized institutions had been allowed to continue lending to companies with low or negative equity, it seems hard to argue that there should have been looser financial supervision—indeed, if this had occurred and exit of insolvent companies had been delayed, corporate and financial restructuring would now be even further from completion.

On the whole, the policies to stabilize the exchange rate—especially the debt rollover—were successful. This stability, together with the replenishment of foreign exchange reserves with the support of the international community, was essential in restoring confidence in the Korean economy. Combined with the easing of macroeconomic policies to support demand and growth, this improved sentiment was a major contributor to the economy's quick recovery from recession.

---

[30]Analysis by Lane *et al.* (1999, Appendix 6.1) suggests that less than one quarter of the swing in GDP growth from 1997 to 1998 can be attributed to the observed deceleration in monetary growth.

Supporting the Recovery—The Conduct of Fiscal Policy

The financial crisis resulted in Korea's worst economic performance in its post-war history. Real GDP fell by 6.7 percent in 1998, with private consumption and fixed investment declining by 11 ½ percent and 21 percent, respectively. The depth of the recession was unanticipated by virtually all analysts, and led to major changes in the focus and operation of fiscal policy. Before the financial crisis, fiscal policy in Korea had been dominated by a culture of fiscal conservatism with the consolidated central government remaining in balance since 1993.[31] Indeed, it has long been a common practice in Korea not to undertake spending commitments until the revenues that finance them have been received. As a result, it required a major shift in the stance of fiscal policy to respond to the unprecedented economic downturn of 1998. Instead of a fiscal policy directed towards budget balance in a time of high growth, the government had to shift to a more supportive stance to provide temporary demand stimulus to a worsening economic downturn.

When the financial crisis hit, the program called for the policy of fiscal conservatism to be continued. The reasons were four-fold: First, the depth of the recession that occurred was not anticipated. Second, the authorities believed that a worsening fiscal position would have placed a greater burden on monetary policy in the overall macroeconomic adjustment. Third, the expected contingent liabilities from the costly financial sector restructuring would require an offsetting policy response in other components of the fiscal balance. Fourth, a tight fiscal policy would provide a positive signal to financial markets and foster a return of confidence. However, as the extent of the crisis unfolded, increasing fiscal support for the economy was programmed to take account of the weaker growth outlook and the need to strengthen the social safety net.

Fiscal policy in 1998

The original 1998 budget, passed in November 1997 before the crisis became full blown, targeted a budget surplus of ¼ percent of GDP based on an assumption of 6 percent real growth (see Figure 11). By early December 1997, however, growth estimates had been downgraded to 3 percent, and consequently the overall balance was expected to worsen to a deficit of around ½ percent of GDP.

---

[31]The consolidated central government includes the general account, 18 special accounts, and 25 extra budgetary funds. In this paper, the consolidated central government deficit and other fiscal aggregates are presented excluding privatization receipts, which are treated as a financing item instead of revenue.

Figure 11. Growth Forecasts and Budget Plans

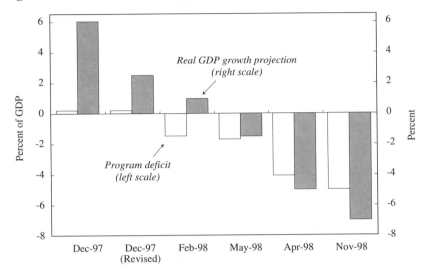

In addition, the interest costs of financial sector restructuring were projected to add a further ¾ percent of GDP to the deficit. Faced with the prospects of a significant turnaround in the overall deficit, it was decided that offsetting policies would need to be implemented with the aim of restoring fiscal balance. Measures were introduced in late 1997 to increase excise and oil taxation, expand tax bases, freeze civil service salaries, and reduce current expenditures.

By the end of December 1997 the extent of the crisis was becoming more clear, leading the government and the IMF to reconsider the appropriateness of the initial fiscal policy response. Rather than trying to maintain a fiscal balance, the revised December program focused on allowing the automatic stabilizers to operate and tolerating a deficit in the short term. It was unlikely that even this policy stance would have provided sufficient stimulus to the economy as the effect of the automatic stabilizers was likely to have been weak given the high proportion of indirect taxes in revenue and the inadequate social safety net.

By early 1998, at the urging of the Fund the government changed the direction of its fiscal policy and started to put greater emphasis on providing fiscal stimulus and lessening the consequences of the crisis on the poor and the unemployed. In February, as a part of the Tripartite Accord (see below), the government concluded an agreement that increased unemployment-related spending by about ½ percent of GDP. This effort, as well as other increases in safety net spending included in the March 1998 supplementary budget, led to an increase in the projected deficit to 1 ½ percent of GDP. This change in fiscal stance provided needed temporary fiscal stimulus to the ailing economy, and also, helped maintain social consensus and support for the government's reform program in the face of economic hardships that were becoming increasingly apparent.

Despite the deeper-than-expected economic downturn and the shift in the official position on fiscal policy, the actual budgetary outturn in the first quarter was one of fiscal balance. Both current and capital outlays were well below projections, partly reflecting difficulties in executing several of the newly implemented social safety net programs and bottlenecks in local government implemented capital projects. However, the balanced fiscal outturn also reflected the traditional emphasis on securing revenues prior to making expenditures; it soon became clear that such old practices would need to be quickly abandoned.

By July 1998, following a sharp fall in output and amid increasing social pressures, the authorities dramatically shifted gears with the introduction of a second supplementary budget. This budget, passed in September, aimed to support the economic recovery by further increasing spending on the social safety net, and by providing assistance to SMEs through guarantees and net lending. Although the thrust of the budget was appropriate, as it increased stimulus at a time of collapsing domestic demand, some elements of the package were questionable. Specifically, the introduction of higher tax rates on interest income and oil products was unnecessary at a time when economic

Figure 12. Actual and Cyclically Neutral Budget Balance

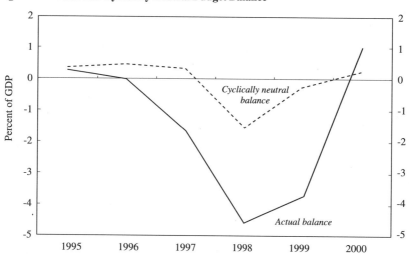

prospects were highly uncertain. In addition, the initiatives on spending could have been better directed towards consumption-generating programs and the further development of the social safety net rather than towards net lending.

By the third quarter of 1998, the economic downturn had moderated and, following the approval of the supplementary budget, government expenditures began to pick-up. Safety net programs in particular were rapidly disbursed, and public works programs were redesigned. By the end of the year central government expenditure had risen from 22 percent to almost 26 percent of GDP and the fiscal deficit reached 4.2 percent of GDP which, although still less than the budgeted level, provided considerable fiscal stimulus to the economy. As Figure 12 shows, although the economic downturn would, in the absence of offsetting policy action, have resulted in the budget moving into a deficit of about 1 $\frac{1}{2}$ percent of GDP, the actual deficit was much larger in 1998.

Fiscal policy in 1999 and 2000

In 1999, the government continued the expansionary fiscal stance. Initially a fiscal deficit, including privatization receipts, of about 5 percent of GDP was targeted. This involved increased spending on the social safety net, greater support for SMEs, and additional interest payments associated with bonds issued for financial sector restructuring. Facing a rapidly rising level of unemployment at the start of 1999, the authorities introduced a supplementary budget in March aimed at reinforcing measures for job creation and protection for the unemployed.

By mid-1999, it was clear that the automatic stabilizers associated with the rapid economic recovery were going to result in a deficit well below the level targeted at the start of the year. In June, the government announced a second supplementary budget that added $\frac{3}{4}$ percent of GDP to the deficit, including measures such as increased deductions and allowances for the personal income tax, corporate tax incentives and preferences, spending to encourage business start-ups, increased funding for subsidized lending and the credit guarantee fund, and expanded programs of free food provision to the needy. However, the continued rapid economic recovery, better-than-expected revenue collections, and lower-than-budgeted capital spending resulted in the deficit falling to 3 $\frac{1}{4}$ percent of GDP in 1999, which fell short of the original deficit target but was still expansionary after adjusting for the effect of the cycle.

In 2000, with the strong economic recovery under way, the Korean authorities intended to redirect fiscal policy towards the process of medium-term fiscal consolidation. In the event, fiscal consolidation proceeded much more rapidly than expected. The budget moved into surplus to the tune of about 1 percent of GDP versus a planned deficit of 2 ½ percent of GDP implied in the supplementary budget, thus achieving fiscal balance four years ahead of the target specified in 1999.[32] The strong performance was partly cyclical (especially the boost to revenue and lower spending for unemployment benefits), and there were also temporary windfall gains (e.g. revenues delayed from 1999 due to Y2K problems). However, overall discretionary expenditure was well below budgeted levels—without any specific directive being given to curtail spending—indicating that the fiscal contraction went well beyond the estimated effects of automatic stabilizers.

Building on the strong performance in 2000, the authorities intend to keep fiscal policy broadly neutral on a cyclically adjusted basis in 2001. With the slowdown of the economy and a rise in unemployment since the end of 2000, they have announced plans to frontload investment spending, as well as new measures to deal with the expected increase in unemployment.

Expanding the Social Safety Net

In Korea, business enterprises have traditionally been the major provider of social benefits. With the high rate of bankruptcy among enterprises following the crisis, one of the most dramatic changes in Korea's policies was the concerted effort directed at putting in place a working social safety net. It became clear early on that the needed financial and corporate sector restructuring was likely to lead to a large increase in unemployment and a deterioration in income distribution. Indeed, unemployment rose from a steady 2-3 percent before the crisis to 8 ½ percent by early 1999, labor force participation fell, and real incomes declined. The government's efforts at instituting a safety net focused on two aspects: (i) providing support for those that had been made redundant and facilitating their rapid return to the workforce; and (ii) providing a minimum level of income for the most needy in the society including the aged, children of the unemployed, and those unable to work.[33] As a result, social safety net outlays increased substantially from 0.6 percent of GDP in 1997 to 1.6 percent of GDP in 1999. The authorities were careful, however, to ensure that in the process of expanding the social safety net they did not create permanent welfare entitlements or distort incentives for job search and work.

To deal with the increase in unemployment, the coverage of the employment insurance system (EIS) was expanded in 1998, first to include all enter-

---

[32]The 2000 Budget originally targeted a deficit for the consolidated central government of 3¾ percent of GDP.

[33]See Martin and Torres (2000) for additional details on social safety net reforms in Korea.

prises with five or more employees, and then further to cover enterprises with less than five workers, part-time workers, and temporary workers. As a result, the proportion of wage workers covered by the unemployment insurance system rose from 33 percent to 70 percent. In addition to expanding benefit coverage, the government also doubled the minimum duration of benefits to 60 days and extended the maximum duration of benefits from seven to nine months.

The government also attempted to reduce unemployment by providing support to firms that retained employees. This support typically involved subsidies for up to six months (later expanded to eight months) for employers that used temporary closures, paid leave, and reductions in working hours to avoid lay-offs. In addition, subsidies were provided for firms that hired workers that had recently been laid-off. Moreover, in July 1998, the Wage Claims Guarantee System was introduced to ensure that workers in bankrupt firms would receive pay for their last three months of work. To facilitate the return of the unemployed back into the workforce, the government also expanded its program of vocational training and introduced a program of loans, up to W30 million, to support small business start-ups.

The government also took steps to provide more direct aid for those most needy and vulnerable in society. This was seen as particularly important as much of the burden of the adjustment fell on this group. Income of the very poorest fell by 17 percent in 1998 and, as the table below shows, the crisis led to a significant widening in the income distribution. Despite such increased inequality, however, income distribution in Korea is broadly comparable to advanced industrial countries.

The public works program was an important component of the safety net strategy. Given the limited coverage of unemployment benefits at the beginning of the crisis, the government created a large number of public works jobs,

Table 3. Korea: Changes in the Income Distribution[1]

	Korea				Canada	Mexico	Sweden	U.S.
	1997	1998	1999 H1	1999 H2	1994	1995	1992	1994
	(percent share of total income)							
Upper 20 percent	37.2	39.8	40.4	40.0	39.3	58.2	34.5	45.2
Lower 20 percent	8.3	7.4	7.3	7.4	7.5	3.6	9.6	4.8
Upper 20 percent/ Lower 20 percent	4.49	5.38	5.54	5.41	5.24	16.17	3.59	9.42
Gini coefficient	0.28	0.32	0.32	0.31	0.32	0.54	0.25	0.40

Source: Korean authorities and World Bank, *World Development Report* (2000).
[1]Based on urban worker households.

drawing from the pool of unemployed—particularly those whose benefits had expired—to perform tasks such as caring for public lands and maintaining public infrastructure, as well as more skilled jobs aimed towards unemployed university graduates. In 1998 public works programs cost the budget over W1 trillion and employed 440,000 persons, with the allocation rising to W2.5 trillion ($\frac{1}{2}$ percent of GDP) in 1999.

More direct social assistance was made available through the livelihood protection program for those who are unable to work and have low income and few assets. This is a means-tested program that provides a below-subsistence level of income support (in 1998 this amounted to up to W152,000 per month plus assistance in paying for medical and education costs) for those unable to work, such as the disabled, the elderly and children. In addition, a variety of programs have been implemented to assist low income, unemployed households. The two most important were the Temporary Livelihood Protection scheme and the Support for Living Costs program (although the one-time benefit in these programs was relatively small).

Finally, the government adopted a number of other programs of social assistance such as providing tuition support for children of unemployed persons, housing subsidies, assistance in paying for medical insurance premiums, and free food programs for children, the elderly, and disabled persons.

In sum, the welfare system in Korea has evolved substantially since the crisis. The government acted promptly to improve the social safety net and limit the rise in poverty. With the economic recovery and decline in unemployment, the focus has gradually shifted from public job creation and layoff avoidance to providing social assistance and encouraging employment with self-support. More importantly, with the passage of the national Basic Livelihood Security Act in October 2000, a comprehensive institutional framework for welfare provision is now being put in place.

Addressing Structural Weaknesses and Increasing Market Orientation

It was evident from the start that the twin crisis that faced Korea in late 1997 was more due to structural weaknesses than to any fundamental macroeconomic disequilibria. Hence, it was clear that the response to the crisis would have to contain a substantial structural component. At the heart of the structural reform agenda were measures to deal with the immediate problems in the financial and corporate sectors and address their underlying weaknesses. In addition, steps were taken early in the program to accelerate capital account liberalization and improve labor market flexibility. Finally, there were measures to foster more timely, transparent, and accurate reporting of key economic data.

The magnitude and timing of the structural program has come under fire, with some critics arguing that it was not necessary because the crisis was largely an external liquidity crisis.[34] According to this view, the program should have just focused on resolving the liquidity crisis rather than including wide-ranging structural policies. This criticism can be rebutted on three levels. First, there was (and remains) a consensus that structural factors were at the heart of the crisis. Hence, the program would not have been credible if it had ignored these weaknesses as the chances would remain high that Korea would suffer from another crisis down the road. In particular, the fact that this was a twin balance-of-payments and financial crisis required urgent attention to the financial sector. Further, as the financial sector would remain weak if corporate creditworthiness and competitiveness were not tackled, corporate restructuring was also a priority. Second, at a more political level, there simply would not have been the massive level of official support or the consensus for rollover by commercial banks in the absence of a substantial structural component that addressed the problems that had been highlighted by the crisis. Third, in many cases the structural reforms were measures that had been discussed or even planned in the years leading up to crisis, in some cases in connection with OECD membership. In light of the strong national desire—especially on the part of the new administration of President Kim Dae Jung, which took office in early 1998—to ensure a durable recovery, it was feasible and desirable to press ahead with many of these measures quickly.

Others have argued that structural reform was necessary, but that reform—especially of the financial sector—should have been delayed.[35] Several of the points in the previous paragraph are again relevant. In addition, if financial institutions with low or negative net worth had been allowed to continue lending at will to companies in similar financial positions there would have been serious moral hazard. The recognition of the losses experienced by the financial sector might have been delayed, but those losses might well have been far larger.

In addition to the measures to stabilize the immediate problems, the structural component part of the program largely consisted of measures that increased the market orientation of the Korean economy. In each case, the focus was on giving greater emphasis to more efficient private sector decision making with reduced role for government in microeconomic outcomes. Market discipline had not traditionally played a major role in the Korean economy, so one of the objectives of the program was to assist the authorities in establishing a framework that would allow market forces to work better.

---

[34]See, e.g., Feldstein (1998) and Radelet and Sachs (1998).

[35]See, for example, Yoshitomi and Ohno (1999).

The extensive structural reform agenda in the programs with the Asian crisis countries has also contributed to the intensification of the debate on the scope and detail of IMF structural policy conditionality.[36] In the case of the Korea program, the vast bulk of structural reforms focused on the core areas of financial and corporate sector restructuring. Measures outside these core areas accounted for a relatively small share of measures listed in extensive policy matrices. Formal structural conditionality—specifically, structural performance criteria—were almost exclusively in the realm of financial sector issues. Nonetheless, in retrospect, the sheer volume and detail of measures listed in letters of intent and policy matrices became widely identified as part of the program's structural conditionality, and streamlining of these matrices would have been possible without a major loss in substance. These issues are discussed in greater detail in Box 3.

Financial sector reforms focused on strengthening regulations and the framework for supervisory oversight, restructuring the financial system starting with the weakest segments (namely the commercial banks and merchant banks), and progressively moving on to the rest of the nonbank financial sector. Reforms in the corporate sector initially focused on improvements in governance and competition policies. Subsequently, the authorities' attention shifted to financial and operational restructuring aimed at reducing debt levels and strengthening the capital structure of Korean corporations. Measures in the areas of financial and corporate restructuring were formulated by the authorities in close consultation with both the Fund and the World Bank.

Reform of the financial and corporate sector also required both greater labor market flexibility and a stronger social safety net. Accordingly, the Tripartite Commission was formed in January 1998. This Commission, with representation from labor, businesses, and government facilitated agreements on layoffs, pay cuts, and reduced overtime and bonuses that were necessary to allow firms to adjust to weaker demand in the wake of the crisis.[37] Labor laws were changed in February 1998 to allow firms to lay off redundant workers in cases of "urgent managerial need." [38] Although the unemployment rate rose sharply,

---

[36]See, for example, Goldstein (2001).

[37]An attempt had been made in late 1996 to introduce such changes, which resulted in a national strike and the abandonment of these plans. The crisis provided the authorities an opportunity to try again and reintroduce labor issues in their reform agenda.

[38]Firms contemplating shedding workers were required to follow strict guidelines aimed at minimizing actual layoffs. Specifically, prior to making a final decision on layoffs, firms are encouraged to maximize efforts to avoid dismissals, including through wage cuts, reductions in working hours, freezing of new recruitment, reduction in the number of temporary workers, early retirement, and temporary shutdown. In addition, the government provided various temporary wage subsidies to firms that retained redundant workers.

Box 3. Structural Conditionality in the Korea Program

The debate about the breadth and depth of structural conditionality in Fund-supported programs has intensified in the wake of the Asian crisis. For example, Goldstein (2001) concludes that "on structural policies the Fund has bitten off more—in both scope and detail—than either it or its member countries can chew" (page 78). A study by Fund staff (IMF, 2001) notes that although experiences regarding the extent of structural conditionality have varied widely across countries, "there are indications that in a significant number of cases, structural conditionality has moved beyond what seems consistent with the principle of parsimony, underscoring the need for streamlining" (page 85). This study also notes that, "with the exception of extended arrangement with Indonesia, the programs in the Asian crisis countries [Korea, Thailand, and Indonesia], which have come to be seen as virtually synonymous with extensive structural conditionality, did not stand out in terms of the number of structural performance criteria, prior actions and benchmarks they included" (page 83). Against this background, this box reviews the nature of structural conditionality in the Fund's stand-by arrangement with Korea.

The Korea program covered a wide range of structural issues in detailed policy matrices.[39] The vast bulk of measures listed in these matrices involved financial sector restructuring, which was seen as essential to restore market confidence, overcome the crisis, and lessen vulnerability to future crises. Corporate sector restructuring, a critical counterpart to the reforms in the financial sector, was also a vital part of the program. As the Fund was not well equipped to deal with corporate sector issues, which were clearly beyond its areas of expertise, close collaboration with the World Bank was necessary for the design of measures in this area. Due to the complexity of the needed restructuring of the financial and corporate sectors, the policy content of the program expanded substantially as the program evolved.

The policy matrices for Korea went beyond the two core areas of financial and corporate sector restructuring. Some of the additional areas covered—such as capital account liberalization, strengthening the social safety net, labor market reforms, and systemic reforms (e.g., institution building, the legal and regulatory framework, and transparency)—were essential to support reforms in the core areas and were therefore important for the achievement of the program's objectives. However, reforms in other areas—such as trade and financial services liberalization, privatization of public enterprises, and tax reform—were probably peripheral.

The measures outside the two core areas, however, were not subject to structural performance criteria (see below) and accounted for a relatively small share of the structural measures listed in the extensive policy matrices. Indeed, these reforms were typically part of the government's broader policy agenda and in many instances were inserted into the policy matrices at the request of the Korean authorities to demonstrate their resolve to enhance flexibility and growth potential of the economy. Nevertheless, as noted in IMF (2001), in view of the ambiguity of the status of the policy matrices that represented programs' letters of intent in the Asian crisis countries, it is perhaps not surprising that all measures listed in them came to be widely identified as part of the program's structural conditionality even though this was not the case.

Monitoring the implementation of structural policies in the Korea program, and hence formal conditionality, relied primarily on program reviews and structural performance criteria, and to a lesser extent on prior actions.[40] This combination of monitoring provided considerable flexibility in adjusting to circumstances, including unanticipated events. Overall, Korea established a good record of policy implementation under the program.

---

[39]The various letters of intent and policy matrices contained in memoranda on economic policies have been published by the Korean authorities and are also available at www.imf.org.

[40]These various monitoring techniques are defined and explained in IMF (2001).

In the initial stages of the program, **program reviews** predominated. Following the approval of the program on December 4, 1997, there were two bi-weekly reviews in mid-December 1997 and early January 1998. Thereafter, there were five quarterly program reviews during 1998 and early 1999, after which the frequency of reviews was reduced to six month intervals. The reviews covered structural issues that were difficult to define ex ante (e.g., ensuring that sufficient public funds were allocated for financial sector restructuring) and also reforms characterized by a series of smaller steps, which were of only moderate significance individually but made an important contribution to meeting the program's objectives when a critical mass was implemented (e.g., tightening regulations on connected lending, large exposure, and financial transactions between affiliates). In addition, the frequent program reviews provided an opportunity to adapt the structural reform agenda and make mid-course corrections to policies in light of developments (e.g., the tightening of regulations on provisioning for exposure to companies undergoing workouts, and defining a strategy for bank privatization). Although this sometimes meant expanding the agenda in response to emerging problems, it also allowed refocusing, with some reforms that were no longer seen as important being dropped from the agenda.

Structural performance criteria focused on measures that were (a) seen as important to the success of the program; (b) could be defined in precise, objectively verifiable terms; and (c) whose implementation in a specific timeframe was important to maintain the momentum of reforms. The three-year program with Korea had a total of 21 structural performance criteria—i.e., an average of seven per year.[41] The performance criteria were almost exclusively in the realm of financial sector issues—the single exception being a criterion on the publication of monthly fiscal data that was aimed at improving transparency—and were generally observed in the timeframe specified. In cases when there were delays—the more notable include delays in obtaining bids for the sale of Korea First Bank and Seoul Bank and in issuing new loan classification guidelines—the Executive Board granted waivers (in the context of program reviews) as it was expected that the performance criteria would be observed in due course.

Prior actions typically related to the completion of reviews and were applied to measures seen as important to keep the structural reform agenda on track. Prominent examples include agreement on steps to enhance the operational independence and autonomy of the supervisory authorities and steps to stabilize the situation in the investment trust sector and also to reform it with the aim of putting the sector on a sound footing in the longer run.

In sum, the structural conditionality in the Korea program was concentrated on the core areas of financial and corporate sector restructuring. The sheer scope of issues to be addressed in these core areas was, however, unprecedented and was a reflection of the complexity of the situation and the interrelationship between various measures. Reliance on program reviews provided considerable flexibility in the monitoring of policies in these areas. In retrospect, although structural performance criteria focused on financial sector reforms, the number of criteria was on the high side, and greater selectivity would have been preferable. Further, streamlining of policy matrices, especially in noncore areas, and greater prioritization based on the importance of structural reforms for the program's objectives would have been more consistent with the principle of parsimony.

---

[41]The Korea program made greater use of structural performance criteria than other stand-by arrangements, which relied more on structural benchmarks that were monitored in the context of reviews rather than being directly linked with purchases. See Tables 6 and 7 in IMF (2001).

labor leaders co-operated with the new administration and labor unrest was limited. In addition, the increase in unemployment (which was subsequently reversed) was limited by a substantial fall in real wages, mainly from reduced overtime payments and bonuses. As discussed above, the strengthening of the social safety net also contributed to improved labor market flexibility.

Capital account liberalization was directed at strengthening market discipline through increased foreign participation in the Korean economy. The initial focus was on easing or eliminating restrictions on foreign investment in Korea. These measures were designed to have an immediate effect in easing the foreign exchange constraint, as well as longer term benefits on the governance and capital structure of companies. By allowing for mergers and acquisitions and imposing the threat of hostile takeovers, the opening of the market to foreigners was intended to strengthen market discipline on managers and owners of domestic companies and help with corporate restructuring. In addition, the foreign exchange regime was substantially liberalized in April 1999 and in January 2001. There was also trade liberalization to enhance domestic competition, including the elimination of trade-related subsidies and of restrictive import licensing and certification.

Overall, the structural program has contributed to an environment where market discipline can now potentially play a strong role in Korea. However, given the broad focus of the structural program, it is not surprising that there are some areas where progress has been slower than hoped, and where there may still remain a tendency for agents to expect government intervention. It will be important that the government's actions demonstrate that market discipline is now well entrenched in Korea. Although the government will always need to monitor and enforce regulations and competition policies, the framework is now in place for market discipline and the market mechanism to drive the process of corporate and financial reform. These issues are discussed in greater detail in the next two sections.

Financial Sector Restructuring

The restructuring of the financial sector was central to the structural reform program. This section outlines the main elements of the strategy adopted, assesses the main achievements, and reviews some of the key items that remain on the agenda.[42]

---

[42]For a review of the structure of Korea's financial system before the crisis see Baliño and Ubide (1999).

Strategy and Implementation

The authorities' strategy comprised four key elements:

- Emergency measures to quickly restore stability to the financial system through liquidity support, a blanket (but time-bound) deposit guarantee, and intervention in systemically important nonviable institutions.
- Restructuring measures to restore the solvency of the financial system by intervention in nonviable institutions, purchase of nonperforming loans (NPLs), and recapitalization.
- Regulatory measures to strengthen the existing framework by bringing prudential regulations and supervision in line with international best practices.
- Corporate restructuring measures to reduce corporate distress and the vulnerability of financial institutions exposed to the highly indebted corporate sector.

Emergency measures

At the height of the crisis, the most immediate need was to restore basic stability of the financial system. The first task was to maintain public confidence in the banking system. Prior to the onset of the crisis, in January 1997, the authorities had introduced a deposit insurance scheme funded by low premium contributions from banks. The scheme provided for full coverage of all deposits not exceeding W20 million per individual depositor. In addition, in August 1997, the government had announced that they would ensure that Korean financial institutions would be in a position to meet their foreign liabilities, effectively guaranteeing these liabilities.

The withdrawal of foreign credit lines in the second half of 1997 suggested that the authorities' external guarantees were not viewed as entirely credible. The guarantee on foreign liabilities of Korean banks was not backed up by any institutional arrangements—a formal guarantee would have required approval by the legislature—nor was it clear as the crisis developed that the Korean authorities had the resources to back up their commitment. Further, the complete implementation of domestic deposit insurance needed legislation, and there was skepticism about the authorities' willingness to deliver on their commitment. Thus further action became necessary and, in mid-November 1997, the government announced that it would guarantee all deposits of financial institutions until end-2000, and would provide liquidity support to banks as necessary. As discussed earlier, in early 1998 the government successfully negotiated extensions of foreign currency debt maturities with foreign banks. Although the assurances to external creditors was initially unsuccessful, the efforts to reassure domestic creditors via the blanket deposit insurance was largely successful and major bank runs were avoided.

The extended coverage of the guarantee was crucial to restore confidence in the system. The guarantees not only included deposit liabilities of banks and their foreign currency obligations, but also some of their trust department liabilities, those of merchant banks, and premiums paid to insurance companies. Appropriately, however, funds invested with Investment Trust Companies (ITCs) were not covered. The guarantees were backed up by the provision of temporary liquidity support by the Bank of Korea (BOK). In September 1997, the BOK provided special liquidity support to merchant banks and to Korea First Bank (KFB), and in December, another facility was established for commercial banks and other financial institutions that had been affected by the suspension of merchant bank operations. With respect to foreign exchange guarantees, the BOK ensured that commitments were met by placing foreign currency with the foreign branches of commercial banks.

Rapid intervention in nonviable institutions was also instrumental in restoring stability of the financial sector. In December 1997 the authorities announced that two commercial banks, KFB and Seoul Bank would be acquired by the government, thereby ensuring that they could continue to meet their liabilities. To deal with the problem of insolvent merchant banks the government announced the suspension of 14 of them in December, and ten of these were closed in January 1998. A bridge merchant bank was formed to take over and liquidate their assets.

Restructuring measures

The next step was to restore the solvency of the financial system. The first element of this process was to distinguish unviable institutions from weak but viable institutions. This involved a systemic evaluation of credit institutions, merchant banks, commercial banks, and specialized and development banks. For nonviable institutions, exit strategies—mergers, sales, or liquidation— were developed and applied. For viable institutions, rehabilitation plans specifying detailed measures to achieve minimum capital adequacy (including fresh capital contributions from new or existing shareholders) and to restructure operations were required. Failure to comply with the performance targets triggered prompt corrective action procedures, including suspension and eventual closure.

The focus of this exercise was the institutions with the greatest systemic importance. This implied giving priority to the insolvent merchant banks and commercial banks. Once these institutions were dealt with, attention shifted to the specialized and development banks and nonbank financial institutions.

Banks

The first wave of public support was targeted at resolving problems with potential systemic consequences. Of the 27 commercial banks at end-1997, 14 had reported capital ratios below the 8 percent requirement, and two were technically insolvent.

- Given their systemic importance, in January 1998 the government nationalized the two large commercial banks that were insolvent (KFB and Seoul Bank).
- In July 1998, five small banks with negative capital ratios were closed. Their operations were transferred to five stronger banks under purchase and assumption agreements.
- The remaining seven undercapitalized banks were required to take remedial action under approved rehabilitation plans to meet the required minimum capital requirement of 8 percent. The banks were given a two-year period in which to attain this level in order not to unduly disrupt the credit process. However, this forbearance was not entirely successful as the banks themselves found they were under increasing pressure from the market to attain the 8 percent ratio as soon as possible.
- During the course of 1999, there were a series of mergers, facilitated by the injection of public funds, involving five of the undercapitalized banks. These mergers resulted in two large government-owned banks (Hanvit and Cho Hung). The other two undercapitalized banks were recapitalized with a combination of private and public funds.
- Banks that were not undercapitalized at end-1997 have undergone diagnostic reviews. Three have been placed under prompt corrective action while the rest have undergone various forms of restructuring, including mergers, downsizing and raising additional private capital.
- The government has also recapitalized the specialized and development banks, which had seen a significant deterioration in their portfolios, and made them subject to regulations in line with those applied to commercial banks.

Nonbank financial institutions

Once the strategy for bank restructuring was in place, the authorities targeted the restructuring of nonbank financial institutions (NBFIs). Priority was initially given to resolving problems in the merchant bank sector as their condition had deteriorated sharply in late 1997. The large concentration of credit risk to the troubled *chaebol* and their affiliates, together with losses in currency, bond, and equity markets, led to widespread distress in this sector. Out of 30 merchant banks before the crisis, only a half dozen remain, the rest being closed, merged with commercial banks, or taken over by the government and consolidated. At this stage the sector has ceased to be a systemic concern; rather the issue now is the role that merchant banks will play in the more liberalized financial sector.[43]

The next step was to close the smaller institutions that had no prospect of viability. These included a very large number of smaller depositary institutions, mutual saving and finance institutions, credit co-operatives, and a large number of more specialized institutions. With the setting up of the unified supervisory system (see below), it became possible to apply similar supervisory standards to these institutions. As a result nearly a thousand smaller institutions have been closed, and it is anticipated that more will follow.

A review of the life insurance sector revealed widespread financial stress. Korea had a large life insurance sector that consisted of 33 companies, estimated to be the sixth largest in the world in terms of premia collected. The industry was also conducting a quasi-banking business, with the average maturity of policies much shorter than is conventional in other countries, and with a large proportion of assets invested in commercial lending. A 1998 review identified 18 weak companies that were requested to submit rehabilitation plans. Seven of these companies had negative net worth; four small companies were closed and the remainder merged or sold. One large company, Korea Life, remains to be dealt with after initial attempts at finding a buyer have failed. The authorities are now seeking to rehabilitate it before making a further attempt to sell.[44]

Following these initial steps, the government implemented a number of measures to strengthen the industry. The EU solvency margin standards for

---

[43]The share of merchant banks in total financial system assets declined from 5 percent at the end of 1999 to 1 percent in June 2000.

[44]In addition, two surety and guarantee insurance companies experienced major difficulties following the default of a large proportion of the corporate bonds that they had guaranteed. The two companies were taken over by the government, merged, and recapitalized as Seoul Guarantee.

life insurance companies were adopted in April 1999, to be phased in over a period of 5 years. New loan classification and provisioning rules similar to those of commercial banks were designed and imposed effective September 2000, and investment guidelines have been tightened to curtail bank-like lending activities. The terms and pricing of policies were liberalized in early 2000. Finally, the insurance business law has been amended to enact the reforms of corporate governance that apply to listed companies.

The leasing sector, said to be the fourth largest in the world, has also been substantially reduced in size following the restructuring measures. Most of the leasing companies were associated with commercial banks, albeit via minority stakes. The bulk have now been closed, with shareholders and creditors absorbing significant losses.

Among other nonbank financial intermediaries, the investment trust industry was perhaps the weakest and posed the most significant systemic risk. This industry—consisting of investment trust companies (ITCs) that were allowed to sell their products and investment trust management companies (ITMCs) that were not—faced twin problems of liquidity and capital deficiency. These institutions were the main purchasers of corporate bonds in Korea. The bottoming out of interest rates and gradual increase in bond yields since early 1999 resulted in mounting unrecognized losses. Initially, the lack of transparency in the sector partly disguised the losses.

The ITC sector suffered from a number of problems. First, the three largest ITCs were insolvent and, although it was illegal, they had been borrowing indirectly from their trust funds to finance operations. They had very large losses in their proprietary trading accounts that were incurred in the late 1980s when the government instructed the ITCs to intervene in the stock market to support falling stock prices. Second, most of the bond funds were not marked to market and inter fund transfers were common given the lax supervisory oversight. With declining interest rates, managers transferred higher yielding paper to new funds in order to offer above-market rates of return and thus attract new investments. The marketing agents of investment trusts essentially offered a guarantee on the funds' rate of return even though this practice was illegal. Third, there was an increasing maturity mismatch in the asset and liabilities. In mid-1999, the average maturity of liabilities was four and a half months compared to the average maturity of assets of 16 months. Fourth, ITCs and ITMCs held a significant proportion of the outstanding debt of the top five *chaebol*, including more than 80 percent of Daewoo's domestic bonds and commercial paper. Finally, the problems had systemic implications because a large proportion of the sector's funding came from financial institutions, including banks, which treated such investments as liquid.

Following the Daewoo crisis in July 1999, redemption pressures mounted as investors became increasingly aware of the losses in ITCs. It became clear then that the authorities' initial approach of delaying the resolution of the industry's problems until the rest of the financial sector had been restored to health, would no longer be tenable, nor would it be possible to avoid the use of public funds.[45] In response the government implemented a number of steps to deal with the liquidity crisis of the sector. These included temporary restrictions on redemptions to slow the withdrawal of funds from the sector, and the creation by the government of a "Bond Market Stabilization Fund" (BMSF) to be funded with contributions from banks and insurance companies. The BMSF's aim was to maintain single-digit bond rates by purchasing corporate bonds and government securities.

These measures temporarily slowed redemptions from bond funds, but the deep rooted weaknesses of the sector required fundamental restructuring efforts. The government responded with a series of measures to accelerate the transformation of the sector starting in November 1999. The two largest ITCs, which did not have large parent company shareholders, were recapitalized. The authorities regarded the third largest ITC, controlled by the Hyundai group, as being in a position to carry out its own recapitalization without the use of public funds. Steps were also taken to move gradually to mark-to-market principles for all bond funds. The ITCs were also instructed to clean up bad assets in their trust funds through write-offs, transfers to sales units (i.e., securities companies), and securitization. The FSS also tightened regulations on disclosure requirements and corporate governance for ITCs. These included disclosure requirements for the performance of fund management, and appointment of non-executive directors, audit committees, and compliance officers to ensure that managements act in accordance with their responsibilities to investors. These efforts stabilized the sector in mid-2000 and the improved disclosure and governance measures started attracting fresh capital from abroad.

---

[45]Indeed, many of the problems of the ITC sector were well recognized by the Korean authorities and the Fund staff before they reached crisis proportions. Thus, the letter of intent for the fourth quarterly review under the stand-by arrangement in November 1998 included measures such as (a) requiring ITCs to mark new funds to market beginning on November15, 1998, and to mark all funds to market beginning on July 1, 2000; and (b) reducing borrowings from their trust funds according to a specified schedule. The authorities, however, were reluctant to push hard on restructuring the sector and these steps did little to prevent the market turmoil that ensued.

NPL purchases

The authorities had announced, in November 1997, a program of nonperforming asset acquisition as a mechanism for delivering official support for bank restructuring. In March 1998, the government estimated the total amount of troubled loans of all financial institutions to be about W118 trillion (about 28 percent of GDP) and targeted W100 trillion worth of loans for immediate disposal through two channels: first, the internal restructuring efforts of financial institutions, and second, purchases by KAMCO at a discount of the face value. Although the efforts of financial institutions took time to bear fruit, KAMCO quickly became influential in the early stabilization of the financial sector by removing a large proportion of the banks' nonperforming assets in exchange for negotiable government guaranteed bonds carrying market related interest rates. These asset purchases helped to stabilize the balance sheet deterioration of the banks and also substituted a more liquid asset for the illiquid assets purchased. In the early stages of the acquisition program the prices paid by KAMCO turned out to be in excess of realizable value of the assets. Thus KAMCO provided solvency support as well as liquidity. Starting in September 1998 KAMCO developed uniform pricing criteria and increased the average discount on its purchases to more realistic levels.[46]

The heavy use of nonperforming asset purchases was controversial at the time because its implications for the use of public funds could not be easily

Table 4. Korea: Asset Quality of All Financial Institutions

Percent of All Loans	Dec-99	Dec-00
Substandard or below	14.9	10.4
Of which: commercial banks	13.6	8.9
Net substandard or below[1]	9.0	4.8
Of which: commercial banks	8.1	3.7
Nonperforming[2]	11.3	8.1
Of which: commercial banks	8.3	6.6
Total loans (in trillion won)	590.9	621.4
Of which: commercial banks	328.3	361.4

[1](Total substandard or below loans-loan loss provisions)/(total loans-loan loss provisions).
[2]Including all loans overdue for more than 3 months and non-accrual loans.

---

[46]After September 1998 the purchase price of secured loans was reduced from 70-75 percent of collateral value to 45 percent. For unsecured loans, a uniform price structure was introduced after September, paying 3 percent of the principal balance, whereas previously doubtful loans and estimated loss credits were purchased at 10-20 percent and at 1-3 percent of face value, respectively.

assessed. Compared with using public funds to recapitalize banks directly, asset purchases did not provide managerial rights to KAMCO, which could have been used to require banks to undergo operational restructuring. In addition, if banks' conditions improved following asset purchases, KAMCO did not benefit from the upside potential. Borrowers were also likely to assign a lower priority to repaying KAMCO as the institution could not provide them with new financing. On the positive side, a centralized approach for asset purchases provided economies of scale in disposition and collection, and freed bank management to focus on the analysis of new loans and other operational issues. Recently KAMCO has also assumed a role in corporate restructuring through its ownership of debt of large corporations that are undergoing debt-equity swaps. Further, KAMCO has used innovative methods to dispose of more than half of its portfolio through various methods with considerable profits. In the process the institution has been influential in nurturing a new market for NPLs both in Korea and also in the region. Following in the agency's footsteps, several financial institutions have become active in the NPL market through strategic partnerships with foreign financial institutions for securitization and disposal of their NPLs.

The stock of impaired loans (i.e., substandard and below) remains high but has been on a declining trend since 1999. As the crisis unraveled, and with the strengthening of loan classification standards, financial institutions' impaired loans reached about 15 percent (W88 trillion) at end-1999 despite KAMCO purchases amounting to W56 trillion (face value). Since then, financial institutions have made significant progress in reducing their impaired loans, with such loans declining to 10 percent (W65 trillion) of total loans as of end-2000. Commercial banks account for about two-thirds of these impaired assets. The decline was mainly due to continuing efforts of institutions to dispose bad loans through sales to KAMCO, via asset-backed-securities (ABS), extensive write-offs, and collections. Questions remain, however, about the magnitude of loans currently classified as "precautionary" (i.e., one category better than impaired) that will likely turn bad.

Use of public funds

A necessary ingredient in the financial sector restructuring process has been the large injection of public funds. This was essential for a number of reasons. First, the history of significant government intervention in financial markets led to expectations of public support, which became self-fulfilling when problems came to light. The government was also unwilling to allow large numbers of Korean citizens to lose their deposits. Second, the share owning structure

Table 5. Korea: Public Funds Used for Financial Restructuring
(As of end-October 2000, in trillions of won)

Form of Support	KDIC	KAMCO	Total
Banks	27.9	17.3	45.2
Nonbanks	15.6	3.2	18.8
Total bond financed funds	43.5	20.5	64
Financed from recoveries	10.5	13.4	23.9
Subtotal	54.0	33.9	87.9
Other public funds	28.9	1.1	30.0
Gross total	82.9	35.0	117.9
Memorandum Item:			
Total recovery	8.9	19.2	19.2

of the commercial banks consisted of institutional portfolio investors and small shareholders, none of which were in a position to be the source of the recapitalization of the sector. Although major corporate groups were substantial owners of non-bank financial institutions (e.g. securities companies, merchant banks, life assurance companies, and investment trust companies), they were barred from owning banks.[47] Third, the size of the problem was obscured by ineffective and misleading accounting arrangements, discouraging private investors from stepping in. Moreover, the scale of the problem was clearly so large as to deter any investor that did not have the backing of the government.

As of end-October 2000, the gross injection of public funds amounted to W118 trillion (22 percent of 2000 GDP). The government's intervention has been channeled through two agencies: KDIC is charged with recapitalization of financial institutions, loss coverage, and depositor protection, whereas KAMCO is responsible for the purchase of impaired assets. The National Assembly has made two separate authorizations for the issuance of government-guaranteed bonds totaling W104 trillion (about 21 percent of average GDP in 1998-2000) for financial sector restructuring.[48] The allocations from the National Assembly have been supplemented by injections of W30 trillion financed from other public sources, including the budget, resources borrowed from international organizations, and asset swaps; of this, about one-third represents an actual or contingent liability for the government. Further, about W24 trillion of recovered funds have been recycled.

---

[47]No shareholder could own more than 4 percent of equity capital of a bank.

[48]The second allocation, which was for W40 trillion, was made in late 2000 and has not yet been fully utilized. Hence, it is not part of the W118 trillion figure of the total injection mentioned earlier.

The use of public funds has been linked to strict criteria to minimize moral hazard. Although initial asset purchases by KAMCO in late 1997 and early 1998 were not linked to specific conditions, once the system stabilized the use of public funds was made conditional on approved rehabilitation plans. In addition, any contribution of public funds was linked to adequate contributions by shareholders. In the case of recapitalization of financial institutions taken over by the government, the shareholder equity has been diluted to avoid moral hazard. A striking example of this was the recapitalization of four smaller banks in late 2000 where all shareholder equity was written down.

In addition, to improve transparency the government published a white paper in late 2000 documenting the use of public funds. The government has also committed to a tight-deadline for the recovery of used public funds through the redemption of preferred shares and privatization of commercial banks no later than 2003, and also through the various asset disposition methods adopted by KAMCO.

The government, by providing the public funds for its past commitments only, is trying to strike a balance between allocating the needed public funds and the moral hazard implications of committing contingency funds for future use. However, further delays in corporate restructuring and additional contingent liabilities of the government may require additional public funds in the future. In addition, the committed amounts so far do not include the contingent liabilities of the government due to the corporate bond guarantee scheme announced in late 2000 (see below). These contingent liabilities may require future use of public funds if the guarantees are called. The remaining challenge for Korea is to speed up the market-based restructuring of the corporate sector without use of public funds and to manage the recovery of public funds efficiently.

Prudential regulations and supervision

Supervisory oversight has been significantly strengthened and prudential regulations have been brought closer in line with international best practice. Steps have also been taken to improve the quality of supervision. Supervision has been consolidated into a single independent agency, the FSC and its executive branch, the FSS. The FSC/FSS now has supervisory as well as regulatory authority for all bank and nonbank financial institutions and also the specialized and development banks. In addition, new legislation makes the FSC (rather than the Ministry of Finance and Economy) responsible for issuing and revoking licenses of all financial institutions. By consolidating many supervisory functions in one agency, the potential for regulatory arbitrage, a problem in the past, has been reduced.

Prudential measures introduced so far have addressed a wide range of concerns, including loan classification and provisioning standards, capital adequacy, accounting and disclosure standards, connected lending, cross guarantees, and foreign exchange liquidity and exposure. Most of the regulatory changes were introduced during 1998-99 with the aim of bringing Korea's prudential regulations closer to international best practice:

- More stringent rules on the classification and provisioning of nonperforming loans have been introduced. The introduction at the end of 1999 of loan classification and provisioning based on "forward-looking criteria," which takes into account the capacity of borrowers to service all obligations rather than focusing on delinquency criteria, was especially noteworthy.
- Large exposure limits for commercial, merchant, and specialized and development banks were reduced, and more comprehensive definitions enacted, which will play a part in limiting the ability of major corporates to gear up excessively.
- Limits on connected lending to large shareholders and their affiliates have been significantly tightened and disclosure requirements strengthened. In addition, since 1999 all connected lending and the terms on which it is provided must be audited and disclosed in annual financial statements.
- Prudential requirements for commercial banks have been extended to specialized and development banks.
- Mark to market accounting has been introduced, including on new funds invested in ITCs, and on all traded securities and derivative positions other than for hedging assets valued at historical cost.
- Controls were introduced for prudent management of banks' foreign currency liquidity. Both commercial banks and merchant banks are now required to report the maturity of their liabilities and assets. In addition, internal liquidity controls based on a maturity ladder approach have been introduced for these institutions. To further improve Korea's external debt profile, the monitoring of external debt and reserves has been strengthened through more frequent reporting and improved coverage.
- Improved arrangements for supervising groups of institutions on a consolidated basis have been established. New arrangements for the supervision of market risk were introduced in 2000.
- Accounting and disclosure standards for banks, securities companies, and insurance companies now fully comply with the requirements of the

International Accounting Standards (IAS 30). Where IAS are silent, the US GAAP will be used as the alternative benchmark.

Achievements

As a result of the crisis and the implementation of the reforms described above, the state of the financial sector has changed radically and its viability has been enhanced. The number of financial institutions has been significantly reduced, some sections of the financial system are much reduced in importance, and the remaining institutions have improved their financial and operational structure. There has been a significant change in ownership and foreign participation as well.

Banks' capital is now in excess of the minimum requirement for almost all institutions. The average capital of commercial banks increased from a reported (but likely overstated) 7 percent of risk-weighted-assets at end-1997 to 10.8 percent at mid-2000 after mergers, closures, and recapitalization. Impaired assets, although still high, are declining and provisions for such loans have been boosted. The restructuring process has also led to a significant consolidation in the Korean banking sector. Mergers have been especially influential in this process. The government's recent restructuring measures include the consolidation of unsound government-owned banks under a financial holding company which will create a large bank with significant market share. This measure has provided an incentive for private banks to follow suit with other mergers.

The government also launched the process of divesting the new stakes it has acquired in the financial sector by selling 51 percent of KFB to a foreign capital group. In addition, Seoul Bank was put under new management with the assistance of Deutsche Bank to prepare it for privatization. The authorities have also committed to the privatization of remaining state-owned banks beginning no later than 2003.

A significant degree of operational restructuring has taken place in commercial bank operations. About one third of the workforce has been cut, along with branch closures, and many remaining employees have had to accept salary reductions. Banks that received government support are also required to set performance benchmarks (e.g., minimum required returns on assets and equity). The restructuring process has also shaken up management culture and is changing the business structure of banks, with positive implications for future profitability. Following the large losses in the immediate aftermath of the crisis, the banking sector reported positive profits before provisions in 1999, and most banks reported positive profits after provisions in 2000. Bank managements are placing an increasing emphasis on profitability rather than asset growth.[49] Most banks now have formal risk management systems in place, although the entrenchment of these techniques into banking operations will take time.

Partial deposit insurance was reintroduced on January 1, 2001 as originally scheduled. This switch from blanket insurance is essential to spur restructuring of the financial sector and reduce moral hazard. The level of insurance has been set at W50 million ($42,000) per depositor, which covers about 40 percent of all deposits and 95 percent of all depositors as of end-August 2000. Noninterest bearing corporate deposits, however, will remain fully covered until end-2003; these deposits are typically used by businesses in their daily operations and the extension of full coverage was granted to minimize the impact of a failure on corporate depositors and their employees and customers.

Among nonbank institutions, the significance of the merchant banking sector has diminished. Out of 30 institutions before the crisis only 4 remain. Although there may remain a niche for small specialist institutions, it is likely to be limited. In addition, many nonviable smaller depository institutions have been liquidated and the remainder do not pose any systemic vulnerability. The ITC sector has undergone a significant change in its business culture. The disclosure requirements and various corporate governance measures, along with mark-to-market pricing of bond funds, have helped to increase investor awareness about risk and the responsibilities of fund managers—necessary first steps for healthy market discipline in the industry.

Finally, significant amount of foreign capital has entered the financial sector, both at banks, securities companies, IT(M)Cs and insurance companies. Although most foreign-owned bank shares remain in the hands of portfolio investors, key strategic partners in large banks are now contributing to significant business decisions. In addition, since early 2000, several foreign financial institutions have formed strategic partnerships or acquired equity holdings in Korean institutions including in ITC(M)s, and securities and insurance companies.

Ongoing Restructuring: A Mixed Picture

Following the initial success in stabilizing the financial sector, the Daewoo crisis revealed further weakness in the financial and corporate sectors and the need for renewed effort in the restructuring process. After an extensive review

---

[49]See Karasulu (2001) for an empirical analysis of the profitability of the banking sector in Korea.

in the latter part of 2000, an independent evaluation committee identified eight weak banks in need of recapitalization.[50] The extension of FLC loan classification and provisioning standards to restructured and workout loans revealed significant capital deficiencies at these banks. Accordingly, in December 2000, the government declared six of these banks technically insolvent and wrote off their entire shareholder capital ahead of public recapitalization. The authorities have also established a financial holding company and brought four of these six banks under the umbrella of the FHC. In addition, four more merchant banks failed in 2000. The government decided against liquidation, and instead provided public funds to normalize operations and merge them for subsequent inclusion in the FHC. The remaining two banks will also receive additional capital injections tied to strict performance criteria that include a freeze on operational costs, targets for NPL disposal and profitability.

The nationalization rather than closure of smaller institutions of no systemic importance was a policy change. This change appears to be partly dictated by political realities—outright closure would have brought forth strong opposition from labor—and partly by cost-benefit analysis of alternative resolution methods. The outright closure of the smaller banks faced strong opposition from labor. However, the decision to include the smaller banks in FHC together with Hanvit could hinder the rehabilitation of all four institutions. In addition, creating financial conglomerates ahead of an adequate governance and regulatory infrastructure may present new vulnerabilities.

The liquidity crunch in the corporate bond market has prompted further government measures. In late 2000, large companies that encounter difficulty in rolling over their bonds became eligible for a scheme, provided they retired 20 percent of the maturing bonds, whereby the state-owned KDB rolls over the remaining 80 percent of maturing amounts for subsequent sale in government guaranteed collateralized bond obligations (CBOs). There was also a sharp increase in the amount of government guarantees provided for bonds of low-rated and small and medium-sized companies when these bonds are included in CBOs. These measures were in response to the exceptional bunching of maturing corporate bonds, the decline of the investment trust sector, the risk aversion of banks, and the strong likelihood that there could be spillovers affecting many viable companies.

---

[50]The group includes four large banks (Cho Hung, Korea Exchange Bank, Hanvit, Seoul) all of which have received significant government support in the past, and four smaller banks (Peace, Kwangju, Cheju and Kyongnam).

The Remaining Agenda

Although much has been done to stabilize the financial system, more needs to be done before its soundness is firmly established. Deeper corporate restructuring will likely reveal additional impaired loans that banks will have to resolve, and a subset of banks remain weak. Indeed, the problems that remain in the financial sector are now largely the result of continuing weaknesses in the corporate sector. Despite the emphasis on creating "clean banks," asset quality problems remain. It is now up to the banks, under the supervision of the authorities, to take an even more aggressive attitude in accounting for asset quality. Only by doing so will banks convince markets that known credit losses have been met and that they are now making operating profits sufficient to meet new credit losses in the future. For balance sheet improvements to be sustained, banks will need to strengthen business practices, especially with regard to risk analysis and lending practices.

A market driven corporate restructuring process will only be truly feasible if it is led by sound and privately owned banks. The privatization of Korea First Bank was a landmark step, and priority will need to be given to privatizing the other nationalized banks and divesting government minority stakes in other banks. The privatization process cannot be done rapidly but it is important that a start be made as soon as the market allows; the costs involved in the government continuing to own these banks for several years outweigh the benefits that might accrue by waiting in the hope that the share price might rise.

Turning to specific issues, first, an immediate priority is the rehabilitation of the banks that, in late 2000, were revealed to have capital deficiencies. The restructuring plans these banks have submitted will need to be vigorously implemented, with special attention to those grouped under the new financial holding company. Second, financial sector consolidation is likely to occur naturally over time through market-driven mergers. The creation of financial conglomerates, however, should be pursued only after an adequate governance and regulatory infrastructure is in place; this will take time to create. And third, the authorities need to be vigilant about the credibility of the supervisory framework; it will be critical to resist pressures for forbearance and ensure operational autonomy of the financial supervisory authorities. Most of the needed improvements in the regulatory framework, or what might be called the "hardware," have now largely been completed. However, important steps remain to be completed to the "software" of the supervisory system. In particular, it will be important to move from a process that emphasizes formal compliance with regulations, which was the tradition of the predecessor organizations of the

Financial Supervisory Service, to one that concerns itself mainly with assessing risk and promoting better risk management.

Finally, the recent intervention by the government in the corporate bond market raises a number of concerns that the authorities will need to address through their actions. First, it will be critical to avoid actions that may create a perception that some corporate groups are "too big to fail," thereby introducing moral hazard and undoing some of the progress of the last three years. Second, it will be important to ensure that the intervention in the bond market contains sufficient safeguards to ensure that corporate restructuring will continue, including the exit of nonviable companies. Third, the use of government guarantees should not become so widespread that the role of the market in assessing and pricing risk is effectively eliminated and replaced with credit decisions by committees of state-owned financial institutions and possible subsidies for borrowers. And fourth, the authorities will need to be watchful of the growing contingent liability that arises from the extensive provision of government guarantees.

Corporate Sector Restructuring

Strategy for Restructuring

In response to the crisis, the government made corporate restructuring one of its key priorities. The main objectives were to restore the health and competitiveness of the corporate sector and address the structural weaknesses that left Korea vulnerable to a financial crisis. Unlike previous interventions, the government tried to limit its role to strengthening the institutions in order to allow investors and creditors to monitor firms and create an environment where market discipline could play a stronger role in driving the restructuring process. However, given the scale of the corporate sector's problems and the use of public funds to restructure the financial system, a substantial government role was unavoidable. The strategy for corporate restructuring had three main elements:

- **Promoting greater competition.** Reforms focused on opening markets to greater competition, both domestic and foreign, by liberalizing the foreign investment regime and strengthening the role of the Fair Trade Commission (FTC).
- **Improving corporate governance.** Measures to improve the corporate governance system included: strengthening investor rights, enhancing

the transparency of financial accounting and disclosure, raising the accountability of managers and major shareholders, and improving the efficiency of bankruptcy procedures.

- **Improving capital structure and profitability.** Through a combination of direct enforcement and market incentives, the government pushed corporations to reduce their excessive debt levels, improve their capital structure, and eliminate cross-subsidization of weaker affiliates. The government adopted a flexible approach to restructuring, depending upon the size, nature of the problem, and available financing options.

Promoting greater competition

Steps to liberalize the capital markets and the foreign investment regime were implemented in the very early stages of the government's reform program. The objective was to give Korean companies direct access to foreign capital markets and to allow for greater competition in the economy. Granting companies direct access to the international capital markets would not only provide them with a wider menu of financing options and lower borrowing costs, but also help shift corporate financing away from an excessive reliance on bank financing.

Figure 13. Gross Foreign Direct Investment in Korea, 1990 - 2000
(In billions of US$)

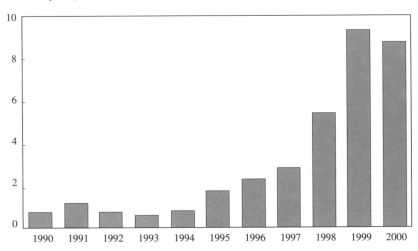

Source: Korean authorities and staff estimates.

The steps to liberalize capital markets and foreign direct investment included: (i) the elimination of ceilings on foreign investment in equity, bond, and money markets; (ii) the lifting of restrictions on corporate borrowing abroad; (iii) the liberalization of foreign ownership in most industries and financial services; (iv) the establishment of a "one-stop service" to simplify the approval process for foreign investment; (v) the easing of hostile takeover rules and other anti-takeover devices to protect existing management; and (vi) the elimination of restrictions on foreign investors to purchase land for investment projects.[51]

These liberalization measures contributed to the strong inflows of portfolio and foreign direct investment, beginning in the first quarter of 1998. Furthermore, in response to the lifting of the restrictions on overseas borrowing, long-term external liabilities of domestic corporations rose from $25 billion at end-1997 to $30 billion by end-June 1999, while short-term borrowings by domestic financial institutions were reduced from $63 billion to $31 billion over the same period.

Improving corporate governance

To strengthen corporate governance, the government addressed a wide range of issues from legal, regulatory, and tax impediments to mergers and acquisitions, asset sales, and spin-offs to improvements in corporate transparency and accounting standards. Several laws and regulations were amended to increase the accountability of management and controlling shareholders. In February 1998, the Korean Stock Exchange (KSE) required that all publicly traded companies have at least one outside board director, and by the end of 1999 fill a quarter of their boards with outside directors. The government also reformed the Commercial Code to clarify the fiduciary responsibility of directors. Steps were also taken to strengthen the rights of minority shareholders to counterbalance the leverage of large inside shareholders. For example, the Commercial Code and Securities and Exchange Act were reformed in February 1998 to lower the threshold for exercising rights to file suit, make proposals at a general shareholders meeting, inspect company's financial accounts, and request the dismissal of directors or internal auditors. In September 1998, restrictions on voting rights for institutional investors were removed, and in December 1998 a limited form of cumulative voting for the selection of direc-

---

[51]For a more detailed review of the government's program to liberalize the capital markets and the foreign investment regime, see IMF (2000).

tors was introduced. The government also announced plans to introduce class action suits against directors starting in 2002.

Considerable emphasis was put on improving the quality and timeliness of financial disclosure and strengthening accounting standards. In February 1998, the government amended the Act on External Audit of Joint-Stock Corporations to bring forward the deadline to 1999 (from 2000) for requiring that all listed companies prepare financial statements that are audited in accordance with international standards (IASC), and to bring financial disclosure standards in line with international best practice. In April 2000, the top 30 *chaebol* were required for the first time to produce combined financial statements that net out intra-group transactions, thereby producing a more complete picture of corporate health.[52] Also in 2000, listed companies were required to release reports quarterly and establish audit committees composed of outside directors, shareholders, and creditors representatives within the board of directors. The government also empowered the Korea Institute of CPAs as an independent professional body for auditing and setting standards by granting it responsibility for regulating and monitoring auditing standards in the profession.

The FTC has played a more active role in enforcing regulations against illegal intra-unit *chaebol* transactions. In April 1998, it prohibited the use of new debt guarantees across affiliates and required that existing guarantees be wound down by March 2000. The FTC has also conducted its own investigations and levied fines on *chaebol* found engaging in illegal intra-unit transactions. In some instances, these investigations have led to lawsuits filed by civic groups and minority shareholders against companies whose actions went against the best interest of shareholders.

Finally, insolvency laws were strengthened to expedite the exit of nonviable firms and facilitate restructuring under court supervision. In February 1998 and again in December 1999, the government amended the insolvency laws to provide a better balance between debtors' and creditors' rights and to improve the speed and efficiency of the court system. To strengthen creditor rights, the government required that creditors' committees be formed and that court-appointed administrators consult with creditors' committees on major issues affecting the administration of the debtor company. Time limits were also introduced to expedite the reorganization process.[53] A specialized ban-

---

[52] "Combined" statements apply the principle of consolidated accounting to companies that do not necessarily have any shareholding links but are under common control. This is a typical form of organization of Korean *chaebol* where control is exerted through family shareholdings in individual companies rather than through a parent holding company (Park, 2000).

[53] Proceeding must commence within one month of filing and be completed within one and half year after filing. Bankruptcy (i.e. liquidation) is automatically triggered if the process is repealed or the reorganization plan is rejected.

kruptcy court was also created in Seoul District with judges assigned predominantly to do insolvency work.

Improving capital structure and profitability: the restructuring framework

The authorities recognized that the changes to the legal and regulatory framework would have little immediate impact on improving companies' capital structure and profitability. In particular, more direct action would be needed to address immediate problems such as the large corporate debt overhang. The Financial Supervisory Commission (FSC) was hence given responsibility for overseeing the restructuring of the corporate sector.

For restructuring, the government separated corporations into three tiers that mirrored the industrial structure of the economy. The first tier was the top-5 *chaebol*—Hyundai, Daewoo, Samsung, SK, and LG—which accounted for a large share of the country's resources and exports.[54] The next tiers were the heavily indebted medium-sized *chaebol* ranked 6 to 64 by asset size, and the cash-strapped small and medium-sized enterprise sector (SMEs). Each group faced similar problems, but differed in the magnitude of their indebtedness, access to capital, and the nature of the restructuring issues.

The restructuring task of the top-5 affiliates was viewed as too large and complex for either the courts or the banks to handle. Because of their large resources, ready access to the capital markets, and the weak conditions of the banks, the government instead pushed the top-5 to restructure on their own, through "voluntary capital structure improvement plans" (CSIPs) that were agreed by the banks, the government, and the companies.[55] The main banks worked with affiliates to draw up plans to monitor progress in restructuring, and the FTC was given greater power to enforce rules against illegal intra-*chaebol* transactions.[56] To help eliminate overcapacity in key manufacturing industries, the government called for a number of mergers and swaps, the so-called "Big Deals." In September 1998, the top-5 agreed on the general terms for merging and/or swapping 17 companies in seven core industries, covering

---

[54]In 1998, the top-5 *chaebol* accounted for roughly 27 percent of manufacturing output, 12 percent of manufacturing employment, and 30 percent of corporate sales.

[55]The CSIPs for the top-5 included steps to: (i) reduce debt-equity ratios to below 200 percent by end-1999; (ii) streamline operations to focus on four or five core businesses, and (iii) cut in half the number of subsidiaries and affiliates.

[56]In 1998, the FTC launched two rounds of investigations on intra-group transactions among the top-five *chaebol*. It found that over 113 firms had provided a total of W6 trillion of support to 56 affiliates. Support came mainly in the form of purchases of subordinated debt or convertible bonds of troubled affiliates at inflated prices. In response, the FTC levied fines of W93 billion.

aircraft, autos, petrochemicals, power generation, rolling stock, semiconductors, and ship engines.

For the more troubled and highly leveraged second tier *chaebol*, the government established an out-of-court workout process modeled after the Bank of England's "London Approach." Unlike the top-5, most of these mid-size companies lacked access to bank credit or the capital markets and needed debt workouts or new loans to have any chance of meaningful restructuring. Many were highly leveraged, with debt in some cases exceeding 1,000 percent of equity, spread across a number of creditors and a variety of debt instruments. They also had complex capital structures with non-transparent collateral pledges and cross-debt guarantees. To address the debt overhang problem of the most troubled *chaebol*, over 200 financial institutions signed in June 1998 a Corporate Restructuring Agreement (CRA) that committed all creditors to abide by specific workout procedures.[57] These procedures typically involved management changes, debt-equity swaps, asset sales, debt rescheduling, performance targets, and new loans. In addition, the government established an arbitration committee, the Corporate Restructuring Coordination Committee (CRCC), to help resolve disputes among creditors or between creditors and debtors.

The government also initiated a number of schemes to help SMEs obtain working capital and trade credit. The financial crisis hit the SME sector particularly hard, with the number of SME failures reaching 8,200 in 1997 and 10,500 in 1998. Support for the SMEs was seen as important not only for political reasons but also as a counterweight in an economy dominated by large conglomerates. Measures included expanding the capacity of the credit guarantee funds and establishing several short-term lending facilities, including through the BOK and KEXIM. Banks were instructed to evaluate the financial status of roughly 22,000 SMEs with outstanding loans of more than W1 billion. Banks classified roughly 40 percent of these as viable, identified candidates for workouts, and set up individual workout departments to review restructuring plans.

Achievements

Progress over the past three years has been mixed; there has been some restructuring, but not enough given the scale of the problem, and there are still significant weaknesses in the corporate sector. On the one hand, aggregate debt-

---

[57]Several candidates for workouts among the second tier *chaebol* affiliates decided to not apply for a workout and instead restructure on their own through CSIPs.

equity ratios have fallen from their excessively high levels; financial disclosure and corporate governance have improved; and the strong economic recovery has helped to improve cash flows. Market discipline is also beginning to play a larger role than before the crisis in punishing imprudent corporate behavior and in separating good and bad companies. On the other hand, Korea's corporate sector still remains highly leveraged and continues to suffer from low profitability, indicating that much more operational restructuring needs to be done. The continued existence of nonviable firms continues to be a drag on the economy, crowding out capital and labor to viable companies. In addition, the recent difficulties with some of the largest *chaebol* affiliates show that they still have the potential to destabilize financial markets.

Progress in restructuring the large chaebol and dealing with the collapse of Daewoo

Under the CSIP, the top-4 *chaebol* (excluding Daewoo) have made progress in reducing the number of subsidiaries and eliminating cross-debt guarantees. The top-4 rationalized 94 affiliates (out of around 190) in 1999 through sales, mergers, or liquidations and largely eliminated cross-debt guarantees by March 2000. The top-4 also met the government's target of a 200 percent debt-equity ratio by end-1999 by lowering their ratios from 470 percent in 1997 to 174 percent in 1999, through asset sales and capital expansion. However, these debt ratios do not account for the effect of cross-equity holdings across affiliates which artificially lower debt ratios without any real debt reduction or capital expansion.[58]

In August 2000, the Financial Supervisory Services (FSS) released for the first time a report on the combined financial statements (CFS) for sixteen large Korean *chaebol* for fiscal year 1999. The release of the CFS represents an important step in improving financial disclosure and transparency and bringing Korean accounting standards closer to international best practices. Not surprisingly, the CFS revealed higher debt-to-equity ratios than what had been reported under the consolidated framework. The average debt-to-equity ratio

---

[58]The large *chaebol* have used cross-equity shareholdings as a way to support weaker affiliates and reduce on paper their reported debt-equity ratios. The government originally placed limits on affiliate's cross-shareholdings, but removed them in 1998 to accelerate consolidation and in response to complaints that they left affiliates vulnerable to hostile takeovers by foreigners. However, the *chaebol* used cross-investments as a way of recapitalizing weaker affiliates without actually investing funds and for lowering debt-equity ratios for the entire group. To limit this, the FTC set a deadline of April 2001 for the top-30 *chaebol* affiliates to reduce their cross-shareholdings to below 25 percent of their net assets.

Table 6. Korea: Key Financial Indicators under CFS, 1999

	Debt-to-Equity Ratio			Interest	Current Assets /
	end-1998	*end-1999*		Coverage Ratio	Current Liabilities[1]
	Original	Original	New CFS	New CFS, end-1999	New CFS, end-1999
	(in percent)				
Hyundai	449.3	181.0	229.7	0.91	0.81
Samsung	275.9	166.3	194.0	3.15	0.96
LG	341.0	184.2	273.2	1.42	0.75
SG	354.9	161.0	227.6	1.47	0.76
Top-4	**352.0**	**173.9**	**225.4**	**1.71**	**0.83**
Total (16)	...	...	**225.5**	**1.42**	**0.81**

Source: FSS.
[1] "Current" refers to assets which can be converted within one year or liabilties with a maturity of one year.

for the conglomerates, excluding financial institutions, was 225 percent at the end of fiscal year 1999 (see Table 6). The higher debt ratios for the top-4 *chaebol* reflected both higher reported debt (by $14 billion) and lower equity (by $10 billion). For the remaining *chaebol*, the debt ratios varied from a low of 82 percent for Lotte to a high of 1,789 percent for Ssangyong.

The CFS also showed that the large *chaebol* were still suffering from poor operating performance. Nine of the sixteen *chaebol* reported an interest-coverage ratio (operating income divided by interest expense) of less than one, indicating that operating income was insufficient to cover their interest payments, let alone their principal obligations. Of the top-4, Hyundai was the worst performer (with a ratio of 0.9) while Samsung (with a ratio of 3) was the best. In addition, the average ratio of current assets to current liabilities was 0.81, implying that in the event of a cutoff in credit lines, many *chaebol* would not be able to cover their short-term debts with current assets that can be liquidated within one year. These figures imply that a majority of these large companies still remain highly leveraged and vulnerable to a rise in interest rates, a cutoff in bank lending, or a slowdown in the economy.

The collapse of Daewoo in 1999 was a result of its failure to address its core problems and delays in restructuring. Daewoo was the country's second largest conglomerate, accounting for roughly 10 percent of total exports. Daewoo's collapse was the largest corporate failure in Korea, and one of the largest and most complex restructuring cases in the world given its huge liabilities ($74 billion or 18 percent of GDP) and large scope of its domestic and overseas operations. Daewoo, like other *chaebol*, suffered from poor cash flow, excessive leverage, and overextension, but instead of selling assets and shedding loss-making businesses, it expanded and borrowed aggressively. As a result, its debt-equity ratio increased from 474 percent at end-1997 to 527 percent at end-1998. By July 1999, Daewoo's financial position became unsustainable.

Fearing the systemic risk from a Daewoo bankruptcy, the government urged creditor banks to roll-over Daewoo's short-term debt and take over its restructuring. Creditor banks eventually placed the 12 Daewoo affiliates under workout programs involving debt for equity swaps, debt restructuring, and new financing, and took over the restructuring of affiliates, by replacing top management and appointing outside auditors.[59] A buyback of just under $5 billion of debt owed to foreign creditors was also negotiated at a price of about 40 cents on the dollar. The takeover of Daewoo by its creditors was an important break from the past and sent a strong signal that no *chaebol* was "too big to fail." The government managed to successfully stabilize the financial system from the fallout, but the implications for the ITC sector, which had been main purchasers of Daewoo bonds, were substantial, resulting in a large fiscal costs.

However, progress has been slow in actually restructuring or selling off the various Daewoo affiliates leading to additional losses and lower values. To date, only small pieces of the group have been sold while creditor banks continue to extend loans ($4 billion in 2000) to keep affiliates operating. Following the collapse in September 2000 of the deal to sell Daewoo Motors to Ford—an event that was a serious blow to market sentiment—and difficulties in securing agreements with labor unions over job cuts, creditor banks decided to put the company into court receivership.

Progress under the workout programs

Workout programs have continued, but have focused more on debt restructuring than asset sales or divestitures. At end-September 2000, 44 companies (including the 12 Daewoo affiliates) were still under workout programs, down from 79 as of end-July 1999.[60] However, many of the workout companies remain deeply distressed and will face uncertain prospects when grace periods

---

[59]Daewoo was later found to have over inflated its assets and hidden debts totaling as much as $34 billion in July 1999.

[60]The change over this period reflects: (i) firms that have "graduated" from the program either through mergers, outright sales, or a turnaround in performance; (ii) firms that have left the program with support of their creditors to seek mergers on their own; and (iii) firms that have been "demoted" and will likely be liquidated or apply for court receivership.

on debt service expire. In some cases, additional workouts were needed after the original programs failed to normalize operations. The strong economic recovery, the stock market boom in 1998-99, and improved liquidity appear to have taken off some of the pressure to restructure.[61]

Banks were slow in pushing for real restructuring and asset sales partly as result of lax provisioning requirements on restructured loans to workout companies and weakness of their own balance sheets. Banks were allowed to classify restructured loans as "precautionary" or "substandard" and subject to provisioning of only 2-20 percent. In addition, banks were allowed to apply less stringent standards on loans to companies under court receivership and to losses resulting from holding secured commercial paper issued by the insolvent Daewoo Group.[62] Preferential treatment was given in order to encourage banks to participate in the corporate restructuring process and to extend new loans to workout companies. However, it subsequently became clear that the lax provisioning requirement was a disincentive for banks to recognize true losses in debt workout cases and led to superficial corporate restructuring with debt rescheduling and long grace periods. In addition, with no real market for distressed assets, pricing was difficult, leading to overvaluation or simply the use of book values. Banks were also constrained by their lack of expertise in corporate management and rehabilitation.

To facilitate the transfer of these distressed assets to investors, the government tightened loan classifications for credits to workout companies, bringing them under the new "forward-looking criteria" (FLC). The elimination of special treatment of loans to workout companies and the subsequent higher provisioning requirement under FLC (starting at end-2000), combined with enhanced accounting standards, have helped banks to take a more realistic view on asset quality. As a result, creditors have already begun selling their interests in some distressed workout companies to specialists with the capacity to realize potential recovery. In October 2000, the government introduced the corporate restructuring vehicle (CRV) system as a way of facilitating this transfer. CRVs take over distressed assets from creditor banks and restructure them using an asset management company with turnaround experience.

Progress has also been slow in resolving firms under court-supervised insolvencies. Thirteen *chaebol* began restructuring under court-supervised reorganizations in 1997. Most remain under court receivership and are being man-

---

[61] See Mako (2001) for a comparison of progress in corporate restructuring in East Asia.

[62] Loans classified as "doubtful" or "estimated loss" require a minimum provisioning ratio of 50 percent and 100 percent respectively. Loans extended to companies under court receivership or mediation procedures were reclassified as "normal" if they fulfilled the requirements as set in their Capital Structure Improvement Plans (CSIPs).

aged by a court-appointed administrator. With the exception of the early large cases, such as Kia Motors, relatively few large corporations have emerged from court-supervised reorganizations or been sold or liquidated.[63] Reasons include the lack of expertise in bankruptcy procedures within the court system, gaps within the insolvency procedures that favored the interests of debtors over those of the creditor, and the small pool of qualified court-appointed trustees.[64] The delays and associated uncertainty also severely hampered the ability of firms under court-supervised workouts to raise capital and compete for new orders.

Corporate governance

Companies have made progress in eliminating cross-payment guarantees and in erecting firewalls between affiliates. As of end-September 2000, only about W1 trillion in debt guarantees for all companies remained outstanding, down from W70 trillion before the crisis.[65] In a break from the past, large *chaebol* affiliates have begun separating themselves from the group. For example, in addition to the forced breakup of the Daewoo Group, the healthier affiliates of the Hyundai group, such as Hyundai Motors and Hyundai Heavy Industries, have taken steps to divorce themselves from their loss-making affiliates.[66]

Although financial disclosure and corporate transparency have improved, gaps in principle and in practice still remain. Korean accounting standards have been brought much closer to US GAAP and international best practices, and creditors, credit rating agencies, and investors have started to scrutinize auditors' reports more carefully. Banks are also using the combined financial

---

[63]In addition to Kia Motors, the exceptions include the sale of Anam Semiconductors to a foreign consortium, the sale of Samsung Motors to Renault, and the emergence of Jinro Coors from the Jinro Group.

[64]For example, changes in the Company Reorganization Act in 1998 which mandated wiping out half of the existing shares if a firm was found to be insolvent merely pushed debtors to apply for the less stringent "composition" procedures which did not mandate a wipeout of equity and allowed debtor management to maintain control of the company (Nam *et al.* 1999).

[65]As many of the remaining guarantees are associated with companies under workout programs or court-supervised reorganizations, the FTC has extended the deadline for eliminating them to March 2002 subject to fines for delays. However, cross-payment guarantees on borrowings from foreign financial institutions still remain.

[66]Using stock market data, Joh (2000) examines market evaluation of corporate governance reforms at the firm level and finds some evidence of improvement. Medium-size *chaebol* affiliates are perceived to be more independent than before the crisis, though group unity for the largest *chaebol* still remains high. In examining the relative performance of common and preferred shares, she finds weak evidence that excess private returns from controlling shares has diminished since the crisis, though the premium remains high compared to other countries.

statements to help classify loans to affiliates of the top *chaebol*. About 8,000 companies, including all listed firms, are now required to produce financial statements audited by independent accountants.[67] To meet the growing demand for corporate information, domestic credit rating agencies have expanded the depth and coverage of their services, and in an effort to deregulate the local credit information industry, the government is preparing legislation to allow international credit agencies to form joint ventures or set up their own operations in Korea.

Shareholder activism is on the rise, although it remains low compared with other advanced countries. Civic groups and minority and foreign shareholders are participating more in shareholder meetings to influence company policy, including through outside directors. Lawsuits have also been filed against corporations for actions that went against the best interest of shareholders. For example, in 1998 the People's Solidarity for Participatory Democracy (PSPD)—a citizens action group—and three large foreign funds won a proxy contest against SK Telecom's board and management, and resulted in the placement of three outside directors on the board, including two appointed by foreign funds. In December 1999, the government amended the Commercial Code and Securities Law to require that 50 percent of directors on boards of large

Figure 14. Percent of Foreign Shareholdings in the Korea Stock Exchange, 1995 - 2000

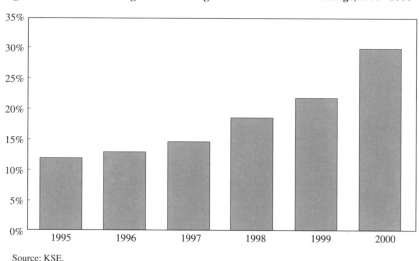

Source: KSE.

---

[67]Auditors who fail to report now face more severe sanctions, including criminal sentencing and large fines.

companies be outside directors and that audit committees be established on the board.[68]

Foreign participation in the Korean economy has risen substantially. For example, foreign ownership in Korean listed companies jumped from 13 percent in 1996 to over 30 percent at end-2000. Many of Korea's leading companies are now majority foreign owned (though not controlled) including Samsung Electronics (57 percent), POSCO (56 percent) and Hyundai Motors (50 percent), though the foreign shareholders are mainly portfolio and institutional investors. In addition, as mentioned earlier, Renault has taken over Samsung Motors, and Daimler Chrysler now owns a 15 percent stake in Hyundai Motors.

Health of the corporate sector

Despite the progress made so far in reducing debt-equity ratios, the corporate sector still remains highly leveraged and continues to suffer from low profitability. The average debt-equity ratio has come down significantly since the crisis but remains high by international standards (see Figure 15). In addition,

Figure 15. Korea: International Comparison of Debt-to-Equity versus Interest Coverage Ratio

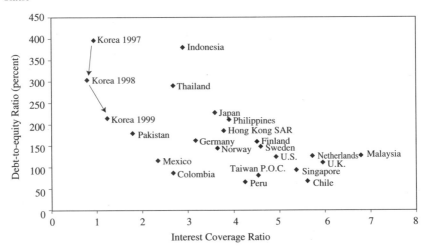

Source: "A Comparative Look of Korea's Corporate Reform," LG Economic Research Institute, 9/21/2000; original data taken from WorldScope DB and the World Bank; Asian Development Bank.
Note: Coverage of companies and the data of observations are not strictly comparable across countries.

---

[68]According to the KSE, as of February 2001 about 49 percent of the directors of the top-4 *chaebol* companies are outside directors.

Table 7. Korea: Indicators of Financial Stability and Profitability in Manufacturing

	Korea			U.S.	Japan	Taiwan, P.O.C.	Germany	Hong Kong, SAR	U.K.
	1997	1998	1999	1998	1998	1995	1996	1996	1996
Debt-equity ratio	396.3	303.0	214.7	158.9	173.6	85.7	163.0	186.0	111.0
Operating income to sales[1]	8.3	6.1	6.6	7.5	2.5	7.3	...	...	...
Ordinary income to sales[2]	-0.3	-1.8	1.7	8.1	2.3	5.1	...	...	...

Sources: BOK, *Financial Statement Analysis*, 1999; national sources.

[1]Operating income is the difference between the revenue of a business and its related costs and expenses, excluding income derived from sources outside its regular activities.

[2]Ordinary income is operating income after losses or gains from interest expenses/income, foreign currency transactions, and disposals of investments and tangible assets.

much of the improvement has been due to issuance of new equity rather than debt reduction. Although cash flows have improved in part due to the economic recovery, profitability continues to suffer, mainly due to high interest payments. This suggests that despite the strong recovery, little operational restructuring has taken place.

The average debt-to-equity ratio for the nonfinancial corporate sector declined from a high of 425 percent in 1997 to 235 percent in 1999. For the manufacturing sector, which accounts for over half the nonfinancial corporate sector, the average debt-to-equity ratio fell from 396 percent in 1997 to 215 percent at end-1999; as of end-June 2000, it stood at 193 percent (see Table 7). Total debt liabilities for the nonfinancial corporate sector fell by only W6.5 trillion in 1999 to W725 trillion (137 percent of GDP). Taking advantage of the rising stock market, equity financing increased sharply in 1999, replacing bond issuances as the primary source of financing.

Manufacturing profitability has improved over the last three years, owing in part to the economic recovery, but it remains weak and is constrained by the large debt service burden. Korea's operating performance compares favorably with Japan, the U.S., and Taiwan Province of China, but after accounting for nonoperating income and expenses, Korean corporate performance suffers markedly. This difference is due mainly to the interest burden on accumulated debt, which accounts for almost all of nonoperating expenses in Korea and is much higher relative to sales than elsewhere.[69] This trend is likely to have

[69]In general, sectors that managed to reduce significantly their debt-equity ratios (information technology, transport, storage and communications) showed better operating performance than those that remain saddled with large debts (construction, wholesale and retail trade).

continued in 2000, when according to preliminary data from the Korea Stock Exchange (KSE), ordinary profits of listed companies fell by 27 percent.

Another important measure of corporate health is the interest coverage ratio (ICR), defined as earnings before interest, tax, depreciation, and amortization (EBITDA) over interest expense. It measures a firm's capacity to cover its interest payments on its outstanding loans and presents a more complete picture of debt sustainability than just debt-equity ratios.[70] If a firm has an ICR of below 1, it is unable to meet its interest payments, let alone its principal obligations, using its current earnings. In the U.S., the average ICR in 1996 was around 8, and in order to earn an A-rating (based upon Standard & Poor's rating requirements), a U.S. company typically must have a ratio of operating cash flow to interest of more than 8.

Despite the improvement in operating performance in 1999-2000, about one in four Korean companies were unable to generate enough cash flow to meet their interest payments.[71] For example, the average ICR in 1999 for the affiliates of the top-64 *chaebol* was 2.3, up from 1.4 in 1998. However, 23

Figure 16. Korea: Amount of Maturing Corporate Bonds, 1999 - 2001
(In trillions of won)

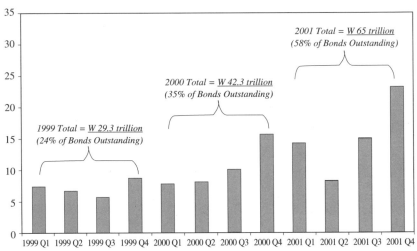

---

[70]For example, although the Hyundai group (along with LG, Samsung and SK) managed to reduce its debt-to-equity ratio to below 200 percent by end-1999 (on a consolidated statement basis), several of its affiliates continued to experience financial difficulties.

[71]The analysis here uses firm level financial data for 496 companies of the top-64 chaebol groups in 1999 (excluding Daewoo) compiled by IFC using data from the Korea Investor Services.

percent of the companies had an ICR below one, including 13 percent which recorded negative EBITDA. Many of the worst performers represented companies in workout programs or in court receivership.[72] The financial position of the medium-size *chaebol* affiliates is much weaker than for the top-4 affiliates. The medium-size *chaebol* had a larger share of companies with an ICR of below one (26 percent), suggesting that they in particular remain vulnerable to adverse shocks.

A broader analysis, which includes principal payments falling due (i.e. a debt service coverage ratio), would likely show that many more firms would be unable to meet their principal obligations with current income. Nearly 60 percent of outstanding corporate bonds mature in 2001; much of this debt was issued shortly after the crisis in early 1998 with a standard three-year maturity. Although some of this is likely to be refinanced or rescheduled, firms with a poor cash flow position will likely face difficulties in rolling over this debt and remain vulnerable to a cutoff in credit lines.

Remaining Agenda

To restore profitability and investor confidence, the corporate sector needs to accelerate deleveraging and undertake deeper operational restructuring. This will require further cost cutting, sales of noncore assets, and strategic alliances. Without these improvements, the corporate sector will remain weak and a source of distress, not of value, in the economy.

In some respects, the difficult part of corporate restructuring still lies ahead—nonviable firms need to be closed, and viable but distressed companies should be subject to rigorous workouts involving debt write downs as opposed to rescheduling. Indeed, the closure of nonviable companies may be a prerequisite for the growth of other companies, as these "zombie" companies are eroding the profit margins and crowding out credit to viable companies. In addition, it will be important for the government to avoid actions that could undo the lesson that no company is "too big to fail." With the improved social safety net, the economy should be strong enough to absorb the temporary dislocation that accompanies restructuring in the short run.

Although bank-led workouts were an important initial response to the systemic crisis in view of the simultaneous distress among dozens of *chaebol* and

---

[72]This result is consistent with BOK's analysis of 3,703 companies in the manufacturing industry, which showed that in 1999 roughly one in four manufacturers were unable to pay their financial costs with their cash income (BOK, 2000). A more recent BOK study of 1,807 manufacturing companies in the first half of 2000 found that about 27 percent still had an ICR of less than one.

insufficient institutional capacity of the courts, their potential as a vehicle for promoting restructuring has diminished. Because of concerns about realizing losses, banks have been unwilling or unable to force necessary divestitures, asset sales, or operational improvements on workout companies. Minority creditors and shareholders have also delayed workout resolutions by holding back support for an agreement until their narrow demands are met (as seen in several Daewoo cases).[73] As a result, relatively few large corporations have emerged from the workouts or from court-supervised reorganization.

To accelerate the restructuring process, attention needs to shift towards greater reliance on court-supervised insolvency. This could help overcome issues such as unrealistic valuations and difficulties with minority participants that have stymied bank-led workouts. Under court supervision, majority creditors would have more leeway to reorganize or liquidate a company. Toward this end, the recent legislation introducing "pre-packaged" bankruptcies should provide greater opportunities for cooperation between debtors and creditors and help simplify and shorten the time needed for liquidation procedures.[74] Additional steps to reform the insolvency system are needed to improve courts' capacity to handle cases effectively and expeditiously. For example, introducing an automatic stay and an "absolute priority rule" for the treatment of different creditor classes could help to encourage and expedite reorganizations, though incorporating such elements may require a broader examination of Korea's bankruptcy system. Insolvency reform is a long-term process, but the governments should press ahead now in anticipation of the next round of reorganizations and liquidations.

Further labor market flexibility would facilitate corporate restructuring. Labor difficulties have not only raised operating costs and created uncertainty, but also discouraged foreign investment and delayed asset sales and mergers. It will therefore be important to develop a national consensus that shifts attention away from preserving old jobs in dying industries to creating new jobs in vibrant growing ones. Some layoffs are inevitable, especially during the current economic downturn, and the government should ensure that provisions under the safety net are adequate to help mitigate their negative impact.

Continued development of capital markets would improve credit allocation, provide a wider range of financing options for companies, and allow

---

[73]Under Korean law, the votes of 80 percent of secured creditors and 66 percent of unsecured creditors are needed to approve a debt restructuring plan.

[74] "Pre-packaged reorganization" refers to the technique whereby an agreement reached between a debtor and a majority of its creditors out of court is then submitted to the court for approval under the applicable reorganization law. Because of the "cram down" provisions of the law, the approval by the court of this agreement makes it binding on dissenting creditors.

investors to play a stronger role in corporate decision-making. In particular, greater access to the capital markets by small- and medium-sized enterprises will lower the barriers to entry into industries long dominated by the large *chaebol*. Developing an active mergers and acquisition market will also facilitate restructuring by avoiding the use of the courts and bank-led workouts, and allowing companies themselves to do the necessary restructuring. This would also help promote further consolidation within industries suffering from excess capacity.

Finally, the campaign to discourage Korea's largest *chaebol* from ill-advised and excessive investments financed by debt will require longer-term efforts. Success will require progress on a number of fronts—strict oversight by investors and creditors, enhanced risk management practices, elimination of anti-competitive practices, stronger and more efficient insolvency procedures, and improved corporate governance. In this connection, recent measures announced by the government—covering issues such as improving the cumulative voting system, a further strengthening of minority shareholder rights, qualifications of outside directors, and transactions with related parties—will be useful. Efforts to further improve financial disclosure and transparency also need to be stepped up. Despite the progress made so far, Korean accounting practices still remain below the level of international best practices, both in principle and in practice. Greater corporate transparency will help to lower the cost of capital, reduce the uncertainty in investing in Korean companies, and allow markets to discipline poor corporate behavior.

The Economic Recovery

Korea's twin crisis resulted in a recession of unprecedented magnitude in 1998 when the economy contracted by almost 7 percent. The recovery in 1999 and 2000, with average growth of 10 percent per year, was also much faster and steeper than expected, and the large output gap was closed by late 1999. In addition, external vulnerability was sharply reduced with the rapid accumulation of external reserves and the reduction in short-term debt. The rebound, however, stalled in the latter part of 2000 with the economy contracting in the fourth quarter. A slowdown from the rapid growth rates of 1999 and much of 2000 was anticipated, and indeed seen as desirable in view of earlier concerns about overheating, but the downturn has been exacerbated by the deterioration in the global environment. Domestic confidence and demand have also been weakened by concerns about the pace of restructuring. The outlook for 2001 is thus for a sharp fall in growth to well below Korea's potential.

Figure 17. Real GDP, 1997-2000

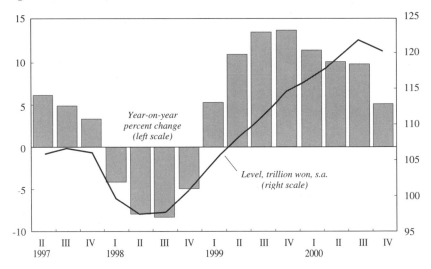

Factors Contributing to Korea's Recovery

Korea's economy bottomed in the second quarter of 1998, half a year after the onset of the crisis. The origin and the nature of the crisis, initial conditions, developments in the external environment, and macroeconomic and structural policies all had significant impact on the recovery path. This section analyzes Korea's recovery by comparing it with other OECD economies that experienced similar crises during the 1990s, with severe external shocks, depreciations of the exchange rate, and banking crises. The comparator countries are Sweden, Finland, and Mexico, and the stylized facts for these countries reveals certain differences that may explain why Korea was able to adjust as quickly as it did.[75]

Initial conditions

Sweden and Finland entered deep and prolonged recessions well before the financial crises of 1992 when their currency pegs were abandoned. Their recessions—which lasted three full years—were triggered by a combination of

---

[75]The choice of comparator countries is always debatable—Sweden and Finland have been chosen because they also have large manufacturing based export sectors. Lee and Rhee (2000) also analyze cross country patterns of recovery following a crisis. They attribute Korea's quick recovery to both the export-oriented structure and swift adjustment of macroeconomic policies.

adverse factors, including the bursting of an asset price bubble and an over-valued exchange rate. Sweden's real GDP contracted by a cumulative 5 percent, Finland's by almost 9 ½ percent reflecting the collapse of trade with the former Soviet Union and a terms of trade shock. The initial recoveries were narrow and externally driven; domestic demand began to strengthen only in late 1994.

Mexico's crisis unfolded in late 1994 and the country experienced a severe recession in 1995 when real GDP contracted by 7 percent. Similar to Korea, Mexico's economy rebounded swiftly. The recovery started about two quarters after the height of the crisis and was driven chiefly by booming exports, benefiting from market-opening trade reforms, strong partner country growth, and an improvement in terms of trade.

Relative to the other countries, Korea's pre-crisis economy enjoyed several advantages—a fiscal surplus; high household savings; a relatively large electronics manufacturing sector that allowed it to benefit from the global electronics boom; and a relatively balanced pre-recession real estate market. In addition, the real exchange rate was reasonably well-aligned with economic fundamentals prior to the crisis. Although there was overinvestment in Korea, this occurred primarily in the tradable goods sectors—namely, shipbuilding, automobiles, electronics, and semiconductors. Fortunately, these sectors received a boost from the significant depreciation of the currency. By contrast, excessive investment in some other crisis economies was concentrated in the real estate sector.

Korea also benefited from its low government debt (9 ½ percent of GDP at end-1996) and a fiscal surplus, which allowed greater latitude in countercyclical policies and in absorbing bank restructuring costs. By contrast, public finances in Sweden and Finland deteriorated rapidly, and were at the core of the crises, leaving less room for fiscal accommodation. In the case of Mexico, because of the higher initial debt level the government sought a fiscal surplus to offset foreign capital outflows and the effects of higher external debt service and bank restructuring costs, dampening its recovery.

With these advantages, Korea's economic turnaround was quicker, stronger and broader based than in Finland, Mexico, and Sweden. Although initially externally driven, the recovery broadened to private consumption and investment in large part due to improved sentiment and a significant recovery in the stock market (mainly in the information technology and communications sector).

External demand

In all countries, the external sector led the recovery and contributed to a sharp turnaround in the current account. But the nature of the external adjustment differed. In Finland, Mexico and Sweden, strong exports led the recovery and current account swing. By contrast, in Korea, although exports were strong, the turnaround in the current account was initially mainly the result of import compression. The net impact was that Korea's current account moved from a deficit of about $1\frac{1}{2}$ percent of GDP in 1997 to a surplus of $12\frac{1}{2}$ percent of GDP in 1998—a swing of almost $50 billion. This turnaround was an important factor in the quick replenishment of Korea's international reserves, which in turn helped restore investor confidence and the restoration of more orderly financial market conditions.

Since the middle of 1998, however, strong exports have played a greater role in boosting Korea's GDP growth. With its open and highly export-oriented economy, Korea benefited from gains in external competitiveness following the substantial depreciation of its currency. The surge in global demand for information technology and electronic equipment was an additional important element. Owing to heavy investment in information and communication technologies since the beginning of the 1990s, Korean producers were well positioned to take advantage of information technology boom in the United States and elsewhere.

Domestic demand

Although strong exports played a pivotal role in Korea's recovery, the contribution of domestic demand to the recovery and subsequent expansion was also important. In fact, Korea's turnaround was broader based than the other crisis-hit countries in the 1990s. For example, despite high unemployment and a decline in real wages, private consumption rebounded very fast in Korea due to an exceptionally high household saving ratio (23 percent average between 1995-97) and low debt burden. By contrast, a revival of private consumption in Finland and Sweden, but also Mexico, was slow to come. Households in those countries were heavily indebted going into the recession, forcing a sharp retrenchment when interest rates rose and credit contracted. This sparked a major increase in household savings, effectively precluding a swift revival of private consumption and prolonging the recession.

The recovery in investment was also swifter in Korea. Initially, however, there was a strong technical element to the rebound. Companies faced a severe liquidity squeeze in 1998 as sales collapsed and banks were reluctant to finance working capital. This forced companies to de-stock rapidly to free up cash and reduce costs. With the rebound in demand and easing of liquidity pressures, restocking to desired levels provided a major boost contributing $5\frac{1}{2}$ percentage points to the 11 percent growth in real GDP in 1999.

Fixed investment also responded surprisingly fast in Korea after a collapse in 1998. Concerns about a drag on investment due to the capacity overhang in several heavy industries and excessive corporate indebtedness were offset by substantial investment to upgrade technology by a number of businesses and equipment investment in new emerging growth industries—such as information technology, telecommunications, and high-tech start-ups. In addition, the recovery in fixed investment may have been faster in Korea than in other countries because the construction sector, where excess supply takes longer to absorb, was not overheated: the construction sector boom of the late 1980s had already unwound when the 1997 crisis hit. By contrast, fixed investment in Sweden and Finland only began to recover three full years after the recession began, reflecting largely the overhang that resulted from the construction sector boom of the late 1980s.

Government policies

Although Korea's spectacular rebound was linked in part to a favorable external environment, the policies pursued by the authorities also played an important role in allowing Korea to take advantage of these favorable external factors.

- First, as discussed in a preceding section, both monetary and fiscal policy switched to an expansionary stance relatively soon after the onset of the crisis.
- Second, the strong efforts to address the structural weaknesses from the outset boosted investor confidence and enhanced the credibility of the stabilization program. Early aggressive efforts to clean up banks' books helped them resume the business of banking relatively quickly. Notwithstanding the major challenges that remain, Korea was widely acknowledged as the front-runner in implementing structural reforms among the crisis-hit Asian countries.
- Third, the opening of the capital account in the midst of the crisis also helped attract foreign capital and reduced reliance by firms on short-term debt and bank financing. Foreign direct investment inflows shot up from less than $3 billion in 1997 to an average of 8\frac{1}{2}$ billion per year in 1999-2000.

- Fourth, the increased flexibility of the labor market also contributed to the adjustment process. There were significant adjustments in both employment and real wages. Given productivity improvements, unit labor costs have fallen sharply thus improving competitiveness.
- Fifth, more generally, both prices and quantities were allowed to adjust, facilitating a quick recovery. Indeed, there was no pass through of the exchange rate depreciation into wages and there was only a first round inflationary impact. After February 1998, month on month inflation was negligible (even though the 12-month rate remained high until February 1999 because of the base effect). If anything, Korean workers seemed prepared to accept lower wages as a result of the crisis. These adjustments facilitated the rapid turnaround, not least because interest rates could start coming down relatively quickly.
- Finally, the high level political commitment to reforms was critical. The new political leadership that took power in Korea in early 1998 made great efforts to solidify the consensus for reforms. By contrast, in economies where confidence in the authorities' commitment to structural reform is less robust, recoveries have been delayed. It also gave rise to much

Figure 18. Manufacturing Labor Productivity, Hourly Wages, and Unit Labor Costs, 1990 - 2000
(1990 = 100)

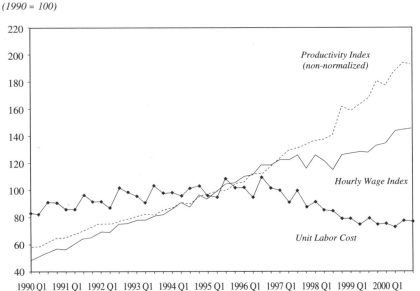

Source: Korea Productivity Center (KPC); and staff estimates.

less uncertainty about the direction of policies than in some of the other crisis countries. These factors undoubtedly contributed to the early return of consumer and investor confidence.

- The various elements discussed above all contributed to the recovery and were mutually reinforcing. Although the positive external environment was a major factor, the policies pursued by the authorities were instrumental in bringing a quicker, stronger and broader based recovery than has been seen in other crisis-hit countries.

Potential Output and the Output Gap

Another perspective on Korea's recovery can be gained from a comparison of actual and potential GDP. To estimate the output gap in Korea since the onset of the financial crisis in 1997 several approaches were employed.[76] Two time series techniques (namely, the Hodrick-Prescott (HP) filter and the cubic spline (CS) smoothing method) were used to derive alternative decompositions of real GDP into its two components: permanent (corresponding to potential output) and cyclical. In addition, a Cobb-Douglas production function (PF) was set up, with physical capital and raw labor as inputs. Using historical data on output and these two inputs, total factor productivity (TFP) was derived and trend productivity growth was estimated. Trend levels of labor were also estimated. Potential output was then estimated by substituting the trend levels of physical capital, labor, and TFP into the production function. Results from the PF approach and projections of trend growth in the labor force and in investment indicate that potential output growth could be approximately 6 percent per year over the period 2000-05.

Table 8. Alternative Measures of the Output Gap and Potential Growth

	1998			1999			2000		
	CS	HP	PF	CS	HP	PF	CS	HP	PF
Output gap[1]	-7.0	-6.3	-8.0	-2.1	-1.2	-1.7	1.2	1.7	1.4
Potential growth[2]	4.5	3.5	2.8	5.1	5.0	3.6	5.8	6.3	6.2

[1]In percent of potential output.
[2]In percent.

---

[76]Further details can be found in Ma (2001).

The three estimated series of the output gap using the various approaches point to broadly the same results. All three series suggest that there was a large

Figure 19. Comparative Recoveries

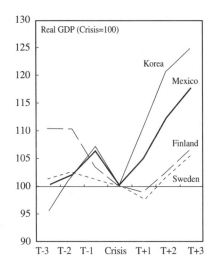

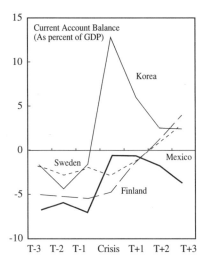

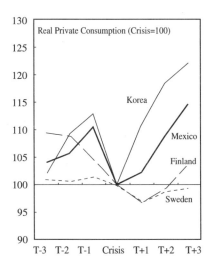

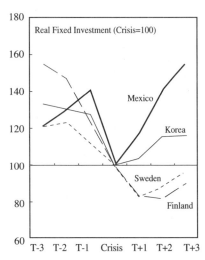

Sources: World Economic Outlook database and staff calculations.
Crisis: Korea = 1998; Finland, Sweden = 1992; and Mexico = 1995.

Figure 20. Actual and Potential Output, 1995-2001

(In trillions of won; logarithmic scale)

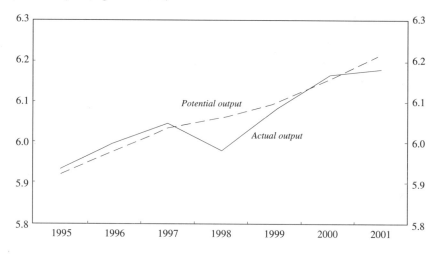

positive gap (i.e., excess demand) in 1997, amounting to 2-4 percent of potential output. Real GDP then fell quickly and substantially in 1998, resulting in
an output gap of about 6-8 percent of potential GDP. The three series suggest
that actual output moved above potential in the second half of 1999. In view
of the strong growth in the first three quarters of 2000, it is estimated that actual
output exceeded potential output in 2000 by around 1 ½ percent. In the earlier
part of 2000 there was concern about possible overheating, but these concerns
were relatively short-lived with the weakening in economic activity in late
2000 and early 2001.

Lessons from the Crisis

The past four years have been among the most turbulent in Korea's recent
economic history. During this period, Korea has not only witnessed severe
turmoil in domestic financial and foreign exchange markets, but also a remarkably rapid stabilization and recovery from crisis conditions. By and large, the
three-year IMF-supported program has been successful and the objectives of
the program have been met. The reforms initiated since the crisis will continue
to yield benefits for years to come and should help restore Korea to the position
of one of the most dynamic and vibrant economies in the world. The credit for
Korea's successful turnaround belongs to the Korean people, who sacrificed
and worked hard, and to Korea's political leadership, who, after the Presiden-

tial election in December 1997, took firm ownership of the stabilization and reform program and implemented it with determination. This section focuses on key lessons from Korea first in the area of crisis prevention and management, and then in the area of structural reforms. It closes with a discussion of the remaining challenges for Korea.

Crisis Prediction and Prevention

The discussion in a preceding section on the origins of the crisis raises the important question of why market participants—including the Fund and other international organizations, credit rating agencies, and investors—were unable to predict the crisis in Korea. Although most observers were aware that there were weaknesses in the system, the savage interaction of these weaknesses was not foreseen.

One explanation for the failure to predict the crisis is that previous crises elsewhere had largely been balance of payments crises, and analysts looking for similar weaknesses in Korea found few of the signs of a classic external crisis. Growth was relatively high; inflation remained low; the real exchange rate was not thought to be overvalued; the current account deficit was within a sustainable range; and the measured fiscal position (which excluded implicit financial sector liabilities) was strong. Moreover, the record of prudent and flexibly applied macroeconomic policies suggested that Korean economic policies would respond appropriately to a large shock. In the event, however, the Korean crisis was the result of mismanagement of companies and banks, not an undisciplined government or poor macroeconomic fundamentals.

From a broader perspective, Korea may also have been a victim of its own success. Although many observers were aware of the growing problems of the highly leveraged corporate sector and a weakened financial system, the fact that these weaknesses had existed for so long while Korea continued to grow rapidly may have created a sense of complacency and confidence that Korea would be immune to a crisis. Korea's model of development worked remarkably well over a sustained period of time, producing an enviable record of development and poverty alleviation. However, as Korea advanced and become more integrated with the global economy, the government- and *chaebol*-led system that had functioned so well during periods of rapid growth proved ill-equipped to deal with new types of shocks to what had become a more developed economy.

Regardless of failures to predict it, the Korea's experience provides some useful lessons for crisis prevention:

- The sequencing of capital account and financial liberalization must be done carefully to avoid the buildup of systemic vulnerabilities. A more balanced approach to capital account liberalization, which would have allowed foreigners to invest long-term in Korean companies, might have limited the potential for liquidity problems and resulted in corporate balance sheets that were less dangerously leveraged. Closer integration with international capital markets also requires that financial supervision and prudential controls be strengthened to ensure that the large capital flows are used appropriately and that incentives for strong corporate governance and market discipline exist. In economies with a history of substantial government involvement the risks of liberalization are commensurately larger in part because of the perceptions of continued implicit government support for companies and financial institutions.
- Greater attention to Korea's external liquidity position probably would have helped to forestall or mitigate the crisis. Although stronger international reserves certainly would have strengthened Korea's external position, more appropriate capital account policies that reduced reliance upon short-term external debt would have been a more direct way to minimize the potential for liquidity problems.
- Greater disclosure of macroprudential indicators and transparency of key macro and financial policies would have alerted markets to these vulnerabilities earlier and perhaps prompted pre-emptive corrective policy measures. Incomplete information on the amount of nonperforming loans, the health of the corporate sector, the maturity profile of external debt, and the level of international reserves allowed problems to go unaddressed, and subsequently intensified the reaction of investors when they suddenly learned the true situation. More complete disclosure to the markets also would have helped investors differentiate between good and bad companies, and created pressures for better corporate governance practices.
- More broadly, the Korean experience suggests that crisis prediction frameworks should pay greater attention to structural vulnerabilities and microeconomic performance. Of course, these factors are harder to quantify, especially consistently across countries. They will hence be difficult to include formally in early warning signals (EWS) models. Crisis prediction (and prevention!) will inevitably retain a substantial judgmental component.

Crisis Management

The rapid emergence from crisis to robust recovery suggests that the response to the crisis was very effective overall. Economic growth resumed just three quarters after the onset of crisis, and output recovered back to potential in less than two years. The following are some key lessons from the Korean experience.

- The early rescheduling of external short-term debt was extremely important. By eliminating the specter of an ongoing drain on foreign reserves and the prospect of imminent default, the rescheduling agreement reduced the reliance on interest rates to stabilize the exchange rate and gave room for expansionary monetary and fiscal policy to address the economic downturn. Korea was caught in a twin crisis for which no simple solutions existed. Raising interest rates to stabilize the exchange rate created distress in the corporate sector, which in turn adversely affected the health of the banks. Eliminating the short-term financing constraint at an early stage allowed macroeconomic policies to shift to supporting the recovery. Indeed, concerted efforts to obtain a rollover agreement with international banks at an even earlier stage would have been preferable.
- The relatively low initial stock of government debt facilitated an appropriate fiscal response, allowing the government to run deficits and provide support for the financial sector. As a result of the healthy starting position, fiscal policy did not need to be tightened and was able to support the recovery. Indeed, Korea's earlier conservative fiscal record allowed an extra degree of freedom in a crisis as markets believed that the fiscal deficits would be temporary. Further, it allowed a substantial expansion of the social safety net, which facilitated structural reform by mitigating the impact on those most affected by the crisis. The switch from the authorities' original relatively restrictive budget for 1998 to a more expansionary stance was rapid. Its actual execution, however, was slower because of the inherent conservatism of Korean budget practices.
- A simple but largely overlooked factor for the strong recovery was that both prices and quantities were allowed to adjust in response to the external shock. Unemployment was allowed to rise and the exchange rate and equity prices fell. Relative prices adjusted, and capital and labor markets were sufficiently flexible so that the large shock could be dissipated quickly across the economy. There was no pass through of the currency depreciation into wages, and inflation was negligible (month-

on-month) after February 1998. If anything, Korean workers seemed prepared to accept lower wages as a result of the crisis. With low inflation, interest rates could be lowered substantially. After the markets stabilized, investors returned quickly when they saw cheap buying opportunities, and labor was able to move to higher productivity industries.

- Despite the initial criticism, the early focus on structural reform was crucial not only for laying the long-term foundations for the continued growth of the economy, but also for boosting the credibility of the government's stabilization program. The primary factors causing the Korean crisis were fundamental weaknesses in companies and banks, not public sector excesses. Without addressing the root causes of the crisis, attempts to regain market confidence through a stabilization program would have been futile, as fears of another crisis would have remained. Without early measures to strengthen corporate governance, foreign investors would have been reluctant to put money back in Korea. It is no surprise that among the Asian crisis countries, foreign money returned to Korea earliest and in the largest amounts.

- In cases where the very stability of the entire financial system is at risk, there may be little choice but to provide a blanket guarantee of bank deposits. In these circumstances, there will be little additional moral hazard from a blanket guarantee—deposits have already been placed in bad banks and bad lending decisions have already been made. But it is important that the authorities rapidly intervene in those banks that have lost their capital, and bring in specialist new management to prevent further erosion.

Structural Reforms

Unlike the rapid recovery of the macroeconomy, progress in structural reform has been slower. This is hardly surprising. Neither a fundamental reorientation of the Korean economy nor the resolution of widespread financial distress were going to be tasks that could be achieved overnight. Nonetheless, there has been very important progress. Some key lessons from the Korean experience include:

- The structural reform program in Korea benefited greatly from its broad support and effective political leadership. The Tripartite Commission of labor, management, and government formed in early 1998 was a useful vehicle for generating social consensus and support for the government's reform program in the face of economic hardships. The commission helped to improve labor market flexibility by facilitating agreement on layoffs and wage cuts and by establishing a social safety net that limited the rise in poverty and helped retrain workers. In contrast with other countries, Korea was fortunate that the presidential election at end-1997 allowed the new government to start with a fresh mandate to implement its economic reform program.

- The government's decision to pursue a centralized approach to restructuring the financial system was justified given the systemic nature of the crisis and perceived inability of the private sector to handle this role. However, having made such a decision, it is important to have an effective exit strategy from involvement in the banking system. Although retaining state ownership may appear to produce a higher recovery rate on the state's investment, delaying privatization may result in large long-run costs if it prevent banks from operating on a commercial basis and from returning to profitability. A market-driven corporate restructuring process will only be truly feasible if it is led by sound, privately owned banks.

- Foreign capital played an important role not only in stabilizing the economy but also in recapitalizing the financial system and transforming corporate decision making. Given the strong need for capital and the limited availability from domestic sources, foreign capital was an important source of funding. The alternative of allowing Korean *chaebol* to increase their control of the banking system could have been disastrous. Without foreign money, financial restructuring would have had to rely upon even more public funds which—for political reasons, and probably appropriately so—became increasingly difficult to secure.

- In cases where nonbank financial institutions play a major role, reform of these may be as important as reform of the banking sector. In the case of Korea, nonbanks (notably life insurance companies and merchant banks) performed many bank-like functions prior to the crisis but were not supervised accordingly. And in the wake of the crisis, supervision of the investment trust companies was not tightened sufficiently quickly. As result, improper management practices and substantial balance sheet growth continued until mid-1999, providing substantial financing to weak companies (most notably the Daewoo group), thereby easing financing constraints and delaying restructuring.

- Realistic valuation of distressed assets is crucial to advance restructuring. Workout programs were an effective initial mechanism for handling the large number of distressed companies but their usefulness waned as their use shifted from a means of dealing with bad assets to a means of attempting to preserve the value of the loans. Although determining a fair price for an unquoted equity is difficult, delaying resolution creates ongoing risks for the system and hence can be more costly than selling at prices that appear to be too cheap. Strict enforcement of loan classification regulations and the threat of bankruptcy are necessary for ensuring that banks and companies have the incentives to pursue realistic valuations and meaningful workout programs. If the government owns a significant portion of the banking system, it can also play an important role in setting an example by selling nonperforming assets, writing off bad loans, or pushing for the exit of nonviable firms—the early sale of Daewoo Motors (for which KDB was one of the lead negotiators) would have been a good precedent.

- Regulatory forbearance must be used carefully to avoid backsliding in restructuring. In Korea, the lax requirements on provisioning for restructured companies under workout programs delayed restructuring and probably resulted in additional losses. At the start, the authorities' preference for forbearance on workout loans was envisaged as a way of encouraging banks to participate in the voluntary workout programs. However over time, forbearance allowed banks to prop up failing companies and avoid recognizing losses. If used, it is important that forbearance be granted on the provisioning *per se* and not on the loan classification standards, and that a clear timetable is announced for its removal.

- Market-based corporate restructuring can only proceed as quickly and as far as supporting market infrastructure allows. Weak accounting standards and financial disclosure can allow firms to hide problems that result in eventual massive losses, as happened in the Daewoo Group, which perpetrated the largest accounting fraud in history. An undeveloped capital market, particularly for corporate control, forces banks to assume responsibility for restructuring instead of shifting it to the companies themselves. An inadequate insolvency system limits the threat of foreclosure and liquidation and delays the exit of nonviable firms. Further, the restructuring process is bound to take longer if the insolvency system favors shareholders over large creditors—it is difficult for banks to steer the process without support from the courts and insolvency system. Finally, it is important to recognize that improvements to market infrastructure and corporate governance take a long time to come to fruition implying that they should be started at an early stage.

- The close link between financial and corporate restructuring requires that the two be undertaken simultaneously, and with an understanding of their implications for each other. The remaining problems in the financial sector are now largely a result of weaknesses in the corporate sector, and the slow progress in corporate sector restructuring is partially due to the unwillingness of creditor banks to write-off bad assets. Progress must be made on both fronts for the process to go forward. In addition, combining the responsibilities for corporate and financial restructuring into one supervisory agency can create a potential conflict of interest, where the regulator may be caught between wanting banks to lend to corporates in distress while at the same time trying to fulfill its supervisory responsibility over the banking system.

The Challenges Ahead

Bold policies and a commitment to reform have led to the overhaul of many domestic institutions and increased the market orientation of the economy. As a result, many of the weaknesses that contributed to the crisis in 1997 have been addressed. But much remains to be done to ensure that the gains endure and that the Korean economy is sufficiently sound and flexible to adapt and prosper as conditions change. Further progress in corporate and financial sector restructuring is imperative to ensure that the remaining problems do not jeopardize what has already been achieved and adversely affect Korea's long-term capacity to grow. Although the economic situation has weakened recently and created new problems for policy makers, there is also considerable upside potential—tangible progress with restructuring, especially in some of the high profile cases, could set in motion a virtuous circle of improved confidence, higher economic growth, and support for further restructuring.

The basic framework for restructuring the corporate and financial sectors is in place, and, looking ahead, the key issue will be implementation and ensuring a stronger role for markets—especially creditors and investors—to drive the process. Indeed, most of the needed "hardware" improvements in the regulatory and institutional framework have now largely been completed, but important steps remain to be completed to develop the necessary "software" of the system in order to change practices and ways of doing business. The government will continue to have a critical role to play in monitoring and enforcement of regulations, but it will now be important for it to step back from intervening in the operation of markets and economic decision making, and instead to rely more—as in other advanced economies—on markets to impose discipline.

Although there is still a long way to go to complete the restructuring and reform process, this is largely a reflection of the magnitude of the necessary changes and should not detract from the major achievements of the last few years. Macroeconomic policy making has achieved much, and must continue to provide a stable environment for ongoing restructuring. Restructuring will be an ongoing, multiyear process, but continued tangible progress is of paramount importance. In sum, the policies adopted by the government are working and have been instrumental in the recovery from the crisis; their continuation is essential to ensure high medium-term growth and reduce vulnerability to shifts in market sentiment and other shocks.

References

Baliño, Tomás, J. T., and Angel Ubide, 1999, "The Korean Financial Crisis of 1997—A Strategy of Financial Sector Reform," IMF Working Paper 99/28.

Bank of Korea, 2000, "Manufacturing Industries: Analysis of Cash Flow During 1999," August.

Basurto, Gabriela, and Atish R. Ghosh, 2000, "The Interest Rate-Exchange Rate Nexus in the Asian Crisis Countries," IMF Working Paper 00/19.

Boorman, Jack, Timothy Lane, Marianne Schulze-Ghattas, Aleš Bulíř, Atish R. Ghosh, Javier Hamann, Alexandros Mourmouras, and Steven Phillips, 2000, "Managing Financial Crises: The Experience in East Asia," IMF Working Paper 00/107.

Borensztein, Eduardo, and Jong-Wha Lee, 2000, "Financial Crisis and Credit Crunch in Korea: Evidence from Firm Level Data," IMF Working Paper 00/25.

Burnside, Craig et al., 2000, "Understanding the Korean and Thai Currency Crisis," *Federal Reserve Bank of Chicago Economic Perspectives* v24, n3, 45-60.

Chinn, Menzie, 1999, "Measuring Misalignment: Purchasing Power Parity and East Asian Currencies in the 1990s," IMF Working Paper 99/120.

Cho, Yoon Je, 1999, "Financial Crisis of Korea: A Consequence of Unbalanced Liberalization?" Paper prepared for World Bank Conference, "Financial Liberalization: How Far, How Fast?" Washington, D.C.

Chopra, Ajai, Kenneth Kang, Meral Karasulu, Hong Liang, Henry Ma, and Anthony Richards, 2001, "From Crisis to Recovery in Korea: Strategy, Achievements, and Lessons," IMF Working Paper 01/154.

Claessens, Stijn, Simeon Djankov, and Giovanni Ferri, 1999, "Corporate Distress in East Asia: The Effect of Currency and Interest Rate Shocks," Note No. 172, Finance, Private Sector, and Infrastructure Network, The World Bank.

Corsetti, Giancarlo, Paolo Pesenti, and Nouriel Roubini, 1999, "What Caused the Asian Currency and Financial Crisis?" *Japan and the World Economy*, Vol. 11, 305-373.

Dekle, Robert, Cheng Hsiao, and Siyan Wang, 1999, "Do High Interest Rates Appreciate Exchange Rates During Crisis?" forthcoming in *Oxford Bulletin of Economics and Statistics*.

Ding, Wei, Ilker Domaç, and Giovanni Ferri, 1998, "Is There a Credit Crunch in East Asia?" *Asia Pacific Journal of Economics and Business* 2 (2), 4-32.

Domaç, Ilker, and Giovanni Ferri, 1999, "Did the East Asian Crisis Disproportionately Hit Small Businesses in Korea?" *Economic Notes* 28 (3), 403-429.

Feldstein, Martin, 1998, "Refocusing the IMF," *Foreign Affairs* 77, 20-33.

Feldstein, Martin, 1999, "A Self-Help Guide for Emerging Markets," *Foreign Affairs* 78, 93-109.

Ferri, Giovanni, and Tae Soo Kang, 1999, "The Credit Channel at Work: Lessons from the Republic of Korea's Financial Crisis," World Bank Policy Research Working Paper 2190.

Ferri, Giovanni, Tae Soo Kang, and In-June Kim, 1999, "The Value of Relationship Banking During Financial Crises: Evidence from the Republic of Korea," World Bank Policy Research Working Paper 2553.

Fischer, Stanley, 1998, "Response: In Defense of the IMF, Specialized Tools for a Specialized Task," *Foreign Affairs* 77, 103-106.

Flood, Robert, and Andrew K. Rose, 2001, "Uncovered Interests Parity in Crisis: The Interest Rate Defense in the 1990s," mimeo.

Frankel, Jeffrey, 2000, "Ten Lessons Learned from the Korean Crisis," Paper prepared for NBER Conference on the Korean Currency Crisis, February 2000.

Furman, Jason, and Joseph E. Stiglitz, 1998, "Economic Crises: Evidence and Insights from East Asia," *Brookings Papers on Economic Activity* (2), 1-135.

Ghosh, Swati R., and Atish R. Ghosh, 1999, "East Asia in the Aftermath: Was There a Crunch?" IMF Working Paper 99/38.

Gobat, Jeanne, 1998, "Corporate Restructuring and Corporate Governance," Republic of Korea—Selected Issues, IMF Staff Country Reports No. 98/74.

Goldfajn, Ilan, and Taimur Baig, 1998, "Monetary Policy in the Aftermath of Currency Crises: The Case of Asia," IMF Working Paper 98/170.

Goldfajn, Ilan, and Poonam Gupta, 1999, "Does Monetary Policy Stabilize the Exchange Rate Following a Currency Crisis?" IMF Working Paper 99/42.

Goldstein, Morris, 1998, "The Asian Financial Crisis: Causes, Cures, and Systemic Implications," Institute for International Economics.

Goldstein, Morris, 2001, "IMF Structural Conditionality: How Much is Too Much?" Institute for International Economics, WP 01-04, April.

Gordon, James, 2001, "The Crisis in Asia: Are There Lessons for Zimbabwe?" in C. Mumbengegwi ed., *Macroeconomic and Structural Adjustment Policies in Zimbabwe*, Palgrawe.

Graham, Edward M., 2001, "The Chaebol and the Continuing Crisis in Korea," draft manuscript, Institute for International Economics.

Hahm, Joon-Ho, and Frederic S. Mishkin, 2000, "The Korean Financial Crisis: An Asymmetric Information Perspective," *Emerging Markets Review* 1, 21-52.

International Monetary Fund, 1999, "Financial Sector Crisis and Restructuring, Lessons from Asia," IMF Occasional Paper 188.

International Monetary Fund, 2000, "Republic of Korea: Economic and Policy Developments," IMF Staff Country Report No. 00/11.

International Monetary Fund, 2001, "Structural Conditionality in Fund-Supported Programs," available at www.imf.org/external/np/pdr/cond/2001/eng/struct/ index.htm.

International Monetary Fund, 2002, "Republic of Korea: Selected Issues," IMF Country Report No. 02/20.

Joh, Sung Wook, 2000, "Control, Ownership, and Firm Performance: The Case of Korea," Korea Development Institute.

Joh, Sung Wook, and Ryoo, Sang Dai, 2000, "Evaluation of Changes in the Corporate Governance System of Korean *Chaebol*," draft paper, Korea Development Institute.

Johnson, Simon et al., 2000, "Corporate Governance in the Asian Financial Crisis," *Journal of Financial Economics* 58, October-November 2000, 141-186.

Johnston, R. Barry et al., 1999, "Capital Account Liberalization in Selected Asian Countries," *Exchange Rate Arrangements and Currency Convertibility, Development and Issues*, International Monetary Fund.

Karasulu, Meral, 2001, "The Profitability of the Banking Sector in Korea," *Republic of Korea—Selected Issues*, Country Report No. 01/101, International Monetary Fund.

Kim, Hyun E., 1999, "Was the Credit Channel a Key Monetary Transmission Following the Recent Financial Crisis in the Republic of Korea?" World Bank Policy Research Working Paper 2103.

Kraay, Aart, 2000, "Do High Interest Rates Defend Currencies During Speculative Attacks?" World Bank Policy Research Working Paper 2267.

Krueger, Anne O., 2000, "Conflicting Demands on the International Monetary Fund," *American Economic Review* (Papers and Proceedings), 38-42.

Krueger, Anne O., 1999, "Why Crony Capitalism is Bad for Economic Growth," mimeo.

Krugman, Paul, 1999, "The Return of Depression Economics," *Foreign Affairs* 78, 56-74.

Lane, Timothy, Atish Ghosh, Javier Hamann, Steven Phillips, Marianne Schulze-Ghattas, and Tsidi Tsikata, 1999, *IMF-Supported Programs in Indonesia, Korea, Thailand: A Preliminary Assessment*, IMF Occasional Paper 178.

Lee, Jong-Wha, and Changyong Rhee, 2000, "Macroeconomic Impacts of the Korean Financial Crisis: Comparison with Cross-country Patterns," Background paper for NBER Conference on the Korean Currency Crisis, February 2000.

Ma, Henry, 2001, "Potential Output, the Output Gap, and Inflation in Korea," *Republic of Korea—Selected Issues*, IMF Staff Country Report No. 01/101, International Monetary Fund.

Mako, William P., 2001, "Corporate Restructuring in East Asia: Promoting Best Practices," *Finance and Development*, Volume 38, No. 1.

Martin, John P., and Raymond Torres, 2000, "Korean Labor Market and Social Safety Net Reforms: Challenges and Policy Requirements," *Journal of the Korean Economy,* Vol. 1, No. 2, 267-300.

Marquez, Jaime, 1999, "Income and Price Effects of Asian Trade," Federal Reserve Board, mimeo.

Nam, Il Chong, Joon-Kyung Kim, Yeongjae Kang, Sung Wook Joh, and Jun-il Kim, 1999, "Corporate Governance in Korea," KDI Working Paper No. 9915.

Park, Yooh-Shik, 2000, "Korea's *Chaebols* Issue Combined Financial Statements for First Time," *Korea Insight*, Vol. 2, No. 8, Korea Economic Institute.

Radelet, Steven, and Jeffrey D. Sachs, 1998, "The East Asian Financial Crisis: Diagnosis, Remedies, Prospects," *Brookings Papers on Economic Activity* (1), 1-74.

Radelet, Steven, and Jeffrey D. Sachs, 1999, "What Have We Learned, So Far, From the Asian Financial Crisis?" Paper prepared for NBER Conference on the Korean Currency Crisis.

Shin, Hyun-Han, and Young S. Park, 1999, "Financing Constraints and Internal Capital Markets: Evidence from Korean Chaebols," *Journal of Corporate Finance: Contracting, Governance and Organization*, June, 169-191.

Yoshitomi, Masaru, and Kenichi Ohno, 1999, "Capital-Account Crisis and Credit Contraction," Asian Development Bank Institute Working Paper 99/2.

3 What Have We Learned from the Korean Economic Adjustment Program?

*Yoon Je Cho**

The Korean economy faced a severe financial and currency crisis in November 1997 and started an IMF program in early December 1997. It fell into a deep recession, with real GDP contracting 6.7 percent in 1998. The economy started a rapid recovery in late 1998, with growth rates of 10.7 percent in 1999 and 8.8 percent in 2000 (Table 1). But the economy started to slow in late 2000, and by mid-2001 a recession appeared likely. Thus, the Korean economy has gone through a full cycle since the 1997 crisis.

The three-year IMF program expired in December 2000. The program has been assessed by many as a success. By the end of 2000, Korea had accumulated foreign exchange reserves of about US$95 billion from less than US$5 billion at the depth of the crisis, becoming number five in the world in terms of foreign reserve holdings. The cumulative current account surplus during the three-year program amounted to US$76 billion, or about 21 percent of annual GDP. Korea also attracted a lot of foreign direct investment as well as portfolio investment. Thus, the Korean economy seems to have fully recovered from the currency crisis.

Nevertheless, its corporate and financial sectors remain weak. Even though the Korean economy has recovered from the currency crisis, it has not fully solved its deep economic problems.

The Korean currency crisis mainly reflected deep-rooted structural problems that had accumulated over many years (see Cho, 1998). Large losses in the corporate sector were concealed by irregular and dishonest accounting practices, and supported by imprudent access to credit. Trade liberalization

*The original draft of this paper was prepared for the international workshop, "Reexamination of Development Strategies: Experience and Lessons of Crisis," organized by the Institute of Developing Economies, Tokyo, March 21, 2001.

Table 1. Macroeconomic Indicators of Korea, 1996-2000

	96	97	98 1/4	2/4	3/4	4/4	Annual	99 1/4	2/4	3/4	4/4	Annual	2000 1/4	2/4	3/4	4/4	Annual
GDP (%)	6.8	5.0	-4.6	-8.0	-8.1	-5.9	-6.7	5.4	10.8	12.8	13.0	10.7	12.6	9.7	9.2	4.6	8.8
Exports	11.2	21.4	25.8	13.6	8.5	7.6	13.2	9.2	14.6	20.0	21.0	16.3	27.1	21.4	22.5	16.4	21.6
Imports	14.2	3.2	-27.3	-25.7	-26.1	-10.1	-22.4	27.3	28.3	32.3	28.0	28.9	31.6	20.6	22.4	8.2	20.0
CPI	4.9	4.5	8.9	8.2	7.0	6.0	7.5	0.7	0.6	0.9	1.0	0.8	1.5	1.4	3.2	3.9	2.3
WPI	3.2	3.9	13.9.	13.3	11.4	8.9	12.2	-4.3	-3.2	-1.1	0.8	-2.1	2.2	1.9	2.6	2.0	2.0
Current Account / GDP	-4.4	-1.7	16.3	14.4	12.0	9.2	12.7	6.8	6.5	6.6	4.9	6.1	1.5	2.4	3.0	2.5	2.35
Real Wage	2.0	2.6	5.6	6.8	7.4	7.4	6.8	8.4	6.6	5.6	4.6	6.3	5.1	3.8	-	-	-
Unemployment (%)	2.0	2.6	5.6	6.8	7.4	7.4	6.8	8.4	6.6	5.6	4.6	6.3	5.1	3.8	3.6	3.7	4.1

Source: Bank of Korea.

limited the ability of monopolistic or oligopolistic domestic chaebol to pass their inefficiency on to customers in the form of higher prices. Financial liberalization increased financial fragility by weakening corporations' financial structure through expanded short-term financing on one hand (Cho, 2001), and by limiting the government's ability to manage bailout programs for already deeply troubled firms on the other.

The immediate causes of the 1997 crisis may have been the severe maturity mismatch between foreign debts and assets of the Korean banking sector, and contagion from neighboring countries. But more fundamentally, the 1997 Korean crisis hit an economy that was in the process of shifting toward a more liberalized and open system from a heavily protected economy with a deep reliance on a government-led development strategy.

The economy was opened and liberalized without properly dealing with long accumulated losses and extremely high corporate debt ratios—the legacy of the past development paradigm—and without changing the old style of economic management. In this paradigm, government, businesses, and banks had formed an implicit risk partnership that facilitated rapid investment expansion and high economic growth. But the development of the necessary institutions and market infrastructure for an efficient and stable market-based economy was lacking. This made the economy extremely vulnerable to external shocks.

The gaps between the speed of changes in the economic environment brought about by liberalization and opening, and the speed with which institutions developed made a crisis unavoidable.

This paper raises four issues regarding the economic adjustment program in a crisis-hit economy based on the Korean experience. First, in the case of a twin crisis—currency crisis and financial crisis—the traditional measures to address the currency crisis such as high interest rate policy can deepen the financial crisis. This effect is magnified in an economy with a high corporate debt ratio. This points to the importance of seeking other measures to stabilize the exchange market complementary to interest rate policy in a twin crisis.

Second, an asymmetric approach to the restructuring and strengthening the regulatory rules among different segments of the financial sector can lead to a rapid shift of funds from the sector in which the regulation is being strengthened to the sector with looser regulation. The Korean investment and trust companies took advantage of poor regulatory oversight in the early stage of financial restructuring and expanded explosively, leaving the overall systemic risk of the financial sector undiminished. This approach to corporate restructuring also had asymmetric consequences for large firms and small firms by contracting bank loans and expanding corporate bond markets. This suggests the need for a careful balance in the approach to the financial restructuring among different segments of the financial system.

Third, financial restructuring and strengthening of regulatory rules have a strong contractionary effect by diminishing the money creation function of the involved intermediaries. During the period of drastic financial restructuring and strengthening of regulatory rules, the actual monetary stance can be affected more strongly by the actions taken by the supervisory authorities than by the policies of the monetary authorities. This suggests a need for close coordination between monetary policies and supervisory policies.

Finally, the Korean experience revives the old question on the speed and sequencing of economic reforms. The Korean corporate and financial sectors faced extraordinarily large problems at the time of the 1997 currency crisis. The introduction of global standards in banking supervision—such as rules on loan classification, provisioning, accounting and disclosure, and BIS capital adequacy ratio—exposed enormous amounts of non-performing assets (NPAs) that had been concealed under lax supervisory rules and poor (or even deceiving) accounting practices. The flood of NPAs has been beyond the capacity of the country's political economy to digest. This pushed the government to forbearance and resort to the old interventionist policies, which compromised its own stated principles of restructuring, thus undermining the credibility of the reform process. This suggests that too ambitious a reform program may backfire. A credible reform program must be based on the economic and political realities in the country.

The paper is organized as follows. The first section deals with the high interest rate policies adopted in the early stage of the IMF program. The second section discusses the impact of the asymmetric approach to the restructuring of the banking and non-banking financial sectors. The third section deals with the effectiveness of monetary policies during the period of financial restructuring. The fourth section discusses the issue of the speed and sequencing of economic reforms.

Dilemma of Interest Rate Policies in Twin Crises

The initial crisis resolution strategy under the IMF program with Korea was composed largely of two parts: macroeconomic policies and structural adjustment measures. The macroeconomic policies were traditional IMF stabilization policies with a tight monetary and fiscal stance. The main goal of these policies was, understandably, to stabilize the exchange market and to improve the current account. The main components of the structural reform policies were financial restructuring and the rapid adoption of global standards in financial supervision, accounting standards, disclosure requirements, and corporate governance. The main goal was to increase transparency and accountability in management and thus to improve economic efficiency.

The direction and goals of each of these policies were admirable . However, the high interest rate policy adopted to deal with the currency crisis aggravated the financial crisis. The 1997 Korean crisis was a "twin crisis" —a currency crisis as well as a financial crisis. At the initial stage of the crisis, the policy response was understandably to quell the currency crisis. But, in the process, it intensified the financial crisis. The initial macroeconomic policies adopted in Korea under the IMF program were essentially the same as the ones adopted in other countries to deal with short-term currency speculation and current account problems.

The Korean crisis was not simply a foreign liquidity crisis, but a deep financial and corporate crisis. The corporate sector had been suffering from severe debt payment problems and long-accumulated losses that had been veiled behind irregular accounting. Corporations relied on continuous credit expansions by banks and foreign creditors for survival. Over-investment, high leverage ratios with heavy reliance on short-term debt, and poor earnings were common to most corporations. This was caused by a distorted incentive structure and misaligned relative prices such as real wages, interest rates and the exchange rate. Lack of adequate competition policies, poor corporate governance, and weak banking supervision allowed reckless investment expansion, which sustained high demand for capital and labor despite deteriorating corporate profitability. This allowed the persistence of high interest rates exceeding rates of return to investment, and high wages exceeding labor productivity (Cho, 1998). The overvalued exchange rate reduced profitability of exporting firms. Poor prudential regulation and supervision failed to curb reckless lending of financial institutions to finance risky investments by corporate firms. Poor accounting and disclosure practices and lack of financial market discipline over corporations contributed to the deterioration in the economic situation.

The Korean economy has experienced three major crises since its take-off in the 1960s: 1971-72, early 1980s, and 1997-98. Each of these crises occurred after a sustained investment boom and a period of lower returns to corporate investment with lower-than-average cost of debt (Figure 1).

In each crisis, the government relied on the "growing-up" strategy, with heavy intervention in the financial system. The common elements of this "growing-up" strategy were the interest rate cuts with massive rescheduling of existing debt under favorable conditions, the extension of new loans, and forced mergers and takeovers of firms supported by favored access to credit and tax exemptions. Currency crises were dealt with mainly by seeking a rollover of debt and new borrowing (including bilateral loans), and by IMF-supported stabilization policies.[1] But the stabilization policies relied mainly on

Figure 1. Return & Cost of Capital Investment of Firms
(In percent)

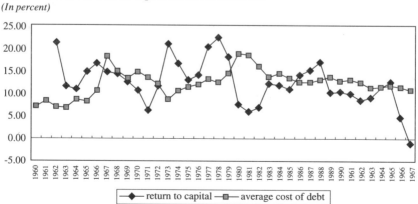

Source: BOK, *Analysis of Financial Statements of Corporate Firms*, various issues.

direct control of credit rather than high interest rates. Interest rates were actually cut substantially in most previous crises (Figure 2).

The 1997 crisis was different. In response to the drastic reversal of capital flows, a key component of the macroeconomic policies under the IMF program was a high interest rate policy (Figure 3). This was needed to curb speculation in the foreign exchange market. But it was extremely costly to

Figure 2. Inflation and Interest Rates
(In percent)

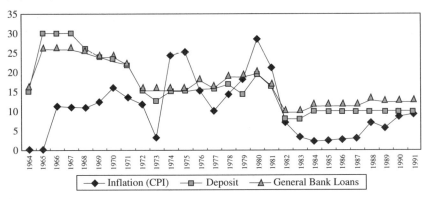

Source: BOK, *Monthly Bulletin*, various issues.

Figure 3. Interest Rates (1995-2000)
(In percent)

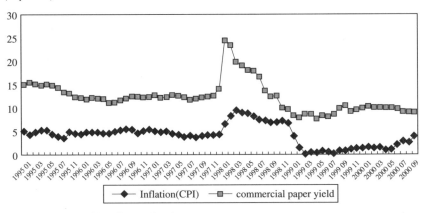

Source: BOK, *Monthly Bulletin*, various issues.

---

[1]In my view, Korea faced currency crises, i.e., the status of near default of foreign borrowing, in the early 1970s when the rapidly increased foreign debt of the second half of 1960s fell due; in 1975 after the First Oil Shock; and again in 1980 after heavy borrowing from the eurocurrency market in the second half of 1970s and the Second Oil Shock.

Figure 4. Interest Coverage and Debt/Equity Ratios

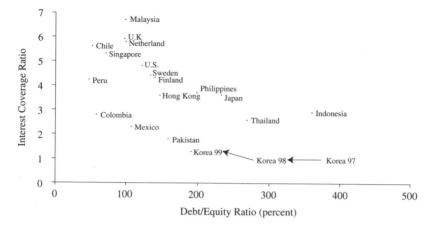

the Korean economy, since Korean firms were extremely highly leveraged (Figure 4).

In Korea, total corporate debt was already more than one and a half times the level of annual GDP,[2] extremely high compared to most economies. About one third of this had been allocated to firms whose earnings before tax were smaller than the interest payment obligation. A sharp increase of interest rates in this situation magnified potential non-performing assets, deepened the financial crisis, and increased the ultimate burden on taxpayers.

The Korean currency crisis was basically a run of foreign creditors on domestic banks in the form of foreign banks refusing to roll over short-term loans. Korea had previously had controls over foreign portfolio investment both inbound and outbound, and hence there was little possibility of a massive outflow of portfolio investment.[3] Several studies (Ohno, Shirono and Sisli, 2000; Goldfajn and Baig, 1998; Furman and Stiglitz, 1998) suggest that the high interest rate policy was not effective in stabilizing exchange rates.[4] In

---

[2]According to Flow of Fund Statistics (BOK, 1998), the corporate sector's total borrowing from financial institutions and direct financing through CPs, bonds, and trade credits exceeded 650 trillion won at the end of 1997.

[3]There was the possibility of speculation on foreign currency by domestic residents, but this could be addressed by temporarily (and partially) limiting conversion of domestic deposits to foreign deposits by residents.

[4]There have been many studies that have tried to examine empirically the effectiveness of interest rate policy in supporting exchange rates (Kraay, 2000; Flood and Rose, 2001). Among them, Basurto and Ghosh (2000) argue that the fact that the coefficient of the real interest rate on the risk premium on Korean bonds issued abroad was positive (although it was not statistically significant) suggests that tightening would have been unlikely to improve the exchange rate and may have been counterproductive.

addition, the overall macroeconomic policy stance did not need to be that tight to improve the current account position, which was already turning to surplus in the last quarter of 1997. Household consumption and investment were also rapidly falling. High interest rates in the Korean case did not stop the foreign banks' run, but perhaps aggravated it by increasing skepticism over the future health of Korean banks.

This suggests that, in dealing with a currency crisis in a highly leveraged economy and with substantial foreign exchange control, the appropriateness of the traditional policy response, especially a high interest rate policy, may need to be reconsidered.

Asymmetric Financial Restructuring and Its Impact

The way financial restructuring was implemented in Korea after the crisis has had important macroeconomic consequences and has affected the subsequent development of financial market structure and the progress of corporate restructuring.

The financial restructuring plan under the IMF program initially underestimated the depth and scope of Korea's financial sector problems. As a result, it concentrated mainly on the restructuring of banks and merchant banking companies (MBCs) in the first year of the program. Strengthening regulatory standards also focused on these institutions. This was not surprising since the origin of the crisis was the run of foreign creditors on Korean banks and MBCs as the asset quality of these institutions became increasingly doubtful.[5] However, the problems were equally or even more serious in other non-bank financial institutions (NBFIs), including investment and trust companies (ITCs), mutual savings banks and insurance companies. When financial restructuring was initiated under the IMF program in 1998, these other financial institutions were largely unaffected by the strengthening of supervision or restructuring. The supervisory authorities benignly neglected the many irregularities in fund mobilization and management by these institutions. As a result, these institutions, especially the ITCs, took advantage of weak or nonexistent regulatory oversight for explosive expansion.

This had both positive and negative impacts. The positive impact was immediate. It mitigated the economic impact of the credit crunch in the banking sector and MBCs as the less regulated non-bank institutions expanded rapidly.

---

[5]In fact, only these two types of financial institutions had been allowed for foreign borrowing business until the crisis.

It allowed many chaebol to obtain finance from this expanding sector to tide over the credit crunch and liquidity crisis. Some chaebol even aggressively expanded their investments during the financial crisis. Overall, this helped spur the quick recovery of the economy in late 1998 and 1999.

The negative impacts were realized in the longer term. The financial restructuring during 1998-99, by shifting funds from the sector over which regulation was strengthened to the sector that remained poorly regulated, did not improve the overall risk in the financial system. The rapid expansion of investment and trust business sustained firms that should have gone bankrupt and increased the level of nonperforming loans in the financial sector. When the investment and trust business imploded, the securities market collapsed, contributing to an economic recession after the short-lived recovery.

In sum, the failure to implement a comprehensive strengthening of supervision and restructuring of the financial sector reduced, intentionally or unintentionally, the degree of economic contraction by sustaining weak chaebol but increased the ultimate cost of financial restructuring. It also had the effect of lengthening the period of corporate and financial restructuring.

Furthermore, the impact of financial restructuring was asymmetric among firms: small- to medium-sized firms, which relied mainly on bank borrowing, suffered more severely than large chaebol, which benefited from the expanding of corporate bond markets during the initial period of financial restructuring.

The total value of assets of the ITCs[6] tripled during January 1998-June 1999, from 84 trillion won to 255 trillion won. Figure 5 compares the actual growth of the ITCs with their 'expected normal' path of growth between 1983 and 1999. The latter was derived by applying the growth rate of total savings (1983) to the volume of ITCs' assets in 1983, which is shown by the dashed line. In the past, the growth of the ITCs had been more or less at the same pace as that of the overall financial sector. But starting in early 1998, its growth far surpassed that of the total financial sector.

The growth of the ITCs came mostly at the expense of banks' trust accounts and the merchant banking industry (Figure 6). By April 1999, total funds mobilized by the ITCs reached about 80 percent of M2, from about 40 percent at the end of 1997.

---

[6]During 1997-2000, two types of investment and mutual companies were allowed: investment and trust companies (ITCs) could mobilize and manage funds; and investment trust management companies (ITMCs) could only manage funds that were mobilized by their affiliated securities companies. Now ITCs have been converted to investment trust securities companies and ITMCs. In this paper, 'ITCs' include ITMCs as well as ITCs.

Figure 5. Actual vs. Expected Normal Volume of Assets of ITCs
(In billions of Korean won)

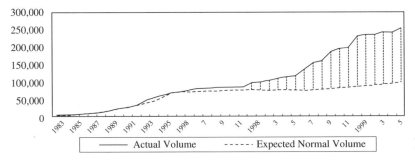

Source: KITCA, *Investment Trust* and MOFE, *Financial Statistics Bulletin*, various issues.
Note: "Expected" is based on the growth rate of M3.

Figure 6. Growth of the Financial Sector
(In billions of Korean won)

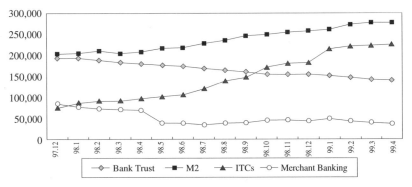

Source: Ministry of Finance & Economy, *Financial Statistics Bulletin*, various issues.

The extraordinary expansion of ITCs during this period reflected at least two factors. First, a sharp reduction of interest rates starting in early 1998 resulted in large capital gains to the funds established by ITCs in late 1997 and early 1998. Second, ITCs used this capital gain to offer higher than the prevailing market interest rates by illegally transferring high yielding bonds from the old funds to new funds. These transfers were neither properly regulated by the supervisory authorities nor monitored by investors. Many ITCs controlled by chaebol aggressively mobilized funds, sometimes with misguiding advertisements, through their affiliated security companies. As Figure 7 shows, the yields of beneficiary certificates offered by the ITCs became substantially higher than the corporate bond yields in the second half of 1998 even though the former was with shorter maturities. This was possible by the illegal transfer of high-yield bonds purchased by previously established funds to the newly established funds. In this way, they attracted many individual investors as well as institutional investors seeking interest rate arbitrage (Figure 8).

This rapid growth took place despite the extremely poor financial status of the ITCs. The ITCs, especially the largest three, had been in negative capital for some time,[7] and their financial situation was further aggravated by the economic crisis (Table 2). Nevertheless, they had not been subject to any

Figure 7. Interest Rate of Time Deposit, Beneficiary Certificate, and Corporate Bond
(In percent)

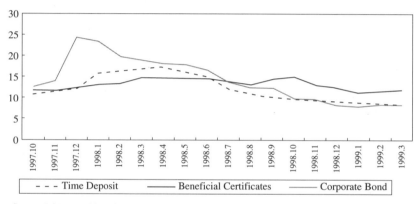

Source: BOK, *Monthly Bulletin*, various issues.
Note: Time deposit is of more than one year and less than two years; beneficiary certificate is of long-term bond fund; and corporate bond is of three years.

Figure 8. Interest Rates and Growth of ITCs

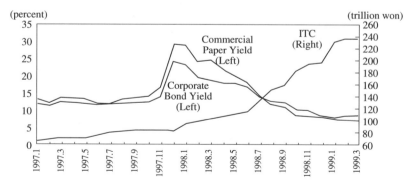

---

[7]The problems of three major ITCs had been aggravated by government intervention in asset management for other policy goals such as sustaining the stock market value and by the lack of professional management.

Table 2. Balance Sheets of ITCs

(In billions of Korean won)

	1997		1998		1999	
	Three ITCs	Regional ITCs	Three ITCs	Regional ITCs	Three ITCs	Regional ITCs
1. Assets	6,805.7	2,748.0	6,570.0	3,809.8	7,705.8	1,132.9
1.1. Current Assets	5,686.1	2,217.9	4,393.6	3,285.4	2,925.0	670.8
1.2. Non-Current Assets	1,119.6	530.1	2,176.1	524.1	4,780.9	462.1
2. Liabilities	7,579.3	2,589.1	10,129.5	3,869.3	10,448.8	1,125.2
2.1. Current Liabilities	7,366.5	2,538.5	10,068.8	3,831.6	8,291.1	1,114.0
(Debt)	(7,057.8)	(2,362.4)	(9,827.9)	(3,379.6)	(5,525.6)	(1,089.9)
2.2.Non-Current Liabilities	212.6	50.5	60.4	37.3	2,157.7	11.2
3. Owner's Equity	**-773.6**	**158.9**	**-3,559.5**	**-59.6**	**-2,743.0**	**7.7**
3.1. Contributed Capital	520.0	600.0	610.2	280.0	610.2	370.0
3.2. Capital Surplus	-1,293.6	-141.1	-4,169.7	-339.6	-3,353.2	-362.3
(Net Income)	(-933.2)	(-104.5)	(-2,966.2)	(-301.6)	(199.1)	(-91.6)

Source: Korea Investment Trust Companies Association.

corrective actions by the supervisory authorities, and were allowed to mobilize and manage funds with benignly neglected irregularities.[8]

Because they did not disclose their asset portfolio and were not audited, the ITCs were not properly monitored by investors or the supervisory authorities. Funds shifted from banks and merchant banking companies to ITCs, leaving the overall underlying risk and distortions in the financial system unchanged or even expanded.

In 1993-96, insufficient regulatory oversight of the commercial paper (CPs) market and the merchant banking industry allowed a rapid expansion of this segment of the financial market, as corporations increasingly financed long-term investment with short-term funds, creating a severe maturity mismatch. Reckless investment was also encouraged since the credit ratings and monitoring of corporate firms by the financial market was extremely poor. The weak financial structure of chaebol eventually led to a string of bankruptcies, contributing to the financial crisis of 1997.[9]

---

[8]The financial insolvency problem of ITCs had dragged the government action to strengthen supervision over the practice of this industry. The government feared the possibility of a run, given a bad financial situation of major ITCs, and has been reluctant to enforce the proper regulatory norms for these institutions.

[9]Cho (2001) discusses how the asymmetric liberalization of interest rates and regulatory oversight led to the rapid expansion of the commercial paper market and 'shortermization' of corporate finance during 1993-97.

The lack of regulatory oversight of the investment and trust industry in 1998-99 was equally dangerous. The ITCs became a channel of funding for some big chaebol-affiliated firms in weak financial health. Many of the large ITCs were owned by chaebol and mobilized about 130 trillion won within a year, equivalent to about one-fourth of the 1999 GDP. The major four chaebol—Hyundai, Samsung, Daewoo, and LG—mobilized 77 trillion won during 1998-99. These funds were used directly or indirectly to support affiliated firms by purchasing the bonds or commercial paper issued by affiliated firms and placing them in affiliated or other ITCs (to circumvent regulatory rules), with the implicit mutual agreement to cross-purchase the bonds or commercial paper of affiliated non-financial firms.

Table 3 shows the amount of commercial paper and corporate bonds purchased by the ITCs for the big five chaebol. As of April 1999, the ITCs held 92 trillion won of securities issued by the big five chaebol compared with 70.2 trillion won financed through the banking sector. It shows that 25 trillion won was used to purchase the Daewoo securities and another 24 trillion won was used to purchase Hyundai securities. These two chaebol increased their domestic debt substantially in the midst of economic crisis and bank restructuring.

The total debt of Daewoo increased by 17 trillion won in 1998. While the banks and other financial institutions were reducing their credit to Daewoo,

Table 3. Trust Assets of ITCs on Big Five Chaebol's Securities
(In billions of Korean won)

	Total	The Big Five Chaebol					
		Sub-total	Hyundai	Samsung	Daewoo	LG	SK
Commercial Paper	51,088	24,797 (48.5%)	8,540 (16.7%)	4,106 (8.0%)	5,938 (11.6%)	4,534 (8.9%)	1,677 (3.3%)
Stock	9,925	4,712 (47.5%)	907 (9.1%)	1,623 (16.36%)	164 (1.7%)	1,018 (10.3%)	998 (10.1%)
Corporate Bonds	154,321	62,633 (40.6%)	14,835 (9.6%)	12,357 (8.01%)	18,846 (12.2%)	10,399 (6.7%)	6,195 (4.0%)
Sub total	215,336	92,143 (42.8%)	24,283 (11.3%)	18,087 (8.40%)	24,950 (11.6%)	15,952 (7.4%)	8,870 (4.1%)
Total trust assets	244,723	(37.7%)	(9.9%)	(7.4%)	(10.2%)	(6.5%)	(3.6%)

Note: As of April 30, 1999.

the investment trust industry provided new financing to Daewoo for their continuous expansion in 1998, and similarly for Hyundai. The force behind the aggressive expansion and avoidance of necessary restructuring for these two chaebol during this period was their control of the investment and trust business.

While the authorities were pushing corporate restructuring by tightening regulations over banks' and other financial institutions' lending, this was undermined by the explosive expansion of investment and trust business, which was almost completely out of the proper regulatory enforcement. Furthermore, the fact that funds shifted to financially troubled ITCs meant that the potential systemic risk in the Korean financial market had not diminished significantly despite hard efforts of the financial supervisory authorities to improve the soundness of the Korean financial system during this period.

About 22 percent of corporate bonds issued between December 1997 and December 1999 became defaulted by the end of 2000 as the companies that issued the bonds went bankrupt (Oh and Rhee, 2001), suggesting that the investment trust sector lacked the capacity to assess risk. As a result, Korea's financial savings were further wasted. Expanding finance to insolvent firms limited the opportunities for more profitable and promising firms to obtain financing, eroding the long-term growth potential of the economy.

The rapid expansion of the ITCs and the corporate bond market during 1998, when domestic interest rates were high, effectively lengthened the period

Table 4. Financing Pattern of Non-Financial Firms
(Average share in percent)

	1981-1985	1986-1990	1991-1995	1996	1997	1998	1999
Bond	10.5	13.6	19.5	18.0	23.9	180.0	72.1
Equity	13.6	22.9	15.6	11.0	7.8	53.0	7.6
Commercial Paper	3.0	5.9	8.1	17.6	3.9	-45.8	-32.3
Sub Total	27.1	42.4	43.2	46.7	35.6	187.4	47.4
Loans	48.0	35.0	38.2	28.3	37.8	-63.9	4.1
Foreign	1.6	3.2	3.5	10.5	5.7	-38.5	19.7
Others	23.3	19.4	15.1	14.5	20.9	15.1	28.8
Total	100	100	100	100	100	100	100

Source: BOK, *Flow of Funds*, various issues.

of high interest payment burden on the corporate sector. As shown in Table 4, corporations paid back short-term loans and commercial paper by heavily issuing bonds, most with a maturity of three years. Corporate bond issues increased sharply during the period of December 1997 to March 1999. This switching from short-term debts to long-term debts during the period when interest rates were relatively high extended the adverse impact of the high interest rate policy adopted after the crisis.

Thus the asymmetric approach to financial restructuring or benign regulatory oversight over the ITCs, whether intended or not, contributed to the quick economic recovery in 1999, but delayed corporate restructuring and deepened financial sector problems. The increased market uncertainty and the resulting collapse of the securities market caused the economic recovery to be short-lived. Since the ITCs expanded most rapidly from mid-1998 to mid-1999, the amount of corporate bonds issued during this period was substantial, with a large proportion of them maturing in 2001 and 2002. In 2001 alone, 65 trillion won of corporate bonds fell due, of which about 25 trillion won were rated below investment grade. Thus, the impact of the ITC debacle has not been fully realized and will continue to exert strain and uncertainty on the Korean financial market.

The above analysis indicates the importance of a careful balance in the strengthening of regulatory rules and in the initiation of restructuring across different financial institutions and market segments to avoid unexpected development in financial markets.

Coordination of Monetary Policy with Supervisory Policies

After the crisis, the actual stance of monetary policy in Korea has been dominated more by the supervisory policies of the financial restructuring authority, the Financial Supervisory Commission (FSC), than by the monetary policy of the central bank, the Bank of Korea (BOK). Money multipliers have been unstable during the last three years. They changed depending on the timing of restructuring of financial institutions (e.g., banks or NBFIs) and the strengthening of regulatory rules and practices over them (Figure 9). In fact, the financial restructuring and strengthening of regulatory rules have themselves had strong contractionary effects.

Loan/deposit ratios have fallen sharply as the banks and other depository institutions became subject to restructuring, and became concerned about their BIS capital ratios and possible runs by depositors. The loan/deposit ratios of commercial banks and mutual savings companies fell significantly after 1998,

Figure 9. Money Multipliers

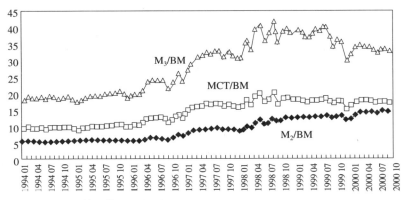

Source: BOK, *Monthly Bulletin*, various issues.

Figure 10. Loan/Deposit Ratio

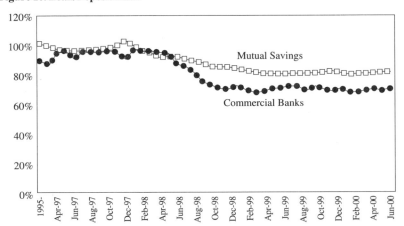

Source: BOK, *Monthly Bulletin*, various issues.

with the timing of each related to the strengthening of regulations and the increased risk of depositor runs (Figure 10).

On the other hand, financial institutions increased their holdings of public securities significantly during this period. Commercial bank holdings of government bonds increased from 6.7 trillion won at the end of 1997 to 19.5 trillion won at the end of 1999, a threefold increase in two years. If all public bonds (including bonds issued by government-owned entities such as KDB, KDIC, and KAMCO) are included, commercial bank holdings increased from 47 trillion won to 110 trillion won during the same period, from 23 percent to 44 percent of their total loans.

Figure 11. Domestic Credit, M3, and Reserve Money
(Billions of Korean won)

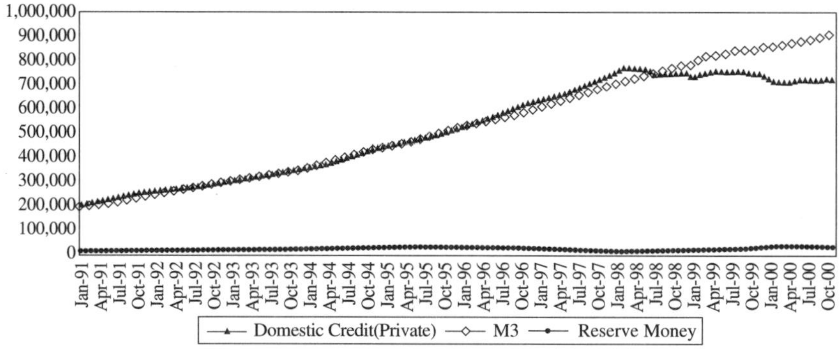

Source: BOK, *Monthly Bulletin*, various issues.

Figure 11 shows the movements of reserve money, M3, and total domestic credit based on the BOK's *Financial Survey*.[10] It shows that, despite rapid growth of M3, total domestic credit to the private sector has been declining since the end of 1997. This reflects the unwillingness of financial institutions to lend to the private sector after the supervisory rules were strengthened and the restructuring of financial institutions was initiated, including by prompt corrective action based on their BIS ratio.

The above experience suggests that the central bank's monetary policy needs to be closely coordinated with the supervisory authorities' policy in order to achieve the intended goal of the monetary policy. It also suggests that, in the future, the macroeconomic and structural reform components of the IMF programs should be carefully coordinated to avoid unexpected macroeconomic consequences. This is especially true in the countries where previously lax regulatory standards and practices are rapidly strengthened by following international standards.

Speed and Sequencing of Economic Reforms

The Korean experience during the last three years highlights the issue of the proper speed and sequencing of economic reforms. The introduction of global standards in an economy where accounting and supervisory practices had been extremely weak pushed long accumulated (but veiled) non-performing assets to the surface at a pace that the political economy of the country could not

---

[10]The *Financial Survey* statistics include assets and liabilities of banks as well as NBFIs.

readily accommodate. A consequence was granting forbearance or exceptions to recently introduced rules, benignly neglecting the rules, or relying on old measures of administrative guidance to roll over credit to troubled firms so that their loans would not be classified as non-performing. All these measures undermined the credibility of the reform program and made future restructuring more difficult.

The Korean experience has also shown that pursuing simultaneous restructuring of the financial and corporate sector is very difficult. Weak banks could not effectively drive corporate restructuring. There was a collective incentive problem that encouraged banks to bail out troubled firms in order to protect their BIS ratios. In a highly concentrated economy like Korea, where chaebol dominate, there are so many financial institutions involved in a single chaebol that coordination is very complicated. The progress of restructuring the corporate capital structure is also limited by the pace of changes in the country's financial market structure.

Political Economy Aspect

In an economy where the initial problems were very deep and the gap between international standards and domestic practice was wide, the speed of reforms, including the opening of the capital market and the introduction of global standards, may have to be tuned with the society's capacity to endure the economic contraction. If a social safety net is not well established to accom-

Table 5. Interest Coverage Ratio and Potential NPLs
(Billions of Korean won for borrowing amount)

	Number of firms (A)	Number of troubled firms (B)	Percentage of troubled firms (B/A)	Total borrowing (C)	Borrowing by troubled firms (D)	Percentage of borrowing by troubled firms (D/C)
Listed Firms			(percent)			(percent)
1995	662	109	16.5	111,462	15,680	14.1
1996	654	158	24.2	137,133	29,554	21.6
1997	641	226	35.3	192,767	65,111	33.8
1998	600	225	37.5	167,941	65,612	39.1
1999	438	94	19.5	136,984	47,549	34.7
Non-listed Firms						
1995	4,623	1,301	28.1	77,580	26,076	33.6
1996	4,722	1,463	31	95,191	32,459	34.1
1997	5,173	1,956	37.8	123,289	52,284	42.4
1998	5,328	1,856	34.8	109,977	52,339	47.6
1999	4,804	1,115	23.2	103,895	49,098	47.3

Source: BOK, *Financial Statement Analysis*, various issues.

modate a sharp increase in the unemployment rate, and if increasing social tension cannot be properly soothed by the political leadership, too ambitious a speed of reform can backfire, putting at risk the reform process itself.

The Korean corporate sector problem was extraordinarily deep. According to a study by Nam (2000), about 25 percent of corporate firms, accounting for 40 percent of total borrowings, had an interest rate coverage ratio below one in 1999 (Table 5). Therefore, in terms of the amount of debt, about 40 percent of firms were not able to pay interest out of their earnings.

Other studies show similar results. According to an analysis undertaken by the BOK of 3,701 companies in the manufacturing sector, roughly one in four manufacturers were unable to pay their financial costs with their cash income in 1997. A more recent BOK study of 1,807 firms for the first half of 2000 found that about 27 percent of firms still had an interest coverage ratio of less than one.

In such a situation, the rapid introduction of global standards in banking supervision (e.g., loan classification based on forward-looking criteria) and accounting caused a flood of NPAs in the financial sector. This in turn would cause the bankruptcy and liquidation of many de facto insolvent firms and a sharp increase in unemployment. In order to deal with these problems properly, an economy must first mobilize sufficient public funds to re-capitalize troubled financial institutions on one hand, and to deal with high unemployment on the other. Otherwise, the resulting social tension may frustrate the reform process itself. Thus, a dilemma is faced in a crisis-hit country regarding the speed of reform: if it is too slow, foreign confidence cannot be recovered quickly; if it is too fast, the domestic political economy cannot digest it.

Difficulty of Simultaneous Restructuring of the Corporate and Financial Sectors

The Korean financial crisis was caused by a corporate debt problem. Thus, the progress of financial restructuring is closely linked to the progress of corporate restructuring. But the simultaneous restructuring of the corporate and financial sector has been very difficult.

Korea adopted a creditor-led, out-of-court framework along the lines of the London approach to corporate restructuring. Workout units were established in eight lead banks, which were responsible for dealing with the problem loans belonging to the second tier, or 6-64, chaebol. In order to reduce the difficulties arising from inter-creditor differences (e.g., between banks and non-banks), the government encouraged 210 financial institutions to sign a Corporate Restructuring Agreement (CRA), based on which Corporate Restructuring Coordinating Committee (CRCC) was empowered to advise on the viability of corporate restructuring candidates, arbitrate inter-creditor differences, and provide guidelines for workout plans proposed by creditors. Although this approach was an appropriate response to a systemic crisis and has achieved some temporary financial stabilization, it has not been a fully effective scheme for promoting real restructuring.

Concerns about realizing losses have made banks unwilling to force necessary divestitures, asset sales, management changes, and other operational improvements. Instead, banks have tended to provide term extensions, rate reductions, grace periods, and conversion of debt into convertible bonds.

It has been difficult to proceed with the progress of corporate restructuring while financial institutions, which themselves are subject to a restructuring program, are heavily burdened with NPAs. Unless a sufficient amount of public funds is mobilized up-front to re-capitalize banks whenever their capital base is eroded due to realistic debt restructurings, and the government is willing to accept temporary, and potentially severe, financial market instability, rapid progress of both corporate and financial restructuring cannot be expected. Furthermore, corporate restructuring will be constrained by the degree of labor market flexibility. If layoffs of redundant workers are difficult for legal or political reasons, the progress of corporate restructuring will also be limited.

Financial Market Structure and Corporate Capital Structure

Korean firms' debt ratios are extremely high by international standards. The average debt ratio of the top 30 chaebol in Korea was estimated at about 570 percent at the end of 1997. If global standards are applied, perhaps a majority of Korean firms will be classified as below investment grade. Therefore, in a country such as Korea, a successful corporate debt restructuring will have to rely heavily on the conversion of debt to equity. But the record so far shows only a very small amount of debt—less than four trillion won out of more than 600 trillion won of total domestic debt—has been converted to equity. This however is not surprising since the debt/equity conversion can be facilitated only when there is a concomitant change in the financial market structure toward a deeper equity market.

During the last three years or so, corporate debt ratios have been reduced. However, this is mainly due to asset revaluations and increases in capital rather than to debt reduction. With a high level of corporate debt, financial institutions of Korea will remain vulnerable to business cycles and external shocks. Thus, the improvement of the corporate capital structure is key to the success of Korea's financial restructuring.

But the corporate capital structure will not be changed significantly unless concomitant changes are made in the financial market structure. And it will take substantial time for the latter to take place.

Total financial debt of Korean companies reached approximately 600-700 trillion won in year 2000.[11] Assuming that the debt ratio of the corporate sector before the crisis was approximately 400 percent, its total capital would be approximately 150 trillion won. To decrease the debt/equity ratio to, say, 200 percent, either capital must increase by approximately 150 trillion won or debt must decrease by 300 trillion won, or some combination of the two. However, it would not be practical to expect that this would happen within a short period of time.

An effective way to expedite the reduction of the corporate debt ratio in the current situation would be a substantial debt/equity conversion. However, the magnitude of conversion of debt into equity that the Korean economy can afford in the short run will be limited, since simply converting loans from financial institutions into equity investment will weaken the cash flow of financial institutions. Thus, in the end, the corporate restructuring must be supported by reconstructing the financial market structure—by developing a deeper equity market. This also requires changes in the patterns of the financial savings by Korean households. In other words, the job of successful financial restructuring in Korea is equivalent to the enormous job of reconstructing the balance sheet of the national economy.

The development of equity markets and changes in the structure of financial markets will also require the establishment of various institutions, including vulture funds, corporate restructuring vehicles, and mutual funds. This means that the improvement in the corporate sector's capital structure will take substantial time, and for the time being, the corporate sector will remain vulnerable to the business cycle and external shocks. Thus the opening of the capital market and adopting global standards overnight can make the overall economy quite vulnerable to a financial crisis.

Concluding Remarks

The Korean economic adjustment experience of the past three and a half years raises many questions regarding the process of structural reforms and market liberalization. Korea, like many other developing countries in East Asia,

---

[11]This is an approximate figure after subtracting "stocks" and "other equities" from "total external financing".

achieved "condensed economic growth". This growth was based on a development strategy with strong government interventions in the market. But now it faces the challenge of having to go through a condensed economic liberalization. It took centuries for the Western economies to industrialize themselves. In the process, they established necessary institutions and market infrastructures through generations and through the learning experience of many crises. The East Asian economies achieved industrialization within a generation or two, and this has been done through heavy protection and government intervention in resource allocation. But their rapid industrialization has coincided with the era of rapid integration of the global economy and the revolution of telecommunication and information technology. They cannot resist the trend of global integration, and this requires them to open and liberalize their domestic economy very fast. But, as discussed above, the lack of necessary institutions, social safety nets, and the economic structure they created make it an extremely challenging task to carry out a rapid transition to a fully liberalized and open economy. The domestic political economy also makes it hard to digest a rapid shift in the economic policy paradigm.

The introduction of global standards under the IMF program has released a flood of non-performing assets that had accumulated for a long time behind loose regulatory standards and accounting practices. This also required massive corporate and bank restructuring, and led to levels of unemployment and public debt, the scale of which the economy had never experienced in the past. This has not been easy to deal with, given the political reality of most of these countries. Either the speed of reform or abiding by the changed rules had to be compromised. In the first case, international capital markets became impatient, putting pressure by responding through adverse capital flows; and in the second case, the credibility of the reform program itself was undermined.

The Korean economy was successful in achieving rapid economic growth during the last several decades. Now it is facing the challenge of rapid and successful economic transition. So far, the economic transition has not been all that smooth and stable.

This paper has not provided solutions to deal with this enormous challenge of economic transition. What it has done is to highlight problems faced in the process of economic adjustment based on the Korean experience during the last three and a half years. But these issues certainly deserve much further study.

References

Basurto, Gabriela, and Atish Ghosh, 2000, "The Interest Rate-Exchange Rate Nexus in the Asian Crisis Countries," IMF Working Paper 00/19.

Cho, Yoon Je, 2000, "Restructuring Financial System in Korea—Key Issues," Sogang Institute of International and Area Studies Working Paper 00-01, October.

_____, 2001, "The Financial Crisis of Korea: A Consequence of Unbalanced Liberalization?" in *Financial Liberalization: How Far? How Fast?* edited by Gerard Caprio, Patrick Honohan and Joseph Stiglitz (Cambridge University Press).

_____, 1998, "The Structural Reform Issues of the Korean Economy," Sogang Institute of International and Area Studies Working Paper 98-01, January.

Dekle, Robert, Cheng Haiao, and Siyan Wang, 1999, "Do High Interest Rates Appreciate Interest Rates During Crisis?" forthcoming in *Oxford Bulletin of Economics and Statistics*.

Flood, Robert, and Andrew K. Rose, 2001, "Uncovered Interests Parity in Crisis: The Interest Rate Defense in the 1990s," mimeo.

Furman, Jason, and Joseph E. Stiglitz, 1998, "Economic Crises: Evidence and Insights from East Asia," *Brookings Papers on Economic Activity* (2), pp. 1-135.

Goldfajn, Ilan, and Taimur Baig, 1998, "Monetary Policy in the Aftermath of Currency Crises: The Case of Asia," IMF Working Paper 98/170.

Goldfajn, Ilan, and Poonam Gupta, 1999, "Does Monetary Policy Stabilize the Exchange Rate Following a Currency Crisis?" IMF Working Paper 99/42.

Nam, Joo-Ha, 2000, "Non-Performing Assets of the Korean Banks," mimeo, Sogang University, September (in Korean).

Kraay, Aart, 2000, "Do High Interest Rates Defend Currencies During Speculative Attacks?" World Bank Policy Research Working Paper No. 2267.

Oh, Gyutaeg, and Changyong Rhee, 2001, "The Bond Market Development After the Currency Crisis," mimeo, January (in Korean).

Ohno, Kenich, Kazuko Shirono, and Elif Sisli, 1999, "Can High Interest Rates Stop Regional Currency Falls?" ADB Institute Working Paper No. 6, December.

Radelet, Steven, and Jeffrey D. Sachs, 1999, "What Have We Learned, So Far, from the Asian Financial Crisis?" paper prepared for a National Bureau of Economic Research conference on the Korean currency crisis.

Comments on Papers 2 and 3

Barry Eichengreen

The commentator's dream is to be presented with a set of papers of uniformly high quality that disagree with one another, providing a controversy to discuss. In this sense the present authors constitute a "dream team" of Olympic caliber. Both papers offer analytical overviews of Korea's crisis and recovery. But while covering many of the same events, they reach quite different conclusions and offer quite different policy recommendations.

Before highlighting their differences, I should emphasize the extent of our authors' agreement. They agree that the Korean crisis reflected a unique conjuncture of macroeconomic and structural imbalances. Korea had been pursuing an investment- and debt-led growth strategy for more than three decades. While this strategy had been eminently successful, it left the economy increasingly susceptible to shocks, owing to Korea's heavy commitment to sectors like semiconductors, its heavy debt load, and its lack of financial transparency. As the rate of return on investment fell relative to the cost of capital, it became clear that this game could not go on indefinitely. Corporate and financial restructuring had been needed even before the crisis to redeploy resources to more profitable sectors, to consolidate or close down financially-troubled enterprises, and to convert debt to equity. Deteriorating macroeconomic and export-market conditions (associated with the collapse of global semiconductor markets in 1996) together with the turmoil in global capital markets (ignited by the crisis in Thailand and its spread to other Asian economies) only brought these realities to the fore. Note that we are no longer debating whether Korea's crisis was caused by structural weaknesses or investor panic. Rather, it was the investor panic, in combination with other factors, that brought the severity of those structural weaknesses to the surface, and the structural weaknesses, in combination with other special factors, that left Korea so vulnerable to investor panic in the first place. Everyone now appears to agree on this interpretation, or so it appears.

Turning now to specifics, I will use Professor Cho's four themes to organize my remarks. Cho's first theme has to do with the destabilizing effects of using high interest rates to stem capital flight and currency collapse in a highly-leveraged economy. Korea's corporate debt on the eve of the crisis was 150 percent of GDP. About a third of these debts were the obligations of firms whose earnings were less than their interest obligations. Against this background, anything that interrupted the flow of new finance or even raised interest rates was extremely disruptive. In particular, interest rate hikes could cause financial distress sufficient to undercut the currency-strengthening effects that the higher interest rates were designed to achieve.

This observation leads Professor Cho to conclude that "in dealing with a currency crisis in a highly leverage economy ... the appropriateness of ... high interest rate policies, may need to be reconsidered." But the need is not just to "reconsider" but to decide what to do instead. *Not* raising interest rates can cause foreign deposits to hemorrhage out of the banking system, force banks to curtail their domestic lending, and lead to equally severe financial distress. Maybe raising interest rates, while painful, is the lesser evil. This is the cautious conclusion of the IMF authors. I agree with them when they say that empirical studies of this question are inconclusive, and not with Professor Cho when he says that studies show that the "high interest rate policy was not effective in stabilizing the exchange rate." That results to date are inconclusive is all but inevitable, in my view, because pinning down the effects of interest rates on exchange rates in this environment is intrinsically difficult, if not impossible. We are essentially estimating the relationship between two endogenous variables. The model is nonlinear, since the effects of small and large interest rate changes are surely very different, and the effects of interest rate innovations are state contingent. These are not circumstances where econometrics are likely to speak clearly.

Even if we believe that the high interest rate policy was counterproductive, the question is what should have been done instead. A larger financing package? Korea's was already an extraordinary 1,900 percent of quota. The imposition of exchange controls to prevent foreign banks from repatriating their balances, as Professor Cho does not state but seems to suggest? This is not an instrument that was available to a country with obligations to the OECD, and in any case its utilization would have had reputational costs. Efforts to bring the banks to the table earlier to negotiate collective forbearance, as the IMF paper suggests? In principle, this may have been the most attractive option. But this observation raises the further question of why it was not pursued. Were the IMF and Korean authorities oblivious of the need to concert the banks before the end of December? I doubt it. I wonder whether this option was in fact feasible in the period of political uncertainty that preceded the installation of the new government. And, even in the absence of the election, would it have been possible to concert the banks before the severity of the crisis was apparent, and before the least patient creditors had been allowed to exit? These issues are not addressed in either of our papers.

In any case, this kind of Monday-morning quarterbacking may not usefully inform policy toward future crises. The ratio of bank debt to new bond issues has declined very significantly since the Asian crisis, and it is infinitely more difficult, as we know, to bring a dispersed bondholder community to the table and negotiate its forbearance.

Professor Cho's second theme is that the incomplete coverage of financial-sector restructuring in Korea allowed financial problems, rather than being solved, to simply shift location, from the commercial and investment banks to the investment and insurance companies. The initial focus on the problems of the commercial banks flowed from the fact that it was they who experienced the decline in foreign deposits at the end of 1997. The problems lurking in the investment trusts, while less visible, were every bit as severe, as the paper by Chopra *et al*. describes. Some investment companies had borrowed illegally from their trust funds. Others held a significant proportion of the debt of the top five chaebol, which put them in a weak position to decline these customers' requests for additional credit. That several were already under water led them to gamble for redemption, explaining the rapid expansion of their balance sheets through the first half of 1999.

So what were the consequences? Professor Cho characterizes these as a mixed blessing. Allowing the liberal provision of credit by investment companies prevented an even more severe credit crunch and plausibly hastened Korea's recovery from the crisis. At the same time, it deepened the problems of the investment trust sector, in turn leading to fears of another financial crisis in the summer of 1999. And it slowed the process of corporate and financial restructuring by easing weak chaebol's continued access to credit.

The key question is what should have been done differently. In retrospect, the implosion of the investment and trust business in 1999, following the Daewoo crisis, creates a prima facie argument for stronger prudential supervision of that sector. But wouldn't clamping down earlier on the investment companies have aggravated the credit crunch and slowed Korea's recovery from the post-crisis recession? Wouldn't doing so have added to the burden of nonperforming loans, risking more intense political backlash against reform? The IMF authors argue that the growth of bond and equity flotations starting in 1998 would have prevented a severe credit crunch even if vigorous regulation had been extended to the nonbank financial sector. This leads them to conclude that tighter regulation of the nonbank financial sector would have been an unmitigated good. But while large firms with access to stock and bond markets would have been relatively unaffected by earlier steps clamping down on the investment company sector, I am not convinced that the same is true of the small firms and start-ups that are arguably Korea's economic future.

Was the answer, then, to combine less forbearance of the investment companies with more forbearance of the banks, so that minimally acceptable levels of bank finance could still be provided to the small firm sector? Our authors do not say.

The third conclusion of Professor Cho's paper is that monetary policy and prudential supervision should be closely coordinated when an economy is restructuring its financial system. In Korea, changes in financial supervision and regulation that led to sharp shifts in the money multiplier were not offset by changes in the money base. The rate of growth of domestic credit declined throughout the post-crisis period, as banks faced with stronger enforcement of prudential rules shunned loans to the private sector in favor of less risky government bonds, while the monetary authorities have done little to offset this. Similarly, there was a sharp decline in the M3 multiplier in the second half of 1999, when the crisis broke in the investment company sector. Professor Cho implies that the Bank of Korea should have pursued a looser policy to offset these developments. Interestingly, the IMF paper does not comment on the role of monetary policy in the recovery (other than to say it was possible to reduce interest rates to low levels at a relatively early date). Nor does it discuss the need to coordinate regulatory policy with monetary policy.

My own view is that the two aspects of this problem should be distinguished. One question is whether the Bank of Korea should have followed a more accommodating policy throughout, to offset the decline in private sector credit. I am skeptical. Hourly wages started pushing higher from the second half of 1998, and more inflation would have created credibility problems for a central bank seeking to demonstrate its ability to operate a stable monetary policy and to maintain a floating exchange rate. On the other hand, the collapse of the M3 multiplier in the second half of 1999 due to the Daewoo crisis and regulatory intervention in the investment-company sector seems like a classic instance of a one-time shock that could have been offset without undermining credibility. Here I would argue that Cho's case for more rapid loosening of monetary policy is on firmer ground.

Finally, Professor Cho argues that the rapid introduction of global accounting standards, which brought the long-submerged problem of nonperforming loans to the surface all at once, backfired in Korea. It slowed financial reform by raising the up-front costs of banking sector recapitalization and creating reform fatigue. The result was pervasive non-application of the newly-promulgated rules. This conclusion is diametrically opposed to that of the IMF team, who argue, if I read them correctly, for even faster application of international standards for accounting, marking assets to market, and classifying loans as nonperforming.

Who is right? This is not a question, alas, that can be answered on narrowly economic grounds. It is also a question of political economy: under what circumstances does the ambition of the reform effort give rise to fatigue and risk a political backlash? Here, you will be aware, we are simply revisiting the classic debate between big-bang and gradual reform. Under what conditions does political sustainability dictate that reform should be spread out over time? And under what conditions do the economic costs of deferring reform militate against delay? As we know from other contexts, this is not a question with a single answer that applies in all times and places. Neither set of authors provides the thorough political economy analysis required to answer it for Korea.

To conclude, this is an exceedingly impressive set of papers. They ask precisely the right questions. If they don't provide convincing answers in each and every case, they at least point us in the right direction.

Jang-Yung Lee

Let me start by commending the IMF's role in helping to overcome the Korean crisis in a relatively short period of time.

There are, of course, questions about the appropriateness of the IMF stabilization policy in the immediate aftermath of the crisis. As pointed out by Chopra *et al.*, the high interest policy was inevitable in that it stabilized the panicky foreign exchange market and helped restore investors' confidence in the Korean won. But many economists have argued that Korea was hit by twin crises—a financial crisis and a currency crisis—at the same time. Undoubtedly, the high interest rates exacerbated the insolvency of large corporations, thereby increasing the amount of nonperforming loans and further deteriorating the soundness of financial institutions. A crisis resolution strategy must, therefore, give careful consideration to the possibility of a vicious circle of increased corporate failures and financial-sector fragility. Looking back, the IMF could have adopted both the principle of flexibility and that of universal treatment when imposing conditionality. This implies that adjustment programs would have taken into account the special economic situation or institutional characteristics of each individual country.

I also think the IMF should have taken a more flexible stance toward interest rate policy in 1998. The high interest rate policy was maintained for too long a period to be justified by the size and duration of macroeconomic imbalances in the Korean economy. The current account deficit of 1996, which amounted to 4.5 percent of GDP, was large, but much smaller than those of other crisis countries such as Mexico and Thailand. And the duration of the external imbalance was relatively short. Furthermore, the level of the current account deficit was not unsustainable for an economy with a potential growth rate of 7 percent.

Even if a strong case can be made for the high interest rate policy, it is crucial to lower the interest rate as soon as market sentiment improves. Admittedly, there were renewed uncertainties in the spring of 1998, when Indonesia's political situation deteriorated further. To cope with these uncertainties and possible spillover effects, the IMF may well have decided to maintain the high interest rate policy in Korea for as long as six months until the Asian countries returned to more stable market conditions.

There was an important structural component to the IMF program. Here, I think the IMF conditionality was a little bit too generous, allowing the Korean authorities to secure a lot of discretionary power. This discretion, however, was not used effectively to facilitate the much-needed reform and restructuring. For example, the exiting of nonviable financial institutions from the market was not done swiftly enough. And there did not appear to be a coherent or a comprehensive restructuring program put in place early in the crisis to ensure adequate liquidity as well as solvency of the banking system.

In a sense, the formal structural conditionality in the IMF program was too weak to support the financial sector restructuring in a timely manner. Although Chopra *et al.* discuss this issue in detail, the paper could benefit from a more analytical discussion of how individual structural performance criteria in the financial sector affected the actual progress of reform and restructuring. In other words, we should ask whether the depth of structural conditionality in the IMF program was optimal, considering the consensus view that one of the root causes of the Korean crisis was financial fragility.

I fully agree with Professor Cho that the delayed restructuring of nonbank financial institutions, such as the investment trust companies (ITCs), led to a typical moral hazard problem. The government's lax response to the liquidity crisis of some ITCs also distorted the incentive structure that determines the behavior of financial institutions as well as their customers. The government's decision to bail out the failing Hannam ITC and five other ITCs, though designed to avoid a run on the ITCs, raised the expectation of public support in a crisis situation and encouraged excessive risk-taking by other weak ITCs.

Another issue is whether the decision to provide fiscal support to the ITCs was appropriate by international standards. As far as I know, the established principles set by the IMF and other international financial institutions holds that the injection of public funds is to be strictly limited to the restructuring of deposit-taking institutions such as banks, not investment institutions such as the ITCs. However, the ITCs continued to be treated like banking institutions due to long-standing market practices and policy pressures. This created a serious moral hazard problem for local investors who accumulated a huge amount of the ITC's bond-type beneficiary certificates without regard to the viability of the ITCs until after the Daewoo group's liquidity crisis in mid-1999. Furthermore, the institutional framework for prudential regulation and supervision was very weak for the ITCs; the system of prompt corrective action, for example, did not exist in the ITC sector.

Despite the significant progress made in corporate restructuring, much of the corporate sector remains highly leveraged by international standards. This indicates that corporate debt should be reduced more actively through asset sales or debt-equity swaps. Only a very small amount of the corporate debt has been converted to equity. Professor Cho is right when he emphasizes the need to develop a deeper equity market to facilitate debt-equity conversion. However, even that will not be enough. It is more crucial to change the mindset of Korean corporations, who are not yet fully adjusted to the new principle of a free market economy and are still resentful of the loss of managerial control to foreign investors. In addition, more incentives should be given to creditor banks who want to enter into debt-equity swaps. In many cases, creditor banks are very reluctant to engage in swap deals because of the negative consequences for their balance sheets.

As Chopra *et al.* note, the structural reform part of the program consisted of measures to increase the market orientation of the Korean economy. And significant progress has been made in this area. However, market discipline is not yet entrenched. In some sectors, there is still a wide gap between global standards and market practices. People's mindsets are not yet fully adjusted to the principles of a free market economy. In this situation, I wonder what should be the optimal role for the government. The Korean government recently announced that it will promote constant, market-driven reform, shifting away from the government-led approach of the last three years. This means that corporate restructuring should be carried out by market forces with the government serving as a system manager or fair referee.

Though desirable, market-driven reform will not be an easy process because it will have to work in a second-best situation in which a significant portion of the market is not functioning properly. The market needs to include a well-functioning financial system that can monitor and weed out potentially insolvent companies in a timely manner. However, the establishment of a well-functioning financial system entails huge administrative, human capital, and legal requirements. In this regard, we should try to support the proper functioning of the market system by improving the still-not-up-to-date managerial software at banks, for example through better training and education of the bank managers. However, the urgency of upgrading operational systems suggests that we must tap other sources of expertise, such as foreign experts who know international best practices in every area of bank management.

4 New Evidence on High Interest Rate Policy During the Korean Crisis

Chae-Shick Chung and Se-Jik Kim

When Korea was hit hard by the financial crisis in 1997, the IMF rescue program included a high interest rate policy for more than three months to stabilize the won/dollar exchange rate. The short-term inter-bank interest rate was raised to 30 percent on December 26, 1997 in response to the exchange rate plummeting from 900 to 2,000 Korean won against the U.S. dollar. As the exchange rate stabilized, the short-term interest rate started to ease following an agreement between the Korean government and the IMF on February 7, 1998. Thereafter the interest rate was gradually lowered as the situation in the foreign exchange market improved. The interest rate fell below its pre-crisis level in the middle of 1998, and has remained low since then.

The high interest rate policy recommended by the IMF for the crisis-hit Asian countries has generated immense public and academic debates. Proponents of the policy such as Fischer (1998) suggest that the high interest rate policy helped stabilize exchange rates during the crisis. By restoring confidence and fostering needed corporate restructuring, the policy encouraged capital inflow to, or discouraged capital outflow from, countries in crisis, which subsequently strengthened their currencies. Opponents of the policy such as Furman and Stiglitz (1998) argue that the high interest rate policy destabilized exchange rates by raising corporate bankruptcies, which accelerated capital outflows.

The debate also stimulated an emerging literature seeking to empirically evaluate the efficacy of the high interest rate policy. The empirical evidence so far is mixed.[1] Some recent studies find that the high interest rate policy helped to stabilize exchange rates. For example, Dekle, Hsiao, and Wang (1998),

---

[1]There are also a few recent theoretical papers, including Lahiri and Végh (2000) and Flood and Jeanne (2000).

137

using weekly Korean data, find that raising interest rates contributed to appreciation during the crisis period. Goldfajn and Gupta (1999), using monthly data for 80 countries for 1980-98, find evidence that high interest rates helped to stabilize exchange rates (see also Cho and West, 2001). On the other hand, Furman and Stiglitz (1998), using data for nine developing countries, suggest that high interest rates had a negative or little effect on foreign exchange stability. Goldfajn and Baig (1998), based on VAR analysis using daily data for crisis-hit Asian countries, find a positive correlation between real interest rates and exchange rates for Hong Kong SAR, Indonesia and Malaysia, but a negative correlation for Korea and Thailand.

Surprisingly, the existing empirical studies yield a mixed result for Korea. The reason for the seemingly inconsistent results from previous studies may be because they do not allow for a nonlinear relationship between interest rates and foreign exchange rates. The purpose of this paper is to evaluate the high interest rate policy during the Korean crisis with a focus on nonlinear effects, in sharp contrast to previous studies. It is important to allow for nonlinearities for the following reasons.

First and most obviously, the relationship between interest rates and exchange rates may, in fact, have significant nonlinear characteristics (Bansal, 1997; Lahiri and Végh, 1999; and Chung, 1998). For example, exchange rate movements may depend on whether the interest rate differential between two countries is large or small.

Second, there may be rich nonlinear dynamics in the time path of exchange rate responses to interest rate shocks stemming from the fact that the relationship between interest rates and exchange rates is affected by a number of other variables, including capital inflows and outflows, corporate bankruptcies, the current account balance, policy credibility, and risk premiums.

Third, the nonlinear model can facilitate the empirical analysis of whether a rise in interest rates has different effects than a fall, something that previous studies have not addressed. The examination of the asymmetric effects is important, particularly because the IMF's high interest rate policy had two phases: a rise in interest rates in the initial period followed by a cutback.

To take nonlinearities into account, we use semi-nonparametric (SNP) estimation, a nonlinear econometric methodology developed by Gallant and Tauchen (1989), followed by nonlinear impulse response analysis developed by Gallant, Rossi, and Tauchen (1993). By applying this methodology to Korean daily data, we compare the reactions of the conditional means of exchange rate changes to various interest rate shocks without relying on a specific parameterization of the mean and variance equations. Intuitively, the methodology can be regarded as an extension of linear impulse response function in VAR analysis to the nonlinear model. By analyzing nonlinearities, however, this model is able to detect potential asymmetries in the response of exchange rates to different types of interest rate shocks. It can also trace out the dynamic path of the exchange rate response, thereby providing a basis for assessing the short- and long-term effect of interest rate changes on the exchange rate.

We derive several important findings. First, the effect of the high interest rate policy on the won changes sign over time. A rise in the interest rate causes the exchange rate to depreciate over a very short period. But the increase in the interest rate induces the appreciation of the won after about four days, and the appreciation continues thereafter without substantial damping.

Second, the low interest rate policy induces a very short-run (less than five days) appreciation, but has no significant effects thereafter. A comparison between the high and low interest rate policies suggests a notable asymmetry in the exchange rate dynamics. Above all, the high interest rate policy induces a substantial appreciation over a long period, say more than thirty days, while the low interest rate policy has no impact on the exchange rate over the same period.

Third, the above results hold regardless of whether the interest rate is at the level of the pre-crisis period or the high interest rate period. This suggests that a further rise in the interest rate during the high interest rate period would have induced a further appreciation of the won, which may imply that the rise in interest rates recommended by the IMF during the Korean crisis was not excessive. It also suggests that a cut in the interest rate to the pre-crisis level could be achieved without causing a depreciation.

These empirical findings suggest that the IMF's interest rate policy during the crisis contributed to the stabilization of the exchange rate. Our results also suggest that the rapid depreciation during the crisis was not temporary, which justifies the high interest rates in the initial period of crisis; and the asymmetric response suggests that a cut of the interest rate back to the pre-crisis level would not induce another serious exchange rate depreciation.

This paper is organized as follows. In the following sections, we discuss the empirical methodology, describe the data, and present the empirical results. We then evaluate the IMF's high interest rate policy and close with some concluding remarks.

Empirical Methodology

In contrast with earlier studies, we adopt the semi-nonparametric (SNP) method proposed by Gallant and Tauchen (1989). The key motivation for choosing a nonparametric model is that it allows us to conduct nonlinear impulse response analysis of the underlying dynamics, including potential asymmetries in the dynamic effects of interest rate policy on the exchange rate.

Semi-nonparametric Estimation of the Conditional Density[2]

Let y_t be the observed data at time t with dimension M, which have a Markovian structure. Markovian structure means that the conditional density of y_t given the entire history $(y_{t-1}, y_{t-2}, ...)$ depends on L lags from the past. Denote the one-step ahead conditional density of y_t as $f(y_t | x_{t-1})$ where $x_{t-1} = (y'_{t-L}, y'_{t+1-L}, ..., y'_{t-1})'$, which is a vector of length $M \cdot L$. Given the history of y_t, one can then determine the conditional density of y_t, $f(y_t | x_{t-1})$, by choosing θ to minimize $s_n(\theta) \equiv -\frac{1}{n} \sum_{t=1}^{n} \log [f(y_t | x_{t-1}, \theta)]$ where n stands for the number of observations or by applying some conventional model selection criteria.

The SNP method is a semi-nonparametric density estimation based on an approximation of $f(y_t | x_{t-1})$ with Hermite series expansion. That is,[3]

$$f(y | x, \theta) \propto [P(z, x)]^2 \cdot n_M (y | \mu_x, \Sigma),$$

where $P(z,x)$ is a polynomial in the standardized error $z = R^{-1} (y - \mu_x)$ and the past data x, $\Sigma = RR' =$ (the variance and covariance matrix), $n_M(y | \mu_x, \Sigma) =$ (Gaussian density), and μ_x is the linear conditional mean function of x_{t-1}, $\mu_x = b_0 + B \cdot x_{t-1}$. The constant of proportionality is $1 / \int [p(z, x)]^2 \phi(z) dz$, which makes $f(\cdot)$ integrate to one. To achieve a unique representation, the constant term of the polynomial part is put to one.

When the density of z does not depend on x, it is a case of homogeneous innovations. When a multivariate polynomial of degree in z, K_z, is equal to zero, one gets $f(y | \theta) = n_M(y | \mu_x, \Sigma)$ exactly. When K_z is positive, one gets a Gaussian density whose shape is modified due to multiplication by a polynomial in the normalized error $z = R^{-1} (y - \mu_x)$. The shape modifications thus achieved are rich enough to accurately approximate densities from a large class that includes densities with fat, t-like tails, densities with tails that are thinner than Gaussian, and skewed densities (Gallant and Nychka, 1987). The tuning parameter K_z controls the extent to which the model deviates from normality.

---

[2] See Gallant and Tauchen (1989) for more detail.

[3] For notational convenience, we use variables with and without time subscript "t" interchangeably.

To approximate conditionally heterogeneous processes, one can apply as above, except letting each coefficient of the polynomial be a polynomial of degree K_x in x. Therefore, the shape of the density depends on x when K_x is positive. All moments, thus, can depend on x, and the density can approximate any form of conditional heteroskedasticity. The tuning parameter K_x controls the extent to which the model's deviations from normality vary with the history of the process.

To capture ARCH/GARCH properties common in most financial variables, one can modify the variance-covariance matrix to depend on the absolute values of the elements of the vectors $(y_{t-L_r} - \mu_{x_{t-1-L_r}}, ..., y_{t-1} - \mu_{x_{t-2}})$. The variance-covariance matrix becomes:

$$\Sigma_{x_{t-1}} = R_{x_{t-1}} R'_{x_{t-1}}$$

$$\text{vech}(R_{x_{t-1}}) = \rho_0 + \sum_{i=1}^{L_r} P_{(i)} \left| y_{t-1-L_r+i} - \mu_{x_{t-2-L_r+i}} \right| + \sum_{i=1}^{L_g} \text{diag}(G_{(i)}) R_{x_{t-2-L_g+i}}$$

where vech (R) denotes a vector of length $M(M+1)/2$ containing the elements of the upper triangle of R, ρ_0 is a vector of length $M(M+1)/2$, $P_{(1)}$ through $P_{(L_r)}$ are $M(M+1)/2$ by M coefficient matrices, $|y-\mu|$ denotes a vector containing the absolute values of $(y-\mu)$, and $G_{(1)}$ through $G_{(L_g)}$ are coefficient vectors with dimension of $M(M+1)/2$. The classical GARCH has $\Sigma_{x_{t-1}}$ expressed in terms of squared lagged residuals and lagged values of $\Sigma_{x_{t-1}}$. Therefore, the SNP version of GARCH is more akin to the suggestions made by Nelson (1991).

Large values of M can generate a large number of interactions such as cross product terms for even modest settings of degrees K_z and K_x. Accordingly, Gallant and Tauchen (1989) suggest two more additional tuning parameters,

Table 1. Semi-Nonparametric Models

Parameter setting	Characterization of $\{y_t\}$
$L_\mu = 0, L_g = 0, L_r = 0, L_p \geq 0, K_z = 0, K_x = 0$	iid Gaussian
$L_\mu > 0, L_g > 0, L_r = 0, L_p \geq 0, K_z = 0, K_x = 0$	Gaussian VAR
$L_\mu = 0, L_g > 0, L_r = 0, L_p \geq 0, K_z > 0, K_x = 0$	Non-Gaussian VAR with homogeneous innovations
$L_\mu > 0, L_g > 0, L_r > 0, L_p \geq 0, K_z = 0, K_x = 0$	Gaussian GARCH
$L_\mu > 0, L_g > 0, L_r > 0, L_p \geq 0, K_z > 0, K_x = 0$	Non-Gaussian ARCH with homogeneous innovations
$L_\mu > 0, L_g > 0, L_r > 0, L_p \geq 0, K_z > 0, K_x > 0$	Full nonlinear non-Gaussian

Note: L_i's are the length for μ=(mean), g=(GARCH), r=(ARCH) and p=(polynomial part), and (K_x, K_z) are polynomial degrees in (z, x).

I_z and I_x, to filter out higher order interactions. $I_z = 0$ means no interactions are suppressed. $I_z = 1$ means the highest-order interactions are suppressed, namely those of degree exceeding K_z-1. In general, a positive I_z means all interactions of order exceeding $K_z - I_z$ are suppressed. Similarly, a positive I_x implies the suppression of all interactions of order exceeding $K_x - I_x$. The relationship between parameter setting and properties of the processes are summarized in Table 1.

Impulse Response Analysis of Nonlinear Models[4]

In this subsection we describe strategies for eliciting the dynamics of the process $\{y_t\}$ as represented by $f(y \mid x)$. The analysis of impulse response functions developed by Sims (1980) has been widely used in the study of the dynamics of a linear process. The basic notion of an impulse response function under VAR analysis is to visualize the dynamic response of the system to a movement of an innovation that is a linear combination of iid innovations, u_t. In the general nonlinear case, however, there are various notions of an innovation, making it difficult to compute an impulse response function. However, if the impulse response function of the linear case is viewed as the perturbation of y_t instead of u_t, then the ideas from the linear VAR extend directly to the nonlinear case, as described in Gallant, Rossi, and Tauchen (1993).

On the assumption that the conditional density of the underlying process depends on at most L lags, the j-step ahead conditional mean profile given initial condition can be expressed by:

$$\hat{y}_j (x_0) = E(y_{t+j} \mid x_t = x_0) = \int y f^j(y \mid x_0) \, dy$$

where $f^j(y \mid x_0)$ denotes the j-step ahead conditional density

$$f^j(y \mid x_0) = \int \cdots \int [\prod_{i=0}^{j-1} f(y_{i+1} \mid y_{i-L+1}, ..., y_i)] \, dy_1 \cdots dy_{j-1}$$

with $x_0 = (y'_{-L+1}, ..., y_0)'$. If x_0 is changed by $x^+ = x_0 + \delta$ or $x^- = x_0 - \delta$, for some vector value δ in the conditional density, the j-step ahead conditional mean profile becomes

$$\hat{y}_j (x^+) = E(y_{t+j} \mid x_t = x^+) \equiv \hat{y}_j^+$$

for $x^+ = (y'_{-L+1}, ..., y_0)' + (0, \cdots, \delta') \equiv x_0 + \delta$, and

---

[4]See Gallant, Rossi, and Tauchen (1993) for more detail.

$$\hat{y}_j\,(x^-) \,=\, E(y_{t+j}|x_t = x^-) \,\equiv\, \hat{y}_j^-$$

for $x^- = (y'_{-L+1}, ..., y'_0)' - (0, \cdots, \delta') \equiv x_0 - \delta$, where $j=1,....,J$. In a similar vein, $\hat{y}_j\,(x_0)$ stands for a baseline, which means the dynamics of conditional means without any perturbation in conditional arguments. Accordingly, positive and negative impulse responses of the J-step conditional mean are $\{\hat{y}_j^+ - \hat{y}_j^0\}_{j=1}^J$ and $\{\hat{y}_j^- - \hat{y}_j^0\}_{j=1}^J$, respectively. These two terms provide a nonlinear impulse response function for shocks on the conditional mean of the system.

Analogously, we can measure the effects of perturbing conditional arguments on the J-step ahead conditional variance matrix. Define the $M \times M$ matrix as $\hat{v}_j\,(x_0) = E[\mathrm{Var}(y_{t+j}|x_{t+j-1})|x_t = x_0)] = \int \cdots \int \mathrm{Var}\,(y_j|y_{j-L-1}, ..., y_{j-1})\,[\prod_{i=0}^{j-1} f(y_{i+1}\,|\,y_{i-L+1}, ..., y_i)]\,dy_1 \cdots dy_{j-1}$ for $j= 1, 2, ...,$ where $x_0 = (y'_{-L+1}, ..., y'_0)'$. The positive and negative impulse responses of perturbations on the volatility are $\{\hat{v}_j^+ - \hat{v}_j^0\}_{j=1}^J$ and $\{\hat{v}_j^- - \hat{v}_j^0\}_{j=1}^J$, respectively.

Data

The data consist of the daily won/dollar spot exchange rate and Korean and U.S. three-month CD rates from January 4, 1995 to September 30, 1998, totaling 897 observations. Both data sets are obtained from Bloomberg. We use daily observations since these are what policymakers watched most closely to formulate interest rate policy during the crisis period, and weekly or monthly data might not yield statistically reliable results given that the high interest rate period was so short.

In our empirical analysis, we divide the overall period into three sub-periods: the pre-crisis period from January 4, 1995 to November 30, 1997; the crisis period (or high interest rate period) from December 1, 1997 to March 31, 1998;[5] and the post high interest rate period from April 1, 1998 to September 30, 1998. The numbers of observations are 709, 76, and 112 for each period. This period anatomy allows us to analyze how the dynamics of interest rates evolved around the crisis. The average levels of the interest rate in each period are used as a baseline initial condition for impulse response function analysis as described in the next section.

We restrict the pre-crisis period to 1995 onward because of structural changes in the won/dollar exchange rate suggested by previous studies. Joo and Kim (1999), for example, argue that exchange rate movements were well

---

[5] We use the terminology "crisis period" and "high interest rate period" interchangeably throughout the paper.

explained by macroeconomic fundamentals after 1995, but not from 1990 to 1995. The timing of the structural break coincides with the Korean government's efforts to liberalize the capital account, such as easing limits on stock investment in non-state owned companies by foreigners from 10 percent to 12 percent and opening the market for non-guaranteed convertible bonds issued by small and mid-size companies. Furthermore, Standard & Poor's upgraded Korea's sovereign credit rating from A2 to A1 in May 1995, which resulted in net capital inflows, an expansionary monetary policy, and won depreciation.

The high interest rate policy (HIRP) period was chosen in accordance with the movement of historical data and previous studies. The beginning of this period coincides with December 3, 1997, the date that the Korean government and the IMF agreed on the first Letter of Intent for the IMF program. As is well known, Korean interest rates rose rapidly around early December 1997. The Korean government also made an upward adjustment of the ceiling on the interest rate from 25 percent to 40 percent, as noted in the Letter of Intent of December 22, 1997. The HIRP period in our analysis is also consistent with Furman and Stiglitz (1998), who suggested that the period of high interest rates in Korea was 113 days long, from December 2, 1997 to late March of 1998.

As the final date of the post-crisis (or post-HIRP) period we choose September 1998, given that the Korean government announced the completion of the first-stage restructuring in October 1998.[6] In the post-HIRP period, the Korean economy was still feeling the aftereffects of the currency crisis and the interest rate was in a downward stabilization trend.

The won/dollar exchange rate and the differential between Korean and U.S. interest rates are illustrated in Table 2. The mean, standard deviation, and difference between the maximum value and the minimum value are largest during the HIRP period. In addition, the exchange rate distribution is skewed to the left during the HIRP period, while the interest rate differential in the same period is skewed to the right. This suggests that the interest rate had an upward trend whereas the exchange rate had an appreciation trend during the HIRP period. Further, during the post-HIRP period, both variables show different characteristics from a normal distribution.

For our empirical analysis, we focus on relation between the percentile change in the won/dollar spot exchange, denoted by *exch* $(= 100 \times \ln[s_t / s_{t-1}])$, and the differential between Korean and U.S. interest rates, denoted by *int*, bearing the interest parity in mind.

---

[6]Of course, it is possible to include the data from October 1998 up until this day for our empirical analysis.

Table 2. Basic Statistics

	Mean	Max	Min	Std. Dev.	Skewness	Kurtosis
KRW/USD						
Whole Period	1038.4	1962.5	753.0	238.6	0.611	2.79
Pre-HIRP	814.5	915.0	753.0	49.2	0.608	1.91
HIRP	1360.5	1962.5	912.6	228.5	-0.311	2.82
Post-HIRP	1173.3	1389.0	1102.5	57.1	1.066	4.18
Interest Rate Differential[1]						
Whole Period	6.16	19.81	0.59	4.25	0.737	3.50
Pre-HIRP	7.79	11.16	4.73	1.27	0.207	2.71
HIRP	12.06	19.81	5.30	4.33	0.155	1.78
Post-HIRP	1.78	6.11	0.59	0.87	1.146	5.07

Note: The pre-HIRP period is between January 4, 1995 and November 30, 1997, the HIRP period between December 1, 1997 and March 31, 1998, and the post-HIRP period between April 1, 1998 and September 30, 1998.
[1]The interest rate differential is between Korean and U.S. interest rates.

Main Empirical Results

The SNP estimation provides information regarding an appropriate statistical model describing the dynamics of the two variables, *exch* and *int*, reasonably well. Based on the estimated SNP specification, the impulse response analysis allows us to see the direction and duration of the effects that changes in the interest rate have on the exchange rate, more precisely on the percent change in the exchange rate.

We conduct the SNP estimation from January 4, 1995 to September 30, 1998 to capture the underlying dynamic structure over the full period since the high interest rate policy during the Korean crisis may have been adopted based on the past behavioral relation between interest rates and exchange rates. At the same time, if policymakers believed that high interest rates could lead to structural changes, they might have a forward looking perspective.[7]

Through the SNP estimation we can identify the parameters driving the dynamics of the model. Given that the SNP approach is based on a truncated Hermite series expansion, we need to determine the key parameters: the degrees of the polynomial (K_z, K_x) and the lag lengths of the mean, the GARCH

---

[7]Fischer (1998) suggests that the high interest rate policy would help restructure an economy as well as restore confidence.

and the polynomial part (L_μ, L_g, L_r, L_p). For this purpose, we use the Bayesian Information Criterion (BIC) as a selection strategy. Table 3 shows the objective surface for SNP estimation and the selected values for the parameters. From the table, we can see that $L_\mu = 4$, $L_g = L_r = L_p = 1$, $K_z = 4$, $I_z = 2$, $K_x = I_x = 0$ are the most appropriate selection based on BIC. This suggests that the model has four lags in the linear autoregressive component, GARCH(1, 1), and non-Gaussian error structure reflected by the fact that a polynomial of degree 4 in z is selected. In summary, the density is a GARCH model with a non-parametric error structure.

Figure 1 presents information on the adequacy of the fit of the estimated model, as in Tauchen (1997) and Chung and Tauchen (2001). A comparison of panels (a) and (d), which show the dynamic behavior of the raw data, and panels (b) and (e), which show the estimated one-step ahead conditional means, indicates that the estimated model does a good job of tracking the mean over the sample period. Panels (c) and (f) are scatter plots of the standardized residuals—the difference between the raw data and the estimated conditional

Table 3. Bivariate SNP Estimation

L_u	L_g	L_r	L_p	K_z	I_z	K_x	I_x	P_θ	S_n	BIC
1	0	0	1	0	0	0	0	9	0.670	0.705
2	0	0	1	0	0	0	0	13	0.598	0.648
3	0	0	1	0	0	0	0	17	0.573	0.638
4	0	0	1	0	0	0	0	21	0.552	0.633
5	0	0	1	0	0	0	0	25	0.546	0.643
4	1	1	1	0	0	0	0	30	-0.911	-0.795
4	1	1	1	4	3	0	0	38	-1.094	-0.948
4	*1*	*1*	*1*	*4*	*2*	*0*	*0*	*39*	*-1.106*	*-0.956*
4	1	1	1	4	1	0	0	41	-1.111	-0.953
4	1	1	1	5	4	0	0	40	-1.097	-0.943
4	1	1	1	5	3	0	0	41	-1.098	-0.940
4	1	1	1	6	5	0	0	42	-1.098	-0.936
4	1	1	1	4	3	1	0	56	-1.130	-0.914
4	1	1	1	4	2	1	0	59	-1.135	-0.908
4	1	1	1	5	4	1	0	62	-1.129	-0.890
4	1	1	1	6	5	1	0	68	-1.136	-0.8742

Notes: L_i's represent the lag length for μ = (mean), g = (GARCH), r = (ARCH), and p = (polynomial part). (K_z, K_z) are polynomial degrees in (z, x). P_θ is the number of free parameters in the model. S_n is the log likelihood value, and BIC stands for Bayesian Information Criterion. Finally, bold and italic characters denote the chosen empirical model based on the minimized BIC value.

mean—of each variable. The scatters are reasonably uniform in the vertical direction, suggesting a good fit.

Within the estimated SNP dynamic structure, we now carry out the analysis of nonlinear impulse response function to investigate the effect of interest rate policy in the pre-HIRP economic environment, when interest rates are lower than they are in the HIRP period. To flesh this out, we empirically investigate how the exchange rate responds to both an upward and a downward adjustment of the interest rate from the average interest rate of the pre-HIRP period. The experiment is expected to provide information on which of the two policies, high and low interest rate policies, would have contributed more effectively to the stability of the exchange rate in the pre-crisis (or the pre-HIRP) economic environment.

Figure 1. Dynamics of Raw Data and SNP Estimation

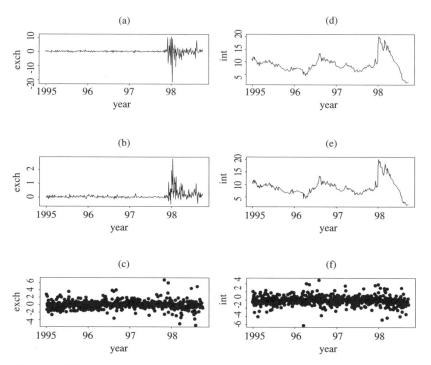

Notes: Panel (a) is a plot of daily observations on the rate of change in the won/dollar exchange rates (*exch*) from January 4, 1995 to September 30, 1998, while panel (d) is a plot of the interest rate differential between Korea and the U.S. (*int*) during the same period. Panels (b) and (e) are plots of the SNP one-step ahead conditional mean for *exch* and *int*, respectively. Panels (c) and (f) are normalized residuals for *exch* and *int*, respectively.

A more precise description of this experiment is as follows. Let $x_0 = (y'_{-L+1},$ ..., $y'_0)'$ be a vector of the averages of *exch* and *int* during the pre-HIRP period. We can then see the effects of an increase in the interest rate differential on the dynamic path of *exch*, which is the rate of change of exchange rates, by changing the conditional arguments x_0 into $x_0^+ = x_0 + (0, \cdots, \delta')' \equiv x + \delta$ where $\delta = (0, y_{int})'$, $y_{int} = \xi \times$ [average level of pre-HIRP interest rate differential], for $\xi = 0.1$, 0.4, and 0.8. That is, we empirically analyze how increases of 10 percent, 40 percent, and 80 percent in the interest rate differential from the pre-HIRP average interest rate differential would affect the change in the exchange rate.[8] We can also easily see the effect on the exchange rate of a decrease in the interest rate differential by putting $\xi = -0.1$, -0.4, and -0.8.

Figure 2 shows the response of the rate of change in the exchange rate (*exch*), to each of the above-mentioned interest rate shocks on the pre-HIRP interest rate differential. From the experiment, we derive the following key findings, which hold regardless of the absolute size of the shock.

First, the effect of the high interest rate policy on the exchange rate changes sign over time. For a very short period, the conditional mean of *exch* stays above zero, suggesting that a rise in the interest rate causes the exchange rate to depreciate. After four days or so, however, the effect is reversed and the conditional mean becomes negative, which suggests that the increase in the interest rate induces an appreciation of the won. The appreciation effect of the HIRP shock is persistent without substantial damping.[9] [10]The dynamic patterns of the exchange rate responses show a remarkable uniformity, especially about the timings of the reversal, regardless of the size of the shock.

Second, the low interest rate policy appreciates the exchange rate only for an extremely short period, but it has no significant effect afterwards. As seen in Figure 2, the low interest rate policy appreciates the won for less than five days. But the effect is almost nil thereafter, at least in terms of deviations from the baseline. This pattern also holds regardless of the size of the shock, with the timing of when the exchange rate effects vanish almost the same for different sizes of the shock.

---

[8]80 percent in this case is the level necessary for the pre-crisis average interest rate to reach the maximum interest rate level during the HIRP period.

[9]In Figures 2 and 3, the chart for the impulse response function is drawn for 30 days, because the shape of the impulse response after 30 days is not much different from the one just before 30 days.

[10]Whether the effect of a shock is persistent or not would depend on the definition of persistency. The responses in the experiment, however, remain at substantial magnitudes, more than 10 percent of the total deviations from the baseline.

Figure 2. Impulse Response Function of Changing Interest Rates in the Pre-HIRP Economic Environment

(i) 80 percent interest rate shock

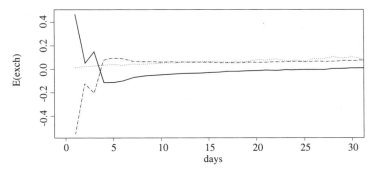

(ii) 40 percent interest rate shock

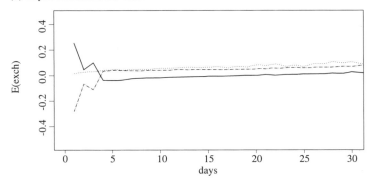

(iii) 10 percent interest rate shock

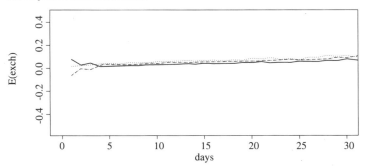

Notes: The y-axis is the conditional mean of *exch*, the percent change in the won/dollar exchange rate. The dotted line (·····) indicates the baseline. The solid line (———) and the dashed line (- - - -) are the responses to a positive and negative shock to the interest rate, respectively.

A comparison between the two policy options, high interest rate policy and low interest rate policy, suggests a notable asymmetry in the exchange rate dynamics. The high interest rate policy induces a substantial appreciation over a long period, say more than thirty days, while the low interest rate policy may affect the exchange rate only over an extremely short period.

Now we look at the effect of interest rate policy on exchange rate dynamics during the HIRP period. More specifically, we examine how the exchange rate responds to an increase or a decrease in the interest rate from the average interest rate of the HIRP period. This experiment is expected to reveal some useful information on the appropriate policy prescription during the crisis period, particularly whether it would have been effective to further raise or cut the interest rate during that period.

In this experiment, we choose ± 0.1, ± 0.3 and ± 0.5 for the value of ξ, the percent increase or decrease in the interest rate differential from the average level during the crisis period. The maximum value for ξ, 0.5, is the ratio of the highest interest rate to the average interest rate during the HIRP period.

Figure 3 illustrates the effects on the exchange rate of shocks on the HIRP interest rate. The key results for the pre-HIRP period hold for the HIRP period. This suggests that a further rise in interest rates during the HIRP would have induced a further appreciation of the won. Thus, it would have been appropriate to continue to raise the interest rate during the HIRP period if policymakers had believed that the exchange rate would have continued to depreciate further. This suggests that the rise in the interest rate recommended by the IMF during the Korean crisis was not excessive.

The results also suggest that a cut in interest rates below the level prevailing during the HIRP period would not have induced a significant depreciation over the three-month period.[11] This appears consistent with the fact that the exchange rate in Korea remained stable even after interest rates were cut back to the pre-crisis level.

The above findings shed new light on the literature on the efficacy of high interest rate policy. In particular, our empirical results may reconcile seemingly inconclusive and mutually inconsistent evidence suggested by the previous studies. Our results suggest that the reason why some empirical studies (for example, Goldfajn and Baig, 1998) using daily data find that the high interest rate policy has little or negative effect on the exchange rate may be because they do not allow for nonlinearities. In addition, our finding that the depreciation effect of the high interest rate policy is reversed after around four days

---

[11]The effect of a decrease in the interest rate seems to revert back to the baseline more slowly during the HIRP period than during the pre-HIRP period.

Figure 3. Impulse Response Function of Changing Interest Rates with HIRP Economic Environment

(i) 50 percent interest rate shock

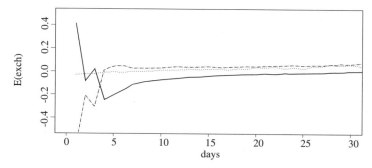

(ii) 30 percent interest rate shock

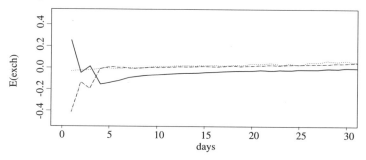

(iii) 10 percent interest rate shock

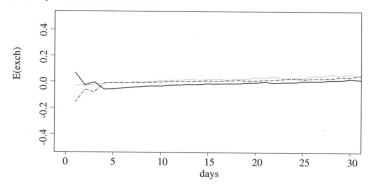

See notes to Figure 2.

suggests that if weekly or monthly data are used (as in Dekle *et al.*, 1998; and Cho and West, 2001), the likelihood of having a positive effect would be higher.

Evaluation of the IMF's High Interest Rate Policy

Our empirical results provide some building blocks to assess whether the IMF's high interest rate policy prescription for Korea during the crisis was appropriate. The assessment would depend partly on how long the underlying trend of depreciation of the won against dollar would have continued. If the depreciation of the won had been very short-lived, less than five days or so, and small, then a low interest rate policy would have been a better policy option. If, however, the depreciation was expected to persist much longer, say one month, then a high interest rate policy would be more effective.

There is evidence that the sharp rise in the won/dollar rate would last for longer than a week, implying that the high interest rate policy was appropriate. In particular, the baseline movements in our impulse response analysis show a depreciation trend for at least a month (see Figures 2 and 3). This implies that our SNP estimation detected the realized depreciation trend of the won/ dollar exchange rate during the pre-HIRP and HIRP periods, which coincide with observed data as shown in Figure 1.

Depreciation pressures lasting for an extended period may reflect the following circumstances at the onset of the crisis. First, there was no easy way to resolve the short-term external liabilities, which acted as a major cause of the currency crisis in Korea,[12] within a short period. This is obvious from the fact that it was three months after the eruption of the crisis before Korea could begin the debt rescheduling process of converting the US\$20 billion short-term liabilities to long-term liabilities. Short-term debts continued to be called in despite financial assistance from the IMF beginning on December 3, 1997.

Second, it took a while for the once-depleted foreign reserves to be rebuilt. As domestic banks, faced with refusal of maturity extension by international creditor banks, were unable to raise funds in foreign currency on their own, the Bank of Korea provided them with contingency funds out of the foreign exchange reserves, which together with excessive foreign exchange market intervention led to the depletion of foreign exchange reserves. The massive re-accumulation of foreign exchange reserves that was obviously necessary

---

[12]This factor is noted as the variable that best predicts the likelihood of a crisis in some empirical analysis. See Park and Choi (1998) and references therein.

to restore investor confidence would have taken more than just a couple of months.

Third, it is not easy for an economy to restore its credit ratings after they have been downgraded. During the crisis, international credit rating agencies quickly downgraded Korea's sovereign credit rating. For instance, Standard & Poor's downgraded Korea's credit rating by ten notches from October to December 1997, and Moody's downgraded six notches on three occasions. The rating of these agencies had an enormous impact on bond and stock investment in Korea, which in turn contributed to the devaluation of the Korean won. Given the difficulty of restoring the credit rating back to its normal level, the depreciating trend of the won was likely to continue for some time.

In sum, our empirical results suggest that the IMF's recommendation of high interest rates was an effective policy for stabilizing the exchange rate. In particular, the asymmetric effects of policy alternatives suggest that raising the interest rate was appropriate at the onset of the crisis while devaluation pressures persisted; and that the subsequent cut in the interest rate was also effective, as the initial uncertainty dissipated.

Conclusion

This study has evaluated the effectiveness of the high interest rate policy in stabilizing the exchange rate in Korea during the crisis. A nonlinear impulse response approach was adopted for a number of reasons. First, the nonlinear model is more general and provides richer dynamics of exchange rate responses to an interest rate shock. In addition, the nonlinear model provides a useful analytical tool to detect potential nonlinearities, particularly the asymmetric response of the exchange rate to an increase compared with a decrease in interest rates.

We found that the effect of the high interest rate policy on the exchange rate changes sign over time. A rise in the interest rate causes the exchange rate to depreciate only for four days or so. However, the increase in the interest rate induces the appreciation of the won afterwards, and the appreciation continues thereafter without substantial damping. We also found that the low interest rate policy appreciates the exchange rate only for an extremely short period, but has no significant effect afterwards. So there is a distinctive asymmetry in the exchange rate response to an interest rate shock. We also suggest that the mixed assessments of previous studies on the efficacy of high interest rate policy in Korea might have their root in the span of the data and the assumption of a linear relationship between interest rates and exchange rates.

Our empirical results also suggest that the IMF's high interest rate policy during the crisis, which was characterized by a sharp increase in interest rates at the onset of the crisis followed by a cutback after several months, was an effective policy prescription for exchange rate stabilization. If the sudden rise in the won/dollar rate was deemed extremely temporary (less than five days), then a low interest rate policy would have been more appropriate. Nevertheless, the economic situation at the time of crisis suggests that the rapid rise in the exchange rate was not temporary. Therefore, the high interest rate policy was appropriate in the situation.

References

Bansal, Ravi, 1997, "An Exploration of the Forward Premium Puzzle in Currency Market," *Review of Financial Studies*, 10, pp. 369-403.

Berg, Andrew, 1999, "The Asian Crisis: Causes, Policy Responses and Outcomes," IMF Working Paper 99/138.

Cho, Dongchul, and Kenneth West, 2001, "Interest Rates and Exchange Rates in the Korean, Philippine and Thai Exchange Rate Crises," KDI and University of Wisconsin.

Chung, Chae-Shick, 1998, "Empirical Anomaly in Exchange Rates and Forward Returns," Mimeo. Korea Institute for International Economic Policy.

Chung, Chae-Shick, and George Tauchen, 2001, "Testing Target Zone Models Using Efficient Method of Moments," *Journal of Business and Economic Statistics*, 19, pp. 255-277.

Dekle, Robert, Cheng Hsiao, and Siyan Wang, 1998, "Do High Interest Rates Appreciate Exchange Rates During Crisis?: The Korean Evidence," Mimeo. University of Southern California.

Fischer, Stanley, 1998, "The Asian Crisis: A View from the IMF," IMF.

Flood, Robert, and Olivier Jeanne, 2000, "An Interest Rate Defense of a Fixed Exchange Rate?" IMF Working Paper 00/159.

Furman, Jason, and Joseph Stiglitz, 1998, "Economic Crisis: Evidence and Insights from East Asia," Brookings Papers on Economic Activity, 2, pp. 1-135.

Gallant, Ronald, and Douglas Nychka, 1987, "Semi-nonparametric Maximum Likelihood Estimation," *Econometrica*, vol. 55. pp. 363-390.

Gallant, Ronald, Peter Rossi, and George Tauchen, 1993, "Nonlinear Dynamic Structures," *Econometrica*, 61, pp. 871-907.

Gallant Ronald, and George Tauchen, 1989, "Semi-nonparametric Estimation of Conditionally Constrained Heterogeneous Processes: Asset Pricing Applications," *Econometrica*, 57, pp. 1091-1120.

Goldfajn, Ilan, and Taimur Baig, 1998, "Monetary Policy in the Aftermath of Currency Crises: The Case of Asia," IMF Working Paper 99/38.

Goldfajn, Ilan, and Poonam Gupta, 1999, "Does Monetary Policy Stabilize the Exchange Rate Following a Currency Crisis?" IMF Working Paper 99/42.

Joo, Sangyoung, and Won-kyu Kim, 1999, "An Analysis of Volatility of KRW/USD Exchange Rate with Macroeconomic Fundamentals During the 1990s," *Korea Trade Review*, 24, pp. 21-37 (in Korean).

Lahiri, Amartya, and Carlos Végh, 1999, "Delaying the Inevitables: Optimal Interest Rate Policy and BOP Crises," UCLA.

Lane, Timothy, Atish Ghosh, Javier Hamann, Steven Phillips, Marianne Schulze-Ghattas, and Tsidi Tsikata, 1999, "IMF Supported Programs in Indonesia, Korea and Thailand: A Preliminary Assessment," Mimeo. IMF.

Nelson, Daniel, 1991, "Conditional Heteroskedasticity in Asset Returns: A New Approach," *Econometrica*, 59, pp. 347-370.

Park, Won-Am, and Gongpil Choi, 1998, "Causes and Predictability of the Korean Crisis," *Korea Economic Panel*, 4 (in Korean).

Sims, Christopher, 1980, "Macroeconomics and Reality," *Econometrica*, 48, pp. 1-48.

Tauchen, George, 1997, "New Minimum Chi-Square Methods in Empirical Finance," in D. Kreps and K. Wallis (Eds.), *Advances in Econometrics, Seventh World Congress*, Cambridge University Press, pp. 279-317.

5 Falling Profitability, Higher Borrowing Costs, and Chaebol Finances During the Korean Crisis

Anne O. Krueger and Jungho Yoo*

Despite the similarities among the countries hit by the Asian financial crisis of 1997, there were some differences. Among them, there were allegations that Korean chaebol had misallocated resources and become overindebted; by contrast, the role of "crony capitalism," in which friends and relatives of the politically powerful received loans that they were not expected to repay, was a focal point.

A number of factors contributed to the crises, and there is no broad consensus as to their relative importance. "Crony," or "chaebol," capitalism, the weakness of banking systems pre-crisis, financial liberalization and opening of capital accounts, and fixity of exchange rate regimes have all been singled out.

While all these factors obviously contributed, their relative importance quantitatively, and the interactions between them, are little understood. It is the purpose of this paper to delve, insofar as is feasible, into the role of the chaebol and the weak banking system in bringing about the Korean crisis. For that purpose, we trace the earlier history of credit rationing, and of the chaebol, the build-up of domestic credit and foreign indebtedness prior to the crisis, and the role of the chaebol in bringing about the crisis. Obviously, the crises in other countries may have had different relative contributions of financial and other variables and the Korean case cannot provide generalizations as to causation. But an understanding of the role of the chaebol and their financing can help, when experience of other countries is similarly examined, to enhance understanding of the vulnerabilities of countries in which the various factors listed above all play a role.

*We are indebted to Jeong-sam Yang, Il-Chong Nam, Inseok Shin, and Duk-Hoon Lee for the generous help they provided in our search for statistics and other data, and to participants in the International Workshop at Stanford University and in the NBER Conference on Currency Crises for helpful comments on the subject matter of this paper.

Such an understanding cannot be achieved, however, without reference to the role and relative importance of each of the key variables and their interaction. For example, if exchange rate depreciation was forced as a consequence of maintaining an unsustainable nominal exchange rate for a long period of time prior to the crisis and was quantitatively the largest factor in leading to the deterioration of the banks' portfolios, resort in the future to a genuinely floating exchange rate and/or preventing uncovered liabilities denominated in foreign exchange should greatly reduce the likelihood of future crises, regardless of the indebtedness of the chaebol. Likewise, if bank lending practices would have resulted in a rapidly increasing proportion of nonperforming loans (NPLs) in the banking system even had the exchange rate not been a significant factor and even in the absence of chaebol indebtedness, the relative importance of improving bank lending practices as a preventive measure for future crises looms much larger. And if rigidities in the banking/financial system, resulting from failure to liberalize and/or regulate sufficiently, were a major contributing factor, the policy lessons would focus on the urgent need for liberalizing and strengthening banking and financial systems in emerging markets.

In a first section, we briefly sketch the roles that each of these factors can play in theory in financial crises. We then provide background on the Korean economy and the evolution of the banking and financial systems, the chaebol, and linkages to the international economy, which are essential building blocks for our later analysis. The third section examines the history of financing of the chaebol and their role in the Korean economy. A fourth section then provides estimates of the extent to which there were NPLs in the banking system prior to the crisis, and the share of the chaebol in those loans. A fifth section examines the role of foreign-currency denominated debt in intensifying the crisis. A final section then provides our best judgment as to the relative importance of the variables widely pointed to as contributing to crisis.

Domestic Credit Expansion, Lending to Chaebol and/or Cronies, Exchange Rate Depreciation, Capital Account Opening, and Crises[1]

The problem for analysis of the Asian crises is not the lack of explanations: it is that there are too many. In those crises, and in the Mexican crisis of 1994,

---

[1]This section draws heavily on our companion paper, "Chaebol Capitalism and the Currency-Financial Crisis in Korea," presented at the NBER Conference on Financial Crises held in January 2001 at Cheeca Lodge, Florida.

a foreign exchange crisis and a financial crisis occurred almost simultaneously, and have come to be termed "twin crises." As will be seen, there are theoretical grounds to anticipate that these twin crises are likely to have a far more
severe impact on a domestic economy than either a financial or a currency
crisis alone, and it is not coincidental that their onset is virtually simultaneous.
In this section, we briefly review the role of each of the possible culprits in
precipitating and intensifying twin crises. Once that is done, focus turns to
interactions between them. Thereafter, we focus on the chaebol, and the likely
orders of magnitude of the interactions of those variables with others frequently blamed for the crises.

Exchange Rate Pegging

Although any nominal exchange rate could, in theory, be associated with the
appropriate real exchange rate,[2] empirical evidence shows that governmental
policies with respect to nominal exchange rates over periods of 3-5 years, if
not longer, significantly affect real exchange rates. Whether this is because of
long lags in adjustment or because of the unwillingness of the domestic authorities to adopt the monetary and fiscal policies consistent with their choice of
nominal exchange rate is not relevant for present purposes.

Empirically, if the authorities intervene in the foreign exchange market
for purposes other than smoothing short-term fluctuations (such as maintaining a fixed nominal exchange rate), the real exchange rate appreciates relative
to major trading partners when domestic inflation exceeds the inflation rate
in the rest of the world. Likewise, if for any reason (such as changes in the
terms of trade or rapid growth of domestic demand for imports) the real exchange rate would adjust in a well-functioning free market but is prevented
from doing so, there can be imbalances between the demand for, and supply
of, foreign exchange. As long as the authorities can meet this demand, buying
or selling foreign exchange as demanded, they can maintain their exchange
rate policy.

All of the countries afflicted with twin crises in the 1990s had intervened
heavily in their foreign exchange market in one way or another to achieve
target nominal exchange rates. In the cases of Mexico and Thailand, the nominal exchange rate had either been fixed, or adjusted according to a formula

---

[2]This would require that the domestic authorities refrain from using monetary and fiscal policies in pursuit of domestic economic objectives and instead allowed inflation or deflation to
occur as the "equilibrium" real exchange rate changed. Thus, if from an initial position of balance, the terms of trade deteriorated and warranted a real depreciation of the currency, the domestic price level would have to be allowed to decline to achieve that real depreciation.

which resulted in significant appreciation of the real exchange rate. In Indonesia and Korea, terms of trade shocks probably called for a significant real exchange rate depreciation at a time when there was some degree of real appreciation—as will be seen below for Korea. For Korea, the American government's concern about its bilateral trade deficit with Korea resulted in significant political pressure to prevent depreciation of the won in nominal terms.

When government officials implicitly or explicitly indicate that they will maintain an exchange rate policy that results in an appreciating currency in real terms, they provide individuals and firms with a strong incentive to access the international capital market—the real interest rate is typically lower than in the domestic market.[3] When domestic residents have access to the foreign capital market, or when domestic banks can borrow abroad, the result is an increase in the nation's liabilities, and the exchange rate policy means that the government is increasing its contingent liabilities. The unsustainability of the nominal exchange rate policy results in a buildup of domestic credit and foreign liabilities until the time when either domestic residents and foreigners anticipate that the exchange rate will alter and attempt to get out of domestic money and into foreign currency and/or the public or private debt-servicing obligations denominated in foreign exchange are not voluntarily met. At that point, either the "run on the currency" results in a "currency crisis" or the prospective inability to continue voluntary debt-servicing forces the same outcome. Resolving the crisis almost always involves an alteration in the exchange rate, and usually in exchange-rate policy.[4]

Of course, there can be a "pure" currency crisis without a financial crisis. This is more likely if there is a reasonably sound banking/financial system or a pre-existing highly restrictive set of capital controls that prevented the buildup of significant foreign indebtedness. Brazil's devaluation in 1999 is one good example of a currency crisis in which there was no serious domestic financial spillover.

---

[3]Lowering the domestic nominal interest rate would result in more domestic inflation and is thus eschewed by the authorities. See Krueger (1997) for calculation of Mexican real interest rates during the pre-crisis period when a nominal anchor exchange rate policy was followed.

[4]It should be noted that not all exchange rate changes will immediately quell the crisis. In the Mexican case, there was already a significant capital outflow when the authorities announced a nominal devaluation. In the view of most market participants, the magnitude of the announced devaluation was too small and the run on the currency intensified. It was not until the exchange rate was permitted to float that the immediate crisis subsided.

Financial Weakness and Crisis

If there is a continuing build-up of NPLs in the banking system, a financial crisis will result unless effective measures are taken to reverse the build-up. NPLs can come about for several reasons: (1) there can be an unforeseen macroeconomic disturbance (originating abroad or domestically) that leads to unfavorable outcomes for borrowers; (2) domestic credit expansion may be so rapid that banks are unwilling or unable to exercise normal prudence in lending and a disproportionate number of borrowers fail to be able to service their debts (often after a macroeconomic downturn); (3) banks may be directed or induced to lend to politically well-connected cronies, who do not service their outstanding loans; and, finally, (4) banks may lend to favored (economically important) enterprises who do not or cannot service their debt obligations. This last case includes the circumstance in which banks provide "evergreen" accounts for large businesses that are indebted to them, rolling over existing debt and extending credits to finance interest payments on it.

For Indonesia, it is thought that the third explanation—obligatory lending to politically well-connected friends and relatives of the President—was a significant factor in the NPLs of the banking system. In Thailand (and to a degree in Korea as will be seen below), rapid expansion of domestic credit contributed. In Japan in the late 1980s, where currency crisis was not a factor, a large negative macroeconomic shock when the rapid inflation of asset prices was reversed, was the trigger for difficulties in the banking system accounts.

Here, the important point is that once NPLs become significant in a bank's portfolios, serious difficulties are likely to result in the absence of sufficient provisioning or capital. A bank with sizable NPLs must charge higher interest rates on its lending in order to cover its costs over a smaller proportion of its business. As such, if it has more NPLs than its competitors, only those unable to obtain cheaper credit at banks with healthier balance sheets will borrow from it, thus increasing the riskiness of its portfolio. At the same time, as depositors learn of the bank's difficulties, they are likely to attempt to withdraw their deposits. And if the banks lend into arrears (so that the NPLs may not even show up as such on bank balance sheets), the problem of NPLs can mushroom rapidly. When many domestic banks have these difficulties at the same time, domestic credit can contract sharply. If there are foreign competitors (or if creditworthy borrowers can borrow abroad), the entire domestic banking system can be threatened.

Domestic Credit Expansion

Domestic credit can expand unduly rapidly because of government direction of credit or because of macroeconomic concerns. But it can also expand rapidly because of the incentives provided by the exchange rate regime, or simply because government monetary and fiscal policy is very loose for whatever reason. Rapid expansion of credit is dangerous: on one hand, it is inflationary, which means that for a while a permissive environment will enable borrowers to service their debts until tighter monetary policy is adopted to curb the resulting inflation; on the other hand, accelerated lending is associated with a deteriorating quality of borrower, both because there are simply not enough sound borrowers to finance such a rapid expansion and because banks do not have the capacity to evaluate lending at such an increasing rate. Rapid expansion of domestic credit was a feature of the pre-crisis period in Mexico, Indonesia, Thailand, Malaysia, and Korea. In the Indonesian case, the expansion of domestic credit exceeded 20 percent of GDP in the pre-crisis years.

Capital Account Liberalization

Many observers have blamed the opening of the capital account for the twin crises of the 1990s. The simple argument goes that without an open capital account, indebtedness could not have built up. However, there have been many experiences with foreign exchange crises in countries where the capital account was relatively closed. The degree to which cross-border financial flows must be regulated to prevent speculative flows when exchange rates are greatly misaligned is more restrictive than is compatible with a relatively open trading regime.

Moreover, there are many countries with open capital accounts that have not experienced the difficulties that the Asian countries did. Economies such as those of Taiwan Province of China and Singapore, where there were current account surpluses and high levels of foreign exchange reserves relative to trade volumes, did not experience difficulties.

To the extent the opening of the capital account results in difficulties, there are more complex avenues than those associated with real appreciation of the currency. First, when the capital account is open and the nominal exchange rate is fixed without appropriate supportive monetary and fiscal policies as discussed above, there are strong incentives for banks and/or private entities to incur foreign-exchange denominated liabilities (capital inflow) because of lower borrowing costs. When they view the government as having guaranteed the exchange rate, they may not match their future foreign exchange liabilities with foreign exchange assets. Second, banks may not have sufficient incentives for appropriate prudence in their lending policies, due either to a lack of capital adequacy (and existing NPLs) or to an absence of appropriate supervision.

The Korean Economy, the Chaebol, Credit Rationing, and Growth

Korean Economic Growth after 1960

Korea's spectacular economic growth from the 1960s to the 1990s is well known. In the 1950s, Korea was one of the poorest countries in the world, and was widely regarded as a country without serious growth prospects. After economic policy reforms began in the early 1960s, Korea began growing at sustained rates previously unheard of in world history.[5] Real GDP grew at an average annual rate of 10 percent per annum in the decade starting in 1963. By the mid-1990s, Korea's real per capita income was nearly nine times what it had been in the early 1960s (Table 1).

Table 1. Korea's GDP, GDP Per Capita, Investment, Savings and Capital Inflows

	Real GDP (billions of 1995 won)	GDP per capita (1995 won)	Investments/ GDP (%)	Savings/ GDP (%)	Net Capital Inflow/ GDP (%)
1960	24,524.5	981.4	10.8	1.4	9.3
1965	33,207.5	1,158.3	14.8	7.5	7.4
1970	56,209.0	1,788.1	25.4	18.2	8.1
1975	82,257.5	2,372.0	28.7	19.4	9.0
1980	114,977.7	3,073.7	31.9	24.2	8.5
1985	167,501.9	4,142.8	30.0	30.6	0.8
1990	263,430.4	6,068.3	37.7	37.6	0.8
1995	377,349.8	8,459.1	37.2	35.4	1.8
1999	436,798.5	9,321.4	26.8	33.5	-6.1

Source: Bank of Korea, *Economic Statistics Yearbook*, various issues and on-line service.

---

[5]Taiwan Province of China's rate of economic growth was equally rapid. Prior to the crisis of the late 1990s, most observers would have claimed that the major difference between the Taiwanese and Korean economies was the relatively small scale of Taiwanese enterprises contrasted with the large share of the Korean chaebol in the Korean economy. But there were other differences: perhaps because of greater strategic insecurity, the Taiwanese held very large foreign exchange reserves in relation to the size of their trade or their economy; the Taiwan dollar showed no tendency for real appreciation; and Taiwan Province of China's current account had been consistently in surplus. The Taiwanese financial system appears to have been considerably sounder than that of Korea in the late 1990s, and the rate of expansion of domestic credit at that time was much lower than that in Korea.

Economic liberalization took place throughout the first 35 years of Korea's rapid growth. In 1960, the country had had the usual developing-country mix of overvalued (and multiple) exchange rates supported by quantitative restrictions on imports (and a black market in foreign exchange), consequent high walls of protection for domestic manufacturers, price controls on many key commodities, credit rationing, a large fiscal deficit, one of the highest rates of inflation in the world, and a huge (averaging around 9 percent of GDP over the period 1953-58) current account deficit financed largely by foreign aid inflows.[6]

First steps in reform included moving to a more realistic (and constant real) exchange rate for exports, and the relaxation of restrictions on importing by exporters. Thereafter, general imports began to be liberalized in the late 1960s and the exchange regime was unified. Other major reforms also took place, including a major fiscal and tax reform in 1964, gradual removal of price controls, and a shift from a regime discriminating against agriculture to a protective one. Quantitative restrictions on imports were greatly eased in the late 1960s, tariffs were lowered in several steps, and further trade liberalization took place in the 1980s. In the early years of rapid growth, however, the banking system remained tightly controlled. Even after a reform in 1965 (which resulted in a positive real rate of interest for borrowers), credit was rationed and the curb market rate was well above the controlled interest rate.[7] Only in the late 1980s did interest rates begin to be deregulated, although the apparent gap between demand and supply of loanable funds was declining over time (see below).

In 1960, Korea's exports were only about 3 percent of GDP, while imports were about 13 percent. Policy makers therefore began focusing on measures to increase exports. They did so by encouraging all exports uniformly,[8] but nonetheless held something that might be regarded as close to an "export theory of value." Any firm that could export was rewarded in proportion to the foreign exchange receipts from exporting. And many of the firms that were initially successful were chaebol (although they were very small at the time

---

[6]See Krueger (1979) and Frank, Kim, and Westphal (1975) for an account of the early period of Korea's rapid development.

[7]See Hong (1981).

[8]All exporters were given an "export subsidy" of a specified number of won per dollar of exports (the number being altered from time to time as conditions were deemed to warrant), an "interest subsidy," and a tax subsidy, each of a given amount per dollar of export. In addition, exporters were permitted to import goods for their use in generous quantities, which undoubtedly permitted some profits by using the excess for domestic sales. To a significant degree, these "incentives" offset the duties and other charges on imports, and resulted in reasonably uniform incentives for import-competing and exportable production.

and some Korean analysts today do not regard the Hyundai, Samsung, etc., of the 1960s as chaebol at all). Because they were successful, they grew rapidly. They received new loans as their exports grew and as they expanded into new exporting activities.[9] Given the underdeveloped state of the Korean financial markets at that time (and in the absence of measures to strengthen them), access to credit was vital for expansion.

The chaebol were successful exporters and, for the first decade or more of Korean growth, were regarded almost as the "heroes" of Korean development. They were rewarded for export performance, and were highly profitable. Hong (1979) estimates the real rate of return on capital to have been about 35 percent or more in the first decade following the start of reforms. The chaebol were generally encouraged to enter whatever export markets they could, but when the authorities wanted a venture undertaken, the chaebol were asked to do so. They undertook these ventures with the implicit guarantee of the government that credit, tax exemptions, and other support would be available to make the venture profitable.[10] But the chaebol were on the whole remarkably profitable and had little difficulty with servicing their (subsidized) debt.

The extent to which the Korean economy changed structure is remarkable (Table 2). Exports and export earnings (the dollar price index of traded goods being stable in the 1960s) grew at over 41 percent annually for the period 1959-69 and continued growing almost that rapidly thereafter. Exports of goods and services as a percentage of GDP rose from 3 percent in 1960 to 14 percent in 1970 to 33 percent in 1980; imports also rose, from 10 percent of GDP in 1960 to 41 percent in 1980. Hence, the Korean economy was becoming much more open.[11]

---

[9]Some of these activities were chosen by the chaebol. On occasion, however, the authorities suggested to chaebol owners that they should move into certain lines of production. This attempt to "pick winners" was not always successful; when it reached its height in the heavy and chemical industry (HCI) drive of the mid-1970s, the rate of economic growth and of export expansion slowed substantially and policies were reversed by the late 1970s. When chaebol incurred losses while undertaking these mandated activities, the banks were directed to extend additional credit to the chaebol, thus setting a precedent for later difficulties.

[10]It is important to underscore that these government "rewards" were there in the context of the export drive. When chaebol could not produce competitive exports, there was little support. Even in the HCI drive—the most industry-specific interventionist phase of Korean policy—the output from HCI industries was to be exported within a specified period. When it became clear that that performance test was not being passed, the entire thrust of policy was reevaluated.

[11]Some of the increase in imports was of course intermediate goods used in the production of exportables. But the percentage import content of exports remained fairly stable at around 35 percent of the value of exports over the period of rapid growth. From 1960 onwards, exporters were entitled to import virtually anything that they might use in producing exportables with little paperwork; in addition, they were permitted to import a "wastage" allowance, which they were free to sell on the domestic market. Thus, the de facto liberalization exceeded that which took

Table 2. Foreign Trade in the Korean Economy

	Exports (Millions of US dollars)	Imports (Millions of US dollars)	Exports/ GDP (%)	Imports/ GDP (%)
1960	116.9	379.2	3.4	12.7
1965	289.8	488.4	8.6	16.2
1970	1,379.0	2,181.7	13.8	23.9
1975	5,883.6	7,997.2	27.2	35.7
1980	19,815.3	25,151.5	32.7	40.6
1985	30,455.4	30,017.0	32.9	32.1
1990	73,295.4	76,360.5	29.1	30.3
1995	147,459.5	154,882.5	30.2	31.7
1999	171,692.4	143,972.5	42.1	35.3

Source: Bank of Korea, *Economic Statistics Yearbook*, various issues.
Note: Exports and imports are those of goods and services on the balance of payments basis.

At the start of reforms, rationed credit financed a large fraction of new investment, especially in the manufacturing sector. The subsidies implicit in this credit served as a stimulus to industry, and permitted much more rapid expansion than would have been possible had companies had to rely on reinvesting their own profits.[12] Exporters were allocated preferential credit based upon their export performance. The real rate of return was so high that all the chaebol would happily have borrowed more had they been able to; most of them, as reported by Hong (1981), borrowed additional funds at the much-higher curb market rates. Thus, lending at controlled interest rates was, at least in the early years, equivalent to an intra-marginal subsidy to the chaebol. However, as the data presented below show, the chaebol did very well even without subsidies. Indeed, given the huge distortions in the economy that prevailed in the late 1950s, it is likely that in the 1960s, at least, almost any reasonably sensible venture into unskilled labor-intensive exportable production had a high real rate of return.

As already mentioned, by 1964 the borrowing rate from the banks was positive in real terms, although below a market-clearing rate. Over the following three decades, the banking system was further liberalized as the real interest rate charged for loans rose, and the gap between the controlled rate and what might have cleared the market diminished (see below). At the same time,

---

place because of removal of quantitative restrictions and lowering of tariffs. With an average tariff rate in the tariff schedule of around 15 percent in 1970, average tariff collections as a percent of imports were about 6 percent.

[12]In much of the public discussion of the reliance of firms in crisis countries on borrowing, what seems to be forgotten is that, starting from very low levels of income and development, there is very little equity and a large fraction of investment must therefore be financed through other channels.

the real rate of return on investments naturally fell as the very high initial returns obviously could not be sustained. We trace the decline in real returns and the increase in the real cost of credit in the next section.

When policy reforms began in the early 1960s, the Korean savings rate was very low—and even negative by some estimates. As growth accelerated and per capita incomes rose, domestic savings began to increase rapidly, rising from around 0 percent of GDP in 1960 to 18 percent by 1970 and to 24 percent by 1980 (see Table 1).[13] But at least until the late 1970s, profitable investment opportunities greatly exceeded domestic savings. As a result, domestic savings were supplemented by borrowing from abroad, equaling as much as 13 percent of GDP in the late 1960s.[14] But, despite the large capital inflows, the debt-service/exports and debt/GDP ratios did not increase because of the rapid rate of growth of export earnings and real GDP.

The Korean government guaranteed these credits, and determined the maximum that could be borrowed, allocating borrowing rights among exporting firms. Since the foreign interest rate was well below the domestic interest rate (especially in the curb market) and the real exchange rate was fairly stable for exporters, there was intense competition for foreign loans.

As domestic savings rose, the proportionate reliance on foreign resources for supplementing domestic savings to finance investment fell. By the 1980s, the domestic savings rate was in excess of 30 percent, and the current account went into surplus for several years in the mid-1980s.[15] Beginning at this time, the American government in bilateral trade negotiations began to pressure the Koreans to let the won appreciate in order to reduce the bilateral trade surplus with the U.S.[16] Most Korean economists by the mid-1990s believed that it

---

[13]In 1960, it is estimated that private saving was a positive 3.2 percent of GDP while government saving was a negative 2 percent of GDP. Foreign sources financed 78 percent of investment, which was 10 percent of GDP (see Krueger, 1979, pp. 206-7). In 1960, most foreign resources were foreign aid.

[14]Most of the capital inflow was from the private sector—largely commercial bank lending—by the late 1960s. Foreign aid had peaked in 1958 and was less than 2 percent of GDP by the mid-1960s. The current account deficit was sustainable because of the profitability of investment and the declining debt-service ratio that resulted from such rapid growth of exports and of real GDP.

[15]Korean policy makers viewed the emergence of the current account surplus as a transitory phenomenon explicable by "three lows" : the fall in oil prices in the mid-1980s, the drop in world interest rates (so that debt-servicing costs declined), and the low dollar (or high yen). The current account turned positive in 1986, rose to a peak of 8.5 percent of GDP in 1988, fell to 2.4 percent of GDP in 1989, turned negative (-0.5 percent) in 1990, and remained negative in the -2 percent range until 1997 when the deficit increased to 4.7 percent of GDP.

[16]Korea was running a bilateral surplus with the U.S. and a bilateral deficit with Japan, and policy makers resisted as far as they could these pressures. One response was to ask the American authorities whether they should devalue with respect to the yen while they appreciated with respect to the U.S. dollar!

would be in Korea's best interest to have some real depreciation of the won, but the pressures not to do so prevented it. While the won exchange rate was not fixed, the range within which it fluctuated was relatively narrow: it appreciated from 890 won per dollar at the end of 1985 to 679 won per dollar in 1989, and thereafter gradually depreciated to 808 won per dollar in 1993, appreciating again to 788 won per dollar in 1995. At the end of 1996 it stood at 844 per dollar, and of course depreciated almost 50 percent in 1997.[17] But, for the decade prior to the 1997 crisis, there had been little change in the real exchange rate.

Thus, by the mid-1990s, Korea had sustained three and a half decades of rapid growth. While there had been periods of difficulty—both slowdowns and overheating—Korean policy makers had met their challenges successfully. As noted by the OECD, the country had come from being one of the poorest developing countries in 1960 to having a per capita income equal to some OECD countries, with a higher rate of economic growth.[18]

The late 1980s had witnessed the introduction of democracy into Korea. The elected governments chose to liberalize further, including especially the financial sector and international capital flows.[19] In 1992-93 there was a "growth recession," as the growth rate slowed to just over 5 percent (contrasted with rates over 9 percent in the preceding two years and an average rate above 8 percent in the preceding decade). One response was to ease monetary policy: domestic credit expanded by over 18 percent in 1994, 14 percent in 1995, and 21 percent in 1996.[20] Real GDP growth responded, exceeding 8 percent in 1994 and 1995. But, as will be argued below, underlying weaknesses were not addressed, and the stimulus to the economy, through expansion of domestic credit and other measures, increased the vulnerability of the financial system later on.

The Crisis

Export earnings failed to maintain their growth rate in 1996, increasing only 3 percent in dollar terms, as falling prices for semiconductors and a number

---

[17]Exchange rates, savings rates, and current account deficit data are all taken from various issues of the IMF's *International Financial Statistics* unless otherwise noted.

[18]For an account of the Korean economy in the mid-1990s reflecting this consensus view, see OECD (1994).

[19]See OECD (1994) for a description of the five-year financial liberalization plan.

[20]This rate was not markedly faster, however, than it had been over the entire preceding decade. Hahm and Mishkin (1999, p. 21) reject the notion that liberalization of the capital account was responsible for the increase in domestic credit, but note that it did play a role in permitting the banks to take on greater exposures to foreign exchange risk.

of other factors resulted in the slowdown. Then, a number of events took place early in 1997 that surely eroded confidence. One of the large chaebol, Hanbo, went bankrupt early in the year. Given that it had been widely believed that the large chaebol were "too big to fail," this in and of itself must have resulted in some loss of confidence and a reexamination of Korea's creditworthiness. Moreover, 1997 was an election year, with the Presidential elections set to be held early in December. That the market anticipated difficulties is reflected in the fact that the Korean stock exchange index fell from 981 in April 1996 to 677 by the end of March 1997 and to 471 at the end of October, even before the outbreak of the currency crisis.

However, while the net and gross foreign (and especially short-term) liabilities of the banking and financial systems were continuing to increase, there was no visible evidence of crisis until the final quarter of the year. The Thai crisis had exploded in June, and the Indonesian crisis had begun during the summer of 1997, but most foreign observers were confident, given Korea's past history, that Korea would not be affected.[21] Korea's offshore banks were holding paper from Indonesia, Russia, and other countries with dollar liabilities, which would further deteriorate the net foreign asset position, but that was not widely known at the time.

Capital flight began early in the fourth quarter of the year. In many instances, it was simply a refusal to roll over short-term debt. But other factors contributed: Korea's sovereign risk status was downgraded by Standard and Poor's in October; reported NPLs in the banking system doubled from the end of 1996 to the fourth quarter of 1998, reaching 7.5 percent of total loans by that time, owing largely to the bankruptcy of six chaebol and the sharp drop in the Korean stock exchange. But, once it became known that reserves were decreasing, others sought to get out of won, and the capital outflow intensified rapidly.[22] Total reserves less overseas branch deposits and other unusable foreign exchange were $22.3 billion at the end of October and fell to $7.3 billion by the end of November.[23] It is reported that, by the time the IMF was approached, gross reserves were being depleted at a rate so rapid that they would have approached zero within 48 hours. In the program presented to the IMF Board,

---

[21]However, many Korean economists and policy analysts were very concerned. One of us (Krueger) was at a conference of Korean economic policy makers in August 1997 and the mood was one of deep gloom. Many of the participants were extremely pessimistic about the chaebol, the state of the financial system, and the potential for reforms of economic policy.

[22]However, even in November, the Finance Ministry was issuing reassuring statements, and private forecasters were minimizing the likelihood that Korea would approach the IMF. For a representative account, see John Burton, "Korean Currency Slide Shakes Economy," *Financial Times*, November 12, 1997, p. 5.

[23]Data are from Hahm and Mishkin (1999), Table 11.

it was reported that usable reserves had dropped from $22.5 billion on October 31 to $13 billion on November 21, and to $6 billion on December 2.[24]

The IMF Program[25]

All three Presidential candidates had declared repeatedly that under no circumstances would they approach the IMF. When the government did approach the IMF, the IMF's problem was complicated by several things: (1) it was not known who the new president would be, and hence with whom the IMF would have to deal on the economics team; (2) there was very little time to put together a program, and both because Korea had been viewed as "sound" until recently and because the candidates had all said they would not approach the Fund, there had been less preliminary work done than was usually the case;[26] (3) the exchange rate was depreciating sharply after the end of October, and when the band was widened to 10 percent on November 19, the rate of depreciation began accelerating rapidly; and (4) as already mentioned, the government was rapidly running out of foreign exchange reserves, and would soon be forced to default on its obligations.[27] The high short-term indebtedness meant that foreigners could get out of won simply by refusing to roll over outstanding debt.[28]

The first (hastily put-together) program set forth as its objectives: "building the conditions for an early return of confidence so as to limit the deceleration of real GDP growth to about 3 percent of GDP in 1998, followed by a recovery towards potential in 1999; containing inflation at or below 5 percent; and build-

---

[24]Other factors also contributed. A financial reform bill, proposed by a blue ribbon committee, had been turned down by Parliament, and it was not clear whether the government had legally guaranteed the foreign exchange liabilities of the financial institutions. While interest rates had risen by about 200 basis points, the Bank of Korea was nonetheless injecting liquidity into the system, which reversed the increase.

[25]The IMF documents cited in this section may be found at http://www.imf.org/external/country/KOR/index.htm.

[26]The fact that the Thai and Indonesian crises had already occurred no doubt diverted some of the attention that Korea otherwise might have received. At that time, too, it must have been anticipated that there would be Malaysian and Philippine programs.

[27]See Boughton (1998).

[28]Hahm and Mishkin (1999, p. 25) point out that "the speculative attack was not in the usual form of direct currency attack to exploit expected depreciation. Due to the tight regulation on currency forwards which should be backed by corresponding current account transactions and the absence of currency futures markets inside Korea at the time, opportunities for direct speculative attack had been much limited. Rather, the drastic depreciation of Korean won was driven by foreign creditors' run on Korean financial institutions and chaebol to collect their loans, and by foreign investors to exit from the Korean stock market."

ing international reserves to more than two months of imports by end-1998." [29] The staff memorandum stated that there were three pillars to the government's program: the macroeconomic framework;[30] restructuring and recapitalizing the financial sector; and reducing reliance of corporations and financial institutions on short-term debt.

For present purposes, the specifics of the Fund program are not relevant. However, understanding those aspects of the program that were important in affecting the severity of the downturn is necessary if an assessment of the role of the various factors leading in the downturn is to be made. In attempting to stem the speculative pressures, the exchange rate was allowed to float, and the won depreciated from the mid-800s level per dollar to almost 1800 per U.S. dollar.[31] The liquidity which had been introduced into the financial system in prior weeks (in an effort to support the chaebol) was removed, and money market rates were raised sharply. In the words of the staff these rates would "be maintained at as high a level as needed to stabilize markets" (p. 5). Day-to-day monetary policy was to be geared to exchange rate and short-term interest rate movements, while exchange rate policy was to be flexible with intervention "limited to smoothing operations."

The 1998 budget as passed by the government had projected a surplus of about 0.25 percent of GDP. But Fund staff estimated that lower growth and the altered exchange rate would reduce the balance by 0.8 percent of GDP, and that it would require 5.5 percent of GDP to recapitalize the banks to meet the Basle minimum capital standards. It was assumed that these funds would have to be borrowed, and interest costs (0.8 percent of GDP) were therefore also included in the altered budget estimates. These factors would, on Fund estimates, have shifted the fiscal account into deficit to about 1.5 percent of GDP in 1998. As stated by staff, "In order to prevent such a deficit and alleviate the burden on monetary policy in the overall macroeconomic adjustment, fiscal policy will be tightened to achieve at least balance and, preferably, a small surplus." The program therefore called for fiscal changes approximately offsetting the negative anticipated changes, and thus for maintenance of the fiscal

---

[29]IMF, Korea, "Request for Standby," December 3, 1997, p. 5.

[30]Much of the controversy surrounding the Korean program centers on whether the program tightened fiscal policy too much. This is discussed below. It should be noted that the Fund staff's introduction of the macroeconomic program indicated that the program would involve "a tighter monetary stance and significant fiscal adjustment" (Request for Standby, p. 5).

[31]As stated in the Request for Standby (pp. 5-6), "The inflation target reflects a very limited pass-through of the recent depreciation of the won to the aggregate price level. In order to achieve the inflation objective, the government will aim to reduce broad money growth (M3) from an estimated 16.4 percent at end-September to 15.4 percent at end-December 1997, and to a rate consistent with the inflation objective in 1998."

stance as anticipated prior to the crisis, with the 1.5 percent of GDP cuts equally distributed between government expenditures and revenues. The government initially raised some taxes to yield about 0.5 percent of GDP.

The second leg of the program was financial restructuring. As already indicated, NPLs were large and increasing prior to the crisis. The depreciation of the exchange rate increased debt-servicing obligations for chaebol and financial institutions, as did the increase in interest rates that came about with monetary tightening. An exit policy was to be adopted to close down weak financial institutions, and the remaining banks were to be recapitalized (through merger or other means). A blanket deposit guarantee was to be phased out at the end of December 2000 and replaced with deposit insurance for small depositors only.[32]

Bank restructuring required a prior, or at least concurrent, restructuring of the chaebols' finances. Given their very high debt-equity ratios (for one chaebol at the height of the crisis, the debt-equity ratio reached 12:1),[33] financial viability where feasible at all would surely require swaps of debt by the chaebol to the banks, giving the banks equity in return. For this reason, it was predictable that it would require time. Data on the finances of the chaebol are given in the next section. The stand-by also addressed corporate governance and corporate-financial-structure issues, focusing on improving incentives and supervision for banking operations and reforming bankruptcy laws. The government also agreed to refrain from providing financial support, providing tax privileges, or forcing mergers for individual companies.

A final issue of concern here is the projected magnitude of the financial support for the Korean program. The current account deficit was expected to decline markedly in 1997 to about 3 percent of GDP, and then—with export growth and won depreciation—to about 0.5 percent of GDP in 1998. However, the very high level of short-term debt was seen to be worrisome. As stated in the standby (p. 12), "It is difficult to estimate with any certainty the likely

---

[32]There were a number of other significant measures, which are less important for present purposes. For example, transparency was to be increased in a variety of ways. Large firms were to be audited by international accounting houses. Supervisory functions were to be reorganized and the Bank of Korea was given much greater independence. Importantly, the government undertook to refrain from attempting to influence lending decisions, leaving those to the financial institutions. But these actions had little impact on the short-run downturn.

[33]These high debt-equity ratios were public knowledge. The *Financial Times* published data on debt-equity ratios for 20 chaebol on August 8, 1997. The highest was Sammi with 33.3 times as much debt as equity; Jinro had 85 times as much debt as equity and Halla 20 times; Hyundai's debt was 4.4 times its equity, and so on. Profits were relatively small as a percentage of assets or sales. In Samsung's case, for example, net profits were 179.5 billion won on sales of 60 trillion won and total assets of 51 trillion won. Nine of the 20 chaebol listed in the *Financial Times* on that day had taken losses.

developments in capital flows ... given the uncertainty surrounding the rolling over of private sector short-term debt and the recent collapse in market confidence... The working assumption is that, on the basis of the beneficial effects on market confidence of the announced program and the large financing package, the bulk of the short-term debt will be rolled over. Under this scenario, the purpose of the exceptional financing would be largely to reconstitute reserves. For this outcome to materialize, it is critical that the financing package provided is adequately large and the program is perceived to be strong. It is anticipated that a comprehensive financing package of about $55 billion will be provided on a multilateral and bilateral basis ..."

The Severity of the Crisis

For at least two weeks after the announcement of the Fund program, questions remained as to whether the downward slide had been halted.[34] By late December, however, the exchange rate had stabilized, and by mid-January, foreign banks announced a $24 billion package of rollovers and new money.[35]

Domestic economic activity slowed markedly in 1998. For the year as a whole, real GDP fell by 6.7 percent, contrasted with the Fund's projected 3 percent. The unemployment rate, which had been 2.2 percent at the end of the third quarter of 1997 rose throughout 1998 and peaked in the first quarter of 1999 at 8.4 percent. The seasonally adjusted industrial production index fell by 15 percent from the end of 1997 to the second quarter of 1998. Thereafter, it rose, reaching its pre-crisis level by the end of 1998 and 144.9 at the end of 1999.

The external accounts improved markedly. There was a sharp drop in imports in immediate response to the crisis, and a much-increased current account balance: while exports were slightly lower in dollar terms in 1998 than in 1997, imports fell 22.4 percent and the current account balance was equal to an astonishing 12.5 percent of GDP for the year. Foreign exchange reserves rose in response, reaching $74 billion by the end of 1999 and $83.6 billion by the end of the first quarter of 2000. The decline in real GDP ended in mid-1998, and by the end of the year, real GDP had exceeded its pre-crisis level. For 1999, real GDP growth exceeded 9 percent, and is projected to attain that same rate for 2000.

---

[34]Because of this, it is very difficult to accept the argument that the Fund program was "too stringent." Indeed, given those uncertainties it is more plausible to argue that the program might have been even more restrictive initially.

[35]*Financial Times*, January 30, 1998, p. 11.

After early 1998, the nominal exchange rate appreciated in dollar terms, entering the year 2000 at around 1100 to the dollar, contrasted with 1800 to the dollar at the peak of the crisis. Moreover, prices at the end of 1998 were about 7 percent higher than at the end of 1997; in 1999 the rate of inflation was just 0.8 percent, as measured by the consumer price index.

Progress in restructuring the financial sector was necessarily considerably slower. Although interest rates had fallen below their pre-crisis levels by the end of 1998, restructuring of chaebol and financial institutions met considerable resistance.[36] Government policy pronouncements and actions have continued to push reforms, but the pace of reform has been much slower than with regard to the balance of payments and external finances.

But by any measure, the negative impact of the crisis and measures to address it were felt most heavily in 1998. By early 2000, the Korean recovery was more rapid and more pronounced than had been anticipated by any.[37]

Estimating the Role of Financial and Other Variables in Leading to Crisis

Subsidized Credits

Financial restructuring was absolutely essential—first to make the reforms credible (or capital outflows would have continued) and second as a prerequisite for economic recovery. And because the devaluation and higher interest rates would both weaken the financial sector in the short run (and this was understood by the markets), failure to address the issue of financial restructuring would clearly have increased the severity of the recession and delayed, if not aborted, the recovery. And financial restructuring could not be satisfactorily undertaken without addressing the very high debt/equity ratios of the chaebol. How much this intensified the downturn however, cannot be addressed until consideration of the finances of the chaebol and the financial system are considered.

Either a financial crisis or a currency crisis must be addressed with measures that will cause economic pain in the short run. But when the two interact, the

---

[36]See, for example, John Burton, "Boxed into a Corner," *Financial Times*, November 23, 1998, p. 17, where the header read "South Korea's chaebol are fighting a stiff rearguard action against government reforms but the conglomerates are being forced to change their ways."

[37]This is not to say that corporate and financial restructuring had been completed. At the time of writing in late 2000, unprofitable chaebol activities, including some large entities are still being closed down, with attendant concerns about a slowing down of the rate of growth in 2001.

resulting costs are much higher. To see how this played out in Korea, we start with an examination of the finances of the chaebol prior to late 1997. An overview of their evolution, and the problems that developed, will be useful before turning to detail. As mentioned earlier, the chaebol had earlier contributed enormously to Korea's rapid economic growth. By the early 1990s, the largest 30 chaebol accounted for 49 percent of assets and 42 percent of sales in the manufacturing sector. While they had received subsidized credit, this implicit subsidy was probably mostly intramarginal in the 1960s and 1970s, and probably simply increased overall profitability and reinvestment rates. However, over time, the chaebols' profitability necessarily diminished, while the real interest rate at which they borrowed was increasing.

Table 3 gives data on lending rates of deposit money banks (DMBs) from 1961 to 1987, the period during which interest rates were controlled. In 1987, the proportion of preferential loans in total reached a peak and began to be reduced, and the Bank of Korea stopped reporting the interest rates by those loan categories separately. To estimate how much of a subsidy was involved in DMB lending, it is necessary to contrast the rates with an estimate of what a market-clearing real interest rate might have been.[38] To that end, Table 4 gives the curb market interest rates, inflation rates, and growth rates over the years from 1961 to 1987. We then construct an estimate of what a realistic real borrowing rate might have been by adding the inflation rate to the growth rate and calculating a three-year moving average.

We then derive estimates of the subsidy through DMB loans in the first column of Table 5. The estimates are made by multiplying the volume of DMB loans with the difference between the reference interest rate and the actual borrowing rate.[39] Also shown in Table 5 are similarly derived estimates of the subsidy through loans to the manufacturing sector from the Korea Development Bank, a nonbank financial institution which lent for investment in public utilities, infrastructure, equipment for manufacturing, and other purchases deemed desirable for developmental purposes. The sum of these esti-

[38]The curb market rate, given in column 1 of Table 4, provides an alternate "reference interest rate." As can be seen, the estimated subsidy to borrowers would be considerably higher if the difference between the borrowing rates and the curb market rate were used. The two move together, however, and it seems reasonable that some part of the curb market rate would have been to adjust for additional risk. Our estimates of the implicit subsidy must, however, probably be taken as a lower bound on the value of loans to their recipients.

[39]The subsidy estimation starts from 1963, as the preferential rate began to be applied to "loans for trade" in the year, and it ends in 1982, as the preferential rates applied to various loans ceased to exist (Table 3). In the early 1980s the government lowered interest rates on ordinary loans more than it did the rates on policy-designated preferential loans, narrowing the gap between the two. Data on the volume of DMB loans is available upon request to the authors.

mates should be compared with the final column of Table 5, which gives all manufacturing firms' ordinary incomes (reported on their balance sheets). As can be seen, the estimated subsidy component of loans exceeded ordinary income in some years, and represented a substantial portion of it in others.

There was almost certainly an element of subsidy in bank lending after 1988 and even in lending at nonpreferential rates prior to that date. Estimating its magnitude is considerably more difficult, as there are no records of the interest rates at which loans were extended. An estimate was made, using the

Table 3. Interest Rates on Loans and Discounts, Deposit Money Banks
(In percent)

	Discounts on Commercial Bills	Loans for Trade	Loans for Machine Industry Promotion	Loans for Equipment of Export Industry	Loans with NIF	"Lending Rate"
1961	13.9	13.9	n.a.	n.a.	n.a.	n.a.
1962	13.9	12.7	n.a.	n.a.	n.a.	n.a.
1963	13.9	9.1	n.a.	n.a.	n.a.	n.a.
1964	14.0	6.8	n.a.	n.a.	n.a.	n.a.
1965	16.5	6.5	n.a.	n.a.	n.a.	n.a.
1966	24.0	6.5	n.a.	n.a.	n.a.	n.a.
1967	24.0	6.3	n.a.	n.a.	n.a.	n.a.
1968	24.3	6.0	12.0	n.a.	n.a.	n.a.
1969	25.2	6.0	12.0	n.a.	n.a.	n.a.
1970	24.3	6.0	12.0	n.a.	n.a.	n.a.
1971	22.9	6.0	12.0	n.a.	n.a.	n.a.
1972	17.7	6.0	10.1	n.a.	n.a.	n.a.
1973	15.5	6.6	10.0	12.0	n.a.	n.a.
1974	15.5	8.9	11.1	12.0	9.2	n.a.
1975	15.3	7.6	12.0	12.0	12.0	n.a.
1976	16.3	7.4	12.4	12.8	12.8	n.a.
1977	16.7	8.0	13.0	14.0	14.0	n.a.
1978	17.8	8.5	14.1	15.1	15.1	n.a.
1979	18.8	9.0	15.0	16.0	14.7	n.a.
1980	24.1	14.8	20.2	21.2	18.2	18.0
1981	19.4	15.0	17.9	18.8	16.4	17.4
1982	12.3	10.8	12.1	n.a.	12.2	11.8
1983	10.0	10.0	10.0	n.a.	10.0	10.0
1984	10.3	10.0	10.0	n.a.	10.7	10.0
1985	10.8	10.0	n.a.	n.a.	10.8	10.0
1986	10.8	10.0	n.a.	n.a.	10.5	10.0
1987	10.8	10.0	n.a.	n.a.	n.a.	10.0

Source: The first five columns are from Bank of Korea, *Monthly Statistical Bulletin*, various issues. "Lending rate" is obtained from *International Financial Statistics*, various issues.

Notes: Bank of Korea stopped reporting DMB interest rates in this format in 1988. "Lending rate" is the minimum rate charged to general enterprises by DMBs on loans of general funds for up to one year. From 1977 it is a weighted average, weighted by loans by nationwide commercial banks. National Investment Fund (NIF) was created in 1973 to help finance policy-favored investment projects.

"lending rate" reported by the IMF in *International Financial Statistics* (Table 3, last column) and taking the difference between the reference rate and that rate times the volume of loans outstanding. The results of those estimates are available upon request to the authors. Unlike the estimates used here, those estimates probably represent upper bounds as to the magnitude of the subsidy implicit in bank loans both because some loans may have been extended at higher interest rates and because the reference rate may overstate the "true" interest rate, especially during periods of falling inflation. Nonetheless, even by our most conservative measure, the subsidy component of lending was

Table 4. Reference Interest Rates
(In percent per annum)

	Curb Market Interest Rate	Inflation, CPI	GDP Growth Rate	Reference Interest Rate
	(1)	(2)	(3)	(4)=(2)+(3)
1961	n.a.	6.5	3.5	10.1
1962	n.a.	7.7	3.3	11.0
1963	n.a.	11.5	5.7	17.2
1964	61.8	18.1	7.3	25.3
1965	58.9	20.4	8.2	28.6
1966	58.7	17.6	9.4	26.9
1967	56.7	11.9	8.4	20.3
1968	56.0	11.0	10.2	21.2
1969	51.4	11.3	10.6	21.9
1970	50.2	13.0	10.9	23.9
1971	46.4	13.9	10.0	23.9
1972	39.0	13.7	7.0	20.7
1973	33.2	9.4	8.6	18.0
1974	40.6	13.0	8.2	21.2
1975	47.6	17.6	8.8	26.3
1976	40.5	21.6	8.4	30.0
1977	38.1	16.9	9.2	26.1
1978	41.7	13.3	10.1	23.3
1979	42.4	14.3	8.7	23.0
1980	44.9	20.5	4.7	25.1
1981	35.3	22.8	3.8	26.6
1982	33.1	19.1	3.9	22.9
1983	25.8	10.6	8.1	18.8
1984	24.8	4.3	8.7	13.0
1985	24.0	2.7	8.5	11.2
1986	23.1	2.5	8.6	11.1
1987	23.0	2.8	9.5	12.2

Source: Bank of Korea, *Economic Statistics Yearbook*, various issues.
Note: Inflation and GDP growth rates shown are three-year moving averages.

Table 5. Estimates of Implicit Subsidy through Deposit Money Bank and Korea Development Bank Loans

(In billions of Korean won)

	Through DMB Loans	Through KDB Loans	Sum of Subsidy Estimates	Ordinary Income, Mfg. Total
1963	0.2	1.1	1.2	4.5
1964	0.5	2.2	2.7	5.6
1965	0.8	3.1	3.9	6.6
1966	1.0	2.9	3.9	11.4
1967	1.5	1.8	3.3	13.4
1968	3.1	2.3	5.5	20.6
1969	5.2	2.7	7.9	24.3
1970	9.7	4.8	14.5	22.9
1971	14.1	6.2	20.3	11.8
1972	15.8	5.7	21.5	56.5
1973	21.9	4.2	26.0	62.3
1974	44.1	10.1	54.2	176.1
1975	82.6	25.0	107.6	169.7
1976	122.1	43.6	165.7	313.6
1977	125.6	47.3	172.9	390.0
1978	135.0	52.2	187.3	615.1
1979	179.4	77.3	256.7	573.9
1980	185.0	86.8	271.8	-55.7
1981	286.4	167.7	454.1	5.6
1982	331.5	215.1	546.6	403.6

Source: The last column is from Bank of Korea, *Financial Statements Analysis*, various issues.

large, and constituted an important element of reported profits for those who had access to bank loans, including chaebol.

Figure 1 shows the rates of return on assets and on equity in manufacturing from 1962 to 1997.[40] For the 1962-82 period for which we have estimates of the subsidy component of loans, estimates are given as to the rates of return that would have prevailed, all else equal, had there been no subsidy implicit in borrowing. Three things should be noted. First, there were declining rates of return over time. Second, there were earlier periods during which the returns to firms would have been negative had it not been for the subsidized credit.

---

[40]Return on assets (ROA) is the ratio of "ordinary income" and average of assets at the beginning and end of a given year, income and assets reported in various issues of *Financial Statement Analysis*. Since "ordinary income" was not available for 1963-75, "net income" was used for the period as the numerator, instead. Return on equity (ROE) is similarly estimated except that the denominator is equity.

Figure 1. Rates of Return, Manufacturing Sector Total

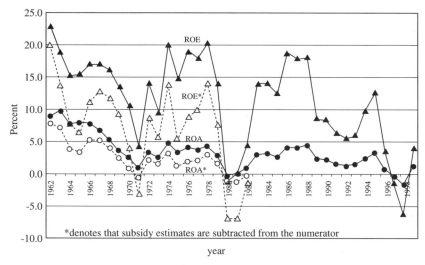

Figure 2. International Comparison of ROA's, Manufacturing

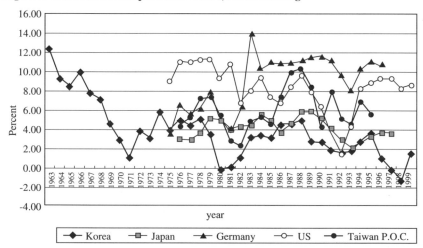

Third, it is small wonder that chaebol and Korean firms in general were highly leveraged: given the incentive to use debt financing entailed in the loans, they were more profitable for doing so, and their founders could retain a stronger controlling interest.

Figure 2 compares the return on assets of Korean manufacturing sector with those in Germany, Japan, Taiwan Province of China, and the United States. The figure shows that the average return for all Korean manufacturing firms fell from above 8 percent in the 1960s, to about 4 percent in the 1970s, under 3 percent in the 1980s, and to 2 percent in the 1990s before the crisis. By contrast, the rates of return in the United States, Germany, and Taiwan Province of China were both higher and more sustained with the exception of the recession years, 1991 and 1992. In Japan, the returns fell but were still about 2.3 percent in 1998—after the impact of the Asian financial crisis. The high rates of return in the 1960s may not have been sustainable for long. They may have been high then, perhaps because many unexploited or under-exploited business opportunities became profitable thanks to policy reforms in the early years of the export drive. And, it may have been inevitable that the rates declined, as better opportunities got exploited first and grew fewer in number. If this had been the only reason, then a decline from 8 percent to 2 percent was too great and the three and half decades have been too long a period for the decline to persist in view of other countries' experience. Not only in the advanced industrial countries but also in Taiwan Province of China, which may be considered more comparable to Korea, the rates of return fluctuate but do not show any long-term declining trend. The only possible exception is Japan in the 1990s, when it had a significantly lower return than in previous decades.

Figure 3 shows highly leveraged financial structure of Korean manufacturing firms compared with their counterparts in the same four countries. The average debt-equity ratio of all manufacturing firms sharply rose from around 1.0 in the early 1960s to above 3.0 in the early 1970s. Since then the ratio usually remained between 3.0 and 4.0, once reaching as high as 5.0. In contrast,

Figure 3. International Comparison of Debt-Equity Ratios, Manufacturing

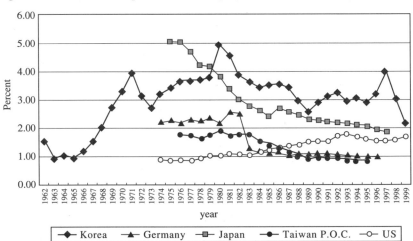

the same ratio in other countries typically remained under two, with the exception of Japan. Thus, the average debt-equity ratio in Korea has usually been two to three times as large as in other countries. Again, this does not seem to have much to do with Korea being behind in economic development compared with industrial countries. A much lower debt-equity ratio has been the rule in Taiwan Province of China as well as in the advanced industrial countries. The credit policy the government followed in pursuit of development objectives provided incentives to rely on debt financing and had a consequence on the financial structure of Korean firms.

Chaebol Finances and Falling Profitability[41]

The next step in the analysis is to consider the chaebol and their profitability in the years leading up to the crisis. For this purpose three groups of firms are identified. Two are groups of chaebol firms: the "Big 5" and the "Big 30," which respectively refer to those firms belonging to the largest 5 and 30 chaebols. The third group is "non-chaebol," refering to those firms that do not belong to the Big 30.[42]

Table 6 shows the average debt-equity ratios of the firms belonging to these three groups in all sectors of the economy and in the manufacturing sector alone, and also the debt-equity ratio of the manufacturing sector as a whole for reference. Clearly, chaebol firms have been much more highly leveraged than non-chaebol firms, whether firms in all sectors of the economy are considered or only those in the manufacturing sector. In the manufacturing sector, the chaebol's debt-equity ratios were greater than 3.5 until the early 1990s, tended to decline somewhat in the middle of the decade, and to climb back above 4.0 just before the crisis. During the period covered in the table, with few exceptions, the chaebol's debt-equity ratio was usually 30 to 60 percent higher than non-chaebol's in the manufacturing sector, and even higher in all sectors. The Big 30 tended to be more highly leveraged than the Big 5, especially when all firms in the economy are considered.

---

[41]The debt-equity ratios, rates of return, and asset growth rates reported in this section were estimated on the basis of financial statements of nonfinancial firms subject to the requirement of external audit, compiled by the National Information and Credit Evaluation agency (NICE). This source is used throughout this paper, unless otherwise noted.

[42]The Fair Trade Commission (FTC) of the Korean government each year designates the 30 largest chaebol in terms of assets and lists the firms belonging to them. The list changes over time. The list used in this paper is the same for each year as that which the FTC designates, and therefore changes over time. The Big 5 includes Hyundai, Samsung, Daewoo, LG, and SK.

Table 6. Debt-Equity Ratios

	All Sectors			Manufacturing Sector			
	Big 30	Big 5	Non-chaebol	All firms	Big 30	Big 5	Non-chaebol
1985	4.62	4.40	3.40	3.49	3.83	3.44	3.07
1986	4.93	4.42	2.48	3.51	4.10	3.87	2.91
1987	4.62	4.45	2.35	3.40	3.92	3.90	2.73
1988	3.32	3.64	2.39	2.96	3.15	3.56	2.55
1989	3.31	3.14	2.00	2.54	3.08	3.08	1.89
1990	3.70	3.61	2.27	2.86	3.43	3.52	2.11
1991	3.89	3.77	2.49	3.09	3.57	3.73	2.30
1992	4.00	3.75	2.66	3.20	3.66	3.62	2.62
1993	3.51	3.17	2.70	2.95	3.10	2.81	2.58
1994	3.59	3.18	2.83	3.02	3.17	2.75	2.70
1995	3.53	3.07	2.97	2.87	3.05	2.57	2.74
1996	3.90	3.54	3.01	3.17	3.49	3.07	2.75
1997	5.24	4.67	3.50	3.96	4.92	4.27	2.98
1998	3.62	3.31	2.89	3.03	3.36	3.16	2.41
1999	2.55	2.73	1.93	2.15	2.06	2.04	1.85

Source: The ratio for "All firms" is derived from Bank of Korea, *Financial Statement Analysis*, various issues. The rest are estimated from firm level data supplied by National Information and Credit Evaluation.

Notes: The estimates for 1987 are not directly comparable with those for other years. "Non-chaebol" refer to the firms not belonging to Big 30.

Obviously, highly leveraged firms are vulnerable to shocks, such as increases in the cost of capital, sharp changes in macroeconomic conditions, and sudden drops in foreign demand. The vulnerability of the chaebol was especially dangerous, given their importance to the Korean economy. The situation was even worse as the chaebol firms were closely linked to each other financially. Firms belonging to the same chaebol tended to invest in each other and guarantee the repayment of bank loans for each other. While this may make sense for the individual chaebol, from the economywide viewpoint, there were risks. Chaebol activities that should have been closed down could continue operating, given financial support from their chaebol affiliates. When difficulties were short-run, this support was evidently warranted. But problems arose because there was little way to determine when difficulties were temporary or more long-term, and components of the chaebol remained in business regardless of their own situation, reducing the profitability of the chaebol as a whole. Because of this, the high leverage combined with close inter-firm links must have resulted in declining rates of return for chaebol over time.[43]

---

[43]It should be noted that the practice not only increased vulnerability and lowered the rates of return for the chaebol, but it also doubtless resulted in the banks turning down loan applications from small firms that might have had very high rates of return.

We turn, then, to Table 7 that compares estimates of the returns on assets and equity between chaebol and non-chaebol firms since the mid-1980s. The returns on assets (ROA) were in general falling during the period except for the years of 1994 and 1995, as we saw earlier in Figure 1. (The sudden surge in external demand for semiconductors and cyclical boom in these two years will be discussed below.) Returns on equity (ROE) show the same pattern, with more pronounced fluctuations.

The rates of return differed much across the three groups of firms. In the mid-1980s the ROA averaged around 4.5 percent for all manufacturing firms, but it averaged 3 percent or less for Big 30, 3-4 percent for Big 5, and above 6 percent or higher for non-chaebol firms. Thus, the non-chaebol firms' ROAs were nearly three percentage points higher than chaebol firms', or twice as high. The rates of return declined from the mid-1980s to the early 1990s. The average return for the manufacturing sector fell below 2 percent. While this decline was taking place, the non-chaebol's ROAs in comparison with chaebol's remained higher, but in absolute terms the gap in profitability between the two narrowed from around 3 percentage points or more to 2 percentage points or less.

In terms of return on equity, too, the gap in profitability was large in favor of non-chaebol. As shown in Table 7, non-chaebol's ROE was typically 50 percent or more higher than Big 30, and 30 percent or more higher than Big 5 until the 1990s. Thus, until the early 1990s, the Big 30 on average had higher debt-equity and lower rates of return on assets than the Big 5, and the Big 5 in turn had higher debt-equity and lower rates of return than non-chaebol.

In 1994 and 1995, however, chaebol firms experienced a sudden rise in the returns on assets and on equity. Consequently, the gap in profitability turned in favor of chaebol. One might wonder, taking an agnostic point of view, if the rise in chaebol firms' returns was a sign of reversal of the long-term decline and beginning of sustained rise in their profitability, which failed to materialize only because of the subsequent crisis. However, it seems quite certain that this was not the case. As Table 7 shows, the sudden rise in returns was most pronounced for the Big 5 chaebol firms in manufacturing. Among them were four major producers and exporters: Samsung Electronics, Hyundai Electronics Industries, LG Semiconductor, and Daewoo Electronics, which benefited greatly from a surge in demand in the world market for semiconductors in 1994 and 1995. When the rates of return were recalculated with these four electronics firms excluded, the returns on assets and equity for chaebol manufacturing firms were more than halved. As shown in Table 7 the return on assets for the Big 5 dropped from 4.8 percent to 2.3 percent for 1994, and from 7.4 percent to 2.4 percent for 1995. The drops in ROA for the Big 30 were similarly

Table 7. Returns on Assets and Returns on Equity
(In percent)

	Return on Assets								
	All Sectors			Manufacturing Sector					
	Big 30	Big 5	Non-chaebol	All firms	Big 30	Big 30*	Big 5	Big 5*	Non-chaebol
1985	n.a.	n.a.	n.a.	3.02	n.a.	n.a.	n.a.	n.a.	n.a.
1986	1.95	3.03	5.23	4.45	3.03	3.01	3.93	4.02	6.66
1987	2.11	2.54	4.47	4.49	2.87	2.90	3.09	3.17	6.08
1988	3.96	4.23	7.44	4.93	4.99	4.88	5.11	4.93	7.91
1989	2.30	2.72	4.44	2.71	2.31	2.05	2.56	2.16	4.44
1990	1.57	1.71	3.74	2.52	1.67	1.84	1.61	1.88	3.65
1991	1.22	1.20	3.66	1.76	0.96	1.04	0.96	1.09	3.21
1992	1.09	1.49	2.86	1.39	1.01	0.90	1.42	1.33	1.97
1993	1.24	1.78	2.69	1.62	1.15	0.66	1.89	1.19	2.24
1994	2.50	3.82	3.05	2.69	2.88	1.24	4.77	2.29	2.79
1995	3.35	5.41	2.42	3.54	4.59	1.37	7.36	2.44	2.71
1996	0.61	1.18	1.29	0.93	0.68	0.47	1.29	1.12	1.45
1997	-0.87	0.37	-0.38	-0.31	-0.88	-0.92	0.48	0.85	0.12
1998	-1.82	-1.33	-0.95	-1.51	-1.94	-2.53	-1.84	-2.74	-1.19
1999	-2.48	-4.06	1.60	1.43	0.95	-0.39	1.10	-0.84	2.82

	Returns on Equity								
	All Sectors			Manufacturing Sector					
	Big 30	Big 5	Non-chaebol	All firms	Big 30	Big 30*	Big 5	Big 5*	Non-chaebol
1985	n.a.	n.a.	n.a.	13.47	n.a.	n.a.	n.a.	n.a.	n.a.
1986	11.33	16.37	19.50	20.02	15.11	14.86	18.42	18.41	26.38
1987	12.20	13.80	15.24	19.99	14.41	14.46	15.08	15.28	23.19
1988	18.76	20.76	25.09	20.48	21.88	21.13	23.83	22.83	28.60
1989	9.94	11.84	14.04	10.08	9.50	8.41	10.94	9.28	13.97
1990	7.11	7.51	11.77	9.39	7.15	7.80	6.95	8.02	10.98
1991	5.86	5.62	12.40	7.00	4.35	4.59	4.46	4.90	10.32
1992	5.40	7.09	10.23	5.78	4.64	4.07	6.62	6.02	6.83
1993	5.87	7.86	9.91	6.56	5.01	2.84	7.86	4.78	8.07
1994	11.38	15.95	11.49	10.75	11.93	5.17	18.02	8.52	10.17
1995	15.26	22.28	9.43	13.94	18.81	5.90	26.86	9.34	10.06
1996	2.89	5.08	5.16	3.73	2.90	2.15	4.93	4.59	5.45
1997	-4.83	1.92	-1.63	-1.41	-4.59	-5.05	2.23	4.15	0.46
1998	-9.61	-6.47	-3.94	-6.71	-9.71	-13.11	-8.49	-12.97	-4.37
1999	-9.98	-16.23	5.36	5.03	3.43	-1.46	3.86	-3.13	8.77

Note: *indicates that estimation excludes four electronics manufacturing firms of chaebol.
See also the notes to Table 6.

drastic. The effect of the change in external conditions on chaebol profitability can also be seen in the returns on equity (Table 7).

The recalculated rates of return for chaebol, although halved, were nevertheless greater than those in the preceding years, still suggesting a possibility of a subsequent upturn in their profitability. However, the economy was in a cyclical upswing in 1994 and 1995.[44] Thus, the rise in chaebol profitability in those two years was a temporary phenomenon reflecting a temporary change in external conditions and the cyclical economic boom. It seems quite certain that the trend of declining profitability for chaebol and non-chaebol was continuing into 1997 when the economy was engulfed by the crisis.

At the same time, the reestimated rates of return show that the profitability gap between non-chaebol and chaebol persisted throughout the 1990s except for the four semiconductor producers in 1994 and 1995. This is a fact, but it is not yet clear if the low profitability is intrinsic to chaebol. It might have something to do with industry-specific factors. For example, it is possible that their profitability was low because chaebol firms were concentrated in those industries that had low profitability. To address this, a simple ordinary least squares regression was run with a dummy for chaebol firms and dummies for industries. The equation without a disturbance term and with the subscripts for firms omitted was:

$$ROA = b_0 + b_1 C + b_2 D_{15} + b_3 D_{17} + \dots + b_{21} D_{35},$$

where ROA is return on assets for a firm, expressed in percentage terms; C is a chaebol dummy equal to one, if a given firm belonged to one of the 30 largest chaebol and zero otherwise; and D_j is an industry dummy equal to one if a given firm is in the j-th industry and zero otherwise. There were 22 two-digit industries in the manufacturing sector, with the classification numbers running from 15 to 36. Of these, the regression included 21 industries, omitting the 16th, tobacco, where no private firm operated.

Table 8 shows the estimated coefficients for the chaebol dummy and the probability that the coefficient takes the estimated value, if it were zero, based on t-distribution. (A more detailed report of the regression results is available upon request to the authors.) When the industry difference in rates of return is taken into account, the chaebol's profitability was still much lower than non-chaebol anywhere between one to five percentage points, usually with

---

[44]As discussed below, the rediscount rate of the Bank of Korea and loan rates of commercial banks were reduced by two percentage points in 1993. Given chaebol's high debt-equity ratios, much higher than non-chaebol's, their profitability would have been still lower, had there been no interest rate cuts.

Table 8. The Effect of Being a ̈Big 30 ̈ Firm on Profitability

	Coefficient	Probability	Coefficient*	Probability*
1986	-3.78	0.0006	n.a.	n.a.
1987	-4.34	0.0000	n.a.	n.a.
1988	-3.66	0.0003	n.a.	n.a.
1989	-3.33	0.0001	n.a.	n.a.
1990	-3.77	0.0000	n.a.	n.a.
1991	-3.24	0.0000	n.a.	n.a.
1992	-2.60	0.0004	n.a.	n.a.
1993	-2.18	0.0032	n.a.	n.a.
1994	-1.64	0.0176	-1.74	0.0126
1995	-1.06	0.1312	-1.45	0.0405
1996	-1.06	0.1564	n.a.	n.a.
1997	-2.92	0.0012	n.a.	n.a.
1998	-4.86	0.0000	n.a.	n.a.

Note: *indicates exclusion of four chaebol semiconductor firms.

very high statistical significance. The statistical significance was lower in the mid-1990s. But it turned highly significant again in 1994 and 1995, when the aforementioned four electronics firms are excluded. Therefore, the low profitability of chaebol firms does not seem due to their concentration in low profitability industries.

Growth of Chaebol Assets, Monetary Policy, and the Financial Conditions of the Banks

Table 9 gives estimates of the assets for all manufacturing firms and the Big 5 chaebol firms. What is striking, given the chaebols' high debt-equity ratios and low rates of returns, is the fact that the growth of their assets has been incomparably more rapid than that of the manufacturing sector as a whole. As can be seen in column 4, the assets of the Big 5 have been growing in value terms at 20 to 30 percent annually since the mid 1980s, while the combined assets of all firms was growing usually around 20 percent per annum or less (column 3). Thus, the Big 5's manufacturing assets in 1997 at the time of the financial crisis was 19 times as large as in 1985, whereas the total assets of the sector was 8.5 times as large. As a result, the chaebol's assets accounted for an increasing proportion of the sector's total. In 1985, the Big 5 chaebol firms held 16 percent of the assets in the manufacturing sector; the proportion rose to 40 percent in the late 1990s.

Table 9. Asset Growth and Asset Share of Big 5 in Manufacturing Total

	Outstanding Assets at Year-end		Asset Growth Rates		Big 5's Asset Share
	All firms (billion won)	Big 5 (billion won)	All firms (percent)	Big 5 (percent)	(percent)
1985	59,602	9,369	17.3	n.a.	15.7
1986	68,024	15,075	14.1	60.9	22.2
1987	83,957	n.a.	23.4	29.1	n.a.
1988	97,785	24,865	16.5	29.1	25.4
1989	119,937	32,671	22.7	31.4	27.2
1990	163,388	43,679	36.2	33.7	26.7
1991	201,015	54,595	23.0	25.0	27.2
1992	222,078	57,795	10.5	5.9	26.0
1993	255,371	63,937	15.0	10.6	25.0
1994	310,605	81,969	21.6	28.2	26.4
1995	358,655	104,684	15.5	27.7	29.2
1996	407,532	126,129	13.6	20.5	30.9
1997	508,985	180,767	24.9	43.3	35.5
1998	518,632	205,725	1.9	13.8	39.7
1999	573,559	209,747	10.6	2.0	36.6

Source: The same as Table 6.
Note: The asset growth rate for the Big 5 in 1987 and 1988 are the averages for the two years.

The disproportionate increase in lending to chaebol by the banks and other financial institutions, despite their lower profitability, seems to reflect the banks' preference for lending to the chaebol in the later period. From the banks' viewpoint, the chaebol were relatively safer borrowers, as they were likely to have better collateral, and repayments were often guaranteed by other member firms of the same chaebol. Indeed, the government intervened and set a minimum quota in bank lending that should go to small and medium-sized firms so that their access to bank credits might not be unduly restricted.

However, government policy was not repressive toward the chaebol. They had come into being supported by policy favors, especially during the so-called Heavy and Chemical Industry Drive of the 1970s. For, as they grew in assets, sales, employment, exports, etc., and increased their relative importance in the economy, they became indispensable and appeared to be "too big to fail."

In this regard, an episode of interest rate cuts in the early 1990s provides an interesting case. In January 1993 and again in March 1993, interest rates were cut. The cuts were the policy response to sharply deteriorating economic conditions, especially falling investments (in part in response to the U.S. recession of 1990-91). But it is noteworthy that these cuts coincided with a period of financial difficulty for the chaebols. The return on assets for both the

Big 5 and the Big 30 was barely one percent in 1991 (see Table 7), and the annual growth rate of assets that used to be around 30 percent or higher dropped to a mere 6 percent in 1992 (Table 9).

In two steps, the Bank of Korea lowered the rediscount rates under its control by two percentage points "to counter the slowdown of economic growth and contraction of firms' equipment investment." In addition to lowering its own discount rate, the Bank of Korea "encouraged" the deposit money banks to lower their loan rates twice, one percentage point at a time. Each time, the their loan and deposit rates were reduced.[45]

This is significant because the 1993 action was similar to those of earlier years when the ROA had fallen (in 1971 and in 1980-82, see Figure 1). If all manufacturing firms, including the chaebol, had had to pay interest two-percentage points more on all their debts, their income would have dropped almost 3.8 trillion won, wiping out their incomes for that year. The interest rate cuts preceded the cyclical boom of 1994 and 1995, when credit expansion in their aftermath resulted in rapid economic growth.

We conclude that, by 1997, the chaebol were highly vulnerable to negative shocks. Their profitability had been falling and was low. In 1996, the Big 30's return on assets was already less than 1 percent, and the Big 5's not much greater than one. Since firms' ordinary income, the numerator of this rate of return, is an income before tax, there was little margin for a reduction in cash flow or an increase in debt-servicing costs. Yet debt-servicing obligations were mounting, and cash flow does not appear to have been increasing commensurately. The large increase in lending by the commercial banks would appear to have had a significant element of "evergreening" to it. Had the interest rate risen in 1994 or 1995 because of macroeconomic conditions, it seems reasonable to conjecture that NPLs would have increased substantially (or evergreening increased significantly) at that time. The chaebol were over-leveraged and vulnerable to interest rate increases.[46]

We turn now to the banking side of the picture. Table 10 shows the rates of return for the commercial banks during the 1990s. As can be seen, total assets of the banks rose dramatically during the 1992-97 period, more than tripling. Net income, however, peaked in 1994 and turned negative by 1997. The rate of return on assets was falling continuously during the period, as was the rate of return on equity.

---

[45]Bank of Korea, *Quarterly Economic Review*, March 1993, p. 12 and June 1993, p. 14.

[46]Most of the chaebol sold large proportions of their products overseas. For that reason, they were almost surely less vulnerable to exchange rate changes, as their won sales would have increased significantly in response to a currency depreciation.

Table 10. Changes in Income, Commercial Banks Total
(In billions of Korean won)

	1992	1993	1994	1995	1996	1997	1998	1999
Gross income	5,336.0	5,995.8	8,332.7	9,339.7	10,418.0	10,505.9	2,909.4	8,367.1
Interest income, net	3,088.1	3,127.0	3,426.7	4,920.2	6,059.5	7,871.2	6,777.2	9,046.8
Interest received	10,471.3	10,109.9	12,308.6	18,321.7	21,755.8	31,892.0	37,943.0	35,017.4
Interest paid (less)	7,383.2	6,983.0	8,882.0	13,401.6	15,696.3	24,072.8	31,165.9	25,970.7
Non-interest income	2,247.9	2,868.9	4,906.1	4,419.5	4,358.6	2,688.7	-3,867.8	-679.6
Fees received	1,250.5	1,551.8	2,480.8	2,249.4	2,281.0	10,299.2	13,266.4	8,210.3
Fees paid (less)	184.1	175.9	237.9	372.8	650.1	8,039.4	11,849.0	5,292.1
Other non-interest income	1,139.7	1,453.1	2,407.9	2,353.9	2,569.1	2,696.9	614.7	444.1
Non-operating incomes	41.8	39.9	255.3	189.1	158.6	-2,268.1	-5,899.9	-4,041.9
Operating expenses (less)	3,176.5	3,649.8	4,362.6	6,033.0	6,982.0	8,093.9	7,587.3	6,445.6
Of which: personnel expenses	2,221.3	2,595.4	3,187.4	4,228.8	4,964.4	5,609.0	5,596.0	2,885.9
Ordinary income	2,159.5	2,346.0	3,970.1	3,306.7	3,436.0	2,412.0	-4,677.8	1,921.5
Increase in loss provision (less)	942.5	1,023.4	2,371.8	2,319.7	2,342.0	6,192.7	7,780.4	7,487.3
Loans	787.6	995.5	2,127.3	1,758.0	1,547.7	3,511.3	8,066.7	7,487.3
Security valuation	95.7	-33.1	183.6	543.5	895.0	2,759.4	-125.8	0.0
Others	59.2	61.0	60.9	18.2	-100.7	-78.0	-160.5	0.0
Income before income tax	1,217.0	1,322.6	1,598.3	987.0	1,094.1	-3,780.7	-12,458.2	-5,565.8
Income Tax (less)	285.5	433.6	550.1	119.2	247.2	139.2	52.4	430.2
Net income	931.5	889.0	1,048.2	867.8	846.9	-3,919.9	-12,510.6	-5,996.0
Total Assets	167,425.1	198,481.3	250,081.2	340,543.0	415,437.8	542,552.8	560,059.7	550,345.3
ROA (%)	0.71	0.62	0.62	0.38	0.31	-1.06	-3.15	-1.42
ROE (%)	6.56	5.90	6.09	4.19	3.80	-14.19	-46.15	-19.62

Source: Financial Supervisory Commission, on-line service.

By 1998 the combined net loss of the banks was 46 percent of their equity. The changes up to and including the crisis year reflect three things: (1) the loss provision for NPLs peaked in 1994 and was declining until it rose sharply in 1997 and 1998; (2) provision for valuation loss on securities was steadily increasing; and (3) the part of non-operating income in non-interest income dropped by more than 2.4 trillion won in 1997.[47]

---

[47]This loss reflects the losses banks suffered when they had to sell their NPLs to Korea Asset Management Company (KAMCO), a public enterprise charged with clearing the financial institutions' balance sheets of their bad loans.

There was little prior indication of the deterioration in the banks' assets. Interest had been paid, although it is difficult to estimate how much of this may have reflected "evergreening" lending to enable chaebol to service their debts. The sudden jump in NPLs in 1997 would seem to suggest that evergreening had been taking place in earlier years.[48]

Not all banks collapsed in 1997, and some had, for all practical purposes, been in difficulty earlier. Table 11 shows the changes in net income in 1993-98 for two of the six largest nationwide commercial banks. As can be seen, Seoul Bank reported virtually zero net income in 1995, and Korea First in 1996 before other banks experienced income losses in 1997. Their plight seems unrelated to the currency crisis in the region or to the sudden and sharp depreciation of won that occurred in the last month in 1997.

There is thus considerable evidence of a weakening of the quality of the banks' portfolios prior to the crisis, in the sense that the financial health of the borrowers was deteriorating. Nonetheless, the proportion of NPLs in their

Table 11. Factors behind the Sudden Changes in Income, Individual Banks
(In billions of Korean won)

	Net Income	Provision for NPLs	Provision for Valuation Loss	Non-operating Income	NPLs, Reported
Korea First					
1993	1,541	913	-36	7	n.a.
1994	1,313	3,168	354	50	14,186
1995	174	2,667	112	188	15,913
1996	62	2,732	871	393	18,697
1997	-16,151	4,514	3,518	-9,064	30,559
1998	-26,149	2,581	n.a.	-6,769	38,323
Seoul					
1993	103	1,712	-19	107	n.a.
1994	531	2,694	33	103	16,958
1995	50	2,216	341	204	16,639
1996	-1,668	2,735	977	208	20,353
1997	-9,166	1,731	3,047	-3,996	24,040
1998	-22,424	3,530	n.a.	-2,266	29,872

Source: Financial Supervisory Commission, on-line service.

---

[48]The NPLs of the commercial banks, as reported by Financial Supervisory Commission, were:

	1991	1992	1993	1994	1995	1996	1997	1998
trillion won	8.27	10.16	11.93	11.39	12.48	11.87	22.65	21.22
percent of loans	7.00	7.10	7.40	5.80	5.20	4.10	6.00	7.40

portfolios was generally stationary or falling until the crisis, although this may in part have reflected the evergreening of accounts. After the crisis, the proportion of NPLs rose sharply, and they were then assumed by the asset management company and the banks booked their losses. The key question is whether those losses were already there and being "evergreened," or whether the events associated with the exchange rate crisis itself precipitated the financial crisis. Certainly, the chaebol were highly leveraged, and a small change in either their profitability or in interest charges would have been enough to tip them into nonperforming status.

The Foreign Currency Vulnerability of the Banks

Table 12 gives data on foreign-currency denominated assets and liabilities of the commercial banks. As can be seen, foreign-currency denominated assets

Table 12. Foreign Currency Denominated Assets and Liabilities, Commercial Banks
(In billions of Korean won)

	Assets			Liabilities		
	Total	Foreign-currency Denominated	Share (%)	Total	Foreign-currency Denominated	Share (%)
1991	161,516.6	18,511.7	11.5	147,736.0	19,169.8	13.0
1992	180,615.6	20,809.4	11.5	165,724.4	20,963.7	12.6
1993	194,988.6	23,787.2	12.2	178,766.0	24,672.2	13.8
1994	228,961.5	30,165.5	13.2	210,044.8	31,313.1	14.9
1995	288,687.8	39,621.3	13.7	267,308.2	40,466.9	15.1
1996	341,558.7	51,861.5	15.2	318,321.7	52,802.2	16.6
1997 J	354,654.9	55,596.3	15.7	325,827.7	55,608.7	17.1
A	360,179.4	56,504.4	15.7	331,075.6	57,767.2	17.4
S	402,529.2	58,197.9	14.5	370,370.1	59,758.2	16.1
O	414,296.5	61,738.5	14.9	381,377.5	64,719.6	17.0
N	435,322.1	72,772.1	16.7	402,357.5	74,440.5	18.5
D	483,498.6	96,448.7	19.9	461,208.8	102,828.2	22.3
1998 J	498,298.8	101,167.1	20.3	467,189.8	113,532.7	24.3
F	504,682.4	110,024.8	21.8	472,441.0	118,551.5	25.1
M	479,636.4	96,407.9	20.1	445,908.6	99,483.8	22.3
A	469,613.1	93,215.7	19.8	435,165.8	96,635.3	22.2
M	471,013.8	97,461.6	20.7	435,140.6	101,132.7	23.2
J	467,583.0	92,560.0	19.8	433,414.5	96,257.4	22.2
J	459,565.3	81,936.0	17.8	425,298.6	85,374.6	20.1
1998 D	469,280.5	72,676.7	15.5	448,765.9	70,633.9	15.7
1999	519,748.6	58,092.9	11.2	493,261.7	55,028.4	11.2

Source: Bank of Korea, *Monthly Statistical Bulletin*, various issues.

were slightly below liabilities throughout the 1990s. At their peak in February 1998—post-crisis—commercial banks' liabilities denominated in foreign currency were 25.1 percent of total liabilities, while assets were 21.8 percent. Interestingly, both the assets and liabilities had risen by about the same percentage during the crisis months, although the gap between them was about two percent wider in early 1998 than it had been in mid-1997.

A question that these data do not answer is the extent to which the quality of the assets and the liabilities were similar. At the time of the crisis, there were reports that many of the loans denominated in foreign currency were to Indonesia, Thailand, and Russia, and that one of the factors precipitating the Korean crisis was the nonperformance of those loans. The data may therefore understate the differential between foreign currency assets and liabilities when risk-adjusted. Even so, it is not evident that the differential was so large that exchange rate changes should have triggered a major decline in the banks' balance sheets. To the extent there was deterioration caused by the exchange-rate change, it would have had to be either in the chaebol's ability to service their outstanding debts or in the failure of foreign debtors to continue servicing their loans to Korean banks.

Conclusions

The chaebol were in a weak financial condition long before the crisis. While the data do not indicate an increase in NPLs, the rapid increase in assets combined with their deteriorating profitability certainly seems to indicate that the banks were "evergreening" the chaebol's outstanding debt. If even a quarter of the net increase in chaebol borrowing from the banks was evergreened, the banks were in very bad shape prior to the Korean crisis in 1997.

In an important sense, the vulnerability of the system was extreme. While very favorable conditions—increased semiconductor prices on world markets, falling world interest rates, a pickup in economic activity in the rest of the world—might have prevented the crisis and enabled the chaebol to regain profitability and reduce the degree to which they were leveraged, their behavior during the boom of 1994 and 1995 does not suggest that they were inclined to do so. Instead, in the boom years, they continued borrowing and increasing their assets, while the rate of return remained low with only a slight cyclical upturn.

The conclusion must be that the Korean crisis was a disaster waiting to happen: when very favorable circumstances did not materialize, the needed increase in evergreening was more rapid than the system could tolerate. The foreign exchange crisis itself probably did not trigger the financial crisis: rather, the increase in interest rates did.

The chaebol's debts to the banks are the chief culprit. And since the chaebol were major exporters, the change in the exchange rate per se probably did not harm their ability to service their debts. However, the increased interest rate clearly did.

In the short run, therefore, more exchange rate depreciation and less interest rate increase—as was in fact the chosen stabilization path—was probably appropriate. Failure to raise the interest rate at all would surely have resulted in larger capital outflows and perpetuated the foreign exchange crisis. Indeed, as was seen, there were doubts over the several weeks after the first IMF program that the package as undertaken was enough. However, further increases in the interest rate (which probably would have reduced the magnitude of exchange rate depreciation) would surely have intensified the financial crisis.

At an analytical level, the impact of the exchange rate depreciation on the banks' balance sheets either directly or indirectly through the ability of the chaebol to service their debts must be deemed to have been relatively small in the Korean case. The fundamental problem was the magnitude of the leveraging the chaebol had had pre-crisis. That, in turn, made the post-crisis workout of the banking system extremely difficult because of the necessity of restructuring the finances of the chaebol first.

Our conclusion raises more questions than it answers. The corporate sector's profitability was declining from the early 1960s to the end of 1990s, while no such long-term decline is discernable in advanced industrial countries or in Taiwan Province of China. Clearly, at the heart of the problem were the highly leveraged financial structure of chaebol and their low profitability. This could have been a small problem had the chaebol's weight in the economy been not so large. As we saw, 40 percent of all assets in the manufacturing sector was in the hands of the five biggest chaebol. This observation raises three related questions: Why did the chaebol keep accumulating assets and expanding business, despite falling profitability? Why did the financial sector, mainly banks, keep financing the chaebol expansion, despite their lower profitability compared with non-chaebol? Why was financial supervision so lax as to allow the system to become so fragile and vulnerable?

As a suggestion for further research, we elaborate the first question. To what extent was the chaebol's falling profitability the result of inevitable forces as Korea developed? Lucrative business opportunities are likely to be exploited earlier than others and grow fewer in number as time passes. In addition, the capital-labor ratio rises and diminishing returns set in. To what extent is the falling profitability the result of constraints or distortions in the incentive system the chaebol faced? Was there an agency problem, as a head (or a family) of chaebol managed all the firms in the group as if he had a complete ownership while he did not?

The profitability of the non-chaebol was also falling, although it was consistently higher than the chaebol's before the crisis. How likely is it that this was due to the same, aforementioned inevitable forces? Given that the chaebol had readier access to bank loans and other credits than the non-chaebol, the difficulty in the access must have been comparatively more important for small and medium-sized firms' falling profitability than were the constraints and other problems that chaebol faced. To what extent is the fall in their profitability related to the rise in chaebol's weight in the economy in the sense that they had to compete against chaebol for resources, especially for financial resources?

We suggested that the government's credit policy provided incentives for the chaebol to rely on debt financing as long and as much as possible. Their consistently high debt-equity ratios compared with non-chaebol suggest that they could borrow more per unit of equity than others. Furthermore, their assets grew faster despite their falling profitability. This suggests that the chaebol were better than others at the game of adapting to and taking advantage of the business environment, including government policy. It is not surprising that one that is better in such a game survives and thrives in business as in nature. So, was the provision of cheap credit the sufficient reason for the rise of chaebol and their eventual domination of the economy? Or, were there other non-economic reasons that explain the rise of chaebol? These are institutional questions, the answer to which may have important policy implications.

Similarly, questions need to be asked and further research conducted regarding, on the one hand, the incentive system in the financial sector, governance and agency problems of banks and other financial institutions, their apparent inability to evaluate risks, and the credit culture in general; and, on the other hand, the reasons why prudential regulations over the financial system had been lax. What happened and why needs to be better understood, if lessons are to be learned and the crises are not to be repeated.

References

Bank of Korea, *Quarterly Economic Review*, various issues.

Bank of Korea, *Monthly Statistical Bulletin*, various issues.

Bank of Korea, *Financial Statement Analysis*, various issues.

Bank of Taiwan, *Zhong hua min guo tai wan di gu gong ye cai wu zhuang kuang bao gao* (Report on Financial Conditions of Industries, Taiwan Province of China), various issues.

Boughton, James M., 2000, "From Suez to Tequila: The IMF as Crisis Manager," *Economic Journal*, pp. 273-291.

Bureau of Census, U.S. Department of Commerce, *Quarterly Financial Report for Manufacturing, Mining, and Trade Corporations*, various issues.

Cho, Dongchul, and Kenneth D. West, 1999, "The Effect of Monetary Policy in Exchange Rate Stabilization in Post-Crisis Korea," KDI Conference on *The Korean Crisis: Before and After* (October 15).

Choi, Sung-No, 1995 and 1996, *The Analysis of the 30 Korean Big Business Groups*, Korea Economic Research Institute, Seoul.

Choi, Sung-No, 1997, 1998, and 1999, *Big Business Groups in Korea*, Center for Free Enterprise, Seoul.

Cline, William R., and Sidney Weintraub, editors, 1981, *Economic Stabilization in Developing Countries* (Washington, D.C.: Brookings Institution).

Cooper, Richard N., 1971, "An Assessment of Currency Devaluation in Developing Countries," in Gustav Rains ed., *Government and Economic Development* (New Haven: Yale University Press).

Feldstein, Martin, 1998, "Refocusing the IMF," *Foreign Affairs* (March/April), pp. 20-33.

Frank, Charles R. Jr., Kwang Suk Kim, and Larry Westphal, 1975, *Foreign Trade Regimes and Economic Development: South Korea* (New York: Columbia University Press).

Furman, J., and Stiglitz, J.E., 1998, "Economic Crises: Evidence and Insights from East Asia," *Brookings Papers on Economic Activity* (2), pp. 1-114.

Hahm, Joon-Ho, and Frederic S. Mishkin, 1999, "Causes of the Korean Financial Crisis: Lessons for Policy," *The Korean Crisis: Before and After* (October; Seoul: Korea Development Institute).

Harberger, Arnold C., 1999, "The Indonesian Crisis Revisited," mimeo (December).

Hong, Wontack, 1981, "Export Promotion and Employment Growth in South Korea," in Anne O. Krueger, Hal B. Lary, Terry Monson, and Narongchai Akrasanee eds., *Trade and Employment in Developing Countries*, Vol. 1, Individual Studies (Chicago: University of Chicago Press), pp. 341-391.

International Monetary Fund, 1995, *International Capital Markets: Developments, Prospects and Policy Issues*, Washington, D.C.

James, Harold, 1996, *International Monetary Cooperation Since Bretton Woods* (New York: Oxford University Press).

Krueger, Anne O., 1979, "The Developmental Role of the Foreign Sector and Aid," *Studies in the Modernization of the Republic of Korea: 1948-1975* (Cambridge, MA.: Harvard University Press).

Krueger, Anne O., 1997, "Lessons for Policy Reform in Light of the Mexican Experience," in Jitendralal Borkakoti and Chris Milner eds., *International Trade and Labour Markets* (Houndmills, Basingstoke and London: MacMillan Press), pp. 44-61.

Little, I. M. D., Richard N. Cooper, W. Max Corden, and Sarath Rajapatirana, 1993, *Boom, Crisis and Adjustment: The Macroeconomic Experience of Developing Countries* (New York: Oxford University Press).

Mussa, Michael, and Miguel Savastano, 2001, "The IMF Approach to Economic Stabilization," National Bureau of Economic Research *Macroeconomics Annual 1999* (Cambridge, Massachusetts: MIT Press), pp. 79-122.

OECD, 1994, *OECD Economic Surveys: Korea 1994*, Paris.

Sachs, Jeffrey, 1997, "The Wrong Medicine for Asia," *New York Times* (November 3).

Williamson, John ed., 1983, *IMF Conditionality* (Washington, D.C.: Institute for International Economics).

Comments on Papers 4 and 5

Myung-Chang Chung

The first paper by Drs. Chung and Kim analyzes the effects of interest rate policy on the exchange rate. The authors conclude that the high interest rate policy in Korea during the crisis contributed to stabilizing the exchange rate.

There are a number of Korean and foreign studies that have tried to investigate the effects of the high interest rate policy during the Korean crisis, but there have been mixed opinions on whether the policy was effective in stabilizing the exchange rate or not. The most distinctive feature of Chung and Kim's paper is its methodology, which allows for a non-linear relationship between the interest rate and exchange rate, in contrast to previous studies that have assumed a linear relationship. In this regard, I think the study makes a significant contribution. In particular, exchange rate movements directly affect inflation in Korea, so the study has implications for the central bank, which is responsible for attaining price stability. Moreover, the study will be a great reference for related studies in the future.

I have a number of specific comments on Chung and Kim's paper:

- First, as pointed out by the authors, the study is based on a bivariate model of the interest rate and the exchange rate, and does not consider other variables that can effect the exchange rate, such as capital flows, the corporate bankruptcy rate, the current account balance, the risk premium, and foreign exchange reserves. The results might have been different if the model included other variables. In this regard, the credibility of the results could have been enhanced if the robustness of its estimation results had been demonstrated, for example by alternatively adding one variable at a time, considering the restriction of the number of observations in a non-parametric estimation.
- Second, the study does not test for the stationarity of the interest rate differentials. The first difference of the exchange rate is used, which can be assumed to be stationary. However, we cannot assume that the interest rate differential between Korea and the United States is stationary.
- Third, the paper analyses only the relationship between interest rate policy and the exchange rate. The paper would be more persuasive if it

included an interpretation of the mechanism through which changes in interest rate policy stabilized the exchange rate.

I would like to thank Drs. Chung and Kim for their excellent work. This paper will allow future studies of the effects of the high interest rate policy on the exchange rate during a crisis to proceed with more depth.

The second paper by Drs. Krueger and Yoo analyses various time series data, including the rates of return on assets and on equity, the scale of assets and their growth in the corporate and banking sectors, and corporate debt ratios. The authors conclude that the "chief culprit" in the Korean crisis was the chaebol's continued heavy build-up of debt despite their worsening profitability. The paper notes that the background to the chaebol's heavy debt accumulation was the incentives provided by the government's credit policy, weak governance, poor credit screening skills of financial institutions, and lax prudential regulation of the financial system.

It may well be true that the heavy debts of the chaebol were one of the important causes of the Korean crisis, and that the aforementioned factors contributed to the rapid increase in chaebol indebtedness. However, the rigidity of the exchange rate system, the accumulated current account deficit, the increased ratio of short-term foreign debt to total foreign debt, and contagion from crises in southeast Asian countries are other factors that affected the outbreak of the Korean crisis.

In this regard, the Korean government has pushed ahead with economic reforms since the crisis. Among them are the adoption of a free-floating exchange rate, lowering of large companies' debt/equity ratios, prohibition of large companies' new payment guarantees that can be used as collateral, lowering of ceilings on financial institutions' credits to a single company, introduction of prompt corrective actions to financial institutions by the supervisory authorities, and strengthening of the standards for accounting and public disclosure. Although we cannot expect that long-established behaviors in the corporate and financial sectors will change in one day with the introduction of these reforms, policy makers in Korea have been trying to put these systems on the right track and will continue to do so.

Drs. Krueger and Yoo argue that the Bank of Korea's easy monetary policy in response to the slowdown of economic growth in the early 1990s also contributed to the large increase in the chaebol's debts. The easing of the monetary policy stance at that time may well have acted as one of the factors resulting in the expansion of financial support to the chaebol. However, the more accommodating policy stance was adopted not only in response to the economic slowdown but also to defuse financial market instability arising from the launch of the mandatory use of real names in all financial transactions in August 1993 and the step-by-step deregulation of interest rates between November 1993 and December 1994.

Finally, I appreciate the authors' attempt to present a comprehensive analysis of chaebol's problems and expect this paper to stimulate further research on the role of the chaebol in the Korean economy.

Bijan B. Aghevli

Before commenting on the two excellent papers by Krueger and Yoo and by Chung and Kim, let me first tell you a fable:

> *Once upon a time and far away, a litter of little tiger cubs was born. And foreigners came from far and wide to admire the cubs, and comment upon the growth potential in their sturdy limbs and the irresistible allure of their shiny coats. The keepers were proud of their small charges, and set up open zoos with no restrictions and invited everyone to come. Foreign visitors rushed in bearing a formula of milk fortified with vitamins and growth hormones for the cubs, and clamored for the privilege of filling their bowls which, fashioned for a trickle, cracked and leaked under the sudden surge. The cubs grew at an astounding rate, and newspapers and scholarly journals marveled at the miracle of their growth. Before long, the cubs were tigers, and still they grew until they burst out of their flimsy cages and roamed unfettered through the streets, howling for the surfeit of milk and hormones on which they had come to depend. Seeing the tigers at such close range, the visitors began to criticize their less-than-perfect coats, their tendency to purr, their unorthodox values. The food which had flowed like a river began to dry up. The keepers, in their confidence that the flow was endless, had not repaired the bowls to safeguard the milk they still had, and watched helplessly as the tigers sickened and gnashed their teeth. Then the IMF doctors were called in to wean the tigers off their rich diet and offer alternative lifestyles. As the tigers limped back into their shattered cages, a rowdy crowd of professors gathered to denounce the cruelty of international civil servants in white coats.*

More seriously, I would like to discuss the causes of the crisis and, in particular, the role of monetary policy during the adjustment, which is the focus of the two papers. Let me start out by agreeing fully with Krueger and

Yoo that "the problem for analysis of the Asian crisis is not the lack of explanations: it is that there are too many." By now, there is a consensus on the
main culprits, but there is still a heated debate on the appropriateness of the
remedies that were adopted. The immediate cause of the crisis was the large
current account deficit in the Asian countries that was financed largely by
short-term debt. Once the crisis hit and financing dried up, exchange rates had
no where to go but to collapse. But the large current account deficit was not
so much the cause as the effect. Krueger and Yoo have outlined the role of
weak financial institutions that led to ever greening of credit to corporations.
They underscore that, in the case of Korea, the corporate sector was already
in trouble by 1996 as rate of return to assets had declined to a low level. Intermediation of large external funds through an inefficient financial system to an
already over-leveraged corporate sector was at the heart of the crisis. Krueger
and Yoo, therefore, support the focus of IMF programs on structural reforms
and, in particular, on financial sector. It is hardly surprising that I fully endorse
their conclusion that: "failure to address the issue of financial restructuring
would clearly have increased the severity of the recession and delayed, if not
aborted, the recovery."

Krueger and Yoo note that, as the corporate sector was over-leveraged,
higher interest rates had a more damaging impact than exchange rate depreciation. This point is, of course, true under normal circumstances. But I would
like to emphasize, as do Chung and Kim, the nonlinear nature of this relationship. While a moderate exchange rate depreciation may not be that damaging
to the economy, the situation changes drastically when, as happened in Korea,
the won moved from 900 to the U.S. dollar to nearly 2000 in a very short
time. In this situation, failure to deal with the exchange rate crisis could quickly degenerate into a vicious cycle of depreciation and inflation. In raising
interest rates, an appropriate balance must therefore be struck between preventing the exchange rate from plunging, while not forcing corporations into
bankruptcy.

Chung and Kim apply a semi-nonparametric method to derive a nonlinear
impulse response function. Applying highly sophisticated econometrics is, of
course, a young man's sport, and I am not in a position to provide critical
comments on their paper. By contrast to their highly technical approach, when
the IMF team arrived in Seoul in late 1997, we relied mainly on back of the
envelope calculations to assist in the formulation of monetary policy. But it
is rewarding to be confirmed by Chung and Kim that our basic intuition was
correct. That is, a sharp increase in interest rates is effective in stabilizing the
exchange rate. I would only make one point on their observation that other
critics of the IMF got the opposite results because they did not use a nonlinear

method. I suspect that those critics would get the results they wanted using any methodology.

Frankly, it's very difficult to see how interest rates can be reduced in the middle of a currency crisis. A number of academics have made the point that, in a recession, the orthodox policy would be to lower interest rates and allow the exchange rate to slide to boost economic activity. For example, one commentator has observed that "we cheerfully let the dollar slide from 240 yen to 140, from three Deutsche marks to 1.8; the Fed even helped the process along by cutting interest rates." But this observation overlooks an important fact: the dollar decline was spread over a period of one and half years, while the drop in the won from less than 1,000 to the dollar to nearly 2,000 took place in only one month. In such an extreme situation, the first priority has to be to stabilize the exchange rate before a vicious inflationary cycle sets in. Once domestic prices begin to skyrocket, the monetary tightening required to re-establish price stability would be extremely costly.

The strategy pursued in these countries was to raise short-term interest rates to arrest the deterioration in the exchange rate, and then gradually reduce it as the exchange rate stabilized. Here, I would like to point out an important fact that has been lost in the debate. Contrary to general perceptions, the initial rise in interest rates in the Asian crisis countries was quite moderate and short lived: in Thailand, short-term rates rose to a peak of 25 percent, in Korea, to 35 percent, and they stayed at these peaks for only a few days before declining rapidly to their pre-crisis level. Furthermore, taking into account the impact of the sharp exchange rate depreciation on inflation expectations, the increase in interest rates was significantly lower in real terms than in nominal terms. Real interest rates (based on the consensus forecast of inflation as a measure of inflation expectations), which were in the range of 7-8 percent before the crisis, rose to short-lived peaks of 20-25 percent before dropping sharply. In both countries, real rates were above 15 percent for only two months, and they are presently about zero. At the same time, both the won and the baht appreciated substantially after the initial crisis, vindicating the approach adopted in these countries.

By contrast, Indonesia's earlier efforts to stabilize the rupiah turned out to be futile. Indonesia's experience, however, is the exception that proves the rule. During the first week of the program, the authorities engaged in unsterilized intervention and allowed short-term interest rates to double to 30 percent. As a result, the rupiah appreciated sharply. But within two days, contrary to understandings with the Fund, Bank Indonesia was instructed to cut interest rates back to their initial level. The subsequent liquidity expansion, together with strong signals from the highest levels of the government that commitments under the IMF program would not be fulfilled, led to the subsequent plunge of the rupiah. The resulting high inflation has necessitated much higher interest rates to reestablish financial stability. The adjustment cost would have been drastically smaller had the government persevered with the original program in November 1997.

To be sure, the weakness of the banking and corporate sectors in the Asian countries constrained the scope for raising interest rates. However, while many critics of Fund programs have pointed to the adverse impact of higher interest rates on domestic borrowers, they have neglected to take into account the impact of exchange rate depreciation on holders of external debt. A precipitous drop in the exchange rate raises the corresponding burden of external debt on the banking and corporate sectors to an intolerable level and undermines financial stability. Thus, the trade-off between exchange rate depreciation and interest rate increase shifts drastically in the presence of exchange rate overshooting. The negative impact of the exchange rate depreciation was particularly pronounced for Indonesia, Korea, and the Philippines, which had a relatively higher ratio of external debt to domestic credit.

I should also underscore that the liquidity squeeze in these countries was not just a consequence of high interest rates. Banks' reluctance to roll over credits also reflected their large nonperforming loans and the weak position of the corporate sector. It is instructive to note that the credit squeeze has not been alleviated even as interest rates in Korea and Thailand have fallen to well below their pre-crisis levels. An even clearer example of this phenomenon is Japan, where even zero short-term interest rates have not restarted the flow of credit.

Finally, I would be remiss if I did not say a few words about Stan Fischer, as he has announced his intention to leave the IMF. The Asian crisis during 1997-98 was an incredibly difficult period for the IMF. As Thailand, the Philippines, Indonesia, and Korea fell in quick succession, IMF staff essentially had to work around the clock. All mission leaders negotiating IMF programs with the Asian countries can tell you many instances of Stan calling them long after midnight to discuss negotiating positions, and then calling them again at the early hours of the next day to be briefed on the results. There is an old adage that no one is indispensable, but Stan comes awfully close. He will be missed by all staff, the current ones as well those who have left.

6 Corporate Restructuring and Reform: Lessons from Korea

*William P. Mako**

Of the countries affected by the East Asia financial crisis of 1997, Korea offers perhaps the most lessons on corporate restructuring in a systemic crisis. One reason is the magnitude of the restructuring challenge faced by over-extended and over-indebted chaebol. Another reason is Korea's record on corporate restructuring. On the one hand, Korea can point to major accomplishments in addressing moral hazard, implementing some operational restructuring, and reducing corporate leverage. On the other hand, legitimate concerns remain about ongoing weakness in the corporate sector. Proceeding from a framework for assessing corporate restructuring in a systemic crisis, the paper highlights a recurring pattern in corporate restructuring activity in Korea since 1997: periodic decisive action by creditors to take over companies; followed by financial stabilization through court supervised insolvency or out-of-court workout; followed by reluctance to pursue more fundamental operational restructuring; and with episodic government initiatives to promote long-term corporate reform and re-energize the corporate restructuring process. From this analysis, the paper identifies lessons more broadly applicable to other countries in systemic crisis and highlights Korea-specific issues and recommendations.

Framework for Corporate Restructuring in a Systemic Crisis

Corporate and financial sector restructuring are two aspects of the same problem. The amount of debt a company can sustain—and on which lenders can

---

*The views expressed in this paper are those of the author and should not be attributed to the World Bank, its directors, or other World Bank staff.

expect reliable debt service—is determined by the company's cash flow (Box 1). Indeed, a company cannot sustain interest payments in excess of its cash flow—that is, when its interest coverage is less than 1:1—let alone make any repayments on principal.

Resolving unsustainable corporate debt

There are a number of ways to resolve unsustainable corporate debt, some better than others. The best response would be for the company to raise new equity and/or undertake "operational restructuring" through the discontinuation of less profitable or loss-making "non-core" businesses, layoffs of excess labor, and other cost reductions to increase the company's earnings and debt service capacity, as well as sales of non-core businesses and real estate or other assets to retire debt. If it appears that operational restructuring cannot reduce corporate debt to a sustainable level, "financial restructuring" becomes appropriate. For example, creditors could convert debt into equity or into lower-yielding convertible bonds. To avoid moral hazard, creditors should contemplate debt write offs *only after* having exhausted all other approaches and should retain some instrument, such as equity, options, or warrants to participate in any recovery.[1] Term extensions may be acceptable, so long as these do not have the practical effect of transforming debt into an equity-like instrument without also giving creditors the rights of equity-holders. Reducing interest below the risk-adjusted rate may also be acceptable, so long as principal is repaid.[2] Grace periods on debt service—especially on interest payments—usually just postpone the day of reckoning for nonviable companies.

Box 1. Measuring a Company's Sustainable Debt

Unless a company is manipulating its earnings, earnings before interest, taxes, depreciation, and amortization (EBITDA) is a reasonable proxy for more complete measures of cash flow. Using a 2:1 interest coverage standard and assuming a market interest rate of 10 percent, for example, a company with EBITDA of $100 million could sustain debt of $500 million.

An EBITDA/interest expense ratio of less than 1:1 is unsustainable. Any ratio below 2:1 is worrisome. For example, Korea's Dong-ah Construction was forced into receivership in 2000 despite 1999 interest coverage of 1.6:1. In the United States, average interest coverage was around 8:1 in 1996, and a higher ratio is needed for an "A" rating from Standard & Poor's.

---

[1]Equity ownership by creditors can create other moral hazard issues, against which the financial supervisor would need to guard.

[2]Governments, however, should discourage rate reductions that provide an undeserved competitive advantage and preserve "zombie" companies from liquidation.

The choice of a forum for such operational and financial restructuring of distressed companies will normally depend on the severity of a company's problems and differences among interested parties. If the company's underlying business is nonviable, liquidation is appropriate. If the company is viable (albeit over-indebted) as a going concern but the parties are separated by wide differences over the apportionment of loss, corporate restructuring may need to proceed via a court-supervised rehabilitation. Otherwise, restructuring may proceed through an out-of-court "workout." A systemic crisis involving hundreds or thousands of cases could overwhelm a nation's courts and create a need for greater reliance on out-of-court workouts.

Link between corporate and financial sector restructuring

Corporate restructuring and financial sector restructuring are two sides of the same problem. The creditor(s) of a corporation under restructuring should provision—and, as necessary, further reduce its capital—to reflect (i) the present value effects of any debt/equity conversions, rate reductions, term extensions, grace periods, and write-offs; and (ii) appropriate provisioning of remaining corporate debt based on international-standard, forward-looking criteria. If a financial institution's risk-weighted capital adequacy falls below some ratio (for example, 8 percent), the government may decide to close and liquidate the institution, merge it with a stronger partner, solicit additional capital from current shareholders, or re-capitalize the institution and take control. Thus, corporate cash flow is linked both to the amount of sustainable corporate debt and to the cost of re-capitalizing financial institutions for losses in resolving the non-sustainable portion of corporate debt. In any case where financial restructuring of a distressed corporation involves a debt/equity conversion, financial institution shareholders will also need to make arrangements for managing the converted equity and plan for eventually exiting from equity ownership. Unless the financial institution has expertise in management of corporate equity, this task should be outsourced.

Corporate restructuring goals

The debtor and its creditors will naturally seek to minimize their losses. For example, the corporate managers and controlling shareholders will seek to avoid loss of control, dilution of their equity, or divestment of favored assets and lines of business. Managers and controlling shareholders of financial institutions will seek to avoid losses on corporate debt restructuring that could necessitate capital write-downs leading to equity dilution, loss of control, and nationalization or liquidation of the institution.

The government will have to balance a variety of conflicting interests. These may include minimizing the costs of bank re-capitalization; protecting workers, suppliers, and subcontractors of failed companies to minimize ripple effects through the economy; minimizing distortions to market competition through excessive debt-rescheduling concessions; avoiding labor strife; and—last but not least—dampening public criticism enough for the government to remain in office.

From the perspective of the distressed company itself, as distinct from its shareholders, one can identify time-phased restructuring goals.

- In the short term (e.g., 3 months), it will be important to achieve a degree of financial stabilization in order to prevent the liquidation of viable, albeit over-leveraged, companies. Non-viable companies should be allowed to fail and exited, for example, through liquidation. In a systemic crisis, however, "strong swimmers" should not be dragged down along with the weak.
- In the medium term (e.g., 6-24 months), operational restructuring should be undertaken to improve the company's profitability, solvency, and liquidity. This will involve steps like those mentioned above.
- Over the longer term, it is important to deter imprudent debt-fueled investment so that companies do not launch non-viable ventures or assume unsustainable debt. Deterrence depends on a demonstration of the ability of wronged creditors to foreclose on assets, liquidate non-viable companies, and take viable but distressed companies away from uncooperative shareholders/managers.

It is relatively easy to financially stabilize distressed companies, for example, through creditor standstills or debt restructuring. Operational restructuring in a systemic crisis is more difficult, since hundreds of firms may be attempting to sell non-core assets, while low stock prices will likely discourage new equity financing. Failure to move beyond financial stabilization, however, and pursue operational restructuring to address operational weaknesses, such as high labor costs, low-margin or loss-making business lines, poor working capital management, or capital tied up in low—or negative-return assets—will diminish long-term competitiveness.

Korea's Recent Experience

Onset of the crisis

The years leading up to the crisis witnessed heavy debt-financed expansion by chaebol into new businesses—often in competitive and cyclical industries—

Box 2. Initial Options for De-Leveraging
The Thirty Largest Chaebol, 1997-99

In early 1998, the government directed that chaebol should reduce their liabilities/equity ratios to 200 percent by end-1999. The following table includes assumptions from early 1998 about opportunities for using court-supervised reorganization or liquidation to resolve insolvent chaebol; and expectations about foreign investment relative to GDP, earnings increases, and new equity issues relative to market capitalization.

Balances	Liabilities	Equity	Liabilities/Equity	Resolution Method
At 12/31/97	351,703	69,122	509%	
	-48,647	-1,947		Court-supervised insolvency
	-12,000			Foreign investment, asset sales
		1,200		"Normal" retained earnings
		2,500		Increased retained earnings
	-8,250	8,250		Domestic equity issues
	-5,250	5,250		Offshore equity issues
Subtotal	*277,556*	*84,375*	*329%*	
		0		Asset re-valuations
	-14,890	14,890		Debt/equity conversions, to 15% of total equity
Subtotal	*262,666*	*99,265*	*265%*	
	-21,250	21,250		Additional debt/equity conversions, debt write-offs, or other debt rescheduling
12/31/99 goal	241,416	120,515	200%	

Sources: Fair Trade Commission for end-1997 balance and *SBC Warburg Dillon Read* for projections of foreign investment and equity issues.

Note: Liabilities and equity in billions of won.

Assuming no asset re-valuations (a practice prohibited since 1999) and 14,890 billion won in debt/equity conversions—which would leave creditors with 15 percent of total equity—the top 30 chaebol would still show liabilities/equity of 265 percent. Thus, an additional 21,250 billion won of debt/equity conversions (or other present value gains to debtors from debt write-offs or other debt restructuring) would be needed to achieve end-1999 liabilities/equity of 200 percent. This analysis is intended not to suggest that 200 percent liabilities/equity was an ideal goal (or better than an interest coverage goal), but rather to illustrate the difficulty of eliminating such a large debt overhang through incremental improvements—instead of a wholesale conversion of debt into equity—within a 2-year period.

and into emerging markets with distant and uncertain profit prospects. During the run-up to 1997, profitability and returns on investment declined, leverage grew, and interest coverage remained razor thin at best. By end-1997, liabilities/equity for Korea's 30 largest chaebol, excluding financial affiliates, was just over 5:1 on average; fifteen of the top 30 chaebol were insolvent or had a liabilities/equity ratio in excess of 5:1.

Estimates in early 1998 raised questions about the ability of Korean companies to achieve sufficient de-leveraging through incremental enhancements, such as asset sales, foreign investment, new equity issues, or increases in retained earnings; this suggested that wholesale reductions in the stock of debt through debt/equity conversions or debt write-offs would be needed. In Korea, liabilities/equity for the thirty largest chaebol was 509 percent at end-1997. There were not enough asset buyers and equity investors, and not enough of an opportunity for immediate operational restructuring, to reduce corporate leverage to the government's end-1999 liabilities/equity target of 200 percent just through incremental measures, such as asset or business sales, issuance of new equity, or increases in retained earnings from operational gains. Hundreds of large corporations were simultaneously exploring the possibility of asset or business sales or equity issues to strengthen their financial position—creating the prospect of an asset glut and fire sale prices. Thus, as illustrated in Box 2, the stock of corporate debt had to be reduced through debt/equity conversions or write-offs to stabilize corporate finances on a lasting basis. Other concessionary debt restructuring—rate reductions, term extensions, or grace periods—could provide temporary financial stabilization for distressed chaebols. But unless they used temporary financial stabilization to implement sufficiently deep operational restructuring, companies might be unable to resume normal debt service upon the expiration of these debt concessions.

Recurring pattern in corporate restructuring

A review of corporate restructuring activity in Korea since 1997 reveals a recurring pattern. Creditors periodically act decisively to take problem companies away from existing management and controlling shareholders while agreeing to some financial stabilization either through a workout or court-supervised insolvency. Subsequent operational restructuring, however, is often delayed because of creditor reluctance to take additional losses on the sale of over-valued assets at realistic prices, reluctance to lay off workers, and different views among creditors. For its part, the government has periodically weighed in with sweeping measures to promote long-term corporate reform or re-energize the corporate restructuring process.

In 1997, 13 chaebol—including such giants as Hanbo Steel and Kia—with cumulative debts of KRW 28 trillion entered court-supervised insolvency. Of these, 11 went into receivership, effectively wiping out existing management and controlling shareholders. While Kia was sold to Hyundai, many companies have languished in receivership or enjoyed the competitive benefits of debt service concessions included in debt composition agreements. In some cases, creditors have been reluctant to sell companies in receivership for less than their outstanding debt. For instance, it was reported that creditors owed $4 billion by Hanbo rejected a $2.5 billion offer for the company from Posco/Dongkuk; a subsequent offer by another investor for $400-500 million was withdrawn, leaving creditors with nothing. As of end-2000, 42 affiliates from the sixty largest chaebol were subject to debt composition proceedings while another 61 were in receivership. Of these 103 affiliates, 54 were designated for rehabilitation, 14 for liquidation, and 35 for sale or merger.

By end-1997, according to one investment bank analysis, another eighteen of Korea's top 30 chaebol (apart from those already under court supervision) were at medium or high risk of insolvency. Simultaneous distress among so many large chaebol was obviously cause for concern, especially since Korea's insolvency system was not capable of rapidly rehabilitating a large number of distressed chaebol, and neither Korea's financial system nor the Korean public were prepared for massive financial sector losses. Between October 1997 and May 1998, Korean financial institutions provided at least KRW 1.9 trillion in emergency bankruptcy-avoidance loans to Haitai, New Core, Jindo, Shinho, Hanwha, Hanil, Dong-ah, Kohap, and Woobang. At least six of these companies subsequently entered court-supervised insolvency or went through one or two workouts. Following two unsuccessful workouts, Dong-ah was designated for liquidation in early 2001.

While it searched for an alternative between potentially cumbersome receivership for resolving distressed companies and "bankruptcy avoidance" loans, the government introduced a number of important initiatives in February 1998 and thereafter. Some would promote general corporate reform: improvements in financial disclosure and accounting standards, including requirements for consolidated and combined financial statements; stronger shareholder rights and enhanced corporate governance standards; relaxation of legal constraints on foreign investment; liberalization of merger and acquisition (M&A) rules; greater latitude for employee layoffs during corporate restructuring or reorganization; improved unemployment insurance benefits; and more streamlined rules on court-supervised rehabilitation. Other reforms sought to impose more financial discipline on large chaebol not in immediate distress: elimination of *domestic* cross guarantees; additional requirements in capital structure improvement programs (CSIPs) to shed non-core affiliates and reduce liabilities/equity ratios to 200 percent by end-1999; tighter exposure limits on financial institutions; and Fair Trade Commission (FTC) action against anti-competitive intra-chaebol transactions. In June 1998, the Financial Supervisory Commission (FSC) encouraged banks to announce a withdrawal of credit, or "exit," from 55 non-viable companies. Soon thereafter, the government announced its support for eight "Big Deals" to consolidate through merger, acquisition, or joint venture businesses in eight sectors suffering from excess capacity. Over the past year, the FTC has been moving to limit to 25 percent of its equity any chaebol affiliate's shareholdings in a related affiliate.

In July 1998, with encouragement from the FSC, 210 local financial institutions contractually bound themselves to the Corporate Restructuring Agreement (CRA) and embarked on "workouts" as an alternative to receivership and uncontrolled "bankruptcy avoidance" loans. The CRA provided for a 2-5 month standstill to accommodate workout negotiations, designation of a lead creditor, a 75 percent threshold for creditor approval of workout agreements, a 7-person Corporate Restructuring Coordination Committee (CRCC) to provide workout guidelines and arbitrate inter-creditor differences if creditors could not agree on a workout plan after three votes, and FSC imposition of fines on creditors for breaching the CRA. The CRCC provided inter-creditor arbitration decisions in 21 cases prior to July 1999.

Between September 1998 and March 1999, CRA workouts involving KRW 34 trillion of debt restructuring and KRW 10 trillion of corporate "self help" (e.g., business/asset sales, new capital, cost savings) were agreed for 41 affiliates of 16 chaebol and 38 medium or large stand-alone companies. Thus, the emphasis was on financial restructuring rather than corporate self-help. Financial restructuring relied mainly on term extensions, rate reductions, and grace periods, along with conversions of KRW 3.6 trillion of debt into equity or convertible bonds. Only KRW 565 billion of debt was to be written off. Controlling shareholders experienced significant dilution as a result of debt/equity conversions and chaebol managements were replaced in some cases. Creditors deployed joint management teams to monitor costs and the disposition of assets. On average, corporate self-help was to be implemented over three years, which was a reasonable goal. It appears that strenuous efforts were made to control costs, but that access to new equity was poor, partly because Hyundai, Samsung, LG, and SK so dominated capital markets, and those sales of non-core businesses and real estate lagged because of unrealistic valuations.

Following an extended period of decline—as evidenced by Daewoo Corporation's negative KRW 12 trillion in cash from operations for 1998—twelve Daewoo affiliates failed in July 1999. Existing management and controlling shareholders were shunted aside, and some were threatened with criminal prosecution. The ability of creditors to displace existing management and controlling shareholders within Korea's second or third largest conglomerate provided some warning that no chaebol is "too big to fail."

By end-1999, CRA workouts had been developed or agreed for the twelve Daewoo affiliates. These had resulted in the restructuring of KRW 59 trillion in debt, mostly through rate reductions and conversions of debt into convertible bonds or equity by early 2001. The CRCC provided inter-creditor arbitration decisions in two Daewoo cases and mediated a proposal—first by Korean creditors, and then by KAMCO—to buy out $4.8 billion in debt owed to foreign creditors by Daewoo Corporation, Daewoo Heavy, Daewoo Motors, and Daewoo Electronics.

Following the financial stabilization of Daewoo companies, momentum for operational restructuring during 2000 was slow to develop. Pre-Ford discussions with General Motors about acquiring Daewoo Motors lapsed. Planned spin-offs of Daewoo Corporation's construction and trading businesses and Daewoo Heavy's shipbuilding and heavy machinery businesses were delayed until the fourth quarter of 2000. These delays reflected the time needed to legislate relief from heavy taxation of the spin-offs and to negotiate preferential terms with public shareholders who, taking advantage of the fact that these workouts were out-of-court, resisted the equity write-downs and share allocations in residual "bad companies" proposed by major creditors. The only sales to occur in 2000 were of Daewoo Telecom's TDX division and of Daewoo Electronic Components. At end-November 2000, Daewoo Motors was put under court receivership. Since then, Daewoo Motors has reportedly laid off 6,400 workers (about 9 percent of its workforce), reduced material costs, and re-negotiated many vendor contracts. Creditors plan to restructure and sell off ten or so units of Daewoo Electronics (DEC), but must first obtain approval from public shareholders, who hold 94 percent of DEC's shares, for a second debt/equity conversion. Despite the fact that DEC had *negative* capital of KRW 27 trillion at end-2000, creditors are continuing—incredibly—to attempt to resolve DEC out of court.

In other ways, 2000 represented a hiatus for the operational restructuring of still-distressed corporations. Business projections used to develop some of the early CRA workouts were clearly unrealistic and, not surprisingly, 18 companies were forced into second-round CRA workouts by mid-2000. These workouts involved additional term extensions, rate reductions, and grace periods, and additional conversions of debt into equity and convertible bonds. An examination of cash flows and creditor descriptions of fantastic assumptions underlying some projections, however, raised doubts about the credibility of these second round workouts.

By mid-2000, there were increasing concerns that regulatory forbearance on provisioning for restructured corporate debt was discouraging financial institutions from pursuing post-stabilization "operational restructuring transactions," such as company sales, transfer to corporate restructuring vehicles (CRVs), asset sales, or liquidation. To encourage financial institutions to agree to CRA workouts, the FSC had provided a special exemption from the general application of forward-looking criteria (FLC). Financial institutions were allowed to provision restructured debt at just 2-20 percent until as late as end-2001. While some financial institutions were more conservatively provisioned in some cases, these may have been the exception. There are also reasons to believe that converted equity was over-valued. A lower-of-cost-or-market rule (instead of, for example, booking converted equity at a nominal KRW 1 per share for illiquid stock) may have allowed banks to carry converted equity at "market prices" that were unrealistically high as a result of thin public floats, legal protections for public shareholders, and agreements among creditor-shareholders not to sell converted equity during the workout implementation period (3 years on average) without unanimous agreement among creditor-shareholders. In cases where sale of a company, transfer of debt/equity instruments to a CRV, asset sales, or liquidation could force a bank to recognize losses on under-provisioned loans or over-valued equity, creditors could be expected to resist such operational restructuring transactions. In mid-2000, the FSC decided to end the special 2-20 percent provisioning for restructured corporate debt and require banks to apply standard FLC to all corporate credits by end-2000.

While required regulations on CRVs were in place by end-2000, no CRV has yet been established. Evidence and anecdote suggest that some banks account less conservatively for restructured corporate debt and converted equity and are less willing to convey these financial assets at realistic transfer prices to a CRV for management. There are also reports that differences have arisen among banks over the relative value of converted equity and debt (e.g., secured vs. unsecured) to be conveyed in exchange for ownership interest in a CRV.

In apparent response to a loss of corporate restructuring momentum, the government sought to reinvigorate its corporate restructuring program in the fall of 2000. During October, twenty-one banks conducted credit risk assessments of just 287 potentially non-viable corporations, of which 69 were deemed problematic but viable with creditor support while another 52 were to be exited. The results were greeted with some skepticism. Only 12 new companies were included on the exit list. The others were mostly "downgrades" from workout to receivership, or from receivership to liquidation. The November 2000 exit list included at least one company from the June 1998 list of companies to be exited. Decisions on two "exit" companies—Hyundai Engineering & Construction (HEC) and SSangyong Cement Industries—were deferred. Our analysis of 1999 interest coverage for 496 large corporations (excluding Daewoo affiliates) based on EBITDA, however, found interest coverage of less than 1.5:1 for 156 of the 496 companies; less than 1:1 for 112; and less than zero—negative cash flow—for 64. This raised additional questions about the adequacy of the October credit risk assessments.

Following HEC's near-default in November 2000, several events raised concerns about a possible bail-out of the company's controlling shareholders: the November roll-over of bank credits through at least end-2000; HEC's announcement of a new "self-rescue" plan (its fifth since May 2000) in which KRW 600 billion of KRW 1,300 billion would be raised from a transfer of HEC's Sosan ranch to state-owned Korea Land Corp; reports that the FSC had asked Hyundai affiliates to end their resistance to supporting HEC's self-rescue, which was seen to be a reversal of the government's policy of requiring chaebol affiliates to stand on their own; and Korea Development Bank's (KDB) "quick underwriting" of KRW 304 billion in HEC re-financing during the first quarter of 2001, with expectations that KDB would underwrite a total of KRW 1.4 trillion of HEC debt during 2001. While it is obviously important to undertake a professional and independent assessment of HEC's businesses— including the profitability and solvency of large construction projects—and preserve whatever is viable, observers worried that such non-market interventions to protect controlling shareholders and management from receivership would negate the lesson—provided at considerable expense—from Daewoo that no chaebol is "too big to fail" and create long-term moral hazard. These concerns were somewhat alleviated by creditor takeover of a bloc of HEC shares and expectations that a debt/equity conversion would severely dilute or eliminate the founding family's equity holdings. However, moves to do a debt/equity conversion ran into familiar problems of potential opposition from secured creditors who wanted to be included with unsecured creditors in a debt/equity conversion and from public shareholders who could insist on preferential terms for write-downs of existing equity. In addition, HEC was slow to implement recommendations from its consultants for cost reductions and other operational restructuring.

Recent moves to support and save Hynix from receivership have created similar concerns. Hynix's end-February 2001 debt was put at KRW 9.1 trillion—KRW 5 trillion with banks and KRW 4.1 trillion with NBFIs. Amounts coming due in 2001 were put at KRW 5.2 trillion. With chips selling for rock-bottom prices, financial institutions—especially the NBFIs—were unwilling to rollover Hynix debt without some emolument. Hynix's lead bank reportedly warned that court receivership would deal a "crippling blow" to the economy. Apparently accepting the argument that current laws and procedures for receivership would harm rather than rehabilitate Hynix, the state-owned financial institutions organized a KRW 5.1 trillion rescue that included creditor bank purchases of KRW 1 trillion in convertible bonds.[3] Under its "quick underwriting" program, KDB has underwritten KRW 840 trillion of Hynix bonds and expects to underwrite a total of KRW 2.9 trillion by end-2001.[4] This rescue plan and other maneuvers have raised issues and criticism. Final recoveries for creditors and post-conversion shareholdings for family members cannot be predicted, so it is impossible to judge this rescue from either a business or a moral hazard perspective. Claiming that Hynix and other Hyundai firms have not undertaken any layoffs, asset sales, or other painful self-rescue steps, one press report suggested that their "insouciance" toward self-restructuring "has triggered a moral-hazard controversy." Indeed, the emphasis is on re-scheduling to the apparent neglect of de-leveraging. Other press reports that the FSS had instructed creditor banks to classify Hynix loans as normal further highlight the conflicts of interest that can arise when a financial supervisor is tasked with managing corporate/financial sector restructuring in a systemic crisis.[5] Reports that Hyundai Heavy, Hyundai Merchant Marine, and Hyundai Corporation had agreed to support Hynix if necessary by purchasing chips from Hyundai Semiconductor of America *at cost plus an 18 percent margin* raise several issues, including the continued existence of cross guarantees (albeit in more creative formats) and the competitive propriety of intra-chaebol transactions.[6]

---

[3]According to reports in the *Korea Herald*, approval for the KRW 5.1 trillion rescue came after 16 investment trust management companies (ITMCs) agreed to participate in a rescue operation organized by Salomon Smith Barney. The ITMCs would purchase KRW 680 billion in Hynix bonds, of which KRW 600 billion would be guaranteed by state institutions. Creditor banks would purchase KRW 1 trillion in convertible bonds and extend the maturity of KRW 800 billion in syndicated debt until end-2003.

[4]Under this program, 70 percent of the bonds underwritten by KDB would go into an asset pool for primary CBOs issued with a 50 percent guarantee from the Korea Credit Guarantee Fund, while creditor banks would take 20 percent, and KDB would keep 10 percent.

[5]Also discomfiting was a report that the Financial Supervisory Service had threatened to fine Hana Bank KRW 6 billion if it fails to provide a promised KRW 11.9 billion of emergency liquidity to Hyundai Petrochemical by April 19, 2001 (*Korea Herald*, April 21, 2001).

[6]For an account of this transaction, see "Changes in the Share Price of HHI Due to Its Purchase Guarantee Agreement of H-A-S Wafers," People's Solidarity for Participatory Democracy Corporate Governance Information Center press release, April 15, 2001.

Perhaps reflecting doubts about the adequacy of the October 2000 credit risk assessments, the Financial Supervisory Service (FSS) recently established a "corporate health checkup system" under which creditor banks have nominated 1,187 domestic firms to undergo credit risk assessments. Those selected had been given "precautionary" or lower credit ratings by creditor banks, recorded an interest coverage ratio of less than 1, or shown other signs of insolvency during the past three years. The number could increase, as it does not include firms under court-supervised composition or receivership. During April 2001 on-site inspections, the FSS reportedly found that most banks had failed to establish detailed and objective criteria for assessing the creditworthiness of companies. Banks were also found to have omitted firms that failed to receive an unqualified audit opinion or that were unprofitable. Firms will be categorized as those to be revived; those suffering from temporary liquidity problems; those suffering from "structural" liquidity problems; and those to be liquidated. Creditor banks are expected to produce results each month and complete this round of credit risk assessments by end-August. The FSS reportedly expects that 200-300 firms will be classified as non-viable.[7]

Results

Looking first at its corporate restructuring performance from a long-term perspective, Korea has done a good job—so far—of establishing precedents to deter companies from making imprudent debt-fueled investments in the future. Through both court-supervised receiverships and out-of-court workouts, the controlling shareholders and managements of many chaebols—including some of Korea's biggest pre-crisis names—have completely lost out or seen their shareholdings severely diluted and their managerial discretion severely circumscribed. The outcome for Daewoo's former managers and controlling shareholders is especially stark. If these precedents are preserved, Korea will emerge from the crisis in a much stronger position than some countries such as Thailand and Indonesia, where gaps in local insolvency/foreclosure systems encouraged rampant "strategic defaulting" and extraordinarily high NPLs. Long-term deterrence of imprudent debt-fueled investments, however, will depend on the treatment of Hyundai's controlling shareholders and managers. If non-market interventions are used to protect them from receivership and loss, the hard-won lesson of Daewoo that no chaebol is "too big to fail" will be lost.

Looking next at short-term financial stabilization to prevent the liquidation of viable albeit over-leveraged companies, Korea has done more than enough

---

[7]*Korea Herald*, May 9, 2001 and May 10, 2001.

for large corporations. Of the 108 companies that had entered the CRA workout process, 36—presumably the "strong swimmers"—had graduated by end-2000. A number of questions can be raised about another 47 companies that remain under workout or which were transferred from workout to receivership or liquidation by March 2001, as well as about the 103 chaebol affiliates that were under court supervision at end-2000.

- Are non-viable companies being identified and liquidated in a timely manner?
- Do creditor stays in court-supervised insolvencies and debt restructuring concessions (e.g., rate reductions and grace periods) in workout MOUs provide market-distorting competitive advantages and preserve "zombie" companies?
- Are viable business assets being allowed to find their highest and best use (e.g., through sale at a realistic market price or transfer to a professionally-managed CRV), or are creditors unreasonably hanging on to workout companies?

It is also worth mentioning that CRA workouts did nothing to financially stabilize Korea's small and medium-sized enterprises (SMEs), which suffered mightily in the crisis. SME failures climbed to 8,200 in 1997 and 10,500 in 1998. The irony is that although Korea's SMEs did nothing to precipitate the crisis, they were surely harmed by their powerful, cash-conserving, late-paying chaebol customers. Lastly, it is important to note that the financial stabilization of large corporations—and the demise of many SMEs—in Korea proceeded according to a rule of law. Korea witnessed none of the unilateral debt moratoria and "strategic defaulting" that have plagued Thailand and Indonesia.

Most questionable is the adequacy of medium-term operational restructuring to improve the profitability, solvency, and liquidity of troubled companies. Anecdotal evidence and fragmentary analysis suggest that there has been some progress, but that more remains to be done. Profitability improved between 1996 and 1999 for most non-workout chaebols, but the situation remains dire for the Daewoo companies and chaebols under workout or court-supervision (Table 1). It is worth noting that GDP growth was 10.9 percent in 1999, slowing just to 8.8 percent in 2000. Despite this still-robust growth, the profits of companies listed on the Korea Stock Exchange decreased 26.5 percent in 2000 and profitability sagged to 1.8 percent. If growth further slows to 3.5 percent or lower in 2001, corporate profitability as well as asset values and corporate valuations could further decline. In retrospect, 1999 may come to be seen as representing a lost opportunity for maximizing gains on the sale or liquidation

Table 1. Net Profitability of Chaebols

Category	Number	1996	1999
Top 4	4	0.9%	3.0%
Daewoo	1	1.0%	-67.7%
6-30	14	0.1%	2.9%
31-64	23	-0.5%	2.4%
Under court supervision or workout	21	0.1%	-25.3%
	63		

Source: KIS.
Note: Profit calculations exclude revaluations of marketable securities and foreign exchange.

of distressed companies, the sale of non-core assets, new equity issuance, inducement of additional capital investment, and conveyance of holdings in distressed companies to professionally-managed CRVs for turnaround and value enhancement.[8]

Changes in liabilities/equity ratios suggest modest progress, but should be viewed with caution. According to the Bank of Korea, liabilities/equity for Korea's manufacturing sector has declined from about 4:1 at end-1997 to 2.1:1 at end-1999. But there has been virtually no retirement of debt. During 1999, the liabilities of Korean companies decreased just 1 percent while assets increased by 9 percent. The great bulk of the KRW 90 trillion in new equity that Korean companies raised or earned during 1999 went to acquire additional assets rather than to retire debt. While 210 percent liabilities/equity represents an improvement, such leverage is relatively high for companies in highly competitive or cyclical business, that is, for most Korean companies.[9] Moreover,

---

[8]The relationship between macroeconomic/asset valuation expectations and corporate restructuring behavior warrants further study. There is ample anecdotal evidence to suggest that Korean companies and creditors, perhaps in anticipation of a "V"-shaped recovery, have had unrealistic expectations and been reluctant to sell assets for less than their purchase price or the book value of outstanding credits.

[9]Korea's construction sector deserves special mention and special attention. According to the LG Economic Research Institute, Korea's construction sector suffers from over-capacity (there are 6,400 construction companies), falling orders, high debt (liabilities/equity of 606 percent), and chronic under-pricing (e.g., 1999 earnings *before interest and taxes* of negative 11 percent). According to industry experts, many construction companies around the world typically price construction contracts at below-cost; rely on change orders to earn a profit; use aggressive progress accounting and invoicing to extract cash from individual projects, which may leave projects insolvent; and require additional projects to get the cash to finish existing projects. Before "rescuing" a distressed construction company, creditors should conduct careful due diligence to ascertain that the company is not engaging in "pyramid" business practices that will simply create a larger financial "hole" in the future. It is very difficult to restructure distressed construction companies and creditor recoveries may be minimal. The greatest benefit from liquidating non-viable construction companies may come from improving the overall health and creditworthiness of the sector.

liabilities/equity ratios have been subject to some manipulation in the past. A few more years of financial reporting according to improved standards will be needed before liabilities/equity ratios can be taken seriously. Even then, liabilities/equity ratios will remain less meaningful than other measures, such as profitability, returns on assets or capital invested, and interest coverage.

Interest coverage (based on earnings before interest and taxes) in Korea has hovered around a razor-thin 1:1 since at least 1997 and Korean companies maintain lower interest coverage ratios than companies in 21 other developed and emerging markets (Figure 1). As indicated earlier, our analysis of 1999 interest coverage for 496 large corporations (excluding Daewoo affiliates) based on EBITDA found interest coverage of less than 1.5:1 for 156 of the 496 companies; less than 1:1 for 112; and less than zero (i.e., negative cash flow) for 64. Without additional equity and/or operational restructuring, such companies run a significant risk of default.

An examination of year 2000 financial statements for 391 companies showed that 24 percent still had interest coverage of less than 1.5:1; that 17 percent had interest coverage of less than 1:1; and that 11 percent had *negative* cash flows. This situation appears to be a slight improvement from 1999, but is still worrisome. Of the KRW 170 trillion in debt (bank loans and bonds) owed by the 391 companies at end-2000, KRW 65.5 trillion (39 percent) was owed by companies with interest coverage of less than 1.5:1. A 1999-2000 comparison of 21 workout companies showed declines in interest coverage from *negative* 0.78:1 to *negative* 1.45:1 and in returns on assets from *negative* 24 percent to *negative* 47 percent. These most-distressed companies should be resolved quickly, probably through receivership or liquidation.

Figure 1. International Comparisons: Liabilities/Equity vs. Interest Coverage

Source: "A Comparative Look of Korea's Corporate Reform," LG Economic Research Institute, 9/21/2000; original data taken from WorldScope DB and the World Bank; Asian Development Bank.

It stands to reason that the easiest operational restructuring measures have already been implemented. The easiest and fastest dispositions of quality assets (often the Korean half of joint ventures with foreign partners) occurred relatively early in the crisis. Examples cited by local equity analysts as corporate restructuring "success stories," such as Hanwha, Doosan, and Hyosung took place outside the CRA workout process. The companies under court-supervision or workout are more problematic. While 6-24 months should suffice to implement substantial operational restructuring at a large corporation, as suggested at the outset, a systemic crisis where hundreds of firms are over-leveraged (see Box 1) and simultaneously attempting to sell non-core assets and raise equity in depressed market conditions poses special challenges. Failure to move beyond financial stabilization and make substantial additional progress on the operational restructuring of distressed corporations could diminish long-term competitiveness.

Lastly, major recognition is due for the implementation of important measures designed to promote general reforms in corporate behavior and impose greater financial discipline: improvements in financial disclosure and accounting standards; stronger shareholder rights and enhanced corporate governance standards; liberalization of M&A and foreign investment rules; tighter exposure limits; and actions to curb anti-competitive intra-chaebol transactions. Progress has not been uniform: gaps in the regulation of investment trust companies (ITCs) added fuel to the Daewoo conflagration; thinly-disguised cross guarantees periodically pop up; and the FTC has yet to prevail in any of its complaints against improper intra-chaebol transactions, which remain on appeal. Overall, however, Korea's efforts to reform the legal and regulatory environment governing corporate behavior should contribute significantly to ongoing reforms in its corporate sector and serve as a model for other countries in the region. Especially heartening are reports that some auditors are being severely penalized for some notable audit failures and, as a result, that auditors were significantly stricter in requiring companies to make adjustments to their year 2000 financial statements.

Lessons and Recommendations

General lessons

The Korean experience offers a number of important lessons for other countries emerging from the 1997 crisis or similar crises in the future.

1. A credible threat of foreclosure/bankruptcy is needed to elicit debtor cooperation with court-supervised rehabilitations or out-of-court workouts. A strong system for insolvency and enforcement of creditor rights can be a powerful tool for rehabilitating viable-but-distressed companies, liquidating non-viable ones, and encouraging debtors to cooperate with out-of-court corporate restructuring efforts. Recent contrasts between Korea and Indonesia and Thailand are instructive. While more remains to be done on the operational restructuring of distressed Korean chaebols, the CRA workouts in 1998-99 did impose significant losses on controlling shareholders and management. The 1997 descent of 11 chaebols into receivership, in which controlling shareholders lost management control and equity rights, provided an incentive for debtors to agree to some losses in CRA workouts. Half a loaf was better than none. In Indonesia, the absence of any credible threat from the country's legal framework for protecting creditors has severely undermined corporate restructuring efforts and encouraged deals that emphasize debt rescheduling and minimize corporate "self help." In Thailand, the lack of a credible threat of foreclosure and liquidation has resulted in anomalous cases of debtors seeking to avoid court-supervised rehabilitation. While Thailand has made significant advances in developing an option for court-supervised reorganization (rehabilitation) and implementation capacity—especially its special-purpose bankruptcy court—the continuing lack of coercive alternatives undermined out-of-court workout efforts.

2. While an efficient framework for out-of-court workouts is necessary in a systemic crisis and can resolve some instances of corporate distress, permanent solutions may require a court-supervised process. An efficient framework for out-of-court workouts is needed both to avoid saturation of the courts and to preserve value. Sole reliance on the courts to restructure hundreds of distressed corporations (not to mention potentially tens or hundreds of thousands of SMEs) in a systemic crisis would overwhelm the courts and legal infrastructure. Evidence from the U.S. and the U.K. also indicates that creditors are likely to receive higher recoveries from an out-of-court workout than from a court-supervised rehabilitation or receivership.[10] The problem increasingly apparent in Korean workouts is that disputes over the allocation of losses and risk—between creditors over (i) the treatment of secured vs.

---

[10]For example, a sample of cases from the US and UK shows that overall creditor recoveries averaged 85 percent in UK workouts versus average recoveries of 51 percent in US court-supervised reorganizations (Chapter 11) and 34 percent in UK receiverships. Peter G. Brierly, "The London Approach to Corporate Workouts," Bank of England, February 2000 presentation, citing J.R. Franks, K.G. Nyborg, and W.N. Torous, "A Comparison of U.S., U.K., and German Insolvency Codes," *Financial Management*, Autumn 1996.

unsecured debt, (ii) the provision of new credits, and (iii) over the sale or transfer of converted equity and restructured credits; and between creditor-shareholders and public shareholders over the allocation of equity losses—are difficult and time-consuming to resolve in an out-of-court process. Delays may impose additional losses on the company subject to workout. Ultimately, resort to a court-supervised process may be needed to resolve such disputes in a timely manner.

3. Forbearance on loss recognition, inconsistent application of provisioning standards, and liberal accounting rules for converted equity may discourage follow-on operational restructuring transactions. Loose linkages between corporate and financial sector restructuring may have encouraged a number of "half measures" in corporate restructuring:

- The heavy reliance in workouts on term extensions, grace periods, rate reductions, and conversions of debt into equity or low-yielding convertible bonds, with negligible debt write-offs;
- The reluctance of creditors to insist on (or agree to) business or corporate asset sales that could force loss recognition on associated corporate loans provisioned at as little as 2 percent;[11]
- The readiness of creditors to agree to second-round workouts in early 2000 for 18 companies of dubious viability who were clear candidates for liquidation;[12]
- The failure of creditors to deal pro-actively with the Daewoo situation, despite signs of increasingly severe corporate distress that were available by end-1998, or Saehan's unanticipated bankruptcy/emergency workout in May 2000;
- The reluctance of creditor-shareholders to put converted equity under professional management, since a professional manager receiving incentive compensation would insist on a realistic transfer price for the converted equity; and
- October 2000 credit risk assessments by banks which turned up an incredibly few companies to be "exited."

---

[11]A good example of this is the case of Hanbo Steel, which has languished in receivership since January 1997—with creditors owed $4 billion having rejected an early $2.5 billion offer from Posco/Dongkuk and another investor group having recently withdrawn its $400-500 million offer. Unrealistic valuations also led creditors to reject a favorable offer from GM for Daewoo Motors in 1999.

[12]Indeed, second-round workout companies were mostly designated for conversion into liquidation or receivership in November 2000.

4. Governments must be ready to impose losses on the shareholders of local financial institutions and force the resolution of over-valued assets. A government's failure to force local financial institutions to pursue financial and operational structuring of their distressed clients will leave companies in a "zombie" state with uncompetitive cost structures, capital tied up in loss-making or low-return assets, and unable to obtain financing.[13]

5. There must be the flexibility and the readiness to lay off excess workers and to accept foreign control over additional companies. Foreign investment can improve the operations of distressed companies and their market access. By providing additional sources of capital, foreign investment can also lessen the losses creditors would otherwise suffer in a systemic crisis. Labor reductions and foreign investment, however, can be the mostly politically contentious—and exploitable—aspect of corporate restructuring. It may be relatively easy for debtors and creditors, seeking to avoid the mutual losses inherent in corporate restructuring, to mobilize workers and the public to oppose layoffs and sales of "national assets" at "fire sale prices" to foreign "vulture investors." In the interests of promoting company rehabilitation and lessening losses to the financial sector, however, it is important to address regulatory and attitudinal impediments to workforce reductions and foreign investment. Development of adequate safety nets and a greater appreciation of the links between foreign investment and sustainable growth should make it easier for governments to address these potentially contentious issues.

6. All significant tax, legal, and regulatory impediments to corporate restructuring must be eliminated, barring some other overriding public policy purpose. Experience from throughout east Asia shows that impediments may include taxation of debtor gains from debt restructuring; the inability of creditors to deduct debt restructuring losses to reduce taxes; immediate taxation of mergers, spin-offs, and other non-cash corporate reorganizations; excessive transfer taxes; unreasonable waiting periods for creditor-review of proposed mergers; legal lending limits; constraints on the ability of state-owned financial institutions to take losses on corporate restructuring; and various protections for public shareholders. Recent experience demonstrates that any one of these impediments can delay a corporate restructuring transaction. Some impediments—such as controls on tax deductions for credit right offs, bank

---

[13]Recent experience indicates that state-owned financial institutions can be just as slow as private financial institutions at loss recognition. While managers/controlling shareholders at private financial institutions will be concerned about possible equity dilution and loss of control, the controlling shareholder (likely to be the ministry of finance) of nationalized or other state-owned banks may want to avoid having to explain additional corporate restructuring losses to the parliament and taxpaying public.

exposure limits, and protections for public shareholders—serve broader public policy interests and cannot be simply swept away. In some cases, waivers may be appropriate (e.g., on legal lending limits). Public shareholder rights to oppose dilutive equity restructuring can be particularly difficult or impossible to override in an out-of-court workout—as seen in recent cases involving Daewoo affiliates. Thus, it may be necessary to rely more on court-supervised processes, such as "pre-packaged" reorganizations, to effect equity restructuring of companies.

7. *Some central body should be responsible for driving financial sector restructuring and making adequate corporate restructuring a condition for bank re-capitalization.* The government should consider forming a special-purpose, temporary, crisis-management team to consolidate responsibility, ensure consistency of work and decisions, provide the necessary specialized skills, and insulate crisis resolution from other official duties and related conflicts of interest. The crisis-management team should report to a governing body that would balance political interests and resolve differences of opinion among the permanent government agencies represented on the team. Since a country's ministry of finance would be the one to issue bank re-capitalization bonds, it should play a leading role on any crisis management team. To avoid conflicts of interest between minimizing costs and safeguarding the nation's financial system, the financial supervisor should normally keep out of financial sector restructuring and focus on supervising financial institutions. The finance ministry and financial supervisor would need to coordinate, however, on questions of regulatory forbearance. To achieve a strong link between corporate restructuring and financial sector restructuring, it would be desirable for the finance ministry to require a professional and independent assessment and certification of the "adequacy" of major corporate restructuring agreements as a pre-condition for making up financial institution losses on the implementation of these corporate restructuring agreements.

Corporate and financial sector restructuring will involve a variety of considerations and costs—including knock-on effects through the economy. The government should seek to minimize *the present value of the multi-year costs of corporate and financial sector restructuring.* But this is easier said than done. Governments often succumb to the temptation to focus only on Year 1 costs, "kick the can down the road," and hope for some macroeconomic *deus ex machina* in subsequent years to lessen the ultimate cost of resolving corporate and financial sector distress. A government's crisis management team would likely benefit from an independent assessment of the net present value costs and effects of alternative strategies for resolving corporate and financial sector distress. Particular attention should be paid to projections of corporate cash flows, unsustainable corporate debt, and bank re-capitalization requirements; alternatives for protecting the workers, suppliers, and subcontractors of failed companies; and the potential effects of below-market interest rates and other debt-restructuring concessions on market competition. To the extent that a government can develop credible cost projections and educate the public on the likely costs of available alternatives, it may be easier for the government to act decisively to resolve corporate and financial sector distress at least cost to the taxpaying public.

8. There must be sufficient implementation capacity to conduct due diligence, structure and negotiate workouts, conclude asset sales, and manage converted equity. Leaving aside thousands of SMEs, the restructuring of hundreds of distressed corporations could absorb every accountant, lawyer, investment banker, workout professional, and receiver in a crisis-stricken country and run up enormous professional fees. Professional support will have to be brought in from outside the country and acclimated to local legal/financial systems. As debtor companies may be unwilling or unable to retain and pay for such professionals, it may be necessary for creditors or the national treasury to pay at least some of these costs. Banks and public asset management companies (AMCs) will lack professionals with requisite experience in corporate workouts and turnarounds. Efforts to develop in-house workout capacity can take time and the results may not be completely satisfactory. Thus, banks and public AMCs would be well advised to retain outside professionals—on some incentive compensation basis, whenever possible—to conduct due diligence, structure and negotiate corporate workouts, and manage asset sales. Lastly, reason suggests and recent experience indicates that corporate restructuring deals in a systemic crisis will leave financial institutions with masses of converted corporate equity. Banks will have enough difficulty in managing themselves in a crisis and will have no experience in managing corporate shareholdings or exercising corporate governance. Thus, the management of converted equity should be outsourced to asset management/corporate turnaround professionals—perhaps through equity partnerships such as those used by KAMCO or proposed CRVs.

9. Crisis efforts to resolve immediate corporate distress should be supplemented with other measures to promote long-term corporate reform. Improvements in financial disclosure and audit standards, corporate governance practices, exposure limits and limits on related-party lending or cross guarantees, and regulation of anti-competitive transactions among related parties can benefit short-term corporate restructuring as well as long-term corporate reform.

Korea-specific recommendations

It is possible to identify five initiatives likely to accelerate the operational restructuring of distressed corporations.[14]

1. Overhaul Korea's insolvency system to facilitate the timely rehabilitation of viable companies and the liquidation of non-viable ones. A host of evidence indicates (i) that out-of-court workout MOUs are an inadequate basis for the post-financial stabilization operational restructuring of distressed companies; and (ii) that greater reliance should be placed on court-supervised insolvency; but (iii) that the current insolvency framework is ponderous and dissuasive to companies seeking rehabilitation. For example, agreement on out-of-court debt/equity conversions is subject to delays due to differences between secured and unsecured creditors. Implementation of out-of-court debt/equity conversions is subject to delay by public shareholders seeking preferential treatment on equity restructurings. It is reported in the press that the FSS—in contravention of its duty to safeguard the soundness of Korea's financial sector—has been pressuring financial institutions reluctant to extend credits to distressed companies as promised in workout MOUs. Under-provisioned or unrealistic creditors are preventing the sale of workout companies or workout company assets, or the conveyance of workout company debt or equity to CRVs for management by turnaround professionals. Composition is too easy on debtors, while receivership/bankruptcy is too stringent. Court-supervised insolvency is too time consuming and uncertain to be useful for rehabilitating companies. Despite incremental reforms adopted since 1997, Korea's insolvency system is still unsuitable. Reluctance to use an unsuitable insolvency system has encouraged excessive reliance on inefficient out-of-court workouts and market interventions as an alternative to receivership.

To develop an insolvency system suitable for the timely turnaround of distressed but viable companies, the Ministry of Finance and Economy (MOFE) working with the Ministry of Justice should give serious consideration to the following:

- Unify current laws on composition (rehabilitation), reorganization (receivership), and bankruptcy (liquidation), and provide clear criteria for commencing each type of case or converting one type of case to another (e.g, from reorganization or receivership to bankruptcy);
- Allow current management—so long as there is no evidence of fraud or gross incompetence—to remain in place in rehabilitation cases under

---

[14]It should also be noted that improved safety nets for laid off workers could provide important support for operational restructuring.

the close supervision of a court-appointed trustee and creditors' committee;

- In rehabilitation cases, give the debtor an exclusive right to file a rehabilitation plan within six months;
- Make trustees (receivers) more responsible to creditors and provide more institutional and professional support to trustees;
- Improve standards for the disclosure of business and financial information about the debtor company to all creditors;
- Adopt an "absolute priority rule" governing distributions of the insolvency estate among senior creditors, junior creditors, and shareholders and a "cram down" rule to make it possible to override dissident creditors or shareholders;
- With improved disclosure standards and an absolute priority rule as prerequisites, adopt procedures to allow court approval of "pre-packaged reorganizations" on an expedited basis, for example, within 45 days;[15]
- Provide for an automatic stay on creditors upon the commencement of insolvency proceedings; and
- Give additional priority to new financing for a company under rehabilitation or receivership.

The emphasis should be on preserving and rehabilitating viable companies. In cases where company managers have engaged in preferential transfers, made fraudulent conveyances, bounced checks, or committed other misdeeds, it should be possible to reverse misdeeds and punish those responsible after the imposition of an automatic stay.

Relatively few large corporations have emerged from court-supervised reorganization or been sold or liquidated since 1997. In pending cases, including new court-supervised cases from among the November 2000 list of 52, reorganizations and liquidations should be implemented as quickly as possible.

2. The Financial Supervisory Service (FSS) should (i) provide guidelines for the latest round of credit risk assessments; (ii) monitor the use of these guidelines to ensure that non-viable companies and companies in need of operational restructuring are identified; and (iii) follow up to ensure that liquidation or restructuring promptly commences, preferably under improved court-supervised insolvency procedures. Guidelines should consider current and projected profitability, interest coverage, and financing needs under more-

---

[15]In cases where a pre-packaged reorganization could be approved within 45 days, it might not be necessary for creditors to classify the debtor company's loans as sub-standard and reserve 20-50 percent of the loan amount.

and less-favorable economic conditions, and provide breakouts by business segment for multi-division corporations. There should be some penalty, such as more stringent on-site reviews, for a bank's failure to use these guidelines or to identify emerging corporate distress. The FSS may protest that it should be the responsibility of the banks to do a professional job of conducting credit risk assessments. The record of Korean banks in identifying and responding to emerging corporate distress, however, is not reassuring.[16] The goals now should be to improve the quality of the August 2001 credit risk assessments and to avoid additional surprises.

3. In the interests of concluding some significant "operational restructuring transactions" of workout corporations, the FSS should work to eliminate over-valuation of assets (corporate credits and converted equity) held by financial institutions. Operational restructuring transactions could include sales of workout companies to strategic or financial investors, sales of non-core businesses or assets of workout companies, or conveyance of workout company debt and/or equity for management by a CRV. Such operational restructuring transactions are needed to create some momentum and move corporate assets into higher and better use. Such transactions could require creditors to recognize losses on over-valued corporate credits or converted equity. Recent discussions indicate that financial institutions may classify the same debt differently, and may provision differently for debt with the same classification. Financial institutions may also differ in how they account for converted equity, with some using a lower-of-cost-or-market rule and others applying more conservative principles to essentially illiquid shares. By investigating discrepancies among financial institutions in how they classify and provision for restructured corporate debt and account for converted corporate equity, and by encouraging less-conservative financial institutions to adopt more conservative practices, the FSS could help create favorable conditions for "operational restructuring transactions." At this point, four years into the crisis and having seen such a macroeconomic rebound in 1999, the time for extended price negotiations and holding out for full recovery on credits or asset purchase prices is past. In those cases where state-controlled financial institutions represent a majority on the workout company's creditor committee, it would seem reasonable for the MOFE to act as a principal in encouraging state-controlled financial institutions to conclude some operational restructuring transactions over the next few months.

---

[16]Notable lapses include Daewoo's developing problems in 1998-1999; Saehan's unanticipated bankruptcy/emergency workout in May 2000; emerging problems at some Hyundai companies during 2000; and under-whelming results from the October 2000 credit risk assessments.

4. Government agencies should not protect controlling shareholders from loss. It is important to distinguish between the distressed company and its management and controlling shareholders. Reasonable steps to preserve the distressed-but-viable company are appropriate. But government agencies can take no action to protect the insiders in any large corporation from loss without negating the lesson from Daewoo that no chaebol is "too big to fail" and giving rise to long-lived moral hazard.

5. *While working through remaining pockets of corporate distress, the government should continue to promote measures that encourage general corporate reform and a shift in corporate emphasis from low-return debt-financed expansion toward greater profitability and financial resilience.* Key measures to promote general corporate reform include improvements in financial disclosure and accounting standards; stronger shareholder rights and enhanced corporate governance standards; and liberalization of rules on M&A and foreign direct investment. Key measures to encourage better financial management at large Korean corporations include loan exposure limits, limits on cross-shareholdings, limits on financing by related non-bank financial institutions, controls on cross guarantees, limited interest expense deductibility on "excessive" debt, and enforcement of Fair Trade Commission fines for unfair business practices. Limits on cross-guarantees and cross-shareholdings may be considered somewhat unusual for a market economy. The current need for such limits reflects the weakness of Korea's financial sector vis-à-vis the chaebols. A privatized and revitalized financial sector should be able to stand up to the chaebol on its own.

7 The Role of Corporate Bond Markets in the Korean Financial Restructuring Process

*Gyutaeg Oh and Changyong Rhee**

It was hardly expected that the initial impact of the Asian financial crisis on the Korean economy would be so severe as to throw the booming economy into a tailspin in such a short period of time. Korea's GDP growth plummeted from the pre-crisis average level of 7 percent in the last twenty years to a negative 6.7 percent in 1998. The recovery process has been no less drastic than the initial free-fall: GDP growth in 1999 and 2000 reached remarkable levels of 10.7 and 8 percent, respectively.

After the short-lived recovery, however, the Korean economy once again headed toward recession and growth in 2001 is expected to be less than 4 percent. Many factors have contributed to such a roller-coaster adjustment process in Korea. This paper focuses on the role of corporate bond markets to illustrate that the flow of funds between the banking sector and the capital market was one of the key factors that determined the post-crisis adjustment process in Korea. There are two government policies that have contributed to the shift of the flow of funds. One is the bank-focused financial restructuring policy and the other is the fluctuation of interest rates that rose to a historical high level and then started falling to single digits from mid-1998.

From the onset of the crisis until mid-1999 when the Daewoo group—the then third largest chaebol—went bankrupt, funds moved from the banking sector to the capital market, especially corporate bond markets. This movement was triggered by the financial restructuring policy, mainly involving banks and merchant banking companies (MBCs). Funds left banks, partly because of increased uncertainty about which banks would survive, and partly

*The authors are grateful to Robert Barro, David Coe, Won-Dong Cho, Se-Jik Kim, Simon Johnson, and other participants for valuable comments. Jongmin Kim provided excellent research assistance.

because banks could not compete with the interest rates offered by investment trust companies (ITCs).

The sharp reduction of market interest rates starting in mid-1998 strengthened the shift of funds. The downward trend of interest rates provided large capital gains to the ITCs, allowing them to offer interest rates higher than the market rates. More investors relocated their money from the banks to the ITCs. This process became a self-fulfilling virtuous cycle in the financial markets: money kept flowing from the banking sector to the ITCs; the ITCs could offer higher rates as the interest stabilized; the interest rates could be stabilized because companies could avoid liquidity problem by issuing corporate bonds. In this way, the corporate bond markets contributed to the prompt recovery of the Korean economy after the crisis.

Unfortunately, the mechanism that produced the virtuous cycle had a critical inherent weakness in that it significantly reduced the chaebol's incentive to restructure. Some chaebol, especially Daewoo, kept on pursuing expansionary strategies financed by bond issues. When the Daewoo group collapsed in July 1999, the mechanism that produced the virtuous cycle broke down completely, posing new challenges to the Korean economy. As a large proportion of corporate bonds issued in 1998 became insolvent, the ITCs failed to deliver the guaranteed rates of return to investors and thus lost their confidence. The direction of financial flows since the collapse of the Daewoo group turned exactly the opposite of what had happened before the Daewoo crisis. The flow of funds shifted from the ITCs to the banking sector, and even to the postal savings institutions.

Banks, thinly capitalized and limited by the BIS capital adequacy standard, still could not extend loans to corporations. Instead of lending to corporations, banks invested in government securities without worrying about their BIS capital ratio. Other investors began to recognize the credit risks associated with corporate bonds and put their money into high-quality bonds. This led to a flight-to-quality with interest rates on risk-free or good-quality bonds dropping significantly. Because of the recent flight-to-quality, companies that avoided the credit crunch three years ago by issuing corporate bonds found it difficult to roll over maturing bonds.

In response to these difficulties, the government intervened in the corporate bond markets in late 2000 with two policies. The first policy was securitization. Securitization reallocates credit risks by slicing cash flows into senior and junior tranches. As long as the government can help place the junior tranches with high credit risks, new credit crunch can be avoided because senior tranches are easily placed to investors despite the flight-to-quality. The second policy was "An Emergency Measure for Swift Underwriting of Corporate Bonds," introduced in December 2000 through the Korea Development Bank. This measure can be regarded as a tool to implement a private workout for troubled conglomerates before they default on corporate bonds.

At this point, it is not easy to evaluate the merits and demerits of the bank-focused financial restructuring policy. Had the government attempted to restructure the banks, the ITCs, and corporations all at once, the economic contraction in 1998 would have been more severe, causing greater economic distress and social unrest. Nevertheless, in retrospect, it can be argued that the bank-focused restructuring policy has produced significant negative side effects. Because the government allowed corporations to issue bonds through the ITCs, the bank-focused restructuring policy unintentionally helped nonviable firms and increased the ultimate costs of financial restructuring to taxpayers.

The purpose of this paper is to quantify the downside of the bank-focused financial restructuring policy by estimating the amount of defaulted corporate bonds that were issued between 1998 and 1999. Our analysis of the corporate bond markets and their default history during the crisis period finds that 22 percent of the total value of corporate bonds issued from December 1997 to December 1999 defaulted during the same period. Of these defaulted bonds, 78 percent were from companies affiliated with the Daewoo group. This demonstrates that the problems of corporate restructuring do not go away just because corporations solve short-run liquidity problems by issuing bonds.

This paper is organized as follows. The next section documents the changes in the flow of funds and developments in corporate bond markets after crisis. We then estimate the amount of defaulted corporate bonds issued between 1998 and 1999. The following section reviews how the government intervened in the corporate bond markets after the Daewoo crisis. We conclude with the policy lessons from our analysis.

The Patterns in the Flow of Funds and the Development of Corporate Bond Markets after Crisis

From the onset of the crisis until the collapse of Daewoo in July 1999, the flow of funds shifted from the banking sector to non-banking institutions, particularly to investment trust companies (ITCs). This pattern was reversed after the Daewoo group collapsed, with the flow of funds shifting back to the banks from the ITCs.

Figure 1. Changes in Deposits between Banks and Other Financial Institutions
(In percent)

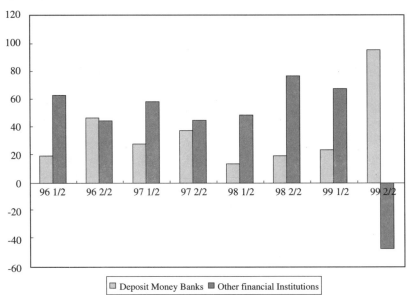

Source: The Bank of Korea, *Monthly Bulletin*, various issues.
Notes: Deposit Money Banks include Commercial Banks and Specialized Banks. Other Financial Institutions include Development Institutions, Savings Institutions, Investment Institutions, Securities Institutions and Public Financial Institutions. Remains of Total Financial Institutions are The Bank of Korea and Insurance Institutions.

The changing direction in the flow of funds is clearly presented in Figure 1.[1] The bars in Figure 1 represent the proportion of the changes in deposits of each institution to the total change in deposits.[2] Since the majority of the deposits in other financial institutions are held by both the ITCs and banks' trust accounts, changes in deposits between deposit money banks and other financial institutions in Figure 1 can be interpreted as a transfer between the banking sector and the ITCs. The share of deposits going to the banking sector, which was about 40 percent in the second half of 1997, dropped to 20 percent in 1998. On the other hand, the share going to the ITCs leaped from 50 percent to 80 percent during the same period. Even though the flow of funds shifted

---

[1] Since the Bank of Korea and insurance institutions are not included in the definition of deposit money banks and other financial institutions in Figure 1, the sum of the shares of the deposit money banks and other financial institutions is not 100 percent.

[2] Deposit money banks refer to commercial and specialized banks, while other financial institutions include development institutions, savings institutions, investment institutions (including banks' trust accounts), securities institutions and public financial institutions.

Figure 2. Corporate Bonds Issued by Credit Ratings
(Billions of Korean won)

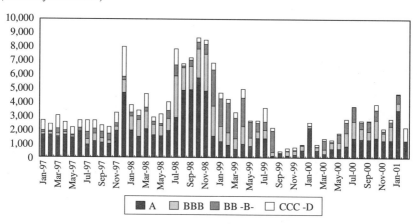

Source: Korea Fixed Income Research Institute database.

from the banking sector to the ITCs, there were no net withdrawals from the banking sector since the ITCs deposited funds back into the banks, and hence the share of deposits going to the banks remained positive prior to the Daewoo crisis. By contrast, share going to the ITCs became negative as the funds shifted from the ITCs to the banking sector in the second half of 1999.

The rise and fall of the corporate bond market is presented in Figure 2. The monthly average amount of corporate bonds issued was less than 3 trillion won prior to the crisis. But it increased to 7 trillion won in the second half of 1998. Only after the government placed a limit on the amount of bonds that chaebol could issue on October 28, 1998, did the amount of corporate bonds issued start to decline. Figure 2 also shows clearly how hard the corporate bond market was hit by the collapse of the Daewoo group in July 1999. After the Daewoo crisis, the amount of corporate bonds issued was almost negligible, as investors became very sensitive to corporate credit risk.

Figure 3 shows the concentration of the maturity structure of corporate bonds. Since the majority of corporate bonds in Korea have a maturity of three years, most corporate bonds issued in 1998 fell due in 2001. More than 65 trillion won worth of corporate bonds, which is about 16 percent of corporate bonds outstanding, will mature in 2001, of which 25 trillion have a credit rating of BBB or lower.

Figure 4 demonstrates how the Daewoo group, which was on the verge of collapse, extended its life by issuing corporate bonds through the ITCs. The Daewoo group issued a minimum of 1 trillion won worth of corporate bonds

Figure 3. The Amount of Corporate Bonds Matured
(Trillions of Korean won)

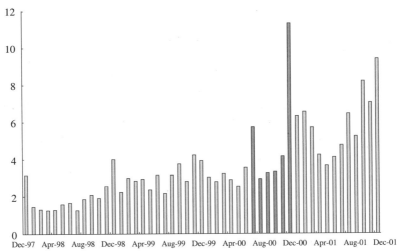

Source: Korea Fixed Income Research Institute database.

Figure 4. Daewoo Group Bonds
(Billions of Korean won)

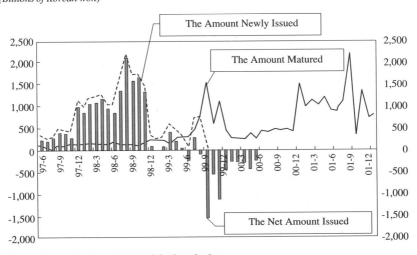

Source: Korea Fixed Income Research Institute database.

during each month of 1998. As a result of this bond binge, the Daewoo group would have had to refinance an average of over 1.5 trillion won each month during 2001, were it still alive. It is also worth noting that the net issuance of bonds became nil as early as in the beginning of 1999. In other words, the Daewoo group already had difficulties in redeeming its matured bonds in the market eight months prior to its bankruptcy. Though not reported, the maturity concentration problem was not limited to the Daewoo group.

Empirical Analysis of Defaulted Corporate Bonds

The bank-focused restructuring policy unintentionally helped nonviable firms to extend their life and increased the ultimate cost of financial restructuring. In this section, we quantify the downside of the bank-focused financial restructuring policy by estimating the amount of defaulted corporate bonds that were issued after the crisis began.

We collected the necessary information for companies that issued corporate bonds from December 1997 to October 2000 and analyzed the characteristics of the corporate bonds that were defaulted during the same period. Our data come primarily from the Korea Fixed Income Research Institute (KFIRI) and contain information on issuer identity, issuance date, maturity, amount issued, yield to maturity, credit ratings, and the existence of guarantee.

Information on default was gathered from various sources, including the Bank of Korea, the Banking Supervisory Authority, the Financial Supervisory Service, and the Korea Securities Computer Corporation. We classified default into seven categories following the definition of the Financial Supervisory Service: bankruptcy, bankruptcy mediation, court receivership, court mediation, workout, private mediation, and estimated loss.

Table 1 presents information on the types and timing of default. Default 2 companies differ from Default 1 companies in that the former still possesses the possibility of resuscitation. During the three-year period from December 1997 to October 2000, a total of 855 companies issued corporate bonds. Of these, 115 companies became insolvent by October 2000, with 40 percent classified as Default 1 and the bulk of the rest as workout cases. If we compare the ratio of each category by the number of bonds or the amount of bonds issued instead of the number of issuing companies, the proportion of workouts increases significantly, whereas the proportion of Default 1 cases decreases. This implies that the workout companies tended to be large. Default was concentrated in 1998. Six companies issued bonds in December 1997 and defaulted in the same month.

Table 2 shows the number of companies that issued corporate bonds and the amount of bonds issued as well as the number of companies that defaulted and the amount of bonds defaulted. From December 1997 to October 2000,

Table 1. Types and Timing of Defaults

December 1997 to October 2000

		Type	Number of Companies	Ratio	Number Of Bonds	Ratio	Amount Issued[1]	Ratio
Defaulted Company	Default 1	Bankruptcy	13	11.30%	17	2.87%	728	0.29%
		Bankruptcy/Mediation	13	11.30%	28	4.73%	1,540	0.61%
		Court Receivership	20	17.39%	52	8.78%	19,246	7.67%
		Sum	46	40.00%	97	16.39%	21,514	8.57%
	Default 2	Court Mediation	4	3.48%	9	1.52%	600	0.24%
		Work Out	63	54.78%	461	77.87%	218,157	86.94%
		Private Mediation	1	0.87%	6	1.01%	1,227	0.49%
		Estimated Loss	1	0.87%	19	3.21%	9,438	3.76%
		Total Sum	115	100.00%	592	100.00%	250,935	100.00%

Number of Companies

Year	Dec-97	1998	1999	2000	N/A	Total
Bankruptcy	1	7	2	3		13
Bankruptcy/Mediation	3	6	4			13
Court Receivership	2	10	6	2		20
Sum	6	23	12	5	-	46
Court Mediation		2		2		4
Work Out		46	13	2	2	63
Private Mediation		1				1
Estimated Loss					1	1
Total Sum	6	72	25	9	3	115

Source: Korea Fixed Income Research Institute database.

[1]Amount issued is in 100 million won.

855 companies issued 3,622 corporate bonds that were worth 127 trillion won.[3] The rapid decline in bond issuance after 1999 shows the drastic effect of the Daewoo crisis on corporate bond markets. During the three years after December 1997, 115 companies out of the companies that issued corporate bonds became insolvent. On average, 22 percent of the total value of the corporate bonds issued from December 1997 to December 1999 defaulted during the same period. Such a high rate of default demonstrates that the ITCs took credit risk with little discipline.

---

[3]Since defaulting companies could issue new corporate bonds, the sum of the number of companies that issued corporate bonds in Table 2 is greater than 855 in the text. Table 2 also excludes asset-backed securities.

Table 2. Proportion of Defaulted Corporate Bonds

Period	97. 12−98. 12			99. 1−99. 12			2000. 1−2000. 10		
Corporate Bond	Number of Issuers	Defaulted Companies	Ratio	Number of Issuers	Defaulted Companies	Ratio	Number of Issuers	Defaulted Companies	Ratio
	571	93	16.29%	517	53	10.25%	295	33	11.19%
	Amount Issued	Defaulted Amount	Ratio	Amount Issued	Defaulted Amount	Ratio	Amount Issued	Defaulted Amount	Ratio
	706,444	192,912	27.31%	325,410	50,510	15.52%	237,125	7,453	3.14%
Financial Bond	Number of Issuers	Defaulted Companies	Ratio	Number of Issuers	Defaulted Companies	Ratio	Number of Issuers	Defaulted Companies	Ratio
	121	35	28.93%	49	11	22.45%	32	4	12.50%
	Amount Issued	Defaulted Amount	Ratio	Amount Issued	Defaulted Amount	Ratio	Amount Issued	Defaulted Amount	Ratio
	411,790	28,443	6.91%	414,431	19,700	4.75%	415,961	1,653	0.40%

Source: Korea Fixed Income Research Institute Data Base.
Note: Excluding ABS. Amounts issued and defaulted are in 100 million won.

Table 3. Defaults by Credit Ratings

Amount Issued (*In 100 million won*)

Credit Rate	Over A-	BBB+ to BBB-	BB+ to B-	CCC+ to C-	D	N/A	Sum	Ratio
1997	-	50	100	200	230	91	671	0.40%
1998	-	-	5,414	6,370	1,616	5,102	18,502	10.97%
1999	84,803	30,615	19,576	311	-	440	135,745	80.47%
2000	-	-	4,270	-	-	50	4,320	2.56%
N/A	-	5,700	3,738	-	-	14	9,452	5.60%
Sum	84,803	36,365	33,097	6,881	1,846	5,697	168,689	100.00%
Ratio	50.27%	21.56%	19.62%	4.08%	1.09%	3.38%	100.00%	

Number of Companies

Credit Rate	Over A-	BBB+ to BBB-	BB+ to B-	CCC+ to C-	D	N/A	Sum	Ratio
1997	-	1	1	1	2	1	6	6.45%
1998	-	-	15	9	1	23	48	51.61%
1999	7	6	10	2	-	2	27	29.03%
2000	-	-	6	-	-	1	7	7.53%
N/A	-	1	3	-	-	1	5	5.38%
Sum	84,803	36,365	33,097	6,881	1,846	5,697	168,689	100.00%
Ratio	7.53%	8.60%	37.63%	12.90%	3.23%	30.11%	100.00%	

Table 3 examines the defaults by credit ratings at the date of issuance. In terms of the amount of bonds issued, about 72 percent of the defaulted bonds were qualified as investment grade bonds with credit ratings over BBB- on the date of issuance.[4] However, this does not necessarily mean that companies with higher credit ratings had a greater likelihood of default during the sample period. The lower half of Table 3 shows the proportion of default in terms of the number of issuing companies rather than the amount of bonds issued. It shows that the proportion of defaulted bonds with credit ratings over BBB- is only 16 percent. The comparison indicates that companies with higher credit ratings tend to issue corporate bonds on a larger scale. Of the 15 companies with credit ratings over BBB- that became insolvent, 14, amazingly enough, were affiliated with the Daewoo group. After the financial crisis erupted, the Daewoo group was responsible for an overwhelming portion of the corporate bonds issued in terms of number and scale. This happened because both credit rating agencies and investors blindly awarded chaebol-affiliated companies with top credit ratings based on Korea's faith in the "Too big to fail" hypothesis.

The influence of the Daewoo crisis on the corporate bond market can be clearly seen in Figure 5. In Korea, small- and medium-sized enterprises are usually unable to issue corporate bonds in the market. They rely on commercial bills as an important financing channel. Therefore, by comparing the number of companies that defaulted with the default rates of commercial bills, we can distinguish the different default histories of large corporations and small enterprises during the sample period. Such a comparison indicates that small- and medium-sized enterprises were hit very hard twice: immediately after the financial crisis in December 1997 and again after the Daewoo crisis in July 1999. But the number of companies who defaulted was relatively evenly dispersed in the second half of 1998 and the period shortly after the Daewoo crisis. However, if we draw the figure again in the lower part of Figure 5 in terms of the amount of bonds instead of the number of companies, we can see that most of the defaulted bonds are concentrated at the time of the Daewoo crisis.

Table 4 shows the reason for this. Of the 25 companies that issued the most defaulted corporate bonds from December 1997 to October 2000, eight companies in terms of the number of defaults and nine companies in terms of the amount belonged to the Daewoo group. The scale of default by the Daewoo group was incomparably larger than that of the other companies listed: not only did the Daewoo group account for 34 percent of the total number of corporate bonds defaulted, they were also responsible for 19.6 trillion won, or 78 percent, of the total value of defaulted bonds. Since the Daewoo group

---

[4]Table 3 does not include guaranteed bonds; including them produces similar results.

Figure 5. Number of Defaulted Companies and the Amount of Defaulted Bonds

Number of Defaulted Companies and Commercial Bill Default Rate

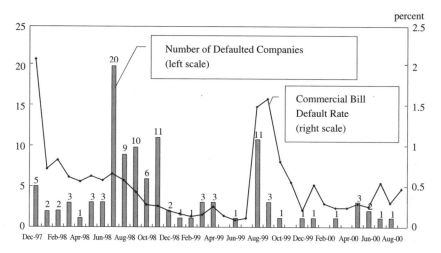

The Amount of Defaulted Bonds and Yield to Maturity

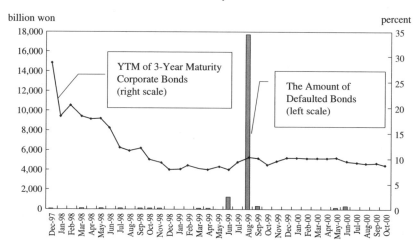

dominated the default list, it is not surprising to see a huge spike in Figure 5 during August 1999.

Blame for the Daewoo group being able to issue such a large amount of corporate bonds should be placed on individual investors and credit rating agencies, as well as on the government.[5] All of them seemed to have believed

---

[5]Oh and Rhee (2001) discuss credit rating migration in Korea after the financial crisis.

Table 4. Top 25 Companies with Defaulted Bonds

Ranking	Firm	Number of defaults	Ranking	Firm	Value (billion won)
1	Daewoo	55	1	Daewoo	9,507.3
2	Shin Ho Paper Mfg	40	2	Daewoo Motors	2,965.0
3	Daewoo Motors	33	3	Daewoo Heavy Industries & Machinery	2,340.0
4	Daewoo Heavy Industries & Machinery	29	4	Daewoo Electronics	1,930.0
5	Jindo	25	5	Renault Samsung Motors	1,300.0
6	Daewoo Electronics	22	6	Daewoo Securities	943.8
7	Shinwon	21	7	Daewoo Telecom	910.2
8	Kohap Corp	20	8	Orion	555.0
9	Daewoo Securities	19	9	Kohap Corp	417.8
10	Daewoo Telecom	18	10	Jindo	354.9
11	Byucksan Construction	12	11	Seahan Group	295.0
12	Orion	11	12	Shinwon	294.1
13	Dong-Ah Construction Industrial	10	13	Shin Ho Paper Mfg	285.4
14	Renault Samsung Motors	10	14	Daewoo Motors Sales Corp	254.0
15	Seahan Group	10	15	Kabool Textiles	175.6
16	Kangwon	8	16	Saehan Media	160.0
17	Shinhan22	8	17	Segye Corporation	160.0
18	ChoongNam Sponning	8	18	Ssangyong Engineering & Construction	122.7
19	Kabool Textiles	7	19	Kangwon	121.6
20	Daewoo Kumsok	7	20	Kabool	120.5
21	Samil Paper Corporation	7	21	Dong-Ah Construction Industrial	112.5
22	Seahan Media	7	22	Daehan Joongsuk	100.0
23	Shinho	7	23	Keangnam Enterprises	98.5
24	Keangnam Enterprises	6	24	Shinhan	98.0
25	Tongkook Corporation	6	25	Tongkook Corporation	86.5
	Total Sum	590		Total Sum	25,087.5

Note: The firms belonging to the Daewoo group are shaded above.

that the chaebol would never go bankrupt. They discounted any possibility of a default by Daewoo. Investors' ignorance of the corporate credit risk is evident in Figure 6, which compares the yield to maturity of bonds issued by the Daewoo group with the market interest rate. For the market interest rate, we

Figure 6. The Yield to Maturity of Defaulted Bonds Issued by the Daewoo Group
(In percent)

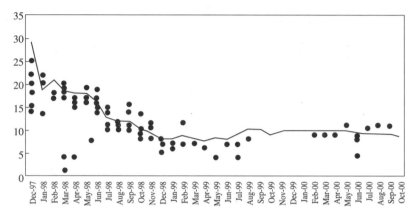

Notes: Dots in the figures indicate the yield to maturity of defaulted bonds at the time of issuance.
The line indicates the yield to maturity of three-year corporate bonds with A+ credit ratings.

used the representative yield to maturity of three-year corporate bonds that possessed A+ credit ratings. The dots in Figure 6 represent the yield to maturity of defaulted bonds on the date of issuance. As can be seen from Figure 6, there was not much difference between the interest rate paid by the Daewoo group and the market interest rate during the sample period. The Daewoo group did not have to offer a higher interest rate than the market rate in order to issue large amounts of corporate bonds.

This finding alone does not mean that the adverse selection problem was due to the high interest rate policy. The high interest rate policy implemented by the IMF immediately after the crisis was harshly criticized. One of the arguments against it was the possible adverse selection problem: a high interest rate policy crowds out healthy companies in the capital market since only the companies with a high risk of default would be willing to pay higher interest rates to raise urgently needed capital. Figure 6 indicates that defaulting companies did not pay higher interest rates than healthy companies. In Korea, this may have occurred due to the lack of reliable credit rating agencies and investors' ignorance of credit risk.

Figure 7 shows that the chaebol also got special treatment in terms of the speed with which their credit ratings were downgraded. The horizontal axis indicates the date when the corporations went bankrupt, while the vertical axis refers to the amount of time it took for a company to declare bankruptcy after its credit rating was downgraded to BB or below. Take, for example, the Tongil Heavy Industry, which is shown in the middle of the figure. Tongil Heavy

Figure 7. Duration between the Downgrading of Credit Ratings and the Default

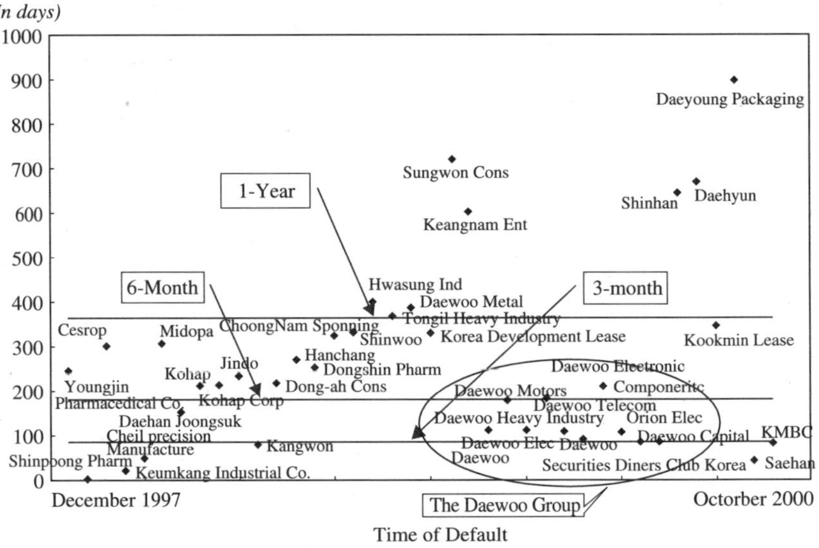

(In days)

Source: Korea Fixed Income Research Institute database.

Industry became insolvent in January 1999, one year after the company's credit rating was downgraded to BB. Except for the Daewoo affiliated companies, most of other companies took at least six months to be declared bankrupt after their credit ratings were downgraded. The Daewoo companies, however, went bankrupt within less than three months after their credit ratings were downgraded. In other words, the credit rating agencies delayed downgrading big companies such as Daewoo until the situation became hopeless. This suggests that not only was the amount of bonds issued a problem, but the speed with which downgrading was declared also made it difficult for investors to respond to Daewoo's default.

Issues in Corporate Bond Markets after the Daewoo Crisis

After the Daewoo crisis, there was a flight-to-quality in the Korean corporate bond market. Once the flight-to-quality began, it became serious due to various institutional constraints. First of all, even though the flow of funds shifted from the ITCs to the banking sector, banks were unable to extend loans to corporations because they were so thinly capitalized. Under the BIS capital requirement, banks preferred to invest in safe government securities.

Secondly, although the mark-to-market accounting practice has been required, the ITCs could not persuade either institutional or individual investors that they could manage credit risks better than the investors could. Furthermore, the ITCs could not clean their non-performing bonds completely, which hindered restoration of investors' confidence in the ITCs. It became quite common for the ITCs, when they launched new bond funds, to promise to invest only in corporate bonds whose ratings were above BBB. As a result, the ITCs, which used to be major purchasers of corporate bonds, merely played a tangential role in corporate bond markets.

Thirdly, other institutional investors, such as public pension funds and insurance companies, typically have investment guidelines that prohibit them from investing in corporate bonds whose credit ratings are below A-. This guideline made sense before the crisis when most corporations had credit ratings above A-. However, after the crisis, credit rating agencies tightened their rating standards and only a few companies maintained a credit rating above BBB. Despite the change in the distribution of credit ratings, the investment guidelines of pension funds and insurance companies remained intact. Hence institutional investors could not funnel their money into corporate bonds whose current ratings were below A- even though they were the same bonds they actively invested in prior to the crisis.

These institutional constraints created a mismatch in the corporate bond market. Most individual and institutional investors wanted to invest in good quality bonds with ratings above BBB. But the number of companies with credit ratings above BBB was very small, and even those companies did not want to issue bonds because they needed to keep their debt-equity ratio below 2-to-1 to meet the government guideline for identifying financially distressed firms. Other companies with credit ratings of BBB or below wanted to issue bonds to roll over their maturing debts. However, few investors wanted to buy them. Even relatively healthy companies whose credit ratings were BBB or below faced difficulty in issuing bonds.

The mismatch in the corporate bond market explains why the asset-backed securities (ABS) markets took off so rapidly in Korea after the crisis (most ABS in Korea are treated as corporate bonds because corporations are usually used as a special-purpose vehicle in the structure).[6] The Korean government laid the legal foundations in October 1998 with the "Asset Securitization Act." The original purpose of the law was to help Korea Asset Management Corpo-

---

[6] In advanced countries, structured financing methods have been developed over long periods of time as financial markets developed. However, in Korea, structured financing methods took off less than two years after they were enacted. See Rosenthal and Ocampo, 1988, and Lederman, 1990.

ration (KAMCO), the Korean equivalent of the Resolution Trust Corporation in the United States, liquidate non-performing loans that were acquired from troubled banks. But, after the Daewoo crisis, it was the ITCs that heavily securitized non-performing bonds to meet their redemption requirement. As a result, collateralized bond obligations (CBO), whose underlying pools were mainly composed of low-quality bonds that the ITCs held, were issued in large volumes.

As shown in Figure 8, the proportion of ABS in the corporate bond market increased rapidly, and accounted for over 60 percent of total corporate bond issuance in 2000. The ABS market developed quickly in Korea because good-quality bonds were in short supply. Adopting the ABS structure, companies and financial institutions were able to issue senior bonds with good credit ratings (usually above A grade). The junior bonds that are difficult to place are usually held by the originators. Thus, after the Daewoo crisis, the traditional corporate bond market shrank rapidly, while ABS senior bonds started filling investors' demand for good-quality bonds.

In addition to being used as a liquidating tool for non-performing bonds, since the middle of 2000, the ABS scheme has been adopted to facilitate the funding needs of companies that have problems issuing bonds because of poor credit ratings. In the "Primary CBO" scheme, securities companies underwrite bonds and then securitize them immediately. In the "Primary CLO (collateralized loan obligations)" scheme, banks make loans and then securitize them immediately. In either, it is not difficult to find investors who want to buy senior bonds even when the flight-to-quality phenomenon plagues the bond

Figure 8. The Growth of the ABS Market
(In trillion won)

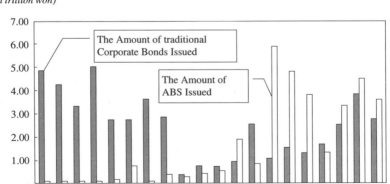

Source: Korea Fixed Income Research Institute database.

markets. As long as junior bonds can be placed, securitization can be used as a powerful tool to overcome institutional constraints that cause the flight-to-quality. After a few securitization deals were tried on a private basis (without the aid of government), however, it became apparent that deals could not continue because it was difficult to find investors for junior bonds.

Government Intervention in the ABS Markets

The government would not have intervened in the corporate bond market if there were enough speculators investing in junior bonds. Unfortunately, under the current institutional settings in Korea, speculators are rare. Unlike the United States, hedge funds are not allowed. Managers of mutual funds or investment trusts have little incentive to take on risk because their fees are not directly tied to their performance. Hence, the government felt obliged to intervene in the corporate bond market in the face of a severe new credit crunch. The ABS schemes turned out to be effective, because the markets were able to place the senior bonds once the government took care of the placement of junior bonds.

One way the government handled junior bonds was to buy them through a government agency. Figure 9 presents an example of a CBO deal done by the

Figure 9. The Structure of CBO

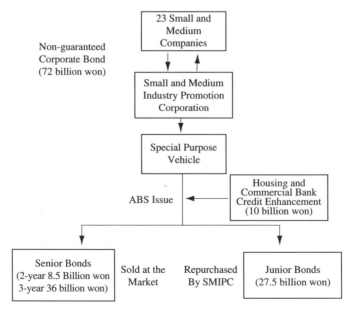

Small and Medium Industry Promotion Corporation (SMIPC). The SMIPC undertook 72 billion won worth of corporate bonds (without guarantee) issued by 23 small- and medium-sized enterprises. The Housing and Commercial Bank provided credit support in the form of liquidity facilities. Using a special-purpose company, the SMIPC created two tranches of asset-backed securities: 44.5 billion won of senior bonds and 27.5 billion won of junior bonds. The junior bonds are not entitled to receive principal payments until the entire principal of the senior bonds has been paid off. The SMIPC was able to sell the low-risk senior bonds to private investors but had to hold the high-risk junior bonds. Through securitization, the SMIPC could provide a total of 72 billion won to the small- and medium-sized enterprises by spending only 27.5 billion won. This demonstrates the effectiveness of the CBO scheme in mitigating the credit crunch.

A second way the government intervened was by providing credit enhancement via the Korea Credit Guarantee Fund and the Korea Technology Credit Guarantee Fund (both of which are public funds in Korea). Considering the low quality of underlying assets, the proportion of junior bonds to the total asset pool should be quite large by U.S. standards. Therefore, in order to reduce the proportion of junior bonds and enhance the funding efficiency of the ABS scheme, the government provided large credit support through Guarantees. As a result, junior bonds were reduced to less than five percent of the total pool asset. Under this scheme, senior bonds (95 percent of the pool asset) were sold to investors, whereas junior bonds were given back to companies that issued the bonds in the pool.

The third way the government intervened was by creating CBO funds through raising money from investors. A CBO fund in Korea has to meet an investment guideline of investing more than fifty percent of its raised money in junior bonds. To compensate for the credit risks involved, the government provided the fund with tax relief on interest income or privilege to get allocation of oversubscribed IPO (initial public offering) stocks listed on the KOSDAQ market. The creation of such funds increased the demand for junior bonds.

These government interventions were aimed at mitigating credit crunch problems and helping relatively healthy companies with credit rating of BBB or below issue bonds. However, they incurred unexpected social costs. From the middle of 2000, when stock prices started to decline sharply, the rates of return of CBO funds that invested heavily in KOSDAQ IPO stocks also fell dramatically. Due to the wrong sweeteners, investors' trust in CBO funds was dampened. Thus, in the first half of 2001 when most corporate bonds issued in 1998 were maturing, the CBO funds could not perform their vital role at all.

Another problem created by these interventions is that credit risks of corporations are now assumed by the government. If the selection of securities in CBO pools is not done carefully, the credit enhancement to CBO that was offered by the government funds becomes a taxpayer burden later on. Therefore, efforts should be made to minimize official credit support to CBO and to end the vicious circle of injecting taxpayers' money to temporarily mitigate pains from the credit crunch.

CLOs and Regulation Arbitrage

The issuance of collateralized loan obligations (CLO) is another example of an effective ABS scheme. CLO differs from CBO in that the underlying assets are bank loans rather than corporate bonds. Figure 10 shows a typical structure of a collateralized loan obligation. In Figure 10, a bank possesses 98.2 billion won of loans. In order to satisfy the BIS capital adequacy ratio, the bank must reserve 7.8 billion won, 8 percent of its total loans. But if the bank securitizes its loans by issuing a collateralized loan obligation, it can increase the amount of loanable funds greatly. For example, after transferring the loans to its trust account, the bank can issue two tranches of asset-backed bonds: 70 billion

Figure 10. The Structure of CLO

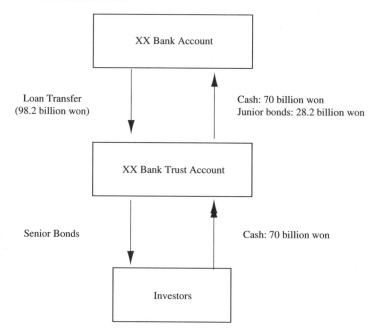

won of senior bonds and 28.2 billion won of junior bonds. The low-risk senior bonds are sold to private investors, while the high-risk junior bonds are taken back by the bank. After the securitization, the bank's holdings of risky assets drop from the initial 98.2 billion won to the 28.2 billion won of junior bonds. Therefore, instead of reserving 7.8 billion won, the bank now needs to reserve only 2.2 billion won.

Of course, the extra 5.6 billion won of loanable funds is the result of a kind of regulation arbitrage. If we consider the risk of junior bonds, the BIS capital adequacy ratio for junior bonds should be increased commensurately. However, according to the current BIS regulation, all corporate bonds, regardless of seniority, are assigned the same 8 percent rule—the source of the extra 5.6 billion won of loanable funds. If the current BIS regulation is a roadblock to overcoming current credit crunch, it may help relax the regulation indirectly by allowing the above regulation arbitrage for the time being.[7] On the other hand, the insufficient capital reserve for covering the credit risks of junior bond increases the possibility that bank insolvencies could reemerge. For the sake of long-run stability, new regulatory policies that can properly respond to CLO scheme should be developed.

Issues on "An Emergency Measure for Swift Underwriting of Corporate Bonds"

As discussed above, big conglomerates in Korea avoided liquidity problems right after the crisis in 1998 by issuing corporate bonds with three-year maturities. As they had to roll over the maturing bonds by issuing new ones, the corporate bond markets faced great uncertainty in 2001. Had the government not intervened in the corporate bond markets, the corporate yield might have skyrocketed in the beginning of 2001. The high yield would have created big losses to the bondholders who held other corporate bonds.

To stabilize the financial markets, the Korean government announced "An Emergency Measure for Swift Underwriting of Corporate Bonds" in December 2000. According to this measure, the Korea Development Bank (KDB) would buy two-year corporate bonds issued by troubled companies that have problems rolling over their debt during 2001. The candidate companies, which would be selected arbitrarily by the KDB, will issue two-year bonds with a face value of eighty percent of maturing debt, with the other twenty percent

---

[7]Another alternative (which has been implemented recently) is for the government to provide a guarantee to the CLO structure in the way similar to the CBO structure. Because of the guarantee, banks can extend new loanable funds without relying on regulation arbitrage. This helps especially when the flow of funds shifts back to banks that are thinly capitalized.

of maturing debt retired using the company's own money. The KDB would later pool the bonds and securitize the cash flows to the pool with credit support provided by a guarantee from the Credit Guarantee Fund. The securitization involves two tranches. A senior tranche that amounts to seventy percent of the pool would be sold to investors. A junior tranche that amounts to the remaining thirty percent would be assumed by both creditor banks of the candidate companies (twenty percent) and the KDB (ten percent).

Although the measure does not specify the candidate companies explicitly, it has actually been used as a tool to implement private workouts for troubled conglomerates orchestrated by the KDB. When troubled companies default on their corporate bonds, it is more difficult to restructure their debts than when they default on their bank loans because ownership structure of bonds is usually more diversely distributed than that of bank loans. Hence, the Emergency Measure tries to mitigate free-rider problems among creditors that may arise in the restructuring process of the troubled companies by replacing the existing corporate bonds with the new bonds assumed by one owner, the KDB. The KDB can initiate a private workout process for the troubled companies before the newly issued bonds mature in two years: either the KDB can arrange a debt-for-equity swap or it can force the troubled companies to restructure according to the pre-specified bond covenants.

Whether the Emergency Measure was the most effective way of stabilizing the financial markets around the end of 2000 is quite controversial. Certainly the government avoided another round of financial market breakdown similar to that caused by the Daewoo crisis. Since the problems of troubled companies were contained by the KDB, other companies were able to refinance their debt by issuing new corporate bonds, thus avoiding the negative externality that might have occurred if troubled big conglomerates had failed. In addition, the ITCs, or investors who put their money in the trusts run by the ITCs, who held a big chunk of troubled corporate bonds, were saved by the Emergency Measure.

The Emergency Measure, however, has several drawbacks. First of all, it is not clear which companies should be selected as candidate companies. When selection is made based on considerations other than economic feasibility of the private workout, social costs (the difference between liquidating value of a firm and the value of a firm as a going concern) associated with the Emergency Measure could be huge. Secondly, the Measure fosters moral hazard problems to investors. Because of the Measure, investors who purchased corporate bonds three years ago from troubled companies for high returns will not be penalized at all when the risks involved materialize. By contrast, investors in the Daewoo bonds redeemed 95 percent of the face value when the

Daewoo crisis occurred. It would be regretful if financial stability were bought in exchange for giving investors a wrong signal that the government will always rescue corporate bondholders. Thirdly, the KDB involvement in the process raises questions regarding whether such a measure violates WTO regulations on government subsidies.

Conclusion

The recurrent credit crunch problems in 2001 show that the problems of corporate restructuring do not go away just because corporations can solve liquidity problems through issuing corporate bonds. The crisis will be overcome only when the firms, properly restructured, become more efficient. In this respect, the bank-focused financial restructuring policy that was implemented in the beginning of the Korean financial crisis cannot get a high grade.

The bank-focused financial restructuring provided the wrong incentives to corporate restructuring. It indirectly allowed some chaebol to expand their businesses instead of restructuring by issuing large amounts of corporate bonds. As a result, the credit crunch problems recurred in the corporate bond markets. In retrospect, the Korean economy might have been better off if the government had restructured banks and the ITCs all at once. By benignly neglecting the ITCs, the government did mitigate the first credit crunch problem in the short run. But the long-run costs of putting the problems aside rather than promptly solving them were too big to justify the bank-focused restructuring policy. Our analysis of defaulted bonds demonstrates that, the negative side effects can overwhelm the good ones.

Another lesson for financial restructuring is that more emphasis should be placed on debt-for-equity swaps rather than debt-to-debt swaps in order to end the vicious circle of credit crunch problems. In the beginning of the financial crisis, when banks refused to extend loans, corporations had to pay back the loans by issuing bonds with higher interest rates. As the maturities of the bonds issued fall due, they have to issue new corporate bonds to roll over the previous ones. As a result of this debt-to-debt swap, the total amount of corporate debt remained virtually unchanged in Korea even though the debt-capital ratios have decreased during the past three years.[8]

The large amount of corporate debt is the main reason for high financial costs and low interest coverage ratios in the Korean corporate sector. No

---

[8]Jang (2000) discusses the changes in the amount of debt and the debt-capital ratios after the financial crisis.

matter how much taxpayers' money is injected in financial restructuring, the chance of another financial crisis is high if the total amount of corporate debt is not reduced. Hence, future financial restructuring policy should focus on inducing corporations to engage in debt-for-equity swaps instead of rolling over existing debts.[9]

The Korean experience also indicates the best way to develop corporate bond markets in a crisis-hit economy. One of the important sources of the Asian financial crisis was the heavy dependence on the banking system in financing corporate investment. As such, the need to develop capital markets as alternative financing sources has been increasingly emphasized in Asia.[10] The Korean experience shows that the ABS scheme can be an effective tool to develop corporate bond markets when a flight-to-quality creates mismatches in the demand and supply of corporate bonds.

The Korean experience also emphasizes the importance of regulatory infrastructures in developing corporate bond markets. Shortly after the crisis, the Korean corporate bond market took off with weak institutional foundations. For example, their rapid expansion owed much to the ITCs that were under loose regulatory supervision. But the boom was short lived. Once the side effects of the weak foundations started to materialize, corporate bond markets created bigger problems to policymakers.

For corporate bond markets to function properly in the long run, investors who are compensated for assuming credit risks should be responsible for the risk when the risk is materialized. Such simple principle, however, has not been observed in the Korean corporate bond markets. By redeeming the bonds defaulted by the Daewoo group, the Korean government subsidized wealthy investors (who blindly pursued high interest income) with the taxpayers' money. The Emergency Measure of putting the Korea Development Bank in action repeated the same mistake. It is important to end the vicious circle of injecting taxpayers' money to temporarily mitigate pains from credit crunch. Instead of trying to make risky bonds less risky by offering various credit supports, the government needs to develop junk bond markets where investors can pursue high-risk, high-return opportunities under their own responsibility.

---

[9]The issuance of CB (convertible bonds) and BW (bond warrants) and the conversion of bank loans to equity should be encouraged as examples of debt-for-equity swaps. It is also important to recognize that the ABS schemes can unintentionally provide wrong incentives for corporations to increase the amount of debt by effectively facilitating the securitization of their non-liquid debts.

[10]Giap (2001) and Yoshitomi and Shirai (2001) summarize the conceptual issues and policy recommendations in developing corporate bond markets in Asia.

References

Giap, T. K., 2001, "Policy Recommendations for Developing Corporate Bond Markets and Balanced Corporate Financing," mimeo (Tokyo: The Asian Policy Forum Report, The Asian Development Bank Institute).

Ingves, S. and D. He, 2000, "Facilitating Bank and Corporate Restructuring: The Role of Government," in C. Adams, E. Litan and M. Pomerleano eds., *Managing Financial and Corporate Distress: Lessons from Asia* (Washington D.C.: Brookings Institute Press).

Jang, Hasung, 2000, "Corporate Restructuring after the Financial Crisis in Korea," mimeo presented at a special conference of Korea Financial Economic Association, November (in Korean).

Kim, Yongtae and Youngsco Park, 1998, "Restructuring Vehicles: Function and Their Relationships," research report, Korea Securities Research Institute (in Korean).

Lederman, Jess, 1990, *The Handbook of Asset-Backed Securities* (New York: New York Institute of Finance).

Lee, Jongwha and Changyong Rhee, 2000, Chapter VII Concluding Evaluation, *Three Years after the IMF Program in Korea*, Korea Institute for International Economic Policy (in Korean).

Oh, Gyutaeg and Changyong Rhee, 2001, "Specialized Funds for Corporate Bonds with BBB Credit Ratings as a Measure to Mitigate Credit Crunch Problems," *Investment Trust*, January, The Korea Investment Trust Company Association (in Korean).

Rosenthal, J. A. and J. M. Ocampo, 1988, *Securitization of Credit: Inside the New Technology of Finance* (New York: John Wiley & Sons).

Yoshitomi, M. and S. Shirai, 2001, "An Analytical Framework for the Development of a Corporate Bond Market in Asia," mimeo (Tokyo: The Asian Development Bank Institute).

Comments on Papers 6 and 7

Simon Johnson

The Korean economic recovery of 1998-2000 raises a major puzzle. How did a country with such a troubled banking system manage to bounce back so fast? The sharp devaluation of the Korean won was clearly helpful in increasing exports. But in an economy like Korea's, it is hard—or perhaps impossible—for manufacturing firms to export without access to at least some credit. Firms need to buy inputs and pay labor in advance of sales. Who provided this essential funding, and on what terms, in the Korean case?

These two papers provide us with important insights into both the Korean recovery and much more general issues associated with financial intermediation during crises. Both are essential reading for anyone interested in helping firms recover or expand after a crisis.

Mako's paper considers Korea financial restructuring in general, while Oh and Rhee focus on the particularly important issue of corporate bonds. The papers are nicely complementary and reading them together makes clear at least three important facts.

- There was enormous pressure for both financial restructuring (i.e., reducing leverage) and operational restructuring (i.e., improving profitability) on the Korean chaebol business groups. Nevertheless, chaebol delayed their restructuring. It is certainly not the case that the Korean recovery was associated with rapid renegotiations of debts or smooth change in firm-level financial and operational arrangements.
- Many chaebol dealt with their short-term financial difficulties by issuing corporate bonds, particularly in 1998 and the early part of 1999. Two companies—Hyundai and Daewoo—issued most of these bonds and soon ran into serious financial difficulty. More generally, issuing bonds probably allowed large firms to postpone necessary restructuring.
- There are also signs that the bond market was effectively propped up in various ways by the government, at least until Daewoo's default in mid-1999. Here the key point is what did the Investment Trust Companies (ITCs) know and when did they know it (and who told them what to do)? There are definite signs that these ITCs were encouraged to buy corporate bonds in general and the bonds of certain companies in particular. In addition, the regulations surrounding bond issues were generally weak

and there was a great deal of regulatory forbearance during the early crisis period.

At least in the Korean case, however, delayed financial restructuring does not appear to have been a major problem. Korea still enjoyed one of the fastest ever economic recoveries. There are suggestions, although no conclusive evidence, that even in the depths of the crisis, firms with good investment and export prospects were able to raise capital in one way or another.

Thinking more generally, immediate liquidation of firms in the first few months of any crisis is difficult. It is very hard to close down the "right" firms when the economy is in disarray and profitability is impossible to predict. Letting some dust settle, if possible, is probably a good idea. More formally, given that bankruptcy is costly, there is clearly some option value to waiting.

At the same time, waiting may increase the costs of failure when it does eventually occur. The scale of the Daewoo collapse, as discussed at length by Oh and Rhee, would surely have been less if it had occurred six months earlier. As Mako argues, slow debt restructuring will delay growth if it prevents capital from flowing to high value projects.

In addition, both papers provide a great deal of compelling detail about the weakness of corporate governance in Korea. Weak corporate governance appears to be associated with high levels of debt both in Korea and elsewhere. We need more research on this issue, but it is quite possible that "institutional" weaknesses, such as a lack of investor protection, create country-level vulnerabilities by encouraging firms and investors to prefer debt over equity.

While the Korean banking system faced severe pressure after the 1997-98 crisis, it did not collapse. However, a careful reading of these two papers leaves one far from sanguine about Korea's ability to avoid another financial crisis in the coming years. Korea's corporate sector has bounced back remarkably well, largely on the basis of an impressive ability to export. Korea's financial sector, particularly its banks, remains weak and unimpressive. Unless further measures are taken to strengthen the banks, we should remain concerned about Korea's ability to withstand shocks.

Taken together these two papers nicely pose the main questions concerning the Korean economic recovery. To what extent was the recovery the result of directed or government-supported credit? To what extent was it due to creative market-based financing solutions that the private sector found for itself? More research is needed to fully answer these important questions of great general interest.

Won-Dong Cho

As one who had participated in Korea's financial and corporate restructuring process at the working level, I am honored to be a discussant for these papers focusing on financial and corporate restructuring.

It is often said that Korea's reform after the 1997 crisis has been conducted on four fronts: public, labor, financial, and corporate sectors. Among them, financial and corporate restructuring have been the core of the reforms. I say this, not to belittle the importance of public sector and labor market reforms. On the contrary, they have laid the foundation on which the real business of restructuring could start. How can one think of restructuring without being able to lay-off? How can one start the costly business of financial restructuring without the backing of fiscal soundness? Nevertheless, these two reforms are basically preconditions for financial and corporate restructuring. While the immediate cause of the crisis was the shortage of foreign exchange reserves, at the end of the day, the 1997 crisis was provoked by the enormous level of nonperforming corporate debt, which became mirrored in a flood of nonperforming loans in the financial sector.

The IMF has been criticized for its remedy of high interest rates and stringent fiscal consolidation at the very initial stage of the crisis. I would argue that such a harsh remedy was inevitable since securing foreign capital was more urgent than solving the domestic credit crunch. In 1997, the Korean authorities had to accept a free-floating exchange regime. But the decision came too late: foreign reserves were almost dried up. Therefore, the immediate problem was how to win back foreign capital that had left the country.

But what was the incentive for foreign investors? They were not sure of the country's future. Even if they thought that reforms and restructuring would be implemented to restore the battered economy, reforms take time for their effects to be realized. Under these circumstances, it was natural for foreign investors to chase after a short-term gain. But even short-term incentives were not easy to find. Under the free-floating regime, the foreign exchange risk suddenly became too much to bear. To accept the FX risk, foreign investors expected a very high return. This situation early in the crisis justified the high interest rate option. Stringent fiscal consolidation was also justifiable because it helped to reduce the FX risk, since it was crucial that the public sector not contribute to expectations of high inflation. Only after successfully rolling over the short-term debt held by foreign financial institutions and launching foreign currency denominated bonds in early 1998, was Korea in a position to deal with problems in the domestic economy.

Having said that, I would agree that the domestic problems worsened during this process. By February 1998, as many as 20,000 firms had gone bankrupt due to the deepening credit crunch, and unemployment was soaring. This was the context in which the government embarked on the restructuring program. But restructuring means more casualties in the short term, although it ensures a brighter future. The authorities had to deal with the credit crunch while pushing ahead with restructuring. Messrs. Oh and Rhee describe the Korean authorities' choice to cope with this apparent dilemma as bank-centered financial restructuring and fluctuating interest rates. Such a policy decision provoked a massive shift of money from the banking sector to the nonbanking sector, mostly to the ITCs. This contributed to a rapid economic recovery, but it was reversed shortly after the collapse of Daewoo, with the economy again slowing.

There are three aspects of the Korean financial markets that are important to help understand the situation at the time. The first concerns the adverse effect of the full deposit guarantee system. With an imminent risk of a bank-run, the previous government hurriedly announced a complete guarantee for principal and interest on bank deposits. Although this prevented a bank-run, the blanket guarantee aggravated the credit crunch by attracting more money into the banking sector.

The full guarantee made it virtually impossible for the government to close large banks since, as guarantor it would have had to pay depositors immediately. Although some public money could be recuperated by selling the assets of the bank, there was a risk that the value of secured assets might erode rapidly. The full deposit guarantee caused moral hazard since banks knew that they would not be liquidated as long as their deposits were large. Indeed, their chance of surviving might increase if they were able to attract more deposits by offering high deposit rates. Some banks actually offered interests rates of more than 25 percent for deposits with maturities of more than one year. It is no wonder that money flooded into the banking sector.

What did the banks do with the money? Even without strengthening prudential regulations, banks did not want to continue corporate lending at previous levels given the high level of nonperforming loans to chaebol. In fact, they did not have to worry about the use of deposits in the first place, because the Bank of Korea repurchased money at a higher rate than their deposit rate, although this higher repurchase rate guaranteed them only short-term profitability. The result was obvious: the money flooding into the banking sector circulated only within the banking sector.

So, the task the new government faced was to redirect money amassed in the banking system to the corporate sector. What the government did to solve this problem was threefold. First, it initiated a full-scale bank restructuring program with 64 trillion won of public money. The process of screening ailing banks at that time was far from perfect. But once the selection was done, the surviving banks could be relieved from the imminent agony of the life-and-death problem, which initiated the credit crunch.

Bank restructuring by itself, however, could not solve the immediate problem since the benefits of reform only materialize with time. Therefore, the second approach the government took was to reduce the incentive to keep money circulating in the banking sector by lowering the Bank of Korea's repurchase rate. With rapidly declining repurchase rates, banks had to either cut their deposit rates or find other uses for their deposits. In the event, the outcome was driven more by cutting deposit rates rather than by increasing corporate lending, which led to a massive shift of funds from banks to the bond market, as noted by Oh and Rhee.

The burgeoning corporate bond market may have been good news for large firms, but it did not help small and medium-sized firms that did not have access to the bond market. To them, the exodus of money from the banks meant it was more difficult to get loans. The government's third approach was to provide loan guarantees through credit guarantee funds, which resulted in sizable losses to the funds.

Let me now turn to the second aspect, which is the nature of Korea's bond market. Not only was its volume small, but also the amount of bonds without guarantee was almost negligible. Most firms were able to issue corporate bonds only after getting a guarantee, mainly from one of the two guarantee insurance companies. In short, Korea's bond market was not credit driven in the normal sense. Although, the corporate bond market had been growing rapidly since mid-1998, it remained a guarantee-driven market. In fact, when new bond issuance virtually stopped at the end of 1997, the previous government retreated from its earlier intention to exclude the two government-sponsored guarantee insurance companies from the coverage of the deposit guarantee system.

This meant that government action toward the bond market was bound to be limited. In order to deal fully with the ITCs, which are major market-makers in the bond market, government would have had to first make public money available. The total amount of bonds guarantee by the two guarantee insurance companies was more than 140 trillion won in early 1998. Paying off that amount was not a politically feasable option. In addition, restructuring the ITCs could have had an even more devastating effect on the market than restructuring the banks.

The government had no choice but to adopt a step-by-step approach. Although I do not want to go into detail, I do want to respond to Oh and Rhee's point on securitization. As they note, the government introduced the primary collaterized bond obligation (P-CBO) and the collaterized loan obligation (CLO) schemes to save the bond market while it carried out a gradual restructuring of the ITCs. The two schemes were successful in securitizing corporate bonds and bank loans with the partial guarantee, as explained clearly by Oh and Rhee. But by the end of 2000, it became increasingly evident that the two schemes by themselves could not save the bond market, which is why the government came up with the KDB bond scheme. This scheme was basically a variation of the previous P-CBO scheme, in the sense that 70 percent of KDB-purchased bonds are securitized through P-CBOs in due course. The KDB's exposure is only 10 percent, since another 20 percent is repurchased by creditor banks; KDB's role in the scheme is more like an underwriter. Furthermore, firms are eligible for the KDB scheme only they were able to pay 20 percent of their existing bonds coming to maturity, so the scheme contributed to lowering the level of corporate debt. While questions were raised about the companies that were eligible, this was a problem in the implementation rather than in the design of the scheme.

The third aspect is related to the observation by some that corporate restructuring has been abandoned in the ups and downs of the bond market. I would argue that this has not been the case. The authorities have made efforts to advance corporate restructuring, even though at times they have had to resort to less market-friendly methods. One example was the Financial Structure Improvement Covenant System. Under this system, each chaebol had to make a covenant with its main bank to cut its debt-equity ratio within a given time. In particular, the top five chaebol were asked to reduce their debt-equity ratio to 200 percent by the end of 1999. It was up to them to decide how to meet the target, but their performance was subject to close scrutiny by their banks on a quarterly basis, with equity improvements due to asset reevaluation excluded. Bonds were issued at the company's discretion, although, as another form of debt, this did not reduce their debt-equity ratio. Firms could opt for equity issuance rather than reducing debt to meet the target of the debt equity ratio. But I would argue that this contributed to corporate restructuring by diluting ownership. In fact, the governing shareholders' equity of the top five chaebol was reduced from 7 percent in 1996 to 5 percent in 1999. It may sound paradoxical but the pace of Hyundai's break-up has been much faster because of the dilution of ownership.

Hindsight always makes people wiser. But one should not forget the actual situation prevailing at the time policy decisions are made. While it is true that some policy options taken by the authorities have not been market-friendly, they have moved the economy in a market-oriented direction. The KDB bond scheme was not completely market-friendly, but it was better than the 100 percent loan guarantees of early 1998 in the sense that it provided only a partial guarantee. The authorities' reliance upon the Financial Structure Improvement Covenant System was reduced as banking supervision was strengthened with, for example, the introduction of foreword-looking criteria in 2000.

Every policy decision has pros and cons which should be weighed carefully. But I would argue that, as long as the pros outweigh the cons, we are moving in the right direction. I believe policy requires more serious deliberation than a simple choice between all or nothing. A swift decision is better than indecision caused by deadlock in the pursuit of an ideal solution.

8 The Korean Labor Market: The Crisis and After

*Dae Il Kim**

This paper documents changes in Korea's labor market during the period of economic crisis. The immediate impact of the crisis on Korea's labor market has been substantial as labor demand shrank to an unprecedented extent, and as many macro and micro policies were deployed in an attempt to survive the crisis. The soaring interest rates and cutback in product demands forced many businesses out of the market, which led to a massive increase in the jobless population. The ensuing economic restructuring program, agreed upon between the IMF and the Korean government, aimed to improve the portfolios of commercial banks and corporations, and included major revisions in labor laws.

In 1999, the Korean economy seemed to have resumed its growth trend. Although it is still debatable whether the recovery reflected successful economic reform or expansionary policies, real GDP grew rapidly in 1999, and both consumption and investment recovered substantially. Capacity utilization reached a record high by the end of 1999, and interest rates, exchange rates, and inflation stabilized. Employment also showed some recovery, although not to the 1997 level.

The empirical analysis of the changes in the Korean labor market in this paper focuses on a few issues. First, it briefly summarizes distinctive features of Korea's labor market with respect to institutions, government policy, and market mechanisms, to help better understand recent changes in the labor market. Second, it documents the changes in employment and wages during the economic crisis and recovery, and investigates the pattern of such changes across sectors and types of workers. In doing so, it attempts to separately iden-

*The author would like to thank Dong-Chul Cho and Gyeong-Joon Yoo for helpful comments and discussion on the topic.

tify market and institutional forces to better understand the mechanisms behind such changes.

Not surprisingly, joblessness rose, particularly among unskilled workers. Unemployment and underemployment rose in terms of both quantity and duration. In the recovery in 1999, the demographic patterns of job gains and wage changes were biased against less skilled workers. Inequality may have increased during the crisis. Some evidence is found for consumption smoothing, especially among poor households.

One of several unexpected and surprising changes was a massive reallocation: many new jobs were created while even more jobs were destroyed. The pattern of job growth shows that, less surprisingly, newly created jobs were inferior to disappearing jobs as indicated by the general decline in wages and the widespread use of non-regular workers. As a result, many of those who formerly had stable, high-wage jobs became either employed in unstable, low-wage jobs, or unemployed. The increase in non-regular jobs does not appear to reflect firms' attempts to reorganize work to achieve long-term efficiency gains, but instead, it seems to reflect their temporary attempts to cut labor costs in the short run.

This paper unfolds in the following way. The next section briefly summarizes key features of the Korean labor market. The following section documents changes in employment, job creation/destruction, unemployment, wages and inequality. The final section concludes with remarks on the implications of the empirical findings.

Institutions and Characteristics of the Korean Labor Market

This section reviews the market structure, institutions, labor supply behavior, and demand conditions in the Korean labor market.

Market Structure

The Korean economy has often been characterized by concentration of economic power among a few large companies. Many have argued that the distorted financial practices by these large firms were at the heart of the 1997 economic crisis. Indeed, a few large firms, previously thought of as too big to fail, went out of business or still are under a severe financial distress.

A market structure focused on a few large firms has a long history in Korea, starting during the period of fast and sustained economic growth in the 1970s and 1980s. The export-oriented economic policy, intentionally and unintentionally, has favored large firms with easier access to foreign markets, as did the Big Push toward heavy manufacturing and chemical industries since the late 1970s, for such industries required large-scale, up-front investments. During the process, commercial banks were guided to finance various projects of large firms without precise evaluation of their profitability.

The dominance of large firms has affected the labor market through various channels, one of which is subcontracting. As indicated in Table 1, more than 70 percent of manufacturing firms with less than 300 employees produced intermediate and final goods for large downstream firms in the early 1990s. The share of such sales in total output exceeded 85 percent among the upstream firms, and 75 percent of such firms supplied more than 95 percent of their output to downstream firms. In other words, upstream firms heavily relied on a single customer, as the largest downstream customer bought an average of 46 percent of these upstream firms' output.

As a large number of small and medium-size manufacturing firms heavily relied on the orders from downstream firms, severe competition for orders placed them at a disadvantage in bargaining with the large downstream firms

Table 1. Subcontracting Among Small and Medium-Size Firms[1]

(1) Frequency of Subcontracting

Firm Size	Total	Subcontracting	Share
All	67,649	49,806	73.6%
5-9 Employees	21,661	14,957	68.8%
10-19 Employees	20,107	15,665	77.6%
20-49 Employees	17,100	12,865	75.2%
50-99 Employees	5,538	3,998	72.7%
100-199 Employees	2,474	1,783	73.7%
200-299 Employees	769	538	71.6%

(2) Extent of Dependency to Downstream Firms

Firm Size	Fraction of Sales on Subcontract[2]		Distribution of Fraction of Sales on Subcontract		
	To All	To Major	<60%	60-95%	95+%
All	85.5	46.4	12.0	13.1	74.9
5-9 Employees	91.4	42.2	9.8	11.5	78.7
10-19 Employees	86.2	45.2	14.2	15.8	70.0
20-49 Employees	86.8	48.7	11.1	11.2	77.7
50-99 Employees	85.7	51.4	14.4	13.6	72.0
100-199 Employees	83.5	45.7	13.6	18.4	68.0
200-299 Employees	73.6	36.7	33.0	13.3	53.7

Source: Kim (1997a).
[1]The sample consists of manufacturing firms with 5-299 employees.
[2]The share of sales to downstream firms in total outputs.

that tended to have monopoly and monopsony powers. Through such subcontracting webs, economic troubles experienced by large downstream firms rapidly spilled over to small upstream firms. The possibility of chain reactions has been the excuse for past interventions to protect large companies in Korea, to which the economic crisis was at least partly attributable. Further, it has served as the rationale for intervention in labor disputes in Korea, as discussed below.

Directly and indirectly, firm size has been associated with workforce composition. Table 2 shows the skill distribution of workers by firm size in 1995 and 1998, where worker skills are represented by their educational achievement. The clearly evident positive relationship between firm size and education level strengthened through the crisis. A part of this positive relationship is accounted for by subcontracting. Small subcontracting firms invested little in product design or R&D, but focused instead on maintaining a stable relationship with the downstream firms (Kim, 1997a). This suggests that their demand for creativity and problem-solving capacity in their workforce was not high. Thus the workforces of subcontracting firms were biased toward unskilled labor.[1] Given that, it is not surprising that small firms were hit hard at the early stage of the crisis and that job losses were concentrated among less educated workers.

Table 2. Skill Composition of Workforce by Firm Size
(In percent)

Firm Size (No. of Workers)	1995 Years of Schooling				1998 Years of Schooling			
	<12	$=12$	$=14$	$16+$	<12	$=12$	$=14$	$16+$
1 to 4	43.5	46.9	4.2	5.5	37.9	48.5	6.1	7.5
5 to 9	37.9	48.5	5.8	7.8	30.2	49.7	8.0	12.1
10 to 19	29.5	50.0	6.7	13.8	24.9	47.7	8.7	18.7
20 to 49	24.8	48.7	6.5	20.0	20.3	46.0	8.4	25.3
50 to 99	20.8	43.0	7.7	28.5	18.1	38.8	8.0	35.2
100 to 299	22.0	47.5	8.5	22.0	15.8	46.1	8.0	30.2
300 to 499	15.8	49.1	9.2	25.9	13.5	44.1	7.7	34.6
500 to 999	16.2	45.6	7.6	30.6	10.4	43.2	8.8	37.6
1,000 or more	11.0	52.4	8.0	28.6	9.2	45.7	8.5	36.5

Source: Author's calculation based on data from the *Survey on Economically Active Population* (1995, 1998)
Note: The sample is limited to wage/salary workers.

---

[1]Kim (1997a) finds that a 10-percentage point increase in the share of firms selling more than 80 percent of outputs on subcontract increases the share of high school graduates or less educated workers among new hires by 1.5 percentage points.

Institutions: Law, Policy, and Unions

Labor Law and Government Policy Responses

The need for economic restructuring led the government to introduce measures both to enhance labor market flexibility and to mitigate unemployment and poverty. Redundancy layoffs and a temporary work agency were legalized, and the government spent 10.1 trillion won in 1998 and 9.2 trillion won in 1999 to fight unemployment. This section briefly summarizes the government's responses to the crisis.[2]

The motivation for the introduction of redundancy layoff came from the common perception that large-scale employment adjustments had historically been difficult in Korea. Flexible employment adjustment was considered important for successful corporate restructuring and attracting foreign investors. The actual implementation of redundancy layoff was not smooth, however. Workers and unions strongly opposed it initially. The Tripartite Commission, established to deal with the issue, reached consensus and put forth the bill for redundancy layoff in early 1998.[3]

There has been criticism, however, that the new law has actually made it more, not less, difficult to adjust employment. Redundancy layoff was not banned before the new law, as the Supreme Court had acknowledged managerial need for layoffs in many previous rulings. The real changes in the new law were the procedures required for a redundancy layoff, and some of them are potentially binding. For example, a firm was required to "exhaust all means to avoid it" before executing a layoff. Such means could include wage reductions, work sharing, not filling vacancies arising from quits or retirement, no new hires, and contract buyout with a bonus. Further, firms were bound to consult "sincerely" with union leaders on how many and whom to lay off. If a firm executed a layoff before going through all these steps, the employer would be subject to a fine and possible imprisonment. The real problem, of course, is that it is always disputable whether a firm has exhausted all means to avoid a layoff, or whether a firm has been sufficiently sincere.

These requirements, intended to suppress excessive and unnecessary layoffs, have imposed costs on firms undertaking restructuring. Mass layoffs

---

[2]The discussion in this section draws mostly upon Ministry of Labor (1998, 1999).

[3]The Commission was called upon by President Kim Dae Jung to shape labor market policies during the crisis. It consisted of union representatives, business representatives, and a neutral party of government officials and professionals. The major issues discussed in the Commission included the introduction of redundancy layoffs and a temporary work agency, and unemployment policies.

almost always brought about confrontations between workers and employers, even under the new law. These costs were not necessarily limited to the affected firms, but spilled over to the economy. In addition to the inefficiency resulting from hostile confrontations, firms often could not restructure their workforce, which in turn distorted labor demands. For example, the clause prohibiting new hiring made it very difficult for a firm to replace existing workers with more productive workers. This led to a significant drop in new hires in the economy, exacerbating the joblessness problem, especially among the young.

A temporary work agency was also introduced to enhance labor market flexibility, allowing employers to outsource workers from manpower agencies on temporary contracts. However, its use has been limited mainly because only professional workers could be outsourced. An employer may not, for example, outsource manufacturing production workers.

Firms were also allowed to replace workers on strike to continue production. This was potentially a very important change for industrial relations in Korea, as strikes have been an effective tool for unions. However, replacement is allowed only within the concerned establishment; replacing workers on strike with those outside the establishment is still prohibited. Firms may reallocate those not on strike to the production site vacated by workers on strike, but as picket-line crossing has been very rare in Korea, strikers have rarely been replaced.

The government attempted to limit job loss by providing various subsidies. Wage subsidies were offered for job sharing (hours reduction) and reemployment of laid-off workers.[4] A subsidized loan program for new businesses was intended to induce new hires, but the program mostly targeted the so-called venture businesses.[5] Training and placement services were expanded as well. The training program covered 301,244 jobless persons in 1998, and 324,623

---

[4]Although the full effects of such job maintenance programs are difficult to measure, they are unlikely to have been large since layoffs have not been the major reason for job losses. For example, among those who involuntarily lost a job in 1998, only 18 percent was through semi-voluntary retirement or layoff from surviving firms. Most job losses were due to bankruptcies. Shedding workers may improve the cash flow of the firms that are marginally under financial distress, but not sufficiently so to change the fate of firms under severe financial distress.

[5]There were at least three problems with this program, including the overly narrow definition of a venture business as one using sophisticated computer technology. Second, the labor demand induced in such businesses, if any, did not match the unskilled workers losing a job. Inflow of capital into the venture sector only led to excessive competition for very high-skilled workers, raising their wages and the wage gap between the skilled and unskilled. Third, the administration of the program has not been efficient because few public officials could properly evaluate the future profitability of highly technical projects, or distinguish between technically complex projects. Not surprisingly, many incidences of fraud have been reported.

persons in 1999; the job placement rate among trainees was 21.2 percent in 1998, and 35.3 percent in 1999.

The quantitative expansion of job training and placement services was mostly an expanded version of what had already been proven to be not very effective. Public sector-provided training was not always linked to market demands, but to the training capacity of the provider. Placement services were also provided by the public sector. As of 1999, only 6.7 percent of job searchers relied on job placement services, public or private, and most of them were older job searchers.

The unemployment policy package also contained programs targeting female and youth unemployment. Starting in October 1998, one-third to one-half of wages was subsidized to employers hiring female heads of household who had recently lost their job. Short-term job opportunities, mostly in social service and child care, were offered to low-income women. The policy also targeted college graduates at the entry level. Approximately 45,000 jobless new graduates were awarded internships for six months in the public sector in 1998.

The coverage of unemployment insurance was expanded from firms with 30 or more employees to firms with ten or more employees in January 1998, to firms with five or more employees in March 1998, and to all firms in October 1998. This expansion of unemployment insurance did not appear to have an immediate impact as eligibility was limited to those who had paid the premiums for at least six months (reduced from one year) at the time of job separation. Approximately 11 percent of people who lost jobs, and an even smaller fraction of the unemployed, were estimated to be eligible for benefits in 1998, because most job losses occurred among small firms.

As unemployment insurance helped only job losers, poverty had to be handled by other measures. Public assistance programs for the poor were expanded to cover an additional 310,000 persons in 1998.[6] A loan subsidy program and public work program for the unemployed were also introduced. The subsidized loan program supported new business start-ups of the unemployed and provided living expenses.[7] Public work programs were one of the most

---

[6]The program classifies the beneficiaries into three groups - home care, institutional care, and self-support. Those under home care received 162,000 won per month in 1998 (22 percent higher than in 1997), and those under institutional care received 125,000 won per month (16 percent higher). Those in self-support programs were eligible for in-kind transfers and subsidized loans, but not for cash benefits as they were considered to be able to work. Among the additional 310,000 people covered, 233,000 people were classified in the self-support program, as most were job losers able to work.

[7]These programs had only a limited impact for two reasons. First, the government intended to finance the program by issuing bonds, but the sale of bonds were far below the target as yields

effective policies. The government spent 1.4 trillion won in 1998 covering 400,000 workers, and 2.3 trillion won in 1999 covering 380,000 workers.[8] More recently, the Basic Livelihood Protection Program was introduced, which pays up to 930,000 won per month—compared with the minimum wage of 361,000 won—to a poor, four-person household.

Labor Unions

It was only in 1987 that labor union activity became an important aspect of Korea's labor market. The union penetration rate rose to as high as 23 percent of wage and salary workers, or 13.8 percent of the total workforce, in 1989, but since then it has gradually declined mostly due to manufacturing's declining share of employment (Kim and Lee, 1997). As of 1998, 14.2 percent of wage and salary workers, or 8.7 percent of the total workforce, were estimated to belong to a union (Korea Labor Institute, 1998).

There are two key characteristics of industrial relations in Korea. First, unions are at the enterprise level, with bargaining between the firm and union over wages and other terms of contract. Second, labor unions in Korea have been regarded as very militant by most domestic and foreign observers, with bargaining often evolving into hostile confrontations and destructive strikes. The role and effect of labor unions appeared to have changed during the crisis, as they sometimes cooperated with firms and the government, especially in the Tripartite Agreement. But at other times they exhibited the same militancy as before.

The characteristics and role of unions in Korea have been affected by legal provisions as well as by economic conditions. The Trade Union Act has prohibited third-party intervention in bargaining, which explains enterprise-level unionism.[9] Union membership has been limited to workers, and thus any

---

were set far below the market interest rate. Second, the loan windows were set up in commercial banks, and the banks applied a set of restrictive conditions on loan approval. For example, applicants for loans were requested to provide some collateral or cosigners, neither of which was easy for a jobless person.

[8]Public work programs also caused some side effects. First, a major portion of the participants in the program had not previously been in the labor force. Second, the compensation level was too generous at 500,000 won per month, which was approximately 50 percent higher than the legal minimum wage. As a result, workers who would have sought employment in small, low-wage businesses tended to prefer public work programs.

[9]During the crisis, the Act was amended so that unions could solicit professional help (for example, from lawyers). The amendment led to an unusual increase in "professionals," mostly from other unions, helping small unions. In that sense, it effectively allowed intervention by other unions in firm-level bargaining. The increase in "professionals" quickly subsided, however.

member becoming unemployed would lose membership. These legal provisions have made it very difficult for workers in small firms to organize. As a result, unions have been concentrated among large firms and public enterprises in Korea.[10]

Despite the low penetration rate, labor unions in Korea remained very strong during the 1990s mainly because they were concentrated among large firms. As mentioned above, economic troubles experienced by large downstream firms had the potential to be spilled over quickly to small upstream firms through the web of subcontracting. This possibility of chain reaction has served as the rationale for intervention in labor disputes in Korea. Prolonged work stoppages in large downstream firms placed small upstream firms at risk because the latter did not have easy access to capital markets, and also because work stoppages often resulted in delayed payments to the upstream firms. The Korean government intervened in labor disputes selectively, often inducing firms to concede to workers in return for favorable arrangements. Repeated interventions led both management and workers to look to the government whenever there were disputes.

Labor disputes have always been important to the government regardless of the causes. Given that, it has been rational for unions to be militant, as the possibility of government intervention increased with the intensity of confrontation. Labor unions in large companies and chaebol in Korea have had a reasonably successful record of wage (and other) bargaining, as they skillfully exploited government intervention. In the process, more often than not, picketing formed against the government, not the concerned firms, and the government usually responded.

The economic crisis in 1997 temporarily changed the behavior of labor unions in Korea. It was an economy-wide demand shock, and the scope of government intervention in the market was severely restricted. There was broad consensus that the labor market needed to become more flexible, and also that workers should bear part of the cost of restructuring, although they might have not been the cause of the crisis. In other words, all parties agreed that the economy would further collapse if the country did not undertake painful restructuring. The Tripartite Commission was formed, and management, workers, and the government reached an agreement on a restructuring program that included redundancy layoff. At this stage and for the following year, labor unions were relatively cooperative.

---

[10]All firms with 15,000 or more employees are organized except for Samsung Inc., but the penetration rate is below 10 percent among firms with fewer than 100 employees (Kim and Lee, 1997).

As the economy started to show signs of recovery in 1999, labor unions started to demand compensation for the concessions they had made during the previous year. Wages started to grow rapidly, retarding the recovery of employment in unionized firms. For example, between the second quarters in 1999 and 2000, real wages grew by 13.3 percent among firms with 300 or more workers, but grew by only 7.8 percent among smaller firms; employment, however, decreased by 8.1 percent in the former while it grew by 4.0 percent in the latter. One may relate the faster wage growth and resulting sluggish employment in large firms to the pattern of job growth during the recovery, which was biased toward unskilled low-wage jobs.

There are two dimensions of the insider-outsider problem that are quite serious in Korea's industrial relations. First, there is the tension between workers and the jobless. As union members lose membership when unemployed, the jobless population's interests are not protected by union members or employed workers. Faster wage growth is a good example: labor demand is reduced by higher wages, so that new hiring does not expand. Second, there is the tension between workers in large unionized firms and workers in small, unorganized firms. High wage growth in large firms limits the expansion of output, and thus fewer orders are placed for small upstream firms. At the same time, those unable to find jobs in large firms because of the high wage growth look for jobs in smaller firms, effectively increasing labor supply to smaller firms. This widens the wage gap between workers in small and large firms. The economic crisis has made the insider-outsider problem more visible, if not worse.

Labor Supply Aspects

Three aspects of labor supply are worth mentioning. First, male labor supply has been quite strong and inelastic with respect to wages. Second, women are less attached to the market, showing a clear age pattern in labor supply behavior. Third, and most importantly, there has been little distinction between unemployment (job search) and nonparticipation.

Figure 1 shows the share of employment in total population by age in 1997 for men and women. For men, the employment share rises until age 30 beyond which it stays above 90 percent until age 50. Thus a substantial fraction of prime-age men works, and an even greater fraction participates in the market, if job searchers are counted. For women, the employment share is much smaller than for men, reflecting a weaker attachment to the market. Further, the age pattern is M-shaped, with a peak at around age 25 and another peak at around age 45, both at about 65 percent. The sudden drop between ages 25 and 30 is approximately 25 percentage points.

Figure 1. Fraction at Work in Total Population by Age

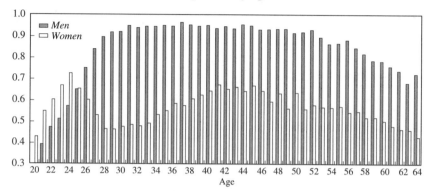

Source: *Survey on Economically Active Population* (1997).

The decline in labor force participation of working women between 25 and 30 years of age is often linked to marriage and childbearing, as the fraction of married women rises equally fast in this age group. However, it is not clear whether the decline is the result of a labor supply decision or discrimination against married women. A relevant feature of female employment is that between ages 20 and 29, 88.2 percent are employed as wage and salary workers, whereas between ages 35 and 54 only 50.9 percent work as wage and salary workers. Most of this difference is accounted for by the increase in the share working as self-employed or unpaid family workers, which is 10.9 percent among the younger population and 43.0 percent among the older population. It is not clear whether this is the result of discrimination or a preference for flexible hours.

The lack of distinction between unemployment and nonparticipation in Korea is basically the issue of response behavior in household surveys. As in many other countries, a non-worker is asked whether he or she has looked for a job during the week prior to the interview.[11] Non-workers in Korea have tended to respond to the question as "not searching," and only a handful of job searchers are found in the data. However, such a response often contradicts the market activity of non-workers. Table 3 shows that only a tiny fraction of job losses have led to unemployment and that an equally tiny fraction of job gains have absorbed unemployment. In other words, a large fraction of the population, reported as non-participants, are expected to maintain market ac-

---

[11]In the United States and other OECD countries, a non-worker is asked whether he or she looked for a job during the previous four weeks. The low rate of unemployment during the 1990s prior to the crisis in Korea has often been considered as reflecting the difference in weeks, but recent data indicate that it is not the number of weeks, but the response behavior.

Table 3. Monthly Transition between Labor Market Status
(In percent)

	Status in the Next Month		
	Employed	Unemployed	Nonparticipating
Status in Current Month			
Employed	96.7 (96.0)	0.6 (21.8)	2.7 (4.4)
Unemployed	28.6 (0.7)	63.3 (65.2)	8.1 (0.3)
Nonparticipating	5.3 (3.2)	0.5 (13.0)	94.2 (95.2)

Source: Kim (2000a).

Note: The i-jth entry represents the fraction of those with status i in a month changing into status j in the next month. The rows sum to 100. The entries in parentheses are the fraction of those with status i in a month who were in status j in the previous month. The columns sum to 100.

tivity. Such marginal participants—those hopping between employment and nonparticipation—are estimated to be as large as 14 percent of the total population above 15 years of age (Kim, 2000a). Workers moving between employment and nonparticipation have been the main reason for low unemployment rates and the small variability of unemployment during business cycles prior to the crisis.[12] As discussed below, however, many more nonparticipants started to report themselves as unemployed during the period of economic crisis, which may be linked to increased assistance to the unemployed in the government's unemployment policy.

Demand Shift toward Educated Labor

The 1980s and the early 1990s have been a period of great wage compression in Korea, especially between the skilled and unskilled workers. The college-high school wage differential, which stood at 96.2 percent in 1985, declined steadily to 55.7 percent in 1995. Most of this decline reflected increases in the supply of college graduates among younger cohorts. However in the mid-1990s, the premium started to grow, suggesting a shift in labor demand toward educated labor.[13]

In Table 4, an estimate of relative labor demands is reported.[14] The ratio of the demand index relative to the 1994 level is calculated for each demographic group of workers.[15] The index has grown faster among educated men

---

[12]Employment has fluctuated substantially during business cycles, however; such fluctuations have been comparable to those seen in other OECD countries (Kim, 2000a).

[13]See Table 8 for the recent changes in college premiums.

[14]The demand indicator is calculated following Katz and Murphy (1992), Juhn, Murphy and Pierce (1993), and Kim and Topel (1995). The index uses changes in sectoral employment, where sectors are defined as industry-occupation cells. The main idea is that if the sectors hiring a certain group of workers more disproportionately expand, this can be viewed as an increase in demand for the group of workers.

than uneducated men, indicating that labor demand has shifted toward skilled workers during the 1990s. This finding is consistent with the literature that shows unemployment duration has increased most among the least educated workers (Kim, 1997b, 1999). The economic crisis in 1997 reduced demand for unskilled workers, or those with no more than a high school diploma, but there is little evidence that it lowered demand for college graduates.

It is notable that there has been a gender gap in labor demand in Korea. The gap can be viewed in two dimensions. First, women have seen a faster increase in labor demand than men in most education groups. Given that the gender premium has also shrunk during the 1990s, this suggests that labor demand has shifted toward women in Korea.[16] Second, unlike for men, there appears to be no discernible education gap in labor demand for women. Between 1994 and 1997, labor demand for women with no more than a high school diploma increased faster than for women with a college degree. Less educated women

Table 4. Estimated Demand Index by Gender/Education Group

(1) Men

	High School Dropouts	High School Graduates	2-Year Colleges	4-Year Colleges
1994	100.0	100.0	100.0	100.0
1995	105.3	105.2	106.1	107.6
1996	107.6	108.3	110.5	112.0
1997	107.6	109.4	128.6	113.4
1998	88.8	97.7	106.1	119.8
1999	89.0	98.2	106.2	117.1

(2) Women

	High School Dropouts	High School Graduates	2-Year Colleges	4-Year Colleges
1994	100.0	100.0	100.0	100.0
1995	109.1	106.1	101.1	105.1
1996	115.6	112.8	105.9	109.2
1997	119.2	117.2	110.6	111.0
1998	107.7	108.9	111.4	120.7
1999	114.4	111.9	111.8	118.7

Source: Author's calculation based on data from the *Survey on Economically Active Population* (1994-99) and the *Survey on Wage Structure* (1994-99).

[15]I report the index for the post-1994 periods only because new industry and occupation classification was introduced in 1994.

[16]See Table 8 for the recent changes in gender premium.

Figure 2. Expansion of College Education in Korea

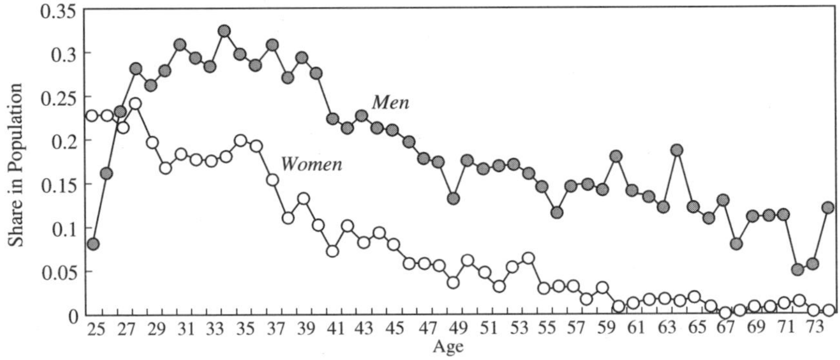

Source: *Survey on Economically Active Population* (1985-99)

experienced a significant decline in demand during the crisis, but the difference between educated and uneducated women in 1999 is much smaller than between educated and uneducated men. In sum, labor demand in Korea has shifted toward women and toward educated men.

The increase in demand for educated workers has been met by an ever-increasing supply of young educated workers in Korea. As shown in Figure 2, the share of college graduates is higher among young age cohorts than older cohorts. The increase in college enrollment was partly due to the expansion of college admission in 1981, and also to the conversion of two-year colleges into four-year colleges in the early 1990s. The rapid increase in college graduates has lowered the college wage premium during the 1980s and the 1990s despite the demand increase (Kim and Topel, 1995). However, as previously noted, the college premium started to rise during the mid-1990s, implying that the increase in demand became more important than the increase in supply.

Changes in Employment, Unemployment, and Wages[17]

The immediate and most obvious effect of the crisis on Korea's labor market was the sharp decline in employment and the rapid increase in unemployment. As illustrated in Figure 3, employment declined by 1.45 million during the

---

[17]The data for the empirical analysis include the *Survey on Economically Active Population* (SEAP: National Statistical Office, 1985-99), the *Survey on Wage Structure* (SWS: Ministry of Labor, 1993-98), *Monthly Labor Statistics* (MLS: Ministry of Labor, 1996-2000), and the *Income and Expenditure Survey on Urban Working Households* (IESUWH: National Statistical Office, 1996-2000).

Figure 3. Changes in Employment and Unemployment

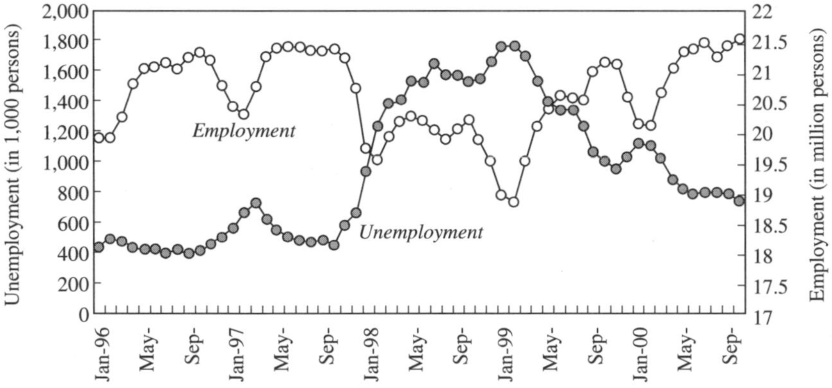

Source: *Survey on Economically Active Population* (1985-99).

five-month period between October 1997 and March 1998. During the same period, unemployment rose by almost a million from 0.45 million to 1.38 million. In addition, the share of households with no earners is estimated to have risen from 6.3 percent in 1997 to 6.8 percent in 1998. This was the period of massive bankruptcies among small firms caught off-guard by soaring interest rates and credit rationing.

Employment, Job Creation, and Destruction

The immediate and massive decline in employment in 1998 and its recovery in 1999 did not affect all sectors and demographic groups the same.[18] For example, manufacturing and construction jointly lost one million jobs in 1998, reflecting that typical firms in these sectors suffered more from the financial crisis due to their high debts. Such massive job losses were also non-neutral among types of workers, affecting unskilled workers more adversely. High school dropouts lost more than a million jobs, and 20-to 29-year-old workers lost 710,000 jobs.

A few developments stand out. First, employment in agriculture/fisheries and public administration, which had been shrinking, recorded substantial net growth of 225,000 jobs in 1998. The increase in agricultural employment implies that the traditional sector has provided some buffer to the shock by supplying additional income sources to hard-hit workers and households. The

---

[18]See Kim and Yoo (2001) for the detailed sectoral and demographic pattern of employment changes.

increase in public sector employment reflects the effect of government responses to soaring unemployment in the form of public work programs and internship.

Second, the pattern of recovery in 1999 differed among sectors and demographic groups. In terms of sectors, the 1999 recovery was generally a mirror image of the 1998 job losses, as manufacturing employment rose by 115,000. Agriculture lost 117,000 jobs, offsetting the previous year's growth. On the other hand, construction lost a further 110,000 jobs, but the extent of job losses was much smaller in 1999 than in 1998. And the public sector showed an even stronger job growth of 118,000 in 1999. In terms of demographic groups, those hardest hit by job losses in 1998 continued to struggle. Despite the generally strong employment growth, jobs for less educated workers grew much slower, and jobs for the 20- to 29-year-old population declined further. An interesting exception is the increase in unskilled laborers in 1999, which rose by 314,000 in 1999, a more-than-sevenfold increase compared to 1996-97. The slower employment growth among uneducated workers and the faster increase in unskilled jobs suggest occupational downgrading during the recovery, as does the fact that newly created jobs were relatively low-paying and required longer work hours.[19]

Figure 4. Job Gains, Losses and Net Job Gains during the Economic Crisis
(In 1,000 persons)

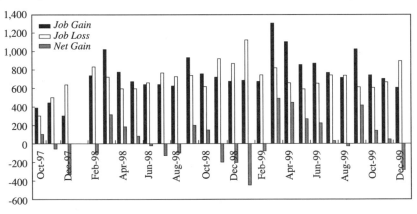

Source: Kim (2001a).

---

[19]See Kim (2001a). Newly created jobs would have paid 6 percent lower wages than destroyed jobs even in the absence of downward pressure from the economic crisis, as most new jobs were retail/service and unskilled jobs while destroyed jobs were high-wage manufacturing jobs. Weekly work hours tended to be longer by 3.7 hours. Such wage and hour gaps between destroyed and created jobs tended to be greater among high-skilled workers, suggesting the possibility of occupational downgrading.

Finally, and more importantly, the post-crisis period brought about an enormous reallocation of jobs, greater than suggested by the changes in employment. Extensive job creation and destruction have taken place during the

Table 5. Net Job Gains and Employment Absorption
(In 1,000 persons)

(A) Net Job Gains by Industry and Occupation

	Period 95/12-96/12	96/12-97/12	98/01-99/01	98/12-99/12
Agriculture/Fishery	-245.3	-14.2	43.1	65.2
Mining	0.5	-1.0	-1.5	0.9
Manufacturing	72.9	-80.1	-189.3	304.3
Public Utilities	-0.5	4.1	-6.8	1.5
Construction	14.9	33.7	-293.4	134.9
Retail/Wholesale	268.1	132.7	68.7	353.5
Transportation/Communication	43.9	24.5	-49.1	25.5
Financial/Insurance/Real Estate	94.2	97.2	16.9	126.5
Services	161.0	125.9	80.2	150.5
Public Adm.	7.6	4.6	27.3	46.3
Managers	-8.0	-12.9	-34.1	-13.7
Professional	24.9	22.2	-12.2	0.7
Technicians	101.1	55.4	-37.9	121.8
Clerks	138.6	60.4	-67.4	137.6
Sales/Service	199.6	167.7	67.3	291.6
Farmers/Fishermen	-230.4	-7.8	10.6	57.6
Craftsmen	14.6	-73.4	-264.5	154.0
Operatives	21.6	-16.8	-108.1	75.2
Laborers	155.4	132.5	142.5	384.3

(B) Employment Absorption by Net Job Gains in Each Sector and Occupation

	Period 95/12-96/12	96/12-97/12	98/01-99/01	98/12-99/12
Total	-207.7	-315.5	42.6	-918.5
Agriculture	-3.5	-6.9	-11.9	-21.7
Mining	0.1	0.1	-0.5	-1.6
Manufacturing	-7.9	-19.8	67.9	-167.2
Public Utility	-0.7	-3.5	2.2	-4.7
Construction	-40.6	-68.1	165.8	-170.1
Retail/Wholesale	-59.0	-80.7	-75.2	-298.5
Transportation/Communication	-26.8	-28.3	4.5	-50.8
Financial/Insurance/Real Estate	-34.5	-41.6	-34.0	-115.9
Services	-29.1	-62.0	-27.0	-137.6
Public Adm.	-5.7	-4.5	-49.2	-51.0
Managers	-1.5	1.8	24.0	-4.9
Professional	-19.5	-16.3	3.8	-23.5
Technician	-24.5	-34.5	4.9	-87.6
Clerks	-49.9	-61.2	-13.7	-149.3
Sales/Service	-26.6	-84.5	-78.8	-226.0
Farmers/Fishermen	-4.1	-5.9	-5.0	-15.8
Craftsmen	-10.1	-25.9	155.6	-162.3
Operatives	-16.0	-24.2	38.9	-76.5
Laborers	-59.2	-64.7	-87.1	-273.4

Source: Author's calculation based on data from the *Survey on Economically Active Population* (1995-99).
Note: The changes in sectoral unemployment are calculated as the number of job losers from the sector entering unemployment minus the number of job gainers in the sector out of unemployment.

period, as shown in Figure 4. As noted above, newly created jobs have been low-paying jobs, while high-wage, good jobs were being destroyed. The government created many new jobs, most of which were for unskilled labor. In 1998, for example, more than half (51.2 percent) of newly created daily-work positions were in the government sector, an enormous increase from 2.8 percent in 1997.

Public sector job growth absorbed a lot of unemployed workers despite its concentration among unskilled jobs, as shown in Table 5. The share of unskilled laborers in the government sector increased, from 10.6 percent in 1997 to 16.0 percent in 1998, and to 27.1 percent in 1999. The share of daily workers in the government sector increased much faster from 3.4 percent in 1997 to 11.0 percent in 1998, and to 26.3 percent in 1999. These are surprising developments because unskilled workers have typically been only marginally attached to the market. Unskilled workers rarely went through an unemployment spell, but rather hopped between nonparticipation and employment (Kim, 2000a). As will be seen below, unemployment rose permanently during the crisis, as the relative value of job search rose. The increase in public sector jobs also contributed to the rise in the value of search, as those jobs were allocated mainly to those "registered as unemployed." It is difficult, therefore, to measure the contribution of increased public-sector jobs to reducing unemployment because they may have induced unemployment in the first place.

Underemployment

Unemployment data understate the deterioration in the labor market caused by the crisis to the extent that the nature of jobs held by employed workers deteriorated. High-wage, good jobs in manufacturing have been replaced with low-wage jobs in trades and agriculture/fishery, suggesting a rise in underemployment. Table 6 reports the distribution of worker types in total employment. Regular employees are those on a labor contract of unspecified length; temporary employees are those on a contract shorter than a year; and daily employees are those employed on a daily basis.[20] Non-employees are employers (hiring employees), self-employed (on own account), and unpaid family workers working no fewer than 18 hours a week.[21]

Although the shift away from regular employees began earlier, the trend was strengthened by the economic crisis, and continued after the crisis. The

---

[20]The Labor Standard Law prohibits fixed-term contracts exceeding a year. Thus regular workers usually have a contract with no indication of duration.

[21]Unpaid family workers working fewer than 18 hours a week are classified as jobless.

Table 6. Distribution of Employment Types and Work Hours

(A) Job Composition (in 1,000 persons)[1]

	1996	1997	1998	1999
Employees				
Regular	7,326.6(36.9)	7,084.1(35.4)	6,402.7(33.7)	6,011.2(31.3)
Temporary	3,787.8(19.1)	4,097.2(20.5)	3,914.9(20.6)	4,081.3(21.2)
Daily	1,690.2(8.5)	1,783.9(8.9)	1,654.8(8.7)	2,172.2(11.3)
Non-Employees				
Employer	1,585.9(8.0)	1,612.4(8.1)	1,405.1(7.4)	1,351.6(7.0)
Self-Employed	3,692.0(18.6)	3,757.9(18.8)	3,797.4(20.0)	3,886.0(20.2)
Unpaid FW[2]	1,749.3(8.8)	1,687.0(8.4)	1,808.4(9.5)	1,724.7(9.0)

(B) Weekly Hours Worked

	1996	1997	1998	1999
Employees				
Regular	51.2	50.3	50.1	51.4
Temporary	52.7	51.7	50.4	51.6
Daily	47.2	45.6	41.1	42.6
Non-Employees				
Employer	58.7	57.9	55.9	57.1
Self-Employed	55.2	54.5	52.9	52.1
Unpaid FW[2]	52.5	51.9	51.1	50.9
All	52.6	51.7	50.5	50.9

Source: Author's calculation based on data from the *Survey on Economically Active Population* (1996-99).
[1]Figures in parentheses are percent of total.
[2]Unpaid family workers working more than 18 hours a week.

share of temporary and daily employees, on the other hand, has risen. The increase in daily employees in 1999 more than offset the decline in regular employees. Self-employment rose during the period of economic crisis, as did unpaid family workers. It is notable that unpaid family workers decreased in 1997, but increased substantially in 1998. It is possible that many small businesses were converted to family businesses in order to cut labor costs, and many job losers may also have become unpaid family workers.

A part of the sharp increase in non-regular workers represents public works program offered to the unemployed. Kim (2001a) shows that the government sector accounted for 51.2 percent of the net increase in daily employment in 1998, which increased from a mere 2.8 percent in 1997. The increase in non-regular workers in the private sector appears to reflect firms' efforts to cut labor costs temporarily. Kim (2001b) shows that an increase in the use of non-regular workers was positively associated with the job separation rate of regular workers among sectors. He argues that the positive correlation is rather inconsistent with the organization-restructuring hypotheses and more consistent with the cost-reduction hypothesis.[22] Choi (2001) also reports a similar result.

Permanent Increase in Unemployment[23]

The massive fluctuations in employment were reflected in equally large fluctuations in unemployment. Unemployment rose from 452,000 in October 1997 to 1.65 million in July 1998, with three-fourths of the increase in a five-month period between October 1997 and March 1998 (see Figure 3). The increase in unemployment was unprecedented in Korea's labor market history in which unemployment fluctuated much less than employment.

Motivated by such a sudden increase in unemployment, a number of researchers have tried to estimate the natural rate of unemployment in Korea. Yoo (1999a) estimates that the natural rate of unemployment may have risen to 6.7 percent in 1998, and Shin (1999) estimates the rate at 5-6 percent in 1998. Yang (1999) argues that the high unemployment rate has shown a tendency to persist. Although unemployment decreased quickly in 1999 relative to 1998, their predictions remain valid; Figure 3 shows that unemployment was much higher at the end of 1999 compared to the end of 1996 while employment is quite comparable between the two points. Further, as of October 2000, employment almost recovered its long-term growing trend, but unemployment is still greater by 200,000 than in the comparable months in 1996 or 1997. The permanent increase in unemployment is an important issue for labor market policy.

The permanent increase in unemployment reflects changes in job search behavior.[24] There are three supply channels affecting the level of unemployment. First, there is the decision by nonparticipants on whether to remain idle

---

[22]Kim (2001b) considered the high-performance organization and core-periphery worker arguments against the cost-reduction hypothesis to explain the increase in non-regular workers.

[23]For detailed demographic patterns in unemployment changes, see Kim and Yoo (2001). This section focuses only on the "permanent" increase in unemployment.

[24]Unemployment increased "too fast," given the magnitude of demand shock. The demand shock placed on the economy by the crisis is roughly comparable to the shock that took place in 1979-80 following the second oil shock. Between 1979 and 1980, real GDP growth fell by 9.8 percentage points and the unemployment rate rose by 1.4 percentage points. Real GDP growth fell by 10.8 percentage points between 1997 and 1998, which was reasonably comparable to the 1979-80 changes, but unemployment rate increased by 4.2 percentage points. Although the two shocks were almost 20 years apart and the level of industrialization differed, the differences in unemployment responses appear too large. Other studies also point out that unemployment rose too fast in 1998. Yoo (1999b) shows that the unemployment rate in 1998 should have been 4.4 percent based on the Okun coefficient from the past three decades.

or search. Second, there is the decision by those who lost jobs on whether to exit the market or search. Third, there is the decision by those who searched for a job but failed to find one on whether to keep searching or exit the market. Figure 5(a) plots the number of nonparticipants starting a job search and their share as a fraction of nonparticipants. Both the number and shares almost doubled in 1998 relative to 1997, and although they subsided, they were still higher at the end of 1999 than in 1997. That is, many more nonparticipants started a job search than before. Figure 5(b) shows that a much greater fraction and number of those who lost jobs entered an unemployment spell instead of exiting the market in 1998. This tendency decreased somewhat in 1999, but it remained still stronger than in 1997. Lastly, Figure 5(c) shows that the number of people who had looked for a job but had failed to find one also increased substantially in 1998, although the share dropped somewhat, reflecting the much greater unemployment in 1998 than 1997. In sum, the first two supply channels increased unemployment, and the last channel somewhat limited the increase in unemployment.

Not all the changes in supply channels were exogenous in the sense that such changes could have been induced by the decline in labor demand through the income effect on labor supply. For example, large-scale job losses had left many households workerless and/or poorer, and previously non-participating members of such households might have been induced to enter the market to supplement household income. Indeed, middle-aged women accounted for a majority of the increase in the numbers initiating a job search after nonparticipation, at least a part of which is the added worker effect. Further, some of the job losers who entered an unemployment spell might have exited the market if their household income had not declined. Some failed job searchers exiting the market might have continued their search if the job access rate had not declined.

Kim (2000b) estimates the counter-factual series of unemployment under the assumption that there were no exogenous changes in supply by the jobless. The estimates account for the direct impact of the decline in demand through higher job separation rates and lower job access rates, and also for the indirect impact through income effects such as the added worker effect. By comparing actual unemployment and the estimated counter-factual unemployment rate, Kim argued that the exogenous change in supply behavior could account for 25-33 percent of the total increase in unemployment between 1997 and 1998.[25] On average, actual unemployment in 1998 was greater by 281,000 than predicted by past search behavior, suggesting that the unemployment rate would have

---

[25]More recently, Nam and Rhee (2001) show that such an effect could be even greater.

Figure 5. Monthly Inflow into Unemployment

(a) Nonparticipants Starting to Search for a Job

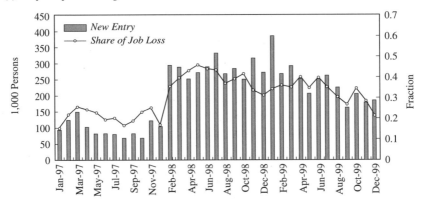

(b) Job Losers Starting to Search for a Job

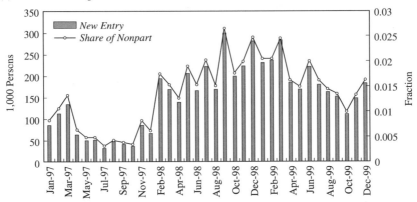

(c) Job Searchers Who Failed to Find, and Are Continuing to Search for a Job

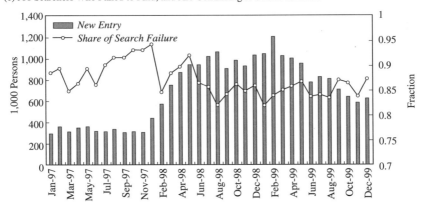

Source: Kim (2000b).

been 5.5 percent rather than 6.8 percent if not for the exogenous supply changes. The changes in supply behavior do not appear to have been induced by the expansion of unemployment insurance, which raised the relative value of job search against nonparticipation for only a small fraction of those who lost jobs. One must look to the forces that may have affected the broader population than those covered by the insurance. Various benefits offered to unemployed workers by the government may have induced nonparticipants to declare themselves as unemployed, to a larger extent than the public work program absorbed unemployment.[26]

Wages and Inequality

The effect of the crisis also shows up in wages. As indicated in Figure 6, nominal wages in firms with ten or more employees doubled between 1991 and 1996, rising an average of 15.3 percent a year. As the annual CPI inflation was 7.2 percent during the period, real wages rose 6.1 percent a year, and were 36 percent higher in 1996 than in 1991. The steep increase in wages stopped in 1998 when nominal wages fell by 5.9 percent between July 1997 and July

Figure 6. Nominal Monthly Wages during the Past 15 Years
(In thousands of Korean won)

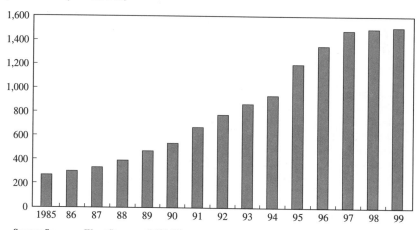

Source: *Survey on Wage Structure* (1985-99)
Note: Firms with ten or more employees are sampled.

---

[26]Kim (2000b) shows that the labor supply increased most among the part of the population that traditionally is detached from the market. This included women, the elderly, and less educated persons. He concludes that they might have remained idle if it were not for the unemployment benefits offered by the government.

1998. This amounted to a 12.5 percent decline in real wages, as the inflation rate was 7.5 percent in 1998.

Wage changes were not the same in all sectors. Industries with the greatest job losses experienced the largest wage declines. As indicated in Table 7, nominal wages fell by 6-10 percent in manufacturing, construction, retail and wholesale trades, and financial, insurance, and real estate (F.I.R.E.) between July 1997 and July 1998. However, nominal wages changed little in transportation, communication, and services, and even rose in public utilities in 1998. Indeed, nominal wages rose as much as consumer prices in public utilities leaving real wages broadly stable.

Three points are noteworthy about wage changes during the crisis. First, nominal wages have been flexible. If not for the wage fall, the decline in employment would have been much greater. Actual wage declines must be greater than indicated in the table because the workforce composition shifted away from low-wage workers due to the concentration of job losses among them. Second, the non-neutrality in wage changes appears less strong than the non-neutrality in employment changes (see Table 5). This suggests that employ-

Table 7. Nominal Wages
(Thousands of Korean Won)

	1996	1997	1998	1999
All	1,401.4	1,491.8(6.4)	1,403.6(-5.9)	1,572.6(12.0)
Men	1,563.8	1,659.7(6.1)	1,549.7(-6.6)	1,747.1(12.7)
Women	985.1	1,055.5(7.1)	997.3(-5.5)	1,133.2(13.6)
Manufacturing	1,322.1	1,357.5(2.7)	1,233.4(-9.1)	1,408.4(14.1)
Public Utilities	1,892.0	2,124.0(12.3)	2,288.1 (7.7)	1,736.1(-24.1)
Construction	1,424.6	1,548.1(8.7)	1,444.5(-6.7)	1,736.2(20.2)
Retail/Wholesale	1,274.9	1,427.0(11.9)	1,292.9(-9.4)	1,472.0(13.9)
Trans./Comm.	1,264.5	1,456.7(15.2)	1,429.9(-1.8)	1,372.4(-4.0)
F.I.R.E.	1,630.5	1,695.2(4.0)	1,578.7(-6.9)	1,958.9(24.1)
Services	1,677.7	1,818.8(4.4)	1,796.5(-1.2)	1,777.5(-1.1)
Size 10-29	1,205.2	1,328.1(10.2)	1,236.6(-6.9)	1,401.3(13.3)
Size 30-99	1,270.4	1,380.8(8.7)	1,321.9(-4.3)	1,477.4(11.8)
Size 100-299	1,336.8	1,430.6(7.0)	1,398.6(-2.2)	1,536.6(9.9)
Size 300-499	1,544.3	1,686.6(9.2)	1,589.1(-5.8)	1,709.1(7.6)
Size 500+	1,755.6	1,777.0(1.2)	1,637.7(-7.8)	1,869.6(14.2)

Source: *Monthly Labor Statistics* (July issues in 1996-99).
Note: Monthly wages in July of each year among firms with ten or more regular employees; figures in parentheses are percentage changes from previous year.

ment adjustments were more important than wage adjustments.[27] Third, the unusual increase in wages in public utilities reflects that most utilities are state owned. Because firms and workers in public utilities were less pressured by the crisis, wages kept pace with inflation.

The recovery in nominal wages in 1999 is a mirror image of the decline in 1998. Those sectors with the greatest wage losses in 1998 recorded the greatest comebacks in 1999, as they did in terms of employment. Nominal wages were actually cut by 24.1 percent in public utilities.[28] This recovery pattern strongly suggests that the increase in wages was to compensate workers for the suffering in the previous year. A similar pattern is also found in the size structure of wages. Nominal wages fell most for small and large firms between July 1997 and July 1998, and then rose most for the same firms between July 1998 and July 1999.

The demographic pattern of wage changes in 1998 can be deduced from Table 8. The gender premium had been declining in Korea before the crisis, reflecting female progress in the labor market, although the decline was relatively slow during the mid-1990s. Between 1996 and 1998, however, the premium declined somewhat faster. Given that employment fell less among men both absolutely and relatively, this suggests that men may have conceded a greater wage cut in return for job stability. The age premium, unlike its declining trend in the past, increased between 1997 and 1998, suggesting that the demand shock was even worse among the young population than indicated by

Table 8. Wage Premiums

	Gender Premium[1]	Age Premium[2]	College Premium[3]
1993	0.758	0.515	0.756
1994	0.717	0.466	0.696
1995	0.706	0.492	0.557
1996	0.693	0.494	0.565
1997	0.671	0.458	0.572
1998	0.648	0.482	0.603

Source: Author's calculation based on data from the *Survey on Wage Structure* (1993-98).
[1]Male/female wage ratio minus 1.
[2]40-54 years old/20-29 years old wage ratio minus 1.
[3]College/high school graduates wage ratio minus 1.

---

[27]Kim and Topel (1995) showed that most sectoral shocks had been absorbed by inter-sectoral shifts in employment rather than by inter-sectoral wage differentials in the 1970s and 1980s. They interpreted the results as indicating that Korea had a single integrated labor market.

[28]In particular, nominal wage cut in public utilities was a result of the pressure imposed on state-owned firms—the wage growth in 1998 was criticized as reflecting poor management in those firms.

the considerable employment loss among them. The college premium had been declining throughout the 1980s and the early 1990s due to the fast-rising supply of college graduates, but this trend reversed in the mid-1990s as the premium rose.

The rise in the age and college wage premiums, together with soaring interest rates during the early phase of the crisis, suggests that income inequality widened during the crisis. Table 9 shows that between the second quarter of 1997 and the same quarter in 1998, urban worker households experienced varying levels of income changes according to their location in income distribution. The poorest 10 percent saw their total earnings and labor income decline by more than 20 percent. In contrast, the richest 10 percent saw their total income increase by more than 10 percent, and their labor income decrease only by 2.0 percent. Among the middle-income group, total earnings and labor income decreased by about 10 percent. This pattern implies rising income inequality.

The changes in consumption expenditure were much more similar among income groups, indicating that low-income groups were engaging in dissaving while high-income groups were still saving, or alternatively that low-income groups had become more insecure financially while high-income groups were cautious in their spending.

The recovery in income in the following year is much less impressive compared with the loss between 1997 and 1998. The recovery tended to favor low-income groups. Most of the recovery took place in labor income, which suggests that the recovery was related to the strong employment gains among unskilled workers in 1999. The recovery pattern in consumption strongly favored the richer households, however, hinting that the 1998 decline in consumption among them was precautionary. The top 60 percent of the distribution recorded two-digit increases in nominal consumption while the bottom 40 percent recorded one-digit increases. That is, as the economy recovered from the early shock, households were re-adjusting their saving (consumption) behavior by doing the opposite of what they did the previous year. The recovery in income and consumption between 1999 and 2000 shows a similar pattern as that between 1998 and 1999, but the magnitudes are much greater in 2000, indicating gains were concentrated in the latter half of 1999.

One should keep in mind that the true increase in inequality, both in income and consumption, is quite likely to be greater than reported in the table because the above results are obtained from urban wage and salary worker households. If households with no labor earnings were added to the sample, inequality would have increased more.[29]

---

[29]The share of households with no labor earnings increased from 6.8 percent in 1998 to 7.9 percent in 1999.

Table 9. Percent Changes in Income and Expenditure by Income Decile

Decile	Variable	Period of Comparisons		
		97.2/4-98.2/4	98.2/4-99.2/4	99.2/4-00.2/4
Bottom	Earning	-23.3	4.3	16.6
	Labor Income	-21.4	3.9	13.0
	Expenditure	-7.3	5.7	9.5
Second	Earning	-14.2	2.1	9.2
	Labor Income	-11.4	-1.4	7.4
	Expenditure	-12.2	12.4	0.7
Third	Earning	-13.1	2.4	8.8
	Labor Income	-11.6	1.0	7.8
	Expenditure	-10.7	8.7	10.9
Fourth	Earning	-11.2	0.8	9.6
	Labor Income	-6.9	0.8	11.9
	Expenditure	-6.4	6.5	22.3
Middle	Earning	-10.0	0.6	8.0
	Labor Income	-8.4	0.8	9.0
	Expenditure	-9.3	11.7	7.6
Sixth	Earning	-9.2	2.2	6.2
	Labor Income	-6.3	2.1	7.2
	Expenditure	-12.7	15.7	8.8
Seventh	Earning	-7.8	2.1	6.0
	Labor Income	-4.5	-0.7	9.8
	Expenditure	-7.6	9.4	4.9
Eighth	Earning	-8.0	2.0	5.7
	Labor Income	-5.7	1.5	6.3
	Expenditure	-10.1	11.8	7.9
Ninth	Earning	-8.1	4.0	5.5
	Labor Income	-8.1	5.0	5.6
	Expenditure	-7.9	13.9	10.1
Top	Earning	11.8	-5.1	1.5
	Labor Income	-2.0	1.4	13.2
	Expenditure	-15.8	23.1	20.7

Source: *Income and Expenditure Survey on Urban Working Households* (1997-2000).

Concluding Remarks

The major impacts of the economic crisis are probably the increase in inequality, underemployment, and the permanent increase in unemployment. Rising inequality reflects labor market demands, which had already started to shift away from less skilled workers in the 1990s. The crisis intensified this trend. Labor income declined most among low-income households, but they were not necessarily those who gained most during the recovery. Although sectoral employment recovery showed a pattern of compensation for the previous year's loss, most job gains were concentrated in low-wage unskilled jobs. In other words, there was occupational downgrading among job losers during the crisis. Such a trend is likely to continue in the future, as the economy is swiftly becoming more knowledge- and computer-based, which is a worldwide phenomenon. Although access to information becomes easier for almost everyone, the winners in market competition will be those who can handle information more creatively and thus more profitably. The reform programs, if successful, will reinforce such competition in the market, and inequality will be pressured to increase.

Legal surroundings and firms' responses are also pointing to an increase in inequality. The share of non-regular employees such as part-time, temporary, and daily workers has increased, and will continue to do so as firms attempt to lower labor costs. Redundancy layoffs, a temporary help agency, and flexible hours are now legalized and will help firms further reduce labor costs. More flexibility in labor markets, coupled with increased capital mobility within and across countries, will increasingly put unskilled workers at a disadvantage.

The permanent increase in unemployment appears to reflect both market forces and changing institutions. The value of job search compared with non-participation has risen due to both income effects and higher unemployment benefits. Rising inequality increases labor supply of those who have been idle in low-income households, as is evident in the increase in labor supply from married women from the relatively poorer households. In some cases, children left school early to enter the job market. The fraction of 15- to 17-year-olds enrolled in school declined by 0.4 percentage point between 1997 and 1999, and the fraction searching for a job increased by 0.2 percentage point during the same period.[30]

Historically, workers have responded to a deterioration in their economic situation in two ways—human capital investment and collective actions. The

---

[30]Estimated from the *Survey on Economically Active Population*.

former is effective and brings long-term benefits, but it is costly. The latter is easier, but efficiency gains are unclear. Little evidence is found, however, for the former. In addition to the above-mentioned decline in enrollment rate, many households reduced educational expenditure during the crisis quite substantially.[31] Such a response may be only temporary, but educational expenditure has not yet recovered to the pre-crisis level.

Collective actions by workers tended to gain momentum during the crisis. As a means of protecting workers, collective actions will lose effectiveness in the future. The labor market will become increasingly more individualized, and the incentive to collude among workers will increasingly be limited to less-skilled workers. Further, as the recent incidences of collective actions have focused mostly on pie splitting, they have been viewed as one of the many obstacles to successful economic reform. Collective actions, at least at this point, do not seem to be the ultimate solution to the problem.

The changes during the crisis and current economic conditions suggest that the Korean labor market should also go through fundamental changes. Both firms and workers will find a way to improve their longer-term prospects given the changes in market conditions. Firms will have to look for new manpower management strategies and workers will have to look for new ways to cope with the changing demand situations. In addition, government will have to provide an environment in which both firms and workers are induced to make efficient choices. Given that firms and workers are optimizing their choices under the institutions provided by government, the role of government can be said to be the most important component in these changes.

Given the shifts in labor demand, labor market policies should focus on job creation, and education and training to induce efficient supply responses, and also on income redistribution policies such as a progressive income tax, an earned income tax credit, an effective placement service, and a stronger social safety net, to name a few. Many countries have been trying to do the same, so the question is not what, but how. Of course, all these must be accompanied by real and fundamental restructuring of the economy: healthy financial institutions and profitable firms are required for job creation, which is the most important policy target.

---

[31]Between the second quarters of 1997 and 1998, educational expenditure declined by 8.7 percent among urban working households. The decline was greater among low-income households: it declined by 13.0 percent among the households in the bottom 40 percent in income distribution, while it declined by only 4.4 percent among the households in the top 40 percent (*Income and Expenditure Survey of Urban Working Households*). If this continues, inter-generational earnings mobility will be seriously impaired in the Korean labor market.

The experience of the crisis in Korea offers an important lesson on how to implement the above measures. It is the coordination of a series of measures that matters, not the measures themselves. Public education should be strengthened (or funded more) to offset the decline in private expenditure. But the educational reform actually implemented hit the wrong target; it simply lowered the mandatory retirement age of schoolteachers, forcing many to leave, which effectively increased student-teacher ratios.[32] The market increasingly requires a skilled workforce, but the Ministry of Education has implemented policies that will discourage talented and hard-working students. An unemployment policy promoting temporary internships of young college graduates at large companies has potentially conflicted with the "no new hire" clause for redundancy layoffs. While the least-skilled workers lost most jobs, high-tech businesses were subsidized under the job creation policy.[33] The public work program paid 150 percent of the minimum wage for a minimal amount of work, attracting workers away from small businesses and hindering the entry of small, low-wage businesses. The newly introduced Basic Livelihood Protection Program guarantees each four-person household 930,000 won per month, which is 257 percent of the minimum wage and 70 percent of the average wage of all wage and salary workers. As argued above, unemployment may have risen permanently due to the ill-designed unemployment policy. These are just a few examples of coordination failure in implementing policies that are expected to have a large and important impact on the labor market.

The coordination failure is most likely to have arisen because some of the policies gave an unbalanced emphasis on temporary pain relief. As well elaborated by Pencavel (1996), product and factor markets are interlinked with each other, and thus policy coordination is a critical issue in dealing with all economic problems. Policymakers need to keep in mind that labor market issues must be dealt with in a more comprehensive framework covering both product and capital markets. Further, potential conflicts must be minimized among policies having various targets. In addition, labor market policies must place a stronger emphasis on long-term issues, especially on improving the skill levels of workers and encouraging human capital accumulation.

---

[32]An increase in class size is likely to lower the quality of education (see, for example, Card and Krueger, 1992; Krueger, 1997; and Lazear, 1999).

[33]Only wages, not jobs, grew astronomically in the sector as newly entering firms competed to attract a limited number of skilled workers.

References

Card, David, and Alan B. Krueger, 1992, "Does School Quality Matter? Returns to Education and the Characteristics of Public Schools in the United States," *Journal of Political Economy* 107.

Choi, Kyung-Soo, 2001, "The Causes of Increase in Non-Regular Employment and Policy Agenda in Korea," unpublished manuscript (Seoul: Korea Development Institute).

Juhn, Chinhui, Kevin M. Murphy, and Brooks Pierce, 1993, "Wage Inequality and the Rise in Returns to Skill," *Journal of Political Economy*, Vol. 101, No. 3.

Katz, Lawrence, and Kevin M. Murphy, 1992, "Changes in the Wage Structure, 1963-87: Supply and Demand Factors," *Quarterly Journal of Economics*, Vol. 107.

Kim, Dae Il, 1997a, "Demand for College Education and the Labor Market Outcomes in Korea," paper presented at the APEC-HRD-NEDM-KDI International Seminar on *Improving the Economic Performance of Education*, November 5-9 (Seoul: Korea Development Institute).

_____, 1997b, "Increase in Unemployment Duration (in Korean)," *Korea Development Institute Policy Research*, Vol. 19, No. 4.

_____, 1999, "Changes in Unemployment Duration during the Period of Economic Crisis (in Korean)," in Fun-Koo Park ed., *Economic Crisis and Changes in the Structure of Unemployment* (Seoul: Korea Labor Institute Press).

_____, 2000a, "Marginal Participants and Unemployment (in Korean)," *Proceedings of Panel Discussions for the Analysis of the Korean Economy*, Vol. 6, No. 1.

_____, 2000b, "Unemployment Dynamics during the Period of Economic Crisis," *International Economic Journal Economics Annual 2000* (conference proceedings) (Seoul: Korea International Economic Association).

_____, 2001a, "The Pattern of Job Growth during the Period of Economic Crisis (in Korean)," *Journal of the Korean Econometric Society*, forthcoming.

_____, 2001b, "Growth in Non-Regular Employment in Korea: Human Resource Management vs. Cost-Reduction Hypothesis," unpublished manuscript, Seoul National University.

_____, and Ju-Ho Lee, 1997, "Labor Market Development and Reforms in Korea," KDI Working Paper No. 9903 (Seoul: Korea Development Institute).

_____, and Robert H. Topel, 1995, "Labor Markets and Economic Growth: Lessons from Korea's Industrialization, 1970-1990," in Richard B. Freeman and Lawrence F. Katz eds., *Differences and Changes in Wage Structures* (Chicago: University of Chicago Press).

_____, and Gyeong-Joon Yoo, 2001, "Labor Market Changes in Korea Since the Crisis," paper presented at the KDI-EWC Conference on "A New Paradigm for Social Welfare in the New Millennium," East-West Center, University of Hawaii, January 11-12.

Korea Labor Institute, 1998, *Korea Labor and Income Panel Study* (micro-data files).

Krueger, Alan B., 1997, "Experimental Estimates of Educational Production Function," NBER Working Paper No. 6051.

Lazear, Edward P., 1999, "Educational Production," paper presented at Labor Studies Seminar, National Bureau of Economic Research.

Ministry of Labor, 1998 and 1999, *No-Dong-Baek-Seo* (in Korean).

_____, 1993-1998, *Survey on Wage Structure* (micro-data files).

_____, 1996-2000, *Monthly Labor Statistics* (in Korean).

Nam, Jae-Ryang, and Changyong Rhee, 2001, "The Economic Crisis and the Changes in Unemployment in Korea (in Korean)," unpublished manuscript (Seoul: Hanyang University).

National Statistical Office, 1985-1999, *Survey on Economically Active Population* (micro-data files).

_____, 1996-2000, *Income and Expenditure Survey on Urban Working Households* (micro-data files).

Pencavel, John, 1996, "The Legal Framework for Collective Bargaining in Developing Economies," Policy Paper, Center for Economic Policy Research, Stanford University.

Shin, Kwanho, 1999, "Changes in Unemployment Rate and Natural Rate of Unemployment in Korea (in Korean)," in Fun-Koo Park ed., *Economic Crisis and Changes in the Structure of Unemployment* (Seoul: Korea Labor Institute Press).

Yang, Joon-Mo, 1999, "A Study on Unemployment Fluctuation in Korea (in Korean)," in Fun-Koo Park ed., *Economic Crisis and Changes in the Structure of Unemployment* (Seoul: Korea Labor Institute Press).

Yoo, Gyeong-Joon, 1999a, "Current Labor Market Development and Equilibrium Unemployment Rate (in Korean)," in Ministry of Labor ed., *Enhancing the Efficiency in Employment Promotion Policy* (Seoul: KDI Press).

_____, 1999b, "Unemployment Projection Based on the Okun Coefficient (in Korean)," *Korean Development Policy Report* (Seoul: KDI Press).

9 Corporate Governance and Corporate Debt in Asian Crisis Countries

Eric Friedman, Simon Johnson, and Todd Mitton[*]

High levels of corporate debt contributed to the severity of the Asian financial crisis in 1997-98. Many Asian companies were more highly indebted and had a greater proportion of short-term debt than their counterparts elsewhere in the world. As a result, even a small shock to the macroeconomy was enough to push them into insolvency. Companies with more debt suffered larger falls in stock prices (Mitton 2001), and countries with more corporate debt suffered larger falls in output during the crisis (Kim and Stone, 1999). Why did the Asian private sector choose to have so much debt?

There are two plausible explanations. The first is that the debt levels of Asian firms were the result of rational choices based on standard financial decision-making. For example, the size, profitability, and growth prospects of a firm may affect its level of debt (see, for example, Titman and Wessels, 1988, and Myers, 1977). In this view, Asian firms were highly leveraged because management and investors were optimistic about the future. Such optimism is hard to avoid in a fast growing country.

The second explanation is that debt levels were high because the country-level institutions protecting investors were weak. La Porta, Lopez-de-Silanes, Shleifer, and Vishny (1997, 1998, 2000) find that weaker investor protection leads to less financial development, particularly to smaller equity markets. As a result, companies have to place greater reliance on debt finance (Rajan and Zingales, 1998a). Rajan and Zingales (1998b, 2001) also emphasize institutions, but place more emphasis on the political allocation of capital. In this view, Asian firms had higher levels of debt because this was how politicians channeled resources to chosen firms. While the institutions-based view is usu-

---

[*]Simon Johnson thanks the MIT Entrepreneurship Center for support. For helpful comments we thank Daron Acemoglu, Stewart Myers, and Andrei Shleifer.

ally presented at the country level, we show below that it has strong testable implications at the firm level. In particular, firms with weaker corporate governance will tend to be more indebted and this correlation should be stronger when country-level institutions protecting investors are weaker.[1]

This paper assesses the financial and institutional views of Asian pre-crisis corporate debt. We find strong evidence at the firm level that standard financial considerations, such as size, profitability, and growth were important determinants of debt levels. But controlling for these variables, we also find that debt was higher when firm-level governance was weaker. Across Asian countries open to capital flows, this result is stronger where country-level institutions are weaker.

Our findings are consistent with and extend the recent literature on corporate debt in Asia. Lee, Lee, and Lee (1999) examine changes in leverage of Korean firms from 1981 to 1997. They find that while debt levels in Korea can be explained partly by standard corporate finance models, even after controlling for factors such as size, growth, profitability, and fixed assets, chaebol firms have higher leverage than non-chaebol firms. Bongini, Ferri, and Hahm (1999) also show that chaebol firms have greater leverage. Kim and Lee (2000) argue that leverage, especially short-term leverage, explains the performance of Korean firms after the Asian financial crisis. Alba, Claessens, and Djankov (1998) argue that weaknesses in corporate governance and capital structure contributed to the crisis in Thailand. Claessens, Djankov, and Lang (1998) show that while vulnerabilities in the financial structure of East Asian corporations existed in the early 1990s, short-term borrowing increased during the 1990s.

At the same time, our findings fit within the broader recent literature on the cross-country effects of institutions. Countries with weaker legal protection for minority shareholders have smaller equity markets, other things being equal, and use less outside finance (La Porta, Lopez-de-Silanes, Shleifer, and Vishny (LLSV), 1997a, 1998, 2000a). Across the world (including Asia), the quality of legal institutions is strongly correlated with "legal origin," meaning whether the country's institutions derive from a common law or civil law tradition (LLSV 1998). Protection for minority shareholders is weaker in countries with a civil law tradition.

Our theoretical link between weak institutions, firm-level governance, and debt builds on the model of expropriation by managers in Jensen and Meckling

---

[1]We use the terms investor protection and corporate governance interchangeably in this paper. The more important distinction is between country-level institutions and investor protection/corporate governance institutions that are chosen by firms.

(1976). Burkart, Gromb, and Panunzi (1998) introduce the assumption that most diversion by management is costly, for example, because it involves legal maneuvers. LLSV (1999b) model the comparative cost of expropriation across countries in a simple static framework. This approach has been developed also by Johnson, Boone, Breach, and Friedman (2000).

Johnson, La Porta, Lopez-de-Silanes, and Shleifer (2000) define tunneling as the legal expropriation of investors by controlling shareholders. We use this term throughout our analysis. We also introduce the term "propping" to indicate the reverse process, i.e., the discretionary but legal transfer of resources into a firm that benefits its minority shareholders and creditors.

The next section provides a simple framework within which we can develop testable hypotheses about the correlation between firm-level corporate governance arrangements and debt. We then describe the corporate governance and financial variables that we use in our analysis, present country- and firm-level regression evidence, and discuss the macroeconomic implications of our findings.

Debt with Tunneling and Propping[2]

A Simple Model

Consider a family or "group" that has one publicly traded firm. This firm is controlled by the group but has separate legal status. The group owns share α of the firm and outsiders own share $1 - \alpha$. Retained earnings are denoted I. In period t, the group tunnels (or expropriates) S_t of retained earnings from the firm and obtains utility of S_t. The expected cost of tunneling is $(S_t^2/2k)$. We assume that $k \leq I$ and k is set outside the control of the firm (i.e., it is the country-level of investor protection). A higher level of k indicates less investor protection and a lower cost of tunneling.

Tunneling is wasteful in the sense that it reduces the amount invested. The group invests what it does not tunnel in a project that earns gross rate of return R_t in period t, and from which it obtains share α. To simplify the analysis, we assume that the support of R_t is contained on $[0, 1/\alpha]$.[3] Also, we assume that the stochastic variable R_t is persistent: i.e., $[R_{t+1}|R_t]$ first order stochastically dominates $[R_{t+1}|R_t']$ when $R_t \rangle R_t'$. For example, one reasonable model could be

[2]This section draws heavily on Friedman and Johnson (2000).
[3]No tunneling occurs if αR is sufficiently high. Given that α is often high in emerging markets, a reasonable economic boom may make it optimal for the group not to tunnel anything.

Brownian motion with mean reversion. We assume that the group observes R_t before choosing S_t.

The publicly traded firm needs to make a debt payment, D, each period.[4] In our simple model this payment does not vary over time. It can be considered as the regular payment due on a long-term bond. The firm's profit in period t is therefore:

$$F(S_t, R_t) = R_t(I - S_t) - D.$$

We assume that if in any period the firm's profit (including debt payment) would be negative then bankruptcy is declared and the firm ceases to operate.[5] This means that there are no future profits or debt payments or opportunities to tunnel these assets.

Intuitively, the group equates the marginal cost and marginal benefit of tunneling. Because the group owns α of the firm, it has an incentive to invest at least some of the firm's assets rather than to tunnel them all. As α rises, the amount of tunneling in equilibrium falls. As k rises, the amount of tunneling in equilibrium grows.

We now solve for the group's optimal behavior by solving the stochastic dynamic program given below.

The group's expected payoff in any period is:

$$\pi_m(S_t, R_t) = \alpha \max[0, F(S_t, R_t)] + S_t - S_t^2/2k.$$

This can be conveniently written as

$$\pi_m(S_t, R_t) = \alpha F(S_t, R_t)* H(F(S_t, R_t)) + S_t - S_t^2/2k,$$

where $H(x)=0$ if $x<0$, and $H(x)=1$ otherwise. Let δ denote the discount factor. Then the Bellman equation for the group's value function (expected discounted present and future earnings) can be written as:

$$V(R_t) = \max_S \{ \pi_m(S_t, R_t) + \delta *E[V(R_t') \mid R] * H(F(S_t, R_t))\}$$

and thus the group's expected payoff is $V(R_0)$.

---

[4]We model the case where the firm has debt, but it could be equity with some debt-like characteristics (e.g., the firm is punished if it has below market "expectations" for earnings.) There just needs to be some incentive to smooth earnings.

[5]We do not deal with the possibility that the debt is renegotiated. As long as both groups and investors lose something when the firm "goes bankrupt," the intuition behind our results holds.

Now we solve this problem. It is easy to see that the value function $V(R_t)$ is strictly positive and non-decreasing in R, as is its conditional expectation $W(R_t) = E[V(R_t') | R_t]$, by persistence. Let

$$S_u(R_t) = \text{argmax}_S \; \alpha F(S_t, R_t) + S_t - S_t^2/2k.$$

Solving the first-order condition gives:

$$S_u(R_t) = k(1 - \alpha R_t)$$

which is the solution for the static model without debt.

First we consider the case when $\delta = 0$ and future payoffs do not matter. Then the group's optimization problem deals only with a single-period:

$$S^*(R_t) = \text{argmax}_S \; \alpha \max[0, F(S_t, R_t)] + S_t - S_t^2/2k.$$

Note that the function to be maximized is continuous with (at most) 2 local maxima. Thus we can show that the optimal policy is $S^*(R_t) = S_u(R_t)$ for $R_t \geq R_m$ and $S^*(R_t) = k$ for $R_t \langle R_m$, where R_m satisfies the equation:

$$F(S_u(R_m), R_+) + \delta w + S_u(R_m) - S_u(R_m)^2/2k = k/2. \tag{1}$$

Note that when $D = 0$, then $R_m = 0$ and we get the same result as in the model without debt, but when $D \rangle 0$, $R_m \rangle 0$. In fact, R_m is strictly increasing in D. Thus, for $R_t \langle R_m$ the presence of debt causes the group to "loot" (i.e., tunnel everything) when rates of return are too low, due to the impending bankruptcy. This "looting" effect of debt is similar to the intuition behind the results in Myers (1977).

Now we return to the case where $\delta \rangle 0$ but for simplicity assume that $R(t)$ is distributed i.i.d., in which case $W(R_t) \rangle 0$ is independent of R. Denote this value by w. In this case, the group's optimization problem is:

$$S^*(R_t) = \text{argmax}_{S_t} \; \alpha [F(S_t, R_t) + \delta w] * H(F(S_t, R_t)) + S_t - S_t^2/2k. \tag{2}$$

Here, the function to be maximized has 2 local maxima and a single downward discontinuity at $S_d(R_t) = I - D/R_t$. Again if $D = 0$, then the firm never goes bankrupt and $S^*(R_t) = S_u(R_t)$.

However, in general the optimal decision policy, $S^*(R_t)$, can take on 2 forms depending on the relationship between R_m (which was defined in equation 1) and R_+, where R_+ satisfies $R_+*(I - S_u(R_+)) = D$, i.e., R_+ is the rate of return at which the firm can just make its debt payment given the amount that the group wants to tunnel. If $R_+\langle R_m$ then the optimal policy is the same as for the case above when $\delta = 0$. However, if $R_+\rangle R_m$, the optimal policy function becomes more interesting as there are 3 regions of behavior.

In the first region, $R_t \geq R_+$, $S^*(R_t) = S_u(R_t)$. In this case the presence of debt does not alter the group's behavior. In the second region, $S^*(R_t) = k$ for $R_t \leq R_-$, where R_- satisfies

$$F(S_d(R_-), R_-) + \delta w + S_u(R_-) - S_u(R_-)^2/2k = k/2.$$

In this case the group tunnels as much as possible (k) from the firm, and we see the "looting" effect of debt.

Interestingly, in the intermediate region, $R_- \leq R \leq R_+$, $S^*(R_t) = S_d(R_t)$. Note that $S_d(R_t)$ is increasing in R_t. In this region, $S_d(R_t) \langle S_u(R_t)$ and thus the presence of debt actually reduces expropriation, as the group is trying to protect his future earnings. We call this the "incentive" effect of debt because the debt induces better performance by groups (from the perspective of shareholders), as argued by Jensen (1986).

These three regions are illustrated in the Figure 1 where tunneling S_t is on the y-axis and R_t is on the x-axis. The dark line is $S^*(R_t)$, the optimal amount of tunneling given the value of R_t. The straight line from $(0,k)$ to $(1/\alpha,0)$ is S_u (R_t), which would be the optimal policy for $D=0$. As mentioned above, the presence of debt may reduce tunneling by the group in the intermediate region, $R_+\rangle R_t \rangle R_-$, in which the group may tunnel less in order for the firm to remain

Figure 1. Debt, Propping and Tunneling

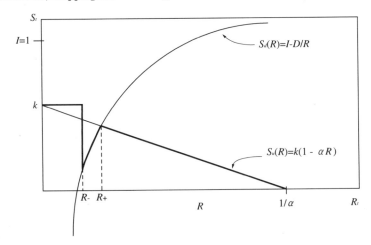

solvent. In this region debt strengthens the group's incentives to act in the interest of shareholders, as suggested by Jensen and Meckling (1976) and Jensen (1986).

Note that in this intermediate region, the group may even tunnel less than 0, i.e., the group puts its own money into the firm to prevent bankruptcy. The explanation is that earnings in the future (both from profit sharing and tunneling) are valuable and the group wants to keep the firm in business in order to have that opportunity. This is "propping."

There is also a region, when R_t is small, in which the presence of debt increases the amount of expropriation by the group since the firm is going bankrupt and thus there is no gain to be had from firm profits. In this region there can be a "debt overhang" that causes groups to expropriate more and thus, as in Myers (1977), hurt the interests of outside shareholders and bondholders.

It is straightforward to show that the qualitative aspects of this analysis are not changed in the general model, where R_t is persistent, but not necessarily i.i.d. In this case equation (2) is changed by replacing w with $W(R_t)$. Since this function is nondecreasing, the solution still breaks into three types of regions: normal, in which there is no effect of debt; looting, where the effect of debt causes increased tunneling; and "anti-theft incentives," where the presence of debt causes the group to tunnel less, in order to protect the firm from bankruptcy. The major difference is simply that the points at which the transition between regions occurs now have to be derived by solving the complete stochastic dynamic program.

In a dynamic context, we have shown the effects of debt on tunneling compared to the 100 percent equity financing case. If the return on investment, R, is sufficiently high, then the presence of debt has no effect. If R is sufficiently low, then the presence of debt can increase the amount of tunneling (a result in line with the intuition regarding "debt overhang" in Myers, 1977). However, if R takes on an intermediate value, then having debt will mean less tunneling, because groups want to keep the firm in business for the future (in this case, the intuition about the effects of debt is similar to that in Jensen and Meckling, 1978 and Jensen, 1986).

In this simple dynamic framework, higher levels of debt can induce better behavior from controlling shareholders (i.e., propping), but it also raises the probability of a collapse with complete looting. The cost of debt is that, in other states, it induces collapses that would not have occurred had the firm been financed just with equity. The optimal choice of debt levels, therefore, depends on the relative costs and benefits of these two considerations.

Extensions

Simple extensions of this model allow us to establish a number of useful results. First, we can allow entrepreneurs to choose the mix of debt and equity when raising capital. Friedman and Johnson (2000) show that under plausible conditions, debt levels will be higher when country-level investor protection (parameter k) is weaker.

We can also allow the entrepreneur to choose his level of firm-specific corporate governance and debt at the same time. An entrepreneur can choose to have stronger corporate governance and less debt or weaker corporate governance and more debt. In this framework, firm-specific corporate governance and debt are substitutes. In cross-sectional firm-level regressions, therefore, we should expect weaker corporate governance arrangements to be correlated with more debt.

A further extension allows debt of different maturities. It seems reasonable to assume that shorter maturity debt is more effective for inducing propping but also more costly in the sense of raising the probability of collapse. The maturity choice is therefore a trade-off between these costs and benefits. It is straightforward to show that maturities will be shorter when country-level investor protection is weaker and when the group chooses weaker firm-specific corporate governance.

Kim (2000) models the broader issue of group formation in a way that is consistent with our approach. In his model, firms borrow from banks and then decide whether or not to form conglomerates in which their debts are cross-guaranteed. After one period, the bank decides whether to liquidate or bailout firms that cannot make an initial payment on the loan. Risk-averse firms have an incentive to join a group, because this will make banks less likely to liquidate them. In this model, groups offer a form of insurance for individual entrepreneurs—in our terminology, they provide the resources necessary for propping, although they also reduce the cost of tunneling.

Macroeconomic Implications

In our model, the distribution of payoffs to outside investors will generally be skewed, with a longer and "fatter" left tail than is usual. Even if the underlying returns, R, are normally distributed, the actual outcomes can have the double hump shape shown in Figure 2. This arises because if returns, R, are slightly low, there is propping, but if R falls below a critical level, then looting occurs.

In this model, weaker legal institutions lead to fewer projects being financed (Friedman and Johnson, 2000). But weak legal institutions can also contribute

Figure 2. Corporate Governance and Crises

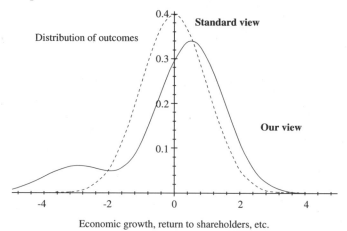

Economic growth, return to shareholders, etc.

to economic crises. Having weak protection of investor rights does not make shocks more likely, but it does mean that negative shocks have larger effects on the overall economy. In this view, institutions matter for a particular aspect of volatility - whether countries can suffer large collapses. Reasonable corporate finance arrangements in a weak legal environment can lead to a bimodal distribution of outcomes, i.e., either the economy does well or it collapses.

Testable Predictions

In this framework, debt acts as a substitute for country-level investor protection and firm-level corporate governance. If more frequent monitoring is helpful to the lender, then short-term debt will be more effective as a governance tool.

There are three testable predictions. Countries with weaker country-level legal protection for investors should have on average more debt relative to assets and, potentially, more short-term debt relative to long-term debt.

Second, within a country, firms with weaker firm-specific corporate governance will have more debt and more short-term debt. This correlation should be stronger in countries where institutions are weaker.

Third, when the political allocation of capital is stronger, there will be more debt, assuming that politicians care about the performance of the firms. Within a country, those with stronger political connections should have more debt.

Measuring Corporate Governance

Country-Level Institutions

La Porta, Lopez-de-Silanes, Shleifer, and Vishny (LLSV 1997a, 1997b, 1998) show that there are systematic differences in the legal rights of investors a-cross countries. LLSV (1998) propose six dimensions—taken from commercial codes or company laws—to evaluate the extent of protection of minority shareholders against expropriation. First, the rules in some countries allow proxy voting by mail, which makes it easier for minority shareholders to exercise their voting rights. Second, the law in some countries blocks the shares for a period prior to a general meeting of shareholders, which makes it harder for shareholders to vote. Third, the law in some countries allows some type of cumulative voting, which makes it easier for a group of minority shareholders to elect at least one director of their choice. Fourth, the law in some countries incorporates a mechanism that gives the minority shareholders who feel oppressed by the board the right to sue or otherwise get relief from the board's decision. In the United States, this oppressed minority mechanism takes a very effective form of a class action suit, but in other countries there are other ways to petition the company or the courts with a complaint. Fifth, in some countries, the law gives minority shareholders a preemptive right to new issues, which protects them from dilution by the controlling shareholders who could otherwise issue new shares to themselves or to friendly parties. Sixth, the law in some countries requires relatively few shares to call an extraordinary shareholder meeting, at which the board can presumably be challenged or even replaced, whereas in other cases a large equity stake is needed for that purpose. LLSV (1998) aggregate these 6 dimensions of shareholder protection into an anti-director rights index by simply adding a 1 when the law is protective along one of the dimensions and a 0 when it is not.

The highest shareholder rights score in the LLSV (1998) sample of 49 countries is 5. Investor protection is significantly higher in common law countries, with an average score of 4, compared with an French-origin civil law countries, with an average score of 2.33. In the LLSV (1998) data, there is no association between a country's level of economic development and its anti-director rights score, but a strong association between the score and the size of its stock market relative to GNP.

LLSV (1998 and 1999a) also find that the legal enforcement of contracts is weaker in countries with a civil law tradition. For example, the efficiency of the judicial system is on average 8.15 in English-origin countries (on a scale

of 1-10, where 10 means more efficient), but only 6.56 in French-origin countries. Legal origin affects investor protection both through the rights available
in the laws and how easy it is to enforce these rights. We use these measures
in our cross-country analysis.

Firm-Level Corporate Governance Measures

Mitton (2001) develops a number of measures that capture important dimensions of firm-level governance. He focuses on three aspects of corporate governance that vary among firms within the same country: disclosure quality, ownership structure, and corporate diversification.

Disclosure quality is an important element of corporate governance. LLSV
(1998) argue that accounting standards play a critical role in corporate governance by informing investors and by making contracts more verifiable. While
LLSV (1998) and Johnson et al. (2000) employ country-specific measures of
accounting standards in their studies, Mitton (2001) proposes two ways in
which disclosure quality can be measured at the firm level. First, he proposes
that a firm will have higher disclosure quality if it has a listed American Depository Receipt (ADR). This higher disclosure quality can emerge formally,
through mandated disclosure requirements of the listing exchange (for level
II and III ADRs), or informally, through a larger pool of investors spurring
increased demand for disclosure and increased scrutiny of the firm's reports
(see Coffee, 1999). Reese and Weisbach (2001) argue that increased protection of minority shareholders is a primary motivation for non-U.S. firms to
cross-list in the U.S. (see also Stulz, 1999). Lins, Strickland, and Zenner (2000)
show that the sensitivity of investment to cash flow falls when an ADR is
issued by a company from a country with a weak legal system and a less-
developed capital market (as defined by LLSV, 1997).

Mitton (2001) also proposes that a firm may have higher disclosure quality
if its auditor is one of the Big Six international accounting firms. Previous
research (e.g. Reed, Trombley, and Dhaliwal, 2000; Titman and Trueman,
1986) has associated Big Six auditors (or Big Eight auditors, for earlier years)
with higher audit quality. The Big Six firms may be more likely to ensure
transparency and eliminate mistakes in a firm's financial statements because
they have a greater reputation to uphold (Michaely and Shaw, 1995), because
they may be more independent than local firms, and because they face greater
legal liability for making errors (Dye, 1993). Additionally, even in cases in
which actual disclosure quality is not higher, Big Six auditors may offer higher
perceived disclosure quality and allay investors' fears because of their prominent, recognizable names (see Rahman, 1998).

The second aspect of corporate governance studied by Mitton (2001) is ownership structure. Shleifer and Vishny (1997) argue that ownership concentration is, along with legal protection, one of two key determinants of corporate governance. Large shareholders can benefit minority shareholders because they have the power and incentive to prevent expropriation. On the other hand, large shareholders can themselves engage in expropriation. La Porta, Lopez-de-Silanes, and Shleifer (1999) find high degrees of ownership concentration in firms from countries with relatively poor shareholder protection, and argue that the conflict between large shareholders and minority shareholders is the primary corporate governance problem in such countries. Morck, Strangeland, and Yeung (2000) and Bebchuk, Kraakman, and Triantis (2000) discuss how controlling shareholders may pursue objectives that are at odds with those of minority shareholders. Concentrated ownership also plays an important role in some European countries. For example, Gorton and Schmid (1999) find that firms are more highly valued when large shareholders own more shares in Germany. In data from 22 emerging markets before the crisis, Lins (2000) shows that large blockholders generally increase firm value, and that divergence between cash flow rights and control rights of controlling management groups and their families corresponds to lower firm values.

The third aspect of corporate governance studied by Mitton (2001) is corporate diversification. While diversification is not a corporate governance mechanism per se, previous research has suggested that agency problems are different within diversified firms. The lower transparency of diversified firms in emerging markets results in a higher level of asymmetric information that may allow managers or controlling shareholders to more easily take advantage of minority shareholders (see Lins and Servaes, 2000; Lins, 2000). If expropriation of minority shareholders increases during a crisis period, then the associated loss in firm value could be particularly pronounced for diversified firms. While diversification can also offer the benefit of improving capital allocation (Stein, 1997), particularly in emerging markets (Khanna and Palepu, 2000), this benefit could disappear in a time of crisis as investment opportunities diminish.

We follow Mitton (2001) in constructing these firm-level corporate governance variables for our sample of East Asian firms. Using data from the Bank of New York, we identify firms that had a listed ADR prior to 1997. Using data from Worldscope, we identify which firms had Big Six auditors prior to 1997. Because of the importance of name recognition, we do not include auditing firms that use local names even if they have affiliations with Big Six firms. (Note that by this definition Korean firms, by and large, are not coded as having Big Six auditors, because the major Korean accounting firms have

Korean names, even though some have affiliations with Big Six firms.) Using ownership data from Worldscope, we identify the percentage shareholdings of the largest shareholder in each firm for which ownership data are available. We further classify shareholdings as "management" shareholdings if the owner is listed as an officer or director of the company. Finally, using data from Worldscope, we classify firms as diversified if they operate in more than one industry, where industries are defined at the two-digit standard industrial classification (SIC) level.

The Determinants of Corporate Debt

We are testing two hypotheses. First, there should be higher levels of corporate debt relative to assets and more short-term debt in countries where institutions are weaker. Second, higher levels of debt and higher levels of short-term debt should be correlated with weaker investor protection at the firm level. This relationship should be stronger within countries where there is less legal protection for investors.

Country Averages

Average levels of debt in the Asian corporate sector were not particularly high compared to other countries. Table 1 shows that long-term debt was 12.9 percent of total assets on average across all Asian countries at the end of 1996, less than in the United States (19.8 percent) or Europe (15.6 percent). Even comparing the most heavily indebted decile of firms across countries, we find a lower ratio of long-term debt to assets in Thailand or Korea than in the United States. More unusual was the relatively high average ratio of short-term debt to assets and the high level of short-term debt for the most indebted firms. In all Asian countries open to capital flows (Korea, Indonesia, Malaysia, the Philippines, Singapore, Hong Kong, and Thailand), short-term debt levels were significantly higher than in other financial markets.

Demirguc-Kunt and Maksimovic (1999) show that firms in countries with a common-law tradition or with better legal systems generally use more long-term debt and a smaller proportion of short-term debt relative to long-term debt. However, this does not appear to be a completely robust result for Asia before the crisis. Table 2 shows that controlling for log GNP per capita, there is only a weak correlation between legal systems (i.e., British or French legal origin) and debt levels. Indeed, the only variable in Table 2 that debt levels are correlated with is French legal origin.

Table 1. Debt Levels of Asian Corporations Prior to the Financial Crisis

	Number of Firms	Long-Term Debt/Total Assets				Short-Term Debt/Total Assets				Growth	Profitability
		Mean	Median	Std. Dev.	90th %ile	Mean	Median	Std. Dev.	90th %ile	Median	Median
China	98	0.076	0.036	0.105	0.225	0.176	0.163	0.105	0.327	12.7%	6.8%
Hong Kong	281	0.104	0.076	0.103	0.244	0.145	0.113	0.152	0.323	11.1%	5.7%
Indonesia	106	0.179	0.146	0.174	0.437	0.167	0.161	0.130	0.355	13.8%	8.8%
Japan	2,083	0.129	0.104	0.120	0.287	0.170	0.142	0.149	0.360	2.4%	2.0%
Korea	211	0.216	0.204	0.156	0.341	0.285	0.281	0.131	0.450	15.1%	4.8%
Malaysia	316	0.111	0.070	0.130	0.269	0.144	0.112	0.143	0.335	17.6%	8.0%
Philippines	68	0.109	0.047	0.128	0.319	0.134	0.105	0.133	0.338	22.0%	7.3%
Singapore	174	0.110	0.056	0.128	0.302	0.120	0.086	0.116	0.275	10.4%	4.3%
Taiwan	193	0.091	0.064	0.096	0.210	0.150	0.119	0.120	0.335	14.4%	6.8%
Thailand	201	0.169	0.137	0.156	0.404	0.257	0.242	0.176	0.499	10.6%	6.1%
All East Asian countries	3,731	0.129	0.094	0.130	0.304	0.175	0.152	0.136	0.360	13.0%	6.1%
Hong Kong, Singapore, and Taiwan	648	0.101	0.065	0.109	0.252	0.138	0.106	0.129	0.311	12.0%	5.6%
China, Indonesia, Korea, Malaysia, Philippines, and Thailand	1,000	0.143	0.107	0.142	0.332	0.194	0.177	0.137	0.384	15.3%	7.0%
Comparative statistics											
United Kingdom	1,269	0.119	0.077	0.213	0.268	0.086	0.048	0.127	0.206	4.0%	7.7%
United States	3,273	0.198	0.157	0.217	0.461	0.047	0.015	0.148	0.111	9.0%	6.9%
Latin America	359	0.133	0.100	0.130	0.282	0.107	0.083	0.115	0.225	15.8%	8.2%
Europe	2,193	0.156	0.130	0.140	0.334	0.096	0.069	0.106	0.209	5.2%	5.4%
Other emerging markets	691	0.112	0.075	0.120	0.250	0.138	0.108	0.124	0.299	22.6%	11.6%

Notes: Data come from financial statements with fiscal year-ends closest to the end of December 1996, and represent all non-financial firms available in the Worldscope database. Growth refers to the one-year growth rate in total assets. Profitability refers to return on assets

Table 2. Corporate Debt and Country-Level Institutions

	Dependent variable is agregate total debt/aggregate total assets			
GDP growth	0.010	0.010	0.010	0.010
	(1.3)	(1.4)	(1.1)	(1.1)
Log GNP	0.007	0.010	0.010	0.010
	(0.7)	(0.8)	(1.1)	(1.1)
Rule of law	0.000	0.000	0.000	0.000
	(0.1)	(0.1)	(-0.8)	(-0.8)
French origin			-0.050**	-0.040
			(-2.1)	(-1.2)
German origin			0.000	0.010
			(0.0)	(0.1)
Scandinavian origin			0.010	0.020
			(0.4)	(0.5)
Creditor rights	0.005			0.000
	(0.5)			(-0.3)
Anti-director rights		0.011		0.006
		(1.5)		(0.5)
Number of observations	40	40	40	40
Adjusted R-squared	0.02	0.05	0.04	-0.02

Notes: The table presents results of OLS regressions of levels of corporate debt on country-level measures of legal protection. The dependent variable is aggregate total debt of all firms in the country divided by aggregate total assets of all firms in the country. All countries with 30 or more non-financial firms in the Worldscope database as of the end of 1996 are included. "Rule of Law", "Creditor Rights", and "Antidirector Rights" are based on scores defined in La Porta, Lopez-de-Silanes, Shleifer, and Vishny (1998). Also estimated but not reported is a constant term. Heteroskedasticity-robust t-statistics are in parentheses, and asterisks denote levels of significance (**=5%).

There appears to be a more robust relationship using data on short-term debt. Countries with a weaker rule of law have higher levels of short-term debt (Table 3). French and German legal origin are also correlated with higher short-term debt levels. Weaker anti-director rights are associated with higher short-term debt levels.

The cross-country evidence, therefore, is broadly supportive of the idea that weak institutions were correlated with higher debt levels for the Asian corporate sector before the crisis, but it is not conclusive. With country-level data it is very hard to distinguish the financial and institutional hypotheses. We therefore turn to firm-level analysis. However, we continue to differentiate between two sets of Asian countries open to capital flows: those with relatively good country-level governance institutions (Hong Kong, Singapore, and Taiwan) and those with relatively weak institutions (China, Indonesia, Korea, Malaysia, Thailand, and the Philippines.)

Table 3. Short-Term Corporate Debt and Country-Level Institutions

	Dependent variable is agregate total short-term debt/aggregate total assets				
GDP growth	0.010	0.010	0.010	0.010	0.010
	(1.3)	(1.5)	(1.4)	(1.4)	(1.2)
Log GNP	0.020	0.020*	0.020*	0.010	0.010
	(1.6)	(1.7)	(1.7)	(1.1)	(1.1)
Rule of law	-0.020**	-0.020**	-0.020**	-0.020***	-0.020***
	(-2.5)	(-2.3)	(-2.3)	(-3.0)	(-2.7)
French origin				0.080**	0.070
				(2.2)	(1.4)
German origin				0.150***	0.130***
				(5.6)	(3.5)
Scandinavian origin				0.080	0.080
				(1.5)	(1.4)
Creditor rights	-0.010		-0.003		0.010
	(-0.7)		-[0.2]		(0.4)
Anti-director rights		-0.030**	-0.030**	0.230	-0.010
		(-2.5)	-[2.5]	(1.5)	(-0.8)
Number of observations	40	40	40	40	40
Adjusted *R*-squared	0.11	0.22	0.19	0.27	0.24

Notes: The table presents results of OLS regressions of levels of short-term corporate debt on country-level measures of legal protection. The dependent variable is aggregate total short-term debt of all firms in the country divided by aggregate total assets of all firms in the country. Short-term means maturity of less than a year. All countries with 30 or more non-financial firms in the Worldscope database as of the end of 1996 are included. "Rule of Law", "Creditor Rights", and "Antidirector Rights" are based on scores defined in La Porta, Lopez-de-Silanes, Shleifer, and Vishny (1998). Also estimated but not reported is a constant term. Heteroskedasticity-robust *t*-statistics are in parentheses, and asterisks denote levels of significance (***=1%, **=5%, *=10%).

Debt and Firm-Level Investor Protection

There is evidence that corporate debt levels in 1996 across Asia were partly determined by reasonable financial considerations. When we pool all 9 countries, Table 4 shows that larger firms had more debt and more profitable firms had significantly less debt. Growth, measured as the one-year percentage increase in assets, is not a significant determinant of debt levels in columns 1-8, but it is significant for Hong Kong, Singapore and Taiwan.

At the same time, our corporate governance variables are also significant. Firms with more concentrated ownership, specifically non-management ownership had lower levels of debt. In column 8, the coefficient on non-management ownership concentration is minus 0.30, which indicates that an increase

Table 4. Firm-Level Corporate Governance and Debt Ratios in Asia

	Nine Asian countries						China, Indonesia, Korea, Malaysia, Philippines, Thailand		Hong Kong, Singapore, Taiwan	
	(1)	(2)	(3)	(4)	(5)	(6)	(7)	(8)	(9)	(10)
Ownership Concentration	-0.20*** (-4.7)									
Mgt. Ownership Concentration		-0.16 (-1.6)					-0.42 (-1.5)	-0.40 (-1.5)	0.05 (0.7)	0.05 (0.8)
Non-Mgt. Ownership Concentration		-0.22*** (-5.1)					-0.32*** (-5.3)	-0.30*** (-4.9)	-0.07 (-1.3)	-0.05 (-1.0)
Diversified			0.03* (1.8)			0.05* (1.7)		0.06* (1.7)		0.03 (1.0)
Big 6 Auditor				-0.02* (-1.7)		-0.03 (-1.2)	-0.02 (-0.5)		-0.04 (-1.6)	
ADR					-0.01 (-0.3)	0.00 (0.2)		-0.05 (-1.1)		0.03 (1.2)
Size (Log total assets)	0.06** (2.3)	0.06** (2.1)	0.07*** (3.5)	0.07*** (3.8)	0.08*** (3.8)	0.05* (1.7)	0.06 (1.4)	0.06 (1.2)	0.04** (2.5)	0.03** (2.0)
Profitability (ROA)	-0.96*** (-3.2)	-0.96*** (-3.2)	-0.98*** (-4.0)	-0.99*** (-4.1)	-0.99*** (-4.2)	-0.95*** (-3.1)	-1.29** (-2.3)	-1.28** (-2.3)	-0.63*** (-5.9)	-0.62*** (-5.7)
Growth (1-yr. % increase assets)	0.03 (1.0)	0.03 (1.0)	0.05 (1.4)	0.05 (1.4)	0.05 (1.6)	0.03 (1.0)	0.02 (0.6)	0.02 (0.5)	0.09*** (3.0)	0.09*** (3.0)
Number of observations	986	986	1427	1427	1525	986	612	612	374	374
Adjusted R-squared	0.25	0.25	0.27	0.27	0.27	0.25	0.24	0.24	0.16	0.17

Notes: The table reports coefficients from OLS regressions of debt ratios (total debt/total capital) on variables related to corporate governance. All non-financial firms from the listed Asian countries with available data in the Worldscope database are included. Data are reported for fiscal year-ends closest to year-end 1996. Definitions: Ownership Concentration is the total stock holdings of all shareholders owning 5 percent or more of the firm; Mgt. (Non-Mgt.) Ownership Concentration is the total holdings of these shareholders who are (are not) listed as officers or directors of the firm; Diversified means the firm operates in more than one two-digit SIC industry; Big Six Auditor means the firm's financial statements are audited by a Big Six accounting firm; ADR means the firm has a listed American Depository Receipt. Also estimated but not reported is a constant, country dummies, and dummies for 11 of 12 industry categories. Heteroskedasticity-robust t-statistics are in parentheses, and asterisks denote significance levels (*=10%, **=5%, ***=1%).

Table 5. Firm-Level Corporate Governance and Debt Maturity in Asia

	Nine Asian countries						China, Indonesia, Korea, Malaysia, Philippines, Thailand		Hong Kong, Singapore, Taiwan	
	(1)	(2)	(3)	(4)	(5)	(6)	(7)	(8)	(9)	(10)
Ownership Concentration	-0.12*** (-5.1)									
Mgt. Ownership Concentration		-0.10*** (-2.7)				-0.09*** (-2.6)	-0.12 (-1.6)	-0.11 (-1.5)	-0.05 (-1.2)	-0.05 (-1.2)
Non-Mgt. Ownership Concentration		-0.13*** (-5.3)				-0.12*** (-5.0)	-0.18*** (-5.4)	-0.17*** (-4.9)	-0.06** (-2.0)	-0.06* (-1.8)
Diversified			0.01 (1.3)			0.02* (1.8)		0.02* (1.8)		0.02 (0.7)
Big 6 Auditor				-0.02* (-1.8)		-0.02 (-1.6)		-0.03 (-1.5)		-0.01 (-0.3)
ADR					-0.01 (-1.0)	-0.01 (-0.5)		-0.01 (-0.7)		0.01 (0.4)
Size (Log total assets)	-0.01 (-1.5)	-0.01 (-1.6)	-0.01* (-1.9)	-0.01* (-1.7)	-0.01 (-1.4)	-0.01 (-1.6)	0.00 (-0.2)	0.00 (-0.1)	-0.03** (-2.3)	-0.03*** (-2.6)
Profitability (ROA)	-0.36*** (-6.6)	-0.36*** (-6.6)	-0.39*** (-7.3)	-0.40*** (-7.4)	-0.40*** (-7.4)	-0.36*** (-6.4)	-0.39*** (-4.8)	-0.39*** (-4.7)	-0.30*** (-4.0)	-0.29*** (-3.9)
Growth (1-yr. % increase assets)	0.01 (1.0)	0.01 (1.0)	0.02 (1.5)	0.02 (1.4)	0.02 (1.6)	0.01 (1.0)	0.01 (0.9)	0.01 (0.8)	0.00 (0.1)	0.00 (0.1)
Number of Observations	985	985	1423	1423	1520	985	611	611	374	374
Adjusted R-squared	0.27	0.27	0.25	0.25	0.24	0.28	0.27	0.27	0.19	0.19

Notes: The table reports coefficients from OLS regressions of a short-term debt ratio (short-term debt/total assets) on variables related to corporate governance. All non-financial firms from the listed Asian countries with available data in the Worldscope database are included. Data are reported for fiscal year-ends closest to year-end 1996. Definitions: Ownership Concentration is the total stock holdings of all shareholders owning 5 percent or more of the firm; Mgt. (Non-Mgt.) Ownership Concentration is the total holdings of these shareholders who are (are not) listed as officers or directors of the firm; Diversified means the firm operates in more than one two-digit SIC industry; Big Six Auditor means the firm's financial statements are audited by a Big Six accounting firm; ADR means the firm has a listed American Depository Receipt. Also estimated but not reported are a constant, country dummies, and dummies for 11 of 12 industry categories. Heteroskedasticity-robust t-statistics are in parentheses, and asterisks denote significance levels (*=10%, **=5%, ***=1%).

of 10 percent in ownership holdings of a blockholder not involved with management is associated with a lower debt ratio of three percent. This result is consistent with the hypothesis that a large outside blockholder has the power and incentive to monitor actions of the firm on the behalf of shareholders. The coefficient on Diversified is 0.06, indicating that diversified firms, on average, had higher debt ratios of six percent. This result is consistent with the hypothesis that agency problems are more severe within diversified firms. While not significant in column 8, the coefficients on Big 6 Auditor and ADR are negative, indicating that firms with higher disclosure quality had lower levels of debt.

Table 5 shows similar results for short-term debt relative to total assets. In this case, firm size is significantly correlated with short-term debt only in columns 9 and 10: larger firms in Hong Kong, Singapore, and Taiwan had less short-term debt. More profitable firms in all countries had lower short-term debt levels. There is no relationship between growth and short-term debt.

The governance results in Table 5 are again consistent with the institutions hypothesis. Firms with more non-management ownership concentration have higher levels of short-term debt. This is a robust result across all columns. More diversified companies have more short-term debt, but only in the countries with relatively weak institutions. Management ownership concentration is correlated with debt but only in the regressions with all nine countries; it is not significant in either of the sub-samples. The magnitude of the coefficient on management ownership concentration in the subsamples fits with the result in the full sample, but the smaller number of observations means that the result is not significant.

Macroeconomic Implications

Firms and countries with weaker corporate governance had higher debt levels before the onset of the Asian financial crisis. How important was debt per se in determining the severity of the crisis across countries and within countries?

We answer this question by assessing the evidence that debt is correlated with adverse outcomes at the firm level during the Asian crisis. Assessing the precise impact of higher debt is made more difficult by the fact that weaker corporate governance likely affects performance both indirectly (via higher debt) and directly (via investor confidence).

Without a valid instrument for corporate debt levels it is hard to determine precise coefficients. In particular, we cannot determine if corporate governance acts on performance directly or just through increased debt levels. This is the subject of our current research, and the results reported below should be interpreted as only preliminary.

Country-Level Outcomes

Why would corporate governance matter directly for the severity of crises? Consider the model presented above with pure equity financing. In this case, the amount of tunneling will be increasing in k, the legal protection of investors. Intuitively, this implies that there will be more tunneling in a downturn when investors have weaker enforceable rights. Johnson, Boone, Breach, and Friedman (2000) discuss this possibility in more detail. They show that if expropriation by managers increases when the expected rate of return on investment falls, then an adverse shock to investor confidence will lead to increased tunneling, and to lower capital inflows and greater attempted capital outflows for a country. These, in turn, will translate into lower stock prices and a more depreciated exchange rate.

Table 6 summarizes some of the accusations regarding expropriation of investors during the Asian crisis. For comparative purposes we also include some notable Russian cases. Clearly there is strong anecdotal evidence that tunneling occurred during the Asian crisis.

There is considerable evidence that countries with weaker investor protection suffered greater adverse effects when hit by the Asian crisis. Johnson, Boone, Breach, and Friedman (2000) present evidence that the weakness of legal institutions for corporate governance had an adverse effect on the extent of exchange rate depreciations and stock market declines in the Asian crisis. Table 7 shows that in simple OLS regressions the extent of legal protection for investors is strongly correlated with the extent of exchange rate depreciation during the Asian crisis. Table 8 shows a similar result with the extent of stock market decline as the dependent variable. Johnson, Boone, Breach, and Friedman (2000) show that corporate governance provides at least as convincing an explanation for the extent of exchange rate depreciation and stock market decline as any or all of the usual macroeconomic arguments.

Looking at a broader set of countries, Pivovarsky and Thaicharoen (2001) find similar results. For all developing countries over the past 40 years, the size of the largest crisis (measured in terms of exchange rate depreciation) and the average size of the largest three crises are larger where institutions are weaker. They find that higher debt levels are correlated with a larger "worst crisis" in some specifications, but their data do not allow them to differentiate between corporate and government debt.

Table 6. Alleged Incidents of Expropriation in the Asian Financial Crisis

Company	Country	Date	Alleged Incident
In Asia			
Bangkok Bank of Commerce	Thailand	1996-97	Bank managers moved money to offshore companies under their control.
United Engineers (Malaysia) Bhd	Malaysia	1997-98	United Engineers bailed out its financially troubled parent, Renong Bhd, by acquiring a 33 percent stake at an artificially high price.
Malaysia Air System Bhd.	Malaysia	1998	The chairman used company funds to retire personal debts.
PT Bank Bali	Indonesia	1997-98	Managers diverted funds in order to finance a political party.
Sinar Mas Group	Indonesia	1997-98	Group managers transferred foreign exchange losses from a manufacturing company to a group-controlled bank, effectively expropriating the bank's creditors and minority shareholders.
Guangdong International Trust & Investment Co	Hong Kong/China	1998-99	Assets that had been pledged as collateral disappeared from the company when it went bankrupt.
Siu-Fung Ceramics Co	Hong Kong/China	1998-99	Assets that had been pledged as collateral disappeared from the company when it went bankrupt.
Samsung Electronics Co.	Korea	1997-98	Managers used cash from Samsung Electronics to support other members of the Samsung group (notably Samsung Motors) that were losing money.
Hyundai	Korea	1998-99	Managers of a Hyundai-controlled investment fund channelled money from retail investors to loss-making firms in the Hyundai group.
Outside Asia			
Tokobank	Russia	1998-99	Creditors who may have been linked to bank managers took control of the bank and its remaining assets following default. Foreign creditors got nothing.
Menatep	Russia	1998	Following Menatep's bankruptcy, managers transferred a large number of regional branches to another bank they controlled.
AO Yukos	Russia	1998-99	Managers transferred Yukos's most valuable petroleum-producing properties to offshore companies they controlled.
Uneximbank	Russia	1999	Following Uneximbank's bankruptcy, managers moved profitable credit-card processing and custodial operations to another bank.

Notes: Reproduced from Johnson, Boone, Breach and Friedman (2000). Sources for the table are: *Wall Street Journal*, May 7, 1999, p. A1; April 17, 1998, p. A12; September 21, 1999, p. A1; August 25, 1999, p. A14; April 4, 1999, p. A1; April 8, 1999, p. A14; The *Economist*, March 27, 1999 and September 11, 1999.

Table 7. Legal Protection of Shareholders and Exchange Rate Depreciation

	(i)	(ii)	(iii)	(iv)	(v)	(vi)	(vii)	(viii)	(ix)	(x)	(xi)	(xii)	(xiii)	(xiv)	(xv)	(xvi)	(xvii)	(xviii)
A. Enforceability of contracts and shareholder rights																		
East Asia Dummy		-0.06 (0.07)	-0.1 (0.09)		-0.005 (0.07)	-0.09 (0.09)		-0.05 (0.07)	-0.13 (0.09)		0.04 (0.09)	0.01 (0.12)						
Judicial Efficiency	0.05** (0.02)	0.05** (0.02)	0.05** (0.02)															
Corruption				0.05** (0.02)	0.05** (0.02)	0.04* (0.02)												
Rule of Law							0.04** (0.02)	0.04** (0.02)	0.03 (0.02)									
Corporate Governance										0.14** (0.05)	0.14** (0.05)	0.13** (0.06)						
Reserves			0.002 (0.002)			0.002 (0.002)			0.003 (0.002)			0.001 (0.002)						
R-squared	0.34	0.37	0.39	0.28	0.28	0.36	0.19	0.2	0.27	0.3	0.31	0.31						
Adjusted R-Squared	0.31	0.29	0.28	0.2	0.21	0.25	0.15	0.12	0.14	0.26	0.22	0.18						
Observations	20	20	20	23	23	23	23	23	23	20	20	20						
B. Shareholder protection, creditor rights, and accounting standards																		
East Asia dummy		-0.06 (0.08)	-0.13 (0.10)		-0.1 (0.10)	-0.11 (0.10)		-0.06 (0.08)	-0.11 (0.10)		-0.1 (0.07)	-0.11 (0.10)	-0.007 (0.03)	-0.06 (0.10)	-0.12 (0.12)	-0.0008 (0.003)	0.03 (0.10)	-0.02 (0.12)
Antidirector Rights	0.06* (0.03)	0.06* (0.03)	0.05* (0.03)															
Antidirector Rights x Judicial Efficiency				0.007** (0.003)	0.007** (0.003)	0.007** (0.003)												
Antidirector Rights x Corruption							0.008** (0.003)	0.008** (0.003)	0.007* (0.003)									
Antidirector Rights x Rule of Law										0.01** (0.003)	0.01** (0.003)	0.01** (0.004)						
Creditor Rights													-0.007 (0.03)	0.007 (0.03)	-0.003 (0.04)			
Accounting Standards																-0.0008 (0.003)	-0.002 (0.01)	-0.005 (0.01)
Reserves			0.003 (0.002)			0.002 (0.002)			0.002 (0.002)			0.001 (0.002)			0.003 (0.002)			0.002 (0.002)
R-Squared	0.17	0.20	0.29	0.26	0.30	0.35	0.25	0.28	0.33	0.29	0.37	0.38	0.00	0.02	0.16	0.00	0.01	0.06
Adjusted R-Squared	0.13	0.11	0.16	0.22	0.22	0.23	0.21	0.20	0.21	0.25	0.30	0.26	-0.06	-0.10	-0.02	-0.05	-0.12	-0.13
Observations	20	20	20	20	20	23	20	20	20	20	20	20	19	19	19	19	19	19

Notes: This table is reproduced from Johnson, Boone, Breach, and Friedman (2000). All results are for OLS regressions, with the dependent variable as the purchasing power of local currency vis-à-vis the U.S. dollar in January 1999 (end 1996=100). Definitions of indices: Judicial Efficiency (0-10, from 1980-83) is higher for more efficient legal systems from perspective of foreign business people; Corruption (0-10, from 1982-95) is higher if less bribery among government officials; Rule of Law (0-10, from 1982-95) is higher for stronger tradition of law and order; Corporate Governance (1-5, from 1998) is higher for better treatment of minority shareholders; Antidirector Rights (0-6, from 1996-97), is higher for better protection of minority shareholders; Creditor Rights (0-4, from 1996-97), is higher for better protection of creditors; Accounting Standards (0-90, from 1990) is higher for more disclosure in company reports. Total central bank reserves in billions of $U.S. at end 1996 is included as a control variable. Number of observations varies if data are missing. Standard errors are in brackets, and asterisks denote significance levels (**=5%, *=10%).

Table 8. Legal Institutions and Change in Stock Market Value

Dependent variable is the stock market value at lowest point in 1998 with end 1996=100

	(i)	(ii)	(iii)	(iv)	(v)	(vi)	(vii)	(viii)	(ix)	(x)	(xi)	(xii)	(xiii)	(xiv)	(xv)	(xvi)
East Asia dummy	2.0 (4.2)		-50.1** (13.6)	-63.6** (15.9)			-48.2** (11.3)	-55.0** (15.0)			-53.8** (10.5)	-56.0** (13.5)			-41.3** (8.4)	-53.4** (10.1)
Efficiency of Judiciary		2.8 (4.5)	1.8 (3.2)	0.003 (3.3)												
Corruption					7.6* (4.3)	9.4** (4.2)	5.9* (3.2)	4.9 (3.5)								
Rule of Law									6 (4.2)	10.0** (4.3)	7.5* (2.8)	7.1** (3.3)				
Corporate Governance													12.9 (7.50)	15.0* (7.60)	6.3 (5.00)	1.7 (5.3)
Macroeconomic Control Variable																
Reserves		-0.3 (0.4)		0.5 (0.3)		-0.5* (0.3)		-0.2 (0.3)		-0.6 (0.3)		0.07 (0.3)		-0.3 (0.3)		0.4* (0.2)
Obs	20	20	20	20	23	23	23	23	23	23	23	23	19	19	19	19
R-Squared	0.01	0.04	0.45	0.52	0.13	0.24	0.54	0.56	0.09	0.26	0.61	0.61	0.15	0.22	0.66	0.73
Adjusted R-Squared	-0.04	-0.08	0.39	0.43	0.09	0.17	0.5	0.49	0.05	0.18	0.57	0.55	0.1	0.12	0.62	0.67
Countries missing	China Czech Hungary Poland Russia	China Czech Hungary Poland Russia	China Czech Hungary Poland Russia	China Czech Hungary Poland Russia	Czech Russia	Czech Russia	Czech Russia	Czech Russia	Czech Russia	Czech Russia	Czech Russia	Czech Russia	China Colombia Greece Portugal Venezuela Russia	China Colombia Greece Portugal Venezuela Russia	China Colombia Greece Portugal Venezuela Russia	China Colombia Greece Portugal Venezuela Russia

Notes: Reproduced from Johnson, Boone, Breach, and Friedman (2000). All results are for OLS regressions, with the dependent variable being the stock market value (IFC Investable Index) at its lowest point in 1998 (end 1996=100). Definitions: Judicial Efficiency is an index from 0 to 10, for the period 1980-83, with a higher score meaning a more efficient legal system; Corruption is an index from 0 to 10, for the period 1982-95, with a higher score meaning there is less bribery among government officials; Rule of Law is an index from 0 to 10, for the period 1982-95, with a higher score meaning a stronger tradition of law and order; Corporate Governance is an index from 1 to 5, for early 1998, with a higher score indicating better treatment for minority shareholders. The East Asia dummy equals one for China, Hong Kong, Indonesia, Korea, Malaysia, Philippines, Singapore, Thailand, and Taiwan. Standard errors are in parentheses. Asterisks denote significance levels (**=5%, *=10%).

Firm-Level Outcomes

If corporate governance and debt matter for the severity of crises, we should expect to find correlations between performance, debt, and our governance measures at the firm level.

Mitton (2001) looks at five Asian countries most affected by the 1997-98 crisis, and finds those firms with larger inside ownership and less transparent

Table 9. Firm-Level Corporate Governance and Stock Returns in Asian Crisis Countries

	Pre-Crisis July 1996 to June 1997		Crisis Period July 1997 to August 1998		Later Period Sept. 1998 to August 1999	
	(i)	(ii)	(i)	(ii)	(i)	(ii)
ADR	-0.008 [-0.11]	-0.039 [-0.45]	0.116** [2.46]	0.104** [1.99]	-1.205* [-1.74]	-0.904** [-2.03]
Big Six auditor	0.022 [0.39]	0.066 [0.98]	0.073* [1.85]	0.045 [1.55]	-2.056 [-1.06]	-0.917 [-1.00]
Largest management blockholder %		-0.113 [-0.25]		0.154 [0.92]		2.777 [1.14]
Largest nonmanagement blockholder %		-0.161 [-0.73]		0.260*** [3.49]		0.191 [0.15]
Diversification*high variation	0.054 [0.98]	0.048 [0.76]	-0.082*** [-3.21]	-0.069*** [-2.77]	0.475 [0.95]	0.373 [0.91]
Diversification*low variation	-0.040 [-0.89]	-0.019 [-0.41]	-0.027 [-0.80]	-0.024 [-0.83]	2.818 [1.21]	0.695 [1.25]
Firm size	-0.025 [-0.36]	-0.007 [-0.09]	0.026 [0.98]	0.061** [2.31]	-0.714 [-1.03]	-0.180 [-0.51]
Debt ratio	0.000 [0.06]	0.001 [0.74]	-0.0031*** [-5.67]	-0.0024*** [-4.14]	0.036 [1.54]	0.014 [1.39]
Number of observations	356	289	384	294	370	288
R-squared	0.213	0.186	0.286	0.337	0.069	0.078

Notes: Reproduced from Mitton (2001). The table reports coefficients of regressions of stock returns over the periods indicated on corporate governance variables for East Asian sample firms. Stock returns are measured in local currency terms adjusted for local price changes. Firms with missing data on ownership, total assets, or debt ratios are excluded from regressions that include these variables. "ADR" means the firm had an American depository receipt listed in the U.S. "Big Six auditor" means the firm's auditor is one of the Big Six accounting firms. Blockholder percentages are classified according to the holder being associated with mangement. Diversified firms are classified based on having above- or below-median variation in investment opportunities. Also estimated but not reported are a constant term, country dummies for four of the five countries, and industry dummies for 11 of 12 industries, as defined in Campbell (1996). Heteroskedasticity-consistent t-statistics are in brackets, and significance levels are: * = 10%, ** = 5%, and *** = 1%.

accounting suffered larger falls in stock price. Table 9 summarizes some of his results. He also finds more diversified firms suffer a greater fall, particularly if they have more uneven investment opportunities (measured in terms of Tobin's Q). This is consistent with the view that firms with weaker corporate governance faced a larger loss of investor confidence. It may also be the case that more diversified firms are less able to allocate investment properly due to internal politics, as suggested by Scharfstein and Stein (2000), and that these political problems become worse in a downturn. At the same time, Mitton (2001) finds that firms with more debt suffered larger falls in stock price.

Lemmon and Lins (2001) confirm Mitton's (2001) finding that firm-level corporate governance was important during the crisis. Using a sample of firms from eight East Asian countries, they show that firm values (as measured by changes in Tobin's Q and stock price) declined significantly more for firms that had a divergence between the cash flow rights and voting rights of the largest owner. They conclude that value declined more for firms in which the incentive for expropriation of minority shareholders was greater.

Obviously a great deal more work needs to be done before we understand exactly when and how firm-level corporate governance matters for performance. Lins and Servaes (1999) also find a discount for diversified firms in seven emerging markets. Claessens *et al.* (1999) find a diversification discount for East Asian firms and worse performance for conglomerates during the East Asian crisis. Following the approach of Mitton (2001), Nalbantoglu and Savasoglu (2000) present evidence that Turkish firms with weaker corporate governance suffered a larger fall in stock price during that country's 1998 crisis.

Institutions, Growth, and Crises

Weaker corporate governance at the firm level is correlated with higher corporate indebtedness. Weaker corporate governance is associated with worse performance at the firm level during the Asian crisis, with potentially both a direct effect and an indirect effect through higher debt. The evidence also suggests that weaker investor protection institutions contributed to worse performance at the country level.

If corporate governance institutions in Asia are so weak, why have most of the economies begun to recover? Are their institutions really too weak to prevent the resumption of sustained growth? If institutions are weak, how did many Asian countries achieve high growth rates over the past 40 years? To answer these questions we have to distinguish between two kinds of insitutions.

The first type of institution offers effective protection against expropriation for entrepreneurs. Acemoglu, Johnson, and Robinson (2001) find that institutions protecting entrepreneurs in the past are an important determinant of institutions protecting entrepreneurs today. Colonies suitable for European emigration developed good institutions, while those with high mortality for Europeans developed more exploitative institutions. More generally, they show that the mortality rates faced by early European settlers are a valid instrument for current institutions, because mortality affected European settlements, settlements determined initial colonial institutions, and these institutions have had persistent effects. Using two-stage least squares estimation, Acemoglu, Johnson, and Robinson (2001) find that variation in institutions that protect entrepreneurs against expropriation account for three-quarters of the income per capita differences across countries (measuring from the first quartile to the third quartile of the cross-country income distribution).

The second type of institution protects investors against expropriation, perhaps by the government, but most importantly by the entrepreneur. It is this type of institution that is represented by parameter k in the model presented above.

The empirical results presented here suggest it is possible to grow with weak investor protection, as long as entrepreneurs feel protected. However, weak investor protection makes an economy vulnerable to collapse. This vulnerability arises from two causes. First, weak investor protection contributes to higher debt levels, as we have documented in this paper. Second, weak investor protection can directly undermine investor confidence, particularly when an economy has just been hit by a negative shock.

The implication is that basic institutions in Asian countries are consistent with economic growth. There is nothing fundamentally wrong with the protection of entrepreneurs in these countries. However, if investor protection continues to be relatively weak in an economy, this creates the potential for repeated severe crises and economic collapse.

Figure 3 provides represents alternative views of Asian growth in a stylized but hopefully useful fashion. Macroeconomic growth rates are on the horizontal axis and probabilities are on the vertical axis. The two graphs on the left-hand side summarize our interpretation of the conventional wisdom. Growth prospects before the crisis were considered good, with relatively small variance. The standard view is now that average growth will be lower and the variance on this forecast is high. In contrast, our view (on the right-hand side of Figure 3) is much more positive, in the sense that we place most of the probability distribution around rapid rates of growth. However, our reading of the evidence from the Asian crisis suggests that this distribution

Figure 3. Alternative Models of Crisis

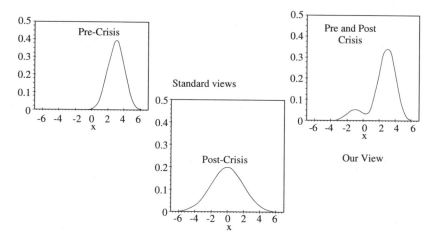

has two humps, so that there is a "fat" left tail to the distribution. It is this fat tail that could be eliminated by strengthening the institutions that protect investors.

Conclusion

There is growing evidence that institutions matter for macroeconomic outcomes in two ways. The fundamental need is for entrepreneurs to feel effectively protected against expropriation by the state. The evidence suggests that many Asian countries have done this relatively well on this dimension and strong "entrepreneur protection" institutions have helped produce impressive growth rates over the past 40 years.

Once entrepreneurs feel secure and are willing to reinvest their profits, a second related set of institutions also matter - the protection of outside investors against expropriation by entrepreneurs. It is possible to attract outside investors even when shareholder and creditor rights are weak, but when these rights are weaker debt will usually be higher. Higher debt levels make countries and companies vulnerable to collapse. Weak investor protection may also undermine confidence at critical moments, such as when the economy has just been hit by a negative shock. Taken together, these two effects of weak investor protection can turn a small shock into a big crisis.

A broader reevaluation of the macroeconomic implications of institutions is underway. For example, Blanchard (1999) argues that institutions in Western Europe were appropriate and well functioning, but could not handle the shocks they received in the 1970s and 1980s. In his view a functional set of institutions became dysfunctional due to a particular set of shocks. Our interpretation of the Asian crisis is similar. More generally, Blanchard (2000) suggests that macroeconomic behavior across countries may depend on the institutions that are in place. The Asian crisis suggests that the precise relationship between institutions and macroeconomic outcomes is of first order importance for economic policy.

References

Acemoglu, Daron, Simon Johnson, and James Robinson, 2001, "The Colonial Origins of Comparative Development: An Empirical Investigation," *American Economic Review* 91, 1369-1401.

Alba, Pedro, Stijn Claessens, and Simeon Djankov, 1998, "Thailand's Corporate Financing and Governance Structures," World Bank working paper.

Bebchuk, Lucian Ayre, Kraakman, Reinier, Triantis, George, 2000, "Stock Pyramids, Cross-Ownership, and Dual Class Equity," in Morck, R. (Ed.), *Concentrated Corporate Ownership*, The University of Chicago Press, pp. 295-315.

Beck, Thorsten, Ross Levine, and Norman Loayza, 2000, "Finance and the Sources of Growth." *Journal of Financial Economics* 58, 261-300.

Blanchard, Olivier, 1999, "European Unemployment: The Role of Shocks and Institutions," manuscript, MIT, January.

Blanchard, Olivier, 2000, "What Do We Know about Macroeconomics that Fisher and Wicksell Did Not?" *Quarterly Journal of Economics*.

Bongini, Paola, Giovanni Ferri, and Hongjoo Hahm, 1999, "Corporate Bankruptcy in Korea: Only the Strong Survive?" World Bank working paper.

Burkart, Mike, Denis Gromb, and Fausto Panunzi, 1998, "Why Higher Takeover Premia Protect Minority Shareholders," *Journal of Political Economy* 106, 172-204.

Choi, Buhmsoo, 1999, "Lessons of Crisis Management from the Korean Experience," paper presented at An International Forum on The Korean Financial Crisis, Harvard University, November 18-19.

Claessens, Stijn, Simeon Djankov, and Larry Lang, 1998, "Corporate Growth, Financing and Risks in the Decade Before East Asia's Financial Crisis," World Bank working paper.

Claessens, Stijn, Simeon Djankov, Joseph P.H. Fan, and Larry H.P. Lang, 1999, "The Benefits and Costs of Internal Markets, Evidence from Asia's Financial Crisis," World Bank working paper.

Coffee, John C. Jr., 1999, "The Future as History: The Prospects for Global Convergence in Corporate Governance and its Implications," *Northwestern University Law Review* 93, 631-707.

Demirguc-Kunt, Asli, and Vojislav Maksimovic, 1999, "Institutions, Financial Markets, and Firms Debt Maturity," *Journal of Financial Economics* 54, 295-336.

Dye, R., 1993, "Auditing Standards, Legal Liability, and Auditing Wealth," *Journal of Political Economy* 101, 887-914.

Easterbrook, Frank H., 1997, "International Corporate Differences: Markets or Law?" *Journal of Applied Corporate Finance*, Volume 9, Number 4, Winter.

Friedman, Eric, and Simon Johnson, 2000, "External Finance with Weak Investor Protection," manuscript, MIT, March.

Glaeser, Edward, Simon Johnson, and Andrei Shleifer, 2001, "Coase versus the Coasians," *Quarterly Journal of Economics* 116, 853-900.

Hoshi, Takeo, Anil Kashyap, and David Scharfstein, 1991, "Corporate Structure, Liquidity, and Investment: Evidence from Japanese Industrial Groups," *Quarterly Journal of Economics* 106, 33-60.

Jensen, Michael C., 1986, "Agency Costs of Free Cash Flow, Corporate Finance and Takeovers," *American Economic Review* 76, 323-29.

Jensen, Michael C., and William H. Meckling, 1976, "Theory of the Firm: Managerial Behavior, Agency Costs and Ownership Structure," *Journal of Financial Economics* 3, 305-360.

Johnson, Simon, Peter Boone, Alasdair Breach, and Eric Friedman, 2000, "Corporate Governance in the Asian Financial Crisis, 1997-98." *Journal of Financial Economics* 58, 141-186.

Johnson, Simon, Rafael La Porta, Florencio Lopez-de-Silanes, and Andrei Shleifer, 2000, "Tunnelling," *American Economic Review* (papers and proceedings), May.

Johnson, Simon, and Todd Mitton, 2001, "Who Gains from Capital Controls? Evidence from Malaysia," *Journal of Financial Economics*, forthcoming.

Khanna, Tarun, and Krishna Palepu, 2000, "Is Group Affiliation Profitable in Emerging Markets? An Analysis of Diversified Indian Business Groups," *Journal of Finance* 55, 867-891.

Kim, Byungmo, and Inmoo Lee, 2000, "Do Agency Problems Explain the Post Asian Financial Crisis Performance of Korean Companies? Chaebol vs. Non-Chaebol firms," manuscript, Korea University.

Kim, Se-Jik, 2000, "Bailout and Conglomeration," Revised version of IMF Working Paper, WP/99/108, August.

Kim, Se-Jik, and Ivailo Izvorski, 2000, "Aggregate Shock, Capital Market Opening, Optimal Bailout and Structural Reform," manuscript, IMF, KIEP and Institute of International Finance, December.

Kim, Se-Jik and Mark R. Stone, 1999, "Corporate Leverage, Bankruptcy, and Output Adjustment in Post-Crisis East Asia," IMF Working paper WP/99/143, October.

La Porta, Rafael and Florencio Lopez-de-Silanes, 1998, "Capital Markets and Legal Institutions," in Shadid Burki and Guillermo Perry editors, *Beyond the Washington Consensus: Institutions Matter*, World Bank, December.

La Porta, Rafael, Florencio Lopez-de-Silanes, and Andrei Shleifer, 1999, "Corporate Ownership Around the World," *Journal of Finance* 54, 471-517.

La Porta, Rafael, Florencio Lopez-de-Silanes, Andrei Shleifer, and Robert Vishny, 1997a, "Legal Determinants of External Finance," *Journal of Finance* 52, 1131-1150.

La Porta, Rafael, Florencio Lopez-de-Silanes, Andrei Shleifer, and Robert Vishny, 1997b, "Shareholders' Rights: Appendix," unpublished appendix to LLSV 1998.

La Porta, Rafael, Florencio Lopez-de-Silanes, Andrei Shleifer, and Robert W. Vishny, 1998, "Law and Finance," *Journal of Political Economy* 106, 1113-55.

La Porta, Rafael, Florencio Lopez-de-Silanes, Andrei Shleifer, and Robert W. Vishny, 1999a, "The Quality of Government," *Journal of Law, Economics and Organization* 15, 222-279.

La Porta, Rafael, Florencio Lopez-de-Silanes, Andrei Shleifer, and Robert W. Vishny, 1999b, "Investor Protection and Corporate Valuation," manuscript, Harvard and University of Chicago, July.

La Porta, Rafael, Florencio Lopez-de-Silanes, Andrei Shleifer, and Robert W. Vishny, 1999c, "Government Ownership of Commercial Banks," manuscript, Harvard and University of Chicago, November.

La Porta, Rafael, Florencio Lopez-de-Silanes, Andrei Shleifer, and Robert W. Vishny, 2000a, "Investor Protection and Corporate Governance," *Journal of Financial Economics*, forthcoming.

La Porta, Rafael, Florencio Lopez-de-Silanes, Andrei Shleifer, and Robert W. Vishny, 2000b, "Agency Problems and Dividend Policies around the World," *Journal of Finance*, forthcoming.

Lee, Jong-Wha, Young Soo Lee, and Byung-Sun Lee, 1999, "The Determination of Corporate Debt in Korea," Harvard Center for International Development working paper.

Lemmon, Michael, and Karl Lins, 2001, "Ownership Structure, Corporate Governance, and Firm Value: Evidence from the East Asian Financial Crisis," manuscript, University of Utah.

Lins, Karl, 2000, "Equity Ownership and Firm Value in Emerging Markets," manuscript, University of Utah.

Lins, Karl, and Servaes, Henri, 2000, "Is Corporate Diversification Beneficial in Emerging Markets?" manuscript, University of Utah.

Lins, Karl, Deon Strickland, and Marc Zenner, 2000, "Do Non-US Firms Issue Stock on US Equity Markets to Relax Capital Constraints?" manuscript, University of Utah and Ohio State University, October.

Michaely, Roni, and W. Shaw, 1995, "Does the Choice of Auditor Convey Quality in an Initial Public Offering?" *Financial Management* 24:4, 15-30.

Mitton, Todd, 2001, "A Cross-Firm Analysis of the Impact of Corporate Governance on the East Asian Financial Crisis," *Journal of Financial Economics*, forthcoming.

Morck, Randall, David Strangeland, and Bernard Yeung, 2000, "Inherited Wealth, Corporate Control and Economic Growth: the Canadian Disease?" in Morck, R. (Ed.), *Concentrated Corporate Ownership*, The University of Chicago Press.

Myers, Stewart C., 1977, "Determinants of Corporate Borrowing," *Journal of Financial Economics*, 5, 147-175.

Nalbantoglu, Osman, and Serkan Savasoglu, 2000, "Impact of Corporate Governance and Foreign Trading on Firm Returns During Crises: the Case of Turkey," manuscript, Harvard University, April.

Pivovarsky, Alexander, 2001, "Does Legal Origin Matter for Financial Development?" Chapter 2 in "Essays on Institutions and Finance," Ph.D. Thesis, Harvard University, May.

Pivovarsky, Alexander and Yunyong Thaicharoen, 2001, "Institutions and the Severity of Currency Crises," Chapter 3 in "Essays on Institutions and Finance," Ph.D. Thesis (Alexander Pivovarsky), Harvard University, May.

Rahman, M. Zubaidur, 1998, "The Role of Accounting in the East Asian Financial Crisis: Lessons Learned?" *Transnational Corporations* 7, 1-51.

Rajan, Raghuram, and Luigi Zingales, 1998a, "Financial Dependence and Growth," *American Economic Review* 88, 559-586.

Rajan, Raghuram G., and Luigi Zingales, 1998b, "Which Capitalism? Lessons from the East Asian Crisis," *Journal of Applied Corporate Finance* 11, 40-48.

Rajan, Raghuram, and Luigi Zingales, 2001, "The Great Reversals: the Politics of Financial Development in the 20th Century," revised manuscript, University of Chicago.

Reed, B., M. Trombley, and D. Dhaliwal, 2000, "Demand for Audit Quality: the Case of Laventhol and Horwath's Auditees," *Journal of Accounting, Auditing, and Finance* 15:2, 183-198.

Reese, W. Jr., and Michael Weisbach, 2001, "Protection of Minority Shareholder Interests, Cross-Listings in the United States, and Subsequent Equity Offerings," NBER working paper #8164.

Scharfstein, David S., and Jeremy C. Stein, 2000, "The Dark Side of Internal Capital Markets: Divisional Rent-Seeking and Inefficient Investment," *Journal of Finance* 55, 2537-2564.

Shleifer, Andrei, and Robert Vishny, 1997, "A Survey of Corporate Governance," *The Journal of Finance* 52, 737-783.

Stein, Jeremy, 1997, "Internal Capital Markets and the Competition for Corporate Resources," *Journal of Finance* 52, 111-133.

Stulz, R., 1999, "Globalization of Equity Markets and the Cost of Capital," Manuscript, Ohio State University.

Titman, Sheridan, and B. Trueman, 1986, "Information Quality and the Valuation of New Issues," *Journal of Accounting and Economics* 8, 159-172.

Titman, Sheridan and R. Wessels, 1988, "The Determinants of Capital Structure Choice," *Journal of Finance* 43, 1-19.

Wolfenzon, Daniel, 1998, "A Theory of Pyramidal Ownership," manuscript, Harvard University.

Wurgler, Jeffrey, 2000, "Financial Markets and the Allocation of Capital," *Journal of Financial Economics* 58, 187-214.

Comments on Papers 8 and 9

Hasung Jang

These are both interesting papers. The paper by Professor Kim deals with the labor market, which experienced the most turbulent changes during the crisis. At the beginning of the crisis, many claimed that high wages and high financial costs were the cause of the weak competitiveness of Korean companies. However, little serious research has been done on the labor market since the crisis. So I was very happy to read the paper, which does a good job of documenting the many structural shifts that occurred during the crisis.

The paper looks at the labor market disaggregated by industry and by the size of companies. However, a comparison of chaebol and non-chaebol companies may reveal more interesting results. For listed companies from 1996-99, for example, the labor force in chaebol companies decreased by about 30 percent, while non-chaebol companies reduced their labor force by only about 5 percent. On the other hand, as Kim notes, wages increased during that period by over 20 percent among chaebol companies while in non-chaebol companies, wages increased only about 8.5 percent. Furthermore, even though the absolute wage has increased, the ratio of labor costs to total expenses has monotonically declined since 1990. This raises questions about whether labor market rigidity or wage rigidity has contributed to lower profitability, or has weakened competitiveness at the microeconomic level.

The paper makes very strong claims in the conclusion that so-called social programs have reduced job seeking on the part of the unemployed, but presents no evidence in support of this claim. The author highlights the basic livelihood protection program, and argues that the high allowance is an obstacle for job creation. Such strong claims should be supported by evidence. The basic livelihood protection program simply replaced the low income family protection program, and I do not believe there has been any increase in the number of the beneficiaries.

Similarly, we have seen a decrease in the participation rate, but I do not know if we can blame that on the public work programs. As the paper notes, more women lost jobs than did men. The author also points out that when we talk about labor market flexibility we always talk about layoff flexibility, not rehiring and re-entering flexibility; we all know that here in Korea, those who work for Daewoo will never get a job in Hyundai. For these reasons, the lower participation rates probably reflect issues related to gender and the class of workers that affected decisions about re-entering the market, rather than the impact of social programs.

Let me turn now to the Friedman, Johnson, and Mitton paper, which I liked very much. Until now, the corporate governance literature has focused on the quality of corporate governance, or the ownership structure, and how that relates to the performance of companies. This paper has taken the argument one step higher to relate corporate governance to macroeconomic issues. I was particularly happy to see the focus on country- and firm-level measures of corporate governance and how they affected macroeconomic outcomes such as the deterioration of exchange rates and the magnitude of economic crises.

One of the interesting results in the paper is that at the firm level, the concentration of ownership turns out to reduce the level of debt, as does non-management ownership. This looks controversial because recent research tends to find that highly concentrated ownership is associated with poor company performance. The explanation may be that owners have concentrated their ownership in the more profitable companies, whereas the less profitable companies are owned by the affiliated companies. It would have been useful to test for the effect of family control by including the discrepancies between cash flow rights and controlling rights.

Finally, it is disappointing that the variable representing disclosure, which is a very important measure for the quality of corporate governance, did not work out as expected, probably because the measure was rather simple. A more appropriate measure of disclosure would, in my opinion, work better than ownership and the other variables in explaining debt levels. There is a more fundamental problem with the data commonly used to analyze the relation between corporate governance and performance: companies with the most serious governance problems perform the worst and fail. This means that they are often not in our data sets. Thus, many papers that claim that corporate governance does not significantly affect company performance may have a serious bias in that the worst companies in terms of governance and performance are not included in the analysis.

The authors emphasize the differing importance of investor protection versus entrepreneur protection at different stages of economic development. The argument is that although entrepreneur protection was one of the main strategies for development policy, with the shift to a more developed market emphasis needs to be put on investor protection. Although I would have liked to see more evidence to support the argument, it is very interesting and important because corporate governance is usually neglected by economists who focus on development policy. The traditional view has been that growth and development needs to be led by the government, often with heavy government intervention. But as the market environment has changed, not only for developing countries but also for emerging market countries, policies to improve corporate governance can be a very effective development policy to induce private sector financial funds, rather than the international financial institutions, to provide financing. It will also be a better mechanism to monitor the implementation of those policies through improved transparency and more involvement of minority shareholders and other creditors. Enhancing the efficiency of development policies is thus another way that corporate governance can have macroeconomic implications.

Zia Qureshi

I will focus my comments on the Friedman, Johnson, and Mitton paper on corporate governance and debt, and attempt to relate some of its findings to the corporate governance reform agenda in Korea. I will also make some brief remarks about Professor Kim's paper on the labor market.

The Friedman, Johnson, and Mitton paper is a valuable addition to a growing body of literature that shows that the institutions of corporate governance matter for macroeconomic outcomes. Some of the econometric results reported in the paper are not very strong, but taken as whole, and supported by corroborating evidence from other recent studies, including at the World Bank, the paper presents a convincing case. Weak corporate governance arrangements—low protection of outside investor rights, family/insider domination of corporate control and interlocking ownership, weak legal enforcement of contracts, lack of financial transparency—tend to produce a corporate financing structure that has a heavier dependence on debt, especially shorter-term debt. These factors also serve to undermine investor confidence, particularly at times of stress. Through both of these effects—higher corporate indebtedness and fragility of investor confidence—weak corporate governance arrangements can render an economy vulnerable to shocks and intensify their impact.

This is indeed what appears to have happened in East Asia. I agree with the authors that weak corporate governance arrangements in these countries provide an important part of the explanation of their vulnerability to the shocks of the late 1990s and of the severity of the economic collapse that followed. Weaknesses in corporate governance also raise agency costs and the cost of capital, and lower corporate value.

These messages were not lost on the governments of these countries. In their policy response to the crisis, improvements in corporate governance were included as an important element of the reform programs they adopted with the support of the international financial institutions (IFIs). Ironically, one criticism of the IMF- and World Bank-supported reform programs that was made soon after the crisis was that they were too broad in scope and encompassed elements such as legal and governance reforms, rather than focusing more narrowly on the immediate task of macroeconomic stabilization. Recent research, of which this paper is a good example, demonstrates that reform of the institutions of corporate governance is germane to the macroeconomic policy agenda, not an unrelated element that can be deferred until much later. Incidentally, these findings are also relevant to the current debate on narrowing the scope of conditionality in IFI-supported programs.

In Korea, the country whose post-crisis reform program I am most familiar with by virtue of my direct involvement in World Bank support for the Korea reform program, substantial progress has been made since the crisis to improve the legal and institutional framework for corporate governance. The corporate governance component of the Korean Government's reform program, which the World Bank actively supported, focused on four main areas: (i) strengthening minority shareholder rights and removing restrictions on the voting rights of institutional investors; (ii) clarifying the role and enhancing the independence of corporate boards of directors; (iii) improving financial transparency by raising standards for disclosure, accounting, and auditing toward international best practice; and (iv) strengthening creditors' rights by improving the bankruptcy system.

Much progress has been made in all of these areas. Indeed, among the East Asian crisis countries, progress on reform has been the quickest in Korea. Yet, a sizable reform agenda remains unfinished. While a further deepening of reform is needed in each of the areas I just mentioned, three elements will be particularly important going forward:

- First, enforcement needs to be strengthened. More explicit investor rights and other governance rules are useful only if there is a credible threat of sanctions under the legal and court system. This includes, for example, removal of obstacles to the prosecution of class action law suits by shareholders; enforcement of penalties and sanctions for breach of rules on disclosure, accounting, and auditing; and making the observance of the Code of Best Practice for Corporate Governance that was issued last year mandatory for companies listed on the Korea Stock Exchange.

- Second, for companies with a large controlling shareholder, typically a founding family, which account for a substantial proportion of listed companies in Korea, a priority is to strengthen legal rules relating to conflict of interest and their enforcement. Compared with companies that are widely held, voting rights of minority shareholders are less effective in protecting their interests in companies with a large controlling shareholder. More important are legal safeguards in dealing with transactions where the actions of managers/directors conflict with their fiduciary "duty of loyalty" to act in the best interests of the company and its shareholders. Examples of such safeguards are board or shareholder approval requirements for transactions with related parties, dissenters' appraisal remedies for M&As, and pre-emptive subscription rights for shareholders.
- Third, market discipline needs to be strengthened to permit market forces to exert greater pressure on firms to adhere to sound corporate governance practices. This includes, for example, further progress in removing obstacles to M&As and strengthening the insolvency system in order to make takeovers or insolvency more credible threats to firms; stronger exercise by the creditor financial institutions of their fiduciary responsibilities in monitoring corporate performance; and strengthening of complementary competition policies and their enforcement to limit non-arm's-length transactions, insider-dealings, and interlocking-ownership that create opportunities for abuse of outside investor rights.

Complementing these improvements in corporate governance, Korea's corporate culture needs to shift in two desirable directions: separation of management from ownership; and maximization of shareholder value rather than corporate size as the main driver of corporate effort. Moreover, Korea needs to continue to move away from the old system of public-private relations characterized by government intervention and provision of implicit insurance (and the associated moral hazard).

Through costly corporate debt restructuring, Korea has made considerable progress in reducing high corporate debt-equity ratios that prevailed prior to the crisis toward levels that are more sustainable. However, unless there are fundamental improvements in the underlying corporate governance regime, this progress runs the risk of being only temporary. If corporate leverage begins to rise again, the systemic vulnerability to crisis would rise with it.

If firms are to reduce their dependence on debt financing, growth will slow if they are then to rely mainly on their own retained earnings, and resources will be less efficiently allocated. A longer-run strategy for sustainable growth must be based on developing equity markets. And if these are to develop, improved corporate governance, including strong protection for minority shareholders, is essential.

I have two additional comments on the Friedman, Johnson, and Mitton paper.

- The paper explains well why weak corporate governance arrangements create incentives for firms to take on more debt than equity. However, what is less clear is why, on the supply side, the providers of debt finance continue to lend large amounts in the face of poor corporate governance practices and rising debt-equity ratios, and hence increasing corporate financial vulnerability. For instance, in Korea in the 1990s, lenders continued to lend heavily to the *chaebol* even in the face of declining corporate performance and mounting debt-equity ratios from levels that were already high. True, being the residual risk bearers, equity owners bear more risk as their claim is only to whatever is left after all prior claims, including those of lenders, have been paid. But lenders face risks too which rise as the financial vulnerability of the borrower rises with increasing indebtedness. I suspect that expectations of a public bailout in the event of loans turning sour provide part of the explanation for the behavior of lenders, both domestic and foreign.
- Second, if this presumption is correct, shouldn't such moral hazard play a more important role in the analysis of corporate indebtedness than it does in the paper? The paper looks briefly at the role of political allocation of lending, but the moral hazard issue I am referring to is broader than that. There is some support for the role of moral hazard in the data. Korea's corporate governance indicators, though lower than those of the advanced economies, have been better than those of most of the other East Asian emerging market countries. Yet, Korea's corporate sector indebtedness has been much higher. Perhaps the traditionally close public-private relations in Korea, and the "too big to fail" phenomenon from which Korea is now beginning to move away, provide part of the explanation.

I turn now to the paper by Professor Kim on Korea's labor market. The paper provides an analysis of labor market changes in Korea since the crisis in impressive detail. I will make only two points:

First, the detailed microeconomic analysis of the labor market would have been more useful if it had been placed in a more macroeconomic and dynamic context. The paper finds that some of the changes in labor market policy, such as liberalization of layoffs and use of temporary labor, have contributed to a rise in wage inequality, and an increase in inferior and less secure jobs at the lower end of the skill range. In a macroeconomic context, these results do not imply that liberalizing layoffs and freeing the use of contract or temporary labor were the wrong policies to adopt. Of course, increased labor market flexibility was a correct policy response, and a necessary part of the reform package in order to allow the needed corporate and industrial restructuring to proceed. Under a proper assignment of policies, increased inequality should be dealt with through other policies, not maintenance of rigidities in the labor market. For example, Kim refers to increased wage inequalities resulting from the rising wages of those with IT skills and declining wages of unskilled workers. The correct policy response to this, of course, is not to prevent such labor market adjustment by limiting labor market flexibility but, more positively, to expand education and broaden access to IT knowledge, as the Korean Government is now trying to do. It would be unwise to overburden labor market policy with a multiplicity of objectives.

Similarly, if the effects of the rise in unemployment and underemployment and the decline in job security are placed in a dynamic rather than static context, one could argue that these negative short-term effects of increased labor flexibility could be more than offset in the medium term by increased efficiency and growth that enhanced labor market flexibility would contribute to. In the interim, of course, it is important to mitigate the impact on the unemployed, especially the poor, by appropriately designed and targeted social safety net programs.

Second, and here I fully agree with Professor Kim, in designing the safety nets, such as defining the level of benefits and the actuarial structure of unemployment insurance, it is vitally important to ensure that these safety nets do not introduce new rigidities and distortions in the labor market that lead to a permanent rise in unemployment—a higher natural rate of unemployment. The unhappy European experience in this area provides important lessons for other countries.

10 Economic Growth in East Asia Before and After the Financial Crisis

*Robert J. Barro**

The Asian financial crisis began with the floating of the Thai baht in July 1997. The crisis then spread rapidly to the Philippine peso and the Malaysian ringgit. In August, the Indonesian rupiah devalued, ultimately by more than any other Asian currency. Relatively small depreciations occurred in the Singaporean dollar, starting in August, and the New Taiwan dollar, starting in October. The South Korean won depreciated substantially starting in November. Japan also had a moderate devaluation between July 1997 and January 1998. No significant devaluations took place in China, which has remained relatively insulated from world financial markets, and Hong Kong, which maintained a currency board linked to the U.S. dollar.

This study focuses on the immediate and long-term effects of the Asian financial crisis on economic performance in east Asia. Specifically, I consider the behavior of economic growth and investment in China, Hong Kong, Indonesia, Japan, South Korea, Malaysia, the Philippines, Singapore, Taiwan, and Thailand.

These ten economies break down naturally into two groups depending on the extent to which they were impacted by the financial crisis of 1997-98. The first group of five countries—Indonesia, South Korea, Malaysia, the Philippines, and Thailand—experienced nominal currency depreciations of more than 50 percent from July 1997 to early 1998. In these countries, offshore nominal interest rates (determined primarily by forward exchange rates) or onshore rates reached at least 25 percent at some point between June 1997 and January 1998. Subsequently, I refer to this group as Asian-crisis countries. The other five east Asian economies experienced nominal

---

*This research has been supported in part by a grant from the National Science Foundation.

depreciations of less than 25 percent, and nominal interest rates remained below 20 percent.[1]

One objective is to assess whether the Asian financial crisis had a long lasting effect on growth prospects and other dimensions of economic performance for the two groups of Asian economies. This task is difficult because only two years' of economic data are available after the ends of the financial crises in 1998. However, I get some information first by looking at recent behavior within the group of east Asian economies, second by imbedding this behavior within a panel analysis of a large number of economies, and finally by using the panel to take a broader view of the impact of currency crises.

Recent Economic Performance in the East Asian Economies

Economic Growth

Figure 1 shows the annual growth rate of real per capita GDP for each of the east Asian economies from 1960 to 2000.[2] The sharp economic contractions in 1998 for the five Asian-crisis countries are evident: real per capita GDP fell by 16 percent in Indonesia, 12 percent in Thailand, 10 percent in Malaysia, and 8 percent in South Korea, but only 3 percent in the Philippines. The other five east Asian economies were less affected: per capita growth during 1998 was -5 percent in Hong Kong, -3 percent in Singapore, -1 percent in Japan, 4 percent in Taiwan, and 6 percent in China.

In 1999-2000, economic recoveries occurred, and the per capita growth rates were positive in all ten economies. Among the five crisis countries, the annualized per capita growth rates were 8 percent in South Korea, 5 percent in Malaysia, 3 percent in Thailand, and 1 percent in the Philippines and Indonesia. For the other five economies, the rates were 7 percent in China, 5 percent in Hong Kong and Taiwan, 4 percent in Singapore, and 1 percent in Japan.

---

[1]Offshore interest rates in late 1997 reached 18 percent in Hong Kong and 17 percent in Singapore. Meaningful data on interest rates are unavailable for China, but the official exchange rate remained virtually unchanged.

[2]The underlying data, in most cases through 1992 (1991 for South Korea, 1990 for Taiwan), are the purchasing-power adjusted values from Summers and Heston (1991 and later years). I updated the Summers-Heston data through 2000 by using information on real GDP from the World Bank, *World Development Indicators*, and the Economist Intelligence Unit, *Country Data*.

Figure 1. Growth Rate of Per Capita GDP

(In percent)

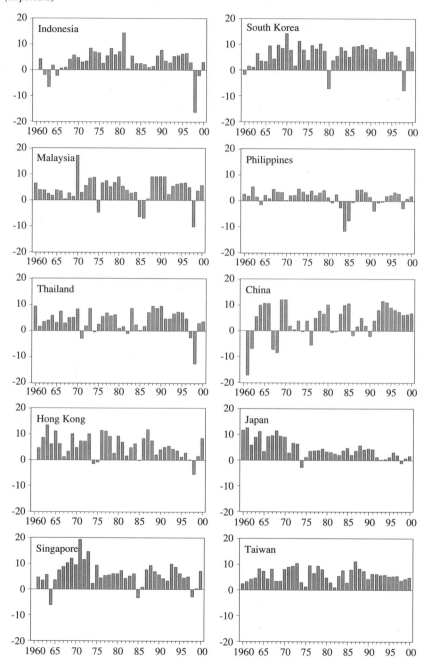

A central issue is whether these recoveries signal a return to the previous patterns of growth. More precisely, even without the Asian financial crisis, projected growth rates in east Asia would have differed from historical ones, partly because the various economies had become so much richer than they were in 1960. Therefore, the question is whether growth forecasts would revert to those that would have been made before the Asian financial crisis. The subsequent analysis quantifies these growth projections and tries to reach some conclusions about the long-term outlook.

Investment Ratios

Figure 2 depicts the investment ratios for the east Asian economics from 1960 to 2000.[3] Four of the Asian-crisis countries—Indonesia, South Korea, Malaysia, and Thailand—showed dramatic declines in 1998, by well over ten percentage points. For the Philippines, which historically had a low investment ratio, the reduction in 1998 was comparatively small. For the four countries in which investment declined sharply, the failure to see substantial recoveries in 1999-2000 suggests that something permanent may have occurred. However, it is also possible that investment ratios tend generally to recover more slowly than rates of economic growth, and the subsequent cross-country analysis supports this viewpoint.

The other five east Asian economies exhibited milder decreases or no decreases in investment ratios during 1998. Hong Kong and Singapore had small reductions from their peak ratios, and little or no decline was seen for China, Japan, and Taiwan. Thus, there is reason to believe that the dramatic falls in the investment ratios in Indonesia, South Korea, Malaysia, and Thailand were specifically related to the Asian financial crisis.

Stock-Market Prices

Figure 3 examines patterns in real stock-market prices. The general idea is that a fall in an economy's stock market likely reflects the market's belief that long-term growth prospects have diminished. In the figures, the real stock-

---

[3]The ratios are for real investment (private plus public) relative to real GDP. The underlying data, in most cases through 1992 (1991 for South Korea, 1990 for Taiwan), are the purchasing-power adjusted values from Summers and Heston (1991). Since 1992, the values were estimated from information on real investment and real GDP from the World Bank, *World Development Indicators*, and the Economist Intelligence Unit, *Country Data*. These numbers were linked to the Summers-Heston values based on a comparison in the overlapping year 1992 (1991 for South Korea, 1990 for Taiwan).

Figure 2. Investment Ratio
(In percent of GDP)

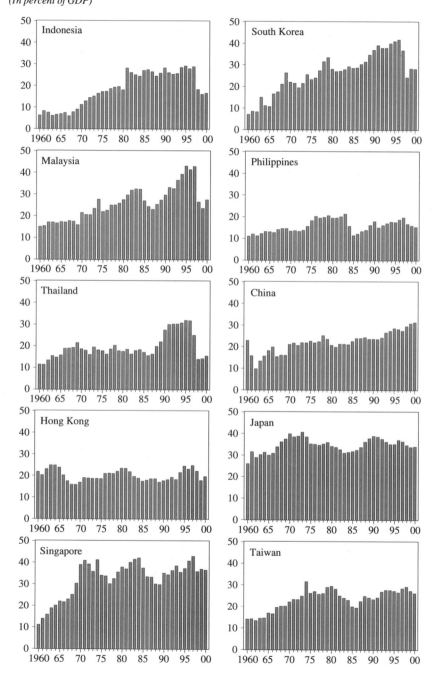

Figure 3. Stock-Market Indexes
(Proportionate scale, Jan. 1998= 1.0)

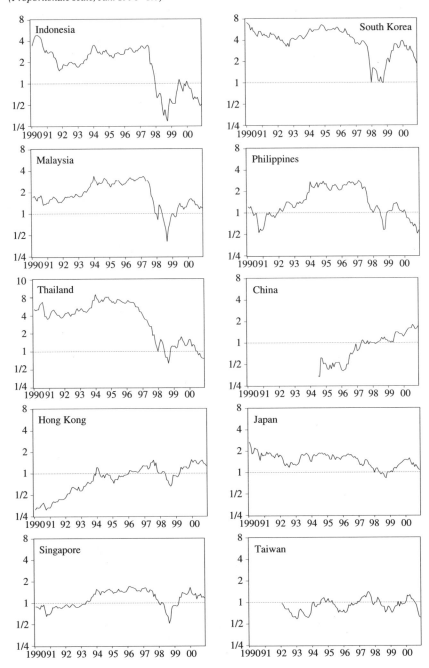

market values are computed by converting local currency values of stock-market indexes to U.S. dollars and then dividing by a measure of the U.S. price level.[4] An alternative procedure would deflate the local currency stock-market indexes by measures of local prices. Shifts in real exchange rates cause the two concepts to diverge.

The five Asian-crisis countries saw sharp declines in real stock-market valuations from the start of the financial crisis in summer 1997 until the fall of 1998. (For Thailand, the drop in the stock market clearly precedes the financial crisis.) For present purposes, an important observation is that valuations at the end of 2000 fall far short of those from early 1997. The ratios of values for December 2000 to those for January 1997 are 0.16 for Indonesia, 0.18 for Thailand, 0.22 for the Philippines, 0.37 for Malaysia, and 0.52 for South Korea.[5] For the five other east Asian economies, the declines in stock-market valuation are less dramatic or did not appear. The ratios of values for December 2000 to those for January 1997 are 0.60 for Taiwan, 0.74 for Singapore, 0.75 for Japan, 1.00 for Hong Kong, and 2.21 for China.[6] It seems reasonable to infer that the sharper declines in real stock market valuation for the Asian-crisis countries reflect effects from the financial crisis itself.

Parts of the declines in real stock-market values, as measured, reflect depreciations of real exchange rates. If the real stock-market values are calculated by dividing nominal stock-market indexes by local consumer price indexes, then the ratios for December 2000 to those for January 1997 are 0.31 for Indonesia, 0.32 for Thailand, 0.34 for the Philippines, 0.52 for Malaysia, and 0.69 for South Korea. For the other countries, the ratios are 0.68 for Taiwan, 0.93 for Singapore, 0.76 for Japan, 1.10 for Hong Kong, and 2.40 for China.

The main conclusion from the analysis of stock-market data is that, from the perspective of the financial markets, events from 1997 through 2000 had permanent negative consequences for the economic outlook of the five Asian-crisis countries. The adverse impacts were less significant for the five other east Asian economies and were not present for China and Hong Kong. The

---

[4]The stock-market indexes, reported in domestic currency units, were converted into U.S. dollars using market exchange rates. These values were converted into real terms by dividing by the U.S. GDP deflator. The natural logs of these values were calculated, the values in January 1998 were normalized to zero, and all values were divided by the natural log of two (to obtain convenient units for the graph). The resulting numbers are plotted in Figure 3, with the values for January 1998 labeled as 1.

[5]Parts of these declines reflect the weak overall stock-market performance during 2000. If the comparisons are between January 2000 and January 1997, then the ratios are 0.34 for Indonesia, 0.38 for Thailand, 0.42 for the Philippines, 0.43 for Malaysia, and 1.12 for South Korea.

[6]In these cases, the ratios for January 2000 relative to January 1997 are 1.02 for Taiwan, 1.04 for Singapore, 1.06 for Japan, 1.23 for Hong Kong, and 1.59 for China.

financial crises that began in summer 1997 were part of the environment that would be reflected in stock-market prices but were, of course, not the entire story. However, the differential market responses in the two groups of economies suggest that the financial crises—and, more specifically, changing perceptions about the long-term consequences of these crises—were significant parts of the story.

Cross-Country Analyses of Economic Outcomes

The general approach in this section is to modify existing work on cross-country analyses of economic growth and other variables to assess the effects of the Asian financial crisis. My recent analysis of the determinants of economic growth has considered a panel of over 80 countries observed over the ten-year periods 1965-75, 1975-85, and 1985-95. See, for example, Barro (2000). For the present study, I updated this sample to include information on growth rates and other variables for 1995-2000. I found the necessary data for 67 countries.

To apply the framework to the period 1995-2000, I modified the panel to consider growth rates over the seven five-year periods 1965-1970, ..., 1995-2000. Thus, any effects of the Asian financial crisis would show up as deviations of economic performance during the final five-year interval from those observed in the earlier intervals. When the data are available, it will be interesting to assess persisting effects on performance in the next five-year period, 2000-2005.

Economic Growth

The framework for determining the growth rate of real per capita GDP is indicated by the baseline system, shown in column 1 of Table 1. Since the general approach has been described elsewhere (such as Barro, 1997) and is likely to be familiar, I include here only a brief discussion.

The dependent variables are the five-year growth rates of real per capita GDP. Estimation is by three-stage least squares, using mostly lagged values of the independent variables as instruments—see the notes to Table 1. Individual constant terms are included for each period; hence, the system does not explain the evolution of world economic growth over time. No country fixed effects are introduced, because this procedure tends to eliminate the bulk of the information in the data, that is, the cross-sectional dimension of the panel.

The first explanatory variable, the log of per capita GDP at the start of each period, reveals the familiar conditional convergence effect: the estimated coef-

Table 1. Panel Regressions for Growth Rate

Explanatory variables	(1)	(2)	(3)	(4)	(5)	(6)	(7)
Log (per capita GDP)	-0.0302	-0.0309	-0.0303	-0.0306	-0.0293	-0.0275	-0.0281
	(0.0031)	(0.0031)	(0.0031)	(0.0031)	(0.0032)	(0.0032)	(0.0032)
Male upper-level schooling	0.0025	0.0030	0.0033	0.0033	0.0025	0.0026	0.0026
	(0.0016)	(0.0016)	(0.0016)	(0.0016)	(0.0016)	(0.0016)	(0.0016)
Log (life expectancy)	0.0541	0.0523	0.0502	0.0506	0.0513	0.0475	0.0485
	(0.0126)	(0.0126)	(0.0126)	(0.0126)	(0.0125)	(0.0125)	(0.0125)
Log (total fertility rate)	-0.0207	-0.0198	-0.0194	-0.0193	-0.0203	-0.0198	-0.0198
	(0.0050)	(0.0050)	(0.0050)	(0.0050)	(0.0049)	(0.0049)	(0.0049)
Government consumption/GDP	-0.094	-0.099	-0.099	-0.100	-0.092	-0.088	-0.090
	(0.021)	(0.021)	(0.021)	(0.021)	(0.021)	(0.021)	(0.021)
Rule-of-law index	0.0153	0.0153	0.0146	0.0149	0.0157	0.0134	0.0144
	(0.0054)	(0.0054)	(0.0054)	(0.0054)	(0.0054)	(0.0054)	(0.0055)
Openness measure	0.0118	0.0148	0.0162	0.0163	0.0140	0.0128	0.0138
	(0.0039)	(0.0040)	(0.0041)	(0.0041)	(0.0039)	(0.0042)	(0.0044)
Inflation rate	-0.0274	-0.0221	-0.0208	-0.0199	-0.0222	-0.0220	-0.0208
	(0.0076)	(0.0074)	(0.0073)	(0.0073)	(0.0073)	(0.0072)	(0.0072)
Investment/GDP	0.074	0.081	0.082	0.083	0.076	0.073	0.075
	(0.022)	(0.022)	(0.022)	(0.022)	(0.022)	(0.022)	(0.022)
Growth rate of terms of trade	0.064	0.066	0.065	0.067	0.063	0.061	0.062
	(0.020)	(0.020)	(0.020)	(0.020)	(0.020)	(0.020)	(0.020)
Group of 5 Asian financial crisis countries (dummy for 95-00)	--	-0.0371	--	-0.0216	-0.0318	--	-0.0182
		(0.0098)		(0.0137)	(0.0100)		(0.0140)
Group of 9 East Asian economies (dummy for 95-00)	--	--	-0.0302	-0.0186	--	-0.0237	-0.0146
			(0.0077)	(0.0108)		(0.0081)	(0.0114)
Group of 5 Asian financial crisis countries (dummy for other periods)	--	--	--	--	0.0109	--	0.0057
					(0.0059)		(0.0086)
Group of 9 East Asian economies (dummy for other periods)	--	--	--	--	--	0.0099	0.0059
						(0.0050)	(0.0074)
Number of countries, observations	84, 550	84, 550	84, 550	84, 550	84, 550	84, 550	84, 550
R-squared values	.46, .36, .30, .25, .44, .21, -.51	.45, .38, .29, .27, .46, .22, -.45	.45, .37, .29, .27, .46, .22, -.43	.45, .38, .29, .27, .46, .22, -.43	.47, .36, .30, .27, .49, .25, -.38	.48, .36, .29, .27, .50, .26, -.33	.47, .36, .29, .27, .50, .26, -.33

Notes: The dependent variable is the growth rate of real per capita GDP. Data through 1992 are from Summers and Heston. Figures were updated through 2000 from the World Bank, *World Development Indicators*, and the Economist Intelligence Unit, *Country Data*. The growth rate is the average for each of the seven five-year periods 1965-1970, ..., 1995-2000.

Individual constants (not shown) are included for each period. The log of real per capita GDP and the average years of male secondary and higher schooling are measured at the beginning of each period. The log of life expectancy at birth is an average for the previous five years. The ratios of government consumption (exclusive of spending on education and defense) and investment (private plus public) to GDP, the inflation rate, the total fertility rate, and the growth rate of the terms of trade (export over import prices) are period averages. The rule-of-law index is the earliest value available (for 1982 or 1985) in the first four equations and the period average for the other equations. The openness measure is the ratio of exports plus imports to GDP, filtered for the estimated effects on this measure of the logs of population and area. The nine east Asian economies are Hong Kong, Indonesia, Japan, South Korea, Malaysia, the Philippines, Singapore, Taiwan, and Thailand. (China is omitted because of missing data.) The five Asian-crisis countries are Indonesia, South Korea, Malaysia, the Philippines, and Thailand.

Estimation is by three-stage least squares. Instruments are the actual values of the schooling, life-expectancy, openness, and terms-of-trade variables, lagged values of the other variables aside from inflation, and dummy variables for prior colonial status (which have substantial explanatory power for inflation). The earliest value available for the rule-of-law index (for 1982 or 1985) is included as an instrument for the first four equations, and the value at the start of each period is included for the other equations. Standard errors are shown in parentheses. The R-squared values apply to each five-year period individually.

ficient is -0.030 (s.e. = 0.003).[7] Also included are two measures of initial human capital, each of which has a positive effect on growth. The coefficient on the average years of school attainment of males aged 25 and over at the secondary and higher levels is marginally significant, 0.0025 (0.0016),[8] and that on the log of life expectancy at birth is significant, 0.054 (0.013). The log of the total fertility rate is significantly negative: -0.021 (0.005).

The next four variables capture aspects of government policies and institutions. The ratio of government consumption (measured exclusively of outlays on education and defense) to GDP is significantly negative, -0.094 (0.021). A subjective measure of the extent of maintenance of the rule of law (an indicator of property rights enforcement) is significantly positive, 0.015 (0.005). Increased openness to international trade also has a significantly positive effect on growth, 0.012 (0.004).[9] Higher inflation, an indicator of macroeconomic instability, is significantly negative for growth, -0.027 (0.008).[10]

Many of the variables just discussed also affect an economy's propensity to invest, as discussed below. However, given the other explanatory variables, a higher ratio of real investment to real GDP still has a significantly positive effect on growth, as indicated by the coefficient 0.074 (0.022). The inclusion of the lagged, but not contemporaneous, investment ratio in the instrument list may allow a causal interpretation of this effect. A higher growth rate of the terms of trade (export relative to import prices) is also expansionary for growth, with the coefficient 0.064 (0.020).

Columns 2-4 of Table 1 show the effects on growth in the period 1995-2000 from dummy variables for being one of the five Asian financial crisis countries and from being one of the nine east Asian economies. (China is excluded because of missing data on some of the explanatory variables.) The five crisis

---

[7]The instrument list excludes the log of per capita GDP at the start of each period but includes earlier values of the log of per capita GDP. If the square of the log of per capita GDP is added as an explanatory variable, there is some indication that the rate of convergence (the magnitude of the marginal effect of the log of per capita GDP on the growth rate) increases as an economy gets richer.

[8]Other measures of school attainment lack significant explanatory power for economic growth.

[9]The independent variable is the ratio of total trade, exports plus imports, to GDP filtered for the typical effect of country size on this trade measure. This last effect was estimated from a system in which the trade-GDP ratio over various periods was the dependent variable. Country size was represented by the logs of population and area, and the system also included effects from import duties and the black-market premium on the foreign exchange. The estimated coefficient of the trade variable on growth arises when the trade variable was included in the instrument list. If only lagged values of the trade variable are included as instruments, the estimated coefficient remains positive but is reduced in size by about 50 percent.

[10]The instrument list excludes inflation but includes measures of colonial heritage. These colony variables have substantial explanatory power for inflation.

countries grew during 1995-2000 at about 4 percent per year below the rate that would otherwise have been predicted by the set of explanatory variables. This growth shortfall is highly significant. For the four other east Asian economies, the estimated growth shortfall was somewhat less than 2 percent per year, and this value is only marginally significant.

Columns 5-7 of Table 1 add the corresponding dummy variables for the six other five-year periods (where the coefficient of the dummy is constrained to be the same for each of these periods). These additional dummy variables have positive coefficients but are only marginally significant. With these variables included, the estimated shortfall of growth during 1995-2000 for the five Asian-crisis countries was a little over 3 percent per year and is still highly significant. The estimated shortfall for the four other east Asian economies was by about 1.5 percent per year and is again only marginally significant.

Table 2. Growth and Investment in East Asian Economies

	(1)	(2)	(3)	(4)	(5)	(6)
Economy	Growth rate 1995-2000	Estimated growth rate, 95-00	Growth rate 1960-95	Investment ratio 1995-99	Estimated investment ratio, 95-99	Investment ratio 1990-94
Indonesia	-0.012	0.034	0.041	0.242	0.262	0.265
South Korea	0.037	0.033	0.066	0.331	0.360	0.380
Malaysia	0.022	0.036	0.045	0.328	0.310	0.318
Philippines	0.013	0.043	0.013	0.171	0.186	0.162
Thailand	-0.006	0.031	0.048	0.222	0.283	0.288
China	0.070	--	0.039	0.268	--	0.236
Hong Kong	0.015	0.038	0.059	0.217	0.216	0.184
Japan	0.011	0.025	0.047	0.360	0.359	0.382
Singapore	0.029	0.047	0.064	0.366	0.350	0.352
Taiwan	0.048	0.023	0.061	0.247	0.237	0.231
Full sample (67 countries)	0.019	0.018	0.022	0.191	0.190	0.182

Notes: The growth rate refers to real per capita GDP. The estimated growth rate for 1995-2000 is from the panel regression shown in Table 1, column 1. The estimated value for the investment ratio for 1995-99 is from the panel regression shown in Table 2, column 1.

Table 2, columns 1 and 2, details the growth shortfall during 1995-2000 for each of the east Asian economies. Column 1 contains the actual growth rates of per capita GDP. Column 2 shows the estimated values from the baseline system in column 1 of Table 1. Note that this system excludes all of the dummy variables for the east Asian economies. In most cases, the estimated values fall substantially short of the historical growth rates, which are shown for 1960-95 in column 3 of Table 2. The main reason for these shortfalls is that most of the economies have become much richer over time, and the convergence effect predicts a reduction in growth rates. This effect is partially offset by the generally favorable and, more pertinently, improving nature of the other explanatory variables that determine economic growth in the system shown in column 1 of Table 1. (The values of the explanatory variables for the east Asian economies are shown in Table 3.) However, the net effect is to predict growth rates below the historical average for most of the east Asian economies. These lowered growth projections would also apply for future periods and would have applied even in the absence of the Asian financial crisis.

As an example, for South Korea, the model's estimated growth rate of per capita GDP for 1995-2000 is only 3.3 percent per year, compared with the 6.6 percent average growth rate experienced for 1960-95.[11] The model predicts similar retardations of growth for the other previously high growing east Asian economies: Hong Kong is 3.8 percent versus 5.9 percent, Singapore is 4.7 percent versus 6.4 percent, Taiwan is 2.3 percent versus 6.1 percent, and Thailand is 3.1 percent versus 4.8 percent. The cutback for Japan, 2.5 percent versus 4.7 percent, is also notable. The only economy in which a growth slowdown was not projected is the Philippines, which has 4.3 percent versus 1.3 percent.[12] However, the main element in this case is the greatly disappointing growth performance during the 1960-95 period.

A comparison of the actual growth rates for 1995-2000 with the model's estimates shows that two of the east Asian countries actually exceeded expectations. These are South Korea, for which the actual growth rate of 3.7 percent beat the model estimate of 3.3 percent, and Taiwan, for which the actual value of 4.8 percent was well above the estimate of 2.3 percent. The other seven

---

[11]This estimated growth rate for South Korea in 1995-2000 exceeds the average value in the sample (0.018) by 0.015. This deviation from the sample mean can be broken down intro contributions from the ten explanatory variables shown in Tables 3 and 4. The results, all expressed as deviations from the sample mean, are as follows: -0.021 for the log of per capita GDP, 0.007 for schooling, 0.001 for openness, 0.008 for government consumption, 0.002 for life expectancy, -0.003 for the terms of trade, 0.000 for the rule of law, 0.008 for fertility, 0.001 for inflation, and 0.010 for investment.

[12]The estimated growth rate for China is unavailable because of missing data on some of the explanatory variables.

Table 3. Explanatory Variables for East Asian Economies

Economy	(1) Log (per capita GDP) 1995	(2) Upper-level schooling 1995	(3) Log (life expectancy) 1995	(4) Log (total fertility rate) 1996	(5) Government consumption/ GDP 1995-99	(6) Rule of Law 1995-1999	(7) Openness measure 1995-1999	(8) Inflation rate 1995-2000	(9) Growth of terms of trade 1995-2000
Indonesia	7.88	1.5	4.16	0.96	0.07	0.57	0.23	0.16	0.037
South Korea	9.12	5.5	4.27	0.54	0.01	0.73	0.06	0.04	-0.043
Malaysia	8.85	3.4	4.27	1.21	0.04	0.77	1.27	0.03	-0.009
Philippines	7.47	2.4	4.18	1.29	0.12	0.67	0.41	0.07	0.098
Thailand	8.52	1.5	4.23	0.58	0.07	0.83	0.37	0.04	-0.018
China	7.71	2.2	4.24	0.65	--	0.83	--	0.02	-0.026
Hong Kong	9.80	4.8	4.36	0.22	0.02	0.90	1.72	0.01	0.004
Japan	9.63	4.3	4.38	0.35	0.03	1.00	-0.32	0.00	-0.027
Singapore	9.65	3.4	4.34	0.54	0.02	1.00	2.08	0.01	-0.004
Taiwan	9.27	3.9	4.32	0.58	0.03	0.73	0.16	0.01	0.011
Full sample (67 countries)	8.43	2.7	4.24	0.95	0.10	0.73	0.01	0.08	-0.002

Notes: Per capita GDP is the PPP adjusted value in 1985 U.S. dollars. Upper-level schooling is the average years of attainment of males aged 25 and over in secondary and higher education. Life expectancy is at birth. The total fertility rate is the number of live births for the average woman over her expected lifetime. The government consumption variable is the Summers-Heston ratio of real government consumption to GDP less the ratios for public spending on defense and education. The values for 1995-99 are estimates based on EIU figures on government consumption and earlier data on the government consumption variable. The rule-of-law measure, from Political Risk Services, is a subjective indicator on a zero-to-one scale, with one the most favorable. The openness variable is the ratio of exports plus imports to GDP less the estimated effect on this ratio from the logs of population and area. These effects were estimated in a panel system in which the dependent variable was the ratio of exports plus imports to GDP over various periods. The mean value of the openness variable was normalized to zero in each period. The inflation rate is for consumer price indexes. The terms-of-trade variable is the growth rate of the ratio of export to import prices.

countries with the available data showed shortfalls of varying sizes, including gaps of 4.6 percent per year for Indonesia and 3.7 percent per year for Thailand.

Investment Ratios

Table 4 contains the results from cross-country estimation of the determinants of the ratio of real investment (public plus private) to real GDP. The dependent variables are the averages of the investment ratios over the seven five-year periods 1965-69, ..., 1995-99. The specification follows the form of Table 1, except that the contemporaneous investment ratio is replaced in the group of explanatory variables by the lagged value of this ratio. Since the investment ratio displays a high degree of serial dependence, this lagged dependent variable has a lot of explanatory power. In the equations shown in Table 4, the estimated coefficient of this variable is in the neighborhood of 0.8 and is highly significant.[13] From the perspective of a partial-adjustment model, the investment ratio can be viewed as adjusting about 20 percent of the way over a five-year period to the target value determined by the other explanatory variables in the system.

The baseline model in column 1 of Table 4 shows a significantly negative effect on the investment ratio from the initial level of per capita GDP. The initial quantities of human capital in the forms of education and life expectancy have positive coefficients, though the one on education is statistically insignificant. The fertility rate has a significantly negative effect.

In terms of the policy variables, the main results are negative effects from government consumption and inflation (which is statistically insignificant) and significantly positive effects from the rule of law and international openness. Changes in the terms of trade have a positive effect that is marginally significant.

Columns 2-7 add dummy variables for the five Asian-crisis countries and the four other east Asian countries (with China again excluded because of missing data). The results show that, for given values of the other explanatory variables, the investment ratios in the five Asian-crisis countries were significantly *higher* than the rest of the sample in the intervals before 1995-99. However, these investment ratios became significantly lower in the 1995-99 period. In contrast, for the four other east Asian economies, the investment ratios did not deviate significantly from those elsewhere in the periods before 1995-99 or in the 1995-99 period. Thus, the Asian-crisis countries differed from the

---

[13]In contrast, if a lagged dependent variable is added to the system for the growth rate in Table 1, column 1, the estimated coefficient differs insignificantly from zero: 0.013 (s.e. = 0.040).

Table 4. Panel Regressions for Investment Ratio

Explanatory variables	(1)	(2)	(3)	(4)	(5)	(6)	(7)
Lagged ratio of investment to GDP	0.809 (0.022)	0.810 (0.023)	0.811 (0.023)	0.810 (0.023)	0.821 (0.021)	0.823 (0.021)	0.823 (0.021)
Log (per capita GDP)	-0.0132 (0.0036)	-0.0138 (0.0036)	-0.0133 (0.0036)	-0.0138 (0.0037)	-0.0098 (0.0034)	-0.0087 (0.0035)	-0.0094 (0.0035)
Male upper-level schooling	0.0021 (0.0016)	0.0021 (0.0017)	0.0022 (0.0017)	0.0021 (0.0017)	0.0012 (0.0015)	0.0012 (0.0015)	0.0011 (0.0015)
Log (life expectancy)	0.037 (0.015)	0.035 (0.015)	0.035 (0.015)	0.035 (0.015)	0.031 (0.014)	0.030 (0.014)	0.031 (0.014)
Log (total fertility rate)	-0.0115 (0.0054)	-0.0120 (0.0055)	-0.0118 (0.0055)	-0.0120 (0.0055)	-0.0104 (0.0050)	-0.0090 (0.0051)	-0.0099 (0.0049)
Government consumption/GDP	-0.100 (0.023)	-0.108 (0.024)	-0.104 (0.023)	-0.108 (0.023)	-0.077 (0.022)	-0.073 (0.023)	-0.073 (0.022)
Rule-of-law index	0.0177 (0.0062)	0.0173 (0.0062)	0.0171 (0.0062)	0.0173 (0.0062)	0.0177 (0.0058)	0.0142 (0.0059)	0.0171 (0.0059)
Openness measure	0.0077 (0.0037)	0.0089 (0.0038)	0.0090 (0.0038)	0.0089 (0.0039)	0.0070 (0.0033)	0.0027 (0.0037)	0.0058 (0.0038)
Inflation rate	-0.0099 (0.0086)	-0.0093 (0.0086)	-0.0094 (0.0087)	-0.0092 (0.0086)	-0.0038 (0.0081)	-0.0075 (0.0083)	-0.0037 (0.0081)
Growth rate of terms of trade	0.055 (0.028)	0.054 (0.028)	0.054 (0.028)	0.054 (0.028)	0.056 (0.028)	0.058 (0.028)	0.057 (0.028)
Group of 5 Asian financial crisis countries (dummy for 95-00)	--	-0.0352 (0.0125)	--	-0.0344 (0.0177)	-0.0265 (0.0125)	--	-0.0271 (0.0177)
Group of 9 East Asian economies (dummy for 95-00)	--	--	-0.0165 (0.0101)	-0.0009 (0.0139)	--	-0.0103 (0.0101)	0.0012 (0.0141)
Group of 5 Asian financial crisis countries (dummy for other periods)	--	--	--	--	0.0263 (0.0048)	--	0.0231 (0.0071)
Group of 9 East Asian economies (dummy for other periods)	--	--	--	--	--	0.0182 (0.0044)	0.0041 (0.0062)
Number of countries, observations	84, 550	84, 550	84, 550	84, 550	84, 550	84, 550	84, 550
R-squared values	.90, .84, .76, .82, .89, .87, .89	.90, .84, .76, .82, .89, .87, .89	.90, .84, .76, .82, .89, .87, .89	.90, .84, .76, .82, .89, .87, .89	.90, .83, .76, .83, .88, .89, .90	.90, .84, .76, .83, .88, .89, .89	.90, .83, .77, .83, .88, .89, .90

Notes: The dependent variable is the ratio of real investment (private plus public) to real GDP. Data through 1992 are from Summers and Heston. Figures were updated through 1999 from the World Bank, *World Development Indicators*, and the Economist Intelligence Unit, *Country Data*. The measure used is the average of the ratio over the seven periods 1965-69, ..., 1995-99. The lagged value of the investment ratio is the average of the ratio over the previous interval. See the notes to Table 1 for other information.

other east Asian economies not only in terms of the adverse shocks to investment in the recent period but also in the sense of having abnormally high investment ratios at earlier times.

Table 2 gives details about the actual and estimated investment ratios in the east Asian economies for the period 1995-99. Among the five Asian-crisis countries, only Malaysia had an investment ratio above the estimated value (by two percentage points). The largest negative gap was six percentage points for Thailand. In contrast, for the four other east Asian economies, most of the gaps were small, with the largest being plus two percentage points for Singapore.

General Effects of Financial Crises

The methodology employed thus far is useful for assessing the contemporaneous effects of the Asian financial crisis on growth and investment for the Asian-crisis countries and for other east Asian economies. When data for 2000-05 and beyond become available, the methodology could also be applied to assess whether effects from the Asian financial crisis persisted beyond the contemporaneous five-year interval.

Another approach, pursued by Lee and Park (Chapter 11), is to regard the Asian financial crisis of 1997-98 not as a unique event but rather as an example of a broader class of crises that have affected numerous countries. The cross-country regression framework can be used to assess the contemporaneous and persisting influences of the universe of currency crises on economic outcomes. The results from this exercise can then be extrapolated to the case of the Asian financial crisis. In this way, inferences can be made about the lasting economic effects of this crisis without waiting for additional data to materialize.

Lee and Park view the Asian financial crises as currency crises. To get a broader perspective on currency crises, they followed the general approach of Frankel and Rose (1996), who identified these kinds of crises with large nominal depreciations of a country's currency over a short period. Specifically, Lee and Park define a currency crisis as a circumstance in which the nominal depreciation of the currency was at least 25 percent during any quarter of the year and exceeded by at least 10 percentage points the depreciation of the currency in the previous quarter. They also use a window of two years to isolate independent crises. According to these criteria, the five Asian-crisis countries all experienced currency crises during 1997-98.

In my analysis, I follow Lee and Park's approach to identifying currency crises, and I use the data for 1970-97 that they kindly provided. I used Economist Intelligence Unit, *Country Data*, to update these figures to 1998-2000 for most of the countries in my sample. I defined a currency-crisis dummy variable for each country during any five-year period to equal one if a crisis occurred during the period and to take on the value zero otherwise.[14] I considered the contemporaneous effects of this variable on economic growth and investment, and I also looked for effects from the presence of a currency crisis in the previous five-year period.

The Asian financial crises were not only currency crises but also involved severe distress for banking systems. To get a broad measure of banking crises, I followed the approach of Caprio and Klingebiel (1996) and Eichengreen and Rose (1998). These authors define a banking crisis as a situation in which bank failures or suspensions led to the exhaustion of much or all of bank capital. The variable I use is a dummy for whether a banking crisis occurred for each country during any five-year period. I again considered the contemporaneous and lagged effects of these crises on economic growth and investment. The underlying data are from Caprio and Klingebiel (1996), as reported on the website of Andrew Rose. These data were supplemented with information in Demirguc-Kunt and Detragiache (1997) and Glick and Hutchison (1999). The resulting data apply from 1975 to 1997. According to these data, the five Asian-crisis countries all experienced banking crises in 1997.

The results from adding the currency-crisis and banking-crisis variables to the systems for economic growth and investment are in Table 5. In column 2, a contemporaneous currency crisis (occurring sometime within the applicable five-year period) is associated with lower per capita growth—by 1.3 percent per year. The corresponding effect for a banking crisis is a retardation of growth by 0.6 percent per year. These effects are statistically significant, and the difference between the two growth effects is significant at the 8 percent level. The results also show that the contractions of growth do not persist into the next five-year period. The estimated coefficients here are *positive*: 0.6 percent per year for a currency crisis and 0.9 percent per year for a banking crisis.[15]

---

[14]I used the interval 1970-74 for currency devaluation to correspond to growth for 1970-75 and to the average investment ratio for 1970-74 and similarly for the other periods. As an alternative procedure, I defined the currency-crisis variable to equal 1 if the crisis occurred in the first year of the five-year interval, 0.8 if the crisis occurred in the second year, and so on. This approach might be preferable if the effect of a currency crisis tended to persist at least for several years. However, this alternative approach generated a poorer fit to the data, especially on economic growth. This finding suggests that the effects of currency crises on economic outcomes are short lived.

[15]Additional persistence would be implied through effects on the independent variables. For example, the reduced level of per capita GDP provides a channel whereby a currency or banking crisis would raise growth in the next period. These effects tend, however, to be small. For instance, if a currency crisis lowers the growth rate of per capita GDP by 0.014 per year for five years, then the log of per capita GDP at the start of the next period would be decreased

Table 5. Regressions with Currency- and Banking-Crisis Variables

Explanatory variables	Economic Growth		Investment Ratio	
	(1)	(2)	(3)	(4)
Lagged ratio of investment to GDP	--	--	0.763 (0.035)	0.732 (0.036)
Log (per capita GDP)	-0.0213 (0.0049)	-0.0220 (0.0048)	-0.0149 (0.0059)	-0.0146 (0.0060)
Male upper-level schooling	0.0020 (0.0020)	0.0024 (0.0020)	0.0019 (0.0023)	0.0021 (0.0023)
Log (life expectancy)	0.027 (0.022)	0.022 (0.022)	0.015 (0.026)	0.024 (0.026)
Log (total fertility rate)	-0.0265 (0.0069)	-0.0267 (0.0068)	-0.0191 (0.0093)	-0.0310 (0.0080)
Government consumption/GDP	-0.102 (0.029)	-0.095 (0.028)	-0.142 (0.034)	-0.145 (0.034)
Rule-of-law index	0.0091 (0.0089)	0.0086 (0.0087)	0.0107 (0.0106)	0.0127 (0.0105)
Openness measure	0.0127 (0.0041)	0.0131 (0.0041)	0.0034 (0.0049)	0.0050 (0.0050)
Inflation rate	-0.0118 (0.0081)	-0.0077 (0.0074)	-0.0191 (0.0093)	-0.0139 (0.0089)
Investment/GDP	0.005 (0.034)	0.038 (0.035)	--	--
Growth rate of terms of trade	0.081 (0.028)	0.087 (0.028)	-0.002 (0.038)	-0.008 (0.038)
Contemporaneous currency crisis	-0.0136 (0.0031)	-0.0134 (0.0030)	-0.0042 (0.0040)	-0.0043 (0.0040)
Lagged currency crisis	--	0.0064 (0.0030)	--	-0.0002 (0.0039)
Contemporaneous banking crisis	-0.0049 (0.0027)	-0.0062 (0.0026)	-0.0102 (0.0034)	-0.0092 (0.0034)
Lagged banking crisis	--	0.0090 (0.0029)	--	-0.0080 (0.0038)
Number of countries, observations	83, 307	83, 307	83, 307	83, 307
R-squared values	.34, .50, .29, -.24	.36, .51, .35, -.24	.81, .90, .88, .89	.82, .90, .88, .89

Notes: Systems 1 and 2 have growth rates of per capita GDP as dependent variables. These systems apply to the periods 1980-1985, ..., 1995-2000. The earlier periods were deleted because of missing data on the currency-crisis and banking-crisis variables. Systems 3 and 4 have average ratios of real investment to real GDP as dependent variables. These systems apply to the periods 1980-84, ..., 1995-99. The currency-crisis dummy variable equals one if at least one of the years in the five-year period features a currency devaluation of at least 25 percent in one of the quarters. Otherwise, the variable takes on the value zero. The banking-crisis dummy variable equals one if at least one of the years in the five-year period features a banking crisis, as defined in Caprio and Klingebiel (1996). (For the last period, this dummy variable is based on information only for the period 1995-97.) See the text for further details. See the notes to Tables 1 and 2 for additional information.

by 0.070. With a convergence coefficient of 0.021, this change implies a higher growth rate in the next period by 0.001 per year. Negative, but quantitatively even smaller, effects involve the persisting influences on investment. Other negative effects on subsequent growth would arise if, as examples, a currency or banking crisis reduces international trade or damages institutions that influence the rule of law. It is also possible that the occurrence of a currency or banking crisis alters the probability of a crisis in subsequent periods and thereby affects the expectation of future growth rates through those channels. These effects have not been investigated.

The broad cross-country analysis indicates that a combination of a currency and a banking crisis would be associated with reduced growth contemporaneously by about 2 percent per year. From this perspective, the recent economic contractions in the Asian-crisis countries look more severe than average. In those cases, reflected in the dummy variables contained in Table 1, growth rates for 1995-2000 were reduced by about 3 percent per year.

For the investment ratio, column 4 of Table 5 shows that a currency crisis is associated with a reduction by about 0.4 of a percentage point, an estimate that is not statistically significant. A banking crisis is associated with a decrease by 0.9 of a percentage point, and this result is statistically significant. The difference between the two effects is not statistically significant—the p-value is 0.36. In any event, although a currency crisis seems to be quantitatively more important than a banking crisis for economic growth, there is no evidence for this pattern with respect to investment.

Column 4 of Table 5 shows that the lagged effect from a currency crisis on the investment ratio is around zero. In contrast, the effect from a banking crisis is a significantly negative 0.8 of a percentage point. Hence, a banking crisis seems to have a persisting negative effect on investment, although such a crisis does not appear to have a persisting negative influence on economic growth (for given values of the investment ratio and other variables).

From the perspective of the broad cross-country analysis, the sharp contractions of investment in the Asian-crisis countries in 1998 were larger than average. In the Asian-crisis cases, reflected in the dummy variables in Table 2, average investment ratios for 1995-2000 were decreased by about 3 percentage points. The broader analysis suggests that a combined currency and banking crisis would typically have been accompanied by a contraction of the investment ratio by about 1.5 percentage points.

Summary

The Asian financial crisis was associated with a sharp reduction of economic growth in east Asia, especially in the five countries that were most directly affected by the crisis. Investment ratios also fell sharply in these crisis countries, though not so much in other east Asian economies. Rates of economic growth in east Asia have rebounded in 1999-2000, but the permanence of this recovery is uncertain. The failure of investment ratios to rebound significantly in the crisis countries suggests that the crisis had a long-term adverse effect. This conclusion is reinforced by the observation that real stock-market prices in the crisis countries have failed to reattain their pre-crisis values.

A somewhat different picture emerges from a broader study of currency and banking crises. This analysis documents the association of currency and banking crises with contemporaneously reduced values of economic growth and investment. However, the magnitude of the typical effect is smaller than that seen in the recent period in the Asian crisis countries. More importantly, the broader evidence fails to detect a persisting adverse influence of currency and banking crises on economic growth. (There is some indication of a persisting adverse effect of a banking crisis on investment.) Thus, if extrapolated to the Asian-crisis countries, the broad evidence predicts returns to the rates of economic growth that would have prevailed in the absence of the crisis.

References

Barro, R.J., 1997, *Determinants of Economic Growth: A Cross-Country Empirical Study*, MIT Press, Cambridge MA.

Barro, R.J., 2000, "Inequality and Growth in a Panel of Countries," *Journal of Economic Growth*, March.

Caprio, G. and D. Klingebiel, 1996, "Bank Insolvencies: Cross-Country Experience," Policy Research Working Paper No. 1620, The World Bank.

Demirguc-Kunt, A. and E. Detragiache, 1997, "The Determinants of Banking Crises: Evidence from Developed and Developing Countries," IMF Working Paper No. 97/106, International Monetary Fund.

Eichengreen, B. and A.K. Rose, 1998, "Staying Afloat when the Wind Shifts: External Factors and Emerging-Market Banking Crises," National Bureau of Economic Research Working Paper No. 6370.

Frankel, J.A. and A.K. Rose, 1996, "Currency Crashes in Emerging Markets: An Empirical Treatment," *Journal of International Economics*.

Glick, R. and M. Hutchison, 1999, "Banking and Currency Crises: How Common Are Twins?" unpublished, University of California Santa Cruz, September.

Summers, R. and A. Heston, 1991, "The Penn World Table (Mark 5): An Expanded Set of International Comparisons, 1950-1988," *Quarterly Journal of Economics*, May. An updated version (Mark 5.6) is available at nber.org.

11 Recovery and Sustainability in East Asia

*Yung Chul Park and Jong-Wha Lee**

Over the three years since the crisis broke out in 1997, the five Asian countries—Indonesia, Korea, Thailand, Malaysia, and Philippines—managed impressive recoveries. The recoveries were faster than expected by anyone. The economies started to bottom out in the second half of 1998. The rebound of growth in 1999 was no less drastic than its free-fall. In Korea, for example, the growth rates showed a turnaround from -6.7 percent in 1998 to 10.7 percent in 1999.

The purpose of this paper is to make an assessment of this speedy adjustment from the crisis in East Asia. In particular, we analyze the macroeconomic adjustment process of the East Asian currency crisis in a broad international perspective. First, we assess the impacts of the crisis on GDP growth using a cross-country data set, which compiled all currency crisis episodes over the period from 1970 to 1995. From these cross-country data, we draw some stylized facts about the adjustment of key macroeconomic variables during the crisis. Then we investigate the critical factors that determine the adjustment process.

Our analysis of cross-country patterns shows that GDP growth rates drop with the eruption of a crisis but then recover quickly to the pre-crisis level in two or three years, showing a V-pattern of adjustment. Thereafter, the GDP growth rates tend to rise slightly above the pre-crisis levels, but then subside back to a more sustainable level. We also compare the adjustment patterns of

*The authors would like to thank Robert Barro, Richard Portes, and participants at the NBER Conference on Management of Currency Crises, Monterey, California, USA, March 2001 for their helpful comments on an earlier draft. Si-Yeon Lee and Do-Won Kwak provided able research assistance.

GDP growth rates between two subgroups of the currency crisis episodes—
one with conditional financial assistance from the IMF and the other without.
We find that the adjustment process was much sharper in the group with the
IMF program, compared to those without. That is, in the IMF program countries, GDP growth rates start to fall precipitously even before the eruption of
a crisis but then recover to its pre-crisis level more quickly in two years.

The macroeconomic adjustment process in East Asia is in general consistent with these stylized patterns. However, the degree of initial contraction
and following recovery has been far greater in East Asia than what the cross-
country evidence predicts. This paper tries to make an evaluation of what
factors contributed to the sharper contraction and the quicker recovery in East
Asia compared with the cross-country patterns.

As discussed in the third section, we believe that a large number of internal
and external factors are responsible for the deeper crisis and the quicker recovery in East Asia. The origin and the nature of the shock, initial conditions,
the development of external environments, and the stabilization and structural
adjustment policies taken must have a significant consequence on the adjustment path as they did in the eruption of the crisis. From cross-country regressions based on the sample of previous crisis episodes, we find that exchange
rate depreciations, expansionary macroeconomic policies, and favorable global environments are the critical determinants of the post-crisis recovery.
Financial assistance from the IMF is found to have no independent impact on
the recovery process.

We find that the quick recoveries in East Asia have been largely driven by
the accommodating macroeconomic policies, favorable external environments,
and more export-oriented structure. After Korea, Malaysia, and Thailand shifted to a relaxation of monetary and fiscal policies by the second half of 1998,
their economies took off. The sharp real currency depreciations must have
had a bigger impact on more open Asian economies. Favorable external developments helped the quick improvement in East Asian exports. In this sense,
the East Asian process of adjustment is not much different from the stylized
pattern from the previous currency crisis episodes over the period from 1970
to 1995. However, the stylized pattern of adjustment cannot explain why the
crisis was more severe and the recovery has been much faster than what was
expected from the previous experiences of crisis. This paper argues that the
sharper adjustment pattern in East Asia is attributed to the severe liquidity
crisis that was triggered by investors' panic and then amplified by weak corporate and bank balance sheets.

The stylized pattern of real GDP growth from the cross-country episodes
displays that the crisis-hit countries can recover their pre-crisis or non-crisis

average growth rate in three years after the crisis. Hence, it raises a question of whether the East Asian economies will be able to return to the pre-crisis trend rate of growth.

Although the financial crisis of 1997 abruptly brought a halt to Asia's period of robust growth, there was little in Asia's fundamentals that inevitably led to the crisis. This paper discusses the long-term prospects for growth in East Asia. From the cross-country regressions, we find that there is no evidence for a direct impact of a currency crisis on long-run growth. This suggests that with a return to the core policies that resulted in rapid growth, the East Asian economies can again return to sustained growth.

The paper is organized as follows. The next section discusses the methodology for our cross-country analysis and presents central features in the macroeconomic adjustments of the crisis-hit countries. Then, using regression analysis based on the cross-country data, we assess the factors that can explain the behavior of GDP growth rates during the crisis. The third section reviews the recent recoveries in East Asia and compares them with the stylized patterns from the cross-country analysis. We analyze the driving forces of the faster recovery in East Asia. The fourth section discusses the issue of the sustainability of the current recovery. Concluding remarks are found in a final section.

Cross-Country Patterns of Adjustment to Currency Crisis

Data

In order to assess the post-crisis adjustment of the crisis-hit countries, one needs first to define a currency crisis. Several alternative indicators and methods have been used in the literature to identify the year when a crisis erupted in each country. Frankel and Rose (1996) and Milesi-Ferreti and Razin (1998) used the nominal depreciation rate of the currency. Sachs, Tornell, and Velasco (1996), Radelet and Sachs (1998), and Kaminsky and Reinhart (1999) combined the depreciation rate with other additional indicators such as losses in foreign reserves, increases in the interest rate, and reversals in capital accounts to identify the crisis.

Each definition has limitations. A large-scale depreciation can occur orderly without a speculative attack. Identifying unsuccessful speculative attacks is a difficult task. Reliable data on reserves and interest rates in developing countries are often unavailable. Reserves or interest rates can change irrespective of an attack. Lee and Rhee (2000) suggest an alternative measure based on the initiation of an IMF stabilization program. But, countries often receive an IMF program after a crisis breaks out or without a currency crisis. Governments may sign an IMF agreement not necessarily because they need foreign exchange, but because they want austerity conditions to be imposed (Przeworski and Vreeland, 2000).

Since the purpose of this paper is not to improve the measure of a currency crisis, we use the conventional nominal depreciation rate of the currency as a benchmark measure. But, in contrast to Frankel and Rose (1996), we use quarterly data, instead of annual data, to define a currency crisis. That is, based on quarterly data, a country is judged to have had a currency crisis in the year when it has a nominal depreciation of its currency of at least 25 percent in any quarter of the year and the depreciation exceeds the previous quarter's change in the exchange rate by a margin of at least a 10 percent. Thus, our definition captures the incidences of currency crises that were severe but short-lived, perhaps due to successful interventions in the foreign exchange market. During the period from 1970 to 1997, the total number of currency crises was 260. We use a window of plus/minus two years to identify an independent crisis. That is, if there were a precedent crisis within two years before a crisis, we count it as a consecutive crisis, but not an independent one. This procedure yields a total of 192 currency crisis episodes.[1]

Then, we divide all crisis episodes into two groups based on whether the crisis-hit countries entered into an IMF program or not. We have compiled data on all types of IMF programs that include stand-by arrangements, extended fund facility (EFF) arrangements, structural adjustment facility (SAF), and enhanced structural adjustment facility (ESAF) over the period from 1970 to 1997.[2] The program is identified by the year when the loans are approved. Thus, if a country received financial assistance from the IMF during or one year after the currency crisis, we consider it as a currency crisis with an IMF program. Note that the decision on participation in the IMF program following a currency crisis can be determined endogenously by various factors. A country may enter into agreements with the IMF when it faces a more severe foreign reserve crisis or a worse macroeconomic situation (Conway, 1994). But, relying on the IMF conditionality may be just a way to impose domestically unpopular austerity policies (Przeworski and Vreeland, 2000).

Table 1 shows a summary of data on currency crises based on our definition during the period from 1970 to 1997. There were 192 currency crisis episodes during this period. The number of crises was increasing over time, from 40 in

---

[1]Lee, Hong, and Rhee (2001) describe the data in more details. We are grateful to Kiseok Hong and Changyong Rhee for sharing their cross-country data set.

[2]The data come from Lee and Rhee (2000), which compiled the information from the IMF, *Annual Report* for each year.

Table 1. Incidence of Currency Crises and IMF Program Participation

Period	Total No.	IMF Program Participation	
		Yes	No
1970-1997	192	71	121
1970-1979	40	12	28
1980-1989	69	24	45
1990-1997	83	35	48

Notes: A currency crisis is defined to occur in the year when a country has a nominal depreciation of currency of at least 25 percent in any quarter of a year and the depreciation rate exceeds the previous quarter's change in the exchange rate by a margin of at least a 10 percent. If the country under a currency crisis received financial assistance from the IMF during the year or one year after the currency crisis, it is classified as a currency crisis with the IMF program participation. Our sample does not include the former Soviet Union countries and counts only independent crises by imposing plus/minus 2 years window.

the 1970s, to 69 in the 1980s and 83 in the 1990-97. The number of countries that experienced at least one crisis was 99.[3] Thus, on average each country had 1.86 crises over the period. Out of the 192 crisis episodes, 71 of them participated in an IMF program.

Macroeconomic Adjustment During the Currency Crisis

On the basis of the currency crisis index, we investigate how the crisis-hit economies, on average, behaved during the five years prior to and following the crisis. We first look at the movement of real GDP growth rates and then investigate the sources of output changes by looking at the movements of GDP expenditure components and major macroeconomic policy variables in the typical crisis-hit country during the period before and after the crisis. We also construct a control group of "tranquil" observations. If a country had not been subject to any crisis within a window of plus/minus two years surrounding a specific year, it is counted as a non-crisis country in that specific year. The behavior of the macroeconomic variables between the two subgroups—one with conditional financial assistance from the IMF and the other without—is also compared.

We use the data for the period from 1970 to 1995. Thus we attempt to draw the stylized pattern of macroeconomic adjustment from the crisis episodes that had occurred prior to the Asian crisis. There are 176 independent currency crises during this period, and in 64 episodes the countries participated in an IMF program.

---

[3]The sample does not include the former Soviet Union countries that experienced currency crises and subsequently received the financial assistance from the IMF in the early 1990s.

Real GDP Growth

Figure 1 shows the movements of average GDP growth rates during the five years prior to and following the crisis; that is, from t-5 to t+5 where t is the year of a currency crisis. For comparison, we include a straight line, which indicates the average GDP growth rate during the tranquil period that did not experience a currency crisis or enter into an IMF program within a window of plus/minus two years.

In general, we find that the growth rates, on average, exhibit a V-type pattern of adjustment over the period before and following the crisis. The growth rates during the pre-crisis period from three to five years prior to the crisis are slightly lower than the average during the tranquil period of 3.5 percent. The growth rate continues to decline over time, from 2.7 percent in t-4 to 1.1 percent in t-1, implying that economic conditions are aggravated prior to the eruption of a crisis.

The growth rate increases slightly in the crisis year, which confirms that most currency crises have indeed been expansionary. As in Gupta *et al.* (2000), we also find that about 70 percent of the currency crises in our sample lead to an output increase in the crisis year. The average GDP growth rate of the crisis-hit countries remains at about 1.9 percent over the crisis year and one year after. But GDP growth recovers to its non-crisis level quickly in three years after the crisis, reaching 4.0 percent in t+3, that is about 0.5 percentage point higher than the average of the non-crisis economies. Thus, the growth rate tends to exceed its pre-crisis or tranquil period average, indicating that after a crisis the country's level of GDP returns to the level of its pre-crisis growth path. Eventually, the growth rate tapers off and returns to the level of the tranquil period in four and five years after the crisis. This V-type pattern and the speed of recovery are broadly consistent with the findings in Hong and Tornell (1999) and Gupta *et al.* (2000).

Figure 1 compares the behavior of the GDP growth rates between the two subgroups- one with conditional financial assistance from the IMF and the other without. We find that the adjustment process shows a much sharper V-type in the program countries than in the non-program countries. The program countries start with lower growth rates of around 1.2 percent in t-4 and continue to slow down. They reach the trough, where the growth rate is -1.2 percent, in one year prior to the initiation of the currency crisis.

This magnitude of decline in growth rates is much larger than that of the non-program countries. At the trough, the growth rate of the crisis-hit program countries is about 4.7 percentage points lower than that of the non-crisis economies. Thereafter, rebounding from the deeper trough, the program countries

Figure 1. Changes in GDP Growth Rates During the Currency Crises

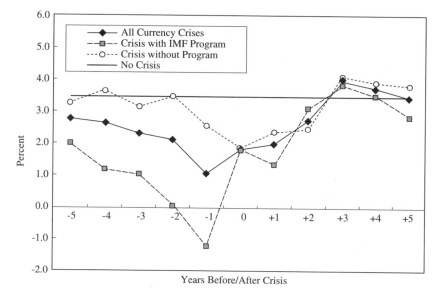

Years Before/After Crisis

show a quicker recovery. The GDP growth rate begins to recover from the crisis year and reaches its pre-crisis level quickly within two years after the onset of a crisis. The non-program countries also begin to recover a year after the crisis and then their growth rates stabilize at the non-crisis level from t+3.

The fact that the program countries have much lower growth rates than the non-program countries confirms that only a very serious macroeconomic situation forces a country to enter into agreements with the IMF. Nevertheless, it is intriguing that the crisis-hit countries show a quicker recovery from a deeper recession with the participation in the IMF program.

GDP Expenditure Components

Figure 2 shows the movements of the components of GDP expenditure during the five years prior to and following the crisis. Panel (a) shows that the share of private consumption expenditure in GDP remains stable over the period. In other words, consumption moves closely with GDP. The adjustment pattern is similar in both program and non-program countries. For the overall period, the consumption to GDP ratio in the crisis-hit economies exceeds the non-crisis tranquil period average, indicating that private consumption is high in the crisis-hit countries and even after a crisis these countries' level of private saving does not increase to the level of the non-crisis countries.

Figure 2. Changes in GDP Expenditure Components During the Currency Crises

(a) Private Consumption in GDP

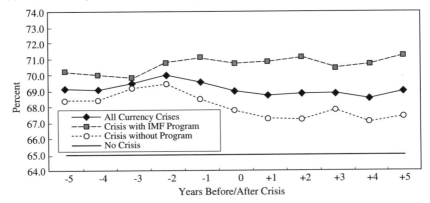

(b) Investment Rate

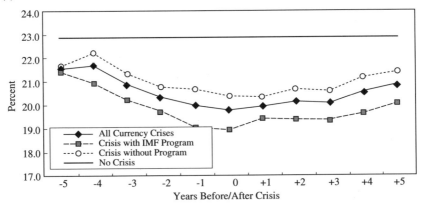

(c) Real Export Growth Rate

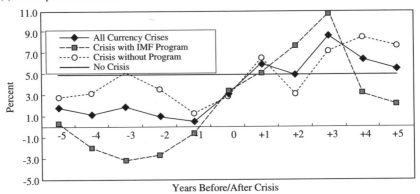

(d) Export Share in GDP

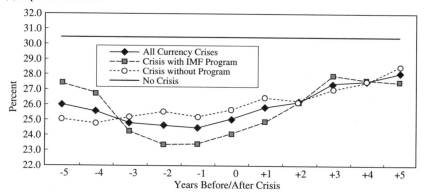

(e) Real Import Growth Rate

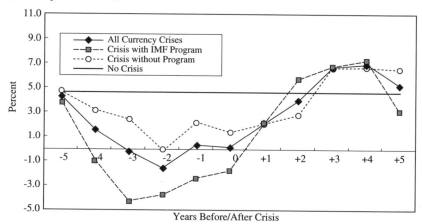

(f) Import Share in GDP

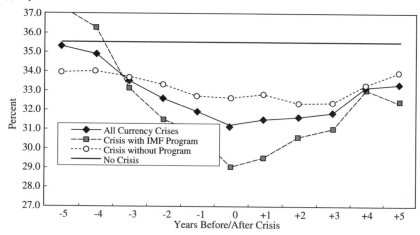

Panel (b) of Figure 2 shows that in contrast to consumption, the investment (private plus public investment) rate shows more fluctuations. The level is no higher in the crisis-hit economies than in the non-crisis countries. For four to five years prior to the crisis, the investment ratio remains below the average level of tranquil observations of 22.8 percent. Thus, a stylized fact is that the crisis-hit countries have had 'over-consumption' but not necessarily 'over-investment,' compared to the level of the non-crisis countries. In the crisis-hit countries, the investment rate tends to decline during the pre-crisis period, reaching 19.8 percent in the crisis year. After the crisis, the investment rate increases gradually but does not return to the level of the pre-crisis or tranquil period, remaining at 20.9 percent for five years following the crisis. A popular claim regarding the role of the IMF conditionality is that the austerity program has an adverse effect on investment. Panel (b) of Figure 2 seems to support this claim. The IMF program countries have experienced a more severe investment contraction than the other group in the pre-crisis period, as the investment ratio declines continuously from 21.4 percent in t-5 to 18.9 percent in t. In the post-crisis period of the crisis-hit countries in which an IMF program is introduced, the investment rate does not recover to the pre-crisis level, remaining at 19.7 percent in t+4 and 20.1 percent in t+5. In contrast, the investment rate returns to the pre-crisis level in the non-program crisis-hit countries in five years after the crisis.

In the crisis-hit countries, domestic expenditure or demand is either slowly recovering or remains permanently below the pre-crisis level. In contrast, export demand shows a quick recovery during the post-crisis period. Panel (c) shows that in the crisis-hit countries, real export growth rates jump from less than 1 percent in t-1, to 3.0 percent in the crisis year and to 5.9 percent in t+1, and then remain at over 5 percent over the post-crisis period. For both program and non-program countries, export growth during the post-crisis period is faster than that of the pre-crisis or tranquil period, and thus leads a strong recovery. Consequently, as shown in Panel (d), after the currency crisis the export share increases permanently above the pre-crisis level. But, note that on average the export share in all crisis-hit countries is still lower than the non-crisis average.

During the early post-crisis period the quick recovery of export growth is accompanied by a contraction of import demand. The pattern of import reduction is more conspicuous in the program countries where import growth rates are negative in the pre-crisis period as well as the crisis year. Panels (e) and (f) of Figure 2 show that although the growth rate of imports recovers to the pre-crisis and non-crisis average in two years following the crisis, its share in GDP remains below the non-crisis average of 35.5 percent. The growth of exports and imports shows that the current account to GDP ratio improves quickly after the crisis. Thus, net exports tend to lead the recovery in the crisis-hit countries.

Macroeconomic Policy Indicators

Public consumption is an indicator of fiscal policy. Panels (a) and (b) of Figure 3 show that public consumption growth rates tend to slow slightly in the

Figure 3. Macroeconomic Policy Indicators During the Currency Crises

(a) Real Public Consumption Growth Rate

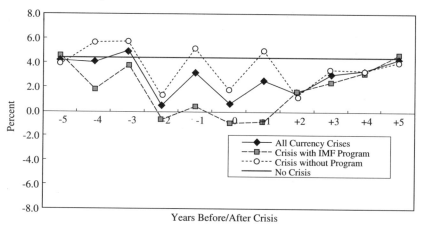

(b) Public Consumption in GDP

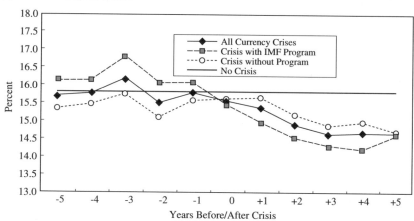

(c) Real Money Supply (M2) Growth Rate

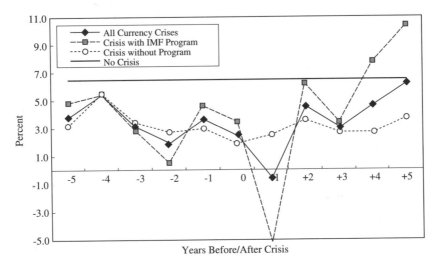

Years Before/After Crisis

(d) Real Bank Credit Growth Rate

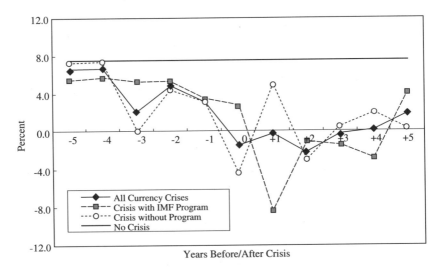

Years Before/After Crisis

crisis year, and then recover to the pre-crisis as well as non-crisis average. But in the first year following the crisis, there is contrasting behavior between the program countries and non-program countries. While the public consumption growth rate is over 5.0 percent for the non-program countries, it is -0.8 percent for the program countries in the year of t+1. This confirms that an agreement with the IMF introduces a contractionary fiscal policy in the program country. Reflecting this sharp contraction in public consumption expenditure, the ratio of public consumption to GDP declines quickly in t+1 with the IMF program. The ratio remains at the level lower than the pre-crisis or non-crisis average in both program and non-program countries even five years after a crisis.

Like fiscal policy, monetary policy of the program countries contrasts sharply with that of the non-program countries. Panel (c) of Figure 3 shows that the real money supply growth rate remains positive throughout the years following the crisis and increases over time to return to the pre-crisis level in five years after the crisis in the non-program countries. In contrast, in the sample of the crisis-hit countries with IMF program participation, money supply growth is negative. Thereafter it returns to the pre-crisis average growth rate. The sharp reduction in money supply in the program countries implies that, as with fiscal policy, participation in an IMF program brings in tight monetary policy in the crisis-hit economy.

It is claimed that a currency crisis often develops into a banking crisis. As international lending declines suddenly, a weak banking sector is unable to play a proper intermediation role. Banks reduce the supply of credit to the private sector. Panel (d) shows that credit supply growth indeed slows down in the crisis-hit countries. For four to five years prior to the crisis, the real credit growth rate is 7.4 percent. Thereafter credit growth rates decline over time, reaching -1.6 percent in the crisis year. Even five years after the crisis, credit growth does not return to the level of the pre-crisis or tranquil period. The slow down of real credit growth is more pronounced in the IMF program countries. The supply of real credit declines by more than 8 percent in the year

Figure 4. Change in Real Exchange Rate During the Currency Crises

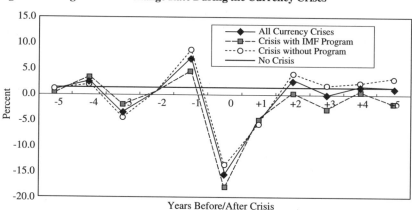

Years Before/After Crisis

following the crisis and thereafter continues to slow down throughout the post-crisis period.

The robust growth of net exports during the post-crisis period is likely to be related to the real exchange rate depreciation associated with (or caused by) the currency crisis. Figure 4 shows that a currency crisis causes a sharp real depreciation of the exchange rate by about 15 percent in the crisis year. The real exchange rate also depreciates by 5.3 percent in the year following the crisis. Thereafter, it appreciates about 2 percent per year. Hence, the real exchange remains depreciated after the crisis. The pattern of adjustment in the real exchange rate is similar in both the program and non-program countries.

Determinants of the Post-Crisis Recovery

We believe there are a large number of factors that determine the stylized pattern of adjustment in real output growth in the crisis-hit countries. Broadly speaking, there are four major factors that influence the adjustment pattern: (i) the origin and nature of the shock, (ii) initial conditions, (iii) domestic policies, and (iv) the external environments.

Origin and Nature of the Shock

The origin and nature of the shock that has provoked a crisis can influence the evolution of the crisis. Many currency crises can be attributed to macroeconomic mismanagement—large budget deficits and consequent monetary expansion in a fixed exchange rate regime—as in the Latin America debt crisis in the early 1980s. In this case, real depreciation of the currency and contraction of domestic absorption help to restore internal and external balance, leading to improvement in the economy.

Investors' panic can intensify the effects of speculative attacks on currency. In particular, when the capital account is liberalized, a bad expectation by foreign investors can easily lead to a sudden reversal of foreign lending, thereby causing a significant contraction of the domestic economy. The adverse impact will be magnified if domestic corporations and financial institutions are heavily leveraged by large, unhedged, and short-term foreign currency debts. When a sharp and unexpected depreciation wreaks havoc with highly leveraged corporate and bank balance sheets, a sudden reversal of capital flows exacerbates the downturn in investment and the economy (Krugman, 1999; Aghion, Bacchetta, and Banerjee, 2000). But, once the investors' panic calms down and foreign capital resumes to flow in, the economy can rebound quickly back to its long-term trend.

Initial Conditions

Differences in initial conditions could result in different patterns of adjustment. For example, structural variables such as per capita output and openness could be important in determining the pattern of post-crisis recovery.

The level of initial per capita GDP can influence the growth rate in the post-crisis period. In growth theory, a country with a lower initial per capita GDP is in a more favorable position for future growth. The fundamental idea is that the gap in existing capital and technology between the current and steady-state levels offers a chance for rapid "catching up," via high rates of capital accumulation as well as the diffusion of technology from more technically advanced economies. In addition, when a currency crisis leads an economy to a lower level of per capita income relative to that of its own trend, the subsequent growth rate by which the economy rebounds to its potential would be higher.

Openness can also influence the speed and extent of the post-crisis recovery. When the economy is more export oriented, a quicker improvement in the current account follows a currency devaluation. Lee and Rhee (2000) argue that the quick recovery of the Korean economy may have been possible because of its openness and export orientation. An export oriented economy benefits more from devaluation after the crisis, and a subsequent improvement in the current account could in turn help restore foreign investors' confidence and hence stability in the foreign exchange market.

Several studies also point out that the behavior of macroeconomic variables prior to the crisis can influence the degree of real output contraction. For example, a rapid expansion of bank credit or lending boom during the pre-crisis periods is critical to the post-crisis recovery (Sachs, Tornell, and Velasco, 1996; and Hong and Tornell, 1999). Gupta *et al.* (2000) find that the higher the size of short-term external debt and the amount of private capital flows are in the years prior to the crisis, the more severe is the contraction of output during the crisis-period.

Policy Factors

Macroeconomic and structural reform policies implemented by the government for crisis management can play a key role in the post-crisis adjustment of real output. Fiscal policy has a direct impact on domestic demand. Monetary policy plays a critical role in determining domestic consumption and investment.

In addition to the macroeconomic stabilization policies, structural reform programs can have significant effects on the adjustment path. It is often argued that structural reforms introduced by the IMF play a catalytic role in resuming foreign trade and private capital inflows, and thus contribute to the fast recovery of a crisis-hit economy as the commitment to the reform program improves foreign investors' confidence in the economy. The critics of IMF programs, however, argue that the implementation of financial restructuring in conjunction with contractionary macroeconomic policies can make a credit crunch more severe than otherwise after the crisis.

For external demand, a larger depreciation of the exchange rate is expected to increase export earnings while cutting down import demand to improve the current account.

External Environment

A global economic environment is also critical to the post-crisis adjustment of crisis-hit countries. Business fluctuations of the world economy can influence post-crisis growth as they have a substantial impact on the terms of trade and export earnings of the crisis-hit country.

To the extent that the relevant data are available, we carry out an empirical assessment of the factors determining the pattern of post-crisis recovery. The explanatory variables that we consider to explain the speed and the extent of post-crisis recovery include per capita real GDP in the crisis year, world economic growth, which is an average of per capita GDP growth rates of a crisis-hit country's trading partners weighted by its trade share, an interactive term of the real exchange rate depreciation with openness (trade-GDP ratio), real public consumption growth, and real money supply growth. We also include the investment rate.[4]

The regression also includes a dummy variable for the IMF program countries to see if participation in an IMF program had any impact on the recovery process. Upon entering an agreement with the IMF, a member government subscribes to the IMF conditionality which typically entails fiscal austerity, tight monetary policy, and currency devaluation. Since we include macroeconomic policies variables separately in the regression, the dummy variable may be able to capture the effect of the IMF program participation in post-crisis recovery.

We also control the differences in country-specific factors that may influence the potential growth path, by including the average growth rate for three

---

[4]The investment rate can be considered as an endogenous variable. The regression results do not change qualitatively when we exclude investment rate in the regressions. Note that investment includes public investment in addition to private investment. The regressions for investment rate are presented in Table 4.

to five years prior to the crisis. However, we do not include pre-crisis macro-economic policy variables in the regressions, for the impact of these variables on the post-crisis recovery are extensively discussed in Hong and Tornell (1999) and Gupta *et al.* (2000). Also, we cannot incorporate any variables that measure structural vulnerabilities of the corporate and financial sectors due to the lack of broad cross-country data.

The dependent variable in the regression is the average growth rate of real GDP during the post-crisis period over k years.[5]

$$(1) \qquad y_{i,t+k} = \frac{1}{k} \sum_{j=1}^{k} (\ln GDP_{i,t+j} - \ln GDP_{i,t+j-1}), \quad i = 1,...,N,$$

where $GDP_{i,t+j}$ is real GDP for country i in the j years after the crisis year (t) and N is the number of crisis episodes in our sample. Then, $y_{i,t+k}$ represents the real GDP growth rate, averaged over the post-crisis period of k years. Because we are mostly interested in short-term recovery, we choose k from 1 to 5. In the previous literature, k was often chosen arbitrarily, and thus cross-section data in which each country had only one observation was used for empirical investigation. Our framework differs significantly in that we use panel data. Thus, we utilize information in both cross-section and time dimensions. Our regression specification is as follows.

$$(2) \qquad y_{i,t+k} = \beta' x_{i,t+k} + \varepsilon_{i,t+k}, \qquad i=1,...,N, \qquad k=1,...,5,$$

where x denotes the vector of the explanatory variables. Note that some independent variables such as real GDP in the crisis year, pre-crisis average growth rate, and an IMF program dummy are identical across all five equations. Fiscal policy variable is included as an average over the period from the crisis year t to the post-crisis year $t+k$, while monetary growth and real exchange depreciation variables are included as an average over the period from the crisis year t to the post-crisis $t+k-1$.

We estimate this system of the five equations by a seemingly unrelated regression (SUR) technique that corrects for heteroskedasticity in each equation and correlation of the errors across the equations.

Table 2 displays our estimates of the basic regression for post crisis recovery at various horizons, based on a total of 101 previous crisis episodes during the period from 1970 to 1995.

---

[5]We have also estimated another specification by using the reversal of GDP growth rate between the crisis-hit (that is, *t-1* and *t*) and the post-crisis period, instead of post-crisis GDP growth, for the dependent variable in the regressions. We find the results do not change much.

Table 2. Determinants of the Pace of Recovery from the Currency Crises: A sample of 101 crisis episodes between 1970 and 1995

	Dependent variable Average GDP growth rate from t+1 to t+k				
(t+k=)	*t+1*	*t+2*	*t+3*	*t+4*	*t+5*
Real GDP per capita at t	-2.037*	-1.240*	-1.028*	-0.817*	-0.816*
(ppp-adjusted, log)	(0.532)	(0.380)	(0.324)	(0.283)	(0.257)
Pre-crisis GDP growth	-0.137	-0.030	0.060	0.057	0.090
(Average, t-3 to t-5)	(0.135)	(0.097)	(0.083)	(0.072)	(0.066)
World per capita GDP growth	0.445*	0.261	0.469*	0.580*	0.541*
(Average, t+1 to t+k)	(0.225)	(0.175)	(0.155)	(0.166)	(0.198)
Investment rate	0.133*	0.136*	0.123*	0.125*	0.104*
(Average, t+1 to t+k)	(0.051)	(0.037)	(0.032)	(0.028)	(0.026)
Real exchange rate change*trade share	0.032	0.004	-0.034**	-0.062*	-0.086*
(Average, t to t+k-1)	(0.023)	(0.020)	(0.019)	(0.023)	(0.029)
Public consumption growth	0.035	0.057*	0.072*	0.078*	0.086*
(Average, t to t+k)	(0.032)	(0.025)	(0.021)	(0.019)	(0.024)
Real money supply growth	0.006	0.012	0.011	0.003	-0.0001
(Average, t to t+k-1)	(0.015)	(0.011)	(0.010)	(0.009)	(0.010)
IMF program participation	-1.042	0.194	0.179	-0.215	-0.040
(dummy)	(0.968)	(0.699)	(0.589)	(0.515)	(0.468)
No. of crisis episodes	101	101	101	101	101
R^2	0.14	0.17	0.24	0.30	0.33

Notes: Standard errors reported in parentheses. Levels of statistical significance indicated by asterisks: *95 percent; ** 90 percent. The system has 5 equations, where the dependent variables are the average real GDP growth rates over k years from the crisis year, t. The system is estimated by the seemingly unrelated regression (SUR) technique, which allows for different error variances in each equation and for correlation of these errors across equations. Each equation has a different constant term, which is not reported. An increase in real exchange rate indicates a real appreciation.

We find a strong and statistically significant negative relation between the initial real per capita GDP and the post-crisis growth rate at all horizons, implying that countries with lower per capita income tend to have larger increases in GDP growth over the period after the crisis. The impact of initial GDP on the post-crisis recovery is much larger in the year following the crisis, but then becomes smaller in the later years of the post-crisis period. The estimated coefficients imply that a 10 percentage point drop in per capita GDP in the crisis year is associated with a 0.2 percentage point (2.04*ln(0.9)) increase in GDP growth in the first year after a crisis erupted, but with a 0.1 percentage point on average over five years after the crisis.

The world growth variable also has a significantly positive coefficient in most of the regressions. The estimated coefficients imply that a one percentage point increase in world per capita GDP growth is associated with about 0.5

percentage point increase in GDP growth of the crisis-hit country in the post-crisis period.

The results also confirm the strong association between investment and GDP growth over the period of adjustment in the crisis-hit economies. The coefficients show that an increase of 10 percentage points in the ratio of investment to GDP is typically associated with an increase in the growth rate of about 1.3 percentage points per year.

Among the macroeconomic policy variables, the fiscal variable (measured by public consumption growth) turns out to be most significant for the recovery in all post-crisis periods except for the year of $t+1$. The estimated coefficients imply that an increase of the public consumption growth rate by 10 percentage points leads to an increase in the GDP growth rate by 0.5~0.9 percentage points.

In contrast to the positive and significant contribution of fiscal policy, monetary policy turns out to be less important for post-crisis recovery. The average growth rates of real money supply are insignificant in all equations. One might argue that the weak effect of monetary policy on real output even in the short run is not credible. However, in our view, the real impact of monetary policy is ambiguous in the crisis-hit economies. Contractionary monetary policy as part of IMF programs can contribute to post-crisis growth as it helps stabilize prices and improve the current account.[6]

The results show that the interactive term between trade share and exchange rate depreciation variables have a significant impact on the post-crisis GDP growth only in a few years following a crisis. The estimated coefficients show that for the country with the average openness ratio of 0.6, a real exchange depreciation of 10 percent raises real GDP growth rate by about 0.4 percentage point per year over the four years after the crisis.

We also examined whether the agreements with the IMF had any impact on the post-crisis recovery. The estimated coefficients turn out to be statistically insignificant. Hence, there is no evidence that IMF programs had any significant impact on the recovery process after a currency crisis, when other factors were controlled.[7]

Macroeconomic policies may have an additional impact on growth by influencing the level of investment. Table 3 shows the results of regressions for the investment rate. We find that both public investment and real money sup-

---

[6]Goldfajn and Gupta (1999) find that the use of tight monetary policy is accompanied with a sharper recovery of output during the currency crises.

[7]A problem can occur in this regression when the participation in the IMF program is endogenously determined. To avoid this simultaneity problem, we need to use an instrumental-variable technique. We do not implement this approach yet due to lack of an ideal instrument.

Table 3. Regressions for Investment Rate in the Post-Crisis Period

(t+k=)	*Dependent variable* Average Investment Ratio from t+1 to t+k		
	t+1	*t+2*	*t+3*
GDP growth in the pre-crisis period	0.281**	0.410*	0.349*
(Average, t-3 to t-5)	(0.152)	(0.141)	(0.156)
Real exchange rate change	0.007	-0.012	0.011
(Average, t to t+k-1)	(0.040)	(0.036)	(0.040)
Public investment-GDP ratio	1.460*	1.319*	1.256*
(Average, t to t+k)	(0.231)	(0.131)	(0.111)
Real money supply growth	0.010	0.085*	0.133*
(Average, t to t+k-1)	(0.036)	(0.040)	(0.046)
IMF program participation	1.002	1.748	1.798
(dummy)	(1.296)	(1.222)	(1.158)
No. of crisis episodes	81	81	81
R^2	0.60	0.65	0.68

Notes: Each equation is estimated by the least squares method. Robust standard errors reported in parentheses. Levels of statistical significance indicated by asterisks; *95 percent; ** 90 percent. Constant term is included, but not reported.

ply growth play a quite significant role in promoting investment from the beginning of the post-crisis period, while exchange rate depreciation is insignificant. The estimated coefficient for public investment suggests that an increase of 1 percentage point in the ratio of public investment to GDP contributes to an increase in the total investment rate by between 1.3 and 1.5 percentage points. Hence, public investment increases total investment more than one for one, implying that public investment does not 'crowd out' equal amount of private investment from domestic sources by competing in product markets or financial markets. Thus, public investment, perhaps by improving the condition of social infrastructure, stimulates private investment and thus contributes to the post-crisis recovery by augmenting capital accumulation. An increase in real money supply growth by about 10 percentage points leads to an increase in the investment-GDP ratio by about 0.9~1.3 percentage points per year over the two years following the crisis.

Assessments of the Recovery Process in East Asia

Macroeconomic Adjustments in East Asia

The economic turmoil that broke out in Thailand in July 1997 swept through East Asia and its devastating impacts were much more severe than anyone had expected. The countries that fell victim to the crisis suffered a sharp reduction in real income. In 1998, the growth rate plunged from the pre-crisis average of 7.0 percent to -13.2 percent in Indonesia, -10.4 percent in Thailand, -7.5 percent in Malaysia, -6.7 percent in Korea, and -0.6 percent in the Philippines. However, since 1999 the five crisis-hit Asian countries have managed impressive recoveries, which have been faster than the similar episodes of recovery in other parts of the world before. The rebounding of the growth rate in 1999 was no less drastic than its free-fall. Korea stood out as the best performer in that year by growing at 10.7 percent. For the other countries, the growth rate ranged from 5.4 percent in Malaysia to 0.2 percent in Indonesia.

With the passage of time, the recovery process has gained momentum. The growth outturn in 2000 is estimated to be higher than that of 1999 in four of the affected economies—Indonesia, Thailand, Malaysia, and the Philippines. In Korea, the growth rate slowed from 10.7 percent to 8.3 percent.

Figure 5 shows the GDP growth rates of the five affected economies. The adjustment process in East Asia that can be inferred from changes in the growth rates seems to be in general consistent with the stylized V-pattern we observe from the previous crisis episodes. However, the East Asian experience is in marked contrast to the stylized pattern of adjustment in GDP growth in that the degree of initial contraction and subsequent recovery has been far greater than what can be predicted from the previous cross-country evidence.

Figure 5. Adjustment of Real GDP Growth Rate in East Asia

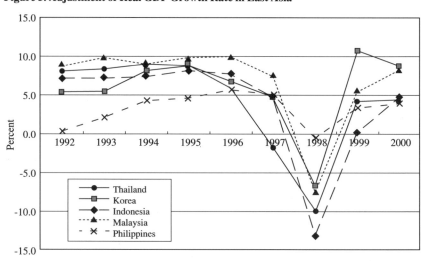

Table 4. Macroeconomic Adjustment in East Asia

a. Indonesia

	1993	1994	1995	1996	1997	1998	1999	2000
GDP growth rate (%)	7.25	7.54	8.22	7.82	4.70	-13.20	0.23	4.8
Expenditure on GDP								
Private Consumption Growth rate	11.77	7.83	12.58	9.72	7.82	-3.32	1.48	3.6
(share in GDP, %)	58.5	58.7	61.0	62.1	64.0	71.2	72.1	67.3
Government Consumption Growth rate	0.19	2.31	1.34	2.69	0.06	-15.37	0.69	6.5
(share in GDP, %)	9.0	8.6	8.0	7.7	7.3	7.1	7.2	7.0
Gross Domestic Investment growth rate	4.88	10.83	11.01	11.97	6.89	-31.81	-15.85	8.9
(share in GDP, %)	29.5	32.0	33.4	32.5	33.0	21.0	17.2	17.9
Exports of goods and services Growth rate	6.81	9.94	7.72	7.56	7.80	11.18	-32.06	27.1
(share in GDP, %)	26.8	27.4	27.2	27.2	28.0	35.8	24.3	--
Imports of goods and services Growth rate	4.65	20.30	20.94	6.86	14.72	-5.29	-40.90	4.1
(share in GDP, %)	23.8	26.6	29.7	29.5	32.3	35.2	20.8	--
Policy Indicators								
Government Capital Expenditure as % of nv.	27.0	23.3	19.7	17.8	14.8	24.1	--	--
Growth Rate of Real M2	10.5	11.5	17.8	19.2	19.0	5.0	-8.0	12.2
Annual Real Bank Credit Growth Rate	13.9	12.2	12.5	14.5	17.2	-25.0	-56.5	--
Real Effective Exchange Rate	--	--	100	109.5	104.5	52.7	74.5	59.1

b. Korea

	1993	1994	1995	1996	1997	1998	1999	2000
GDP growth rate (%)	5.49	8.25	8.92	6.75	5.01	-6.69	10.66	8.8
Expenditure on GDP								
Private Consumption Growth rate	5.60	8.19	9.60	7.07	3.50	-11.43	10.32	7.1
(share in GDP, %)	54.4	54.4	54.7	54.9	54.1	51.3	51.2	57.3
Public Consumption Growth rate	4.58	1.90	0.81	8.17	1.45	-0.41	-0.60	1.3
(share in GDP, %)	11.1	10.4	9.7	9.8	9.5	10.1	9.1	10.2
Gross Domestic Investment growth rate	5.87	8.55	9.37	7.50	-1.44	-16.68	2.90	8.0
(share in GDP, %)	34.4	36.4	37.2	37.9	33.4	22.0	26.0	28.7
Exports of goods and services Growth rate	11.30	16.08	24.59	11.21	21.44	13.25	16.35	19.9
(share in GDP, %)	24.6	26.4	30.2	31.5	36.4	44.2	46.4	--
Imports of goods and services Growth rate	6.21	21.58	22.36	14.25	3.18	-22.40	28.94	34.0
(share in GDP, %)	25.1	28.2	31.7	33.9	33.3	27.7	32.3	--
Policy Indicators								
Government Capital Expenditure as % of Inv.	6.0	6.7	8.6	10.0	11.0	21.6	18.8	17.3
Growth Rate of Real M2	11.8	12.4	11.2	10.9	9.7	19.5	26.6	23.1
Annual Real Bank Credit Growth Rate	6.8	13.7	10.3	14.4	14.4	4.3	18.8	--
Real Effective Exchange Rate	--	--	100	104.5	100.3	83.1	90.8	92.5

c. Malaysia

	1993	1994	1995	1996	1997	1998	1999	2000
GDP growth rate (%)	9.89	9.21	9.83	10.00	7.54	-7.50	5.42	8.3
Expenditure on GDP								
Private Consumption Growth rate	6.25	9.39	11.66	6.87	4.31	-10.80	2.53	12.2
(share in GDP, %)	48.3	48.4	49.2	47.8	46.4	44.7	43.5	42.6
Government Consumption Growth rate	8.43	7.87	6.06	0.73	7.63	-7.84	20.08	1.7
(share in GDP, %)	13.0	12.9	12.4	11.4	11.4	11.3	12.9	10.6
Gross Domestic Investment growth rate	15.41	14.14	19.04	6.71	8.87	-36.29	0.54	27.9
(share in GDP, %)	41.7	44.9	49.2	47.3	48.9	30.2	26.9	26.8
Exports of goods and services Growth rate	11.54	21.91	18.96	9.23	5.42	-0.21	13.76	16.1
(share in GDP, %)	80.3	89.7	97.1	96.5	94.6	102.0	110.1	--
Imports of goods and services Growth rate	15.04	25.64	23.7	4.89	5.74	-19.37	11.58	25.7
(share in GDP, %)	83.3	95.9	108.0	102.9	101.2	88.2	93.4	--
Policy Indicators								
Government Capital Expenditure as % of Inv.	13.5	12.4	12.9	12.0	11.9	23.8	--	--
Growth Rate of Real M2	23.0	7.9	16.8	20.8	14.7	-6.7	14.2	8.4
Annual Real Bank Credit Growth Rate	7.1	10.2	26.5	16.9	19.9	-2.2	0.5	4.5
Real Effective Exchange Rate	--	--	100.0	106.5	105.5	86.8	87.6	72.9

d. Philippines

	1993	1994	1995	1996	1997	1998	1999	2000
GDP growth rate (%)	2.13	4.39	4.67	5.85	5.19	-0.59	3.32	4.0
Expenditure on GDP								
Private Consumption Growth rate	3.05	3.72	3.82	4.62	4.99	3.45	2.64	3.5
(share in GDP, %)	78.8	78.3	77.7	76.8	76.6	79.7	79.2	70.7
Government Consumption Growth rate	6.15	6.13	5.62	4.10	4.67	-1.95	5.41	-1.1
(share in GDP, %)	8.0	8.1	8.2	8.1	8.0	7.9	8.1	12.8
Gross Domestic Investment growth rate	8.00	7.14	4.94	9.94	9.77	-9.00	-0.11	2.3
(share in GDP, %)	22.7	23.6	23.3	24.8	26.3	22.2	21.1	17.8
Exports of goods and services Growth rate	6.26	19.77	12.04	15.40	17.15	-21.04	3.65	8.7
(share in GDP, %)	34.9	40.1	42.9	46.8	52.1	41.4	41.5	--
Imports of goods and services Growth rate	11.48	14.51	16.03	16.73	13.49	-14.71	-2.79	2.1
(share in GDP, %)	43.9	48.2	53.4	58.9	63.6	54.5	51.3	--
Policy Indicators								
Government Capital Expenditure as % of Inv.	15.0	13.7	13.4	8.1	8.0	8.0	11.0	--
Growth Rate of Real M2	20.2	16.0	16.2	14.2	20.2	-1.2	9.4	--
Annual Real Bank Credit Growth Rate	30.7	19.2	31.8	38.8	20.2	-15.4	-6.3	--
Real Effective Exchange Rate	--	--	100.0	110.4	111.0	94.0	100.8	69.0

e. Thailand

	1993	1994	1995	1996	1997	1998	1999	2000
GDP growth rate (%)	8.38	8.95	8.90	5.93	-1.68	-10.17	4.16	4.4
Expenditure on GDP								
Private Consumption Growth rate	8.43	7.87	7.55	6.83	-1.05	-12.33	3.49	4.6
(share in GDP, %)	55.8	55.2	54.6	55.0	55.4	54.0	53.7	56.4
Government Consumption Growth rate	5.11	8.19	5.37	11.91	-3.03	1.94	2.82	6.5
(share in GDP, %)	8.3	8.2	7.9	8.4	8.3	9.4	9.3	11.5
Gross Domestic Investment growth rate	8.55	10.83	10.04	8.08	-18.59	-35.17	-1.72	11.8
(share in GDP, %)	40.9	41.6	42.7	43.0	33.7	19.0	20.5	22.7
Exports of goods and services Growth rate	12.74	14.25	15.50	-5.53	8.41	6.72	8.86	19.5
(share in GDP, %)	42.4	44.4	47.1	42.0	46.3	55.1	57.5	--
Imports of goods and services Growth rate	11.78	15.75	19.87	-0.52	-11.38	-22.28	20.24	24.6
(share in GDP, %)	44.9	47.7	52.5	49.3	44.4	38.4	44.4	--
Policy Indicators								
Government Capital Expenditure as % of Inv.	12.9	13.4	12.0	16.6	23.4	29.3	23.1	17.7
Growth Rate of Real M2	15.1	7.7	11.3	6.8	10.9	1.6	5.1	-0.9
Annual Real Bank Credit Growth Rate	18.6	24.6	15.1	9.4	13.6	-11.3	-6.0	-17.3
Real effective exchange rate	--	--	100.0	109.2	102.4	90.0	93.5	73.6

Source: Asian Development Bank on-line country data (http://www.adb.org/Statistics/country.asp).
Note: The share of expenditure components in GDP is constructed based on data in constant prices.

The initial GDP contraction in 1998 was largely caused by the collapse of investment: the level of domestic capital formation plummeted in all five countries in 1998. The contraction amounted to more than 30 percent in Indonesia, Malaysia and Thailand, 17 percent in Korea, and 9 percent in the Philippines (Table 4).

Compared to investment demand, private consumption fell to a lesser degree. The consumption-GDP ratio remained mostly stable in the crisis period, which is consistent with the cross-country stylized pattern. On the contrary, the investment-GDP ratio dropped sharply. In Korea, for example, it fell from 33.4 percent in 1997 to 22.0 percent in 1998. Investment demand started to recover somewhat in 1999 in Korea and Malaysia, but it has continued to decline in the other countries.

While domestic demand was sluggish, a large increase in net export paved way for the initial recovery of the Asian economies. Import demand declined in all of the crisis-hit countries in 1998 by a substantial amount, ranging from 22 percent in Korea and Thailand to 5.3 percent in Indonesia, while exports continued to grow or remained unchanged in all countries except the Philippines.

It is therefore clear that net exports led the recovery in East Asia. Figures 6 and 7 data demonstrate the pattern of adjustment in more detail. A close examination of the quarterly rates of GDP growth shows that both Korea and Thailand reached the trough as early as the second quarter of 1998, and Indonesia, Malaysia, and the Philippines two quarters later. Overall, the recession in East Asia bottomed out in the second half of 1998, less than a year after the crisis had broken out. As shown in Figure 7, the subsequent recovery in 1999 was led mostly by a surge in net exports. Over the post-crisis period the private consumption to GDP ratio has remained stable in all countries except Indonesia. In Indonesia, private consumption expenditure rose in 1998. In Korea and Malaysia, the investment rate started to increase from the latter half of 1998, whereas in the other countries the investment rate declined.

An increase in public investment appears to have contributed to the resurgence of total investment expenditure in Korea and Malaysia. Table 4 shows that in both countries the fraction of government capital expenditure in total investment jumped from 11 percent in 1997 to over 21 percent in 1998.

The large depreciation of currency has backed up the quick surge of net exports since 1998. Table 4 and Figure 8 show that the level of real effective exchange rates in the five crisis-hit East Asian countries depreciated by 22 percent on average, ranging from 12 percent in Thailand to 50 percent in Indonesia in 1998.

Figure 6. Quarterly Changes of Real GDP Growth in East Asia
(In percent, year over year)

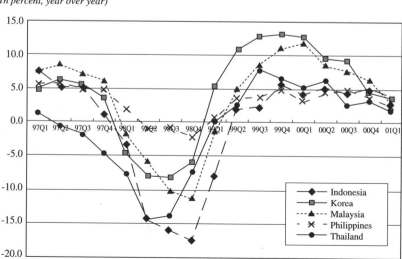

Figure 7. Quarterly Movements of GDP Components in East Asia

(a) Private Consumption in GDP (%)

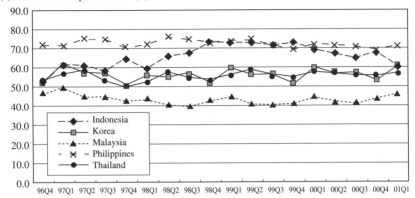

(b) Investment Rate (%)

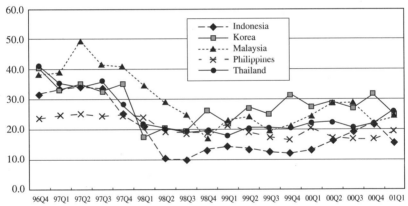

(c) Real Export Growth Rate (%)

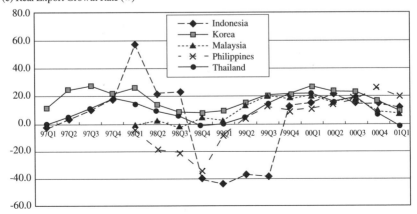

(d) Real Import Growth Rate (%)

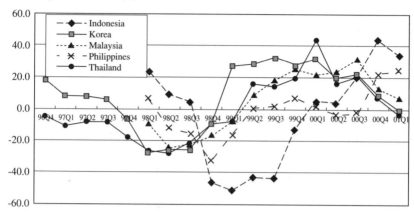

Figure 8. Real Effective Exchange Rate in East Asia

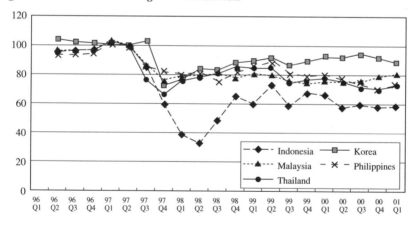

Factors behind the Speedy Adjustment in East Asia

A large number of internal and external factors are likely to have contributed to the pattern of macroeconomic adjustment to the crisis in East Asia. On the basis of the cross-country evidence and available information on the pattern of macroeconomic adjustment in East Asia, we attempt to identify some of the factors that have engineered the post-crisis recovery.

Macroeconomic Factors

According to the empirical examination of the stylized pattern of adjustments from the previous 160 currency crisis episodes over the period from 1970 to 1995, which show a V-type adjustment of real GDP growth, a large real depreciation, expansionary monetary and fiscal policy, and an improvement in the global economic environment have been responsible for the upturn of the crisis-hit countries. In this sense, the East Asian process of adjustment is not much different from the stylized pattern. The same factors contributed to the quick post-crisis recovery of the East Asian economies.

An important structural factor driving the speedy adjustment in East Asia may have been the region's higher level of openness. With a relatively large trade sector and export-orientation, these economies benefited from a large depreciation of the real exchange rate. The level of openness in terms of the share of exports and imports in GDP ranges from 200 percent in Malaysia to 60 percent in Indonesia. Thus, compared to other crisis-hit economies before, the depreciation is likely to have had a bigger impact on the more open East Asian economies. Note that the size of real exchange depreciation in the East Asian countries was comparable to the average depreciation rate in the previous crisis episodes.

One special feature of the East Asia crisis is that compared to the cross-country evidence, the impact of depreciation on real output showed up as early as one year after the crisis. The large real exchange depreciation therefore restored external balance without much delay in East Asia. The flexibility in the labor market may have facilitated this swift adjustment, since the shift of resources from the non-tradeables to the tradeables sector elicited by the massive real exchange rate depreciation requires flexible factor markets.

The quick improvement in East Asian exports has been supported by favorable external developments. The global economy was strong in 1999. The U.S. economy has been able to absorb a large amount of exports of the East Asian economies. U.S. per capita GDP growth rates were 3.3-3.4 percent in 1998 and 1999, and jumped to 4.4 percent in 2000, which by far exceeded the average growth rate of 2.0 percent over the period from 1970 to 1995. As we saw from the cross-country regressions, global economic growth has a strong impact on the post-crisis recovery, particularly in the early years following the crisis. The deterioration in the terms of trade that precipitated the crisis thus reversed in 1999. In particular, the increase in the prices of semiconductors helped to boost Korean, Malaysian, and Thai exports.

Concerning macroeconomic policy management, the swift change in policy stance toward expansion has supported a quick recovery of the crisis-hit

Figure 9. Policy Indicators in East Asia

(a) Real Public Consumption Growth (%)

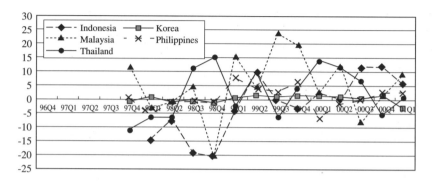

(b) Real Money Supply Growth (%)

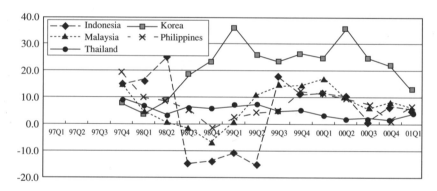

(c) Real Credit (1997, Q2=100)

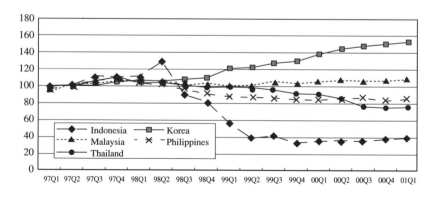

economies. In Korea relaxation of monetary and fiscal policy began around in April of 1998. A comparison of the turning points in the adjustment process measured by growth rates of the quarterly GDP with the timing of policy changes, broadly confirms that easing of monetary and fiscal policy has quickened the pace of recovery in both Thailand and Malaysia (Figure 9). Thailand shifted to a modest relaxation of macroeconomic policy in June 1998, and its economy took off in the fourth quarter of the same year after zero growth in the preceding quarter. In particular, public consumption expenditure increased significantly in the latter half of 1998. It was not until the third quarter—the end of August—of 1998 that a relaxation of monetary and fiscal policy was announced in Malaysia, and its economy moved out of the trough a quarter later. In Indonesia, on the contrary, because of the continuing weakness of the Rupiah, monetary policy remained contractionary until the second quarter of 1999. But public consumption increased sharply in the third quarter of 1999. This expansion boosted output growth in 1999. In Philippines, monetary policy was slightly contractionary over the post-crisis period, while public consumption expenditure has been growing since the first quarter of 1999.

The positive role of expansionary macroeconomic polices in the post-crisis recovery raises the question of whether the initial tightening of monetary and fiscal policy was too harsh, and maintained for too long, and as a consequence deepened the crisis. In order to deal with the crisis itself—stopping bank runs, protecting the payment system, and stemming capital outflows, the IMF prescribed tight monetary policy together with fiscal austerity, which initially led to a sharp increase in interest rates. The contractionary monetary and fiscal policy has been criticized by many, including Radelet and Sachs (1998) and Feldstein (1999), as having been unnecessary because these countries were suffering from a liquidity problem. They imply that the traditional IMF prescriptions may have done more harm than good as they drove many highly leveraged but viable firms out of business, thereby deepening the downturn of the economy. The contribution of the initial IMF austerity programs remains controversial. On the other hand, it is quite clear that the swift change of macroeconomic policy stance toward an expansionary one helped these economies recover quickly. Fiscal policy had become contractionary immediately after the crisis, but was reversed quickly to be expansionary. The change in monetary policy stance then followed. Once the depreciation of the currency was arrested and stability returned to the foreign exchange market, the authorities of the crisis countries were able to adjust gradually the interest rates downward and expand the money supply.

Panic and Balance Sheet Effect

The contraction of real income in the East Asian countries that suffered the crisis was much larger and the subsequent recovery of these countries has been much faster than what can be predicted from the previous crises. There must be additional factors that have contributed to the deeper contraction and the quicker recovery in East Asia. We consider that the East Asian crisis has an aspect of a severe liquidity crisis caused by investors' panic. This nature of the crisis must have an important role in the macroeconomic adjustment during the crisis.

There is general agreement that a fixed peg to a currency basket dominated by the U.S. dollar when the current account was piling up deficits was one aspect of policy mismanagement that triggered the crisis in Thailand. In a recent paper, Williamson (2000) shows that had it been implementing a BBC (basket, band, and crawl) rule, Thailand might have staved off its crisis, because the country was suffering from a balance-of-payment crisis. However, the Thai crisis was contagious, as shown by Park and Song (2001a, 2001b), and even a good exchange rate management using the BBC rule could not have saved other crisis victims like Indonesia and Korea from the contagion.

Although macroeconomic policies and economic fundamentals of Korea and Indonesia were regarded sound and credible, many foreign investors simply moved out of East Asian financial markets when they realized that most of the East Asian countries would suffer from similar macroeconomic and structural problems that were driving Thailand to the brink of debt default. With the withdrawal of foreign lenders and investors from the region, other East Asian countries experienced a sharp liquidity crisis and balance sheet problems associated with a large currency depreciation, causing a region-wide crisis explicable by second and third generation crisis models. That is, the contagion of the Thai crisis set in motion a crisis characterized by self-fulfilling prophecy and balance sheet deterioration in other East Asian countries, which did not have serious balance-of-payment problems. Once hit by contagion, the BBC system was simply unable to stave off the crisis because the band could not be maintained.

Why did foreign portfolio investors panic so much and exhibit herd behavior? They initially moved into East Asia with large sums of money to be invested in all types of local securities and real assets by the mistaken notion that rapid growth in the region would be sustained or that their investments would be protected by government guarantees. Most of the foreign investors paid little attention to the structural problems of the financial and corporate sections that began to haunt East Asia before moving in. When these problems came to light in the midst of currency depreciation and interest rate increases, they were startled. The ensuing fear of losing their investments then drove them to a state of panic, and every investor was scrambling to the exit.

Thus, one critical factor that could explain both the initial sharper contraction and faster recovery is related to changes in the expectations of foreign investors and both domestic households and firms on economic prospects of the crisis countries. When foreign investors began to lose confidence in East Asian economies, capital flows abruptly reversed. As shown in Table 5, in 1997 private net capital flows reversed by $115 billion (from a $120 billion inflow in 1996 to a $5 billion outflow). It is no wonder that this large-scale shift in financial flows provoked deep contractions, huge depreciations and financial embarrassment. And the argument goes that once investors' panic calms down and foreign capital inflows resume, the economy rebounds to its long-term trend.

Immediately after the crisis, there was rampant speculation that the crisis countries might not be able to avoid foreign debt default and hence might have to declare a debt moratorium. The international financial community, including the international financial institutions, also did not hesitate to lay the blame on the East Asian countries for the crisis. With the emerging consensus that the crisis countries had profound problems that were more serious than had been realized before, the prospect for recovery in East Asia turned from bad to worse. Many were skeptical whether these countries had institutional capacity and political will to carry out the necessary structural reforms. Even if

Table 5. Capital flows to the Five Asian Economies
(Billion U.S. dollars)

	1996	1997	1998	1999	2000e
External financing, net (A+B)	118.6	39.5	-15.2	-4.9	-1.2
A: Private flows, net	119.5	4.9	-38.7	-5.2	-3.8
Equity investment	16.8	5.2	16.8	30.1	15.6
Direct equity	4.8	6.8	12.3	14.6	9.5
Portfolio equity	12.0	-1.7	4.5	15.4	6.1
Private creditors	102.7	-0.3	-55.5	-35.3	-19.3
Commercial banks	69.6	-17.4	-48.8	-29.3	-15.3
Non-bank private creditors	33.2	17.2	-6.7	-6.0	-4.1
B: Official flows, net	-0.9	34.6	23.5	0.2	2.6
International financial inst.	-1.9	22.7	19.7	-4.6	2.5
Bilateral creditors	1.0	11.9	3.8	4.9	0.1

e- estimate
Note: The five countries include South Korea, Indonesia, Thailand, Malaysia, and the Philippines.
Source: IIF, January 2001.

they had, the skeptics pointed out that these crisis countries would take many years to put their houses in order. Under these circumstances, it is quite possible that the households and firms as well as foreign investors came to believe that the crisis was a permanent shock which would lead to a new lower equilibrium in terms of output and employment than when the crisis was seen as a temporary shock. And this perception of permanency may have induced domestic consumers and investors to cut down their spending a lot more than otherwise during the first six months of the crisis. However, the extensive criticism of East Asia diminished and gradually gave way to a more optimistic outlook for the crisis economies, and the realization that the crisis might be a temporary phenomenon started sinking in the minds of consumers and investors, thereby encouraging their spending.

In restoring the confidence of foreign investors, large support packages by the IMF made some contribution. The funding helped to reduce the short-term liquidity constraints of the economies and provide resources to stem the exchange rate depreciation. There were other turning points. Korea, for example, reached an agreement with its creditor in February of 1998 to lengthen the maturities of the short-term foreign currency loans (Radelet and Sachs, 1998).[8] After the agreement was reached, at least some of foreign credit facilities including trade credit were restored. With this restoration of credit, the fear of a debt default abated considerably.

A large decrease in aggregate investment demand during the crisis period suggests that corporate distress was one of the main factors responsible for the sharper contraction in output in East Asia. Structural weaknesses in corporate and bank balance sheets were often pointed out as the main channel through which the effect of foreign disturbances was magnified in the East Asian crisis (Krugman, 1999; and Stone, 2000).

The reversal of capital inflows combined with a sudden downward shift in expectations could lead to a sharp depreciation of the exchange rate. The large unexpected depreciation was much more disastrous in East Asia because most firms were highly leveraged. When the bulk of corporate debts are denominated in U.S. dollars while revenues and assets are in local currency, the depreciation deteriorates the balance sheets of firms and inflicts large losses. Table 6 shows that foreign exchange losses of the Korean firms amounted to more than 17 trillion won in 1997, which was about 3.8 percent of GDP.[9] These losses together with the increase in foreign debt financing costs result in a

---

[8]They did not do so voluntarily, but at the urging of the G-7 governments and the IMF, and only when they were convinced that they would be repaid with handsome returns.

[9]According to Hahm and Mishkin (2000), the foreign liabilities accounted for about 16% in total corporate debt in 1997 in Korea.

Table 6. Foreign Exchange Losses of the Korean Corporate Sector
(Billion won, percent)

	1997	1998	1999
Gains on Foreign Exchange Transactions (A)	-2,692	-784	203
Gains on Foreign Exchange Valuation (B)	-14,571	-1,026	2,533
Total Gains (A+B)	-17,263	-1,810	2,736
Percent of Total Assets	-2.4%	-0.2%	0.3%
Percent of GDP	-3.8%	-0.4%	0.6%

Source: Authors' estimates based on the Bank of Korea, *Financial Statement Analysis.*

decline in the present value of the equity of the corporate sector. Gray (1999) estimates that a 50 percent depreciation would have reduced the equity value of Korean corporations by 9 percent and that of Indonesian corporations by 21 percent. The lower equity value leads to lower investment.

Balance sheets of financial institutions were also very vulnerable to the currency depreciation. Since in East Asia banks had a large amount of foreign liabilities in their balance sheets, they suffered losses emanating from the currency mismatch.[10] In June 1997 the ratio of foreign liabilities to foreign assets of the banking sector ranged from 1.3 in Korea to 6.8 in Thailand (Table 7). Maturity mismatches also created another vulnerability. Korean data shows that short-term foreign liabilities were more than twice as large as short-term foreign assets (Table 8).

Table 7. The Ratio of Foreign Liabilities to Foreign Assets of the Banking Sector[1]

	1996.12	1997.3	1997.6	1997.9	1997.12	1998.3	1998.6	1998.9	1998.12
Indonesia	1.4	1.7	1.8	1.8	1.5	1.2	1.0	0.8	0.8
Korea	1.3	1.3	1.3	1.3	0.9	0.8	0.8	0.8	0.9
Malaysia	2.6	2.5	2.8	2.3	2.1	1.6	1.4	1.3	1.7
Philippines	1.8	1.7	1.9	2.0	1.7	1.8	1.7	1.6	1.4
Thailand	6.9	7.3	6.8	5.5	4.7	4.2	3.2	2.5	2.3

[1]Gross foreign liabilities and assets of deposit money banks.
Source: ADB based on data from IMF, *International Financial Statistics.*

---

[10]In 1997 the foreign liabilities accounted for about 55% of banks' total liabilities in Korea, 27% in Thailand, and 15% in Indonesia (ADB, 2000).

Table 8. Foreign Assets and Liabilities Outstanding at Financial Institutions in Korea
(Billion U.S. dollars)

	1996.12	1997.3	1997.6	1997.9	1997.12	1998.3	1998.6	1998.9	1998.12
Assets									
Total	67.2	70.4	72.1	72.0	72.0	70.5	71.2	68.1	63.9
Long-term	30.6	33.2	33.2	32.5	27.3	25.9	27.1	26.0	24.7
	(46)[1]	(47)	(46)	(45)	(38)	(37)	(38)	(38)	(39)
Short-term	36.6	37.2	38.9	39.5	44.7	44.6	44.1	42.1	39.2
	(54)	(53)	(54)	(55)	(62)	(63)	(62)	(62)	(61)
Liabilities									
Total	116.5	126.2	129.4	127.1	89.9	83.8	79.8	74.0	70.9
Long-term	43.5	46.0	48.1	51.7	47.5	45.0	58.6	55.6	52.0
	(37)[2]	(36)	(37)	(41)	(53)	(54)	(73)	(75)	(73)
Short-term	73.0	80.2	81.3	75.4	42.4	38.8	21.2	18.4	18.9
	(63)	(64)	(63)	(59)	(47)	(46)	(27)	(25)	(27)
Net Liabilities									
Total	49.3	55.8	57.3	55.1	17.9	13.3	8.6	5.9	7.0
Long-term	12.9	12.8	14.9	19.2	20.2	19.1	31.5	29.6	27.3
Short-term	36.4	43.0	42.4	35.9	-2.3	-5.8	-22.9	-23.7	-20.3
Long-term Asset /Liabilities(%)	70.3	72.1	69	62.8	57.4	57.5	46.2	46.7	47.5
Short-term Asset /Liabilities(%)	50.1	46.3	47.8	52.3	105.4	114.9	208	228.8	207.4

Source: Bank of Korea.
[1] Percentage of total assets.
[2] Percentage of total liabilities.

Once banks and non-bank financial institutions suffer a sharp decline in profits and hence a substantial erosion of their capital base, they are downgraded by the rating agencies and often denied access to international financial markets. As experienced by many money-losing financial institutions in East Asia, foreign banks and other institutional investors simply cut the lines of credit they had offered through the inter-bank loan market and refused the rollover of short-term loans when their client institutions were in trouble. This refusal created serious liquidity as well as balance sheet loss problems at the East Asian financial institutions. Faced with the liquidity problem, many banks and non-bank financial institutions had to reduce their supply of loans in both local and foreign currencies drastically even to their viable loan customers.

The mounting losses caused by the deterioration of bank balance sheets was bound to increase the country risk premium of the crisis-hit countries. A rise in the country risk premium in turn pushes up the cost of capital and lowers the present value of the equity of the corporate sector. Gray (1999) estimates an 8 percent temporary rise in the country risk premium for a year leads to a drop of 7 percent in the present value of corporate equity in Korea and 2 percent in Indonesia.[11]

An increase in the interest rate and currency depreciation together with other shocks can reduce the equity value of the corporate sector below a threshold that triggers widespread default. The risk of default was higher in East Asia where firms were highly leveraged with a large amount of short-term liabilities. The firms with a larger share of short-term debt faced more difficulties in financing and were unable to service their debts: bankruptcies soared, thereby magnifying the crisis.

In the recovery process, macroeconomic stability plays a crucial role for the normal operation of viable firms. Stabilization of the exchange rate and interest rate improves the equity value of the corporate sector and thus promotes investment. Improved confidence leads to an increase in spending. The restructuring of the corporate sector is necessary in order to reduce the vulnerability of the corporate sector and thus prevent the future crisis. However, in the short run, a quick recovery can not be engineered unless there is resurgence of domestic demand.

Structural Reform and Recovery[12]

At the beginning of the crisis, there was widespread belief that the crisis countries' commitment to structural reforms would be critical to the recovery in East Asia. The reforms were expected to help East Asia emerge from the crisis with more stable, transparent, and efficient financial and corporate sectors. This expectation of reform espousing a market-oriented system would then improve long-term growth prospects and, at the same time, restore market confidence, thereby inducing the return of foreign lenders and investors to the region.

Three years into the reform process, the crisis countries have accomplished a great deal in improving the soundness and profitability of financial institutions and alleviating corporate distress. The World Bank (2000, p.7) argues that "assertive structural adjustment helped restore credit flows and boosted consumer and investor confidence." Yet, it is not clear whether and to what extent financial and corporate restructuring has contributed to the ongoing recovery. Most of the serious structural problems that were identified as the major causes of the crisis in Indonesia, Korea, Malaysia, and Thailand could

---

[11]The high domestic interest rate, which aims at stemming rapid depreciation, has the same devastating effect on the value of corporate sector equity and thus investment.

[12]See Park (2001a, 2001b) for more details.

not have been resolved over a span of two years. In fact, banks are still holding in their balance sheets a large volume of non-performing loans and remain undercapitalized in all four countries. Many corporations in the region are still unable to service their debts. As for institutional reform, new banking and accounting standards, disclosure requirements, and rules for corporate governance have been introduced, but they are not rigorously enforced. It will take many years for the new system to take root.

Since the crisis countries are not even half-way there in restructuring their financial institutions and corporations, it would be presumptuous to argue that the reform efforts have established a foundation for sustainable growth in East Asia. Nor, would it be correct to assert that the gain in efficiency through the restructuring, which is difficult to measure at this stage, has been one of the principal factors driving the recovery. The improvement in efficiency is likely to be realized and translated into high growth over a longer period of time, certainly longer than two years.

The available pieces of evidence also do not support the contention that market-oriented reforms have contributed to restoring market confidence in the East Asian crisis countries; it certainly did not appear to have during the first two years of the crisis. International credit rating agencies report that reforms in the banking sector in the crisis countries have not gone far enough to ensure that these economies would be able to forestall another financial crisis. Only toward the end of 1999, Moody's and S&P upgraded the sovereign credit ratings of Korea and Malaysia to the lowest investment grade from speculation grade. By that time, the recovery was in full swing in East Asia. Journalistic accounts have abounded with similar concerns and continued to raise doubts regarding the effectiveness of the reform in the crisis countries. Under these circumstances, most foreign investors would find it risky to return to the crisis countries, but they have. Many of the foreign investors appear to have been lured back by the rapid recovery and substantial improvements in external liquidity resulting from large surpluses on the current account.

Reflecting recovery rather than ratings improvement, capital inflows in East Asia have been rising. Since policy changes and structural reforms are subject to many uncertainties and require a long time to take effect, international banks and global institutional lenders do not seem to have either the patience or ability to monitor and assess the effects of structural reforms. This is particularly true when they are preoccupied with the short-term performance of their portfolios.

Differences in Post-Crisis Performance among the Asian Countries

The five Asian countries most affected by the Asian financial crisis experienced a speedy recovery that was faster than anyone had expected. But the extent of the recovery from the crisis differed among the five countries. By the end of 1999 only Korea had surpassed its pre-crisis peak level of GDP. Malaysia and the Philippines did so later in 2000, while Thailand and Indonesia still need another year or so to recover to their pre-crisis output level.

Table 4 indicates that the difference in the post-crisis recovery in 1999 reflects mainly the difference in the performance of investment and export growth among the Asian countries. While the annual growth rate of export in 1999 amounted to 16.4 percent in Korea, 13.8 percent in Malaysia, and 8.9 percent in Thailand, it was -32.1 percent in Indonesia. After investment ratios had dropped sharply in the five Asian countries in 1998 due to the crisis, they showed a slow recovery in 1999 in both Korea and Malaysia. By contrast, in the other three Asian countries investment ratios contracted further in 1999.

The investment contractions reflect the significant distress in both the corporate and financial sectors. The financial crisis caused deterioration of firms' balance sheets. Then, the deterioration of the balance sheets of firms caused a massive accumulation of non-performing loans at banks and other non-bank financial institutions. The accumulation of bad loans cut into profits and consequently decreased the equity value of the financial institutions. Decapitalized financial institutions as a result of the mounting losses were forced to curtail their lending to both viable and non-viable firms, thereby exacerbating the downturn of investment.

In a bank oriented financial system that characterizes the financial structure of the crisis-hit countries in East Asia, the repercussion of bank failures is much more pervasive and felt throughout the economy. Because of their dominance, therefore, banks are likely to bring down many viable firms than otherwise when they are not able to function as intermediary.

Data show that the investment and output contractions in the Asian countries are closely associated with the sluggish bank lending. Although the money supply began to expand in 1999 for the five Asian economies, the supply of bank credit in real terms continued to slow in three of them—Indonesia, Thailand, and the Philippines (Panels (b) and (c) of Figure 9). In fact, more than three years after the crisis, real credit supply remains below the pre-crisis level in those three countries. The investment ratio recovered most quickly in Korea where real credit increased at the highest rate over the post-crisis period.

Prospects for Long-term Growth in East Asia

As the recovery continues in East Asia, there is a growing hope that these economies will be able to return to the pre-crisis level of robust growth. In this section, we make an assessment of the long-term growth prospects for East Asia.

Impacts of a Currency Crisis on Long-Term Growth

We investigate the impact of a currency crisis on long run growth based on a cross-country regression framework. We control for all important growth determinants and then examine whether a currency crisis has had any independent impact on GDP growth in the long run.

A wide variety of external environment and policy variables will affect growth prospects by changing the long-run potential income and the rate of productivity growth. Based on the results from previous empirical research, we consider the following variables as the important determinants of long-run per capita income growth: (1) initial income, (2) human resources, (3) the investment rate, (4) exogenous terms of trade changes, and (5) institutions and policy variables including government consumption, rule of law, and openness.[13] To measure the stock of human capital, we use the average years of secondary and higher schooling for population aged 15 and over, available from Barro and Lee (2001). The rule of law index is a measure of the quality of institutions, which is based on the evaluation by international consulting firms that give advice to international investors. The openness measure is based on Sachs and Warner (1995). This index is calculated as the fraction of years during the period that the country was considered to be open to trade and thus sufficiently integrated with the global economy. The evaluation of the country's openness is made on the basis of four dimensions of trade policy: average tariff rates, quotas and licensing, export taxes, and the black market exchange rate premium.

Table 9 presents the results of regressions for per capita real GDP growth rate using the explanatory variables just described. The data are a panel set of cross-country data over the two decades, 1975-85 and 1985-95. The system of two equations is estimated by a seemingly-unrelated-regression (SUR) technique, which allows for the correlation of the errors across the equations.

The regressions show that most of the controlling variables are significant determinants of long-term growth. For instance, the coefficient on the log

---

[13]Our specification closely follows Barro (1997) in selecting the explanatory variables.

value of initial GDP is highly significant. Thus it provides strong evidence for conditional convergence: that is, a poor country with a lower initial income level grows faster, when the variables influencing the steady-state level of income are controlled. Specifically, the coefficient in column 1 of Table 9 imply that a country at half of income level of another country grows by 1.4 percentage points ($=2.0*\ln(2)$) faster than the richer country.

We add to the regression a variable that measures the occurrence of currency crises. The variable is constructed with the number of currency crises that each country experienced during the past decade. We have used the number of crises over the period of 1970-75 for the first equation and over the period of 1975-85 for the second equation. Thus we test if an experience of a currency crisis can have an impact on growth in the next decade. The estimated coeffi-

Table 9. Long-Run Impact of Currency Crisis on Per Capita Growth Rate

Equation	(1)	(2)
Estimation method	*Seemingly-Unrelated Regression*	
Initial GDP per capita(log)	-1.965	-1.975
	(0.360)	(0.365)
Years of schooling	0.350	0.357
	(0.246)	(0.247)
Investment rate	0.084	0.085
	(0.033)	(0.032)
Terms of trade change	0.084	0.086
(% per annum)	(0.036)	(0.037)
Government consumption	-0.139	-0.140
(Percentage in GDP)	(0.032)	(0.032)
Rule of law index	1.212	1.195
	(0.830)	(0.829)
Openness	2.726	2.708
(1= most open)	(0.482)	(0.485)
Currency crisis	0.043	0.211
(no. of crises in previous decade)	(0.033)	(0.436)
Currency crisis with IMF program		-0.386
(no. of crises in previous decade)		(0.670)
R^2	.54, .37	.54, .37
Number of observations	84, 82	84, 82

Notes: The system has two equations, where the dependent variables are the growth rate of real per capita GDP for each of the two: 1975-85 and 1985-95. The estimations use the SUR (seemingly-unrelated) estimation technique, which allows the error term to be correlated across the two periods and to have a different variance in each period. Each equation is allowed to have a different constant term (not reported). Standard errors are shown in parentheses. The R^2 values and the number of observations apply to each period separately.

cient turns out to be statistically insignificant, implying that there is no direct impact of currency crises on growth in the long run. In column (2) of the regression, we add a variable that represents the number of currency crises with the IMF program participation. We also found no significance for this variable.

Although there is no direct impact of a currency crisis on long-run growth, it would be possible that a currency crisis or IMF program can have an indirect impact on long-run growth by influencing the controlling variables. For instance, if the investment rate becomes permanently lower because of the post-crisis stabilization program in the crisis-hit countries, it would have a negative impact on growth in the long run. On the contrary, if IMF structural reforms improve the quality of institutions, then a currency crisis with the IMF program participation can have a positive impact on growth.

Sustainability of East Asian Growth

The quick turnaround of the Asian economy from the 1997 crisis has brightened the region's economic prospects. Despite the impressive record of the recovery, however, not everyone is sanguine about East Asia's future prospects. The World Bank and IMF, for example, are not optimistic about the prospects of these countries sustaining the ongoing recovery, largely because weaknesses of financial institutions and balance sheet problems of corporations still remain unresolved in the region.

The macroeconomic performance of the crisis countries in 2001 will provide important clues to the question of whether these countries will be able to return to the pre-crisis trend rate of growth. Up to 2000, the pattern of recovery in East Asia has been quite similar to that of Mexico after its crisis in 1994.

Although the financial crisis of 1997 abruptly brought a halt to Asia's period of robust growth, there was little in Asia's fundamentals that inevitably led to the crisis. The key to the Asian crisis was too much short-term capital flowing into weak and under-supervised financial systems. This suggests that with better financial management and a return to the core policies that resulted in rapid growth, the East Asian economies can again return to sustained growth (Radelet, Sachs, and Lee, 2001). The major factors that have brought the relatively high growth in East Asia were high rates of saving, good human resources, trade openness, and maintenance of good institutions. In terms of these fundamentals, East Asia still has strong potential for a sustained growth.

But, in the long-term, the growth rate will be lower than the previous pre-crisis average of 7 percent. The convergence factor, which was found to be quite strong in the cross-country growth regression in the last section, implies that the faster growth in the last decades will force the East Asian economies to grow at a slower pace in the next decade. That is, the East Asian countries now have a much smaller gap in reproducible (physical and human) capital and technical efficiency from their long-run potential levels than they had in the last decades. Hence, the East Asian economies will face a smaller chance for rapid "catching up" through high rates of capital accumulation as well as the diffusion of technology from more technically advanced economies in the next decade, and inevitably become adjusted to a lower growth path.

The coefficients in the cross-country growth regressions imply that the convergence factors alone makes the Asian economies grow by about 1.5 percentage points slower over the next decade, compared to the last decades in which they had started with less than a half of their current income. Hence, unless the economies could achieve substantial improvements in other fundamental factors, such as quality of institutions, real GDP would grow at about 5 percent per year.

Concluding Remarks

The contraction of real income in the East Asian countries that suffered the crisis that erupted in 1997 was much larger and the subsequent recovery of these countries has been much faster than what can be predicted from the previous episodes of crisis elsewhere. The purpose of this paper has been to identify some of the factors that may explain the severity of, and rapid recovery from, the crisis. According to our empirical examination of macroeconomic developments following the crisis in East Asia, including a V-type adjustment of real GDP growth, a large real depreciation, expansionary monetary and fiscal policy, and an improvement in the global economic environment have been responsible for the upturn of the crisis-hit countries. In this sense, the East Asian process of adjustment is not much different from the stylized pattern observed from the previous 176 currency crisis episodes over the period from 1970 to 1995. However, the stylized pattern of adjustment cannot explain why the crisis was so severe and why the recovery has been so much faster than what was expected from the previous experiences of crisis. This study argues that the East Asian financial upheaval was in a large measure a liquidity crisis caused by investors' panic. Once the liquidity constraint was eased as it was during the first half of 1998, domestic demand has since surged again and the crisis countries have been able to move toward the pre-crisis path of growth.

References

Aghion, Philippe, Philippe Bacchetta, and Abhijit Banerjee, 2000, "Currency Crises and Monetary Policy in an Economy with Credit Constraints," Working Paper, Economics Department, Harvard University, forthcoming in *European Economic Review, ISOM Volume.*

Asian Development Bank, 2000, *Asian Recovery Report 2000*, March, Asian Development Bank (Manila, Philippines).

Barro, Robert, 1997, *Determinants of Economic Growth: A Cross-country Empirical Study*, Cambridge MA, MIT Press.

Barro, Robert, and Jong-Wha Lee, 2001, "International Data on Educational Attainment: Updates and Implications," *Oxford Economic Papers* 53(3), pp. 241-263.

Conway, Patrick, 1994, "IMF Lending Programs: Participation and Impact," *Journal of Development Economics*, 45, pp. 365-391.

Feldstein, Martin, 1998, "Refocusing the IMF," *Foreign Affairs*, Vol. 77, pp. 20-33.

Frankel, Jeffrey A., and Andrew K. Rose, 1996, "Currency Crashes in Emerging Markets: An Empirical Treatment," *Journal of International Economics*, 41, pp. 351-366.

Goldfajn, Ilan, and Poonam Gupta, 1999, "Does Monetary Policy Stabilize the Exchange Rate Following a Currency Crisis," IMF Working Paper 99/42.

Gray, Dale, 1999, "Assessment of Corporate Sector Value and Vulnerability: Links to Exchange Rate and Financial Crises," World Bank Technical Paper No. 455.

Gupta, Poonam, Deepak Mishra, and Ratna Sahay, 2000, "Output Response During Currency Crises," mimeograph, IMF and World Bank, forthcoming in *IMF Staff Papers.*

Hahm, Joon-Ho, and Frederic Mishkin, 2000, "Causes of the Korean Financial Crisis: Lessons for Policy," NBER Working Paper 7483.

Haque, Nadeem Ul, and Mohsin S. Khan, 1998, "Do IMF-Supported Programs Work? A Survey of the Cross-Country Empirical Evidence," IMF Working Paper WP/98/169.

Hong, Kiseok, and Aaron Tornell, 1999, "Post-Crisis Development of Asia," Korea Development Institute, mimeo.

Kaminsky, Graciela, and Carmen M. Reinhart, 1999, "The Twin Crises: The Causes of Banking and Balance-of-Payments Problems," *American Economic Review*, 89(3), pp. 473-500.

Krugman, Paul, 1999, "Balance Sheets, the Transfer Problem and Financial Crises," in *International Finance and Financial Crises: Essays in Honor of Robert P. Flood Jr.*, edited by Peter Isard, Assaf Razin, and Andrew Rose, International Monetary Fund and Kluwer Academic Publishers (Washington, DC and Norwell, MA, USA).

Lee, Jong-Wha, and Changyong Rhee, 2000, "Macroeconomic Impacts of the Korean Financial Crisis: Comparison with the Cross-country Patterns," Economics Department, Korea University Working Paper, forthcoming in *World Economy.*

Lee, Jong-Wha, Kiseok Hong, and Changyong Rhee, 2001, "The Macroeconomic Adjustment during the Currency Crises," *Kyung Je Hak Yon Ku*, 49(2), pp. 227-253, in Korean.

Milesi-Ferreti, Gian Maria, and Assaf Razin, 1998, "Current Account Reversal and Currency Crises: Empirical Regularities," IMF Working Paper 98/89.

Park, Yung Chul, 2001a, "East Asian Dilemma: Restructuring Out or Growing Out?," *Essay in International Economics*, No.223, Princeton University (Princeton, NJ, USA).

Park, Yung Chul, 2001b, "A Post Crisis Paradigm of Development for East Asia: Governance, Markets, and Institutions," Korea University, Economics Department, mimeo.

Park, Yung Chul, and Chi-Young Song, 2001a, "Institutional Investors, Trade Linkage, Macroeconomic Similarities, and the Contagious Thai Crisis," *The Journal of Japanese and International Economies*, 15, pp. 199-224.

Park, Yung Chul, and Chi-Young Song, 2001b, "Financial Contagion in the East Asian Crisis—With Special Reference to the Republic of Korea," in *International Financial Contagion*, edited by Stijn Classens and Kristin Forbes, Kluwer Academic Publishers (Norwell, MA, USA), pp. 241-265.

Przeworski, Adam, and James R. Vreeland, 2000, "The Effect of IMF Programs on Economic Growth," *Journal of Development Economics*, 62, pp. 385-421.

Radelet, Steven, and Jeffrey Sachs, 1998, "The East Asian Financial Crisis: Diagnosis, Remedies, Prospects," *Brookings Papers on Economic Activity I*, pp. 1-74.

Radelet, Steven, Jeffrey Sachs, and Jong-Wha Lee, 2001, "Determinants and Prospects of Economic Growth in Asia," *International Economic Journal*, 15(3), pp. 1-30

Sachs, Jeffrey, and Andrew Warner, 1995, "Economic Reform and the Process of Global Integration," *Brookings Papers on Economic Activity I*, pp. 1-118.

Sachs, Jeffrey, Aron Tornell, and Andrei Velasco, 1996, "The Collapse of the Mexican Peso: What Have We Learned?" *Economic Policy*, 22, pp. 13-56.

Stone, Mark, 2000, "The Corporate Sector Dynamics of Systemic Financial Crises," IMF Working Paper WP/00/114.

Williamson, John, 2000, *Exchange-Rate Regimes for East Asia: Reviving the Intermediate Option*, Policy Analysis in International Economics No. 60, Institute for International Economics.

World Bank, 2000, *East Asia: Recovery and Beyond*, May.

Comments on Papers 10 and 11

Charles Adams

These two papers raise important questions about the 1997-98 crisis and its possible long-run effects on the affected economies. In my comments, I want to focus on two interrelated issues: (i) what the evidence presented in the papers can tell us about the possible long-run impact of the 1997-98 crisis on Korea's growth rate; and (ii) why the output declines during the Asian crisis were much larger than in other currency crises. In addition, my comments will touch briefly on the evidence presented by Park and Lee on the short-run behavior of crisis economies with and without Fund programs.

Long-term growth prospects. When the Asian crisis first erupted, there were many observers who wondered whether it signaled the end of the (so-called) Asian miracle. Either because of the damaging effects or, most likely, because the crisis was seen as reflecting deep-seated problems plaguing affected economies, skeptics were quick to start hammering the nails in Asia's coffin. Subsequently, as the crisis economies began to bounce back quite quickly in 1998-99, questions were raised about the sustainability of the recoveries (a "dead-tiger" bounce?). There was, in short, a fair degree of concern in some quarters about the outlook for Asia in the aftermath of the crisis. Against this background, Barro's paper provides a useful overview of the factors underlying the very favorable long-term growth performance of the Asian economies and both papers shed light on what the experiences from other currency crises can tell us about the long-run effects of the Asian crisis.

The approach adopted to assess whether the crisis will have long-run effects on growth is to look at a large number of currency-crisis episodes (defined in terms of the size and abruptness of the change in the exchange rate), and whether they have tended to be accompanied by persistent effects on real GDP. Periods of currency crisis are captured through dummy variables. The main (and, in my view, somewhat surprising) finding is that currency crises, on average, have not lead to long-run changes in growth and investment, once allowance is made for trend changes related to convergence and other effects.[1]

---

[1]Given the way equations are formulated, the Barro tests also implicitly consider whether there are long-run effects on the level of real GDP. On average, there are no effects on either the long-run level or growth rate of real GDP.

Applying this result to Korea would thus make one relatively optimistic about long-term economic prospects, at least in so far as the crisis would not be seen as causing damage.[2] Notwithstanding this relatively sanguine conclusion however, it should be noted that the Korean stock market does not yet appear to be pricing in a sustained bounce back and investment rates are still to recover to pre-crisis levels, notwithstanding the pick up of the economy from the sharp slowdown in 1997-98.

What is one to make of the relatively benign conclusion on the long-run effects of currency crises on growth? There would seem, in my view, to be at least four reasons for caution.

- First, there is the question as to how to interpret the results given that growth and the occurrence of currency crises should ideally be determined endogenously in a fully specified model. In short, there is a question about the conditions under which the effects of a crisis can meaningfully be assessed through adding "exogenous" dummy variables to growth equations. One possibility is that the crisis dummies are capturing the impact of unobserved variables that influence both the occurrence of crises and (potentially) long-run GDP growth. But, if this is the case, these variables should ideally be identified and included as independent variables in the equations explaining long-run growth. Alternatively, the specification may be capturing potential feedback between crises and growth. For example, crises may encourage political or economic change (for good or bad) that, in turn, influences the determinants of growth. Alternatively, the growth process itself may influence the probability of crises such as might be the case, for example, if a crisis was caused by over investment over a sustained period.

- Second, the methodology used is obviously based on the premise that currency crises are, in some sense, alike and that findings can be generalized. Clearly, however, currency crises are not all alike and average results can conceal wide differences in outcomes. For example, in some cases, currency crises have been accompanied by banking crises or external debt problems and, in others, by political change or upheaval. My prior would be that the degree of persistence would likely depend on whether crises have been accompanied by problems in these other areas. In particular, currency and external debt crises seem to have had quite

---

[2]Somewhat surprisingly, Barro's paper implies that the trend growth rate of the Korean economy had already declined sufficiently sharply by the latter half of the 1990s that actual growth over this period (including the effects of the crisis) was above trend. As best I can tell, this reflects the effects on trend growth of the sharp decline in Korea's terms of trade in 1996/97 as well as convergence effects.

persistent effects on growth, as was the case, for example, in Latin America during the 1980s. And currency crises involving banking problems seem also to have large and quite persistent effects, especially when banking problems are not promptly addressed. Beyond this, there is also the possibility that currency crises may have different effects across different types of economies according to the currency denomination of external debt. In particular, the short-run effects of such crises may be positive in mature economies that borrow in their own currencies but negative in emerging-market countries that only borrow abroad in foreign currencies (see Krugman, 1999). For all of the above reasons, the zero long-run average effect might well conceal a wide range of different experiences across countries that it would be useful to understand before applying the "average" effect to other crises.

• Third, although they incorporate many of the standard determinants of growth, the estimated equations include few of the variables that have figured prominently in recent discussions of the Korean (and other Asian) crisis episodes. Most notably, there is no direct allowance for the structure and efficiency of financial intermediation, corporate governance, transparency etc. These are factors that have been emphasized, in particular, by Chopra *et al.* at this conference as potentially important for understanding the crisis in countries such as Korea. Since no direct allowance is made for these variables, the equations cannot easily be used to assess the implications of "reforms" in these areas for the long-term growth outlook and hence how the crisis—by spurring reform—could have long-lasting effects on growth. Moreover, if, as some at this conference have argued, these "new" structural variables are more important for growth than has been assumed in the past, their exclusion from the estimated equations raises the possibility that the equations have been misspecified.

• Finally, another reason for caution is that the Korean and other Asian crises clearly differ from the average experience in terms of the severity of the output declines and the failure of investment to thus far recover significantly. Part of the reason for this may be that the Asian crisis was both a banking as well as currency crises. But, until the reasons for the differences are better understood, care should be used in extrapolating from other crises. In addition, we need to understand better whether the failure of investment to rebound in Asia since the crisis signals potential problems down the road for growth or is simply the reflection of past excesses. An important question, in this connection, is whether it will be possible for rapid growth to resume in Asia with less investment than before the crisis. This might be the case, for example, if structural reforms are successful in improving the efficiency of financial intermediation and would imply that the weakness of investment need not be cause for concern.

Severity of output declines. As noted, the output declines during the Asian crisis were much larger than during the average currency crisis. Park and Lee, in particular, argue that the large output losses reflected the interaction between investor panic, liquidity problems, and the structure of balance sheets, specifically, currency/maturity mismatches and high leverage. In essence, the story is one in which economies were shifted from a "good" to a "bad" equilibrium by (self-fulfilling?) investor panic, leading to very large output losses. The degree of investor panic in Asia, including the very large reversal of capital inflows of over $100 billion in 1997-98, is well documented by Park and Lee, and the argument made that the "fragile" structure of balance sheets rendered Asian economies particularly vulnerable to the associated liquidity problems. The argument appears consistent with other work that has sought to identify the vulnerabilities that may have turned a potentially "minor" crisis into a "major" event. As is well known, however, it is not easy to allocate "responsibility" across liquidity problems caused by investor panic and more deep-seated weaknesses and insolvency problems. Even though many would agree on the importance of balance-sheet structure, there continue to be differences of view on its role in explaining the severity of the Asian crisis. More substantively, however, a key question is whether balance sheet effects would make the Asian crisis fundamentally different from other crises and lead to long-run effects different from those in the "average" crisis. My impression is that Park-Lee see the Asian crisis as very different from many earlier crises but, if this is the case, it is not clear whether the earlier crisis experiences will necessarily provide a good guide to assessing the effects of the Asian crisis.

Finally, let me turn to the question of the behavior of crisis countries with and without Fund programs. The Park and Lee paper suggests that there have tended to be some potentially large differences in the short-run behavior of currency-crisis economies with and without Fund programs. Most notably, countries under Fund programs on average have tended to experience larger output contractions during crises, but seem also to enjoy sharper bounce backs. Although they recognize that care is needed in interpreting the results—including because countries with programs may have more severe problems than those without—Park and Lee suggest that the differences reflect a tendency for more contractionary policies to be adopted under Fund programs. Having made these observations, however, it is striking that Park and Lee do not make much of the fact that these differences between program and non-program cases do not apply in the Asian crisis countries. Looking at the data provided on the five Asian crisis economies (Table 4 in their paper), the range of outcomes for the 1997/98 output collapse is spanned by two countries with Fund programs: Indonesia (where the decline is largest) through the Philippines (where the decline is smallest). Interestingly, however, the output declines in Thailand and Korea (with Fund programs) do not appear very different to that in the one crisis country without a Fund program (Malaysia). This raises questions as to the reasons for the similarities and how they can be reconciled with the results for other crises. Possible questions include: Were the outcomes similar because Malaysia actually followed similar policies to those advocated by the Fund, at least until capital controls were imposed in late 1998? Alternatively, were the output declines similar, notwithstanding different approaches to crisis resolution, because of common factors across the Asian crisis economies? Did all these economies face the same panic-induced liquidity problems the authors regard as important? Although Park and Lee present charts on the behavior of different demand components and policy indicators in the crisis economies, the data do not point to a clear answer as to whether similar policies were followed and why short-term outcomes for output were similar.

Let me conclude by complementing the authors for these two interesting papers on the crisis. Even though we are not yet in a position to reach firm conclusions about the effects of the crisis, the papers have done an excellent job enhancing our understanding of the possible long-run implications for growth as well as short-run crisis dynamics.

Yong Jin Kim

I am honored to comment on papers by such distinguished scholars as Professors Barro, Park, and Lee. I will first briefly summarize their results and then comment on their papers.

Both papers analyze panel data for a large number of countries using the standard cross-country growth methodology. Professor Barro concludes from developments in the five Asian-crisis countries' stock markets and the investment share in GDP, which was relatively high before the crisis and low after the crisis, that there may be long-lasting impacts from the crises. Barro finds that a somewhat different conclusion emerges from a broader study of currency crises, which suggests that the five Asian-crisis countries could experience a rapid V-type recovery. Thus, his expectations about the long-run impact of the crisis on the Korean economy are mixed.

Professors Park and Lee also show that countries that went through currency crises, including the five Asian-crisis countries, tend to have a rapid V-type recovery. They identify the recovery mechanism as follows: Currency crises depreciate exchange rates, thus increasing exports, and expansionary monetary and fiscal policies increase domestic absorption, contributing to the rapid recovery. Trade partners' economic growth, changes in the terms of trade, and export-oriented policies are additional factors that can contribute to a rapid recovery. Park and Lee find that the recovery of investment tends to be rather slow. Developments in the five Asian crisis countries were similar to those in other countries that experienced currency crises, but with a deeper economic contraction right after the crises and a faster recovery. Based on panel regressions for many countries, Park and Lee also find that the experiences of crises, with or without an IMF program, do not affect economic growth rates over the following decade. The authors' results are quite exact and clear.

I have three comments, which are mostly complementary to both papers. The first is that a fast recovery is one thing, but making an economy less vulnerable to crises is another. The second comment concerns how to measure the cost of a crisis. From a theoretical perspective, if the cost of a crisis is as negligible as the cost of a business cycle as argued by Lucas (1987), why are we bothered with crises. My last comment attempts to reemphasize the importance of the proper design of institutions, as Friedman, Johnson, and Mitton argue in their paper for this conference.

As we all know, there is a heated debate among economists and policy makers in Korea. Some argue that the post-crisis restructuring process has not corrected the flaws in the organization of firms and financial institutions that caused the crisis. Others argue that, evidenced by the strong macroeconomic data, the Korean economy is on the right track. The disagreement is not about the current state of the economy, but about whether the economy is healthy enough to not have another crisis in the future. With data available for only two years after the crisis, it will be very difficult to discriminate between these two arguments.

Just before the crisis strong Korean macroeconomic performance suggested a sound economy that was resistant to crises. The crisis was unexpected. This suggests that we should be very cautious about interpreting the rapid recovery to imply that the Korean economy is less vulnerable to crises in the future. We can construct a simple model in which the probability of having a crisis depends on firms' debt-equity ratio, and given this probability, the crisis is caused by investors' herd behavior, as in Kim and Lee (2001). In this setup, fiscal and monetary policies can speed up the economic recovery from the crisis, but do not decrease the probability of having a crisis in the future, unless those policies decrease the debt-equity ratio. Expansionary macroeconomic policies can even increase the probability of crisis by subsidizing insolvent firms with higher debt-to-equity ratios. As this model illustrates, a fast recovery and making the economy resistant to crises may be quite different problems.

Other studies imply that increasing transparency is essential to reduce the probability of having a crisis. Frankel and Rose (1996), for example, show that higher levels of foreign direct investment lower the probability of a crisis, as in Hong Kong and Singapore. Similarly, Wei and Wu (2001) show that corruption or poor public governance is associated with a higher loan-to-FDI ratio, and this is related to a higher incidence of a currency crisis.

In this context, it would be interesting to do nested tests linking macroeconomic performance with microeconomic data representing the quality of financial institutions, firms' governance structure, and so on. Papers such as King and Levine (1993) show that the quality of financial institutions has a significant impact on economic growth.

My second comment is that if there is a trade off between the two goals of a fast recovery and making the economy more resistant to crises, how should limited government resources be allocated between them to maximize welfare. If making an economy completely crisis-free is very expensive, then there exist an optimal allowance of crises. To design an optimal allowance of crises to maximize agents' welfare, calculations of the cost of crisis and the probability of having a crisis over a set of different economic systems will be unavoidable.

My third comment is related to how to restructure the organizations of firms and financial institutions to minimize agency costs. We have learned from the crisis that the agency problems of chaebol and financial institutions have had large economic costs. These phenomena are well phrased by "too big to fail," "bet the bank," and so on. Economic theory says that resources are allocated through two channels, organizations and markets, as Coase (1937) noted. In this context, the strategy of introducing more competition into the markets will not, by itself, result in a more efficient allocation of resources. As the cases of Hanbo, Daewoo, and Hyundai chaebol exemplify, more severe competition without properly designed governance, incentives, and monitoring systems will induce the owners of firms to invest more resources into cheating activities, than into productive activities. Some argue that if chaebol owners behave this way, they will fail in the future due to the mechanism of competitive markets. This may be true, but for the owners it is optimal to cheat.

Without the proper incentive mechanism, cheating will continue and the welfare costs will be continuously borne by other agents. This is very obvious theoretically and empirically. In this context, making markets more competitive should go hand in hand with making organizations more transparent. The history of capitalism shows that better designs of organizations, mostly to deter agency problems, have continuously and painstakingly evolved. Can developing countries skip over this process simply by encouraging competitive markets and decreasing new regulations?

Let me summarize the third point. We should design the governance system such that it will provide the proper incentives through explicit rules of law, not relying on owners' moral spirits, nor politicians' discretion. Becker (1968) shows that criminals are rational agents maximizing their utilities, using all kinds of means, including illegal ones, and measuring costs and benefits rationally. Thus, his therapy is simple. Raise the cost for wrongdoings, by increasing the penalty and/or the probability of being caught.

References

Coase, Ronald, 1937, "The Nature of the Firm," *Economica*, pp. 386-405.

Becker, Gary S., 1968, "Crime and Punishment: An Economic Approach," *Journal of Political Economy*, Vol. 76, pp. 169-217.

Frankel, Jeffrey, and A. Rose, 1996, "Currency Crashes in Emerging Markets: An Empirical Treatment," *Journal of International Economics* Vol. 41, pp. 351-66.

Kim, Yong Jin, and Jong-Wha Lee, 2001, "A Model of Self-fulfilling Crises," mimeo.

King, R., and R. Levine, 1993, "Finance and Growth: Schumpeter Might Be Right," *Quarterly Journal of Economics*, Vol. CVIII, pp. 681-737.

Krugman, Paul, 1999, "Balance Sheets, the Transfer Problem, and Financial Crises," in *International Finance and Financial Crises: Essays in Honor of Robert P. Flood, Jr.*, ed. by P. Isard, A. Razin, and A. Rose (International Monetary Fund and Kluwer Publishers).

Lucas, Robert E. Jr., 1987, "Models of Business Cycles," Basil Blackwell.

Wei, Shang-Jin, and Yi Wu, 2001, "Negative Alchemy? Corruption, Composition of Capital Flows, and Currency Crises," *NBER* Working Paper No. 8187.

12 Restructuring Korean Banks' Short-Term Debts

*Woochan Kim and Yangho Byeon**

This paper provides detailed accounts of the Korean banks' debt restructuring process in the first half of 1998. This event deserves our attention not only because it significantly relieved the Korean economy of its immediate shortages of foreign exchange, but also because it provided a turning point from which the Korean economy started to regain foreign investors' confidence, and thus to overcome the crisis. Reflection upon this event also has a special meaning at the time of writing as Korean banks have recently repaid in full the debts that had been extended up to three years in early 1998.

The objective of this study is fourfold. First, the paper aims to serve as a future reference for those who might later face a similar problem. Although the Korean experience was unique in many regards and is not likely to be replicated by other countries, we believe that the knowledge of this event will better equip those facing similar problems. To this end, the paper turned out to be a case study with detailed accounts of events, explanations of major decisions, and the logic behind them, and some anecdotes. In particular, we tried to cover in detail the administrative aspects, which might be more useful

*Special thanks go to Mark Walker at Cleary, Gottlieb, Steen, & Hamilton, Hong-Sung Moon at the Korean Ministry of Finance and Economy, Min-Seop Song at the Korea Exchange Bank, and David Behling at the KDI School of Public Policy and Management for their useful comments. Thanks also go to Sang-Jin Han at Cleary, Gottlieb, Steen, & Hamilton, Adam Cooper at Ernst & Young, and Yong-Soo Park at the Korea Development Bank for providing useful data sets. The views expressed herein are those of authors and do not necessarily reflect the views of the Ministry of Finance and Economy, or of any other organization with which the authors are or have been affiliated to, or of the people who provided help. A more detailed version of this paper can be found from the KDI School Working Paper No. 01-06 (http://www.kdischool.ac.kr/library/wpaper_in.html).

for those who are actually implementing a debt-restructuring process. Appendix 1 shows the list of information sources used in this paper.

Second, the paper aims to give a detailed account from the debtors' perspective. Existing publications seem to have covered the event from the perspective of creditors or of international organizations. Such approaches, however, left out many important aspects of the debt restructuring process. The paper pays special attention to issues such as how the government set the strategy to win favorable terms from the creditors, how the government organized its delegation in the midst of a power shift from the old administration to the new, and what considerations were taken when it determined its positions on various negotiation items.

Third, the paper aims to uncover an important aspect of the debt restructuring process that is not well known to outsiders. The agreement reached in New York in late January 1998 was no doubt an important step forward for both the debtor and the creditor. However, the agreement was tentative and only involved thirteen creditors. During the following two months, it was up to the Korean government to persuade the rest of the creditors to join the maturity extension program. The paper provides information about this endeavor.

Lastly, the paper attempts to provide some useful statistics regarding government guarantees and the effectiveness of the debt exchange program. In particular, we analyze if the moral hazard problem reemerged among creditors and debtors due to government guarantee. We also analyze if restructuring of bank debts triggered a withdrawal of credit from the corporate sector, and if small creditors or creditors that were not involved in the New York negotiation had a lower participation rate in the debt exchange program than others.

Events Running Up to the New York Negotiation

Background

In mid-December 1997, the US$57 billion rescue package put together by the international community did little to restore investor confidence in Korea. To add insult to injury, international rating agencies went into a frenzy of competitive downgrading. In addition, given the large but uncertain amounts of looming non-performing loans, banks had extreme difficulty in rolling over short-term debts, let alone obtaining new loans. To prevent a series of bank defaults, the Bank of Korea had been lending foreign exchange to ailing banks, reducing official reserves. On December 18, usable foreign exchange reserves only amounted to US$4 billion, down from US$22 billion at the end of October.

The domestic political scene exacerbated the financial crisis. On December 18, a new president had been elected but would not take office until February 25, 1998. Until then, the defeated government remained in charge. To foreigners, it was not clear who was in charge of the economy. With a lower sovereign credit rating, government bond issuance became a remote possibility. Instead, it became more practical and urgent to extend the maturity of short-term debt falling due and to work with international credit rating agencies to forestall any additional downgrades.

Government Starts to Take Action

In mid-December 1997, discussions took place between Man-Soo Kang, Vice Minister of Finance and Economy and the heads of foreign bank branches in Seoul on ways to roll over short-term credit lines to Korean banks. The meetings, however, could not lead to any concrete results since Seoul branches did not have enough influence over their headquarters regarding the decision to roll over.

On December 19, to prepare for meetings with major credit rating agencies in mid-January, the Korean government (hereafter government) appointed Goldman Sachs & Co. and Salomon Smith Barney as its joint financial advisors. They were to provide advice on the possible issuance of government bonds, although they were not yet appointed as official lead managers. Gerald E. Corrigan, Managing Director of Goldman Sachs & Co. and former New York Federal Reserve Bank chairman, was also invited to act as strategic adviser to Chang-Yeul Lim, Deputy Prime Minister and Minister of Finance and Economy (hereafter Deputy Prime Minister), on reform of the financial system.

On December 22, 1997, the Korean National Assembly approved a bill submitted by the government to provide a guarantee for foreign currency debt that had been incurred in 1997 and would be incurred in 1998 by domestic banks. According to a statement in the bill, the guarantee would help alleviate the nation-wide foreign exchange liquidity problem by facilitating new borrowings (including rollovers) by domestic banks. The size of the guarantee was limited to a maximum of US$20 billion plus interest, and the maturity was limited to three years. Thirty-three domestic banks, including state-owned banks and specialized banks, were eligible to apply for the guarantee. The Bank of Korea and merchant banks, however, were not. On the same day, the National Assembly also approved the issuance of sovereign bonds up to a maximum of US$10 billion by the government.

International Community Makes a Move[1]

Concerned that the announcement of a US$57 billion rescue package put together by the international community did not immediately improve confidence toward Korea, the U.S. Treasury wanted to make an early disbursement. But this could not be done before the private-sector banks had rolled over their credit to Korean banks. In response to the request made by the U.S. Treasury and the IMF, William McDonough, Chairman of the Federal Reserve Bank of New York, convened a meeting in New York on December 22, 1997, to convince key U.S. banks to roll over their maturing inter-bank loans to Korean banks.

During this meeting, it was emphasized that failure to roll over credit would trigger a systemic risk to the world financial system, and that if agreement were reached, the official community would extend additional accelerated resources to the Korean government. On December 24, Christmas Eve, a second meeting was convened. McDonough repeated the official view that the banks should agree to roll over their credit. The banks agreed.

A similar meeting took place in London. The Bank of England summoned a meeting on Christmas Eve and it was agreed that HSBC would act as the country coordinator. The U.K. banks' position was to roll over short-term credit until March 31, provided every creditor agreed to do the same. In Frankfurt, the Germans had some trouble coordinating as they had more banks lending to Korea than the British. The first meeting between German banks and the Bundesbank took place on December 29. The German position was to roll over credits falling due by the end of 1997 for an extra month.

On December 24, 1997, the participating countries in the supplemental financial support package for Korea announced that they would be prepared to support the disbursement of a substantial portion of that package—about US$8 billion—contingent on a voluntary program by bank creditors to extend the maturities of existing claims on Korea.

In New York, roles were assigned to bring some order to the roll over process. Chase Manhattan Bank was to coordinate smaller banks in the U.S.; J.P. Morgan & Co. was to work on a plan for the second stage—restructuring debt falling due beyond the first quarter of 1998 and raising new money; and Citibank was to work with non-U.S. banks.

In working with non-U.S. banks, William Rhodes, Vice Chairman of Citibank, was instrumental. One of his major tasks was to work with Japanese banks, the group that had the largest exposure to Korea and yet was among

---

[1]Most of the information in this part is taken from Lee, "Korea Stares into the Abyss," *Euromoney* (March 1998).

the slowest to coordinate their own response. At that time, the Japanese banks were having their own funding problems. Their domestic bad debts were growing and their capital was being eroded with the fall of the Nikkei. After meeting with heads of top ten banks and Eisuke Sakakibara, Japanese Vice Minister of Finance, Rhodes finally was able to convince the Japanese banks to roll over lines falling due at the year-end until at least January 5.

On December 29, major creditors gathered at J.P. Morgan and confirmed they would roll over their credit falling due by the end of 1997, though for varying periods. This temporary extension provided a valuable window for the creditors and the Korean government, on behalf of the debtors, to engage in a debt restructuring negotiation. The IMF also accelerated its disbursement to Korea: instead of waiting until the next scheduled disbursement date (January 8, 1998), the IMF Executive Board approved a US$2 billion disbursement on December 30, 1997.

Government Appoints Legal Advisor for Debt Restructuring

In Seoul, on December 28, 1997, Cleary, Gottlieb, Steen & Hamilton (hereafter Cleary) informally showed interest in becoming a legal advisor to the government to help the banks in rolling over short-term debt. Initially, the law firm was approached by the creditors and was asked to be their legal advisor. However, as the law firm was already advising the government on the issuance of the government's sovereign bond, Cleary wanted to be on the debtor's side instead of the creditors'. The government responded positively and appointed Mark Walker and Robert Davis of Cleary to be the legal advisors.[2]

J.P. Morgan Takes an Initiative

At the December 29 creditor meeting, J.P. Morgan & Co. unveiled its plan for a longer-term solution to Korea's liquidity crisis. A document titled "Korean Financing Proposal: Indicative Terms and Conditions" described the proposal in detail. The proposal basically called for (i) the exchange of part of the short-term debt of Korean banks falling due during 1998 for government issued bonds (the exchange offer), and (ii) the issuance of additional government bonds for new cash (the new cash offer).

The package had two distinctive features. One was to make the exchange and the new cash offer simultaneously, which was not in accord with the

---

[2]Mark Walker was known to have represented the Mexican government in its external debt matters during the crisis of 1995.

government's original intention. The package also prevented additional new offerings for a certain period of time. The second feature was to set the interest rate via a modified Dutch auction in which new cash and exchange offer participants would be requested to submit the interest rates at which they would be willing to accept the securities. The bids would be accepted starting from those with the lowest interest rates. The interest rate of the last bid that fills the target amount would then be applied to all the accepted bids. The same interest rate would be applied to both offers. The aim of this market-based pricing mechanism was to encourage as much voluntary participation as possible from the creditors.

J.P. Morgan's Proposal Reaches the Government

The government, which was not present at the December 29 meeting in New York, received J.P. Morgan's proposal on December 30 (Seoul time). The proposal immediately raised a number of concerns to the government. First, the simultaneous offering seemed to have a lower chance of a success in raising new cash in comparison with a sequential offering that would extend the maturity of existing loans first and then issue a sovereign bond for new cash. The latter strategy obviously gave more time to prepare a bond issue, and the bond could be issued in more favorable circumstances after the debt maturity had been extended.

Second, pricing via a modified Dutch auction was likely to result in a higher interest burden for a number of reasons. According to such mechanism, the debtor does not have any voice in determining the interest rate, naturally leading to a high interest rate. Moreover, it would not be the average interest rate of the accepted bids, but the interest rate of the last bid that fills the target amount that would be applied to the offering. According to this scheme, creditors do not know how much of the original loans would be replaced by Korean government debt before the bidding. Such uncertainty would also induce investors tendering for the new cash offer to bid a higher price than they would if the question of existing loans was already resolved.

Third, replacing bank debt with government debt had the risk of terminating the close working relationship domestic banks previously enjoyed with their foreign counterparts. In fact, several Korean branches of international banks had expressed their preference for a government guarantee to a complete replacement by government bonds.

Lastly, there was a technical problem with J.P. Morgan's proposal. While government only had a US$10 billion approval from the National Assembly to issue a sovereign bond, J.P. Morgan's proposal required a much larger bond issue.

Government Seeks Outside Advice

Before finalizing its position on J.P. Morgan's proposal, the Korean government asked for advice from the two joint financial advisors—Goldman Sachs & Co. and Salomon Smith Barney—and from the IMF. A memorandum sent to the Ministry of Finance and Economy on January 2, 1998, best describes the position held by the two investment banks. In the memorandum, they were basically in favor of a sequential approach: restructuring the existing bank debt first and then attempting to issue a large sovereign bond. As for the exchange offer, they were concerned that a Dutch auction mechanism is a very public and a high profile transaction, which effectively eliminates any possibility for the government to re-negotiate the terms.

The stance taken by the IMF regarding J.P. Morgan's proposal can be learned from the letter sent by Stanley Fischer, First Deputy Managing Director of the IMF, to the Ministry of Finance and Economy. In a letter dated January 4, Fischer took a neutral stance, advising the government not to reject any financing or restructuring proposal for the time being, and to quickly seek advice from a financial advisor who knows the market well and who has an objective view.

Ambassador Chung Visits the United States

Between January 4 and 6, 1998, In-Yong Chung, Korean Ambassador of International Finance, visited the U.S. and met with the IMF, major creditor banks in New York and their regulators, the U.S. Treasury, and the New York Federal Reserve Bank. The meetings were mainly for fact-finding. The following findings were noteworthy. First, Japanese banks were more in favor of debt maturity extension than of converting the existing debt into longer-maturity government bonds. Second, it was reconfirmed that countries participating in the supplemental financial support package would accelerate their disbursement only if the debt maturity was extended, making this an urgent matter. Third, major creditor banks and their supervisors were all expecting an official action on debt maturity extension by the government no later than the end of January. To the date of Ambassador Chung's visit, debt rollover was discussed only among creditor banks without the presence of any Korean entity. Fourth, many creditors called for a neutral financial advisor to be appointed by the government. Fifth, many creditors emphasized the importance of having one voice from Korea after the presidential election.

Government Starts to Draft Its Own Proposal

Given all the criticism raised against J.P. Morgan's proposal and fact-findings by Ambassador Chung, the government started to draft its own proposal on January 5, 1998. In a meeting held at the Deputy Prime Minister's office on January 7, 1998, the Korean government came up with three principles regarding its own proposal. The first principle was to take a sequential approach and initially concentrate on extending the maturity of existing bank debts. The second was to use government guarantee as a way of extending the maturity. This was different from J.P. Morgan's proposal, which suggested replacing existing loans with government issued bonds. The third was to set the interest rate via negotiation.

In that meeting, government also decided to send a working-level delegation to attend the meeting with creditor banks, scheduled to be held on January 8 in New York. The delegation's tasks were to convey the message that the government would make its own proposal to the creditors by mid-January and to gather information on each creditor's position regarding J.P. Morgan's proposal.

Government Meets Major Creditors in New York

The meeting with creditor banks took place at Citibank's New York headquarters. Ten banks, each representing a geographical region, and observers participated in the meeting. The Korean delegation was composed of Yangho Byeon (Director, International Finance Division, MOFE), Mark Walker and Robert Davis (legal advisors from Cleary, Gottlieb, Steen & Hamilton), and others. The meeting started with a telephone briefing by Stanley Fischer on the Korean economy. The key message of his briefing was that Korea would need foreign exchange amounting to US$44 billion during 1998, and that the situation called for close cooperation from the major creditors.

After Fischer's briefing, Director Byeon explained the three principles the government had set out earlier on the financing/restructuring package and promised that the delegation would come back to New York with a more complete proposal in the week of January 19. Director Byeon also noted that the three principles were only initial thoughts and that the government would welcome any proposal from the creditors. There was no strong opposition from the creditors at the meeting.

During their stay in New York, the delegation found that Citibank and Chase Manhattan Bank were basically in accord with the government's position. In particular, they found that Citibank was in favor of rolling over all existing loans up to late March.

Government Organizes a Unified Team for the New York Negotiation

On January 11, 1998, at a meeting between Yong-Hwan Kim, Co-Chairman of the Joint Presidential Committee on Economic Policies (hereafter JPC), and Chang-Yeul Lim, Deputy Prime Minister, the government decided to establish a special subcommittee and a working-level task force to prepare for negotiations with creditors in New York. Great care was taken to ensure that the subcommittee and the task force included individuals associated with President-Elect Dae-Jung Kim. This was to prevent any confusion from having multiple voices speaking for Korea. President-Elect Dae-Jung Kim established the JPC immediately after his victory on December 18, 1997, to take charge of economic policy before his term started in February.

It was decided that the special subcommittee would be headed by Yong-Hwan Kim and be composed of the Deputy Prime Minister, the Governor of Bank of Korea, the Chief Secretary to the President on Economic Affairs, and one person to be appointed by the committee chairman. The subcommittee was empowered to make final decisions on the Korean proposal and compose the delegation to be sent to New York. It was decided that the working-level task force would be headed by Duck-Koo Chung, Deputy Minister for International Finance and Economy (hereafter Deputy Minister), and was to be staffed by JPC officials, Ministry officials, investment bankers from Goldman Sachs & Co. and Salomon Smith Barney, and Mr. Mark Walker. The task force was mandated to draft the Korean proposal and come up with detailed negotiation strategies.

Government Revisits the Basic Principles of the Proposal

At the same meeting on January 11, 1998, the government revisited the basic principles of its restructuring/financing proposal. First, the government again made clear that it would decline J.P. Morgan's proposal. The proposal was regarded as serving only the interests of creditors, and risked aggravating the moral hazard problem among creditors. Creditors would not only have their non-performing loans to near-bankrupt Korean banks replaced by government bonds with a much higher market value, but they would also have the right to charge a high interest rate. According to the scheme, existing creditors would hardly pay a price for their misjudgment in lending to Korean banks.

Second, on sequencing, the government decided to begin with a debt maturity extension. A syndicated loan would follow immediately after that in February, if possible, and a sovereign bond would be issued only in a favorable market situation. It was emphasized that existing creditors should be treated differently from new creditors that would participate in the bond issuance: the former had made a misjudgment and consequently should pay some penalty on rolling over existing obligations into new bonds or loans; the latter were starting fresh. So, to be fair, the former should receive a lower interest rate than the latter. J.P. Morgan's proposal, however, did not make this distinction and allowed existing creditors to charge the same interest rate as the new ones.

Third, the government made a number of decisions on the details of the debt maturity extension. Only the short-term debt of banks coming due in 1998 would be eligible for extension. Long-term debts, merchant bank debts, bonds, off-balance sheet items, overnights, and trade financings would be excluded. Long-term debt falling due in 1998 was relatively small amounting to US$ 10.7 billion. A joint investigation conducted in early January with the IMF and the Federal Reserve Bank of New York revealed that the size of off-balance sheet items was relatively modest and that the maturity structure was well matched. Overnight loans were excluded because their maturity by nature could not be extended to one or more years. Trade financing was excluded because it was a safe credit in the first place with its underlying physical transaction and by nature could not be extended to one or more years.

Since the economic situation was improving, the maturity would be extended only up to five years, preferably under three years. The interest rate would be determined by negotiation between the two parties. Instead of issuing a government bond or the government taking a loan, as a way to extend the maturity, Korean banks would receive government guaranteed bank loans from the creditors, although voluntary extensions without government guarantee would be encouraged.

Government Lays Out a Negotiation Strategy

During January 13 and 14, 1998, at meetings between Yong-Hwan Kim and Chang-Yeul Lim, the government discussed its strategies and tactics for the negotiation in New York. Three points were noteworthy.

First, the government decided to have individual meetings with the core banks and their supervisors before the negotiation started on January 21. The goal was not only to persuade them to accept the government's proposal, but also to update the government's proposal after having identified the position of each bank. In-Yong Chung was to visit Europe (January 13-15) and Woo-Suk Kim, Director-General of International Finance at the Ministry, was to visit Japan (January 15-16). It was important to soothe the feelings of Japanese and European banks that felt they had been excluded from the recent talks despite the fact that they had more exposure to Korean banks than did the U.S. banks.

As for the U.S. banks and their supervisors, Yong-Hwan Kim and Jong-Keun You, the President-Elect's Economic Advisor, were to visit Washington D.C. and New York immediately before the negotiation on January 18-19. They were to meet key U.S. banks, the Treasury Department, the Federal Reserve Board, and the IMF. These meetings were to be held confidentially so as not to provoke any annoyance from the banks that were not contacted. Mark Walker was also to meet banks in the U.S., Japan (January 10-14), and Europe (January 15-18).

The second point was in regard to how the negotiation meetings should be organized. Mark Walker advised the government to ask William Rhodes, Vice Chairman of Citibank, who Walker had previously worked with, to preside over the meeting at Citibank, and suggested which bank representatives to invite. Stanley Fischer, First Deputy Managing Director of the IMF, would be asked to attend the meeting; Michel Camdessus, Managing Director of the IMF, would be asked to participate by phone; and William McDonough, President of the New York Federal Reserve Bank, would be asked to deliver a speech. Yong-Hwan Kim would deliver a speech on the Korean economy and Duck-Koo Chung would outline the Korean proposal. It was intended to make sure that the discussion centered on the Korean proposal rather than on J.P. Morgan's.

The third point was to organize a team of Korean bankers to assist the negotiation team on interest rate matters. Bankers from the Korea Development Bank and the Korea Exchange Bank were to be recruited to form a back-up team to provide relevant data and analysis during the New York negotiations.

A moratorium as a negotiation strategy was considered but rejected without much disagreement. It was expected that existing debt could be rescheduled with a very low interest rate if Korea announced a moratorium. The government, however, had to consider the side effects. Korean firms were expected to suffer greatly in overseas transactions with a government moratorium. They would not only have a hard time financing capital from abroad but also would be forced to settle payments in cash. This would greatly constrain imports of raw materials necessary for Korea to survive and to export out from the coming recession.

Government's Foreign Exchange Cash Flow Projections

In preparation for the negotiation meeting, the government updated the foreign exchange cash flow projections for 1998 (Table 1). The financing gap was

Table 1. Foreign Exchange Cash Flows Projection for 1998
(In billions of U.S. dollars)

Foreign Exchange Needs	68.2
Financial Institutions	36.4
Short-term Debt	25.0
Long-term Debt	10.7
Commercial Paper	0.7
Reinforcing FX Reserve	31.8
Foreign Exchange Funding	38.4
Disbursement from IMF	24.7
Current Account Surplus	3.2
Foreign Investment	7.0
Net Borrowing by the Corporate Sector	3.5
Financing Gap	29.8

Source: Ministry of Finance and Economy, ROK.

estimated to be US$29.8 billion. Out of US$68.2 billion of total foreign exchange needs, short-term debt falling due to financial institutions was estimated to be US$25 billion. The rest came from long-term debt, commercial paper, and foreign exchange needed to reinforce official reserves. Out of US$38.4 billion of total financing, borrowing under the IMF program was estimated to be US$24.7 billion. The rest came from a projected current account surplus, foreign investment, and corporate sector borrowing. The financing gap of US$ 29.8 billion was to be addressed by short-term debt maturity extension (US$ 15 billion) plus new money from syndicated loans (US$5 billion) and a sovereign bond issue (US$10 billion).

Reactions from Europe and Japan

The visits by In-Yong Chung, Woo-Suk Kim, and Mark Walker to Europe and Japan revealed that banks in those regions were more in favor of the Korean proposal than of J.P. Morgan's. Part of the reason came from their resentment toward U.S. banks, which they thought were monopolizing the discussions. This meant the creditors were starting to fracture, while the Koreans were showing unity.

Another reason was that the European and Japanese banks were commercial banks that put more value on preserving traditional business relationships with Korean banks than did J.P. Morgan, which was acting more like an investment bank. In particular, they criticized J.P. Morgan's proposal of a 20-year government bond with no call option, which would require the government to pay high interest rates for too long. They opposed the modified Dutch auction mechanism for fear that rates might come out so high that there would be a political backlash in Korea against the whole deal. With these visits, the government was able to correct the perception of Japanese and European banks that Korea tended to talk only with the U.S. creditors.

On January 16, 1998, major creditors officially completed a plan to roll over short-term loans to Korean banks through March 31. This gave creditor banks and the government time to sit down and work out a long-term agreement in the following week. A fax message from Citibank Vice Chairman William Rhodes informed the government that Citibank had received confirmation from all regional coordinating banks that the banks in their constituencies supported the program to roll over short-term maturities to Korean financial institutions through March 31. The fax noted that David Pflug, Vice Chairman of Chase Manhattan Bank acting as regional coordinator for the U.S. banks, had advised that all of the U.S. banks were participating.

Delegation and the Official Directive

On January 17, 1998, President Young-Sam Kim approved the Korean delegation and the official directive given to them. Given the technical nature of the negotiation, the delegation was divided into high-level and working-level groups. The first group, headed by Yong-Hwan Kim, was to meet with core U.S. banks and their supervisors outside the negotiation table. The second group, headed by Deputy Minister Duck-Koo Chung, was to lead the actual negotiation.

The directive included all the major principles discussed earlier. Three new items were noteworthy. First, it allowed the creditor banks to shift their loans from weaker to stronger banks. Second, it allowed the debt to be denominated in major currencies other than the U.S. dollar. Third, the directive included the option of prepayment of debt. In case the delegation could not abide by the directive, it had to ask for a revised version from the Deputy Prime Minister, who would be staying in Seoul during the negotiations. As for matters not specified in the directive, the delegation had discretion to make its own decision. Given the technical nature of the negotiations, Mark Walker took charge of preparing the term sheets. Also, to minimize any mistake from the delegation, it was decided to go through Mark Walker when communicating negotiation terms with the creditor banks.

The New York Negotiation

Day One: January 18

Part of the Korean delegation, including Yong-Hwan Kim, Jong-Keun Yoo, In-Yong Chung, and Duck-Koo Chung, arrived in New York. In the afternoon, they discussed a Lehman Brothers proposal that the government set up a paper company to purchase short-term loans from creditor banks and issue securities backed by these loans. The paper company was to be capitalized by government bonds, gold, or cash. The size of the capital was estimated to be 25-30 percent of the debt to be purchased. The proposal, however, was rejected on the basis that it did not necessarily help in extending the maturity of existing debts.

Day Two: January 19

The Korean delegation had individual meetings with major U.S. financial institutions: Jon Corzine, Chairman of Goldman Sachs; D. Maughan, Chairman of Salomon Smith Barney; Douglas Warner III, Chairman of J.P. Morgan; and William Rhodes, Vice Chairman of Citibank. As expected, Corzine, Maughan, and Rhodes were quite supportive of the government, while Warner was not.

In the morning meeting with Goldman Sachs, Jon Corzine supported the government's strategy of separating the exchange offer from the new cash offer. He expected that a successful negotiation in extending debt maturity would trigger rating agencies to place Korea at a higher credit rating. Referring to the *New York Times* article on January 17 by Thomas Friedman, he mentioned that the U.S. Congress was concerned that creditor banks might be completely bailed out from the crisis. He mentioned that this concern, together with the move on January 16 by Standard & Poor's to change the rating outlook from "negative" to "developing," would work in favor of the government at the negotiation table. He also thought that the President-Elect's direct dialogue with the public that was televised live on national networks on January 18 had contributed to improve foreign investor confidence.

Chairman Maughan of Salomon Smith Barney basically said the international capital market was not ready for a bond issue worth US$25 billion and that it would be wise to postpone the bond issuance until credit ratings had improved. He also expected that a successful debt maturity extension would trigger Standard & Poor's to raise the Korean credit rating three steps from B+ to BB+. Moreover, a successful debt maturity extension would flatten the currently inverted yield curve, which, in turn, would permit the government to later issue a sovereign bond with a shorter maturity of three to five years.

In terms of the government's leverage at the negotiation table, Chairman Maughan mentioned four points. First, the government guarantee had reduced credit risk. Second, the yield curve was flattening. Third, the Basel Accord on capital adequacy allowed creditor banks to free capital once an OECD sovereign guarantees the debt. Fourth, in the long run, creditor banks can make profits by keeping the relationship with Korean banks. He even told the Korean delegation that a rate of LIBOR+200-250 basis points would be possible for the extended debt.

At the meeting with J.P. Morgan in the afternoon, the delegation confirmed that J.P. Morgan was not in favor of the government's proposal. Chairman Warner stressed that a comprehensive approach of carrying out exchange and new cash offers simultaneously is more appropriate at a time when Korea urgently needs foreign exchange. Although he showed some flexibility regarding the determination of interest rate by giving up the modified Dutch auction J.P. Morgan had originally proposed, he emphasized the need for any debt maturity extension to be voluntary. He also mentioned the need for off-balance sheet items to be included in the debt eligible for government-guaranteed extension. In response, the delegation made clear that off-balance sheet items would not be included in eligible debt.

The rest of the delegation arrived on January 19. At the law office of Cleary, the negotiation team headed by Duck-Koo Chung prepared for the meeting on January 21. The Cleary office became the base camp of the delegation throughout the negotiation.

Day Three: January 20

Part of the delegation headed by Yong-Hwan Kim visited Washington D.C. and met with major opinion leaders: Alan Greenspan, Federal Reserve Chairman; Joseph Stiglitz, World Bank Chief Economist; Fred Bergsten, Institute for International Economics Director; Robert Rubin, Treasury Secretary; Stanley Fischer, IMF First Deputy Managing Director; and Charles Dallara, Institute of International Finance Managing Director.

In the morning meeting, Alan Greenspan thought that the Korean economy would recover as long as the government accelerated its structure reforms, particularly those leading to a reduction of corporate debt. On debt maturity extension, however, he recommended that the negotiations should be completed as soon as possible even if that meant somewhat unfavorable interest rate terms. In the following meeting, Joseph Stiglitz expressed concern that the IMF program would bring a credit crunch, and suggested that the government make sure trade financing was not curtailed. He told the delegation that the

United States also experienced a credit crunch in the early 1990s despite the successful resolution of the S&L crisis in the late 1980s.

Fred Bergsten hosted a luncheon. Referring to the atmosphere at the U.S. Congress, he stressed that creditor banks needed to take a haircut as a way of assuming part of the responsibility. He was also interested in what effect the depreciated currency would have on exports. In the afternoon meeting, Treasury Secretary Robert Rubin suggested that the government take a comprehensive approach by making exchange and new cash offers simultaneously. He was also concerned with Korean banks' off-balance sheet obligations. In the following meeting, Stanley Fischer suggested that the government limit the amount of debt that could be converted to a one-year loan.

At the Cleary office in New York, the rest of the delegation made final preparations for the next day's meeting. Final touches were made on the term sheet, the presentation slides, and the speech.

Day Four: January 21

In Seoul, the National Assembly approved a bill submitted by the government to guarantee foreign currency debt of US$15 billion plus interest. While the National Assembly had passed a similar bill in December 1997, amounting US$20 billion plus interest, it did not cover debt that the Bank of Korea would incur from the countries participating in the supplemental financial support package, and thus was not enough to cover all the debt eligible for maturity extension. Out of a total of US$15 billion, US$8 billion was intended to guarantee the Bank of Korea's debt and US$7 billion was to guarantee maturity-extended debt of commercial banks, state-owned banks, and merchant banks not covered by the previous bill. The bill was passed on the condition that the government guarantee would be extended only to viable financial institutions.

On the same day in New York, the delegation had additional meetings with the banking community before the official negotiation started in the afternoon. A breakfast meeting was arranged with New York Fed President, William McDonough. During the meeting, he fully acknowledged the government's position, but also emphasized that it was in Korea's interest to expedite the negotiation since the situation in Indonesia was worsening. He stressed that it would be inappropriate for the government to guarantee off-balance sheet obligations, and agreed that creditor banks should refrain from asking for high interest rates on the grounds that it would only aggravate moral hazard. During a meeting with Chase Manhattan Chairman Shipley, he emphasized that the interest rate should be determined on a voluntary basis through a market-based solution, indicating that Korean banks might have to pay a high interest rate.

The first negotiation meeting with creditors took place between 2:00 and 4:30 p.m. in the second floor boardroom at Citibank's Park Avenue headquarter in New York. Yong-Hwan Kim headed the Korean negotiation team. Fourteen creditor banks from eleven countries participated the meeting. Terrence J. Checki, Executive Vice President at the New York Federal Reserve Bank, also attended. Duck-Koo Chung presented foreign exchange projections for 1998 and the government's proposal to address the financing gap; Mark Walker, legal advisor, made additional explanations as to the details of the government's proposal. Stanley Fischer briefed the banks by telephone. The Korean delegation proposed a list of ten creditor banks to represent all the creditors and negotiate on their behalf. The ten banks were chosen on the basis of their credit exposure and geographical representation.

Thanks to the government's marketing effort before the meeting and the resentment from European and Japanese banks toward the U.S. banks, the overall mood was favorable toward the delegation and the discussions centered on the government's proposal instead of J.P. Morgan's. Although J.P. Morgan continued to push its plan arguing that the Dutch auction was the best method for price discovery, the argument did not last long. Morgan had limited leverage, and could not refuse to do the rollover just because the Koreans would not raise new money through the Dutch auction.

Among the items discussed during the meeting, three points in particular were noteworthy. First, creditor banks raised the concern that if the debt maturity was to be extended, the participating banks would exhaust all their exposure to Korean banks and this would make it difficult for any new business to take place with the Korean banks. To this, the delegation made clear that the extended loans would be transferable. Also, they emphasized that a successful debt maturity extension would significantly ease the foreign exchange liquidity problem and would reduce credit risk toward Korean banks, which, in turn, would allow a greater exposure to them. Second, creditor banks asked if loans to merchant banks were also to be eligible for a guarantee and maturity extension. To this, the delegation replied that the government guarantee would apply only to those merchant banks that are financially viable. Since investigation on the viability of merchant banks was still in process, the delegation was not able to name which merchant banks would be eligible obligors. Third, some creditor banks were concerned that a sovereign bond issuance later, at a lower rate, would discount the value of loans extended earlier. To this, the delegation argued the opposite: a concurrent new cash offer would allow existing debt to be extended only at a high interest rate.

It was agreed that the creditor banks would come up with a list of 10-15 banks that would represent all creditors based on the list suggested by the

Korean delegation. The next meeting was scheduled on January 23 to discuss the details of the debt maturity extension. Creditor banks needed some time to consult with the banks in their constituencies. A one-page press release stated that the discussions were very positive and constructive.

Day Five: January 22

The negotiation team led by Duck-Koo Chung discussed strategies for the meeting next day. Yong-Hwan Kim and Jong-Keun Yoo flew back to Washington D.C. to meet with Michel Camdessus.

During the strategy meeting in New York, four issues were discussed. First, for the time being, it was decided that merchant banks were to be excluded from the eligible obligors. Second, it was decided to cap the one-year extension within 20-25 percent of the total obligation being extended. It was not certain that the Korean economy would normalize within a year and it was not wise to let debt obligations be concentrated in a particular year. Third, the team decided to consult experts at Bears Stern, which did not have any exposure to Korea, on the interest rate. Experts from the Korea Development Bank and the Korea Exchange Bank suggested a spread of LIBOR+150-190 basis points as a starting point at the negotiations. This spread was obtained by surveying the rates applied to loans to a sovereign with a comparable credit rating. Fourth, the delegation requested Citibank to include more banks from Japan and Germany to represent the creditors, while excluding ING Bank, which was more like an investment bank. Japanese and German banks were perceived to be more favorable to the government's proposal. The request was accepted and Citibank included Sanwa Bank and West Deutsche Landesbank, while excluding ING Bank. Deputy Prime Minister Chang-Yeul Lim subsequently approved these decisions by telephone.

Day Six: January 23

The second meeting with creditors took place between 2:00 pm and 6:00 pm. Deputy Minister Duck-Koo Chung headed the Korean negotiation team. Thirteen banks from seven countries attended the meeting as official representatives. Terrance Checki, Executive Vice President of the New York Federal Reserve Bank, also attended as an observer.

The discussions centered on the following five issues. First, creditor banks were suspicious that the real debt figures falling due in 1998 for Korean merchant banks was much higher than what was reported by the Korean delegation. They also noted that it was likely that British banks would not participate in the maturity extension agreement if merchant bank debts were not included in the eligible debt. To this, the delegation suggested that this matter should be taken up separately after the viability investigation was completed on the merchant banks.

Second, creditor banks questioned whether it was guaranteed that all Korean banks would accept any agreement reached in New York. They warned that Korean banks' full participation was critical for the success of the maturity extension. To this, the delegation promised to immediately re-confirm with the Korean banks as to their acceptance and inform the creditor banks at the next meeting (January 26).

Third, creditor banks raised the interest rate issue for the first time and suggested the IMF's Supplemental Reserve Facility rate of LIBOR+350 basis points as the basis of discussion, noting that the current yield on bonds issued by the Korea Development Bank, which then prevailed at LIBOR+585 basis points. They also tried to leverage the worsening Indonesian situation to get concessions from the delegation regarding the interest rate. The Korean delegation responded that it would bring its own interest rate proposal to the next meeting.

Fourth, to enhance tradability, the creditor banks suggested to exchange existing floating rate note (FRN) loans for transferable loan certificates (TLC). They also argued that the prepayment option should be restricted so as not to limit the tradability of the claims. Specifically, they suggested that there should be no option for one-year maturity claims and to allow the option for longer maturities only after a certain period had lapsed, say one year for two to three-year maturity claims and two years for five-year maturity claims. The delegation refused the exchange of FRN loans on the basis that it would be difficult to maintain existing business relationships between the Korean banks and the international banks.

Fifth, the creditor banks suggested that loans be denominated either in U.S. dollars or in Japanese yen. Japanese banks said that they expected more than half of the existing exposure would be denominated in yen once existing loans were replaced by longer-maturity loans. The next meeting was scheduled for January 26.

Days Seven and Eight: January 24 and 25

During the weekend, the negotiation team gathered at the Cleary office and reviewed the issues raised at the meeting of January 23. On the merchant bank issue, the delegation decided, with approval from the Deputy Prime Minister, to allow merchant banks' existing debt be eligible for maturity extension for those merchant banks judged viable by the government by March 31, 1998.

Given that many merchant banks had foreign owners, the delegation decided to exclude from eligible debt the obligations owed to certain foreign banks that had 20 percent or more of the capital of an eligible obligor or had influence over the eligible obligor's management. On the tenor issue, the delegation decided to limit the one-year offerings within 20 percent of the total offering, so as not to have obligations concentrated too much in the following year. They also decided to limit the size of the five-year offerings to US$5 billion, so as not to be locked in with high interest rates for a large amount of debt.

On the currency denomination issue, the delegation decided to allow yen-denomination, provided that the eligible debt was originally yen denominated. On the tradability issue, the delegation decided to refuse the issuance of FRN, but to allow creditor banks to change the debtor bank on the first interest payment date, provided that it be informed no less than 90 days before, and that both the existing debtor and the replacing debtor consent to the trade.

On the interest rate issue, the delegation consulted with Bears Sterns and the Korean bankers that accompanied the delegation. They decided to propose a semiannual rate equal to six-month LIBOR plus a spread of 140, 155, 170, and 180 basis points, respectively, for a medium-term loan of one, two, three, and five-year maturity.

The following five principles were developed to back up the proposal. First, applicable margins had to reflect loan spreads available at that time to borrowers with comparable credit ratings. At that time, spreads applicable to syndicated loans to institutions with credit ratings comparable to Korea's (Moody's Ba1; S&P B+) ranged from 62.5 (five-year maturities) to 197.5 basis points (six-year maturities). Thus the proposed applicable margin of 180 basis points for a medium-term loan with a 5-year maturity was a relatively high spread. A few days before, S&P had upgraded its credit rating outlook with respect to Korea from "negative" to "developing," which further suggested that the proposed applicable margins were not unreasonable or unrealistic.

Second, prevailing bond yields were not an appropriate benchmark for the applicable margin since there are fundamental differences between the bank-lending market and the debt capital market. Pricing in the bank loan context take into account long-term business relationships, which do not exist in the public bond markets. In addition, bond spreads are intended to compensate for the relatively higher volatility in the debt capital markets. Two recent examples of disparities between sovereign bond yields and loan interest rates were provided.

Third, prevailing spreads on bank loans obtained by Korean banks were not an appropriate benchmark for the applicable margins since participation in the proposed exchange program would provide existing creditor banks with significant benefits. First of all, the creditor banks would benefit from reduced default risk, due to Korea's guarantee of the medium-term loans. Next, the creditor banks would benefit from increased BIS capital ratios. Lastly, the creditor banks would benefit from reduced country default risk, due to the coordinated extension of maturities of short-term bank debt under the exchange program.

Fourth, spreads applicable to the Supplemental Reserve Facility (SRF) provided to Korea by the IMF were not an appropriate benchmark for the applicable margins. The emergency funds provided by the 13 countries, as well as the SRF, carried relatively high interest rates. However, such rates were deliberately fixed at a high level for policy reasons. As explained by Mr. Geithner, the U.S. Assistant Treasury Secretary, "The IMF is providing loans at substantial premiums to maximize assistance, minimize use, and ensure quick repayment."

Fifth, high applicable margins were undesirable in light of the moral hazard problem, and also damaging for political reasons. Without a haircut, creditors risk falling into the habit of blind lending. Also, if the applicable margins were set at an excessively high level, emergency funds provided by the thirteen countries might be channeled to service the medium-term loans. There was a risk that such channeling of public funds for private profit would create a negative public perception of the exchange program and result in a political backlash in the thirteen countries.

As a negotiation strategy the delegation decided to discuss the pricing issue only after a certain degree of agreement had been reached on all other matters. This separation was intended to prevent the creditor banks from linking other matters with the pricing issue. Deputy Prime Minister, Chang-Yeul Lim, confirmed that the Korean bankers would fully participate in any agreement that would be reached between the creditor banks and the government delegation.

Day Nine: January 26

Prior to the third meeting with the entire creditor bank representatives the delegation met with J.P. Morgan, Citibank, Tokyo-Mitsubishi Bank, Société Générale, and Commerzbank. A significant gap still seemed to exist between the delegation and the creditors regarding the pricing issue. Vice Chairman Stern of J.P. Morgan regarded the SRF rate as a benchmark and suggested a spread of LIBOR+300-450 basis points. In the following meeting, Vice Chairman Rhodes of Citibank was concerned about Jong-Keun Yoo's interview with the *Wall Street Journal*, where he stressed that creditor banks should also take a haircut. Japanese and European banks emphasized that the spreads should be set at a level acceptable to the market participants.

The negotiation meeting with the creditor bank representatives took place at Shearman & Sterling, a law firm advising the creditors, from 11:00 a.m. to 5:00 p.m. The meeting started with a short speech from Duck-Koo Chung, who clarified the Korean government's position on issues other than pricing. Mark Walker then presented the revised term sheet, which was discussed after lunch.

On the merchant bank issue, creditor banks, the British and German banks in particular, strongly argued that merchant banks should not be treated differently from other banks. They questioned why only merchant banks, but not commercial or state-owned banks, had to go through the government's viability assessment. They also noted that creditor banks did not discriminate merchant banks from commercial banks when they extended debt maturity until the end of March, and argued that the government should abide by its August 25, 1997 announcement to guarantee all debt incurred by Korean financial institutions, including merchant banks.

On the prepayment issue, the delegation explained that restricting the exercise of option during the first year, the government intended to limit banks from refinancing high-cost medium-term loans with low-cost short-term loans, which would increase the fraction of short-term loans. On FRN, some banks continued to request it even after it was clear that they would have more enhanced tradability by having the option to change debtor banks.

The rest of the afternoon session mainly concentrated on the pricing issue. After short comments by the Deputy Minister, Mark Walker detailed the pricing proposal and the rationale behind it. After an hour of discussion among themselves, the creditor banks came back and told the delegation that the proposed spreads were unrealistic and that the delegation should reconsider its proposal. The meeting ended with a decision to meet the following day.

After the meeting with creditors, the delegation members gathered at the Intercontinental Hotel and further discussed their strategies regarding the pricing issue. It was expected that the creditor banks would make a counterproposal. In this case, it was decided that the delegation request a one-hour recess and suggest a revised proposal with spreads higher by 30-40 basis points. With rounds of counterproposals, it was expected that the gap would narrow and agreement be reached. The SRF rate of LIBOR+350 basis points was set as the reservation rate.

Day Ten: January 27

At 5:30 a.m. the delegation received news that Indonesia had temporarily ceased to service its debt. Although Indonesia insisted that it had not declared a moratorium, many believed that a moratorium was already in effect, given that many companies had ceased servicing their debts. This made it urgent to conclude the pricing negotiation as soon as possible.

The fourth meeting with creditor bank representatives took place at Shearman & Sterling and lasted more than seven hours. Mark Walker started by going through the Korean proposal again, stressing that creditor banks must take into account the fact that loans were being guaranteed by the government, and that pricing proposals should be backed by market data. In response, the creditor banks requested a recess and after 40 minutes of discussion, came up with their first counter proposal of spreads of 275, 325, 350, and 380 basis points, respectively, for one, two, three, and five-year maturity loans. These spreads were 135-200 basis points higher than the Korean proposal.

In return, the delegation requested a recess and made a revised proposal with spreads of 175, 190, 200, and 215 basis points, which were 100-165 basis points lower than the spreads proposed by the creditors. European banks argued that they would be unable to continue the negotiation based on the low interest rates proposed by the Korean delegation, which would require them to increase loan-loss provisioning. The creditors also reminded the delegation that the deal had to be sold not just to the banks in the negotiation room, most with long-term commitments to Korea, but also to over 200 other lenders around the world, some with little at stake in Korea other than getting their money back.

In the afternoon session, the creditor banks came up with their second proposal. They suggested excluding the five-year maturity loan from the negotiation, incorporating the delegation's argument that the spread on the five-year maturity loan was too high. They lowered the spreads and proposed 275, 300, and 325 basis points, respectively, for one, two, and three-year maturity loans. The delegation asked for a recess and discussed whether it would make another proposal or accept the offer. A number of factors pointed toward accepting the proposal. Most of all, the spreads proposed by the creditors were below the reservation rate of LIBOR+350 basis points. Also, the worsening situation in Indonesia mandated an early conclusion. Lastly, it seemed that the creditor banks had no room to concede any further. Despite these considerations, the delegation decided to make one last proposal. They proposed 185, 200, and 220 basis points, respectively, for one, two, and three-year maturity loans. To this, the creditor banks responded that agreement could not be reached, and suggested another meeting the following day.

Since it was likely that agreement would be reached next day, the delegation prepared for a press release after the meeting. The term sheet was revised to exclude a five-year maturity extension. The delegation was told to consult with the Deputy Prime Minister before they committed to a final agreement with the creditors.

Day Eleven: January 28

The fifth meeting with creditor bank representatives took place at Shearman & Sterling at 10:00 a.m. The meeting started with negations on matters other than pricing. Most of the discussion took place between the lawyers for each side. No significant gap emerged between the delegation and the creditors. After a ten-minute break, the creditors made their third pricing proposal. They suggested 225, 250, and 275 basis points, respectively, for one, two, and three-year maturity loans. The figures were 50 basis points lower than the previous proposal across all three maturities. The gap from the delegation's proposal was also only 40-55 basis points. They stressed that any lower spread will trigger loan-loss provisioning, which would preclude any further discussion.

During the recess, the delegation gathered at the Cleary office and discussed their next move. There was consensus that the creditor banks no longer had room to lower the spreads any further. So, it was decided to seek a more favorable deal in terms of prepayment rather than in terms of pricing. The Deputy Prime Minister approved the directive to accept the interest rate offer, but at the same time to request that prepayments be allowed after six months from the loan exchange date for the two and three-year maturity loans.

The meeting resumed at 7:00 pm and the Korean delegation accepted the pricing proposal made by the creditor banks. It was declared that an agreement had been reached and a joint press release was prepared. In the press release, Deputy Minister Chung said, "The plan agreed today will provide a stable source of funding to the Korean banks on commercial, market terms, and on a voluntary basis. As such, the achievement marks a critical step in the efforts of Korea to surmount its current liquidity crisis and to restore stability to the Korean banking sector. We look forward to a successful completion of the exchange offer with the participation of all creditor banks." Vice Chairman Rhodes added, "Today's agreement is a key step toward Korea's goal of returning shortly to the international capital markets."

The Term Sheet

The final term sheet was titled "Proposal with Regard to the External Debt of Korean Commercial, State-Owned, and Specialized Banks (Including Overseas Branches, Agencies, and Certain Foreign Banking Subsidiaries) and Certain Merchant Banks." The term sheet consisted of three parts: (i) definitions, (ii) terms and conditions of new loans, and (iii) exchange procedures.

On definitions, eligible debt covered inter-bank deposit obligations and short-term loans, other than excluded debt, owed to foreign banks and financial institutions by eligible obligors and maturing during calendar year 1998. Excluded debt covered trade finance, publicly traded securities (including securities sold pursuant to Regulation S or Rule 144A), commercial paper, overnight deposits, call money, contingent obligations such as derivatives and guarantees, and obligations owed to controlling shareholders of eligible obligors. Repurchase obligations were included, provided that the Bank of Korea's monetary stabilization bonds or other won-denominated securities of Korean governmental issuers backed them.

Eligible obligors included thirty-three Korean commercial banks, state-owned banks, and certain specialized banks including their foreign banking subsidiaries and their overseas branches and agencies, but excluding their non-bank subsidiaries. Eligible obligors also included merchant banks, but not their subsidiaries, provided that they had been determined by the government to be commercially sound and viable prior to the commencement of the exchange offer.

According to the final term sheet, new loans guaranteed by the government had the following terms and conditions. New loans could have final maturity of one, two, or three years from the exchange date at the election of the holder of eligible debt at the time of the tender for exchange. A holder of eligible debt was not able to elect to exchange more than 20 percent of the eligible debt tendered by it for new loans with a final maturity of one year. Interest on the new loans had to be paid semiannually and interest was to accrue from the exchange date. The semiannual rate was equal to six-month LIBOR plus applicable margin of 225, 250, and 275 basis points, respectively, for one, two, and three-year final maturities.

New loans had to be denominated in the U.S. dollar, except that eligible debt denominated in the Japanese yen or the deutsche mark on December 31, 1997, may, at the option of the holder, be exchanged for new loans denominated in those currencies. Each eligible obligor had the right to prepay its new loans having final maturities of two or three years in whole or in part on any interest payment date, beginning with the first semiannual interest payment date, without premium or penalty.

In the event of the acquisition of an eligible obligor by another bank, the new loans of the acquired eligible obligor had to become obligations of the successor bank. In the event of a liquidation of an eligible obligor, its new loans would have to be assumed by the government or by another eligible obligor that agreed to such assumption. New loans were to be in the form of transferable loan certificates, in minimum denominations of US$250,000, transferable to other banks and financial institutions. The governing law for the new loan was the law of the state of New York.

On exchange procedures, the eligible obligors and the government had to invite holders of eligible debt to exchange their eligible debt for new loans of the same eligible obligor. On the first interest payment date for any new loan, the holder had the right to exchange such loan for a new loan of the same tenor and principal amount to a different eligible obligor designated by such holder not less than 90 days prior to such first interest payment date, with the consent of both the existing eligible obligors and the proposed substitute eligible obligor. No restriction was imposed on the transferability of eligible debt prior to the end of the exchange period.

New loans issued in exchange for each item of eligible debt had to have a principal amount equal to the principal amount of such eligible debt. Interest accrued and unpaid on eligible debt through the effective date had to be paid on the effective date. Each creditor tendering eligible debt had to agree to roll over until the exchange date of all eligible debt tendered. Each tendering creditor had to specify the final maturity and currency of the new loans that it wishes to receive in exchange for its tendered eligible debt. All tenders were considered irrevocable unless the Korean government amended the terms of the exchange offer in any material respect.

Since the Korean government's objective was that substantially all eligible debt be exchanged for new loans in order to alleviate the liquidity shortage, the consummation of the exchange offer was subject to the receipt by the eligible obligors of tenders to exchange not less than US$20 billion of eligible debt. The exchange period was two weeks from the date on which the exchange offer is made, subject to extension for up to an additional two weeks at the election of the government.

Day Twelve: January 29

The delegation had a working-level discussion at Shearman & Sterling's office on the details of the debt exchange with thirteen creditor banks and the two legal advisors. A schedule was tentatively agreed upon: three weeks were given to finish various documentations; the exchange offer was to be sent to the creditors on February 23, and two weeks were given for them to tender the offer; four weeks were allocated for reconciliation; and finally, debts were to be exchanged for new loans on April 7. The whole process would be finished in approximately two months.

Figure 1. Time Table for Debt Exchange

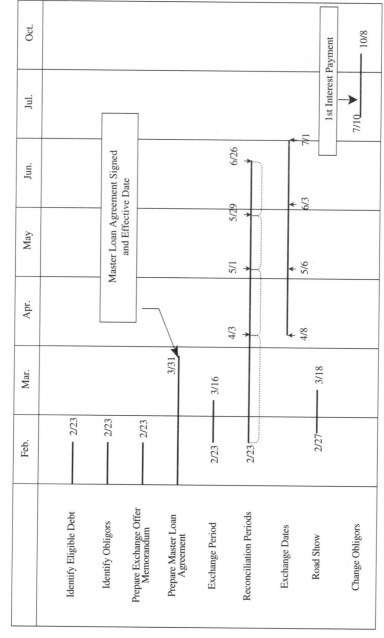

To facilitate the exchange process, the Korean government needed to identify eligible debt as soon as possible. To this end, the government also agreed to identify the list of eligible debt holders, the list of subsidiaries and branches of obligors, and the finalized list of merchant banks eligible for debt exchange. It was also agreed to appoint various agents necessary for the debt exchange. As for the exchange agent, Citibank showed strong interest, and given Vice Chairman Rhodes' leadership in the international banking community, no objection was raised to Citibank's appointment.

The Debt Management Team[3]

Establishment of the Debt Management Team

To implement the debt exchange, a task force—the Debt Management Team for Korean Financial Institutions (hereafter DMT)—was established on February 9, 1998. Se-Pyo Hong, Chairman and President of the Korea Exchange Bank (hereafter KEB), headed the DMT, for KEB had the largest eligible debt among the obligors.

The DMT had to manage the whole debt exchange process. The most urgent task was to identify eligible debt by various categories (by obligor, by debt holder, by country, and by debt category). To this end, it had to obtain a list of contact points in all the debt holding institutions, identify numerous subsidiaries and branches of the obligors, and monitor new borrowings and repayments by obligors. During the exchange period, creditors' participation rates were identified on a daily basis. The DMT also had to:

- Appoint various agents including reconciliation, calculation, and syndicate agents;
- Review documents by the legal advisors;
- Conduct a series of road shows during the exchange period to maximize the amount of tenders;
- Administer the issuance of a government guarantee to the obligors; and
- Decide how to share the administrative costs among the obligors.

To effectively disseminate information regarding the debt exchange, the DMT issued a newsletter five days a week between February 18 and March 13. The

---

[3]See KDI School Working Paper No. 01-06 for more detail on the activities of the debt management team.

newsletter was distributed via fax to all obligors, to relevant government ministries, and to supervisory institutions.

From February 27 to March 8, government and obligor banks conducted a series of road shows covering almost all the headquarter cities of creditor banks. During the presentations, government delegations noticed that perception on the Korean economy was improving. Moreover, they discovered that most of the creditor banks were favorable toward the exchange offer. Besides regular presentation meetings with creditor banks, individual meetings were also arranged with government ministries or central banks to ask for their cooperation in persuading creditor banks under their jurisdiction to roll over.

Changes to the January 28 Term Sheet

Since the term sheet agreed upon on January 28 was only a tentative agreement with a limited number of creditors, three additional documents had to be prepared to formally enter an agreement with all the participating creditors. First, an Exchange Offer Memorandum had to be prepared and sent to each eligible debt holder on February 23. The memorandum had to explain in detail the terms of the exchange and ask if an eligible debt holder would like to participate in the debt exchange. Before sending out the memorandum, more discussion had to take place at a technical level on the scope of eligible debt and the exchange procedure.

Second, a Letter of Acceptance (including the supplemental schedule) had to be prepared so that each eligible debt holder, having read the Exchange Offer Memorandum, could notify the exchange (or reconciliation) agent as to how it would like to participate in the debt exchange. A Letter of Acceptance was designed so that an eligible debt holder could notify in a common format its intention to participate in the debt exchange, the maturity, and the currency denomination of the new loan.

Third, a Master Loan Agreement had to be prepared so that all the parties involved (obligors, debt holders, guarantor, and agents) would be able to enter a formal agreement with a single contract. This approach of entering a single contract was considered to be more efficient than to enter hundreds of contracts for each debt exchange.

The DMT held two conference calls with creditors on February 4 and 10, to discuss some remaining technical issues regarding the debt exchange, and then legal advisors had another documentation meeting on February 19 in New York. In those meetings, a number of changes were made to the January 28 term sheet regarding the scope of eligible debt, the debt incurred by overseas subsidiaries, and the details of debt exchange. The changes were reflected in the Exchange Offer Memorandum that was sent to creditors on February 23. Many of the changes were motivated by concerns that the size of the tendered debt might be less than US$18 billion. On the scope of eligible debt, seven more items were included:

- Overnight deposits that were originally eligible debt but had been converted into overnights with the same eligible obligor on or after December 24, 1997, and remain outstanding, became eligible;
- Call money became eligible as it was considered to be a short-term loan;
- Repurchase obligations were included as eligible even if backed by securities issued by local governments, state-owned banks, or specialized banks;
- Floating rate certificate of deposits (hereafter FRCD) were interpreted as not constituting a publicly traded security, making a FRCD with a maturity of one year or less eligible;
- Long-term loans and long-term FRCDs with annual put options were considered as short-term loans and became eligible;
- Banker's acceptances (B/A) that were money market lines in disguise, with no underlying physical transaction, were considered as a short-term loan and became eligible; and
- Syndicate loans became eligible. If some of the creditors in the syndicate were not an eligible debt holder or were not willing to roll over, they were required to submit a waiver.

The January 28 term sheet had to be adjusted to address a loophole in the government guarantee that excluded debt incurred by overseas subsidiaries. From the creditors' point of view, it was necessary to switch the obligor from the subsidiary to its parent to receive the government guarantee. This could be done in three ways. First, the parent bank was allowed to assume the loan incurred by its subsidiary before the exchange period (e.g. before February 23, 1998). Second, when submitting the letter of acceptance, creditors could choose the option to switch the obligor from a subsidiary to its parent. This, however, took effect only when a written agreement among the three parties (creditor, subsidiary, and its parent) was submitted to the agents (exchange and reconciliation) and reconciliation was successfully completed. Third, the parent bank could guarantee the obligation of its subsidiary, with the government in turn guaranteeing the obligation of the parent guarantor, including its guarantee obligation.

A number of issues were confirmed about the details of debt exchange. First, new loans incurred during the exchange period were also considered eligible, whereas initially only the loans existing as of February 23 were eligible. Second, the maturity of existing debt, once tendered, was automatically extended to the exchange date of April 8. If reconciliation was not completed by April 8, the maturity was to be automatically extended to the next exchange date. Third, since the maturity of reconciled eligible debt expired on April 8 regardless of the original maturity, a breakage fee had to be paid by the obligor to the holder of new loan. The payment, however, was restricted to those debts incurred before December 24, 1997, and expired after February 23, 1998. For debt expiring after June 30, 1998, a breakage fee was not given if it was transformed into a one-year loan.

Fourth, given some skepticism that the total tendered debt might be less than US$18 billion—the original trigger point requiring creditors consent for the exchange to take effect—the trigger point was changed to US$17 billion. A suggestion to change the trigger point to US$16 billion was rejected for fear that this might have a negative effect on investor confidence. Fifth, in case the government as a guarantor had to pay the debt, it was decided to make payments from the Foreign Exchange Stabilization Fund and then replenish the Fund from the government budget. This was necessary since there might be a time lag if payment was made directly from the government budget.

Lastly, creditors were told which merchant banks were commercially sound and viable on March 2, 1998. Out of eleven merchant banks that had eligible debt, nine were determined to be commercially sound and viable. As of February 23, their eligible debt outstanding was US$1.37 billion. Two merchant banks that were deemed nonviable had US$47 million of debt.

Letters of Acceptance & Master Loan Agreement

Letters of Acceptance started to arrive on March 4. The exchange period was originally supposed to expire on March 12, but it was extended up to 5:00 p.m., March 16, 1998. Letters of Acceptance were received from 134 creditors from 32 countries amounting to US$21.84 billion. This was 100.7 percent of the eligible debt outstanding at the beginning of the exchange period (February 23) and 96.4 percent of the eligible debt outstanding on March 16. Exchange to one, two, and three-year maturity loans took up 17.2 percent, 45.0 percent, and 37.8 percent, respectively. The 20 percent cap imposed on one-year maturity loan was not fully exhausted.

The signing ceremony of the Master Loan Agreement was held on March 31, 1998 at Hotel Lotte in Seoul. Seventy-six people, from the Korean government, the IMF, legal councils, lending banks, and borrowing banks, attended the ceremony. From 11:40 a.m. to 12:10 p.m., short speeches were delivered by Kyu-Sung Lee, Minister of Finance and Economy; Yong-Hwan Kim, Vice President of the United Liberal Democrats; and Jong-Keun You, Economic Advisor to the President, gave speeches representing the government. William R. Rhodes, Vice Chairman of Citibank, delivered a short speech on behalf of the lenders, and Se-Pyo Hong, Chairman and President of the Korea Exchange Bank, gave a speech on behalf of the obligors.

The signing took place at 12:10. The Master Loan Agreement was an agreement among seven parties: the obligors, the parent guarantors, the Republic of Korea, the lenders, the syndicate agents, the calculation agent, and the exchange agent. It set forth terms and conditions on the exchange of loans, interests, principals, payments, guarantees, events of default, changes in obligors or parent guarantors, assignments, agents, and so on. Each obligor bank submitted a power of attorney to the DMT, stating that it delegated its right to sign the Agreement to the Korea Exchange Bank. The lenders, by submitting the Letter of Acceptance to the exchange agent, in effect, had already delegated their right to sign the Agreement.

Reconciliation & Government Guarantee

Having received the Letters of Acceptance by March 16, the first round of reconciliation took place from March 17 to April 3. The first exchange date was scheduled to be on April 8, 1998. Ernst & Young, as a reconciliation agent, had to check if each debt tendered by a creditor fell in the eligible debt category, and if the principal amount tendered matched with the information provided by the corresponding obligor. According to the Exchange Offer Memorandum, the reconciliation agent had to report an itemized list of reconciled/unreconciled debts (reconciliation statement) to the three related parties (each eligible debt holder, the Korean government, and each obligor) by April 3, 1998. Only the reconciled debt was assumed to be effectively tendered and be exchanged to a new loan on April 8, 1998. Unreconciled debt had to be reconciled and be exchanged in the later rounds.

A government guarantee was given to new loans (and interest) converted from the eligible debt that had been tendered and reconciled. The guarantee, however, did not cover new loans toward overseas subsidiaries. The total amount of government guarantee was US$21.74 billion plus interest.

The government guarantee process started with drafting of the Guarantee Agreement, describing the details of the guarantee, including the guarantee fees and the sinking fund. This Agreement was sent to each obligor for its signature. The obligor then sent back the signed Agreement to the DMT with the government guarantee application form, the debt repayment schedule, and the debt repayment schedule in case of a default. Upon receipt of these documents, the government reviewed the application. By signing the Master Loan Agreement on March 31, 1998, the government guarantee became legally binding on all relevant parties, and on the first exchange date (April 8, 1998) the guarantee became effective.

Measures to Mitigate Moral Hazard

The government took three measures to minimize moral hazard. First, it charged guarantee fees from the obligors. Second, it required obligors to participate in establishing a sinking fund. Third, obligors were required to submit debt repayment schedules, including prepayments.

Yearly guarantee fees were set to be from 0.2 percent to 1.5 percent of the outstanding debt, depending upon the credit rating and the BIS capital ratio of the obligor concerned. This measure was to address the moral hazard that can arise by giving government guarantee regardless of the obligors' financial situation. However, it was also important to keep the fee within a reasonable level. It was feared that the borrowing cost including the high guarantee fee would later become a benchmark rate, and thus set the general borrowing costs of the Korean financial institutions.

An obligor with a credit rating equivalent to that of a sovereign was levied 0.2 percent, 0.4 percent, 0.6 percent, 0.8 percent, and 1.0 percent of guarantee, if its BIS capital ratio was above 8 percent, 7-8 percent, 6-7 percent, 5-6 percent, and below 5 percent, respectively. An obligor with a credit rating lower than that of a sovereign was levied 0.3 percent, 0.6 percent, 0.9 percent, 1.2 percent, and 1.5 percent of guarantee fee if its BIS capital ratio was above 8 percent, 7-8 percent, 6-7 percent, 5-6 percent, and below 5 percent, respectively. A credit rating was considered to be equivalent to that of a sovereign if either rating from Moody's or Standard & Poor's was the same as that of a sovereign. Guarantee fees in the Korean won were collected every six months on each interest payment date. The amount of revenue collected from this guarantee fee totaled approximately US$150 million.

A sinking fund was established by requiring each obligor to deposit 3 percent of its outstanding debt at the Foreign Exchange Stabilization Fund in U.S. dollars. Contributions to the fund started on May 7, 1998, with 0.25 percent of outstanding debt being contributed each month until April 7, 1999. Obligors were allowed to retrieve their deposits as they made repayments. There was also a penalty for late deposits, the penalty being an additional deposit of one-year LIBID+100 basis points times the delayed amount. The deposit was remunerated once a year, the amount being one-year LIBID at the time of initial deposit times the average deposit outstanding. The deposits could not be provided as collateral.

Loan Transfers & Prepayments

According to the Master Loan Agreement, lenders were allowed to transfer their loans to other financial institutions. In the first three years, there were 124 transfers amounting to US$1.2 billion, or over 5 percent of total new loans. A significant amount of that, however, was inter-branch transfers within the same bank. There were also changes in obligors as banks merged and overseas branches were liquidated.

As of April 2001, all loans that were exchanged in April 1998 have been fully repaid: there were no defaults. Instead, obligors prepaid significant amounts of loans in advance. This indicates that obligors did not suffer from moral hazard. Banks strived to prepay loans with interest rates higher than prevailing market rates. According to the initial debt repayment schedule, obligors had to repay US$3.76 billion by April 1999, US$9.79 billion by April 2000, and US$8.20 billion by April 2001. By exercising the prepayment option, the obligors instead repaid US$4.18 billion in April 1999, US$8.75 billion in October 1999, US$6.76 billion in April 2000, US$2.12 billion in October 2000, and US$0.26 billion in April 2001.

Ex post, such prepayments also lowered the effective spreads. By replacing the original loans into lower-spread loans, the obligor banks were able to lower the effective spreads to 231 basis points for the two-year tranche and 217 basis points for the three-year tranche compared with original spreads of 250 and 275 basis points, respectively.[4]

Analyses of the Restructuring Program

Government Guarantee and Moral Hazard

One of the unique aspects of debt restructuring in Korea was the provision of a sovereign guarantee. Although it was acknowledged that a government guarantee was an effective tool to encourage creditors to participate in the program, it raised concerns that it might aggravate moral hazard among the

---

[4]KDI School Working Paper No. 01-06 explains how the effective spreads are calculated.

debtors and the creditors. In this section, we examine the data to see if these concerns actually materialized.

Our approach is to guess the kinds of behavior creditors would have taken if they fell back into the habit of blind lending due to the government guarantee. Three testable outcomes were considered.

- First, before committing to the maturity extension program, creditors would not bother to switch their short-term loans from poor to better quality debtors. That is, from the time creditors knew about the existence of government guarantee at the end of 1997 until the last day of the exchange period on March 16, 1998, creditors would not withdraw their loans from poorer quality banks to lend to better quality banks.
- Second, when tendering the maturity extension offer, creditors would not discriminate between poorer quality banks and better quality ones. In this case, creditors' average participation in the maturity extension program would be no greater for better quality debtors than for poorer quality debtors.
- Third, once creditors have tendered the maturity extension offer, they would choose the length of maturity independent of the banks' quality. That is, the average maturity creditors tendered would not be longer for better quality banks than for poorer quality banks.

Figures 2, 3, and 4 show the results. Figure 2 depicts the average growth rates of eligible debt over a period between December 31, 1997, and March 16, 1998. Comparison is made between those banks with a BIS ratio above 8 percent and those with a ratio below 8 percent. On average, eligible debt increased by 5 percent in banks with a high BIS ratio, while it decreased by 23 percent in banks with a low BIS ratio. As a robustness test, the growth rate of eligible debt is recomputed over the February 23 - March 16 sub-period. During this period, which corresponds to the exchange period, eligible debt on average increased by 34 percent in banks with a high BIS ratio, while it increased by only 7 percent in banks with a low BIS ratio.

Figure 3 depicts creditors' average participation rate to the maturity extension program. Three obligor groups are considered: nationwide commercial banks, local commercial banks, and merchant banks. Value-weighted averages are computed to control for the possibility that creditors with small eligible debt might show lower participation rates. The participation rate is measured by dividing the amount of loans tendered and reconciled as of April 3, 1998, by the amount of eligible debt as of March 16, 1998, the last day of the exchange period. For each obligor group, the creditors' participation rate is

Figure 2. Growth Rate of Eligible Debt
(In percent)

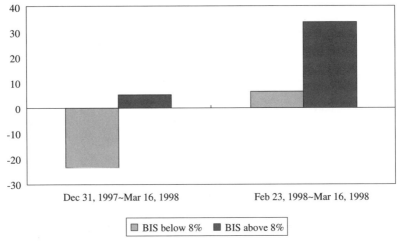

Source: Ministry of Finance and Economy, ROK.

Figure 3. Participation Rate by Obligor Group and BIS Ratio
(In percent)

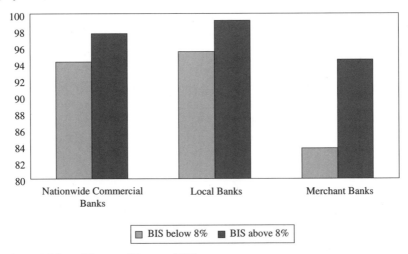

Source: Ministry of Finance and Economy, ROK.

higher in those banks with a high BIS ratio than in those banks with a low BIS ratio.

Figure 4 depicts the average maturity of newly tendered loans. The value-weighted average maturity is computed separately for obligors with participation rate below 95 percent and those above 95 percent. Regardless of the participation rate, the average maturity of new loans is greater in banks with a high BIS ratio than in banks with a low BIS ratio.

These results show that creditors were not blind to the quality of banks when making their decisions on lending, withdrawing, extending maturity, and choosing the maturities. Although the differences are relatively small and we did not formally test the statistical significance of the differences, the pattern is persistent enough to suggest that creditors did not fall back into the habit of blind lending. Despite the government guarantee, it seems that creditors did learn a lesson and became more cautious toward banks with poor quality.

As another way to shed light on the moral hazard issue, we examined if the short-term debt ratio started to creep up again after the government guarantee. If moral hazard actually took place, debtors would not mind taking short-term debt, since the government would step in and guarantee the payments in times of trouble, and creditors would not mind short-term lending if they believed that the government would step in and guarantee the payments when debtors face a problem.

Figure 4. New Loan Maturity by Obligors' Participation Rate and BIS Ratio
(In years)

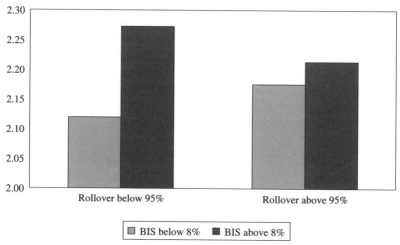

Source: Ministry of Finance and Economy, ROK.

Figure 5 shows a time-series of the ratio of short-term debt to total debt in the Korean banking sector including the merchant banks. Before the end of 1996, the ratio was near 60 percent. In the first half of 1997, the ratio started to fall and this trend accelerated in the second half as foreign banks refused to roll over the maturing loans. Then, in April 1998, the ratio dropped again as US$21.74 billion of short-term loans were exchanged into one, two, or three-year loans. The short-term debt ratio started to creep up again in early 1999, mainly due to the repayment of new loans provided as a part of the maturity extension program. Since the second half of 2000, the ratio has stabilized at about 35 percent, considerably lower than in the midst of the crisis in late 1997.

For moral hazard to take effect, the interest rate applied to new loans should not be set at a penalty rate, so that debtors would not have any incentive to make prepayments. However, Korean banks made significant prepayments during the past two years, which indicates that the interest rates were set at penalizing levels. Figure 6 shows this. Originally, obligors had to repay US$ 3.76 billion by April 1999, US$9.79 billion by April 2000, and US$8.20 billion by April 2001. Instead, by exercising the prepayment option, they repaid US$4.18 billion in April 1999, US$8.75 billion in October 1999, US$6.76 billion in April 2000, US$2.12 billion in October 2000, and US$0.26 billion in April 2001. These prepayments were encouraged by the measures the government introduced to minimize moral hazard among the debtor institutions, as explained above.

Figure 5. Short-term Debt Ratio of Commercial & Merchant Banks
(Ratio of short-term debt to total debt)

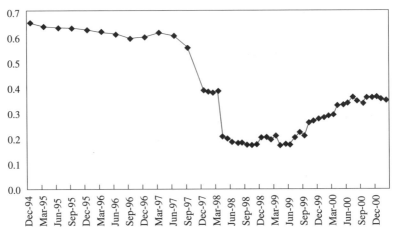

Source: Ministry of Finance and Economy, ROK.

Figure 6. Debt Repayment by Interest Payment Date
(In billions of U.S. dollars)

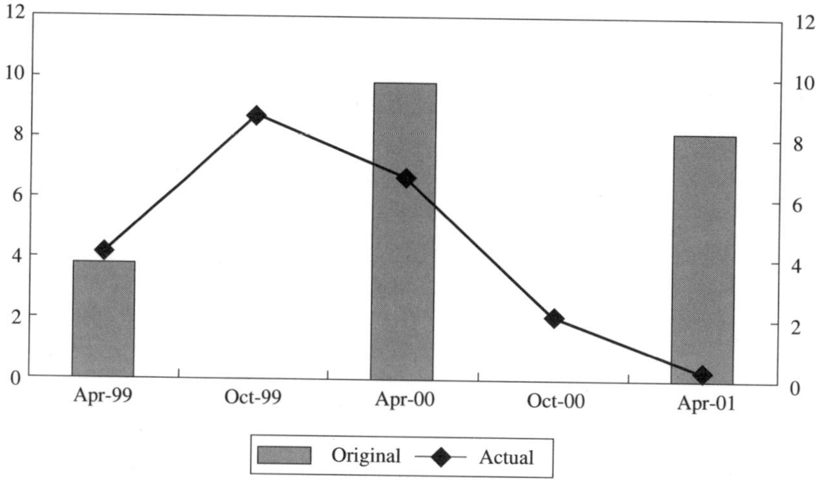

Source: Ministry of Finance and Economy, ROK.

Effectiveness of the Restructuring Program

Another unique aspect of debt restructuring in Korea was that it rescheduled only bank loans. Other forms of credit such as corporate loans were not covered. This raised concerns that foreign creditors might withdraw from the corporate sector as their exposure to Korean banks increased with the maturity extensions. Figure 7 shows that the financial sector's long-term debt (LTD) increased with the maturity extensions in early 1998, but this only seems to have reduced the financial sector's short-term debt. The corporate sector's long-term debt remained stable. Although the corporate sector's short-term debts have been decreasing, the drop seems to have taken place before the maturity extension in April 1998, with most of the drop between the end of 1997 and March 1998. Even if this drop was a preemptive measure to reduce exposure in advance, the magnitude was moderate, and did not pose any threat to the success of the restructuring program.

Another concern during the exchange process was that creditors with relatively small amounts of eligible debt would have a low participation rate. Three reasons were behind such concern. First, those creditors would not think their withdrawal would trigger systemic risk to the world economy. Second, those creditors usually did not have any operation other than their loans. Third, the Debt Management Team and the central banks in creditor countries must

Figure 7. External Debt by Obligors
(In billions of U.S. dollars)

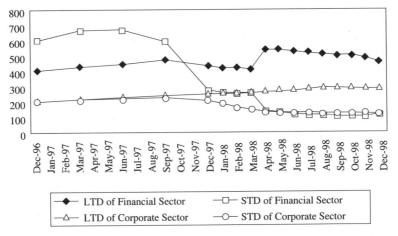

Source: Ministry of Finance and Economy, ROK.

have paid more attention to those creditors with large eligible debt. The value-weighted average participation rate among creditors with eligible debt below US$100 million was 78 percent, while the average participation rate among creditors with eligible debt above US$100 million was 98.15 percent.

Creditors that did not participate in the New York meeting in late January showed lower rollover rates than those who did participate in the meeting. Among the nine countries with eligible debt between US$100 million and US$ 500 million, only Canada and Switzerland participated in the New York meeting. Canada and Switzerland had a 99.1 percent average participation rate while the other seven countries had only 85.6 percent participation rate.

Concluding Remarks

A number of factors contributed importantly to the success of the Korean debt restructuring process.

First, it was wise for the Korean government to forcefully oppose the proposal made by J.P. Morgan. Making exchange and new cash offers simultaneously would have lowered the possibility of success compared with the sequential approach supported by the Korean government. The modified Dutch auction mechanism proposed by J.P. Morgan would have led to a much higher interest rate. Persuasive efforts conducted by the Korean government before the New York negotiation paid off and J.P Morgan's proposal lost center stage at the negotiation tables.

Second, it was wise for the Korean government to speed up the process of negotiation and documentation. The negotiation took less than a month and the documentation took only two months. By delaying the process or, at the extreme, declaring a moratorium, the Korean government could have obtained more favorable terms on existing debts. But to eliminate economic uncertainty and restore investor confidence, it was better to accelerate the process.

Third, the government guarantee of rolled over debt may have helped. It not only made the loans relatively safe, it also freed capital that would have been set aside to abide by the BIS rule. Given that Korea was an OECD member country, the sovereign guarantee transformed rolled over loans into assets with zero percent risk weighting. This was especially attractive to those creditor banks that had suffered capital erosion due to poor performing local stock markets.

Fourth, unlike Mexico, Korea is not endowed with natural resources such as crude oil that could be readily sold for foreign exchange. This suggests that some creditors may not have considered the government guarantee to be fully credible. There must have been other reasons why creditor banks participated in the restructuring program. The size of the Korean economy is one candidate. During the crisis, the G-10 central banks explicitly told the banks under their jurisdiction that any failure to roll over credit lines to Korea would trigger a systemic risk to the world's financial system. Another candidate is the confidence in the Korean economy. More than thirty years of outstanding economic performance may have imbued a belief in the creditor banks that the Korean economy would successfully recover from the crisis.

Fifth, aggressive road shows conducted to maximize the number of creditor banks participating in the debt maturity extension program were instrumental. The tentative term sheet agreed upon in New York only involved thirteen creditor banks from seven countries. This meant that Korea had to persuade the remaining creditors to have a meaningful amount of debt rolled over. Later the total number of creditor banks participating in the program turned out to be 134 from 32 countries. Such a good result would not have been achieved without the carefully organized and well-conducted road shows by the government and the obligors.

Sixth, the Korean government made sure that debtors receiving a government guarantee did not fall into the trap of moral hazard and resume excessive short-term borrowing. It charged debtor banks guarantee fees according to their risk profiles, it required debtor banks to participate in establishing a sinking fund, and it required debtor banks to submit debt repayment schedules, including prepayments. As a result, the Korean banking sector was able to keep its short-term external debt at about 35 percent of total debt, and make significant prepayments on the rolled over debts. Creditors did not fall into the habit of blind lending because of the guarantee.

Seventh, it was helpful to link the supplemental financial support package with the voluntary maturity extension by the international banking community. From the participating governments' point of view, it would have been politically damaging if the tax money provided to Korea were only used to pay back Korean banks' debts to international banks. As such, the participating governments made it clear that the disbursement from the package was contingent on the creditors taking a haircut in the form of voluntary maturity extensions. This, in turn, had the effect of telling the creditor banks that once they extended the maturity of their loans, a significant amount of money would be set aside to make these loans safer.

Eighth, Korea was fortunate to have two outstanding veterans on emerging market debt restructuring: William Rhodes, who chaired the negotiation process in New York and who later accompanied the Korean delegation on many road shows, and Mark Walker, who worked as the legal advisor to the Korean government. It also helped to have appointed outside financial advisors at an early stage and to have worked closely with the IMF.

Korea's experience in debt restructuring during a crisis makes the proposals suggested by the Korean government in April 1999 regarding private sector involvement more convincing.[5] In essence, the Korean proposal is to create a pre-established program for debt restructuring and establish a common channel through which the international financial community communicates with the debtor government. The Korean government believes that if there had existed such a mechanism at the time of the crisis, it would have saved significant amounts of time, energy, and money.

Specifically, the government proposed establishing an ad hoc committee for debt workout comprised of representatives from the debtor and creditor governments, central banks from G-7 nations, the IMF, and other relevant international organizations. The committee would deliberate and reach collective decisions on existing private sector debts. In the 1998 restructuring, the discussion initially started among G-7 governments and the IMF. With their persuasion, creditor banks became involved. And lastly, the Korean government representing the debtor banks participated in the deliberation. If such a

---

[5]Ministry of Finance and Economy, New International Financial Architecture: Korea's Perspective (April 1999).

committee were pre-established, deliberation between the creditor and debtor banks could have started much earlier.

The government also proposed that the provision of emergency funding by the IMF be linked to the debt workout program arranged by the ad hoc committee. In the 1998 restructuring, the US$57 billion rescue package was initially not linked to debt restructuring by the private banking community. Later, as a way of inducing voluntary rollover and also as a way to avoid political damage, the countries participating in the supplemental financial support package made it clear that disbursement was conditioned on voluntary debt restructuring by the international banking community.

In order to provide the needed time for negotiations, the government also proposed that the committee recommend an automatic standstill for three months. In the 1998 restructuring, creditor banks initially rolled over their credit maturing at the end of 1997 until the end of January. In mid-January, they extended the maturity again until March 31, 1998. The rollovers, however, were not automatic. Nor were they legally binding. Many creditor banks withdrew their loans despite the decision by a number of large banks to roll over loans.

The government also proposed to form a sub-committee of creditors where decisions on debt workout issues could be made either on a majority basis or by a consensus of two-thirds. In the 1998 restructuring, the Korean government spent more than two months contacting each individual creditor institution. If the debt workout decision was made collectively under such a sub-committee, it could have saved significant amounts of time and resources.

Lastly, the government proposed that international financial institutions provide an advisory group of experts to help the committee in terms of legal and technical assistance in the debt restructuring process. Such was not the case in the 1998 restructuring. The Korean government had to employ a team of international experts on its own.

The Korean government believes the above proposals will help ensure constructive private sector involvement in future crisis.

Appendix 1
Sources of Information

Information used in this paper mostly came from internal documents of the Korean government, mainly the Ministry of Finance and Economy. A number of selected documents are listed below.

Documents in Korean
- Progress Report on Debt Maturity Extension: December 1997 - January 1998
- Progress Report on the Activities of Debt Management Team
- Bill for Approval on the Sovereign Guarantee of External Foreign Exchange Debt by Domestic Banks Incurring in 1997 and 1998
- Bill for Approval on the Sovereign Guarantee of Foreign Exchange Debt by Bank of Korea and Foreign Exchange Banks Incurring in 1998
- Official Directive on the Negotiation for Debt Restructuring
- Government Guarantee Agreement
- Establishment of Sinking Fund Regarding the Guarantee on Foreign Exchange Debt

Documents in English
- J.P. Morgan & Co., Korean Financing Proposal (various versions)
- Korea's Financing Plan for 1998
- Term Sheet (various versions)[6]
- Lee, Peter, "Korea Stares into the Abyss," *Euromoney*, (March 1998)
- Debt Maturity Extension Program: Questions and Answers
- Exchange Offer Memorandum
- Letters of Acceptance
- Master Loan Agreement
- Eligible Debt by Obligors & Creditors
- Tendered Debt by Obligors & Lenders
- Ernst & Young, Reconciliation Statement
- Ministry of Finance and Economy, *New International Financial Architecture: Korea's Perspective* (April 1999)
- IMF, *Involving the Private Sector in Forestalling and Resolving Financial Crisis* (April 1999)
- IMF, "Private Sector Involvement in Crisis Prevention and Resolution: Market Views and Recent Experience," *International Capital Markets (September 2000)*

---

[6]The title of the January 28 version is "Proposal with Regard to the External Debt of Korean Commercial, State-Owned and Specialized Banks (including Overseas Branches, Agencies, and Certain Foreign Banking Subsidiaries) and Merchant Banks."

13 Strengthening the International Financial Architecture: Open Issues, Asian Concerns

Barry Eichengreen*

This paper assesses measures taken or under consideration to reform the international monetary and financial system.[1] The analysis of efforts to strengthen the international financial architecture, as these initiatives are colloquially known, has grown into a considerable industry.[2] The literature is now so large and unruly as to all but elude systematic assessment. I therefore organize my analysis around a pair of questions. First, how meaningful are the changes to the international financial architecture currently underway—are they merely cosmetic or do they constitute a significant attempt to modify the structure and management of the international financial system? Second, do the initiatives under consideration address Asia's concerns with, inter alia, the volatility of financial markets, the structure of policy conditionality, and the operation of the exchange rate system?

The relevance of these questions will be evident to those familiar with the reform debate. Calls for radical changes (Soros, 2000; Eatwell and Taylor, 2000; Meltzer *et al.*, 2000) have not borne fruit. Instead, the proposals that have received the most serious attention from the official community all work within the structure of existing markets and institutions.[3] This has led the critics to dismiss official initiatives as doing too little to enhance the efficiency and stability of the international financial system. Others would counter that even incremental changes can have a large cumulative effect if they all work

*I thank Morris Goldstein for helpful comments. This paper was updated in the spring of 2002 to reflect post-conference events bearing on its arguments.
[1]It can be read as the latest instalment on a series of papers on this subject, the most recent of which was completed in May 2000 and published as Eichengreen (2000).
[2]Two recent examples of the genre, on which I draw, are Goldstein (2001) and Park and Wang (2001).
[3]The G-7's 1999 Cologne Communique is a clear statement of the intent to work within the existing framework and a rejection of radical departures.

in the same direction. Thus, Goldstein (2001) describes current reform efforts as the most significant attempt to strengthen the international monetary system in more than 40 years. Whether these reforms are having a large or small effect—and whether they will significantly enhance the efficiency and stability of the international financial system—is thus the most fundamental question concerning the architecture debate.

That this agenda should raise concerns among Asian observers is not surprising. It was the Asian crisis, after all, that provided the impetus for the current wave of reform efforts. Those who regard the operation of international capital markets as a factor in the outbreak of the Asian crisis and see the subsequent spread of economic difficulties as evidence of the instability of global finance have been in the vanguard of those calling for radical changes in financial regulation. Others, critical of multilateral intervention for having done more to aggravate than to contain Asia's crisis, have taken the lead in calling for reform of the international financial institutions. At the same time, there are reasons to be skeptical that the prevailing agenda is compatible with the Asian approach to development. Is it compatible with the Asian model of bank-centered finance, high debt gearing, and close industry-government relations? Does it address Asian concerns with market manipulation and exchange rate volatility? Will it speak to complaints that rapidly growing Asian economies have insufficient voice in the deliberations of the multilateral financial institutions?

In the following section, I analyze efforts to address these concerns through the development of international standards for macroeconomic and financial development. This standard-setting initiative is the most prominent and ambitious item on the architectural agenda; arguably it is the one for which the most far-reaching results are promised. Thus it is important to ask whether this initiative is sensibly conceived, whether it is adequately focused, and whether it will deliver the goods.

Official opinion on the remaining topics is more divided. In the third section I consider reform of the exchange rate system in light of dollarization in Ecuador and El Salvador, inflation targeting in Brazil, and recent proposals for reestablishing pegged exchange rates at the regional level. While there has been little progress in agreeing on redesign of the global exchange-rate system, I ask whether discussions to date can be seen as delineating a limited menu of options for exchange rate management, with different entrees to accommodate the tastes of different regions. In the subsequent section, I revisit the case for regional monetary and financial cooperation, including the swap lines of the Chiang Mai Agreement, proposals for a common basket peg, and the idea of an Asian Monetary Fund. The conclusion is an assessment of where we stand.

Standards

Standards and codes for sound financial management are the aspect of the architectural agenda to which the official community has devoted the most effort and to which it most regularly points as evidence of its commitment to reform. Standards have been developed for everything from macroeconomic policy and data dissemination to institutional and market infrastructure. The IMF compiles a list of initiatives taking place under this heading, has developed a Special Data Dissemination Standard that covers key economic data, and has promulgated codes for transparency in monetary and fiscal policy. It has prepared and published several rounds of Reports on the Observance of Standards and Codes (ROSCs) and cooperated with the World Bank in developing a joint Financial Sector Assessment Program (FSAP) to identify the vulnerabilities of national financial systems. The Financial Stability Forum, created in 1999 as a venue for discussing common financial problems and sharing information on regulatory best practice, has convened a Follow-Up Group on incentives for fostering the implementation of standards. In all, official compendia list upwards of 64 standard- and code-related initiatives.[4]

International standards for sound practice at the national level are an obvious vehicle for addressing challenges for collective stability in a world of sovereign states. It can be argued that they are the only viable approach to providing the collective good of stable financial markets in the absence of a super-national body with the power to override national monetary and financial decisions.[5] To an extent they have always been the focus of efforts to enhance financial stability. In the late 19th century, such standards were limited to the monetary arena.[6] That we refer to the dominant monetary arrangement of that period as the gold *standard* is no coincidence, in other words. The gold standard was the internationally accepted standard for sound financial management: adhering to it was necessary and sufficient for a country to participate actively and constructively on international capital markets (Bordo and Rockoff, 1996).

Standard setting limited to the regulation of monetary affairs sufficed so long as there was little pressure to use monetary policy to achieve goals other

---

[4]See Financial Stability Forum Task Force on Implementation of Standards, Issues Paper (March 2000), Annex 9, Part 2.

[5]And in a world where domestic financial problems can spill across borders—this assumption is implicit in the notion that financial stability is a global public good (Wyplosz, 1999).

[6]Actually, the spread of the international gold standard was part of a broader movement for international standardization in areas other than the financial, which can be dated from the 1860s (Eichengreen and James, 2001).

than currency stability and no fully articulated theory of stabilization policy. It was viable as long as financial integration was limited mainly to purchases of government and railway bonds. The early decades of the 20th century saw a challenge to this limited agenda. Fiscal and monetary instruments had been directed toward other objectives during World War I, leading to recognition of the need to extend standards into additional areas. With the failure of efforts at the Brussels and Genoa Conferences of 1920 and 1922 to develop standards for fiscal policy, central bank independence, and international cooperation in the conduct of monetary policy, countries retreated into financial autarky, soon followed by the outbreak of the Great Depression. International standards for financial practice were rendered redundant by tight regulation of financial transactions, international financial transactions in particular. Thus, the standards to which countries were held by the Bretton Woods Agreement were essentially limited to exchange rates (IMF members were obliged to declare par values and to consult regarding their adjustment) and current account convertibility. These obligations were fundamentally oriented toward stabilizing and sustaining international trade rather than international finance.

The recovery of market-based financial transactions was responsible for the subsequent expansion of these functions. The growing cross-border repercussions of national economic policies, transmitted by unprecedentedly large capital flows, led to the Second Amendment of the IMF Articles of Agreement empowering the IMF to conduct "firm surveillance" of its members' macroeconomic policies. The Herstatt crisis led to the Principles for the Supervision of Banks' Foreign Establishments (the Basle Concordat agreed to in 1983), while the debt crisis, which created worries that international banks were dangerously undercapitalized, led to the Basle capital adequacy standards for internationally-active banks (the Capital Accord published in 1988). The subsequent growth of international capital markets then elicited widespread recognition of the need for more far-reaching changes in national financial practice. Ultimately, this effort foundered on the attempt to amend the Articles of Agreement to oblige IMF members to render their currencies convertible on capital account, an incompletely thought through attempt to apply the "gold standard solution" of unilateral liberalization to a world where the preconditions for successful financial liberalization were more complex.

But there was no denying that international financial markets had become more liquid and deeply integrated.[7] The range of claims traded internationally

---

[7]In a series of recent papers (for example, Bordo, Eichengreen, and Irwin, 1999), I have attempted to cast doubt on the notion that financial markets were as deeply integrated, at least in ways that are relevant for current policy discussions, in the late 19th century as today.

was greater than ever before; no longer were these dominated by government and railway bonds. The number of banks, corporations and governments able to fund themselves offshore was larger than before World War I (the prior period of financial globalization) or in the immediately succeeding years. Short-term capital movements were larger. More credit was available to highly-leveraged institutions. As a result of these changes, there were more points along the chain of financial transactions where things could go wrong, with negative effects not just for the country in which the problem originated but for its neighbors and potentially the world as a whole.

This recognition led in the first half of the 1990s to a broadening of IMF conditionality to encompass institutional reforms related primarily to the operation of financial markets.[8] It inspired Morris Goldstein's proposal for an international banking standard and to the creation of the Fund's Special Data Dissemination Standard in 1996.[9] But it was the Asian crisis that sealed the case for international standards. As interpreted by G-7 governments and the multilaterals, that crisis reflected weaknesses in prudential supervision and regulation, auditing and accounting, bankruptcy and insolvency procedures, corporate governance, and financial transparency. Preventing the recurrence of such crises required steps to upgrade national practice in these areas. The absence of other mechanisms and experience with the Basle Accord pointed to standards as the logical means of achieving this end. And applying peer pressure, conditioning multilateral assistance on progress in these areas, and encouraging market participants to focus on countries' adherence to these standards were obvious ways of encouraging conformance in the absence of a global regulator with enforcement powers.

This historical digression is meant to suggest that there is a logic for the current approach to strengthening the financial architecture. The globalization of finance renders countries vulnerable to the destabilizing repercussions of financial problems abroad. Because integration is even more extensive than a century ago, so too is the scope for destabilizing spillovers. Increasingly, financial regulation has the character of a global public good. But in the absence of a global financial regulator with enforcement powers, the only mechanism for supplying this public good is national initiatives to upgrade supervision, regulation, and practice. Standards are a focal point for the peer pressure, conditionality, and market discipline that provide the incentives to carry out this task.

---

[8]I return to the debate over IMF conditionality below.

[9]Which in turn provided impetus for the IMF's Framework for Financial Stability and the Basle Committee of Banking Supervisors' Core Principles for Effective Banking Supervision, published in 1997.

To say that this process has a logic is different from saying that it will necessarily have the desired effect. For one thing, there are worries that the standard-setting process has already lost its focus. The international policy community has promulgated or recognized upwards of 60 standards, raising the question of whether governments will take any of them seriously. Morris Goldstein (2001) has reasonably asked whether officials have created a bureaucratic Frankenstein.

Recognizing this problem, the Financial Stability Forum has designated 12 standards as deserving priority in implementation.[10] These are concerned with macroeconomic policy and transparency (with corresponding standards for monetary and fiscal policy transparency, data dissemination, and data compilation), institutional and market infrastructure (with standards for insolvency, corporate governance, accounting, auditing, payments and settlement, market integrity, and market functioning), and financial regulation and supervision (with standards for banking supervision, securities regulation, insurance regulation, and financial conglomerate supervision).[11] Although this is a step in the right direction, the process would be more effective with even more attention to priorities and less effort to be comprehensive.

Then there is the question of whether these standards are suited to the circumstances of the countries to which they are applicable. Although Hong Kong and Singapore are represented in the Financial Stability Forum, low- and middle-income emerging markets are not. Private-sector standard-setting bodies like the International Accounting Standards Committee have subcommittees responsible for addressing the problems of emerging markets, but standard setting is still dominated by the G-7 countries, their regulators, and their market participants. To the extent that these individuals lack familiarity with the Asian model of bank-centered finance, industrial policy insulated from rent seeking, and reciprocal control, they may underestimate its viability. And standards requiring arm's-length dealing between banks and corporations, Western-style prudential regulation and supervision, and resource allocation guided by asset prices may be corrosive of a bank- and government-led development model with a track record of success.

My own view is that the Asian crisis and historical experience generally have shown that financial integration implies the need for a degree of institutional harmonization. Asian countries cannot sell corporate securities to international investors without requiring their issuers to employ international stan-

---

[10]See http://www.fsforum.org/Standards/HowOrganized.html.

[11]The Bank and the IMF currently focus on standards in 11 areas, which are more or less coincident with this list (IMF and World Bank, 2001, p. 16).

dards for auditing, accounting, and financial reporting; otherwise, even a rumor about the condition of the issuer, however ill founded, may provoke panic and destabilize the market. They cannot allow banks to fund themselves offshore without removing implicit guarantees and applying internationally-recognized regulatory standards; otherwise, foreign lenders will have no reason to discipline borrowers, who will respond by levering up their bets. Governments cannot borrow abroad unless they are prepared to provide information; otherwise revelations about the public finances may lead panicked investors to herd out of the markets all at once. The choice, then, is whether to participate actively on international financial markets, in which case international standards along the lines of those developed by market-led economies like the United Kingdom and the United States are the only game in town, or to limit such participation, in which case a variety of other institutional arrangements are possible. My own reading is that Asian policy makers see their economies as exiting the phase of government-led extensive development for a subsequent phase of more heavily market-led development in which financial market integration will play a prominent role, creating irresistible pressure for institutional convergence around international standards of the sort currently being promulgated.

Even if Asian countries opt for financial integration and embrace internationally-recognized rules and procedures, standards are unlikely to contribute much in the absence of appropriate institutions. Pastor (2000) makes this point for legal rules. The law is a system of interdependent concepts; few legal rules and concepts can be understood and applied without reference to other legal rules and concepts. A rule will not deliver efficient and equitable outcomes in the absence of a body of precedent, reflecting accumulated knowledge of its functioning in the context of a living legal system. Hence, standardized rules are unlikely to be effective where a complementary body of law does not exist. IOSCO's standards for securities regulation will not have their desired effect in the absence of an adequate body of commercial law (governing, inter alia, the duties of company directors and officers, takeover bids and other transactions intended to change control, and private rights of contract and property). Similarly, an international standard for the equitable and efficient determination and resolution of insolvency will not be workable in a country that lacks an independent judiciary.[12]

The objections in the preceding paragraph are really of two types. One is that standards will not work when the institutions required for their application

---

[12]While a few standards can simply be airlifted into a country (auditing practices as carried out by the Big 6 accounting firms), they are exceptions to the rule.

are absent. Legal standards will not work when an independent judiciary and rule of law are absent. Financial standards will not work in the absence of sanctions against corruption and malfeasance—including the dissemination of blatantly false and misleading balance-sheet information. But this is not just a critique of standards: it is a challenge to viability of a market economy, which cannot function in such an environment. International standards may be just a small part of the solution to these problems, but they are part of the solution just the same. This objection is not a fundamental critique of the standard-centered agenda, only a reminder that it is just a small part of the larger task.

The other objection is that rigid and detailed international standards discourage experimentation and the adaptation of best practice to local conditions. Superior arrangements compatible with the local legal culture and economic context tend to be discovered through a trial-and-error process informed by local knowledge. Attempting to micro-manage institutional arrangements at the international level stifles local innovation.[13] The counter is that the standards promulgated by the international community are general: they set broad benchmarks for minimally acceptable practice but allow governments to meet those desiderata in different ways. This is a caution that standards that are too specific can be counterproductive. It suggests that standards that take the form of broad principles (such as the Basle Committee's Core Principles for Effective Banking Supervision) offer a better model than those setting out detailed methodologies (such as the IMF's Special Data Dissemination Standard, or SDSS).

Then there is the issue of resource cost. Studies of the cost of implementing WTO commitments—only a small subset of the relevant standards—have found that these can be very substantial for developing countries (see, for example, Finger and Schuler, 1999). Collecting and processing data and strengthening regulatory and supervisory standards require technicians and data processors, computer programmers and bank inspectors. However commendable the effort, these investments may come at the expense of programs supporting socially vulnerable groups and risk eliciting a political backlash in cash-strapped economies (Soludo and Rao, 1999; Park and Wang, 2001).[14] If the G-7 and the multilaterals are serious about investments in standards, then they should consider earmarking grants for this purpose.

---

[13] "The supply of ready-made standards to domestic law makers does not facilitate, and may actually impede, the acquisition of this knowledge," as Pastor (2000, p. 3) puts it.

[14] There are also presumably benefits in the form of lower borrowing costs, but these accrue down the road, making them difficult for poor countries with high discount rates to invest in.

Finally, what incentives are there for countries to take ownership of the relevant standards—to implement them, as distinct from simply voicing the intent? Those incentives are of four types: surveillance, conditionality, regulation, and market discipline. I leave the discussion of IMF conditionality to a subsequent section. Suffice it to say that the notion that the IMF should be actively involved in this process is controversial. This would encourage the further expansion of IMF surveillance and conditionality and entangle the Fund even more deeply in the economic and social affairs of its members, something to which its shareholders and Managing Director have both declared their opposition. There is more sympathy for the notion that ROSCs, FSAP reviews, and the Fund's quarterly reports on progress of countries subscribing to the SDDS provide an objective basis for the financial surveillance conducted by Article IV missions, in the context of which the relevant warnings can be issued and congratulations extended.[15] The Financial Stability Forum's willingness to name names in its review of offshore financial centers and the readiness of the Financial Action Task Force to do the same for money laundering suggest a new resolve to provide candid assessments.[16] Still, it is hard to imagine that standards-centered surveillance not backed by standards-related conditionality would do much to alter the behavior of governments.

Conditionality applies only to countries with programs. This raises the question of how to apply official incentives to the others. The policy community has backed away from direct regulatory incentives.[17] Whereas the early proposal for revising the Basle capital adequacy standards proposed heavier charges on loans to countries failing to comply with the relevant standards, the revised proposal omits this recommendation.[18] The recommendation of

---

[15]Although this would be inconsistent with the notion that adherence to these standards and codes is voluntary, which remains the official IMF position, adopted to assuage countries skeptical of the whole endeavor. In addition, there remains some confusion about the precise way in which these assessments should feed into surveillance activities. Currently, ROSCs and Article IV surveillance occur at different times and periodicities. Moreover, countries volunteer for ROSCs (not all, it must be noted, with equal enthusiasm), while Article IV surveillance is obligatory of members (IMF and World Bank, 2001).

[16]Although these will surely continue to fall short of numerical ratings.

[17]About the only explicit step in this direction is the decision by IMF directors that compliance with financial standards should be a consideration when the decision is taken of whether to prequalify a country for a Contingent Credit Line. And the fact that no country has applied and that the Fund's recent efforts to render the facility more attractive have had little effect (for good reasons, as I argue below) has rendered this initiative largely irrelevant.

[18]The following objections to the proposal carried the day. First, that this could be seen as second-guessing the risk management systems and credit policies of domestic institutions. Second, that it could create moral hazard if lower capital charges for certain jurisdictions were viewed as an official seal of approval for their policies. Third, that it would be hard to quantify conformance with standards and hence map them onto capital charges. And, fourth, capital

the Financial Stability Forum that implementation should be fostered by "encouraging" regulated institutions to take information on standards into account, that regulators should urge caution in dealing with counterparties located in jurisdictions which have gaps in their observance of standards, and that they should require issuers to disclose information on the observance of standards in prospectuses for international sovereign bond issues, is weak soup in comparison.

Given all this, if there is to be pressure to comply, it will have to come from the markets. A review by the Financial Stability Forum (2000) suggests that institutional investors and fund managers have rather limited familiarity with these standards and codes (Clark, 2000). That Standard and Poor's is now producing corporate governance ratings for individual firms based on the OECD principles is a promising development, as is the fact that two commercial agencies have offered to rate countries' compliance with a variety of other standards. But whether the market has the requisite attention span remains to be seen.

Exchange Rates

The crises of the 1990s, including Asia's in 1997-98, made it impossible to deny that "intermediate" exchange rate arrangements—those lying between very hard pegs and relatively free floats—are fragile and crisis prone. These crises provided compelling evidence of the costs when pegged rates collapse. The decline in the value of the currency, when it comes, is "larger, more rapid and more unanticipated than when a depreciation occurs under a floating exchange-rate regime" (Mishkin, 2001). The distress suffered by banks and firms with unhedged foreign currency exposures is greater. There is at least impressionistic evidence that the associated output losses are larger.

These effects can be understood as consequences of the build-up of unhedged foreign exposures among banks and corporations led to believe that they are insured against currency fluctuations by the authorities' commitment to peg the rate, and of the shock to confidence that results when the anchor for monetary policy, namely the one and same exchange rate peg, is withdrawn abruptly. A more prudent arrangement, the conclusion follows, would be to move to a more flexible rate voluntarily rather than under duress. Currency fluctuations would then remind borrowers of the need to limit their borrowing and

---

charges are designed to address credit risk, but standards are designed to address other forms of risk as well. This author, for one, does not find these objections particularly compelling.

hedge their exposures, and the central bank and government would have to develop independent sources of credibility. Alternatively, the country could adopt a hard peg to a foreign currency or make that foreign currency the exclusive circulating medium and legal tender, eliminating currency risk and allowing policy credibility to be imported quickly rather than laboriously grown at home.

This wisdom became increasingly conventional following the Asian crisis. In an April 1998 speech on international financial reform, then-U.S. Treasury Secretary Robert Rubin declared that the IMF should no longer provide financial assistance to support overvalued currency pegs. His successor, Lawrence Summers (2000, p. 8), stated that "the choice of appropriate exchange rate regime for economies with access to international capital markets, increasingly means a move away from the middle ground of pegged but adjustable fixed exchange rates towards the two corner solutions of either flexible exchange rates or a fixed exchange rate supported, if necessary, by a commitment to give up altogether an independent monetary policy." Stanley Fischer, drawing on IMF staff's assessment of the de facto exchange rate regime in IMF member countries, showed that the proportion with intermediate arrangements (neither hard pegs nor floats) was significantly lower in 1999 than 1991 (34 percent versus 62 percent for all countries, 42 percent versus 64 percent for emerging markets).[19] Fischer's testimony to the Meltzer Commission forecast that more countries would move to the corners.[20] IMF staff's most recent paper for the Executive Board on exchange rate arrangements (Mussa *et al.*, 2000) similarly concludes "for developing countries with important linkages to modern global capital markets ... the requirements for sustaining pegged exchange rates have become significantly more demanding. For many emerging market econom-

---

[19]Fischer (2001, Figure 1). Some would dispute that these numbers are informative, arguing that a non-negligible share of emerging markets that claim to float independently or to operate a managed float in fact intervene heavily to limit the variability of the rate (Calvo and Reinhart, 2000). Since Fischer's tabulations are based on IMF economists' assessments of the de facto regime, and not the regime announced by the authorities, it is necessary to argue that they are subject to capture in the context of Article IV and program negotiations. I return to this below.

[20]In fairness, I should note that there remain defenders of intermediate arrangements. Frankel (1999, p. 30) argues that "intermediate solutions are more likely to be appropriate for many countries than are corner solutions." Williamson (2000), while acknowledging the fragility of intermediate arrangements, argues that these can be redesigned so as to limit their vulnerability of speculative pressures. Leaving aside countries that have not yet gained access to international capital markets, which are a species that will presumably grow increasingly endangered over time, this is not an argument for which I have much sympathy. In my view, the evidence of movement away from the middle is incontrovertible. As Goldstein (2001) observes, the list of countries that have been able to maintain a fixed rate for five years or longer is now very short; at the time of writing it is composed of just two: Argentina and Hong Kong.

ies, therefore, regimes that allow substantial exchange rate flexibility are probably desirable. Some emerging market countries, of course, may go in the other direction—toward hard currency pegs (such as currency boards), supported by the requisite policy discipline and institutional structures."

Thus, an international system of hard pegs and relatively free floats is seen as the monetary component of the new international financial architecture. For members of the "missing middle school," this consensus, together with the observed movement away from intermediate arrangements, is an area of real progress in rationalizing the international financial system (see for example Fischer, 2001).

Less heartening is that many countries—most recently Turkey—have moved away from intermediate arrangements not in a measured way but as the result of a crisis. Also disturbing is the suspicion that a not insignificant number of emerging markets that claim to operate floating rates intervene heavily to damp currency fluctuations, in practice operating what amounts to soft ("noncredible") pegs (Calvo and Reinhart, 2000). Insofar as the authorities have changed the name but not the reality of the exchange rate regime, firms and banks, still confident that they are protected from large currency fluctuations by the authorities' implicit commitment to stabilize the rate, may fail to hedge their exposures, while the authorities, for their part, will fail to invest in the development of a new monetary anchor and a source of credibility independent of the exchange rate. The crisis problem may have been disguised, in other words, but it has not been eliminated.

It is not hard to understand why countries are reluctant to abandon intermediate exchange rate arrangements. Abandoning the national currency for the dollar (or the euro) is a symbolic sacrifice, as acknowledged even by those who believe that dollarization (used henceforth as a generic term) has more benefits than costs. Abandoning a peg for greater flexibility will be a shock to the balance sheets of both the public and private sectors. It will undermine confidence if the exchange rate had previously served as the anchor for monetary policy and if the commitment to peg it had been an important source of policy credibility for the government and the central bank. Knowing that exiting from the peg will be a shock to confidence and it may precipitate a recession, governments are understandably inclined to put off the decision.[21]

It follows that if countries are not going to exit voluntarily from soft pegs, the IMF needs to counter this status-quo bias. The Council of Foreign Rela-

---

[21]Eichengreen and Masson *et al.* (1998) show that exits from pegs have typically been associated with significant recessions. Eichengreen and Rose (2001) provide supporting evidence, generalizing the sample to include de facto as well as de jure pegs and focusing on exits that take place in response to speculative pressure.

tions Task Force on Strengthening the International Financial Architecture (Council on Foreign Relations, 1999) argued that the Fund should provide the appropriate incentives by committing not to provide large-scale financial assistance to governments intent on defending overvalued currency pegs. But the qualification that the Fund should not support "overvalued" currency pegs provides a convenient pretext for exceptions, and the pressure to make exceptions on political grounds will remain great. In other words, the CFR did not explain how such a commitment could be made credible. The Meltzer Commission, while urging the more active use of Article IV consultations to remind countries of the risks associated with pegged rates, did not propose that their abandonment should be a precondition for IMF assistance.

The reality is that the IMF is an institution of many members. Reflecting their diverse structures, histories, and circumstances, there is no consensus among them about the appropriate exchange rate arrangement, forcing the Fund to qualify its recommendations. Nor is it clear that the IMF is any better placed than governments to trade off the political and economic costs of recession now for the benefits of a more robust exchange-rate regime later. The Fund's own status-quo bias is clear in the recent cases of Argentina and Turkey. The institution was a strong supporter of Argentine convertibility until the final months of 2001, reflecting fears that abandoning that regime would be a sharp shock to confidence. In the case of Turkey, the 2000 IMF program sought to sustain the lira's crawling peg regime for 18 months rather than moving immediately to a more flexible rate.

This last case is revealing of the underlying dilemmas. Diagnoses of Turkey's problems were informed by the Asian crisis. The banks had received implicit guarantees as the price of being used as instruments of the government's industrial and agricultural policies. The combination of a pegged exchange rate and an open capital account encouraged them to leverage their bets. A more flexible exchange rate could solve this problem by encouraging the banks to more prudently manage their exposures, but a sudden change in the rate would disturb balance sheets and confidence. Hence, the IMF program sought to move gradually in the direction of greater flexibility over a period of 18 months, at the end of which the banks would have limited their exposures sufficiently that neither they nor the Turkish economy would be destabilized.

The Turkish crisis showed that this program was shaped by wishful thinking. The preconditions for holding the exchange rate stable are formidable when political commitment is tenuous and banks are weak. The knowledge that the authorities plan to move to greater flexibility in the future creates the perception of a one-way bet. And hopes that the banks will hedge their exposures today in response to the knowledge that the exchange rate will be allowed to float more freely tomorrow will be dashed if those banks are public or well connected politically and if tomorrow is not scheduled to come for 18 months. In the end, Turkey is just another example of the difficulties of operating an intermediate arrangement for even a limited period of time.

Post-Asian crisis statements by the U.S. Treasury recommended that emerging markets move toward more flexible rates. This reflected worries that widespread dollarization might create political and diplomatic complications if the Federal Reserve did not adjust U.S. monetary policy to accommodate the needs of the newly dollarized economies, together with skepticism of the workability of monetary union. Europeans have always been more sympathetic to pegs, reflecting lessons drawn from the currency turbulence of the 1930s, and more optimistic about the prospects for monetary union. And now that a European Monetary Union exists, joining it provides an obvious solution for Eastern European countries seeking to eliminate the exchange rate problem.

The IMF, for its part, has overcome its initial skepticism regarding currency boards, dollarization, and monetary unification, having been influenced by the successes of these arrangements in the 1990s. IMF economists on the way to the staff cafeteria traverse a corridor lined with cases displaying the currency notes of the institution's members; throughout the 1990s they regularly referred to this fact, proclaiming that the rule of "one country, one currency" was one of the most robust regularities in monetary economics. Europe's success in launching the euro would appear to have rendered this conviction less firm.[22] And, while not exactly an enthusiast of dollarization, the Fund did not resist Ecuador's decision to adopt the U.S. currency.

But if only the corners are viable, who should move to which one? In Europe, where there is a commitment to political as well as economic integration, monetary union is the best option. Each country enjoys currency stability vis-à-vis its principal trade and financial partners but flexibility useful for facilitating adjustment against the rest of the world. The commitment to political integration allows the creation of institutions of shared governance, in turn enabling each member to have a voice in the common monetary policy. This is a luxury not enjoyed by an El Salvador that unilaterally adopts the dollar or a Hong Kong that pegs to it via a currency board. Absent a comparable commitment to political integration in Latin America and Asia, there are reasons to question whether there exist realistic prospects for monetary union on those continents in coming decades.[23]

---

[22]See for example Asante and Masson (2001), where two Fund economists provide a sympathetic discussion of the case for a monetary union for the Economic Community of West African States (ECOWAS).

[23]I return to this question, with Asia in mind, below.

A hard peg is the obvious solution for small countries with ties to larger neighbors and/or weak institutions. Small countries that trade heavily with a single larger partner and rely on it for external finance satisfy the classic optimum currency area criteria for pegging. It makes eminent sense from this point of view for El Salvador to adopt the U.S. dollar and for Estonia to peg to the euro.[24] Similar arguments can be made for countries with underdeveloped financial markets that leave firms and banks unable to hedge against currency fluctuations, and with weak institutions, chronic budget deficits, and banking-sector problems that prevent the authorities from credibly committing to low inflation. Advocates of dollarization will argue that we have just described the universe of emerging markets. In other words, since all emerging markets are characterized by these conditions, the world is destined to move toward three currency blocs centered on the dollar, the euro, and the yen.[25]

Even leaving politics aside, there are reasons to doubt this forecast. The collapse of Argentina's currency board is indicative of some of the problems with wider dollarization. Brazil, not the United States, is Argentina's most important trading partner. Argentina attracts foreign investment (or hopes to!) from Spanish banks and European bond markets. Hence, its single-currency peg created serious difficulties for the economy when the euro or the real depreciated against the dollar. Asia faces a similar dilemma, as evidenced by the near-fatal consequences in 1997 of the combination of dollar pegs and dollar-yen fluctuations.[26]

Thus, there remains a case for independent floating by countries with the capacity to operate such a system, assuming—contrary to the assertions of the advocates of dollarization—that these countries exist. Such countries will presumably have diversified trade and financial linkages. They will have independent central banks, well regulated financial systems, efficient fiscal institutions, and stable political institutions. These preconditions should enable monetary policy makers to acquire credibility and encourage them to follow sound and stable policies without orienting monetary policy around a particular value for the exchange rate. As their commitment to do so gains credibility, the volatility of the exchange rate (which reflects uncertainty about future policy) will diminish accordingly.

---

[24]Similar arguments can be made for small Caribbean island economies, some Pacific Island economies, and the members of the CFA franc zone.

[25]Unilaterally in the short run (via dollarization or its equivalent) or in more concerted fashion in the long run (via a proliferation of monetary unions).

[26]Frankel and Wei (1994) estimate the implicit weights of the dollar and the yen in the exchange rate targets of Asian countries, and find that the weight attached to the dollar in the most of their currency baskets was 0.9 or higher.

This requires the authorities to articulate and implement an alternative monetary policy operating strategy.[27] The leading candidate is inflation targeting. Inflation targeting entails an institutionalized commitment to price stability as the primary goal of monetary policy, mechanisms rendering the central bank accountable for attaining its monetary policy goals, the public announcement of targets for inflation, and a policy of communicating to the public the rationale for the decisions taken by the central bank.[28] Central bank independence is needed to give the monetary authorities the leeway necessary to commit to price stability. And a stable fiscal policy and banking system are needed to avoid problems of fiscal dominance that would otherwise prevent the central bank from subordinating other goals to the objective of price stability or cause its independence to be undermined.

The multi-dimensional nature of this definition explains why there is no consensus about which emerging markets practice inflation targeting. Brazil, Chile, the Czech Republic, Israel, South Africa, Poland, Colombia, Thailand, Mexico, the Philippines, and South Korea are all cited in this connection. While the length of this list would appear to pose a challenge to those who argue that floating backed by inflation targeting is not viable in emerging markets, there is the question of whether these countries are actually practicing inflation targeting or are really just covertly pegging their currencies. That some, like Israel, also maintain bands for their exchange rates, while others, including South Korea, intervene to limit or offset exchange rate fluctuations, has been pointed to as evidence that they are really covert peggers. And since a soft commitment to peg the exchange rate is the worst of all arrangements, it follows according to this view that these countries would be better off dollarizing.

But the fact that their central banks alter monetary policy when the exchange rate moves may not in fact mean that they are not inflation targeting. Insofar as depreciation is a leading indicator of inflation, the standard inflation targeting framework suggests tightening monetary policy when the exchange rate weakens. This is the prescribed response when there is a change in the direction or availability of capital flows due to, say, a rise in foreign interest

---

[27]Floating, as Calvo (2000) has put it, is not a monetary strategy; it is the absence of a monetary strategy.

[28]This definition, and the subsequent discussion, follows Eichengreen (2001). The policy-relevant case is flexible inflation targeting, when there is also a positive weight on other variables besides inflation—output, for example—in the central bank's reaction function. Strict inflation targeting, in contrast, is when only inflation enters the objective function. Since few central banks and polities are prepared to disregard all other variables under all circumstances, flexible inflation targeting is the policy-relevant case.

rates, or a deterioration in foreign investor sentiment toward the country. A higher foreign interest rate implies less capital inflow for a given domestic interest rate and therefore a weaker currency. As the exchange rate weakens, higher import prices are passed through into inflation. The appropriate response is thus to raise interest rates. This is not because the central bank cares about the exchange rate in and of itself, but because it cares about inflation.

If the disturbance is to the foreign component of aggregate demand (to the terms of trade or export demand), again the exchange rate will weaken, since export revenues will have declined while nothing else affecting the foreign exchange market will have changed in the first instance. In addition, demand will decline, since foreigners are demanding fewer of the country's exports. Now there are two offsetting effects on inflation: while higher import prices will be passed through into inflation, weaker aggregate demand will be deflationary. If the second effect dominates, then inflation will decline with the growth of the gap between potential and current output, and the appropriate response for an inflation-targeting central bank will be to cut interest rates regardless of the weight it attaches to output variability. The more policy relevant case is probably the one in which this shock, by depreciating the exchange rate, is inflationary on balance. If the central bank attaches a high weight to output variability, it still may want to cut interest rates. If, on the other hand, it attaches a high weight to deviations of inflation from target, it may instead raise interest rates to limit currency depreciation and inflation in the short run, while still allowing the exchange rate to adjust eventually to its new long-run equilibrium level. In other words, it will acknowledge that the weakness of demand requires a weaker exchange rate, but it will still smooth the downward adjustment of the currency by leaning against the wind in order to prevent a sharp spike in inflation.

This framework suggests a test of whether countries like South Korea have really begun to practice inflation targeting. Find instances where the shock is to commodity rather than capital markets, since these are the cases where the weakness of output creates a case for interest rate cuts and allowing the exchange rate to adjust. Consider not just the tendency for the central bank to lean against the wind in the short run but also its willingness to allow the exchange rate to adjust subsequently. 2001 is a useful data point insofar as the shock to the Korean economy is mainly from commodity markets (reflecting the U.S. recession, continuing Japanese difficulties, and the high-tech slump). An inflation targeting central bank will tighten as inflation heats up, but it will also allow the exchange rate to adjust if the slump persists. My reading of Korean experience is that the central bank, while concerned with inflation, nonetheless allowed the won to depreciate in 2000-01 with the slowdown in the global electronics industry and therefore in domestic growth. This does not look like fear of floating to me.

A final characteristic of emerging markets that may affect their ability to target inflation is liability dollarization. In many emerging markets, the obligations of banks, corporations, and governments are denominated in foreign currency, while the bulk of their revenues are domestic-currency denominated.[29] When the exchange rate depreciates, their balance sheets suffer, and this "financial accelerator" significantly depresses output and employment.

The simplest way of thinking about liability dollarization is as reducing the response of output to currency depreciation.[30] While depreciation renders domestic goods more competitive, as before, now it also weakens the balance sheets of banks, firms, households, and governments, depressing consumption and investment. Consider the response to a negative shock to capital markets. Weaker consumption and investment due to adverse balance-sheet effects now imply less inflation in the intermediate run. An inflation-targeting central bank will therefore feel less compelled to raise interest rates in order to push up the exchange rate and damp down the increase in import prices. If the shock to the exchange rate emanates instead from commodity markets, higher import prices will still be passed through into inflation, but now aggregate demand will be even weaker than before because of the adverse balance-sheet effects. Since output is lower and inflation is no higher than in the absence of liability dollarization, again there will be less pressure to hike interest rates in order to stabilize the currency and damp down inflation, and more incentive to cut interest rates to stimulate production. Surprisingly, this suggests, regardless of the source of shocks, that reluctance to let the exchange rate adjust will be *less* in the presence of liability dollarization.

While this may seem counterintuitive, it is just a specific illustration of the general point that when the central bank worries more about variables other than inflation, either because those variables have a heavier weight in its objective function or because the parameters of the model cause those other variables to be displaced further from their equilibrium levels (where the latter is the case presently under discussion), it will move more gradually to eliminate discrepancies between actual and target inflation. Because the exchange rate must move more to increase output and employment, and because measures which would limit its fluctuation and thereby reduce im-

---

[29]Insofar as banks and other intermediaries close their open foreign-currency positions by issuing dollar-denominated loans, the liability dollarization of their customers will be greater still.

[30]As it turns out, this is not precisely what those concerned with the perverse effect of exchange rate changes in the presence of liability dollarization have in mind, as I explain momentarily.

ported inflation tend to destabilize the economy, the now weaker tendency for depreciation to stimulate activity means that the central bank will do even less to limit depreciation.[31]

Clearly, those who argue that liability dollarization creates fear of floating have something else in mind, presumably that the balance-sheet effects of currency depreciation are so strong that a cut in interest rates, which weakens the exchange rate, depresses output on balance. In this case, a negative shock to capital markets still fuels inflation through higher import prices, encouraging the authorities to raise rates. But now, in addition, it lowers output through the adverse balance-sheet effect. The appropriate response, which damps down inflation *and* stabilizes output by limiting balance-sheet damage, is to raise interest rates and push the exchange rate back up toward its preshock level. "Fear-of-floating" type behavior results. If the disturbance is instead to commodity markets, the weaker exchange rate again means more imported inflation and lower levels of output.[32]Again, interest rate hikes are the appropriate response to both problems, since a higher interest rate that strengthens the exchange rate not only damps down inflation but also strengthens balance sheets. Again, the central bank will not hesitate to raise interest rates. Again, its response will resemble fear of floating.

This formulation has some peculiar implications. For one, a negative commodity market shock that reduces export demand and depresses output must be offset in the new equilibrium by an appreciated exchange rate, not a depreciated one. This is a world where overvaluation is good for output because its favorable financial effects dominate its adverse competitiveness effects, even in the long run, which hardly seems realistic.

A possible reconciliation is that when the exchange rate depreciates by a large amount, the adverse balance-sheet effects dominate, but when it depreciates by a small amount, the favorable competitiveness effects dominate. Large depreciations cause severe financial distress because they confront banks and firms with asset prices for which they are unprepared while doing little to enhance competitiveness because of the speed with which they are passed through into inflation. For small depreciations, the balance of effects

---

[31]The same is true when the problem in the financial system is maturity mismatches rather than currency mismatches. Again, the more the central bank fears that an interest rate hike designed to damp down inflation will cause financial distress (because the maturity of banks' liabilities is shorter than their assets, or because higher interest rates will increase default rates among bank borrowers), the less sharply it will raise interest rates in the intermediate run to strengthen the exchange rate and limit inflation.

[32]The decline in output is even larger than before because the direct effect of the decline in foreign demand is reinforced by the indirect effect of exchange rate depreciation via its adverse impact on balance sheets.

is the opposite. Small depreciations are more likely therefore to satisfy the conditions for an expansionary devaluation.[33]

If the exchange rate falls sufficiently to enter the first range, then an inflation-targeting central bank will raise interest rates sharply with the goal of pushing up the currency and minimizing the financial damage to banks, firms, and households. But if the depreciation is modest, so too will be the rise in interest rates; the central bank will allow the currency to fall to a new lower level so long as the competitiveness effects continue to dominate the balance-sheet effects.[34]

Thus, whether emerging markets can implement an inflation targeting regime that allows the exchange rate to fluctuate more freely depends on the precise extent and effects of their liability dollarization. If even a small depreciation of the exchange rate threatens to destabilize balance sheets and the macroeconomy (that is, the country immediately enters the zone where depreciation and lower interest rates are contractionary and destabilizing financially), then the central bank will not be willing to let the exchange rate move. Although the preceding propositions for how the central bank should respond flow directly from the standard inflation-targeting framework, inflation targeting and a hard peg are basically indistinguishable under these conditions. If the perceived advantage of inflation targeting is that it permits greater exchange rate flexibility, then the advantages of inflation targeting are correspondingly less in highly dollarized economies. Inflation targeting then has no obvious advantages over a hard peg, which has the merits of simplicity, transparency, and credibility.

For countries where the adverse balance sheet effects dominate only when exchange rate movements exceed a critical threshold, inflation targeting will be viable so long as shocks and exchange rate fluctuations are small, while the desire to intervene and stabilize the exchange rate will dominate when they grow large. The additional exchange rate flexibility promised by inflation targeting will be feasible, but the central bank's appetite for indulging in it will have limits. When those limits are reached, intervention to stabilize the exchange rate will become its overriding objective.[35]

---

[33]This nonlinearity in the effect of the exchange rate on output might seem arbitrary, but in fact it is precisely the way authors like Aghion, Baccheta, and Banerjee (1999) and Krugman (2001) model the interplay of competitiveness and balance-sheet effects: the former dominate for small depreciations but the latter dominate for large ones, producing a nonlinear aggregate demand equation of precisely the sort being assumed here.

[34]In fact, heavy intervention when the exchange rate drops precipitously but light intervention when it fluctuates around normal levels is not unlike the observed behavior of many central banks.

[35]Observe that this commitment to prevent the exchange rate from moving further when it

This discussion suggests that exchange rate arrangements consistent with the new architecture will vary not by region but with the characteristics of individual countries. Small countries that depend heavily on trade and financial transactions with a single larger partner will prefer to peg rigidly or perhaps even to adopt the latter's currency. Larger countries where the extent of liability dollarization is limited, fiscal institutions are reasonably strong, and the political commitment to price stability is firm will prefer to practice inflation targeting and allow the exchange rate to vary. There are examples of both kinds of arrangements in Latin America (contrast El Salvador and Brazil) and Asia (contrast Hong Kong and Korea). The present perspective does not suggest that exchange rate arrangements will be uniform within regions or vary in some systemic way across them. It does not suggest a distinctively Asian solution to the exchange rate problem.

Regional Responses

The previous point notwithstanding, calls are frequently heard for a regional response. The Asian crisis elicited proposals for a new institution to free Asian countries from dependence on the IMF. IMF financial assistance, in the Asian view, was too little, too late, and the Fund's conditions were not well suited to the Asian model. The IMF's insistence on high interest rates as a means of restoring confidence proved counterproductive, given the high debt-equity ratios of corporations in the region. Requiring governments to close problem banks in the midst of the crisis produced a credit crunch, given the dependence of Asian economies on bank finance. The Fund's call for tax increases and public spending cuts was inappropriate for countries that did not enter the crisis with fiscal imbalances and only served to aggravate the recession. IMF surveillance failed to place sufficient weight on the dangers of premature and poorly sequenced capital account liberalization and on the special risks posed by large players in small financial markets. And the Fund's infatuation with flexible exchange rates was incompatible with Asian countries' preference

---

reaches the edge of this band should be credible, since the central bank will not be sacrificing something else in order to stabilize the rate. In the conventional model (without liability dollarization), stabilizing the currency by raising interest rates sacrifices output and employment. In the present model, in contrast, raising rates at this point will be good for output and employment as well as the exchange rate. All this assumes, implicitly, that liability dollarization is an immutable fact. If, on the other hand, it is something that countries can grow out of by strengthening their institutions and policy credibility, and therefore cultivating the ability to borrow in their own currency, then the range of emerging markets for which floating and inflation targeting is a viable option will increase further with time.

for trade-friendly pegs. In response, the concept of an Asia Fund was tabled by the Japanese government soon after the outbreak of the crisis, leading to the negotiations that ultimately culminated in the so-called Chiang Mai Agreement on an Asean+3 network of currency swaps.

As the preceding paragraph makes clear, there are several rationales for institution building at the regional level. The fact that crises have a regional component (Glick and Rose, 1999) sharpens the incentive for neighboring countries to engage in mutual surveillance and to extend assistance to one another in the face of potentially contagious threats to stability. Because intraregional trade is of growing importance (a quarter of Asean's trade is within the grouping and another 17 percent is with Japan) and many Asian countries sell into the same markets outside the region (whether measured by the geographical direction of trade or the similarity of its commodity composition), unilateral exchange rate depreciation can seriously erode the competitiveness of a country's neighbors.[36] The popular perception is that many of these countries have similar economic structures and, by implication, vulnerabilities; in conjunction with the fact that they have common creditors, this implies that difficulties in one can undermine investor sentiment and the availability of finance to the others.

The subtext here is that the conditions attached to foreign assistance would be better attuned to the realities of the Asian model were they formulated by Asian countries for Asian countries. Asian policy makers, the argument goes, better understand the distinctive characteristics of the Asian model, allowing them to reach appropriate conclusions about the structure of assistance and conditionality. Obviously, this is a disputable point: it is difficult to think of three economies whose structures differ more than South Korea, Hong Kong, and China.[37]

It is hard to quibble with the argument for a market in ideas. The IMF has no monopoly on macroeconomic and financial wisdom. Regional funds are presented as a mechanism for intensifying this competition and allowing good ideas to drive out bad. But would they? Here it is important to distinguish between technical assistance and financial assistance. There is no reason to discourage countries from taking technical assistance from the provider with the best track record.[38] But development assistance is not the core competency

---

[36]These data are for total exports in 1998.

[37]In addition, this argument may itself sow the seeds of contagion: by advancing the notion that there is such a thing as the Asian model, it may encourage the belief that similar problems lurk in other Asian countries when one of them succumbs to financial difficulties.

[38]Information asymmetries may make it difficult for governments to quickly identify the most efficient supplier, but with time one imagines that they will be able to judge by results.

of the IMF; rather, it is domain of the World Bank, the regional development banks (including the Asian Development Bank), national agencies such as USAID, and nongovernmental organizations.[39] There is already a market for ideas, in other words. But in the case of financial assistance in these of crisis, it is not clear that competition among funding agencies will result in the good ideas crowding out the bad. Governments will have an incentive to shop around for the most generous assistance and the least onerous terms. Only if one is convinced that IMF conditionality is uniformly too strict and its terms too paltry will competition guarantee better outcomes. Those who see the IMF as too willing to lend and the resulting moral hazard as corrosive of market discipline will not be convinced.[40]

Among the most vocal proponents of a regional response are those who advocate a cooperative exchange-rate stabilization arrangement for Asia. The most prominent proposal is for a common basket peg with weights on both the U.S. and Japanese currencies.[41] The basket structure of the peg would absorb many of the effects of yen-dollar fluctuations, insulating Asia's economy from an important source of shocks from outside the region, while common weights in the different baskets would rule out intra-regional exchange rate fluctuations due to fluctuations in non-Asian currencies.[42] The second element in particular presupposes cooperation at the regional level.

---

[39]One may argue that the technical assistance needed by governments to gather and disseminate information on fiscal and financial affairs is part of the IMF's core competency. But once one moves from here only slightly, for example to technical assistance for the development of prudential supervision and regulation, there is at least as strong an argument for delivery by other institutions like the World Bank.

[40]Thus, to reassure those concerned with the scope for moral hazard, proponents of an Asian Fund have always insisted that this new arrangement would complement rather than substitute for IMF assistance and conditionality. But the implicit tensions remain. They are evident, for example, in the latest incarnation of the Asean+3 swap arrangement. The agreement at Chiang Mai provided that only 10 percent of the total bilateral swap could be disbursed without linking it to an IMF agreement. Malaysia reportedly lobbied for a much larger fraction but was forced to give way in the face of an opposing consensus. But the Malaysians reportedly obtained the signatories of the final agreement to agree that all swaps would consider the "economic conditions" of the countries requiring them, which may open the door to swaps not linked to IMF conditionality.

[41]Variants of the common-basket-peg proposal focusing on the need for agreement on the weights of the basket and less on the need for swaps and surveillance are Kwan (1998) and Williamson (1999).

[42]But there are some difficult issues lurking here, like the appropriate choice of weights. Williamson distinguishes weights based on trade shares and trade elasticities. One might also ask whether weights related to trade flows or financial flows are more appropriate in a financially globalized world and wonder how to calibrate the latter. I see no reason to discuss here schemes for an Asian monetary union (and even schemes for an Asian Monetary System as a stepping stone to a monetary union, as in Dieter, 2000), which are political non-starters.

But dollar-yen fluctuations are not the only source of shocks to Asian financial markets. Intra-regional exchange-rate fluctuations are not the only transmission belt. In a world of high capital mobility, simply declaring common basket pegs is not enough to ensure their viability. It does not insulate the economies in question from all disturbances, nor does it ensure the robustness of the resulting exchange rate system. Sustainability may require very extensive financial assistance to protect the participating currencies against speculative pressures. This, in turn, presupposes institution building to lend credibility to that commitment and to render it incentive compatible. And to the extent that currency pegs can be laid low by financial problems internal to the region (banking-sector problems, for example), robustness will require measures strengthening prudential supervision and regulation.[43] This presupposes institutions of mutual surveillance to render this commitment credible and incentive compatible. The countries extending the swaps will be prepared to do so only if they believe that those receiving them will not follow reckless policies leading to reckless demands for support—and only if they believe that they will be paid back.

Thus, financial support on the scale needed to sustain a regional exchange rate stabilization agreement is likely to be forthcoming only if mechanisms are developed compelling the participants to strengthen their financial policies and systems, together with institutions to monitor their compliance and sanctions for failure to comply. By implication, the hope that a regional arrangement of this sort would not have to be burdened by the oversight and conditions that accompany IMF programs is likely to be disappointed.

The Asean+3 system of swaps and credits illustrates several of these dilemmas. Swap agreements already existed between some Asean members at the time of their 1997 crisis, but these were ineffective in containing the crisis. One diagnosis of this failure was that their scale was inadequate; hence, the new arrangement, encompassing not just Asean but also China, South Korea, and Japan, marshals more than $800 billion of reserves. This is an impressive number, but it pales in comparison with the financial resources of investors worldwide. Under what conditions, then, can such a system deliver the promised exchange rate stability? Only when its members pursue financial reforms that limit the likelihood that their reserves will have to be utilized.[44] In particular, only when they have strong financial systems will they be able to raise interest rates to defend their currencies (without ratcheting up the pressure on

---

[43]Kaminsky and Reinhart (1998) have shown that banking sector problems tend to precede currency crises: often it is the former that play the casual role in twin crises.

[44]This is the conclusion of *Financial Times* (2001).

already fragile financial institutions to intolerable levels) rather than immediately appealing for foreign support. It is no coincidence, then, that the Chiang Mai Initiative committed its signatories to cooperation on prudential supervision and mutual surveillance of their banking systems.[45] Whether this commitment will be pursued with vigor is not yet clear. But if the signatories are serious about extending significant financial assistance to one another through their network of swap lines, then there will be pressure to move in this direction. It is also revealing that the Asean+3 countries linked the expansion of their swap arrangements to the development of an Early Warning System designed to identify the need for policy adjustments that might avert or minimize the need to draw. With the expansion of the swap network to include China, South Korea, and Japan, there is now predictable discussion of the need to expand the Early Warning System. One wonders whether the members would be willing to extend financial support for the exchange rates of countries that did not heed their early warnings, and if so what conditions would be attached to such assistance.

It is not clear, in other words, that this arrangement will ultimately oblige its participants to meet fewer conditions than its IMF analog. One waits to see what conditions the strong-currency countries attach when they are asked to extend significant credits.[46]

This brings us finally to IMF conditionality. The expansion in the number and range of conditions attached to IMF loans became a bone of contention following Asia's crisis. The feeling was that the Fund's structural conditions

---

[45]Government of Japan (2001, p. 5).

[46]My skepticism that a system of collective pegs will be sustainable even if Asian countries take very significant steps in the direction of stronger surveillance is well known (see Bayoumi, Eichengreen, and Mauro, 2000). The exceptionally large intergovernmental loans needed to sustain such a system in a world of high capital mobility require a very high level of political commitment. In a world of sovereign states, there is no guarantee that the borrowing country will make the adjustments necessary to pay the money back. And, with the financial stakes so high, this will render the countries extending it reluctant to lend. These pressures were evident even in Europe in 1992-93, where the commitment to political integration was unrivaled and the strong currency countries participating in the European Monetary System were officially obliged to provide the weak currency countries unlimited support. Thus, I doubt that an Asian system of common basket pegs or bands would be sustainable. Rather, it would heighten fragility. It would be a move in precisely the wrong direction. Its defenders will object that the Chiang Mai Agreement commits its signatories to provide financial support but not to repeg their currencies. However, there is a danger that the existence of this swap network could encourage the participants to consider the restoration of their pegs if they are confident of foreign support. In this sense, this arrangement is a potentially serious source of moral hazard. I see this danger as implicit in some of the published remarks by finance ministers to the Third Asia-Europe Finance Ministers' Meeting in Kobe in January 2001, and in the discussion paper jointly prepared by French and Japanese staff for that meeting (Government of Japan, 2001).

were invasive, that they were formulated without reference to the government's capacity to muster support for reform, and, to the extent that they pointed out structural weaknesses of the program countries, that they did more to destroy than to strengthen confidence. The 1997 Indonesian program is seen as typifying the problem: its loan conditions dealt with reforestation, the national car program, local content programs for motor vehicles, the compulsory 2 percent after-tax charitable contribution, restrictive market agreements for cement and paper, the forced planting of sugar cane, the introduction of a micro-credit scheme for small businesses, and the elimination of the Clove Marketing Board.[47] An Asian Fund would be less invasive, the argument runs, given the tradition in the region of non-interference in other countries' economies.

Although the number of structural conditions attached to IMF programs peaked in 1997, the increase in such measures was not specific to Asia's crisis. The number of structural conditions per program more than doubled between the late 1980s and early 1990s and doubled again between the first and second half of the most recent decade (IMF, 2001a, p. 3, Figure 1). Explanations for the trend include the priority that came to be attached to restoring growth in highly-indebted countries in the 1980s (complaints that the Fund placed too much weight on stabilization and therefore was too tolerant of recession led to this emphasis on growth, which in turn required structural reform) and the emphasis on structural transformation and institution building in formerly centrally planned economies in the 1990s.[48] While these experiences help to explain why the Fund became accustomed to giving growth-related advice and applying structural conditions, they do not justify its preoccupation with micro- and sectoral reforms in East Asia, a region with an admirable record of growth and no history of deep structural problems. They do not explain why the conditions attached to the Fund's 1997 and 1998 programs with Indonesia, South Korea, and Thailand were so numerous and detailed.

In a sense, the fact that most Asian countries had not entered their crisis with chronic macroeconomic imbalances was the very observation that motivated the emphasis on structural reforms. If macroeconomic imbalances were not the problem, then macroeconomic performance criteria were not the solution. If it was structural weaknesses in Asian financial markets that caused the crisis

---

[47]See Goldstein (2000).

[48]The irony is that the demand for more emphasis on supply-side structural reforms came from the developing countries themselves, which now see the IMF's emphasis on structural reforms as excessive, but were then critical of the Fund as being to demand- and short-run oriented (Goldstein, 2000). To an extent it is also true that national legislatures and NGOs increasingly saw IMF Letters of Intent as a vehicle for leveraging their preferred agendas in developing countries, a strategy that some of them now presumably regret.

to take such a toll, then it was structural reform of financial markets that was called for. The argument for structural conditions on loans extended in response to the crisis is then the same as the argument for international standards to encourage the upgrading of financial markets and institutions before the fact.[49] That the Asian crisis, like many other recent crises, was a capital-account crisis rather than a current-account crisis inevitably blurred the line between measures that were needed to address the underlying instabilities and measures that were not. Solving a current-account crisis simply requires measures that will reduce absorption, while solving a capital-account crisis requires restoring confidence, which is a much more nebulous matter.

Still, if it is crises in financial markets that the IMF is in the business of averting, and flaws in the structure and regulation of financial markets that are the problem, then it is hard to justify conditions related to government policies remote from financial markets, such as reforestation or clove marketing. In principle, there is a line between structural measures that promise to significantly strengthen financial institutions and markets and others that are only peripherally related to macroeconomics and finance. The IMF, not unaware of the backlash that some of its more invasive conditions provoked, has attempted to take this distinction on board.[50] To raise the consciousness of staff and management, it has circulated an Interim Guidance Note on Streamlining Structural Conditionality that emphasizes "the need to limit conditionality to those measure that are critical for achievement of the program's macroeconomic objectives."[51]

---

[49]What we can call the "new institutional macroeconomics," which responded to evidence of chronic macroeconomic imbalances (and the manifest failure of program countries to meet the Fund's macroeconomic performance criteria) sought to discover deeper determinants of macroeconomic policies, and found them in institutional arrangements like central bank independence and the centralization of fiscal policy making processes, also led the Fund increasingly to emphasize institutional reforms as a way of increasing the likelihood that countries would be able to sustain the macroeconomic adjustments recommended in the course of Article IV surveillance or required as conditions of IMF loans.

[50]A recent IMF review of conditionality acknowledges that "in many cases, conditionality has been applied (or has been construed as applying) to reforms that are not really critical to the Fund's decision of whether to continue its financing" (IMF, 2001a, p. 5). And the Fund's new managing director has clearly signaled his desire to streamline Fund conditionality, as has the new U.S. Treasury Secretary.

[51]This statement (IMF, 2001b, p. 31) is overly restrictive, in my view, since it appears to emphasize the macroeconomic to the exclusion of the financial, or at least to fail to elaborate the links between the two. Others have gone still further in the restrictive direction. Thus, the Meltzer Commission essentially recommends abolishing program conditionality, arguing that the IMF should instead prequalify countries for assistance (on the basis of the strength of their banking systems and fiscal policies) and then lend to the qualified unconditionally at high interest rates.

But determining precisely which measures are critical for macroeconomic balance and financial stability is easier said than done.[52] Some would go as far as to argue that reform of the Indonesian timber monopoly was essential to signal a new resolve to root out cronyism and corruption, and that the confidence of financial markets could not be regained in the absence of that resolve. Even the Indonesia program, in this view, was not overly ambitious or detailed. But even those who criticize these conditions as going too far would acknowledge the difficulty of devising general rules for what kinds of reforms are and are not needed for the restoration of investor confidence.[53] We know to be suspicious of a consensus—in this case in favor of simplified conditionality—when we see everyone from the Meltzer Commission to the Council on Foreign Relations to the Group of Twenty Four to the IMF chiming in. We suspect that they really have different things in mind, at least when it comes to moving from principle to practice.

Moving from process-based to results-based criteria is an obvious way of streamlining conditionality. The IMF's continued willingness to lend could be based on the authorities' observed success in recapitalizing the banking system, for example, rather than on the specific steps taken with regard to problem banks. This would avoid micro-management of reforms and give the national authorities more leeway to adopt measures appropriate to local circumstances. But insofar as results take time to materialize, it would be inconsistent with the G-7 preference for shorter-duration loans to discourage chronic borrowing and for front-loading IMF disbursements to strengthen confidence.

The proof of the pudding is in the eating: one may ask, for example, whether the Fund's recent programs for Argentina and Turkey are significantly leaner than their predecessors. This is hard for those on the outside to judge: we have access only to the Letter of Intent (LOI), which describes not only policy measures on which the Fund's financing is conditional but also other aspects of the authorities' policy program. For what it is worth, Argentina's December 2000 LOI, together with the attached Memorandum of Economic Policies, describes measures designed to update and strengthen antitrust legislation, a

---

[52]The Financial Stability Forum's 12 standards deserving priority of implementation presumably qualify, since they are directly related to macroeconomic policy and transparency, financial market infrastructure, and prudential supervision and regulation. Yet there is deep suspicion in developing countries of proposals for extending IMF conditionality into these areas. See, for example, Mohammed (2000).

[53]The Fund's 1979 "Guidelines on Conditionality" (IMF, 1999) similarly called for parsimony, the need to limit performance criteria to the minimum, and the importance of paying regard to a country's social and political objectives and circumstances; look what happened subsequently.

new regulatory framework to support development of the ports system, the consolidation of three nutritional programs, and a new regulatory framework for the telecommunications sector.[54] Turkey's LOI of January 2001 includes provisions related to reform of the tobacco sector and the rolling out of tax identification numbers.[55]

Thus, efforts to refocus and streamline IMF conditionality are one place where Asia's message has been heard.[56] But only time will tell whether the Fund can successfully implement the principle. Could a regional fund do better? There is no obvious reason for thinking so.

Summary Assessment

I now return to the questions posed at the outset: how meaningful are the changes to the international financial architecture currently underway—are they merely cosmetic or do they constitute a significant attempt to modify the structure and management of the international financial system? Different readers will have different views of whether the glass is half empty or half full. Mine is that the effort to extend international standards to areas beyond the strictly monetary is, or at least promises to become, a very significant development affecting the structure and stability of the international financial system. Upgrading macroeconomic policy and transparency, financial market infrastructure, and financial regulation and supervision is essential for stability in a financially integrated world. And international standards, with pressure to comply to be applied by multilateral surveillance, IMF conditionality, regulation, and market discipline, are the only available means to this end in a world of sovereign states. Significant obstacles remain before this initiative can be operationalized: the design of the relevant standards is contested, there is resistance to their use in IMF conditionality, and the markets have not yet displayed a readiness to rely on them when making lending decisions. Still, I can

---

[54]It enumerates a total of 18 structural benchmarks.

[55]The May 2001 LOI and attached Memorandum of Economic Policies are more tightly focused on banking sector reform, fiscal policy and transparency, debt management and privatization, but they include a total of 27 structural policy conditions.

[56]The cost and term of IMF loans is a different story. The Fund's September 2000 changes shorten the repayment period and increase the cost of borrowing. While these changes are designed to discourage repeated and extended borrowings, which is not a situation in which Asian countries have found themselves in the past and not one they presumably expect to find themselves in the future, these reform are still moves away from the more liberal lending terms that many Asian governments presumably had in mind.

imagine looking back years from now and seeing the standards-centered initiatives of the late 20th and early 21st century as a significant turning point.

The question of whether the glass is half empty or half full also applies to changes to the exchange rate system. My view is that the observed tendency for countries to evacuate the middle ground between very hard pegs and relatively free floats is important progress. It is a step in the right direction. Less reassuring is continued disagreement about the appropriate exchange rate arrangement for countries in particular circumstances, the reluctance of emerging markets to allow their currencies to fluctuate, and the impulse to restore soft pegs and bands on a regional basis. Hopefully it will not take another round of crises to demonstrate which of these tendencies are positive and which are not.

Reforms of IMF lending and conditionality are clearly in the manner of fine tuning rather than radical changes. Modest increases in interest rates and reductions in term are unlikely to do much to modify the propensity for governments to borrow from the Fund. A higher threshold of relevance to program objectives, more reliance on institutions like the World Bank in areas that are outside the core competency of the Fund, and a modest reduction in the number of structural benchmarks that a country must meet hardly represent a radical recasting of IMF conditionality. They fall short of the recommendations of the Meltzer Commission, and for good reason. My view is that this is unavoidable—that conditionality must be broader and therefore fuzzier in a financially integrated world where crises are driven by capital-account problems.

Do these initiatives address Asia's concerns about the volatility of financial markets, the structure of conditionality, and the operation of the international monetary system? The answer is "incompletely, at best." A more satisfactory outcome requires that Asian countries represent their views more effectively and that the multilaterals reform their voting procedures and deliberations to better enable those views to be heard. But it also requires understanding that the volatility of financial markets, the fragility of pegged exchange rates, and the breadth of IMF conditionality are unavoidable in a world of financial integration. No changes in the international financial architecture that fall short of turning back the clock on globalization can change these uncomfortable facts.

References

Aghion, Philippe, Philippe Bachetta, and Abhijit Banerjee, 1999, "Capital Markets and Instability in Open Economies," unpublished manuscript, Study Center Gerzensee.

Asante, R.D., Paul Robert Masson, and Jacqueline Irvine, 2001, "The Pros and Cons of Expanded Monetary Union in West Africa," *Finance and Development*, No. 38 (Washington, D.C.: International Monetary Fund), March.

Bayoumi, Tamim, Barry Eichengreen, and Paolo Mauro, 2000, "On Regional Monetary Arrangements for ASEAN," *Journal of the Japanese and International Economies*, No. 2, pp. 121-48.

Bordo, Michael, and Hugh Rockoff, 1996, "The Gold Standard as a Good-Housekeeping Seal of Approval," *Journal of Economic History*, No. 56, pp. 389-428.

Bordo, Michael, Barry Eichengreen, and Douglas Irwin, 1999, "Is Globalization Today Really Different than Globalization a Hundred Years Ago?" *Brookings Trade Forum*, pp. 1-72.

Calvo, Guillermo, 2000, "Capital Markets and the Exchange Rate, with Special Reference to the Dollarization Debate in Latin America," unpublished manuscript, University of Maryland at College Park.

Calvo, Guillermo, and Carmen Reinhart, 2000, "Fear of Floating," NBER Working Paper No.7993 (Cambridge, Massachusetts: National Bureau of Economic Research.)

Clark, Alistair, 2000 , "International Standards and Codes," *Financial Stability Review* (December), pp. 162-168.

Council on Foreign Relations, 1999, *Safeguarding Prosperity in a Global Financial System: The Future International Financial Architecture* (New York: Council on Foreign Relations).

Dieter, Heribert, 2000, "Monetary Regionalism: Regional Integration Without Financial Crises," CSGR Working Paper No. 52/00 (University of Warwick: Centre for the Study of Globalisation and Regionalisation).

Eatwell, John, and Lance Taylor, 2000, *Global Finance at Risk: The Case for International Regulation* (New York: New Press).

Eichengreen, Barry, 2000, "Strengthening the International Financial Architecture: Where Do We Stand?" *ASEAN Economic Bulletin*, No. 17, pp. 175-192.

_____, 2001, "Can Emerging Markets Float? Should They Inflation Target?" unpublished manuscript, University of California Berkeley, http://emlab.berkeley.edu / users/eichengr/website.htm.

Eichengreen, Barry, and Harold James, 2001, "International Monetary Reform in Two Ages of Globalization (and In Between)," paper presented to the NBER Conference on Globalization and History, Santa Barbara, May 4-6.

Eichengreen, Barry, and Paul Masson, with Hugh Bredenkamp, Barry Johnston, Javier Hamann, Esteban Jadresic, and Inci Otker, 1998, *Exit Strategies: Policy Options for Countries Seeking Greater Exchange Rate Flexibility*, IMF Occasional Paper No. 168 (Washington, D.C.: International Monetary Fund).

Eichengreen, Barry, and Andrew Rose, 2001, "Does It Pay to Defend Against a Speculative Attack?" in Michael Dooley and Jeffrey Frankel (eds.), *Currency Crises in Emerging Markets* (Chicago: University of Chicago Press).

480   *Barry Eichengreen*

Financial Stability Forum, 2000, "Report of the Follow-Up Group on Incentives to Foster Implementation of Standards," http://www/fsforum.org/Reports.htm (August 13).

Financial Times, 2001, "Asia Links Up" (April 9), p. 12.

Finger, J. Michael, and P. Schuler, 1999, "Implementation of the Uruguay Round Commitments: The Development Challenges," unpublished manuscript, the World Bank.

Fischer, Stanley, 2000, "Presentation to the International Financial Institution Advisory Commission," unpublished manuscript, IMF (March).

_____, 2001, "Exchange Rate Regimes: Is the Bipolar View Correct?" Distinguished Lecture on Economics in Government, *Journal of Economic Perspectives*, Vol. 15, (Spring), pp. 3-24.

_____, 2000, *The International Financial System: Crisis and Reform,* Robbins Lectures, delivered at the London School of Economics, 29-31 October (processed).

Frankel, Jeffrey A., 1999, "No Single Currency Regime is Right for All Countries or at All Times," *Essays in International Finance* No. 215, Princeton University: International Finance Section, Department of Economics.

Frankel, Jeffrey A., and Shang-Jin Wei, 1994, "Yen Bloc or Dollar Bloc? Exchange Rate Policies in East Asian Countries," in Takatoshi Ito and Anne Krueger (eds.), *Macroeconomic Linkages: Saving, Exchange Rates, and Capital Flows* (Chicago: University of Chicago Press).

Glick, Reuven, 2000, "Fixed or Floating: Is It Still Possible to Manage in the Middle?" paper prepared for the conference on Financial Markets and Policies in East Asia, Asia-Pacific School of Economics and Management, ANI, Canberra (September 4-5).

Glick, Reuven, and Andrew Rose, 1999, "Contagion and Trade: Why Are Currency Crises Regional?" *Journal of International Money and Finance,* No. 18, pp. 603-617.

Goldstein, Morris, 2000, "IMF Structural Programs," in Martin Feldstein (ed.), *Economic and Financial Crises in Emerging Market Economies* (Chicago: University of Chicago Press).

Goldstein, Morris, 2001, "An Evaluation of Proposals to Reform the International Financial Architecture," paper presented to the NBER Conference on the Management of Financial Crises, Monterey (March 28-30).

Government of Japan, 2001, "Exchange Rate Regimes for Emerging Market Economies," discussion paper jointly prepared by French and Japanese staff for the ASEM Finance Ministers' Meeting, Kobe (January), http://www.mof.go.jp/english/asem1aseme03i2. htm.

International Monetary Fund, 1999, *Selected Decision and Selected Documents of the International Monetary Fund,* Vol. 24 (Washington, D.C.: International Monetary Fund).

_____, 2001a, "Conditionality in Fund-Supported Programs— Overview" (February 20), www.imf.org/external.

_____, 2001b, "Conditionality in Fund-Supported Programs—Policy Issues" (February 16), www.imf.org/external.

International Monetary Fund and World Bank, 2001, "Assessing the Implementation of Standards: A Review of Experience and Next Steps," approved by Jack Boorman and Kemal Dervis (January 11).

Kaminsky, Graciela, and Carmen Reinhart, 1998, "The Twin Crises: The Causes of Banking and Balance-of-Payments Problems," *American Economic Review,* Vol. 89, pp. 473-500.

Krugman, Paul, 2001, "Crises: The Next Generation," unpublished manuscript, Princeton University.

Kwan, C.H., 1998, "Yen for an Anchor: Asia in Search of a New Exchange Rate Regime," in Ramon Moreno and Gloria Pasadilla (eds.), *Monetary Problems of the International Economy* (Tokyo: Asian Development Bank Institute).

McKinnon, Ronald, 2000, "After the Crisis, the East Asian Dollar Standard Resurrected: An Interpretation of High-Frequency Exchange-Rate Pegging," unpublished manuscript, Stanford University.

Meltzer, Alan, et al., 2000, *Report of the International Financial Institution Advisory Commission,* (Washington, D.C.: International Financial Institution Advisory Commission).

Mishkin, Frederic, 2001, "Financial Policies and the Prevention of Financial Crises in Emerging Market Countries," NBER Working Paper No. 8087 (Cambridge Massachusetts: National Bureau of Economic Research).

Mohammed, Aziz Ali, 2000, "The Future Role of the IMF: A Developing Country Point of View," in Jan Joost Teunissen (ed.), *Reforming the International Financial System: Crisis Prevention and Response* (The Hague: Fondad), pp. 193-209.

Mussa, Michael, Paul Masson, Alexander Swoboda, Esteban Jadresic, Paolo Mauro, and Andrew Berg, 2000, *Exchange Rate Regimes in an Increasingly Integrated World Economy,* IMF Occasional Paper No. 193 (Washington D.C.: International Monetary Fund).

Park, Yung Chul, and Yunjong Wang, 2001, "What Kind of International Financial Architecture for an Integrated World Economy?" paper prepared for the Asian Economic Panel, Cambridge, Massachusetts (April 26-27).

Pastor, Katherina, 2000, "The Standardization of Law and its Effect on Developing Countries," G-24 Discussion Paper No. 4 (New York and Geneva: United Nations).

Soludo, Charles C., and Musunuru Sam Rao, 1999, "Potential Social Impacts of the New Global Financial Architecture," unpublished manuscript, University of Nigeria.

Soros, George, 2000, *Open Society: Reforming Global Capitalism* (New York: Public Affairs Press).

Summers, Lawrence H., 2000, "International Financial Crises: Causes, Prevention, and Cures," *American Economic Review Papers and Proceedings,* Vol. 90, pp. 1-16.

Williamson, John, 1999, "The Case for a Common Basket Peg for East Asian Currencies," in Stefan Collignon, Jean Pisani-Ferry, and Yung Chul Park (eds.), *Exchange Rate Policies in Emerging Asian Countries* (London: Routledge), pp. 327-344.

Williamson, John, 2000, *Exchange Rate Regimes for Emerging Markets: Reviving the Intermediate Option,* Policy Analyses in International Economics No. 60 (Washington, D.C.: Institute for International Economics).

Wyplosz, Charles, 1999, "International Financial Stability," in Inge Kaul, Isabelle Grunberg, and Marc A. Stern (eds.), *Global Public Goods: International Cooperation in the 21ˢᵗ Century* (New York: Oxford University Press), pp. 152-189.

14 A Framework for Exchange Rate Policy in Korea

Michael Dooley, Rudi Dornbusch, and Yung Chul Park

The monetary policy and exchange rate regime that served Korea well for many years ended in crisis in 1997. The regime that collapsed was characterized by a tightly managed nominal exchange rate and domestic financial markets that were controlled by the government and largely closed to international transactions. The practical question for authorities over the next few years is what monetary and exchange rate regime will best promote the objectives of maintaining economic and financial stability as financial markets are liberalized.

Our basic proposal is that the powerful policy tool, interest rate policy, be used to attain a "flexible" inflation target. Flexibility in this context means that the authorities also care about short-run fluctuations in domestic output and employment. The less powerful policy tool, sterilized intervention in the foreign exchange market, would be used to limit day to day changes in exchange rates.

We argue that the government should continue to be an important *participant* in the foreign exchange market but not attempt to establish a *level* for the exchange rate. Our proposal will involve intervention that is triggered by exchange rate volatility but constrained by an announced target for the government's overall net foreign asset position. The objective of this regime is to allow the government to participate in the foreign exchange market in a way that contributes to economic stability and promotes the development of the private sector's participation in foreign exchange and financial markets.

The 1997 crisis was, in our view, caused by the inability of the exchange rate regime to coexist with a more open and competitive financial market. There are many historical precedents for the sequence of financial liberalization, crisis, and reform of exchange rate and monetary policy arrangements. Industrial countries experienced a very similar sequence in the early 1970s and, like Korea today, were forced to adapt to the new reality with very limited information about how the new system would work.

The question now is how exchange rate arrangements should evolve in order to insure a sustained economic recovery. It is important that the *interim* regime promote economic stability and growth and that it be consistent with a wide range of monetary regimes that might become available in the future.

At present the Korean government has considerable discretion in managing the exchange rate and financial policy. In order to improve policy transparency and credibility, market intervention should be carried out according to a set of rules. The rules proposed in this study have the following three components:

(i) Sterilized intervention—changes in the composition of the central bank's assets between domestic assets (won) and foreign assets (denominated in foreign currencies) will be relied on to moderate volatility in daily nominal exchange rates in excess of three percentage points against a basket of the dollar, Euro, and yen. This rule could be extended to resist cumulative movements of more than 6 percent in one week.

(ii) A target level for net foreign assets (foreign exchange reserve net of foreign currency liabilities and derivative positions) would be established. Deviations in the level of reserves generated in limiting exchange rate volatility would be eliminated over a six-month period according to an announced rule. The target level of reserves should be large enough to meet a bank run initially, but with accumulation of the experience in managing reserves, the level could be adjusted to balance the cost and benefit of maintaining a large stock of foreign assets.

(iii) A flexible inflation-targeting rule would be established. A short-term interest rate would be used as an intermediate target to stabilize output in the short run and inflation in the long run.

In the current situation the government has considerable discretion in managing exchange rate and monetary policy. In our view, rules are needed for three reasons. First, Korea's exchange rate policy is important to its trading partners. It is necessary, therefore, to effectively communicate what the policy is and how it will be carried out. Because the government will be an active participant in the foreign exchange market, it is crucial that its intentions be clear both to private market participants and to its trading partners. One of the attractions of the adjustable peg system was that the government's objectives were clear and summarized by the target for the nominal exchange rate. Indeed it is easy to forget that the Bretton Woods system that served the industrial countries well before their financial markets were liberalized was initially seen as a way to avoid competitive devaluation.

Second, the success of a regime that accepts some level of nominal exchange rate volatility depends on the private sector's ability and willingness to provide liquid and efficient foreign exchange markets. Markets can deal with volatility if market participants are free to profit from trading strategies that exploit volatility. This is more likely if the government's intervention in the market is limited. The market's ability to limit movements in exchange rates away from fundamentals requires clear and steady economic policies. Clearly, markets are likely to function better if the government's objectives and policies are clearly understood and consistently pursued.

Finally, in the absence of a tightly controlled nominal exchange rate the authorities will need to explain their monetary policy objectives and performance in terms of some variable or set of variables other than the exchange rate. We argue below that a flexible target for inflation has many advantages for Korea.

The rules we propose have three components. Changes in the *composition* of the central bank's assets between domestic assets (denominated in won) and foreign assets (denominated in foreign currencies) would allow the central bank to *participate* in the foreign exchange market without altering the monetary base. The objective of this participation, sometimes referred to as sterilized intervention, would normally be to moderate volatility in daily nominal exchange rates in excess of one to three percentage points against a basket of the big three currencies. The rule could be extended to resist cumulative movements of more than 3-6 percent in one week. This rule would be symmetric for appreciation and depreciation of the won as long as net reserves remain within a normal range. The authorities would not be obliged to intervene if they considered large changes in the rate an appropriate reaction to changes in the economic environment.

A target *level* for net foreign assets (foreign exchange reserves net of foreign currency liabilities and derivative positions) would be established. The statistical definition of net foreign assets follows directly from the objective for intervention. In altering its net foreign asset position the government is imposing a mirror image change in the private sector's net currency exposure. The basic idea is that if private market participants are forced to take a larger net position in a currency they will be less likely to push the exchange rate to levels that are likely to be reversed. Standard accounting practice for measuring currency exposure for private entities are comprehensive in that they consider conventional financial assets and liabilities as well as derivative positions that affect the financial net worth of the firm when exchange rates change. These accounting practices are easily adapted to measure the net foreign currency position of the government.

Altering the intervention rule would reverse deviations in the level of reserves generated in limiting exchange rate volatility. If reserves deviate by more than 25 percent from their target level the intervention rule would become asymmetric. If reserves fall (rise) by more than 25 percent subsequent daily depreciation (appreciation) of the won up to 3 percent would be permitted. If reserves deviate by more than 50 percent the rule would be again adjusted to 3 percent in the direction that moves away from their target level and 0.5 percent in the direction that moves reserves toward their target level.

An asymmetric intervention rule could generate losses for the government. Clearly if the public knows that the government will be a net seller of domestic currency bonds in order to rebuild reserves this will, other things equal, depress the exchange rate. But this is appropriate since the initial intervention artificially supported the currency. Moreover, there is no guarantee that the exchange rate will ever rise to levels that make the intervention profitable. But there is no one way bet typical of a regime in which the authorities are obliged to defend a currency peg.

We would expect that in establishing its target the government would balance the cost of maintaining a stock of liquid foreign assets against the benefit of being able to mitigate the effects of swings in private capital flows. In the early days of an interim regime the desired stock of reserves might be quite large by historical standards. Recent experience suggests that net reserves of 50 percent of GDP would not be unreasonable.

Changes in the *level* of the central bank's total assets, and therefore the monetary base, would allow the central bank to determine a short-term interest rate in Korean financial markets. The practice of using a short-term interest rate as an intermediate target to stabilize output in the short run and inflation in the long run has become widely established in both industrial and developing countries. Inflation targeting would be fully consistent with the objective of liberalizing and strengthening domestic financial markets.

Policy Challenges

The Current Account, Net Debt, and Capital Flows

We argue above that a simple set of rules for intervention can go a long way toward insuring that Korea's financial market will develop and that Korea's trading partners will not see the exchange regime as injuring their interests.

A necessary condition for such rules to be credible is that the current account or, what is the same thing, the change in net debt of the Korean economy generated by private investment decisions must be acceptable to the government of Korea.

The logic of this proposition is simple and unavoidable. If the private sector is free to borrow and lend, market forces will determine the level of the exchange rate, net capital flows, and the current account balance. As a participant in international capital markets the Korean government can mitigate the volatility of this process but it cannot hold back the tide of international capital flows unless, of course, it decides to reimpose controls.

Policy makers are sometimes impatient with this constraint arguing, for example, that it is not politically feasible to allow the country to fall into debt or to give up the benefits of export-led growth. We do not believe that a macroeconomic policy regime can resolve this potential conflict. The constraint on the government's objective for the current account is not a "theory." It is an identity. If the private sector determines the scale and direction of net capital flows free of controls, the government cannot also determine the scale and direction of net capital flows.

We recognize that private capital inflows to emerging markets have not always been beneficial. Financial crises have been a frequent and painful feature of the international monetary system in recent years. The obvious welfare costs of crises have led to a general reevaluation of strategies for opening repressed financial systems to international competition. There is a growing recognition that greater reliance on market forces to coordinate financial markets has apparently contradictory implications for policy makers. On the one hand, liberalization reduces the direct role of the government in domestic credit markets. State owned or directed financial systems have done a poor job of allocating resources, and this blueprint for economic development has been decisively, and rightly, rejected by the government of Korea. It is the complexity of credit allocation that gives market mechanisms the decisive edge over planning.

On the other hand, we have ample evidence that badly structured and poorly regulated private financial markets can also misallocate resources. The limitations and fragility of private credit markets in emerging markets should not have been a surprise. Credit markets in industrial countries are highly regulated and there is a very large and sophisticated literature on the distortions to private incentives that make this regulation necessary. A balanced assessment of these arguments suggests to us that successful liberalization of credit markets will severely limit the government's direct participation in financial markets and at the same time require a substantial expansion of the government's role in supervision and prudential regulation. In the transition to a fully liberalized domestic financial system, restraints on the liability management of resident financial and nonfinancial institutions may be a useful component of the government's overall strategy. In some circumstances such limitations might take the form of controls and taxes on international capital flows.

An overriding short-term challenge facing policy makers in emerging markets is to establish policy regimes that are immune from financial crises. The unhappy fact seems to be that a stable macroeconomic environment may be necessary but not sufficient to coax the desired outcomes from liberalized financial systems. But we want to emphasize the idea that monetary policy should not be assigned the task of offsetting capital movements generated by distorted or inefficient private incentives. Moreover, sterilized intervention may be useful over short time horizons but in most cases intervention "papers over" the problem without altering the incentives behind private capital flows. As a result the authorities can offset private capital flows for a while but it is clear that this encourages more private capital flows.

For similar reasons we are also unconvinced that fiscal policy is an effective policy tool for influencing private capital flows. While fiscal policy might in very special circumstances be used to influence net capital flows we do not believe that the government's net debt position should be determined by developments in international capital markets.

Our conclusion is that if there is a problem with private capital flows the government should directly limit such transactions, and at the same time, work to alter the incentives that may have generated capital flows not in the country's interests. A liberalized financial system means that although the government is not directly setting quantitative restrictions on capital flows it will have to work very hard to insure that net private capital flows are not distorted and are consistent with prudent financial management of private investors and debtors.

Volatility

Free financial markets are volatile. It would be very helpful, therefore, if the authorities would clearly link their objective for a market-oriented financial system to their acceptance of an appropriate amount of volatility in financial prices, including exchange rates. The appropriate level of volatility, in turn, depends on the ability of financial and nonfinancial institutions to adjust to this new environment. Although we believe that private market participants will eventually provide the stabilizing speculation needed to insure the performance of a market-determined system, these institutions are not yet fully developed in Korea. There is no doubt that the ultimate success or failure of this interim regime will depend on the behavior of the private sector.

What can the government do to promote stabilizing speculation? The most important ingredient is to allow substantial volatility from day to day in exchange rates. This provides the profit incentives for speculators to smooth rates and the incentive for other market participants to hedge exposures.

The initial weakness of corporate and bank balance sheets following the 1997 crisis has made it difficult for firms to adjust to highly volatile exchange rates. An important tradeoff is that some measure of volatility is *necessary* to make private speculation profitable. But excessive volatility will be a serious problem for financial and nonfinancial institutions with weak balance sheets.

The key to this problem, however, is how balance sheets evolve over time. This will be strongly influenced by expectations about intervention policy. If the authorities are perceived as having an objective for the *level* of the nominal exchange rate, private investors will structure their balance sheets to take advantage of such a guarantee. There is no need for a private firm to hedge dollar liabilities if the government is expected to use its reserves to liquidate all or most of the private sector's dollar liabilities at some floor level for the exchange rate.

The tendency for the private sector to increase its vulnerability to exchange rate changes when it believes that the authorities have an objective for the level of the exchange rates is a very important reason for establishing rules for floating. If the private sector believes that they are insured against depreciation they will borrow in foreign currencies and this will, in fact, make it difficult for the government to stand by when there is downward pressure on the currency. The rules suggested here would have two positive effects. First, it will send a clear message to the private sector that they are responsible for the financial risks they take on. Second, when the policy is tested by a fall in the exchange rate the government has a clear policy to stick to.

It is never easy to stand by when markets punish firms that have made bad decisions. In our view the only way to insure that private risks are avoided is to allow firms to fail. This, in turn, requires efficient procedures for liquidating firms that make bad decisions. Many observers have argued that this "credit culture" will be difficult to implement in Korea and other emerging markets. We agree but would add that, if this is really the case, liberalized financial markets cannot work. The decision to move to market-determined financial markets is the decision to strictly limit the government's intervention designed to save individual firms from the market's judgment.

Exports

One of the most difficult problems with volatility is that export industries that have enjoyed the protection of managed exchange rates are also not well prepared to cope with greater volatility in exchange rates. The key question is whether or not exporters will adapt to the new system and at what cost. Experience in other countries suggests that exchange rate volatility has not reduced the growth of international trade.

But this does not mean that exchange rate volatility will be welcomed by exporters. Export industries will carefully observe the government's intervention behavior in order to assess their risks in concentrating on export markets and the benefit of hedging their exposure to exchange rate changes. No business that is accustomed to protection from uncertainty by the government will welcome a more volatile environment. If the government is believed to have an objective to resist appreciation of the currency, firms will exploit the guarantee by focusing on production for export and by not hedging the domestic currency value of receipts. The success of an interim regime will depend on the authorities' ability to balance the needs of exporters and other market participants.

Small and medium-sized businesses do not have credit ratings that allow them to use many hedging techniques. In most hedging instruments there is significant counterpart risk and this risk makes participation expensive and, in many cases, impossible. Options are a good alternative since the firm pays a fee and does not need further credit. But the option exchange itself must be well capitalized to ensure participants that large rate movements will not generate default. The authorities could participate in the options exchange perhaps through a capital infusion.

The Optimal Stock of Gross Reserves

The optimal stock of gross reserves, or the ratio or gross reserves to GDP, is difficult to quantify. In focusing on the net foreign currency position of the government we have left the optimal composition of gross assets and liabilities and derivative positions in the background. Suppose, for example, that the Bank of Korea borrows dollars and invests in liquid dollar assets. Gross reserves have increased but the government's net foreign currency position has not changed. Thus we would not call this intervention. In fact, the rules for floating outlined above put no constraint on the level of gross reserve assets, gross foreign currency liabilities, and derivative positions, but only on the government's net exposure. Nevertheless "borrowing in advance of need" might help stabilize market expectations and discourage speculative runs on the currency. It follows that, within the guidelines set out here, the government is free to balance the advantages of a borrowed war chest against the carrying cost of borrowing long in order to lend short.

Our main point here is that the government of Korea has a legitimate need for reserves and an accumulation of large stocks of gross or net reserves is not a threat to the interests of other countries. To the contrary, an appropriate stock of reserves can be an important contribution to the stability of the international monetary system. The problem is that this objective is difficult to distinguish from the objective of trying to control the level of the exchange rate or the current account balance. This is a legitimate concern both for foreign governments and private investors.

A Safety Valve: Concerted Intervention

Allowing exchange rate volatility also opens up the way for noise traders, or worse, for those that would attempt to manipulate the rate of a small open economy for their own advantage. The importance of such behavior in practice has been debated for as long as there have been markets. We will not settle such matters here much less the more difficult question of the tradeoff between market-determined prices and the costs of destabilizing speculation. But we do need to provide a mechanism for the authorities to react to such behavior when they are convinced it is dominating markets.

It follows that a prudent regime incorporates a safety valve that allows governments to step in and take a strong stand concerning the appropriate level of the exchange rate. Such interventions should be infrequent and, to insure that governments' participation in the market is decisive, it should be the result of a formal agreement among governments, perhaps through regional swap agreements or the BIS. There is some evidence that concerted intervention by governments of industrial countries has been effective in stabilizing exchange rates and we see no reason for limiting such policy moves to industrial countries.

If the exchange rate is clearly being manipulated or if a movement in one direction is thought to be a speculative bubble, the governments involved should be able to agree to a concerted intervention and to share the exchange rate risks associated with such an intervention. In the case of Korea, bilateral negotiations with the big three would not be practical but consultation with other Asian governments would be an attractive alternative.

This consultation process is crucial in defusing a political reaction from trading partners. It would also signal to the private sector that the intervention is funded by deep pockets and is likely to be successful in stabilizing the exchange rate. The reserve targets would be relaxed but not eliminated following concerted intervention. If fact, it would be much easier to gather agreement for such an intervention if the terms for unwinding each government's position were set out in advance.

Inflation Targeting

Overview

By assigning the currency composition of the government's net assets to smooth exchange rates we have left free the more powerful policy, namely changes in the monetary base and associated changes in short-run interest rates. The benefits of freeing this important tool depend on a coherent policy framework. Our suggestion is that flexible inflation targeting with an intermediate interest rate target would be appropriate for Korea. This is an appealing regime for several reasons. First it allows an "additional" role for the exchange rate in policy making. Nominal exchange rate changes have predictable effects on subsequent inflation. It follows that the appropriate policy response to exchange rate depreciation is a tightening of monetary conditions. As emphasized above, the central bank is not backed into a corner of defending a given level for the exchange rate but is, nevertheless, expected to react to mitigate the inflationary and deflationary effects of changes in nominal exchange rates.

Second, by clearly communicating its inflation objectives and forecasts the government provides a clear justification for its nominal interest rate instrument. This will allow the government to build a track record and, in that way, increase its credibility.

Third, the fact that the government will certainly miss its inflation target from time to time is actually an advantage of the system because it provides an opportunity for the government to explain its understanding of what part of the forecast went wrong and why. It is our view that credibility does not come from the particular nominal target chosen. Credibility comes from the demonstration that the government has a consistent policy framework and can explain and learn from past errors in the context of that framework.

The operating procedure associated with inflation targeting is simple to formulate and communicate to the private sector. The first step is to calculate a "normal" real interest rate that is neutral with respect to the business cycle. The second is to quantify an inflation forecast conditional on policy. Third, the inflation forecast plus some part of the percentage difference between the expected and desired inflation rate is then added to the normal rate to obtain the short-term interest rate target. There are many judgments to be made in this procedure and a great deal of discretion and judgement can be incorporated into the process.

Svensson (2000) provides an explicit model of a small open economy and evaluates alternative inflation targeting procedures in the context of the model. There are important issues that would have to be resolved before such a model could be applied to Korea. In particular the fact that the exchange rate has an immediate effect on output and prices in a small open economy has to be taken carefully into account in designing the regime. These important questions are beyond the scope of this paper but we do provide a very simple description of how our policy regime would react to shocks to the economy in Appendix I. An extended version of the Svensson (2000) model that explicitly introduces the current account is presented in Appendix II.

We believe that there are no serious technical barriers to successful inflation targeting in Korea. Moreover, the regime has several advantages. First, the interest rate is clearly visible to the private sector every day. Second, when errors occur the authorities have a simple framework within which errors can be decomposed and can communicate how the procedure will be modified to insure better future performance. Third, and most important, this procedure requires the central bank to pursue the one policy objective it has the power to achieve in the long run, the rate of inflation.

Credibility and Inflation Targeting

Some observers have argued that exchange rate regimes similar to that described above are unlikely to serve the interests of emerging-market countries. Calvo (2000a) and Calvo and Reinhart (2000b), for example, have argued that there are good reasons for countries that started out floating following a crisis to quickly return to a de facto fixed rate regime. This tendency has been called "fear of floating" and is a clear empirical regularity among developing countries. The more difficult question is why this has been such a common phenomenon and what, if any, lessons are applicable for Korea.

One approach is to argue that floating exchange rates are, in fact, not optimal for emerging markets. This argument is based on the idea that a fixed exchange rate is the only credible and verifiable nominal anchor for monetary policy in developing countries. If this is true then there are certainly strong reasons for adopting a fixed exchange rate. Our view is that this assumption does not fit Korea well at all. Countries with histories of high inflation may find it difficult to convince the private sector that they can be trusted to hit an inflation target. But the government of Korea, we believe, would be more credible if it announced an inflation target. An inflation target would provide a superior anchor for private expectations about monetary policy in Korea because the relationship between the monetary base, short-term interest rates, and inflation is much better understood than the relationship between the exchange rate and any variable over which the authorities have control. It is exactly a commitment to defend an exchange rate that has become, in the market's view, over or under valued that makes an adjustable peg regime unstable. Even in inflation-prone countries such as Brazil and Mexico inflation targeting has been quite successful in stabilizing inflationary expectations. Moreover, uncertainty about the level of the exchange rate that is consistent with price stability means that a commitment to a fixed exchange rate might destabilize the price level.

Alternative Intermediate Regimes

Although our preferred regime does not call for an important role for the level of the nominal exchange rate we recognize that there are good arguments for a regime in which the exchange rate plays a more central role. In this section we discuss regimes that capture the important elements of such alternatives.

The central focus of the basket-band-crawl (BBC) regime is three-fold. First and foremost, it is designed to maintain competitiveness. Over time, the exchange rate will depreciate at a pace such that the countries' inflation differential (beyond what is induced by the Balassa-Samuelson-Komyia effect) is offset by nominal depreciation. Second, where there is no dominant trading partner, the reference point is a basket of currencies rather than a single reference currency. Third, there is room for exchange rate fluctuations to free up, within limits, domestic monetary policy and to have some market-based signaling role for exchange rates. Clearly, the regime is not a panacea: domestic monetary and fiscal policies matter for performance, but the arrangement is sufficiently stabilizing for capital markets to elicit substantially stabilizing speculation.

When inflation rates are high, fixed or unchanging nominal exchange rates can not be sustained. This leads to the first part of the proposal: crawling. The notion of crawling was first practiced in Latin America. It clearly involves a trade-off: indexing the exchange rate means inflation is more nearly perpetuating itself than coming down under the force of a (fixed) nominal exchange rate anchor. However, in exchange, there is no loss of competitiveness and the associated risk of recurrent devaluation crises declines. The higher the rate of inflation, the more important the emphasis on the crawl.

The second part of the scheme is the basket feature: because trade with the dollar block and with Europe is a significant portion of Asian commerce, the exchange rate regime should be diversified. In that way another source of major swings in competitiveness—external currency movements rather than domestic inflation—is contained. Any trend inflation and productivity adjustment aside, external currency changes affect the central parity. For the Korean won, weights might be 0.3 for the U.S. and the ERM combined and 0.6 for Japan. Whenever the dollar appreciates 10 percent on the yen and the euro, there is an offsetting appreciation of the Won by 3 percent on these currencies. As a result, weighted average competitiveness is preserved: a gain in the dollar markets of 7 percent and a loss in the euro and yen markets of 3 percent. The adjustment is clearly not neutral across firms, but it is the best that can be done under the circumstances. Firms can go further in seeking stability by using forward contracts. From an inflation point of view, the rule maintains the stability of the average price level.

The basket feature does not mean that there is a need to intervene in all reference currencies. In practice, the foreign exchange market is run in terms of one of the reference currencies, say the dollar. The central dollar rate then is adjusted in terms of the trend factors and the corrections deriving from external rate movements among the basket currencies.

The third feature involves the band aspect. The band idea is a lesson drawn from flexible rate experiments. The lesson comes in two ways. First, that fully flexible rates may not be stable rates, and more so, that the more fundamentals (like monetary policy) are not fully exogenous. Second, market determined rates might play a useful role in signaling the need for realignments of the central parity. Between the market signaling and policy makers learning and reacting, there may be the potential for gradualist change in the central parity. That offers more flexibility than a fixed rate and more stability than a fully flexible rate. It thus tries to blend the best of both worlds.

There are two critical questions in the design of the target zone scheme. One is the issue of the band width. There is no scientific basis to determine a good band width. Williamson (2000) recommends a 7-10 percent range on either side. His basis for these numbers is that less is too little and more is too much. Ultimately, band width has to be calibrated on the stability of the central parity real exchange rate and on the stability of domestic financial policies. The more stable each of these is, the more stable the expected exchange rate and, hence, the narrower the plausible range of fluctuations and the defensible range. By contrast, if the equilibrium real rate is subject to substantial fluctuation, wide margins are essential, and even that may not be enough. Clearly, in the latter case, there is an urgent need to bring financial policies under control since that, not intervention, is the only way to stabilize the foreign exchange market. An unstable equilibrium real exchange rate in turn calls for an extra arrangement that makes the real central parity significantly flexible over time. Here, in fact, is a key challenge for regimes that feature the nominal exchange rate as an explicit policy objective.

A key ingredient in getting good performance is a realistic assessment of the equilibrium real exchange rate. This is all the more important, the more significant is structural change in the trade and capital markets. The prevalent model for calculation of real equilibrium exchange rates takes as given a current account target:

$$x = f(R, Y, Y^*, ...) \quad \text{or} \quad R' = \lambda(x', ...) \tag{1}$$

where R is the real exchange rate, Y and Y^* are home and foreign output, x is the current account, and x' the target level. The dots represent other relevant policy variables. For given paths of output and policy variables that have a bearing on the current account, and for a given current account target, we arrive at the equilibrium real exchange rate, R'. This brief discussion makes clear two points: first, there needs to be a current account target to know what an equilibrium exchange rate is. Without a target concept, anything is possible—5 percent of GDP deficits or even 10. As the example of Mexico reminds us, what seems plausible one day—and is easily rationalized as the wonders of reform and modernization—the next day is called unsustainable.[1]

There are no hard and fast rules for allowable or sustainable deficits. The more a deficit reflects investment rather than consumption the more plausible the case for allowing it to go forward. The more a deficit is financed by direct investment, the more plausible a larger number. But when everything is said and done, large deficits create vulnerability, and that is why a target may be appropriate.

The second point, which is just as important, is that the current account does not depend exclusively on the real exchange rate. Other policies need to be consistent to take weight off the real exchange rate. Thus, we cannot have full employment, a large fiscal expansion, and a small deficit without expect-

---

[1]It would be interesting to explore the fate of all large deficits. We know from the work of Goldfajn and Valdes (1997) that large real appreciations have little chance of going away without a crash. One surmises the same fate befalls their mirror image, large deficits. As the bankers say, it is not speed that kills, it is the sudden halt.

ing high real interest rates and a major real appreciation. They might create the right size current account, but they are not sustainable because the real interest rate will attract capital and the real appreciation will harm the traded goods sector. Since these outcomes are inconsistent with medium-term stability, any target zone arrangement built around them is bound to be challenged. In that sense, BBC-style exchange rate arrangements—or any exchange rate arrangement for that purpose—are not a panacea to deal with bad policy.

Williamson (2000), perhaps the most ardent advocate of intermediate regimes, claims that a well-managed BBC regime could have forestalled the Thai crisis in 1997, although such a regime could not have saved other countries from contagion of the Thai meltdown. Why is the BBC regime unable to ward off the contagion effects? The band element of the BBC makes it potentially crisis prone, that is, the obligation to intervene at the edge of a conventional band can trigger a crisis. For this reason, Williamson (2000) argues that emerging market economies in East Asian may consider moving to an intermediate regime with no obligation to intervene at the edge of the band.

These new intermediate regimes include: the reference rate proposal in which the authorities do not have to defend a parity but are not allowed to push their currencies away from the parity. A soft margin arrangement in which the nominal rate is maintained within a band around a moving average of current and past market exchange rates. And finally, monitoring bands that require hands-off policy within a pre-announced band but allow intervention without obligation to intervene once the rate goes out of the band.

The modified versions of an intermediate exchange rate regime may reduce the vulnerability of emerging market economies to speculative attacks. Nevertheless, they are subject to the fundamental objection that they require a judgement concerning the equilibrium real exchange rate. We do not believe that it will be possible to identify an equilibrium exchange rate and in the absence of such knowledge such regimes in practice will evolve to traditional looking fixed exchange rate regimes.

The Currency Board Arrangement

Overview

The past 20 years have brought a fundamental transformation to monetary management. Independent central banks with transparency and some inflation target, more or less explicit, are now standard. In many emerging economies, such as Korea, we also now observe independence of central banks and, where rates are flexible, some variant of an inflation-targeting policy approach.

At the same time, monetary integration is a live theme. In Europe this has become a fact with the creation of the European Monetary Union; and that experience is growing with the increasing incorporation of countries in the East, a handful as early as 2004 and quite a few on the waiting list beyond. Indeed, membership in the European Union comes automatically with membership in the monetary union and some form of representation at the European Central Bank. But even though membership in the European Union is clearly on the horizon, the larger candidate countries so far remain attached to discretionary exchange rate regimes, forsaking the readily available option and benefits of unilaterally adopting the Euro.

In Asia, the discussion of monetary arrangements is picking up at the behest of Japan. Noting the European developments and some discussion of dollarization in Latin America, and the fragmentation of the region in response to the Asian crisis, Japan is exploring what kind of monetary arrangements might make sense (see Ogawa and Ito, 2000). As a concept, this goes far beyond the discussion of an Asian IMF or the establishment of central bank swap lines that are already in place.

Traditional Challenges

Six arguments make up the case against currency board arrangements. They are, respectively, sovereignty, the loss of seigniorage, the loss of monetary policy, the loss of lender of last resort, the loss of fiscal preparedness, and abandonment of the exchange rate. On the surface, each argument is persuasive; on closer scrutiny none really is. Sovereignty is beyond discussion: when it comes to the quality of money the argument does not come up; when it comes to national pride it should not come up in most countries.

The loss of seigniorage is, of course, a critical issue for public finance. The inability to pursue an optimal inflation strategy to extract maximum revenue (as a function of the inflation sensitivity of money demand and the growth rate) limits public sector revenue and forces either spending cuts or recourse to possibly more distortionary forms of taxation. This argument is more appropriate for full dollarization, but even in the case of a currency board it does apply with the only mitigation that interest is earned on foreign exchange reserves. This limits the seigniorage issue to the spread between a country's borrowing and lending rates times reserves—we can imagine reserves being borrowed to support the currency on a long term basis but invested short term. The spread is a reality and the seigniorage issue accordingly is real. But there is an important offset to the loss of seigniorage from the reduction in public debt service costs that result from reduced interest rate—more on this below— and this factor is surely far more significant than the 1 percent or so of GDP in seigniorage loss. Of course, any kind of stability-oriented monetary policy will yield some bonus but currency boards and dollarization presumably command the highest bonus.

The loss of monetary policy is, on the surface, very obvious: if money creation is tightly and mechanically linked to reserve flows, the external balance not the local central bank determines interest rates. But there is surely an illusion here: what central bank in say Latin America can cut interest rates below New York, or what central bank in Eastern Europe can go below Frankfurt. Their fondest hope is to get down to these levels and the safest way to get there is to foreswear all and any kind of independence. In principle there might be some scope for deeply undervalued currencies, expected to appreciate, to achieve lower nominal interest rates than New York but achieving such levels of undervaluation is unseen in the region except in the immediate aftermath of a collapse at which time inflation fears typically abound.

The loss of the lender of last resort function is intriguing. It is based on the assumption that the central bank, not the treasury or the world capital market, is the appropriate lender. There is surely nothing encouraging about the scene of money printing to save banks that are facing an external drain— the brief Turkish experience of December 2000 with this strategy starkly reminds us that this is an express train to currency collapse. In that situation, the central bank poured money into failing banks even as that money poured out of the country, cutting central bank reserves at the pace of a billion dollars a day and more. At most then the lender of last resort issue has to do with substituting good credit (not money) for bad credit. That is intrinsically a treasury function or, if the treasury can not be a source of good credit, a function for the good part of the banking system, if any, or for the rest of the world. It may be the case that there is not good credit available and that as a result bank closure is inevitable; much better to recognize this than to conceal the fact in a process of money creation that blows up the currency and the good banks too. Lender of last resort, more often than not, is failed or failing banking policy.

A surprising argument in questioning currency boards is fiscal preparedness. Of course, at an elementary level there is a point here: the central bank must be cut off from the treasury, all back doors must be closed. It is hard to see how a discretionary monetary and exchange rate policy can accommodate a lack of a good fiscal situation better than a fixed rate. At the most extreme level this may just be an argument about the government being unable to do without seigniorage revenue. As argued above, the savings on debt service from lower interest rates under a currency board amply compensate and take away much of the sting of this argument. But if it is not that, there is no argument. To believe that inflation and devaluation are constructive solutions to a fiscal problem is contradicted by much of financial history. Indeed, from a political economy point of view one might argue that the favorable political and growth effects following upon a shift to a currency board might offer a quite unique opportunity to implement an important fiscal reform.

The most serious and contentious point about a currency board is the abandonment of the exchange rate. This objection comes in two ways. First, in response to an unfavorable disturbance, a flexible exchange rate offers an easier way of adjusting relative price levels and hence competitiveness than general deflation. Second, a fixed rate sets up a one-way option that is bound to be a target for speculative attacks.

Consider first the loss of easy relative price flexibility. This argument can be overdone in a number of ways. First and importantly, most disturbances are temporary rather than permanent. As a result they should for the most part be financed rather than adjusted to. But before we even get to that discussion, there is, of course, the question of whether exchange rates are, in fact, a short-run stabilization tool. With low short-run elasticities it is entirely possible that rate movements could destabilize the current account and employment. That view is more relevant the more the discussion focuses on temporary disturbances as the target of rate movements.

But the more substantial issue is to view the response to disturbances in a context of intertemporal optimization including an explicit role for capital markets. In a world where there are international capital markets, cyclical disturbances at home or abroad or temporary terms of trade fluctuations do not require offsetting movements in relative prices so as to maintain current accounts balanced. On the contrary, from a perspective of intertemporal optimization, partial adjustment of consumption or investment and current account financing should be most of the buffer. But if current account adjustment is not part of the script, where is the need for relative price adjustment? Of course, this overstates the point because there will typically be some adjustment of consumption or investment and, as a result, some need for relative price changes to deal with full employment. To some extent this need is met by flexibility of wages and prices but that flexibility may be incomplete, more so in a new regime. That leaves a bit of an exchange rate issue but it also puts it in a cost benefit perspective. In terms of the models used in new classical economics, the exchange rate can be used as a "fooling device" to create unexpected changes in real factor rewards but these will last only as long as expectations and wages and prices can not adjust.

At the same time, the option to fool agents comes at a cost in the capital market. If recourse to unexpected movements of the exchange rate are part of the regime they will translate into a premium in interest rates and hence the cost of capital. That in turn translates into a loss of competitiveness, which must be made up by lower equilibrium real wages. (This discussion assumes that capital is mobile and labor is not.) The point of the discussion is to say that the devaluation option has limited scope in labor markets, as new classical economics warns, and it surely has a cost in the capital market. Closing the circle suggests that a regime with the devaluation option translates into lower average equilibrium real wages compared to a hard peg.

For the case of permanent or highly persistent disturbances the role of exchange rates becomes, of course, more prominent. Here it is an issue of adjustment rather than financing. This adjustment of the relative prices would, of course, seem to be favored by exchange rate movements. But it is also true that price-wage adjustment can do much the same. If they can not, because of "rigidities," it stands to reason that the exchange rate will rarely do the job without some complication. That certainly has been the experience of Latin America where inflation-devaluation cycles have been the centerpiece of the monetary regime.[2] If anything, the exchange rate has been the dominant instrument of destabilization.

It takes a very special kind of money illusion that accepts real wage cuts from a large and perfectly obvious devaluation but can not generate a fall in wages or prices. Perhaps it says more about the monetary authorities' unwillingness to create the conditions for deflation but their willingness and ability to get by with real wage cutting by depreciation and inflation. After all, the wage-price regime is not written in stone but rather is mostly written by the central bank's systematic policy conduct.

The Gains from Currency Unions and Boards

The gains from a currency board or dollarization come in the financial area and derive from a far enhanced credibility in the exchange rate regime, and hence in inflation performance. The gains come in two forms. First and most obviously, there is a dramatic decline in interest rates with all attendant benefits. That gain is, of course, more important the more debilitated a country is

---

[2]Martinez, Sanchez, and Werner (2000), for example, note that pass-through from the exchange rate to prices is as high as 65 percent, of which 50 percent occurs within two quarters.

financially (see Giavazi and Pagano, 1998, who called it the gain "from tying one's hands"). In the case of Greece or Italy becoming part of the EMU they were altogether striking. In countries that are not outright fragile, the gains are still significant since in a modern financial setting a cost of capital difference of a percentage point or two are decidedly relevant. But the gains from abandoning national money are inversely proportional to its quality, past, current, and prospective.

As important are the transformation of the financial sector and the lengthening of agents' horizons. With low inflation and stable inflation, and a stable currency, economic horizons lengthen. The lengthening of horizons, in turn, is conducive to investment and risk taking which translates into growth and this closes a virtuous circle. Moreover, once an economy moves out of crisis or state of siege mode, distortions and inefficiencies become far more apparent and can become the target of public policy. There is ample evidence that inflation hurts growth, and high and unstable inflation does so with a vengeance. Hence a monetary regime that delivers and maintains low inflation, other things equal, will help growth. While these points are quite obvious—and were behind the case for low inflation targets on the part of central banks in advanced economies—on the periphery and notably in Latin America they are still to be reaped. In sum, doing away with inflation is a step toward pervasive and deep reform.

A Currency Board for Korea?

The preceding discussion on the advantages and disadvantages of the currency board arrangement suggest that the system deserves a careful examination as an alternative regime in the long run for the East Asian countries instead of dismissing it outright as an arrangement politically unacceptable. The ASEAN plus the three northeast Asian countries have been working together to create a regional arrangement for financial cooperation which may be a first step toward establishing an East Asian currency union.

Although monetary integration in East Asia is far off in the future, the discussion on regional financial cooperation renders credence to the currency board as a viable alternative to either the flexible or intermediate regime for East Asia. However, in the short run or during the transition period, we seriously doubt that Korea should entertain the idea of adopting a currency board arrangement.

There are two considerations that make a currency board not an appropriate regime for Korea at this time. The fundamental problem is that Korea may need real exchange rate flexibility to soften the impact of changes in world demand for Korean output and exports. Moreover, we believe that the Korean authorities do not need to give up real exchange rate flexibility in order to enjoy a credible low interest rate regime. This may be a problem for countries with a history of high inflation, but this is not the case for Korea.

Recent Experience in Korea and other Emerging Markets

A number of recent studies have suggested that nominal exchange rates fixed at untenable levels were one of the major causes of financial crises in emerging markets. The IMF view is that the intermediate regimes may serve as temporary systems, but in the long run the choice for these countries comes down to either floats or hard pegs. Nevertheless, many countries in East Asia have apparently been reluctant to accept the advice of the IMF and the economic profession in general. Malaysia decided to adopt a fixed exchange rate system in the midst of a crisis, China continues to adhere to what they call a managed floating system, and other East Asian countries intervene extensively to stabilize their nominal exchange rates.[3]

Volatility

Baig (2000) and Hernandez and Montiel (2001) show that the currencies of the East Asian crisis countries have been relatively more stable since early 1999 compared with a representative sample of other floating currencies. Their interpretation of this evidence is that the crisis countries have reverted back to the old regime of pegging their currencies to the dollar. As put by Williamson (2000):

> Where the authorities of a country do not announce any objectives that would permit a judgment that they had succeeded or failed, but where they nevertheless have views about where the exchange rate ought to be, and are prepared to act on those views. They announce no parity or band, but they typically worry if the rate depreciates a lot, and they intervene, or change interest rates, or sometimes seek to influence the flow of capital, with a view to having an impact on the exchange rate. And they may certainly worry about the exchange rate appreciating so much as to threaten their country's competitiveness, as has been the case in Korea.

---

[3]See Park, Chung, and Wang (1999) for the evidence of intervention in Korea.

Figure 1. Real Exchange Rate Movement in the East Asian Crisis Countries
(1989= 100)

A. Korea

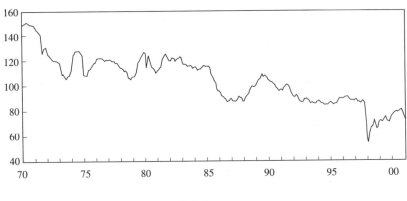

B. Indonesia

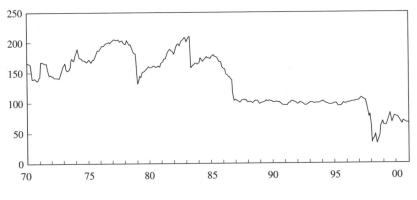

C. Thailand

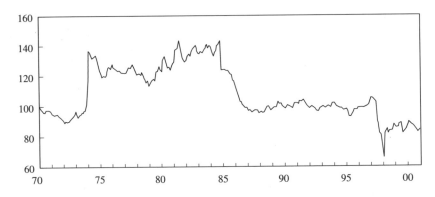

Table 1. Exchange Rate Movements in East Asia
(Mean and standard deviation of percent changes in exchange rate of local currency against the U.S. dollar)

Period	Indonesia		Korea		Thailand		Japan	
	Mean	Stdv	Mean	Stdv	Mean	Stdv	Mean	Stdv
Pre-Crisis	0.02	0.15	0.03	0.25	0.01	0.10	0.08	0.64
Post-Crisis	0.05	1.53	0.01	0.43	0.04	0.52	0.68	0.84

Table 2. Volatility Change
(Standard deviation of daily changes in exchange rates)

	Indonesia		Korea		Thailand		Japan	
	Pre-Crisis	Post-Crisis	Pre-Crisis	Post-Crisis	Pre-Crisis	Post-Crisis	Pre-Crisis	Post-Crisis
Depreciation(A)	0.14	1.07	0.20	0.34	0.07	0.36	0.46	0.48
Appreciation(B)	0.12	1.17	0.18	0.28	0.07	0.38	0.46	0.52
A/B	1.67	0.91	1.11	1.21	1.0	0.95	1.0	0.92

As can be seen in Figure 1 and Tables 1 and 2, the volatility of the nominal exchange rates of the East Asian countries has increased a great deal since 1998, compared with the pre-crisis period. Nevertheless, the currencies of these countries have been less volatile since January 1999 than the yen and other floating currencies outside of East Asia. Baig (2000) also shows that while the volatility of exchange rates has increased, the volatility of interest rates and reserves has decreased in the crisis countries. It is not clear how these two different developments should be interpreted, but an index of exchange rate flexibility (the standard deviation of exchange rate changes divided by that plus the standard deviation of the ratio of changes in reserves to lagged monetary base) suggests that Korea and Singapore have returned to the pre-crisis degree of inflexibility.

One explanation for the increase in instability in the foreign exchange market may be related to the shift from managed to free floating, itself, and a simple statistical test—a regime dummy in a conditional variance equation—bears out the significance of the regime shift.

In addition to the regime shift, deregulation of capital account transactions appears to have contributed to the increased volatility of the won-dollar exchange rate. Capital market opening has increased both the volume and volatility of capital movements in and out of Korea's financial markets. As shown

Table 3. Volatility of Portfolio Capital Flows

	Indonesia	Korea	Thailand
Absolute Rate of Changes	2.5	8.6	14.7
Absolute Changes	3.1	2.2	0.9

Note: Standard deviation in the post-crisis period (1999:01-2000:12) to the standard deviation in the pre-crisis period (1995:05-1997:04). Quarterly data are used for Indonesia due to data limitations.

in Table 3, the ratio of the standard deviation of capital flows in the post-crisis period to that in the pre-crisis period suggests that volatility of capital flows rose markedly since deregulation took effect in 1998.

Capital account liberalization has also increased integration of Korea's capital markets into the markets of major international financial centers including New York. As a result of the increased pace of integration, external shocks originating in New York and Tokyo are almost instantaneously transmitted to Korea's financial markets, particularly the equity market. Reflecting the growing trend of integration, for example, the coefficient of correlation between the U.S. and Korean stock prices rose to 0.57 after the crisis from -0.86 during the pre-crisis period (Table 4).

Finally, a number of recent studies provide some evidence that foreign portfolio investors operating out of the equity market in Korea have exhibited a tendency to engage in positive feedback trading: buying when the market is booming and selling when it is slumping. These studies also suggest that

Table 4. Financial Integration with U.S.
(Correlation coefficients with the U.S. of daily prices and rates)

	Stock Price	Interest rates
Indonesia		
Pre-crisis	0.92	0.30
Post-crisis	0.59	-0.71
Korea		
Pre-crisis	-0.86	0.01
Post-crisis	0.57	0.21
Thailand		
Pre-crisis	-0.88	0.06
Post-crisis	0.31	0.17

foreign investors are prone to moving together in a herd in East Asian financial markets (Choe, Kho, and Stulz, 1998; Kim and Wei, 1999; and Park and Park, 1999). The positive feedback trading and herd behavior of foreign portfolio investors, who as a group hold more than 30 percent of the total valuation of the equity market in Korea, are likely to have contributed to increasing instability of the stock market, which appears to have spilt over into the foreign exchange market, amplifying volatility of the nominal exchange rate.

Intervention and Policy Objectives

A number of recent studies on exchange rate policies have shown that policymakers in developing and emerging market economies have been reluctant to let their exchange rates fluctuate freely for fear of a large depreciation. One of the policymakers' fears with floating is the potentially devastating effect of sudden large changes in the currency as well as the effect of maturity mismatches on the balance sheets of banks and corporations laden with large U.S. dollar-denominated short-term debts (Calvo and Reinhart, 2000a and b; Eichengreen and Hausmann, 1999; Goldfajn and Olivares, 2000; and Mussa et al., 2000). The more serious these balance sheet effects are, the larger is the amount of currency mismatches between dollar-denominated assets and liabilities. According to Calvo and Reinhart (2000a) and Eichengreen and Hausmann (1999), the possibility that the emerging economies face negative balance sheet effects at the time of a large depreciation is high since their banks and corporations usually do not have proper tools to hedge their exchange risks, even though they have large dollar liabilities. Calvo (2000a), Mussa et al. (2000), and Goldfajn and Olivares (2000) also point out that the low volatility of the exchange rates may encourage more currency mismatches by discouraging hedging attempts.

Another possibility is that a large depreciation may complicate inflation management, while it could downgrade their sovereign ratings and consequently reduce their accessibility to international financial markets (Goldfajn and Werlang, 2000; Calvo and Reinhart, 2000b; and Hausman et al., 1999).

Calvo and Reinhart (2000b) find that the sovereign ratings of developing countries were significantly downgraded following the currency crises, and that the magnitude of their downgrade was far greater than that of developed countries. They thus argue that this credibility problem has been pervasive in developing countries. Since the loss of access to international lending may cause disruptive effects on developing economies that heavily depend on foreign capital for investment, the central banks minimize the volatility of the exchange rates by intervention in the foreign exchange markets or adjustments in monetary policies.

Central banks of developing countries that are reluctant to allow higher volatility of exchange rates are concerned about the effects of depreciation on domestic prices. In particular, central banks of economies with a high degree of exchange rate pass-through try to minimize the inflationary effects of depreciation by controlling the downward pressure of local currencies. According to the empirical findings of Goldfajn and Werlang (2000) and Calvo and Reinhart (2000b), the degree of pass-through is higher in developing countries than in developed countries. Thus, the fear of floating due to the fear of inflation would be more common in developing economies. In addition, central banks would be more concerned about the pass-through, and hence the volatility of exchange rates, if they pursue inflation targets or if the economy has de facto wage indexation (Goldfajn and Olivares, 2000; Hausmann *et al.*, 1999).

These arguments may be able to account for only a part of the reality. The first three (the balance sheet effect, credibility problem, and fear of inflation) are valid only when the value of the local currency depreciates. They are, however, not valid when the exchange rate tends to appreciate and at the same time, exhibits low volatility. Although an appreciation of the local currency improves balance sheets and credibility as well as lowers inflationary pressures, central banks are likely to intervene to restrain further appreciation in order not to lose export competitiveness. Thus, it would be more appropriate to argue that the first three factors are the reasons for "the fear of large depreciation" or devaluation rather than the fear of floating.

A prima facie evidence of market intervention in East Asian countries is, of course, the massive accumulation of foreign exchange reserves by buying current account surpluses. In Korea, the level of reserves increased to 21 percent of GDP in 2000 and was more than twice as large as the volume of short-term foreign debt (Table 5). Between 1998 and 2000, the current account recorded large surpluses ranging from 12.6 percent to 2.4 percent of GDP each year.

Had the authorities abstained from market intervention, the nominal exchange rate might have appreciated much more than otherwise, possibly choking off the ongoing recovery from the crisis. Therefore, a market intervention designed to mop up current account surpluses could account for the authorities' intervention and the reserve gain.

Have the authorities also intervened when they thought the country's export competitiveness was being eroded or price stability was threatened? Measures of market intervention developed by Bayoumi and Eichengreen (1998) and Glick and Wihlborg (1997) suggest that policymakers in Thailand and In-

Table 5. Foreign Exchange Reserves and Current Account Balance in Korea

	Foreign Exchange Reserves		Current Account Balance	
	In millions of U.S. dollars	In percent of GDP	In millions of U.S. dollars	In percent of GDP
1996	34,037	6.5	-23,005	-4.4
1997	20,368	4.2	-8,167	-1.7
1998	51,975	16.2	40,365	12.6
1999	73,987	17.8	24,477	5.9
2000	96,131	21.0	11,040	2.4
2001[1]	105,191	23.5	6,000	1.3
2002[1]	119,323	23.9	2,000	0.4

[1]Estimates by the International Institute of Finance.
Source: Institute of International Finance, Inc. and the Central Bank Website

donesia have intervened less forcefully. For Korea indices of market intervention hardly changed between the two different exchange rate regimes. However, it is normally expected that the regime shift would result in a substantial decrease in these indicators, but this is not apparent in East Asia.

Using high frequency data it has also been shown that the Korean authorities have been active in managing the won-dollar exchange rate (Park, Chung, and Wang, 1999). Using intra-day data over the 10 days from September 10-20 in 1999, the authors show that large changes in the nominal exchange rate disappeared within a few minutes. Unlike other free-floating regimes, the intra-day exchange rate movements did not show any volatility clustering, suggesting that the Korean authorities were actively managing the nominal exchange rate.

The evidence discussed above suggests that, like many other emerging market economies, Korea, Thailand, and Indonesia have adopted an intermediate exchange rate regime. What have been the objectives of market intervention in these countries? The analysis of intra-day data suggests that market intervention has been geared to stabilize high-frequency exchange rate movements in Korea. But there may have been other motives behind management of the local currency-dollar bilateral exchange rates in the three countries.

Smoothing operations for high frequency exchange movements may be necessary after a crisis, to stabilize market expectations. Under such a circumstance, the authorities' smoothing operations could help market participants establish their expectations on the future movements of both the real and nominal exchange rates by minimizing the effect of noise trading (Hernandez and Montiel, 2001).

If stabilizing the nominal exchange rate is the main objective, then Hernandez and Montiel (2001) argue that exchange rate smoothing would lead to substantial fluctuations in the stock of foreign reserves around a certain level that is deemed appropriate for intervention and achieving other objectives. However, they do not find any evidence that Korea and other East Asian crisis-hit countries have used their reserves to conduct smoothing operations; instead, the stocks of reserves have exhibited a systematic tendency to increase over time in these countries.

Surprisingly, the volatility of foreign exchange reserves has declined substantially during the post-crisis period in Korea. The Korean authorities, it appears, have not resorted to the use of reserves to moderate the movements of the nominal exchange rate. Instead, they have relied on a few state-owned banks to intervene in the market, using their own holdings of foreign exchange, which are not counted as part of the central bank foreign reserves. Our proposal for a reserve target would clearly require that such operations be included in the authorities' net foreign assets. If their interventions were not effective, the authorities made it known that they would step in through sterilized intervention to reduce instability in the foreign exchange market. When the yen depreciation recently led to a parallel depreciation of the Korean won, the central bank was able to clamp down the market by simply announcing their intention of conducting sterilized intervention.

The three crisis countries may not have been as concerned about stabilizing their dollar exchange rates as much as they were about stabilizing either the nominal or real effective exchange rate. These countries may have had good reasons to peg their exchange rates or to manage them against a basket of currencies of the countries with which they have extensive trade relations. Hernandez and Montiel (2001) speculate that the East Asian countries may have preferred basket pegging to fixing to the U.S. dollar because the importance of the U.S. as their trading partner has declined, and they may want to use the exchange rate as a nominal anchor.

However, Hernandez and Montiel do not find any evidence that any of the East Asian countries which they analyze were managing their bilateral exchange rates vis-à-vis the U.S. dollar to stabilize a nominal effective exchange rate. They do not identify the currencies included in their basket, but assuming that the basket contains the U.S. dollar, yen, and the euro, the authorities would manage the won-dollar exchange rate to offset fluctuations in the U.S. dollar-yen or the U.S. dollar-euro bilateral exchange rates. When the yen depreciates, for example, vis-à-vis the U.S. dollar as it has in recent periods, one would expect an intervention to engineer a depreciation of the won-dollar exchange rate so that the nominal effective exchange would remain relatively stable.

Since Korea and other crisis-hit countries in East Asia have followed export-led development strategies and are likely to continue to rely on exports for growth, one might conjecture that Korean policymakers have intervened in the foreign exchange market to stabilize the real effective exchange rate. Once again, Hernandez and Montiel do not find any evidence to support that conjecture. If the Korean authorities were as sensitive to maintaining export competitiveness as they are often claimed to be, then one might conjecture that they would intervene more actively when the exchange rate appreciates than where it depreciates. To examine this possibility, we have estimated the conditional probability that the authorities are more likely to step in to reverse the exchange rate movement, when it appreciates than otherwise. Our estimation results do not provide any evidence to support such an asymmetric pattern of intervention.

In summary, what were the Korean policymakers trying to achieve by intervening in the foreign exchange market? The empirical evidence provided by Park, Chung, and Wang (1999) and Hernandez and Montiel (2001) suggests that their objectives have been: to stabilize day to day volatility in the won-dollar exchange; to resist appreciation of the real effective exchange rate after the crisis; and to build a reserve buffer to financial vulnerabilities the economy may have to face while undergoing financial and corporate restructuring.

Although Hernandez and Montiel de-emphasize the significance of the first objective, in a country like Korea where hedging facilities are expensive and limited to a few firms in the trade sector, the authorities have been under constant pressure to moderate fluctuations in the won-dollar exchange rate (Park, Chung, and Wang, 1999).

Finally, one advantage of the flexible exchange rate system is that it allows the monetary authorities a measure of independence in conducting monetary policy to attain domestic policy objectives of low inflation with a high level of employment—which may in turn help stabilize indirectly the nominal exchange rate. While there is little evidence that Korea and other East Asian countries have gained any noticeable monetary autonomy, it is not clear whether this is the result of market intervention or other developments.

Our interpretation of recent experience is that for Korea our proposed regime would be a natural extension of policies that have developed since the crisis. The authorities have intervened in the foreign exchange market while allowing substantial changes in rates over time. What is needed now is to move forward with a regime that clarifies the objectives and procedures consistent with a managed floating environment.

Concluding Remarks

The purpose of this paper has been to develop a framework for monetary and exchange rate policy appropriate for Korea. Our main conclusion is that Korea should stay with the managed float it introduced in the aftermath of the 1997 crisis, but should add inflation targeting and should make the criterion for sterilized intervention explicit.

Sterilized intervention should be assigned the task of limiting day to day volatility in the value of the won against a well-defined basket of major foreign currencies. Intervention designed to limit volatility will generate deviations in the government's net reserves from their target level. In this event the intervention rule will become asymmetric so as to move toward the target level for net reserves.

We recommend that changes in the monetary base be assigned the task of hitting a short-term interest rate derived from a Taylor rule. We do not think that the Korean authorities will have difficulties in establishing a credible regime along these lines.

The key assumption behind our proposal is that international capital flows will be consistent with current account balances and the evolution of net debt for Korea that are acceptable to the authorities. This, in our view, will require very active prudential regulation of domestic financial markets in addition to a stable macroeconomic policy environment.

While there are good arguments both for intermediate regimes and hard pegs we do not believe that these regimes are consistent with Korea's current circumstances. In the absence of explicit rules for floating and inflation targeting it seems to us likely that that policy will drift toward a return to an adjustable peg regime prone to crises.

Appendix I: Examples of Policy Reactions Under Inflation Targeting

Example 1: Suppose a domestic boom increases imports and the current account deficit. If this were not financed by an increase in private capital inflows at the initial interest rate, the nominal exchange rate would tend to depreciate. Our regime would automatically lean against the exchange rate depreciation for three reasons.

- First, the fall in the output gap rule would require a rise in the target interest rate.

- Second, the exchange rate depreciation would increase actual and expected inflation and the target interest rate would rise.
- Third if the exchange rate depreciates rapidly the central bank will be a net buyer of domestic currency. Sterilization would increase domestic credit and reduce international reserves.

It follows that some of the current account deficit would be financed by a decline in reserves. If the exchange rate depreciates slowly and markets remain orderly, intervention would not be called for.

Example 2: The effects of a decline in domestic activity would be symmetric. A domestic recession would generate a current account surplus, a stronger currency, lower domestic interest rates and a fall in reserves.

Over the course of a business cycle international reserves would return to their target level.

Example 3: Suppose world demand for Korean goods declines because of a fundamental demand shift away from Korean goods or a decline in activity in the rest of the world. This is sometimes called a change in the terms of trade. If the current account deficit were not offset by an increased capital inflow the exchange rate would tend to depreciate.

In this case an increase in the output gap would tend to lower the domestic target interest rate.

The expected inflation effect would tend to fall with output but rise with the depreciation of the exchange rate. The net effect from the inflation target rule is uncertain.

Intervention would tend to lean against the exchange rate depreciation. The decline in international reserves would finance some of the current account deficit.

Example 4: A shift toward Korean exports would have symmetric effects. The current account surplus would be associated with exchange rate appreciation and higher domestic interest rates. The surplus would be in part financed by an increase in reserves.

Reserves would return to their target level if the change in the demand for exports was caused by the business cycle abroad but would not return if there was a permanent shift in the relative demand for Korean goods.

A permanent demand shift would generate a permanent deviation from the reserve target and would have to be reversed by asymmetric intervention. Even though intervention is reversed it may not be a mistake since slowing the adjustment in the exchange rate may permit a less costly adjustment to the permanent change in the demand for exports.

Example 5: Suppose with no cyclical or relative demand shocks that private capital inflows increase because investment in Korea becomes relatively attractive. This is sometimes called the capital inflow problem. This puts upward pressure on the exchange rate and, in turn, generates a current account deficit. The appreciation of the exchange rate limits the capital inflow since it reduces expected profitability.

The domestic output gap will fall and this will tend to raise the target domestic interest rate, reducing domestic expenditure and making room for the current account deficit, but encouraging the capital inflow.

The expected inflation rate would fall and this would require a decline in the domestic interest rate.

Intervention would tend to resist the appreciation and international reserves would rise. In this case the current account is more than matched by a private capital inflow. The international reserves increase is financing a capital inflow rather than a current account deficit. In this case the build up of international reserves would not be automatically reversed and would have to be reversed by asymmetric intervention. Again the intervention may not be a mistake since it spreads the real effects of the capital inflow over time.

The important question is whether or not the investment is productive and prudent. That is, the current account deficit is the real transfer that allows an increase in the capital stock and the efficient utilization of foreign savings. If distorted incentives or irrational exuberance generates the capital inflow it would of course be better to completely insulate the economy. The problem is that in deciding to open the capital account the government has given up the only effective way to do this. Exchange market intervention to defend temporary exchange rate pegs are themselves serious distortions for private capital flows. Distortions to domestic credit markets are magnified by capital flows. But capital flows are magnified by sterilized intervention.

Example 6: If private investment in Korea becomes less attractive the effects are symmetric to those described in example 5. Exchange rate depreciation is associated with a current account surplus.

The effects on the domestic interest rate target are uncertain and the depreciation is associated with a decline in reserves.

The fall in reserves is permanent and would have to be reversed by asymmetric intervention.

While all the situations outlined above involve changes in current accounts but there is no sensible way to target the current account itself. In practice, we do not observe the shocks that jointly determine the current account, the exchange rate, domestic output, and inflation. The best we can do is put in place a policy regime that sets out a predictable government reaction to changes in market conditions.

Appendix II. A Model for a Small Open Economy with Inflation Targeting[4]

The general points made in Appendix I can be made more precise with a model of a small open economy with inflation targeting developed by Svensson (2000). We extend this model by including explicitly the current account, which depends upon income, the real exchange rate, and foreign income. This model will then be used to evaluate the viability of a macroeconomic policy regime with a free floating exchange rate, free capital mobility, and inflation targeting.

The model consists of a Philips curve, an aggregate demand equation, a policy objective function in the form of the Taylor rule, an interest rate parity condition, and a specification of the current account. We also follow Svensson in specifying the determination of the foreign variables in the model. There is also an equation describing government expenditure policy; following Fischer (2001), it is assumed that fiscal policy is activated to remove any large imbalances in the current account.

Model

Aggregate supply (Philips curve)

$$\pi_t = \beta \pi_{t+1/t} + \lambda(y_t - y_t^n) + \alpha_\pi \hat{q}_t + \varepsilon_t \tag{1}$$

π_t is domestic inflation in logarithm in period t, i.e.,

$$\pi_t = p_t - p_{t-1}$$

where p_t is the log domestic price level, y_t is the log level of output, and ε_t is a zero-mean productivity shock.

y_t^n is the log level of natural output defined as

---

[4]Prepared with Kwanho Shin.

$$y^n_{t+1} = \gamma^n y^n_t + \hat{y}^n_{t+1} \tag{2}$$

where $0 < \gamma^n < 1$.

$\hat{q}_t = q_t - 1$ where q_t is the log real exchange rate defined as $q_t = s_t + p^*_t - p_t$ where s_t is the nominal exchange rate and p^*_t is the log foreign price level.

The disturbance term, ε_t obeys

$$\varepsilon_{t+1} = \gamma_\varepsilon \varepsilon_t + \hat{\varepsilon}_{t+1} \tag{3}$$

where $0 < \gamma_\varepsilon < 1$ and $\hat{\varepsilon}_t$ is an i.i.d. random variable with zero mean and variances σ^2_ε.

In this model, CPI inflation π^c_t is defined as:

$$\pi^c_t = w\pi^f_t + (1-w)\pi_t = \pi_t + w(q_t - q_{t-1})$$

where π^f_t is the foreign inflation rate and w is the share of foreign goods in consumption.

Aggregate demand (IS Curve)

$$y_t - y^n_t = y_{t+1/t} - y^n_{t+1/t} - \phi(i_t - \pi_{t+1/t}) + g_t + CA_t + \alpha_y \hat{q}_t +$$

$$\alpha^*_y y^*_t + \eta^d_t \tag{4}$$

where i_t is the nominal rate of interest, which is the instrument of monetary policy, y^*_t is the log foreign output level, and g_t is government expenditure. The disturbance term η^d_t is a demand shock that follows:

$$\eta^d_{t+1} = \gamma_\eta \eta^d_t + \hat{\eta}^d_{t+1} \tag{5}$$

where $0 < \gamma_\eta < 1$ and $\hat{\eta}^d_t$ is an i.i.d. random variable with zero mean and variances σ^2_η.

Taylor rule

$$i_t = f_\pi \pi_t + f_y(y_t - y^n_t) \tag{6}$$

Interest rate parity condition in real terms

$$\hat{q}_{t+1/t} = \hat{q}_t + i_t - \pi_{t+1/t} - i^*_t + \pi^*_{t+1/t} - \varphi_t \tag{7}$$

where φ_t is a foreign exchange risk premium and i_t^* is the nominal interest rate in the foreign country.

Current account

$$CA_t = -c_y y_t + c_{y^*} y_t^* + c_q q_t \qquad (8)$$

Government expenditure policy

$$g_{t+1} = \gamma_g g_t + c_g CA_t + \hat{g}_{t+1} \qquad (9)$$

Foreign variables

Following Svensson (2000), foreign variables and φ_t are assumed to be explained by AR processes:

$$\pi_{t+1}^* = \gamma_\pi^* \pi_t^* + \hat{\pi}_{t+1}^* \qquad (10)$$

$$y_{t+1}^* = \gamma_y^* y_t^* + \hat{y}_{t+1}^* \qquad (11)$$

$$\varphi_{t+1} = \gamma_\phi \varphi_t + \hat{\varphi}_{t+1} \qquad (12)$$

where $0 \langle \gamma_\pi^*, \gamma_y^*, \gamma_\pi \langle 1$ and $\hat{\pi}_{t+1}^*, \hat{y}_{t+1}^*$, and $\hat{\varphi}_{t+1}$ are i.i.d. random variables with variances, $\sigma_{\pi^*}^2$, $\sigma_{y^*}^2$, and σ_φ^2.

The foreign interest rate i_t^* follows a Taylor rule in the foreign country

$$i_t^* = f_\pi^* \pi_t^* + f_y^* y_t^* + \xi_t^* \qquad (13)$$

The disturbance term, ξ_t^* obeys

$$\xi_{t+1}^* = \gamma_\xi^* \xi_t^* + \hat{\xi}_{t+1}^* \qquad (14)$$

where $0 \langle \gamma_\xi^* \langle 1$ and $\hat{\xi}_{t+1}^*$ is an i.i.d. random variable with variance $\sigma_{\xi^*}^2$.

Results of Optimal Policy

In order to describe the dynamics and to obtain solutions of the model, we have assumed values of the parameters that are *a priori* reasonable (Table A1). Figure A1 shows changes in the endogenous variables over time in response to an exogenous demand shock with the Taylor rule specified as $i = 1.5\pi$. For the set of parameter values we have selected, the model is stable and converges to new equilibria.

Table A1. Parameter Values

$\beta = 1$	$\alpha_y = .1$	$f_y^* = .5$
$\lambda = 1$	$\alpha_y^* = .1$	$c_y = 1.5$
$\alpha_\pi = .1$	$\gamma_\eta = .9$	$c_y^* = 1.5$
$\gamma_n = .9$	$f_\pi = 1.5$	$c_q = 1.5$
$\gamma_\varepsilon = .9$	$f_y = .5$	$\gamma_g = .9$
$\phi = 2$	$f_\pi^* = 1.5$	$c_g = .1$

Figure A1. Demand Shock

$i = 1.5\pi$ g=exogenous

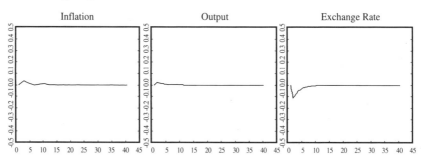

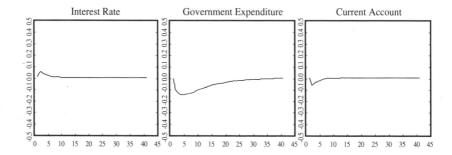

References

Baig, T., 2001, "Characterizing Exchange Rate Regimes in Post-Crisis East Asia," IMF Working Paper WP/01/152 (Washington, D.C.: International Monetary Fund).

Borensztein, E., and J. Zettelmeyer, 2001, "Monetary Independence in Emerging Markets: Does the Exchange Rate Regime Make a Difference?" IMF Working Paper WP/01/01 (Washington, D.C.: International Monetary Fund).

Calvo, G., 2000a, "The Case for Hard Pegs in the Brave New World of Global Finance," unpublished manuscript, University of Maryland.

Calvo, G., 2000b, "Testimony on Dollarization," Subcommittee on Domestic and Monetary Policy, Committee on Banking and Financial Services (June 22).

Calvo, G., and C. Reinhart, 2000a, "Fear of Floating," *NBER Working Paper* No. 7993.

Calvo, G., and C. Reinhart, 2000b, "Fixing for Your Life," in S. Collins and D. Rodrik, eds., *Policy Forum* 2000 (Washington, D.C.: Brookings Institution).

Choe, H., B. Kho, and R. Stulz, 1999, "Do Foreign Investors Destabilize Stock Markets? The Korean Experience in 1997," *Journal of Financial Economics*, Vol. 54, No. 2 (November): 227-264.

Dornbusch, Rudiger, 1998, "Lessons from the European Monetary Union for Latin America," at http://www.mit.edu/~rudi.

Dornbusch, Rudiger, 1999, "The Target Zone Controversy," mimeo, February.

Dornbusch, Rudiger, and F. Giavazzi, 1998, "Hard Currency and Sound Credit," at http://www.mit.edu/~rudi.

Edwards, S., 2000, "Exchange Rate Regimes in Emerging Economies," unpublished manuscript, UCLA.

Edwards, S., and M. Savastano, 1998, "The Morning After: The Mexican Peso in the Aftermath of the 1994 Currency Crisis," *NBER Working Paper* No.6516.

Eichengreen, B., and R. Hausmann, 1999, "Exchange Rate and Financial Fragility," *NBER Working Paper* No. 7418.

Feldstein, M., 1998, "Refocusing the IMF," *Foreign Affairs*, Vol. 77, pp. 20-33.

Fischer, S., 2001, "Exchange Rate Regimes: Is the Bipolar View Correct?" *Journal of Economic Perspectives*, Vol. 15, No. 2, pp. 3-24.

Frankel, J., 1999, "No Single Currency Regime is Right for All Countries or at All Times," *Princeton Essays in International Finance,* No. 215 (August).

Furman, J., and J. Stiglitz, 1998, "Economic Crises: Evidence and Insights from East Asia," *Brookings Papers on Economic Activity II.*

Ghosh, A., A.-M. Gulde, and H. Wolf, 2000, "Currency Boards: More Than a Quick Fix?" *Economic Policy,* No 31 (October).

Giavazzi, F., and M. Pagano, 1988, "The Advantage of Tying One's Hands," *European Economic Review,* 32, 5, pp. 1050-1082.

Glick, R., and C. Wihlborg, 1997, "Exchange Rate Regimes and International Trade," in B. Cohen, ed., *International Trade and Finance: New Frontiers for Research* (Cambridge University Press), pp. 125-156.

Goldfajn, I., and G. Olivares, 2000, "Can Flexible Exchange Rates Still Work in Financially Open Economies?" Studies on International Monetary and Financial Issues for the Group of Twenty Four.

Goldfajn, I., and R.O. Valdes, 1997, "Are Currency Crises Predictable?" IMF Working Paper WP/97/159 (Washington, D.C.: International Monetary Fund).

Goldfajn, I., and S. Werlang, 2000, "The Pass-Through from Depreciation to Inflation: A Panel Study," Working Paper No. 423, Department of Economics, PUC-Rio.

Hanke, S., and K. Schuler, 1994, *Currency Boards for Developing Countries: A Handbook,* San Francisco, ICS Press.

Hanke, S., L. Jonung, and K. Schuler, 1993, *Russian Currency and Finance: A Currency Board Approach to Reform,* Routledge, London.

Hausmann, R., M. Gavin, C. Pages-Serra, and E. Stein, 1999, "Financial Turmoil and the Choice of Exchange Rate Regime," Inter-American Development Bank, Working Paper No. 400.

Hernandez, L., and P.J. Montiel, 2001, "Post-Crisis Exchange Rate Policy in Five Asian Countries: Filling in the "Hollow Middle?" IMF Working Paper WP/01/170 (Washington, D.C.: International Monetary Fund).

Kim, W., and S. Wei, 1999, "Foreign Portfolio Investors Before and During A Crisis," NBER Working Paper No. 6968.

Martinez, L., O. Sanchez, and A. Werner, 2000, "Consideraciones Sobre la Conducción de la Política Monetaria y el Mecanismo de Transmisión en Mexico," Banco de Mexico, unpublished manuscript.

Mill, J.S., 1894, *Principles of Political Economy*, Vol. II, London, Macmillan.

Mishkin, F. S., and M. Savastano, 2000, "Monetary Policy Strategies for Latin America," NBER Working Paper No. 7617 (March).

Mussa, M., P. Masson, A. Swoboda, E. Jadresic, P. Mauro, and A. Berg, 2000, "Exchange Rate Regime in Increasing Integrated World Economy," Occasional Paper No. 193 (Washington, D.C.: International Monetary Fund).

Ogawa, E., and T. Ito, 2000, "On the Desirability of a Regional Basket Currency Arrangement," NBER Working Paper No. 8002.

Park, Y.C., C.S. Chung, and Y. Wang, 1999, "Fear of Floating: Korea's Exchange Rate Policy After the Crisis," in Y.C. Park and Y. Wang, eds., *Exchange Rate Regimes in Emerging Market Countries* (Seoul: Korean Institute for International Economic Policy), forthcoming in *Journal of Japanese and International Economy*.

Park, Y.C. and I.-W. Park, 1999, "Who Destabilized the Korean Stock Market?" presented at the Workshop on Capital Flows organized by Institute of Development Studies at the University of Sussex, Brighton, UK, September 13-14, 1999.

Roubini, N., 2000, website on global macroeconomics at http://www.stern.nyu.edu/globalmacro/

Svensson, L., 2000, "Open-Economy Inflation Targeting," *Journal of International Economics*, Vol. 50, pp. 155-183.

Williamson, J., 2000, *Exchange-Rate Regimes for East Asia: Reviving the Intermediate Option,* Policy Analysis in International Economoics No. 60, Institute for International Economics.

Comments on Papers 12, 13, and 14

Anne O. Krueger

I like the paper by Kim and Byeon. The account of the negotiation and restructuring of Korea's debt after the crisis is very interesting and will serve as a valuable reference work, as the authors intended. We owe them a debt of gratitude.

I have only a few comments. The first is that it would be useful to include balance sheets as of, for example, September 30, December 4, and December 31, 1997, to give context to why it was necessary to restructure the debt. Table 1 does report the "foreign exchange needs" for 1998, but there is very little discussion of where those "needs" came from; more than one half of the "financing gap," for example, is the need to build up reserves, although there is no explanation of how this figure was arrived at. It would also be useful to contrast these *ex ante* estimates with the financing needs that actually emerged in 1998. This would be particularly interesting because everybody was pessimistic at the beginning of the year, but by the end of the year the targets had been overachieved.

My second comment is that I am skeptical of the idea of preorganizing creditors in order to be ready for the next crisis, unless all countries do it. If the Korean government were to announce that it was going to preorganize their creditors in order to be ready for the next crisis, the message received by the market might not be the one Korea wanted to send. Such a plan would only work if it was done through concerted international action. There could also be problems because circumstances change, outstandings change, and even within the same group of creditors relative positions may shift over time. So I am a bit skeptical about the value of this in any sense other than as one of the committees of major creditors that has been set up in the past.

Eichengreen's paper is, as always, very good, on the mark, and well balanced. I have only a few comments. I am sympathetic with his view that standards are fine, but there may be too many, and there may be problems for some countries to implement standards quickly. A possible solution for countries that are not already heavily engaged in capital markets, which may include countries with many capital controls, could be a convention that allowed a longer time period to adopt standards. The incentive for these countries to adopt the standards is that until they do so, they have less access to the international capital markets. In this case, there may not be as much of a problem as much of the discussion in the paper implies.

The author notes that there may be some conflict between the IMF's standards and the Asian "model" of bank-centered development. It seems to me that one of the things that has to happen is that the Asian model, which worked so well in the past, is not working that well anymore and has to be changed. Accordingly, I am less concerned than Eichengreen about a possible conflict between IMF standards and various aspects of the Asian "model."

On exchange rate policy, I share the view that we have had a hollowing out in the middle. On the whole, this is desirable as it strengthens the system, and may indeed be the single biggest change. I tend a little bit more to the floating end of the spectrum than Eichengreen, and I am a little bit more skeptical of dollarization under normal circumstances. For example, the author cites the CFA franc with approval. Those who were in on the discussions know that it took years and years to get the authorities to devalue the CFA franc, despite the fact that there were relatively large price level increases in the CFA franc area. There was a very long time when the economies in the CFA franc zone were having great difficulty because the French were covering the gap and keeping the wrong exchange rate in ways that created a lot of problems.

Similarly for Turkey, where I think there was more to the nominal exchange rate anchor and less to the banks' problems than suggested in the paper. Turkey, after all, had an inflation rate over two years that was something like 30 percent above the rate of nominal depreciation. While Turkey is not fully open, it is open enough so that the resulting real appreciation was a huge problem. I see the weak banks as having been a factor that made their problems more difficult, but I would put more weight on the exchange rate regime as a precipitating factor.

Eichengreen argues that a hard peg is the obvious solution for small countries with ties to larger neighbors and/or weak institutions. Even here, I lean toward a floating rate. Consider the experience of the Mexican economy, which after all is not that different in size to Korea. Until 1996 most of the authorities were very skeptical as to whether floating would work. Only after they had been pushed into it did they go to anything like a clean float. Indeed, the Governor of the Bank of Mexico, who earlier argued that floating would not work, now argues that floating has made the conduct of domestic monetary policy much simpler and more straightforward. The Bank of Mexico no longer is looking at the exchange rate as one of the guides that it uses for policy, although they will intervene a bit if they think there is a big fluctuation; instead, they announce domestic credit targets. The judgment to date is that it has been a very successful emerging market solution to many of their problems. Now

Mexico still has a weak banking system and they have a number of other problems that need to be addressed. But from all reports and evidence, the management of the exchange rate as an issue has just gone from the table, to almost everybody's satisfaction. There is, however, some suspicion that with the higher oil revenues, some intervention may have crept back in, but this is a criticism about intervention not about the floating exchange rate policy.

So basically I share the hollowing out of the middle hypothesis. However, I suspect the political conditions and the economic institutions, by which I mean particularly a flexible wage rate setting mechanism, under which you could go to dollarization of any form—the hard peg—are relatively limited. Estonia is a good case in point: they were coming from a fixed regime and were quite willing to peg to the deutschemark; there was not, if you like, a legacy of anything other than a hard peg.

On regional funds, I just have two comments. The first is that big countries tend to have problems with their neighbors. The United States certainly has been seen as a big country relative to Mexico, Canada, the Caribbean, and Central America; I don't need to go further. India is seen as the giant that thwarts ambitions in Nepal, Bangladesh, Pakistan, and Sri Lanka. Other big countries in the same way are seen to be problems to their neighbors. Proposals for Asian monitoring of each other run some of the risks of heightened sensitivities between big and small countries that we see in other regions, particularly when the big countries are economically stronger. My second comment is that if you want to have a fund to ensure against risks, you need a pool of countries that face different risks so that you can diversify risks across that pool. Yet I would have thought that most Asian countries are likely to be on the same side of future economic shocks. That is like having a bunch of farmers, all of whom live along the same flood-prone river, getting together to provide themselves flood insurance.

The paper by Dooley, Dornbusch, and Park is the hardest to comment on. While I agree with most of the paper, I am not sure I agree with the proposed exchange rate intervention rule. When one is moving away from managed intervention, markets have to learn. In the Mexican case, I think the learning process went astonishingly smoothly in part because, after the Bank of Mexico had gotten burned in every conceivable way, it realized it had no alternative. The Bank of Mexico was so desperate, it was credible, which is one reason the transition was as smooth as it was. If this interpretation is correct, then any kind of rule that would smooth things in the market will also slow down the learning process. Do you want that, or do you simply want inflation targeting?

I am also worried about intervening in reaction to special events. I agree there are a few times when intervention has been successful, but I recall instances when interventions have not been successful. Moreover, once you say that you are going to allow the rate to float except in special cases, you have to define the special cases, which puts you almost right back into the soup you were trying to get out of. I am not sure there are never any special cases but, on the other hand, there are Type-1 and Type-2 errors. Especially when you have a history of lots of intervention, it is probably preferable to go very clean to let the markets learn and develop. If markets evolve in ways that still require some fine tuning, this can be done at a later date. But the more the fine tuning happens at the beginning, I assert, the longer the learning process is likely to be and the less satisfactory it is likely to be.

Jun Il Kim

The paper by Kim and Byeon contains a wealth of information on the debt negotiation between Korea and foreign creditors in 1998. The detailed documentation of the negotiation procedure is important reference material for the future study of financial crises, and as such has considerable historic value. Because this paper is more or less a case study, my comments will focus on the issue of moral hazard and the authors' conclusions.

The authors claim that the provision of government guarantees did not result in severe moral hazard problems on either the side of the creditors or the debtor. They identify three testable outcomes that would have been observed if creditors and debtors succumbed to moral hazard, and provide some evidence against the identified testable outcomes. While the testable hypotheses are nicely setup, the empirical analysis is too primitive to provide statistically reliable results. The simple comparisons of average participation rates or rescheduled loan maturity across groups of debtor banks presented in Figures 2-5 need to be supported by a more sophisticated statistical analysis.

The authors note in their conclusion that the Korean government's guarantee may not have been as good as that of Mexico, which has natural resources such as oil reserves as an effective collateral for the guarantees. And based on this, they argue that there were other reasons why creditors participated in Korea's debt restructuring programs. Their answer is a combination of a "too-big to-fail" hypothesis on an international level and the international confidence in Korea based on past economic successes.

I would emphasize another factor, which is that the high degree of openness of the Korean economy gave credibility to the government guarantees. In general, an economy with a large external sector, both in absolute size and relative to GDP, tends to have a large capacity to generate external liquidity through current account surpluses in a short period of time. Indeed, Korea had current account surpluses of more than US$86 billion in 1998-2000, thanks to the sharp depreciation of the won coupled with the high interest rate policy imposed by the IMF. It would not have been unreasonable for foreign creditors to expect the Korean economy to generate such external liquidity at the time of the external debt restructuring in 1998.

The authors claim that Korea's successful debt restructuring in 1998 is a leading example of private sector involvement. But it should also be noted that this was only possible with the provision of the sweetener of government guarantees plus an interest premium.

My final comment is that the paper would have been more interesting if it had provided an analysis of Korea's bargaining leverage at the time of debt rescheduling negotiation, including the potential cost of a payment moratorium to an economy heavily reliant on international trade and with limited access to international capital markets.

Eichengreen's paper is well organized and very informative about recent discussions and progress in strengthening the international financial architecture. I agree in principle with the author's assessment in most areas discussed in the paper. I also believe that the valuable insights and intuitions provided by the author with respect to the nature of interplay among standards, institutions, and practices will be of great help in understanding the scope and depth of the future challenges faced by the international financial community. Nonetheless, I would like to add several points related to discussions of the international financial architecture.

First, there is little question that the conditionality associated with IMF rescue packages needs to be streamlined and made more focused, as argued by the author. But we also need to recognize the role of conditionality with respect to the political economy of structural reform. Korea's past experience provides a good reference in this regard. Most structural reform measures swiftly implemented or deliberated after the crisis under the auspices of the IMF had long been discussed in Korea before the crisis, particularly over the course of Korea's accession to OECD. But there was no action.

I think the IMF conditionality worked as a pivotal force in the implementation of reforms that would otherwise have been very difficult to implement. Indeed, many Korea watchers, including foreign investors, academics, and the press, have argued that the pace of structural reforms in Korea has significantly slowed since 1999 due to not only the macroeconomic recovery but also to the reduced influence of the IMF in line with the repayment of the money borrowed under the Special Reserve Facility.

Second, we need to remember that for every reckless borrower there is a reckless lender. Therefore, the issue of moral hazard should be addressed not only on the debtor side, but also on the lender side. In this regard, I believe that advanced countries should also strengthen their efforts to improve standards for supervision, prudential regulation, risk management, and financial soundness, and to strengthen enforcement of the upgraded standards. In addition, an incentive-compatible mechanism needs to be devised to increase private sector involvement, including the introduction of Collective Action Clauses in global bond offering by emerging market economies.

Third, discussions on the international financial architecture should recognize that lending by foreign banks tends to be a more volatile source of financing than portfolio investment in bonds and equities, not only in crises but in general, and particularly since the 1990s. One reason rests in the difference in adjustment mechanism of bank lending and portfolio investment to shocks. Specifically, the market value of bank loans does not constantly adjust to shocks as their prices are rigid, while that of portfolio investment does. Consequently, banks tend to pull out their money from countries at the time of increased risks, rather than adjusting prices, resulting in high volatility in bank lending flows. This fact implies that as capital markets are replacing banks as the main capital intermediaries, the shift to capital markets will increase international financial stability, *ceteris paribus*. In the mean time, however, discussions on reforms to the international financial architecture need to pay more attention to bank lending.

Let me close with some comments and suggestions on the paper by Dooley, Dornbusch, and Park. This paper proposes for Korea a system of managed floating, coupled with flexible inflation targeting, as an interim exchange regime until either a fully flexible exchange rate or a credible peg can be established in an environment with well-developed financial markets. The proposed framework includes three main components: 1) sterilized intervention, 2) a target level for net foreign assets of central bank, and 3) flexible inflation targeting. The basic intuition underlying the proposed system is that monetary policy enjoys a substantial degree of independence and that sterilized intervention can be used to limit excessive exchange rate volatility.

The proposed regime seems to be reasonable, in principle, for Korea. Neither excessive exchange rate volatility nor too little volatility, which could lead to excessive taking of unhedged positions, would be desirable. I agree with the authors' view that neither a currency board nor a BBC system is appropriate for Korea currently given the need for real exchange rate flexibility for stabilization purposes, and that Korea does not have a credibility problem with regard to establishing price stability.

Nevertheless, there may be difficulties, as well as side effects, to actually implement the proposed regime. First, it may be hard for the government or central bank to know *a priori* whether large changes in the exchange rate are "appropriate" reactions to changes in the economic environment, in which case the authorities are not obliged to intervene. In order to make such a judgment, the authorities would need to know the nature of the underlying shocks (e.g., real versus monetary, domestic versus external, etc.). A more formal modeling would be desirable to better understand the working mechanism of the proposed framework and to answer questions such as the following: Should the authorities resist upward and downward pressure on the exchange rate regardless of the nature of shocks? Should the authorities react differently to temporary versus permanent shocks? What is the optimal threshold of exchange rate movement that should trigger intervention?

Second, the reserve-targeting rule suggested in the paper may generate long swings in the exchange rate, although it may stabilize it in the short run. The targeting rule prescribes currency depreciation (appreciation) over an extended period after the fall (rise) in reserves by more than 25 percent from the target, where the change in reserves occurred because of market intervention to smooth high frequency movements in the exchange rate. This process of restoring reserves to a target level may increase the volatility of low-frequency movements in the exchange rate, which could be costly to the tradable goods sector.

Third, maintaining net foreign reserves of 50 percent of GDP, as suggested in the paper, seems to be a formidable challenge to emerging market countries like Korea; it means net foreign reserves of more than US$200 billion for Korea! The proposal is not clear how to achieve such a level of net foreign reserves. Given the current level of base money, the accumulation of net foreign reserves up to 50 percent of GDP would mean either a dramatic increase in the money supply, a squeeze in domestic credit, or both. If it is accompanied by an increase in the money supply, the exchange rate will be under substantial pressure, increasing volatility. Another implication of holding large net foreign reserves would be the quasi-fiscal cost stemming from the interest rate differential between home and foreign assets. I believe the analysis should address these two problems in a more operational framework.

Finally, the proposed framework implicitly assumes the use of capital controls for prudential purposes if necessary to keep current account deficits at an acceptable level to the government. This aspect may create frictions with the existing progress in capital account liberalization since the crisis. If, however, the risk premium on domestic assets is positively correlated with increases in current account deficits, the need to rely on capital flow restrictions could be reduced. Nevertheless, it would have been helpful if the authors also addressed the implications for monetary and exchange rate policy of distortionary costs and the effectiveness of capital controls.

Conference Program

Friday, May 18

Welcome and Opening Remarks: *Kyung Tae Lee and Yusuke Horiguchi*

Session 1: Overview of the Korean Crisis and the Crisis-Resolution Strategy

Moderator - *Il SaKong*

Ajai Chopra, Kenneth Kang, Meral Karasulu, Hong Liang, Henry Ma, and Anthony Richards, "From Crisis to Recovery in Korea: Strategy, Achievements, and Lessons"

Yoon Je Cho, "What Have We Learned from the Korean Economic Adjustment Program?"

Discussants - *Barry Eichengreen, Jang-Yung Lee*

Session 2: Monetary Policies

Moderator - *Stephen Grenville*

Chae-Shick Chung and Se-Jik Kim, "New Evidence on High Interest Rate Policy During the Korean Crisis"

Anne O. Krueger and Jungho Yoo, "Falling Profitability, Higher Borrowing Costs, and Chaebol Finances During the Korean Crisis"

Discussants - *Myung-Chang Chung, Bijan B. Aghevli*

Session 3: Financial and Corporate Reform

Moderator - *David T. Coe*

William P. Mako, "Corporate Restructuring and Reform: Lessons from Korea"

Gyutaeg Oh and Changyong Rhee, "The Role of Corporate Bond Markets in the Korean Financial Restructuring Process"

Discussants - *Simon Johnson, Won-Dong Cho*

Session 4: Labor Markets and Corporate Governance

Moderator - *Sung Hee Jwa*
Dae Il Kim, "The Korean Labor Market: The Crisis and After"
Eric Friedman, Simon Johnson, and Todd Mitton, "Corporate Governance and Corporate Debt in Asian Crisis Countries"
Discussants - *Hasung Jang, Zia Qureshi*

Reception: Remarks by Deputy Prime Minister and Minister of Finance and Economy, *Nyum Jin*

Saturday, May 19

Session 5: After the Crisis

Moderator - *Kyung Tae Lee*
Robert J. Barro, "Economic Growth in East Asia Before and After the Financial Crisis"
Yung Chul Park and Jong-Wha Lee, "Recovery and Sustainability in East Asia"
Discussants - *Charles Adams, Yong Jin Kim*

Session 6: Implications for Future Crisis Management and the International Financial Architecture

Moderator - *Tarrin Nimmanahaeminda*
Woochan Kim and Yangho Byeon, "Restructuring Korean Banks' Short-Term Debts"
Barry Eichengreen, "Strengthening the International Financial Architecture: Open Issues, Asian Concerns"
Michael Dooley, Rudi Dornbusch, and Yung Chul Park, "A Framework for Exchange Rate Policy in Korea"
Discussants - *Anne O. Krueger, Jun Il Kim*

Session 7: Lessons from the Korean Crisis and Recovery

Moderator - *Yusuke Horiguchi*
Panelists - *Robert J. Barro, Pyung Joo Kim, Yung Chul Park, Hak Kil Pyo, and Eisuke Sakakibara*